Alaska Fishing

The Ultimate Angler's Guide, 3rd Edition

ISBN (Paperback): 1-929170-11-4
ISBN (Hardback): 1-929170-29-7
LCC Number: 2004105516

Publishers Design Group, Inc.
Roseville, California
1.800.587.6666
www.publishersdesign.com

Printed in China

Alaska Fishing

The Ultimate Angler's Guide, 3rd Edition

Compiled by

Rene Limeres & Gunnar Pedersen

PUBLISHERS DESIGN GROUP, INC
ROSEVILLE, CA 95678

ACKNOWLEDGEMENTS

In compiling the information used in the various editions of *Alaska Fishing*, we consulted with hundreds of folks all across Alaska—guides, charter boat captains, lodge owners, pilots, biologists, sport anglers, tackle and fly shop owners, etc.—who were kind enough to share their expertise to help us "fill in the blanks" on the vast and varied fishing possibilities in our behemoth state. To attempt to mention all who provided assistance over the years would be a massive undertaking, certain to fill many pages of this publication (and no doubt still miss many important individuals), so a giant heartfelt "Thanks!" must suffice here for those who helped with the earlier editions.

Among the many we are indebted to for this new book, foremost is the wonderful group of collaborators and advisors who worked long and hard on *Alaska Fishing III*. Special thanks must go to those who went above and beyond in their generosity answering countless questions and providing all kinds of material and necessary critique to make this book most complete, accurate, and comprehensive: Tony Weaver, Tom Cappiello, Gary Souza, Peter Hardy, Kurt Iverson, and others. Also worthy of mention are the great photographers who so willingly (and expeditiously) submitted so many of their most stunning images for consideration, many of which made it in to the pages of *Alaska Fishing III*: Brian O'Keefe, Tony Weaver, Nick Jans, Chlaus Lotscher, Greg Syverson, Tom Cappiello, Chris Palle, Doug Wilson, Bob Butterfield, Dave Vedder, Mark Emery, Corey Schwanke, Andy Hahn, Bill Buckley, Dody Morrison, and others.

We want to thank all the individuals who so graciously provided information and photos of record catches for the interesting sidebars that appear in some of the species chapters: Paul Kanitz, Daniel Thorsness, Ted Rainer, Larry Hudnall, Rick Thynes, and Les Anderson.

A very special thanks to William Hickman, who spent countless hours laboring on the many fine maps and other numerous illustrations used in this new edition. For all your hard work and untiring support, Bill, a debt is owed that can never be fully repaid.

Gunnar Pedersen did a remarkable job of researching much of the original material that *Alaska Fishing III* is based on, and helped tremendously in updating and critiquing this new edition. We are very grateful for his involvement and the authority it adds to the book.

Countless individuals and businesses involved in the Alaska sport and commercial fishing industries shared generously of their knowledge of local waters and conditions, to whom we are most grateful. (Many are listed under "Recommended Services" throughout the locations descriptions sections of the book; please give them your support whenever you can.)

Numerous personnel—far too many to mention—within the Alaska Department of Fish and Game, U.S. Forest Service, Fish and Wildlife Service, and other agencies were extremely forthcoming with assistance, providing considerable information on local fisheries. We are most grateful for all their help.

It would be remiss not to mention the considerable support and patience of our loving spouses and significant others through the long and difficult process of getting this book together. We couldn't have done it without you; love to you all!

Last, but certainly not least, this book would never have happened without the extremely competent guidance and expertise (not to mention saintly patience) of Robert Brekke of Publishers Design Group, who oversaw the project from initial design to publication to fulfillment. To him, and his talented staff, we are indebted tremendously.

Alaska Fishing
The Ultimate Angler's Guide, 3rd Edition

CONTENTS

Alaska Fishing

The Ultimate Angler's Guide, 3rd Edition

Major Contributors
Rene Limeres
Gunnar Pedersen
William Hickman
Tom Cappiello
Peter Hardy
Tony Weaver
Gary Souza
Ken Alt
Kurt Iverson
Les Palmer

Compilation
Rene Limeres/Gunnar Pedersen

Editing
Rene Limeres

Maps/Illustrations
William Hickman

Fish Illustrations
Dan Mills
William Hickman

Photo Research
Rene Limeres

Senior Design
Robert Brekke

Line Art Drawings
Mark Whitfield
Chris Ceccarelli

Editorial Assistance
Rebecca Kellyhouse
Robin Sullivan

Proofreading
Midge James

Advisors
Peter Hardy
Tony Weaver
Robert Farmer
Gary Souza
Kurt Iverson
Paul Fitzgibbons
Barry Reynolds
Rich Culver
Bill Huntington
Nick Jans
Ken Alt
Dean Williams
Tom Cappiello
Bill Stoabs

ALASKA'S MAJOR SPORT SPECIES

THE CONTRIBUTORS

This new version of *Alaska Fishing* builds on two earlier editions that were compiled, edited, and written in large part by Rene Limeres and Gunnar Pedersen, with contributions by Ken Alt, Thomas Cappiello, Gary Souza, Peter Hardy, Steve Wottlin, and Robert Farmer.

Rene Limeres

Principal editor and major contributor for the new book. Has been involved in Alaska sportfishing and the media for years, as a professional guide (Southwest Alaska), outdoors writer/ photographer, publisher of the award winning *Alaska Hunting and Fishing Calendar,* and former editor of *The Alaska Professional Hunter.* Many of his photographs appear throughout the book as well.

Gunnar Pedersen

Spent his childhood in Norway and adolescence fishing the rivers, lakes and bays of Southcentral Alaska. Eventually became a top notch guide and successful author/publisher of the best selling fishing book on the 49th state (*The Highway Angler*). Provided updates and compiled new information for many of the chapters in this new book.

Thomas Cappiello

Biologist and lifelong hardcore sport angler (and IGFA World Record holder), he has over twenty years experience fishing and researching in Alaska. He provided updates on Cutthroat Trout and two new, detailed chapters on Rockfish and Lingcod, in addition to many superb photographs that appear throughout the book.

Gary Souza

Resides in Ketchikan, a confirmed steelhead, trout, and salmon addict, who has fished extensively throughout the Northwest, conducted steelhead seminars, fly casting clinics, and been a guide, charter boat captain (and minister) in Southeast for many years. For this new edition, he revised and expanded his excellent Steelhead chapter, and generously shared his expertise to make the Saltwater Salmon chapter more complete and accurate. His assistance in checking facts in many of the southern Southeast locations descriptions was invaluable.

Alaska Fishing

The Ultimate Angler's Guide, 3rd Edition

Peter Hardy

A lifelong Alaskan of Anchorage, the state's "Halibut Guru" and extremely knowledgeable salmon fisherman (and super nice guy), he updated his thorough chapter on Halibut and provided information and critique on the King Salmon chapter and others.

Kurt Iverson

Lives in Juneau and has many years experience as a fishing guide, commercial fisherman, fish and wildlife technician, and currently fisheries analyst with the Commercial Fisheries Entry Commission. With his extensive expertise, he did a beautiful job revising and expanding the section on northern Southeast Alaska.

Les Palmer

Outdoors writer and avid angler of Sterling, has been living in and fishing Alaska for forty years. He writes a weekly column for the *Peninsula Clarion* and contributes regularly to *Alaska Magazine*. We were delighted to have him write a chapter on Salmon Sharks.

Tony Weaver

Resides in Anchorage and is a well recognized authority on flycasting and flyfishing Alaska. The Alaska Council President for the Federation of Fly Fishers (FFF) and Certified Master Fly Casting Instructor, Tony is also chief technical editor for *Fish Alaska Magazine*. He's fished extensively all around Alaska and the world and, for this book, we were proud to have him as general flyfishing advisor and author of many of the flyfishing sections that appear in the species chapters.

William Hickman

Resides in Anchorage, and is a talented illustrator and retired Alaskan homesteader. From his initial renderings for the first two editions, Bill spent considerable time developing the many color illustrations and maps used in the new book.

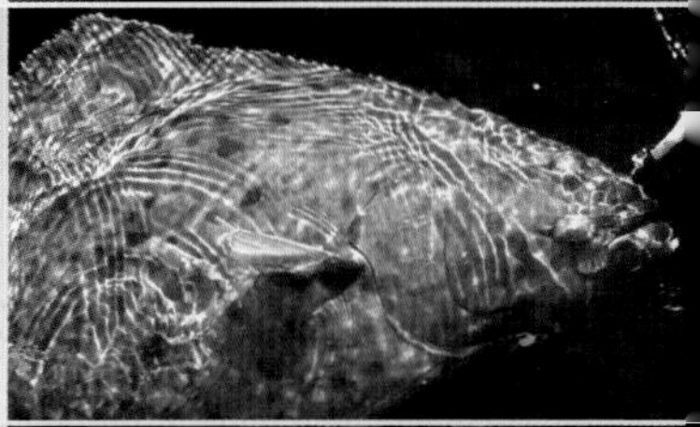

Ken Alt

Resides in Fairbanks, and did pioneer fish inventories and research in western Alaska for ADF&G. He is now a fisheries consultant and, for this new edition, he updated his excellent chapter on Sheefish and critiqued many of the chapters.

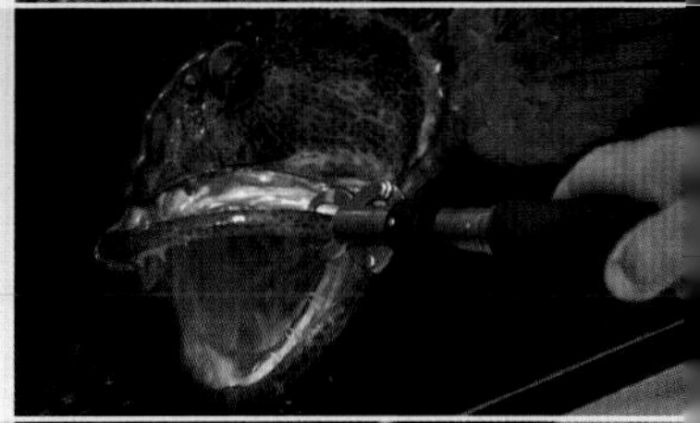

ALASKA'S MAJOR REGIONS/LOCATIONS

Photo illustrations of lures courtesy of: Luhr Jensen, Yakima Bait Company, Rapala Normark, Mepps, Mann's Bait Company.

Filleting and Knot Illustrations (pages 430-435) used with permission to reprint from *Pier Fishing in California: The Complete Coast and Bay Guide, 2nd Edition* (2004 Publishers Design Group). Illustrations by Chris Ceccarelli.

Although the authors and publisher have made every effort to ensure the information contained in *Alaska Fishing, The Ultimate Angler's Guide, 3rd Edition* is correct, certain inaccuracies may be unavoidable with the uncertainty of Alaska's fish runs and rapidly changing economic factors. (As this book went to press, oil prices were reaching record highs with predictable impact on nearly every facet of Alaska's tourist industry.) We apologize for any inconvenience or travel disruption caused by errors or omissions, but assume no responsibility for factors beyond our control that may affect the accuracy of this book.

We would appreciate if readers would call our attention to any errors or outdated information they find in the book by writing us at:

Publishers Design Group
P.O. Box 37
Roseville CA 95678
(916) 784-0500
Fax (916) 773-7421
books@publishersdesign.com

Information Updates
The authors will be making periodic updates to *Alaska Fishing III*, available through the web by following links at *www.ultimaterivers.com*. Readers are encouraged to check for the latest changes in fishing regulations (including license fees), revised visitor services' costs and contact information, trophy fish updates, new techniques, etc., to best help them plan for their upcoming Alaska fishing adventures.

PREFACE

This guide is the latest version of a book that had its beginnings during a long, snowbound winter over ten years ago, with an idea born among some Alaskan fishing guides to create a complete and authoritative reference on fishing their state.

The remoteness and immensity of Alaska place some very real limitations on anyone's ability to fully experience (and write accurately about) the vast range of fishing possibilities available across this state. For this reason, the plan from the start was to have a collaborative effort of experienced resident fishing guides, outdoors writers, biologists, hard core sport anglers, etc., sharing their expertise to create a level of comprehensiveness, accuracy, and insight never before achieved in a guide to fishing Alaska's many waters.

There are many resources available for anyone who wants to take the time to research information on Alaska's fisheries. Like others who have written on Alaska's sportfishing, for baseline information on species' ecology, major fisheries, harvests, status, etc., we relied heavily on the published research, management reports, inventories, annual surveys, personal communications, etc., of the Alaska Department of Fish and Game, the U.S. Fish & Wildlife Service, U.S. Forest Service, Bureau of Land Management, and other agencies, state and federal.

Beyond that, however, for the detailed technical sections and much of the information that appears in the many locations descriptions, we drew more from the input of our collaborators and dozens like them—air taxi pilots, charter boat skippers, fishing guides, lodge owners, outfitters, etc., from across Alaska. Their years of experience over a wide range of conditions has given them a practical knowledge of local fishing that is second to none.

In our original development of the book, we wanted to give readers a much more complete and holistic understanding than could be conveyed through the standard rundown of major species and techniques, so we broadened the scope to include overviews of the state's six geographic regions and the various settings (and challenges) they provide for sportfishing. To be more thorough (and to please our publisher), we included detailed descriptions of the most important fishing locations—over 250 river, stream, lake, bay, island, and strait hotspots across Alaska.

With its encyclopedic treatment, including many appendices and cross-referenced index, *Alaska Fishing* broke new ground as the first truly complete and integrated reference of its kind. The response overall from the public and critics was very positive; many hailed it as a definitive angling guide, the new "Alaska fishing bible." The book sold out and a revised second edition was released a few years later, which proved equally popular.

Now with this long overdue, completely updated, expanded, and reformatted *Alaska Fishing The Ultimate Angler's Guide, 3rd Edition*, we have fully realized the original dream by creating a guide that is most complete, comprehensive, and attractive, covering all major sport species in Alaska's fresh and salt waters, with many new locations, dozens of new maps and charts, and hundreds of color illustrations, including many gorgeous photos that capture the grandeur, beauty, and excitement of sportfishing in Alaska. We hope you find it very useful and enjoyable.

—Rene Limeres
Anchorage, 2004

INTRODUCTION

Alaska looms in our imagination as a vast northern frontier, rich in mystique and natural wonders. The former prize of Russia, home of the Eskimo (and Tlingit and Athapascan), land of gold rush dreams, and America's last great wilderness, it has always been (and perhaps always will be) a place to inspire wonder and the adventurous spirit in us all.

Much about the 49th state is superlative and unique. It has North America's tallest mountains, largest rainforests, biggest glaciers, most awesome scenery, largest animals, etc., and just about every school kid can tell you it's more than twice the size of Texas. But less known, perhaps, is that—due to its location, physiography, lack of development, and the divine grace of Nature—Alaska sustains some of the most remarkably abundant and diverse cold water fisheries on the planet. While the rest of the world's fishing regions yield only a shadow of their former wild bounty due to the ravages of man, Alaska's waters continue to produce a staggering surplus of prime food and game fishes.

For sport anglers, this richness is spread out over a vast, diverse, and challenging environment. There are countless rivers, streams, creeks, lakes, and ponds, and a coastline longer than that of the contiguous states, filled with an amazing variety of coveted species, in terrain that can vary from lush coastal rainforest to barren arctic tundra.

Understandably, the state's immensity, remoteness, notorious conditions, and seemingly limitless fishing possibilities can overwhelm and even intimidate potential Alaska anglers. Faced with so many options, confusing claims and misinformation, even seasoned world anglers may find it difficult, if not impossible, to make intelligent choices in their trip planning.

For these beleaguered, would-be Alaska anglers and for the armchair dreamers of the world, we offer this, the third edition of the most comprehensive and insightful guide to fishing the world's ultimate coldwater angling destination. In its pages you will find everything you need to know (and a whole lot more) to sort through the hype and fill in the gray areas on the how, when, and where of fishing America's greatest state.

Beyond the basic information that any decent guide should provide, *Alaska Fishing III* delves into fish behavior and habits, regional geography and climate, trophy and record fish information, fishing ethics, cultural and historical significance of fisheries, and many other topics that, hopefully, will give greater knowledge and awareness of Alaska and its remarkable fisheries.

But just as fishing Alaska is about so much more than catching fish, this new guide, in its writing and graphics, attempts to convey a sense of the considerable romance involved in fishing the Last Frontier. With its undiminished wild fish populations, magnificent, unspoiled landscapes, and solitude, Alaska is unique in a world of put-and-take hatchery fishing, crowds, and urban blight.

In researching and compiling this book, we were constantly amazed by the diversity of fishing experiences possible in Alaska, each with its own flavor and possibilities. You can visit remote lakes in the Brooks Range and share the same camps, fishing, and timeless vistas as ancient Eskimo hunters did millennia ago, fish sparkling southwest rivers where fat rainbow trout and charr fight each other for your fly (while thousand-pound brown bears ply nearby shallows for dinner), or lose yourself for days on a Huck Finn log raft adventure down a giant Interior river, with fabulous pike, sheefish, and grayling opportunities around every bend. And then there are the countless sheltered bays along the southern coast, where you can heave out some pots, drop a line or two and, in short order, have the makings for a feast fit for an emperor.

(Just as interesting, perhaps, are the colorful characters who run the lodges, air taxis, and guide and outfitting services in some of these far-flung places. They are the last of a vanishing breed, Alaska's true pioneers.)

There is all this and more, of course, in the vast territory of fishing dreams that stretches from the coast of British Columbia to the Arctic Ocean. There are endless, fish-till-you-drop summer days, frosty, aurora-filled nights on fall trout safaris, an amazing pageant of wildlife through the seasons to liven every outing, and a feeling of being connected to something so much bigger than the humdrum of everyday life back in "civilization."

May it always be so.

It is our sincerest hope that you find this guide useful in furthering your understanding, appreciation, and exploration of one of the last truly great places for the adventure angler.

HOW TO USE THIS BOOK

This book is a comprehensive guide for anyone seeking greater knowledge on angling in Alaska, regardless of previous fishing experience. It is designed and written to be an easy to use, integrated reference on the state's major sport species, regions, and best fishing locations. It is highly recommended that you read it in its entirety. However, if time and desire dictate otherwise, you can easily navigate through the various sections to access information on a particular species, region, or location of interest. If you know the name of the area you'd like to fish (bay, inlet, lake, creek, river system, etc.), use the index in the back of the book to find the corresponding page. If you'd like to travel to a particular part of Alaska and want to find out what kind of fishing is available there, turn to the region chapters to read about that area. If you're interested in knowing which areas provide good fishing for a particular species, turn to the appropriate species chapter and consult the summary pages at the end for a list of the of the major sportfishing locations for that species (many of which will be described in detail in the appropriate locations section).

Species Chapters

We expanded the Alaska Species Section to include all major gamefishes in the state's fresh and salt waters—17 species—plus a chapter on the specific conditions and techniques involved in fishing Alaska's saltwater salmon. We have purposely omitted any detailed information on fishes of minor importance—burbot, whitefish, greenling, cod, etc. This certainly does not imply that you'll find no good opportunities to fish these species in Alaska. Readers who want more information on any of the minor sport species available in Alaska should contact the Alaska Department of Fish and Game (local, regional, and state offices listed throughout the book).

The species chapters can be an invaluable resource for trip planning. In addition to comprehensive information on the life histories, status, and habits of Alaska's major game species, and the most effective techniques and gear used, they feature tips on the best locations and times for fishing. For each species, we provide a list of top trophy specimens and the locations they were captured; this information is compiled from 40 years of records gathered by the Alaska Department of Fish and Game under their annual Trophy Fish Awards program. Keep in mind that, because of the vastness of the state and remoteness of many of the fishing locations, not all trophy hotspots are listed, and there may be some yet to be discovered. Detailed species summaries are provided at the end of each chapter, along with a list of the major Alaska locations where they are found.

Locations Descriptions

For each region, we describe in detail the major sportfishing areas and the very best lake, stream, and marine fishing locations. To aid in trip planning (and save space), we list the following useful information at the beginning of each location description:

Location Name/Rating: The name of a lake, stream, river, bay, or strait, plus three or four star rating if it ranks among the best in Alaska.

Location: The distance and direction of each location from reference points, usually major cities or towns.

Access: The major access options for locations.

Facilities: The available public/private facilities for each location.

About River Running

For many rivers we use the following international scale to rate difficulty for floating (by raft, canoe, kayak):

Class I: Moving water with some riffles and waves, suitable for beginners.

Class II: Small rapids with standing waves to three feet high, for boaters of some experience.

Class III: Rapids with high waves, may require scouting or difficult maneuvering; for intermediate boaters.

Class IV: Long, difficult rapids, canoe or small open boat unsafe; for high level experienced boaters.

Class V: Extremely hazardous, long and/or violent rapids, requiring "lining" or portages; for experts only.

Class VI: Extreme white water, usually floodwater conditions and rare locations; top experts only.

This general scale is for normal water levels; Alaska river conditions can change swiftly and dramatically, so caution is the rule.

Highlights: The major highlights of each location. (Here and elsewhere throughout the book we may use a variety of adjectives such as: "outstanding," "superb," "excellent," "great," "decent," "good," and "fair" to describe the fishing, which hopefully will be meaningful and not too subjective for most folks. Keep in mind that this is Alaska, where even "fair" fishing can far surpass anything most people are used to in home waters.)

Major Species: The major species of interest that each location is known for. (For a complete list of all the species available at each location, consult the fish charts at the end of each location section.) To save space, the following abbreviated versions of fish species are used:

KS-king salmon	**SS**-silver salmon
RS-red salmon	**KO**-kokanee
PS-pink salmon	**CS**-chum salmon
RT-rainbow trout	**CT**-cutthroat trout
ST-steelhead trout	**CHR**-charr
DV-Dolly Varden charr	**LT**-lake trout
NP-northern pike	**SF**-sheefish
GR-arctic grayling	**HT**-halibut
LC-lingcod	**RF**-rockfish

BF-bottomfish (halibut, lingcod and rockfish)
SHK-salmon shark

Additional information is compiled at the end of each locations section to help with trip planning: U.S. Geological Survey topographic contour map (scale 1:63,360) and, where applicable, National Oceanic and Atmospheric Administration (NOAA) Nautical Chart references for each listing; a list of recommended local contacts for services (guides, outfitters, air taxis, charters, etc.); state and federal contacts for public lands information; and a brief summary of pertinent area/regional Alaska Department of Fish and Game Regulations and contact information. We have made every effort to include the most current contact information, including web addresses. When planning your trip, please consult these contacts for assistance with your vacation planning.

Many of the rivers and lakes listed are on public lands, incorporated into national wildlife refuges, parks, forests, preserves or part of our Wild and Scenic River System. Contact the agencies listed (see appendix also) for important information on access, use and management of these waters.

Note: *Use the information given on locations only as a general guide for trip planning. Conditions vary from year to year, even from month to month, on many Alaska waters. Consult with local sources before making any final trip arrangements. Check with the Alaska Department of Fish and Game for the latest Regulations Information and Emergency Orders that may affect your fishing.*

Region Overviews

The region overviews provide synopses of the salient features and highlights of the state's six major fishing regions as pertains to the terrain, weather and fishing conditions, fisheries, and availability and relative costs of visitor services. Regional maps, climate tables, and run timing charts provide additional useful information for trip planning.

For the purposes of this book, the state is divided into six separate regions, following, more or less, the standard physiographic provinces recognized by the state's geographers:

Arctic: (ARC) The north slope of the Brooks Range to the Arctic Ocean, from Point Hope to the Canadian border.

Interior: (INT) The central part of the state between the Alaska and Brooks ranges, bounded by the Middle Fork of the Koyukuk River on the west and the Canadian border on the east.

Northwest: (NW) The drainages of Norton and Kotzebue sounds and the Chukchi Sea, south of Point Hope, including the lower Koyukuk and western Brooks Range lakes (southern slope).

Southwest: (SW) The Alaska Peninsula and Aleutians, Bristol Bay, and lower Kuskokwim and Yukon rivers.

Southcentral: (SC) Alaska's North Gulf Coast drainages from Cape Suckling to Shelikof Strait, including the Kenai Peninsula and the Kodiak/Afognak/Shuyak Island complex.

Southeast: (SE) The Panhandle from Dixon Entrance to Icy Cape (and coastal streams to Cape Suckling).

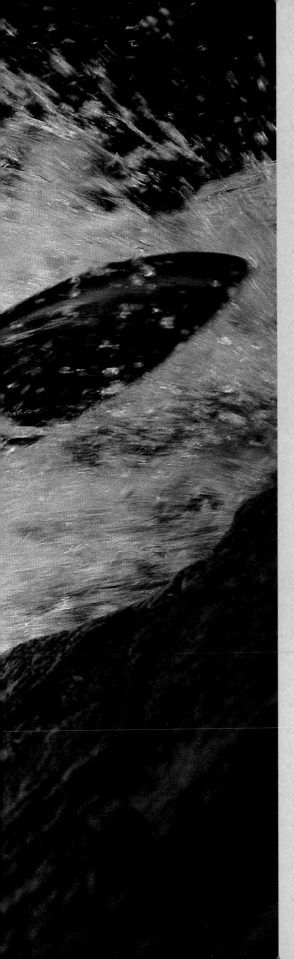

Gamefishes of Alaska

O f the 17 major Alaska gamefishes detailed in this publication, twelve belong to one of the world's most significant and successful families of coolwater fishes, the salmonids—the salmons, charrs, trouts, whitefishes, graylings, and three other lesser groups of fishes (70 species in all), native to oceans, lakes, and streams of the northern hemisphere. Besides their preference for clean, cold, highly oxygenated water, all fishes of this family possess similar physical characteristics, like streamlined bodies, forked tails, and adipose fins (the small rounded fins topside just ahead of the tail), and live in fresh water or split their life residence between rivers and the sea (called anadromy). Alaska, encompassing most of the rich northeast Pacific basin, has an abundance of suitable habitat and forage to support large numbers of these coveted food and game fishes, much to the envy of the rest of the world.

1

Alaska's Pacific Salmon

No species are more synonymous with Alaska's bountiful fisheries or, for that matter, the culture of the entire Northwest, than the amazing Pacific salmon. Part of an ancient lineage that traces its beginnings some 40 million years ago, Pacific salmon (genus *Oncorhynchus*) as we know them probably evolved during the Pliocene (the period before the glaciers, over a million years ago) into the seven species now found in the North Pacific. (Five occur in Alaska.) Their historical success is due to remarkable life history adaptations that allow them to exploit the region's abundant cool streams for protected spawning and rearing habitat, and the rich coastal and off-shore marine waters to quickly attain adult size and the reserves needed to complete their strenuous life cycle.

The saga of the salmon is nothing if not a metaphor for life's perilous fight for survival. From the moment the eggs are laid, these fish face constant attrition from all manner of depredations. Other fish, including juvenile salmon, will actively seek out the rich roe for food and feed heavily on emerging fry or migrating smolts. Diving birds like terns, loons, king-fishers, and mergansers also take their toll. Alaska's capricious weather and fluctuating river conditions devastate great numbers of young as well. Out at sea,

salmon are at risk from larger pelagic fishes like sharks, giant halibut, and lingcod, along with marine mammals (fifteen species of seals, whales, dolphins and sea lions prey on them) and high seas fisheries interception. On their return to fresh water, they face the cruelest gauntlet of all, Alaska's inshore commercial fishing fleet after which, if they survive, they must still negotiate rapids, throngs of sport anglers, marauding bears, and what have you before they can hope to complete their life cycle. Of the thousands of eggs laid and fertilized by a breeding pair, only precious few offspring survive to return as mature adults to spawn and continue the cycle. (Breeding is terminal for all Pacific salmon, with rapid deterioration and death following the mating act.)

The annual return of millions of Pacific salmon into countless rivers, lakes, and streams along the southern and western coasts of Alaska has significance far beyond the immediate economic value to fishermen and native subsistence users. These fish essentially drive the coastal ecosystems, providing sustenance for myriad wildlife that would be hard pressed to survive Alaska's long winters without the concentrated food they provide (whether salmon flesh, roe, or young) and, through their carcasses, adding essential elements to the food chains of waters that would otherwise be quite sterile and unproductive.

Salmon-Steelhead Life Cycle Glossary

Alevin: newly hatched fish with yolk sac still attached.

Fry: post-alevin juvenile fish stage.

Parr: post-fry juvenile fish stage, prior to smolting.

Smolt: young salmon preparing to enter the sea (2-5").

Buck/Cock: a sexually mature male fish.

Hen: a sexually mature female fish.

Jack: a precocious, sexually mature male fish.

Kelt: outmigrating, spawned out steelhead or Atlantic salmon.

Milt: salmon sperm.

Redd: salmon nest.

Roe: salmon eggs.

Alaska's Trout and Charr

Among the many creatures that benefit from the presence of so many salmon are Alaska's fabulous trout and charr populations, unequalled anywhere else in the world for their variety and abundance (except perhaps the northeastern coast of Siberia and the Kamchatka Peninsula). Closely allied with the salmon, Alaska's five species (*Oncorhynchus spp.* and *Salvelinus spp.*) share many of the same traits, including anadromy in some instances, and include some of our continent's most prized gamefishes (steelhead, rainbow, and cutthroat trout).

Except in waters of the Arctic and isolated lakes and ponds, most of Alaska's trout and charr have life histories that are intertwined with those of the Pacific salmon. Their feeding habits and seasonal movements revolve around the salmon life cycle activities, and many of the angling strategies used to entice them are similar, if not identical. (This aspect is covered in great detail in the species chapters that follow.)

Alaska's Grayling and Whitefishes

This important group of salmonid fishes (comprised of two subfamilies) includes some eight species or more in Alaska, with only two of significant sportfishing potential, the Arctic grayling, *Thymallus arcticus*, and the world's largest whitefish, the sheefish, *Stenodus leucichthys*. These fish differ somewhat from the salmon, trout and charrs, having larger scales, smaller teeth and, except for grayling, an absence of markings. Their distribution in Alaska is widespread.

Alaska's Pike

Alaska's sole representative of this unique worldwide group of fishes (order *Esociformes*) is the northern pike, *Esox lucius*. An important sport species, very widespread, particularly in the vast lowland habitat of Alaska's Interior (and parts of Southwest and Northwest), the northern pike has a distinctive appearance and demeanor that endears it to many anglers.

Alaska's Saltwater Gamefishes

(For the purposes of this publication, the various species of salmon taken in saltwater are grouped together in the Alaska Saltwater Salmon chapter.)

The rockfishes are a very large and important group (family *Scorpaenidae*) of shallow to deep water, long-lived ocean fishes, with more than 30 species found along the southern coast of Alaska. Recognized by their bass-like shape, attractive coloration and spiny (venomous) fins, rockfishes are significant to Alaska sport anglers because of their abundance, eagerness, and fine eating qualities.

The Pacific halibut, *Hippoglossus stenolepis*, is perhaps the most prized species of flatfish in the world because of the size it attains and unexcelled eating qualities. In Alaska it is pursued diligently by a well developed commercial and charter fleet along the southern coast. It can be taken with simple techniques and stout gear in a variety of waters throughout the year.

The fearsome lingcod, *Ophiodon elongatus*, is an interesting bottom dweller and important sport species found throughout the open waters along Alaska's rocky Pacific and North Gulf coasts (usually occupying similar habitats as the ubiquitous rockfishes).

Salmon shark, *Lamna ditropis*, is a streamlined, high speed predator attracted in seasonal localized concentrations by the great numbers of returning salmon along the North Gulf Coast. It has only recently been recognized as a sport species, with a growing interest from the sport and charter fleets.

Chinook
King of Salmon

You may find yourself someday, in your wildest fish dream come true, on the wind-whipped coast of the Bering Sea, at one of a handful of small native villages that lie at the mouths of the great rivers there. A kindly old man with sparkling eyes and a face like shoe leather waits to greet you warmly, then listens intently to your request. With an affirmative nod and a toothless grin, he motions to his grandson to fetch the skiff and run you upriver. The smiling boy quickly takes you around a few bends to a big fork, where he deposits you and your gear on the gravel and is gone in a flash. For the next few days and sleepless nights—for there is no real night this far north in June—you are caught up in the magic of one of the greatest yearly miracles to befall these desolate coasts: the stirring arrival (in numbers undiminished) of the first and most awesome of the Pacific's five salmon of summer. It's a fish prized through the ages for its size, gaminess, and good eating—the one they call chinook, the king of salmon.

Not given to recklessness like its cousin the coho, and certainly not the same class of fighter as the exalted steelhead, the chinook, in sheer size and strength alone, supremely outclasses any of its peers. Husky from summers out in the rich North Pacific, a king will tip the scales at 30, 40, or 50 pounds or more—a formidable adversary, especially when fresh from the sea. When an ocean-bright 30-pounder slams your fly and rips into half your backing, you'll swear you've snagged a whale. The ensuing grudge match can last hours (a Minnesota man fought a monster Kenai River king for a day and a half!), during which the brawny lord of all salmon will test you and your gear to the limit. But if you're tough and lucky enough to slug it out to the end, you'll stagger ashore with a prize definitely worth the trip to these waters. For the only thing more impressive than the fight of a big king salmon is the magnificent sight of one up close: immense, full-bodied, with sides of buffed platinum tinged with purple, and muscular flanks that taper into a broad and powerful tail. It is a countenance both awe-inspiring and humbling, one of nature's most exquisite expressions of a sea-roaming, fish-eating, river-running machine.

Heading out to king camp—lower Kanektok River, Southwest Alaska

CHINOOK: KING OF SALMON

More than an angler's prize, of course, the king of salmon, *Oncorhynchus tshawytscha*, has been an inseparable part of Pacific Northwest culture for centuries. The first white explorers of the region, beginning with the epic voyages of Vitus Bering more than 250 years ago and, later, Lewis and Clark and Alexander Mackenzie, encountered elaborate rituals that native coastal people performed to celebrate the annual return of the great chinook (the name derived from the Chinook Indian tribe of the Columbia River basin). In their mythology, these fish were the embodied spirits of supernatural beings from the sea, who ascended rivers to sacrifice themselves for the survival of their captors who, in turn, harvested and consumed these first salmon of summer with great ceremony and respect.

The region's rich bounty of kings provided white settlers a thriving commercial fishery which was, until the tragic debacle of the great dams, one of the cornerstones of the Pacific Northwest's vibrant economy. Yet despite man's many ravages over the years, the chinook has managed somehow to survive and, in Alaska at least, retains a measure of its former glory.

Here in the Last Frontier, the mighty king salmon is somewhat of a pop icon. We have made it our state fish and used its name and image shamelessly to promote businesses; to glorify towns, streets and subdivisions; and to create countless works of folk art. As the focal point of a multimillion-dollar sportfishing industry (hooking and landing a big king salmon will always be the quintessential Alaska angling experience) and a prized commercial and subsistence species, the chinook's significance and stature are elevated beyond any measure.

DESCRIPTION

Chinook are the largest of the Pacific salmon, routinely reaching 30 pounds or more, and lengths of 45 inches, though their average weight in Alaska is around 18 pounds. The International Game Fish Association (IGFA) sport-caught world record is 97 1/4 pounds, taken from Southcentral's Kenai River in 1985. Fish exceeding 100 pounds are occasionally snared in commercial fishing nets. (A 126-pound giant was taken by fish trap at Stikine River near Petersburg in 1949, and kings up to 135 pounds have been reported from Southcentral's Cook Inlet.)

A mature chinook, when fresh from the sea, is similar in general appearance to other Pacific salmon, particularly the coho or silver, *Oncorhynchus kisutch*. It has a fusiform body with sides of bright silver, a deep purplish-blue back, white belly and scant, cross marks along its back and top fins. Distinguishing features other than its generally large size include an overly broad head and jaws (up to 20% of body length or more); a deep, somewhat compressed body and broad tail, with markings across both lobes. (This, along with a black gum line on the lower jaw, helps distinguish smaller king salmon from the coho.) Teeth on mature chinooks are well developed, especially in breeding males.

Spawning fish undergo moderate changes in physical appearance. Both sexes turn dusky red to copper or brown (sometimes with blackish or purple shading), while males develop hooked jaws, ridged backs and more dramatic markings/coloration. Juvenile king salmon are hard to distinguish from other small salmon, trout or charr, but normally have wider parr marks, tinted edges on the adipose fins, and moderately forked tails.

The flesh of a king salmon is usually a deep orange-red color, but can vary to pink or even white in some locations, depending on diet, time of year, and other factors. Rich and flavorful, it is prized for eating—grilled, fried, baked, smoked or canned—and ranks along with the red or sockeye salmon as one of the North Pacific's most valued food fishes.

RANGE, ABUNDANCE & STATUS

King salmon were originally distributed along the north Pacific coast, from Hokkaido, Japan to the Anadyr River in Asia, and from Kotzebue Sound to central California in North America. The least abundant of the Pacific salmon, they have historically been most concentrated in larger river systems (the San Joaquin-Sacramento River system of California and Washington's mighty Columbia each supported runs in excess of a million fish at one time). Today, king salmon are found in greatest numbers from British Columbia north to the Yukon River. In Alaska, chinook runs occur along most of the southern and western coasts, from Dixon Entrance in Southeast to Point Hope in Northwest, with the most significant populations occurring in the state's great rivers—the Yukon, Kuskokwim, Nushagak, Susitna, and Copper.

Though the chinook has not fared well throughout most of its range (the Columbia and other once-great salmon rivers of the Pacific Northwest have runs so depleted they are now under protection of the Endangered Species Act), its status in Alaska has remained relatively more stable. In recent years, commercial catches have exceeded half a million fish annually, along with sport harvests of 100,000 to 200,000.

The future of Alaska's wild chinook, along with the other Pacific salmon, remains far from secure. Overfishing, climate fluctuations, and a growing dependence on hatchery-enhanced runs (which now contribute a significant percentage of the commercial and sport harvests noted above—up to 20% or more in parts of Southeast and Southcentral Alaska) threaten the long-term viability of these last great wild stocks.

LIFE HISTORY & HABITS

Chinook are, in many ways, the most ecologically diverse of the Pacific salmon. They are the longest-lived, and can return sexually mature at anywhere from two to nine years of age, which allows them to attain the greatest size of any salmon (to 100 pounds or more). They also show the widest variation in run timing; within their range from California to Alaska, there are discrete stocks that return to spawn nearly every month of the year. In Alaska, chinook generally spend a year or two in freshwater as fry, then three to five years at sea, before returning in early summer to their rivers of origin. Their wanderings are potentially among the most extensive of any fish species, involving forays into the far reaches of the North Pacific and river migrations of more than 1800 miles (upper Yukon River).

Like all salmonids, Alaska chinook need clear, cold (less than 60° F. preferred) stream habitat for breeding and rearing. They begin active life from eggs hatched in gravel stream bottoms in late winter or early spring, remaining in the protection of the gravel as alevins for two to three weeks until the yolk sac is absorbed and they emerge as fry. Newly emerged fry feed on insects, plankton, and crustaceans. They school in pool edges, under cutbanks and around aquatic vegetation and logjams, for protection from predators and strong currents. Growing rapidly, they remain in streams until the spring of their second year of life (or occasionally their third year), when they "smolt up" and proceed en masse to the sea. Remaining close to shore these adolescent, estuarine chinook feed on small fish, crustaceans, and mollusks, rapidly increasing in size until they are large enough to venture into the open sea. Some stocks, particularly those found in Southeast Alaska, may spend their entire lives in protected inshore waters, providing the basis for year-round local fisheries. These are called "feeder kings." Others will make extensive migrations into the North Pacific and Bering Sea during their third year of life.

While in the open sea, chinook feed almost exclusively on other fish—particularly herring, sandlance, eulachon, pilchards, pollack, smelts, and anchovies—with seasonal binges on squid, crab larvae, euphausids, and amphipods rounding out their diets. Chinook salmon have been found in a great range of depths, from just below the surface to more than 300 feet, depending on the season. They are subject to the same predation as the other members of the Pacific salmon clan. Fry get eaten by charr, rainbow trout, coho, terns, mink, etc.; older fish in the sea are at risk from larger pelagic fishes, marine mammals (seals, whales and sea lions) and, of course, man.

A king's final year in the ocean brings a substantial size increase, and for Alaska fish this can occur at anywhere from two to seven years of age or more. Precocious male fish, called "jacks," can become sexually mature at age one onward and are a well-known, frequent phenomenon in some river systems. Generally, however, in Alaska, most returning fish are four to six years old. Mature Alaska kings begin entering freshwater in May (earlier in Southeast), with peak periods of river inmigration occurring in June and early July. Because of their size, they are inclined to move and hold deeper than other salmon and, in rivers, they can

Alaska's kings provide year-round, nearshore sportfishing opportunities throughout much of the coast. (See chapter on saltwater salmon for details on Alaska's ocean king fishing.)

better utilize the main channels and faster flows for migrating and spawning. They are known to linger in estuaries and lower rivers for a time in early summer, waiting for optimal tide, temperature, and water flow conditions before ascending. (Some fish even return to sea, then reenter a completely different watershed.) Generally, fish that show earliest will complete the longest river migrations, which may be considerable in systems such as the Yukon, where a significant number of chinook travel the entire river length to spawn in headwaters in Canada (a journey of nearly 2,000 miles).

Variations in run timing occur throughout Alaska, with some larger systems containing a variety of tributary habitat occasionally receiving more than one run during a season.

Early runs, dominant in Southcentral and the larger rivers of Southeast, typically occur in relatively cold, coastal runoff drainages. Starting as early as mid-April, these fish enter estuaries, with a peak inmigration between late May and mid-June, tapering off by late July. Common weight is 12 to 30 pounds, occasionally exceeding 50 pounds.

Middle runs are the most common throughout Alaska and usually occur in slightly warmer rivers and streams, such as those connected to lakes or lowland habitat. These kings enter freshwater in late May, peaking in numbers from mid-June through early July, with the migration ending by mid-August. Common weight is 15 to 40 pounds, but may exceed 60 to 70 pounds or more.

Beyond the Southeast Panhandle, most king salmon fishing is done in rivers, such as the Nushagak (SW), shown here.

Much less common are the late runs, known to occur only in a handful of larger, more temperate, lake-associated drainages. These runs typically begin in mid-June, peak from mid-July through early August, and conclude by mid-September. Common weight is 30 to 50 pounds, with some specimens up to 90 pounds. Some late-run drainages, such as the Kenai River, can produce kings over 100 pounds.

The timing of king runs in inland waters, especially those of interior Alaska, may be delayed considerably by extensive river migrations (Although considered early run fish when they enter the mouth of the Yukon River, kings don't reach Fairbanks until four to six weeks later, in July and August.). In addition, ocean-bright kings may appear as late as October in a few coastal areas that otherwise are dominated by early or middle runs.

Actual spawning in Alaska takes place predominantly during July and August (but has been observed as early as the first part of June or as late as November); and, as with the other Pacific salmon species, is instigated by the female's digging of the shallow nest, or redd, which can be quite substantial in size. Nest location is influenced by a variety of factors but, as noted, kings seem better able to utilize the larger substrate and greater stream flows of main channels, probably because of their larger size. The number of eggs varies from several thousand to well over 15,000, which are deposited in bouts of egg laying and male fertilization that may last for several days. As in all Pacific salmon, breeding is terminal, with rapid physical deterioration and death soon following. However, a few specimens may delay spawning by several months or survive the process only to re-enter saltwater and eventually expire in the sea.

In temperament, king salmon are generally more reserved than the rambunctious coho, though they certainly can attack prey and lures with great aggression at times. Probably because they are the least abundant of the Pacific salmon, kings tend to be not as social as the other species, so you are more likely to encounter the solitary individual in your angling efforts. Other chinook habits that are well-known and important to fishermen are their sensitivity to light and tolerance for deeper waters. In the ocean, they tend to feed during the darker hours of the day and move into deeper waters as the light intensifies. (They are generally taken by sport anglers at greater depths than other salmon.) Much of this behavior extends into freshwater, as they actively move up rivers during the wee hours of morning or late at night, and seek out deeper channels and holes during midday.

Alaska's King of Kings

World Record King salmon, 97 lbs., 4 oz.
Caught May 17, 1985, Kenai River (SC)

Living along the world's most famous trophy king salmon river for over 35 years, longtime Alaskan Les Anderson of Soldotna has had his share of big fish, but none to compare to the whopper that didn't get away that fateful spring day in 1985. Fishing with his brother-in-law above Eagle Rock, a popular hole on the lower Kenai river, Anderson hooked the behemoth salmon on a Spin-n-glo and eggs drifted along bottom. Using a custom rod setup and 25-lb. line, Les played the giant for over an hour before he and his brother-in-law were able to somehow beach it. Anderson's IGFA World Record fish, just shy of the century mark, has gone unchallenged now for almost 20 years.

FISHING FOR ALASKA'S KING SALMON

Sportfishing for the king of salmon is serious business in Alaska, with the annual catch approaching or exceeding one-half million fish in recent years. During the long, sunny days of June, armies of anglers flock to the state's major rivers, and fleets of boats ply the popular fishing drags along the coast.

In Southeast, almost all chinook angling effort occurs as a saltwater intercept fishery, targeting mature salmon bound for streams in Canada, the Pacific Northwest states, and other parts of Alaska. Major spawning occurs in only a handful of large river systems there—like the Taku, Alsek, and Stikine—with about a dozen or so lesser rivers supporting small runs of several thousand fish or less. Hatchery enhancements augment the fishery considerably in certain areas, and non-breeding, immature king salmon, called "feeders," can be caught in most Southeast waters year round. Most of the kings are taken by trolling from boats, with a very limited amount of shore fishing in certain locations; flyfishing opportunities are even more rare. (See chapter on saltwater salmon for details.)

Farther north into Southcentral are found the state's most popular and intensively managed king salmon stream fisheries, like the fabulous Kenai with its giant fish (to 70 pounds or more), and the clearwater tributaries of the Susitna and Copper rivers. There, most effort is spent drift fishing or back trolling from boats, with a significant amount of bank fishing in some areas. Saltwater angling for kings occurs in lower Cook Inlet, Kachemak and Resurrection bays and, to a lesser extent, Kodiak Island and Prince William Sound. The remote, clear-flowing streams of Southwest's Bristol Bay and lower Kuskokwim River hold Alaska's most abundant opportunities for shore casting and stalking the mighty king on a fly rod, although a significant amount of boat fishing occurs on the larger rivers like the Nushagak, Alagnak, Naknek, Togiak, and others. Farther north, the silty Yukon's substantial kings are usually intercepted in clearwater tributaries and sloughs, with sporadic opportunity for sportfishing occurring far up the coast, to Norton Sound and beyond.

Freshwater Methods & Gear

From the north Gulf Coast to Norton Sound, most of the fishing effort for Alaska's king of salmon involves drifting, trolling or casting lures or bait in freshwater. In the big rivers, this is most effectively done from boats, but significant innovations in gear and increased access to prime waters have made spin, bait or fly casting from shore more popular than ever. Here's a rundown on the most effective techniques/ gear:

Drifting & Trolling: Alaska's most deadly chinook lure happens to be nothing more than a bright, buoyant plastic whirligig, commonly called a drift bobber. Rigged off a swivel on a short section of stout leader with a lead dropper, and drifted along bottom, the bobber or Spin-N-Glo (as the most popular style is called for its spinning action and bright color) is deadly for several species of salmon, as well as for big trout and charr. For kings, the larger sizes (#0 to #4 and Super Spin-N-Glo) in bright fluorescent colors (chartreuse, red, orange, pink, and yellow) are the standard on all major Alaska salmon rivers from the

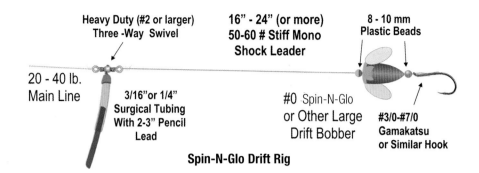

Heavy Duty (#2 or larger) Three-Way Swivel

16" - 24" (or more) 50-60 # Stiff Mono Shock Leader

8 - 10 mm Plastic Beads

20 - 40 lb. Main Line

3/16" or 1/4" Surgical Tubing With 2-3" Pencil Lead

#0 Spin-N-Glo or Other Large Drift Bobber

#3/0-#7/0 Gamakatsu or Similar Hook

Spin-N-Glo Drift Rig

Klutina to the Unalakleet. The addition of flashy hook skirts, colored yarn, drops of fish scent or cured salmon roe (attached with an egg loop hook snell) considerably enhances their appeal.

Most Alaska river king anglers fish these drift bobber rigs from a skiff, drifting or trolling them off 25 to 75 feet of line, depending on water depth and current. Since the drift bobber is buoyant, it's nearly impossible to foul on bottom, and is effective fished slow or fast. The important thing is to have enough lead rigged to keep it on bottom. You'll see the rod tip twitch with each bounce if it is properly weighted. You also need razor-sharp hooks, as chinook have superhard mouths. Anglers generally wait on the strike until the fish takes the rod down hard, especially when fishing with bait.

Next to drift bobbers, plugs are the most commonly used lures on Alaska's king rivers; you'll see

034 Hot Shot

great boxes crammed full of them in guides' boats along the Kenai, Naknek, Gulkana and other popular big salmon rivers. Large diving plugs (like Magnum Tadpollys, Wiggle Warts, Hot Shots, T-55 Flatfish and K14-K16 Kwikfish) in colors of silver (with green, chartreuse, fire red-orange, pink or blue highlights) or solid metallic red, green, blue and chartreuse, are the most used.

Large, "flasher type" spinners like the Jensen Teespoon (size #5 and #6) or Skagit Special (size #6 to

Teespoon

#8) in hammered nickel, brass, fire red, chartreuse or rainbow blades can also be fished with great effect under the right conditions. They are usually rigged like a drift bobber with a lead dropper and short leader off a

three-way swivel, either alone or with bait like salmon roe. Dragging them behind a boat requires more attention than with a drift bobber, as the big blades will hang on bottom or foul if worked too slowly.

Back trolling is a very efficient and frequently used technique, particularly on large, fast rivers like the Kenai. For this, the skiff is pointed upriver, with motor, oars, or anchor used to slow or halt the drift, so that the lure is essentially working in the current with little or no actual movement. The idea is to probe the bottom much more slowly than in drifting, to better entice kings holding around structure or moving up deep channels. Drift bobbers, eggs, plugs, and spinners are the most commonly used enticements. They are usually rigged off a jet diver, a fan-shaped, plastic diving device that planes downward in the current when pulled behind the boat. (Plugs with deep diving lips—like Hot Shots, Magnum Wiggle Warts, and Tadpollys—can usually be fished alone, under most conditions.)

There are two ways to rig the jet diver. You can run it attached directly to the main line or, with a short piece of strong mono or bead chain, to a plastic slide on the main line. (The slide rigging allows a big fish to be played unimpeded by the action of the diver.) The large divers will pull a lure down 20 to 40 feet and are most commonly used on the deeper, faster Alaska chinook rivers like the Kenai. (They come in a variety of bright colors and can even be rigged alone as lures.)

Between 30 and 50 feet of line (or more depending on depth and current) is usually played out to reach bottom when back trolling. You can hold and wait for fish moving up the river or drift slowly down and probe bottom; either way will produce strikes. Note that most anglers will wait for the fish to bury the rod tip before setting the hook. If you back troll with plugs, always check the action of your rig beforehand,

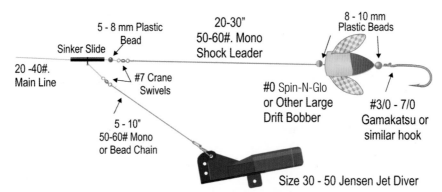

Back Trolling Rig

to ensure that your lure is swimming upright in a straight line. You may have to "tune" the action with a pair of pliers, especially if you are using a plug and bait combination. To do this, bend the eye on the nose of the plug to compensate for the direction of lean so that the lure swims upright. Adjustments can also be made on the eye holding the hook, if the plug is out of balance. Check the lure's action at fast speed.

Most anglers with little or no experience on Northwest rivers have difficulty imagining just how strong a big Chinook can be, especially in Alaska's big, brawling waters. To give yourself half a chance with these giants when drifting or trolling the state's big salmon rivers, use a heavyweight (rated for 15 to 30-pound. line), fast action salmon rod with plenty of power in the butt section. This should be matched with a high quality, heavy freshwater or light saltwater casting reel (made by Daiwa, Shimano, Ambassadeur, etc.) capable of holding around 200 yards of 17 to 20-pound test line. Use only the highest quality line (17 to 40-pound test mono or braided) and terminal tackle (swivels, snaps, hooks, etc.). Check frequently for wear.

Back Bouncing: Back bouncing is an intensive technique similar to back trolling that can be very effective in the slower water of deep holes or eddies. The boat is faced upstream and motored or anchored against the current. The lure is fished off the back, not passively, but with a jigging motion, raising and lowering off bottom and playing more line out as it is worked farther and farther away from the skiff. The rigging can be virtually the same as used for drifting, though many anglers use a shorter, stiffer rod, along with less leader and usually more weight (up to six

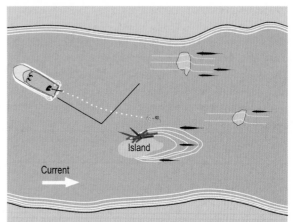

In back bouncing, boat is worked across and down stream using motor or anchor to slow drift. Angler uses jigging motion to bounce lure-usually drift bobber/eggs- along bottom into deep holding areas and around structure.

ounces or more, depending on current, and with a sliding sinker setup usually more efficient than swivel rigging). The boat can be slipped backwards in a strong current to help keep the lure on bottom. Drift bobbers, plugs, and eggs are most commonly used. Like in jigging, most fish taken by back bouncing will be hooked on the upstroke, so a quick and powerful motion is required and hooks must be kept razor-sharp by frequent honing or replacement.

Shore Casting: Under the right conditions, casting and working lures from shore can be a more productive and enjoyable way of fishing Alaska's river kings. On smaller, shallower waters like the clearwater tributaries of the Susitna, the Karluk River in Kodiak, Kenai's Anchor, or some of the salmon rivers in Southwest, a considerable percentage of anglers prefer to stalk king salmon this way, using lighter tackle.

For this kind of fishing, lighter, longer, more moderate action rods than those used for drifting/back trolling are matched to medium salmon or heavy steelhead class reels loaded with 12 to 17-pound test line. Large, well-balanced spinners (like the Super Vibrax, Bolo, or Mepps Giant Killer), or spoons (like big Pixees, Krocodiles or Hotrods) in silver or gold with bright highlights (yellow, red, chartreuse, orange, pink, green) cast well with the lighter gear and are very effective, along with plugs (like small Hotshots, Tadpollys and Rapalas), in similar colors. A rigged drift bobber can also be fished from shore, using "quartering" casts upstream and steady retrieve to reel in slack as the rig bounces along bottom. (You can prolong the drift considerably by walking downstream as you reel, if conditions allow.) Side planers can also be used to work the main channel from shore.

The trick is to fish slowly and deeply, right above bottom. Depending on the current, depth, and lure used, additional weight may be required in the way of rubber core sinkers (1/4 to 1/2 ounce) attached above the lure, or a lead dropper rigged off a swivel, the same as for fishing a drift bobber.

Likely areas to target are stream mouths, confluences, pools, sloughs, cutbanks, drop-offs, behind islands, etc., anywhere the big fish might hold on their upriver migration. Of course, don't overlook the main channels if they are not too deep or swift. Keep in mind the tradeoff for this more enjoyable, light tackle fishing is that if you hook a really big king from the bank, there is the very real possibility of a downriver chase to keep from losing the fish.

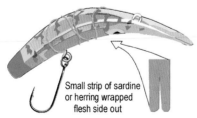

Small strip of sardine or herring wrapped flesh side out

Bait Fishing: In glacial or other turbid waters where the use of bait is still allowed, its effectiveness on kings is unmatchable, either alone or as an attractant on lures. Most anglers use cured salmon roe, herring, sardines, and even shrimp. Spin-N-Glos and cured salmon roe have perhaps taken more Alaska kings than any other lure and bait combination, but big spinners and even plugs benefit immensely from the addition of a "natural sweetener." A short strip of herring or sardine, wound flesh-side-out with fine thread to the bottom of a plug, is a standard enticement used by many Southcentral river guides. (Remember that you'll definitely need to "tune" the plug before fishing it in this manner.) Scented oils and other liquid attractants can also be used to increase fish appeal; they are usually applied to a short piece of bright yarn tied to the hook. (Be sure to check latest fishing regulations, including any emergency fishing orders, before using bait or scents with your lures.)

THE FIGHT OF A KING

Alaska chinook generally don't take as hard as coho or chums in freshwater. Frequently they'll pick up a lure or bait as they move upriver and you'll feel only a tightening resistance on the end of the line. For this reason, and because of their extremely hard mouths, getting a good hook set is essential. Keep your hooks honed to razor sharpness, and fish only super-strong, single siwash or bait hooks, size 3/0 to 7/0. When you feel solid resistance that might be a fish, tighten down and wait for a headshake or movement to confirm you are not snagged, then bury the hook with a hard upward jerk of your rod, tighten down and set the hook again. Then hang on!

Once the salmon feels resistance from the line, it will panic and make an explosive break (usually downstream) into the main channel. A fair-sized king in moderate current can exert an unbelievable amount of pressure and take you well into your backing in a matter of seconds, so you must act quickly to slow the fish before it gets too far into heavy water, if you can. Your drag should be tightened and rod held high to create maximum resistance during those initial runs, using a pumping motion to regain line whenever possible. You may have to follow the fish downstream if it starts getting away from you. This is an easy matter with a powerboat, but much more difficult for bank fishermen, who may be hindered by obstructions, deep water, or other hazards.

Drastic measures are necessary if the salmon takes more than 75 yards of line in moderate to heavy current, and you are fishing without a boat and unable to pursue downriver any farther along shore. Most anglers, at this point, will tighten the drag all the way, reef back on the rod and wait for the inevitable. However, some find that they can regain control by lowering their rod to horizontal and pulling laterally to steer the fish toward the bank, rather than trying to

Working the Aniak River (SW) from shore. Many of Alaska's mid-sized or small king rivers can be fished effectively this way.

lift and turn it from a vertical angle. Another last-ditch measure that sometimes saves a fish is to let off pressure entirely, until the fish calms and follows instincts to swim back upriver.

You'll need a large, strong landing net and a big pair of heavy-duty pliers (needlenose vise grips work best) for subduing and unhooking any Alaska kings you do manage to bring in. Fish you intend not to keep should be kept at all times in the water. (See the catch and release section in the Appendix for more details on handling/releasing trout and salmon.) Any badly bleeding or overly fatigued salmon should be kept.

FLYFISHING ALASKA'S RIVER KINGS

Hooking and landing the king of salmon on a fly-rod is one of angling's great accomplishments. The development of high performance gear, along with continued exploration and experimentation by guides and serious sport anglers has opened opportunities that were unheard of not too long ago. Though landing one of these brutes with a long, limber stick is certainly just as much a feat as it's ever been, at least today it can be done with some regularity.

Ideally, your best chances of hooking an Alaska king on a fly are in productive salmon streams with fairly clear, not too deep or swift water, preferably close to the sea. (The closer to salt, the brighter and more aggressive the salmon.) The best areas will be in accessible holding water—river mouths and confluences, small pools, tailouts, edges of sloughs, under cutbanks, ledge pools, behind islands, etc. Keep in mind that kings usually don't have any problem moving up through the main channel, so any water that isn't too deep or fast should be considered.

The greatest challenge for the flyfisher is to have the proper line, rigging, and presentation to put the fly in front of the noses of the bottom-hugging kings in the wide variety of conditions typically encountered on Alaska's rivers. In shallow waters (six feet or less) of slow to moderate current, this usually involves fishing a weight forward floating or intermediate line and 7 to 9-foot leader, with perhaps some additional weight in the form of a split shot or two. Deeper and/or faster waters will require sinking lines and shorter leaders (see next section and accompanying illustrations for details).

Locating fish by sight is preferred, but certainly not always possible in most Alaska waters. Far more common is to look for signs of showing fish, or to just fish blindly, in likely holding areas like those described. Most of the time you won't have to make elaborate casts; just a 20 to 50-foot lob and a basic streamer swing and strip, only slower and deeper. It cannot be stressed enough that the single most important thing in flyfishing kings is to present the fly at the proper depth and speed, for kings will seldom pursue an enticement very far and almost never if it passes any distance above them in the water column. Use a short, slow strip for retrieve in most situations, along with weighted flies, sinking leaders and, if need be, split shot or wrap lead to help get the fly down to proper depth. On your sinking line presentations, you can keep your leader/tippet length short (four to five feet, or even less), as kings are not leader shy.

King salmon on a fly, Kenai River (SC).

In most Alaska rivers in early summer, holding water may contain a mix of salmon—sockeyes, chums, and kings, quite often in that order of abundance (along with scattered charr, rainbow trout, and perhaps even grayling). Your king fly may attract some of these accompanying species so, unless you are sight fishing or working the main channel of large, fast rivers, be prepared for incidental hookups before you get a chance at your intended quarry.

The take of a king on a fly in fresh water can vary, from a bump that might be mistaken for bottom, to a hard strike that sets your heart thumping, but, generally, kings are not very aggressive takers. They develop very hard mouths once they enter fresh water, so you must keep razor-sharp hooks and use a very hard set when you feel a fish. A fly has a definite advantage over hardware in its holding ability, with little mass to aid the fish in throwing the hook. It almost goes without saying that high quality line and leaders/tippets, strong hooks, and sound knots are essential to your success in these challenging conditions. (You'll want to check and maintain those terminal components frequently because of the abuse they sustain from the fish and river bottom.)

Fatigue in the wrist and forearm is a major limiting factor for fly anglers waving big sticks and giant flies. Having lightweight, high performance gear and knowing how to cast properly and play big fish effectively will go a long way in alleviating cramping and soreness. Two-handed Spey rods, more difficult to master than conventional gear, allow for less tiresome casting, more line control, and greater leverage on the fish, advantages that can make flyfishing these big salmon much more enjoyable and productive.

Gearing up for flyfishing Alaska's river kings

For flyfishing kings in Alaska's rivers, you'll need sturdy, high quality gear. For rods, that means a high performance, ten or eleven-weight (or twelve-weight for fishing deep, fast waters or for trophy fish), medium-fast action, heavy salmon or medium saltwater fly rod, 9 to 10 feet long, with a fighting butt section. Match that with a large salmon or tarpon class fly reel capable of holding the line, plus a minimum of 150 yards of 30-pound backing. Two-handed Spey rods, 10 to 12-weight, 13 to 15 feet long, are also used with increasing frequency on Alaska's larger king rivers. A minimum of three basic line setups will get you through most of the conditions you'll encounter: a weight forward, high performance taper, full float line; a short (5 to 15 feet), medium density (Type 3 to 4) sink tip; and a high density (350 to 550 grain), sinking line (24 to 30 feet tip) for extreme conditions. Interchangeable tip systems and shooting heads are versatile, economic alternatives to carrying extra reels and/or spools.

A versatile, effective leader/tippet system (see illustration) for flyfishing kings in most Alaska river situations can be fashioned from high quality, stiff but flexible, low stretch monofilament (for proper presentation, abrasion resistance and good hook setting). Those without time or inclination can choose from a wide variety of manufactured leaders specially designed for fishing big salmon, in lengths of 6 to 9 feet, and tippets from 12 to 22 pounds.

King salmon flies developed on some of the state's more popular salmon rivers have traditionally been big, gaudy creations of marabou, mylar, chenille and tinsel tied on super-sharp, strong hooks, size 2 to 3/0, in colors of bright cerise, orange, pink, yellow, chartreuse, green, and purple. The more commonly used and most productive are large marabou flies (Alaskabou, Popsicle, Showgirl, etc.); oversize versions of common attractor patterns like Flash Fly, Wiggletails, Polar Shrimp, Egg Sucking Leech, etc.; giant egg/flesh flies (King Caviar, King Killer, Bunny Bug); oversize leech or leech-like patterns (Bunny Leech, Zonkers, Matukas, etc.); versatile saltwater patterns like the Clouser Minnow and Lefty's Deceiver; gaudy Tarpon-tied streamers like the Outrageous; and classic saltwater forage patterns like the Herring Fly, Candlefish, and Shrimp. For shallower, clear water streams like the Kanektok, Goodnews, Karluk, etc., king patterns of more subdued size and color are more useful.

A strong set of pliers and sturdy landing net are essential

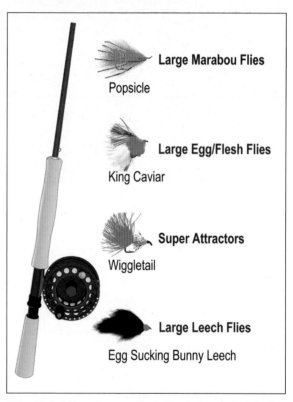

Large Marabou Flies
Popsicle

Large Egg/Flesh Flies
King Caviar

Super Attractors
Wiggletail

Large Leech Flies
Egg Sucking Bunny Leech

Taking Alaska's king salmon on a fly requires stout gear: a ten to twelve-weight, two-handed Spey or single-handed rod with fighting butt section, matched with a heavy salmon or tarpon class reel loaded with sufficient backing and the appropriate floating or medium to high density sink line. Large marabou, attractor and egg/flesh flies are the traditional enticements.

Alaska's Best Rivers for Flyfishing Kings

Goodnews (SW); Kanektok River (SW); Arolik (SW); Karluk (SC); Ayakulik (SC); Talachulitna (SC).

Top Fly Patterns for Alaska Kings

Leech (Egg Sucking, Bunny, Strip, etc.), Zonker, Popsicle, Alaskabou, Herring Fly, Wiggletail, Outrageous, King Caviar, Deceiver, Bunny Fly, Flash Fly, Everglow, Alaska Candlefish, Seaducer, Clouser Minnow, Shrimp, Tarpon Fly.

Top Ten Alaska Trophy King Salmon

97 lbs., 4 oz.	Kenai River (SC)	1985
95 lbs., 10 oz.	Kenai River (SC)	1990
93 lbs.	Kelp Bay (SE)	1977
92 lbs., 4 oz.	Kenai River (SC)	1985
91 lbs., 10 oz.	Kenai River (SC)	1988
91 lbs., 4 oz.	Kenai River (SC)	1987
91 lbs.	Kenai River (SC)	1995
90 lbs., 4 oz.	Kenai River (SC)	1995
89 lbs., 4 oz.	Kenai River (SC)	2002
89 lbs., 3 oz.	Kenai River (SC)	1989

Alaska King Salmon Trophy Timing

Kenai River (SC)	mid-late July
Cook Inlet (SC)	late June–mid-July
Willow Creek (SC)	mid-June–early July
Klutina River (SC)	mid-late July
Kasilof River (SC)	mid-late July
Talkeetna River (SC)	late June–early July
Lake Creek (SC)	mid-June–early July
Salisbury Sound/Peril Strait(SE)	mid-May–mid-June
Sitka Sound (SE)	mid-May–mid-June
Eastern Frederick Sound (SE)	late May–late June
Eastern Passage (SE)	mid-May–mid-July
Gulf of Esquibel (SE)	mid-May–early July
Bucareli Bay (SE)	mid-May–early July
Revillagigedo Channel (SE)	early-late June

Simple Leader Setups for Alaska King Salmon

For six feet of water or less, slow to moderate current. Additional weight (split shot, wrap lead, etc.) may be needed to get fly down to bottom.

For deeper water (to 12'), slow to moderate current. Use 5-12 foot tip, medium density (Type III-V); keep leaders short, fine tune with extra weight on tippet.

For Alaska's deepest and fastest water (lower Kenai, Nushagak, Alagnak, etc.). Use long (24-30 ft. tip), high density (350-550 grain) sink lines and very short leaders.

For trophy fishing in extreme conditions and tippet class fishing. No more than 12" shock tippet (last 12 inches to fly, any test allowed) or less than 15 inches class tippet allowed by IGFA.

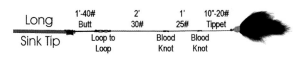

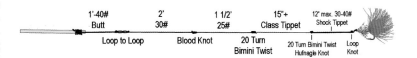

King Salmon
Oncorhynchus tshawytscha

SPECIES SUMMARY

Alaska common names: King, king salmon, chinook, chinook salmon, jacks (precocious spawning males); feeders or shakers (coastal immature).

Description: The largest Pacific salmon. Full-bodied, with purple-blue to black topsides, silver sides and silver-white belly when fresh from the sea. Irregular, small black markings on back, dorsal fin, and entire caudal fin. Black gumline in lower jaw. Breeding males are dusky red, copper or brown, with blackish shading, jaw elongated, teeth enlarged; spawning females less dramatic. Flesh orange-red to white.

Size: Average 18 lbs., length 32-36 inches; to 50 lbs. and 48 inches (or more).

State/World record: 97 lbs., 4 oz., Kenai River (SC), 1985, Les Anderson.

Habits: Aggressive piscavore; feeds, moves and spawns in deeper waters than other salmon.

Notes: Light sensitive; moves and feeds mostly in subdued light.

Meristics: Gill rakers 16-30; vertebrae 67-75; pyloric caeca 90-240; lateral line scales 130-165; branchiostegals 13-19; dorsal fin 10-14 rays; anal fin 13-19 rays; pectoral fin 14-17 rays; pelvic fin 10-11 rays.

Range: Coastal Southeast to Point Hope (NW) and all interior drainages except North Slope. Numerous introduced landlocked lake populations, SC-INT.

Preferred Habitat: Large, deep, extensive rivers for rearing and spawning; rich coastal and offshore environments for maturing adults.

Best waters: Large, clearer flowing, coastal river systems SC-SW; nearshore bays, straits, channels, points, islands, and canals, SE Panhandle to North Gulf Coast.

Best times: Immature saltwater fish available year-round; mature spawners freshwater peak May–July, later in north.

Best Bait/Lures/Flies: Herring, salmon roe; large drift bobbers, spoons, spinners and plugs; big gaudy marabou, egg/flesh, attractor, baitfish and leech flies.

Best Trophy Areas: Kenai River and Lower Cook Inlet saltwater (SC); SSE saltwater (Ketchikan/POW).

RECOMMENDED GEAR

Baitcasting: 7 1/2 - 8 1/2 ft., Graphite, medium-fast action, heavy salmon rod (rated 15-30 lb. line); matching heavy freshwater or light saltwater reel with 200 yds. of 20-30 lb. test mono or braided line.

Spincasting: 7 1/2 - 8 1/2 ft., medium-fast action, heavy salmon spinning rod (rated 12-25 lb. line); matching heavy freshwater or light saltwater spinning reel with 200 yds. 15-25 lb. test monofilament line.

Flyfishing: 10-12 wt., 9-10 ft., medium-fast action flyrod with fighting butt section; large salmon or tarpon class reel with 150 yards 30 lb. backing. Or 9-12 wt., 13-15 1/2 ft. Spey rod, matching Spey reel with 150 yds. 30 lb. backing. WF full float or sink tip Type III-VI lines or T-series, 350-550 grain lines, or equivalent, with heavy steelhead/salmon or tarpon leader, 12-20 lb. tippet. Interchangeable tip system lines for Spey rods.

ALASKA'S MAJOR KING SALMON LOCATIONS

SOUTHEAST

Sportfishing effort here is almost all a saltwater intercept fishery. Feeder kings are available year-round; mature, stream-bound fish, from mid-April to mid-July (timing varies from NSE-SSE; also, outside waters fish longer than inside for prespawners). In some locations, hatchery fish extend the season and even provide a few scattered shoreline fisheries. Among the many straits, sounds and bays listed below, each can have a number of concentration points for feeding and migrating king salmon.

Yakutat: Yakutat Bay; Situk and Akwe rivers.

Haines: Chilkat and Chilkoot inlets.

Skagway: Taiya Inlet.

Juneau: Lynn Canal, Favorite and Saginaw channels, Stephens Passage, Cross Sound, Icy and northern Chatham straits.

Sitka: Sitka and Salisbury sounds; Whale, Branch and Khaz bays; Peril and lower Chatham straits.

#3/0 King Flash Fly   Rigged Herring   #6 Teespoon   #0 Spin-N-Glo and Eggs   7/8 oz. Pixee Spoon

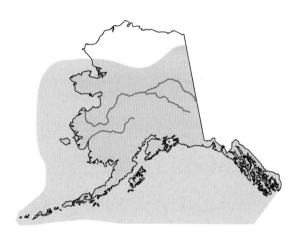

Petersburg: Frederick Sound, Wrangell Narrows/Blind Slough and Duncan Canal.

Wrangell: Eastern Passage (including Narrows and Earl West Cove); Stikine, Zimovia and Sumner straits; Ernest Sound.

Ketchikan: Behm Canal (Bell Island, Neets Bay, Helm Bay, Clover Pass, etc.); Tongass Narrows (including Mountain Point); Clarence Strait (Niblack-Caamano points, Vallenar Point-Dall Head); Percy, Ship and Skin islands; Carol Inlet, Herring Bay/Cove and Revillagigedo Channel.

Prince of Wales: Bucareli/San Alberto bays; Gulf of Esquibel (Heceta and Noyes islands); Dall Island; Lower Clarence Strait (Kasaan Bay); Lower Sumner Strait (Point Baker, Warren Island, Coronation Island).

SOUTHCENTRAL

Angling for chinook here is mostly freshwater, and includes the state's most heavily targeted, world-famous trophy fisheries of Kenai River and surrounding Cook Inlet. Feeder kings are available year-round; mature stream-bound fish from late April to late July. Some shoreline opportunities exist, primarily for hatchery fish. Run timing for freshwater fisheries is usually May into August; most locations peak from late May to early July.

Upper Copper River: Klutina, Gulkana, Tonsina and Tazlina river systems.

Kenai Peninsula: Lower Cook Inlet saltwater (Whiskey Gulch, Deep Creek, etc.); Kachemak Bay (Homer Spit, Halibut Cove, Seldovia Bay); Kenai, Moose, Anchor, Ninilchik and Kasilof rivers; Deep Creek.

Lower Cook Inlet: Chakachatna & McArthur river systems.

Upper Cook Inlet: Little Susitna, Chuitna, Lewis, Ivan and Theodore rivers; Beluga River tributaries.

Matanuska/Susitna Valleys: Landlocked (Matanuska, Memory, Prator, Knik and Finger lakes); clearwater tributaries (Deshka, Talachulitna and Talkeetna rivers; Lake, Montana, Willow, Little Willow, Sheep, Peters & Alexander creeks); sloughs and stream mouths of Susitna River (including Yentna River).

Knik Arm: Eklutna tailrace.

Anchorage: Ship Creek; Landlocked: (Jewel, Mirror, Sand, DeLong, Clunie, Beach and Taku-Campbell lakes).

Kodiak: Karluk and Red (Ayakulik) rivers; Monashka Creek and Bay; Chiniak Bay; Sitkadilak Island/Strait; Marmot Bay/Strait; Shelikof Strait.

PWS: Resurrection Bay, Passage Canal/Whittier Harbor (Shakespeare Creek); Valdez Arm/Harbor & Orca Inlet/Fleming Spit.

SOUTHWEST

Presently, with little developed saltwater sportfishing, this area has the state's most abundant, highest quality stream fisheries, with unexcelled opportunities for flyfishing. The run timing is June and July; peak mid-June to early July.

Bristol Bay: Alagnak, Naknek, Wood, Togiak and Nushagak river systems.

Alaska Peninsula: King Salmon (Ugashik), Chignik, Meshik and Sandy rivers; Nelson Lagoon system.

Kuskokwim: Goodnews, Arolik, Kanektok, Aniak and Holitna river systems.

Lower Yukon: Andreafsky and Anvik rivers.

NORTHWEST

Most drainages from Yukon to Kotzebue Sound support some spawning populations; only a few (in Norton Sound) are noteworthy. The run timing is mid-June to mid-July, peaking in late June or early July.

Norton Sound: Unalakleet, Shaktoolik, Inglutalik, Tubutulik and Kwiniuk rivers.

INTERIOR

Most fish this far inland are in less than prime condition. However, good fishing can be found in and below nearly every clearwater confluence and slough of the Yukon River. The run timing is late June to early August (peak mid-July). A few area lakes (Birch, Chena, Quartz) have stocked, landlocked chinook.

Tanana: Salcha, Chena and Chatanika rivers; Nenana River clearwater tributaries.

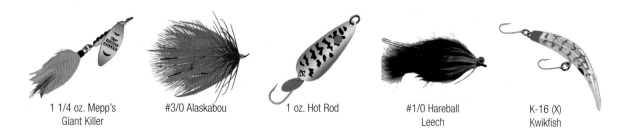

1 1/4 oz. Mepp's Giant Killer   #3/0 Alaskabou   1 oz. Hot Rod   #1/0 Hareball Leech   K-16 (X) Kwikfish

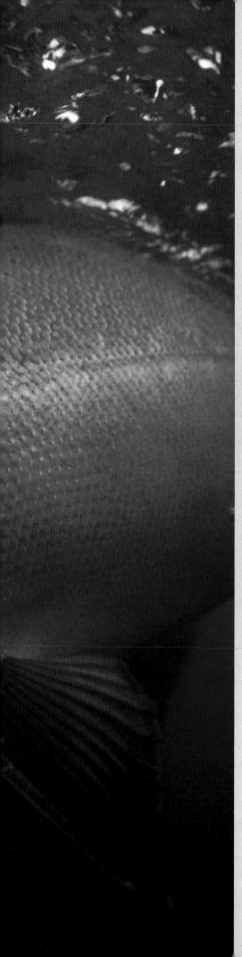

Silver
August Salmon

It is the height of the short northern summer, and fireweed stands tall as corn next to old Charlie Wassilie's gear shed. From this vantage point high above the Kuskokwim, he scans a landscape little changed since his ancestors' arrival eons ago, then offers me a chunk of smoked salmon and some of his thoughts.

"Fishing should pick up, soon—Freddie's caught some out in the Bay already—but with the river so low, I don't know. I remember when I was a boy, one summer we didn't get any until September."

Charlie's been busy these last few weeks, using this special lull time—when the rivers ebb with the last of the runoff and the big runs of king and chum subside—to fix gear, smoke fish and work on boats. He has faith that soon enough, Alaska's late summer rains will flood the rivers, and on the crest will come frantic hordes of salmon, pumping new life into the land. For Charlie and his people, the arrival of these last salmon of summer means the completion of crucial food stores necessary to carry them through the long winter. But for "gussocks," or white men like me, these fish have a significance that goes far beyond their food value. Silvers (or coho salmon) are the punchiest fighters of the entire Pacific salmon clan. Nothing gets the adrenaline flowing like the thought of bright, rambunctious coho, and the sweet torture they can inflict on a fly and an eight-weight rod. The show of these August salmon marks the end of Alaska's glorious summer—a bittersweet but exhilarating time for Alaska anglers and a call to embrace some of the best and last fishing of the season.

Silver salmon action, Tsiu/Tsivat River, North Gulf Coast

SILVER: AUGUST SALMON

The aggressive and acrobatic silver or coho salmon, *Oncorhynchus kisutch,* gets high marks from Pacific anglers, who pursue it with a passion perhaps second only to that shown for the mighty chinook. Found in great numbers along the coast of Alaska from Southeast to Norton Sound, the silver has traditionally been an important commercial and subsistence species, as well as the cornerstone of Alaska's fabulous late summer sportfishery. The arrival of these fish along the coast in late July kicks off a wave of excitement, as dozens of fish derbies get underway and countless sport anglers prepare for what many consider the high point of Alaska's fishing season.

A reckless and voracious predatory nature—important to its success as a species—is what sets the silver apart as a world-class gamefish. No other salmon takes a lure as vigorously or predictably, even long after it has stopped feeding in fresh water. And once hooked, the August salmon fights spectacularly, with long, hard runs and vigorous leaping. With big fish of 12 to 15 pounds or more on a fly rod or medium-weight spinning tackle, the battle can be one of freshwater angling's most challenging.

DESCRIPTION

The Alaska silver is a powerful, medium-sized salmon. When fresh from the sea, it has a steel blue, black, or gray back, chrome sides and whitish belly, with (faint) irregular black markings along the topsides. It can easily be mistaken for a small chinook, although a silver's tail is usually less forked, smaller and spotted only on the upper lobe, and the silver does not have the dark gumline of a king salmon. Like other Pacific salmon, silvers undergo dramatic changes in appearance once they enter fresh water to breed, particularly males. There is a deepening of the body, the sides darken and become imbued with dark red or greenish bronze and, in males, the head and jaws become enlarged (kyping) and shaded with greenish-black hues .

The third largest of the Pacific salmon, Alaska's silvers can attain weights of up to 20 pounds or more, though generally they average six to nine pounds (more in certain areas of the state). For many years, the world's largest silver salmon came from Southeast Alaska and the coast of British Columbia (up to 30 pounds); but recently, transplanted stocks in the Great Lakes have surpassed the largest specimens caught

In Alaska, silvers are found continuously from Dixon Entrance below Ketchikan, to Norton Sound, then sporadically to Point Hope (68 degrees north latitude), with their greatest numbers concentrated from Kuskokwim Bay south. The Kuskokwim River is the state's largest producer, with runs of up to a million fish in peak years.

This mid-sized salmon has a noted preference for short, coastal streams, and you'll find it at its best in the rugged, well-watered terrain of Kodiak Island, the North Gulf Coast and Southeast Alaska. (There are over 2,000 known silver salmon streams there alone.) Silvers in these waters routinely reach weights of 12 pounds or more—with 20-pounders not uncommon. Via the immense Yukon and Kuskokwim rivers, the silver salmon is able to penetrate the state's vast interior and utilize the abundant glacial gravels of the Alaska Range, spawning inland as far as tributaries of the upper Tanana River. Through intensive stocking and propagation efforts by the Alaska Department of Fish and Game (and other agencies), numerous landlocked, enhanced and "terminal" (non-breeding) populations of silver salmon currently exist, providing increased opportunities, particularly for urban anglers.

Even though enhanced runs now comprise a significant part of Alaska's total sport catch (up to 20% or more in certain areas, like Southeast), overall the status of the state's wild silver salmon runs remains remarkably stable. This means that anglers can expect to encounter some of the world's most productive fishing for the species for years to come, in thousands of rivers, lakes, and bays.

from the species' natural range. The current IGFA world record is a whopping 33 1/4-pounder caught in Pulaski, New York, in 1989, while the biggest sportfish caught in Alaska's waters was a 26-pound silver taken from Icy Strait (NSE) in 1976.

Besides providing some of the greatest sport to be had on rod and reel, silver salmon also make for some of the finest eating of any fish in the North Pacific. Their flesh is orange-red, firm, and flavorful, not as rich or as prized as that of the sockeye or chinook, but in many ways more suited for grilling, frying, smoking, or canning.

RANGE, ABUNDANCE & STATUS

Silver salmon have a potential range that encompasses most of the North Pacific basin, from Hokkaido, Japan (and scattered points farther south), north to the Anadyr River, across the Bering Sea, and south along the North America coast to Monterey Bay, California. Comprising only a small portion of the total Pacific salmon population (less than 10%) they are much more abundant along our coast than in Asia, and have had their range extended considerably through extensive propagation efforts.

LIFE HISTORY & HABITS

Silvers, like the rest of the salmon, have interesting life histories and habits. Hatching sometime in mid-winter, young coho quickly move into stream margins, side channels, and small pools to feed on small insects and plankton. Territorial and voracious, they display the same aggressive tendencies that will distinguish them as great sportfish later in life. (The small fry that congregate under cutbanks in most Alaska streams are usually coho.) Minnows, smolt, and even their own kind are subject to their depredations, and they can inflict serious damage on other important species like sockeye salmon and rainbow trout.

From data available, it seems that Alaska's silvers spend a year or two (rarely three) in fresh water, before "smolting" and heading to the ocean in spring or early summer (May to July). While at sea, they feed heavily and grow rapidly on steady diets of fish (herring, sandlance, smelt, and other small salmon) and invertebrates (crab larvae and shrimp), generally preferring the top 100 feet of the water column. Spending their entire ocean existence near shore or in circular wanderings far out into the Gulf of Alaska, Alaska's silver salmon mostly return to spawn at the end of their second summer at sea, at three or four years of age. A significant percentage of oddball age classes—precocious, two-year-old fish called "jacks," or five or even six-year-old fish—can occur at times in some systems. Timing and duration of runs in Alaska varies, as the fish seek optimum stream flow and water temperatures before entering fresh water.

Spawning silvers undergo dramatic physical changes—such as shown here—particularly the males.

Early runs commonly occur in cold, runoff rivers and creeks and fast-flowing mountain streams throughout much of their range. Southcentral Alaska has many drainages with early strains (such as the Northern Cook Inlet systems), in contrast to Southeast which has very few. Early runs also occur in Southwest, yet are largely non-existent in Northwest. These early-run fish may begin showing in late June, with numbers peaking from late July through mid-August, and tapering off in late September. Silvers of this strain are notably quite small on average, weighing four to eight pounds, with very few specimens exceeding twelve pounds.

The dominant strain in much of Alaska runs somewhat later, and is found in a wide variety of water, from coastal systems to inland drainages, especially marshland streams and waters associated with lakes and ponds. The Northwest, Southwest, and all of Gulf Coast Southcentral support these later summer runs, as do a good many areas of Southeast. Spawning fish from the Interior initially enter fresh water at the same time as these middle-run timing fish. The runs commence in mid-July, peaking from mid-August through early September, and come to an end by mid-October. Common size is 6 to 11 pounds, with fish up to 16 pounds; a few populations produce coho of 18 pounds or more.

Late runs are mostly associated with relatively warm systems consisting of large, deep lakes, streams with upwelling springs or ground seepage (as is the case in many rainforests), and sections of glacial rivers. Southeast has significant habitat capable of supporting these late runs, probably more so than any other region of the state. However, late runs are also common in coastal areas of Southcentral, particularly Kodiak Island. Late runs begin in mid-August, peak mid-September through early October, and usually end by late November. Perhaps as a result of favorable growth conditions of juveniles and adults alike, average weight tends to be on the heavy side, 10 to 15 pounds, with 20-pounders not unusual. Late runs are known to yield trophy and record specimens up to 25 pounds.

While these timing characteristics for Alaska's silver salmon are fairly accurate for most populations in the state, deviations do occur. There are true winter runs in a few locations. The Chilkat River in Southeast (best known for its concentration of bald eagles) is home to a run of coho peaking in October and November, with catches possible into January and February. Southcentral's famous Kenai River has a most unusual winter run, with a peak inmigration to the upper river in October and a significant component coming in strong through December. Bright fish are present as late as March in any given year, with spawning commonly lasting into spring (April). On the other hand, fresh coho have been reported in at least a couple of streams as early as May and June (likely anomalies). Thus, anadromous silver salmon may be present in Alaska's fresh water just about any month of the year.

Actual spawning usually takes place in late fall (October and November), but can occur as early as August or as late as January (or later) in some populations. Mating and depositing fertilized eggs in a manner similar to other salmon, silvers die soon after

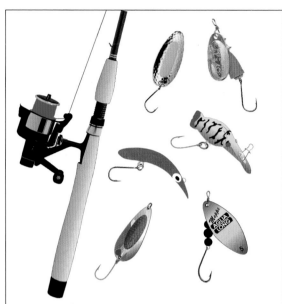

Gearing up for Alaska's silvers: A medium-weight salmon rod and reel combo, 8 to 15-pound test line and bright spinners, spoons, and plugs.

breeding, leaving some 1,400 to 5,700 fertilized eggs per breeding hen buried in several gravel redds.

While landlocked coho are almost exclusively the result of stocking efforts, naturally occurring populations are found here and there. These fish are most often blocked from exiting lakes or ponds in their migration to the sea and end up living up to two years or more in fresh water before attaining prenuptial coloration associated with mature adults. As silvers require flowing water (unlike kokanee) and complete physical maturity for propagation, the stunted fish do not spawn, with the population eventually dying off completely.

As is the case with other salmon species, silvers have a reputation for entering drainages for a certain amount of time before exiting back into salt water and continuing their migration to the stream of birth. Although these forays usually do not extend much beyond the tidal regions, some fish are known to stray several miles inland.

Generally more social than kings, but not as gregarious as the sockeye or pink salmon, prespawning silvers will congregate extensively in bays, river mouths, lake outlets, pools, and sloughs, and show themselves frequently, making easy targets for sport anglers. But it is their temperament and feeding behavior more than anything that is their undoing in encounters with the sport angler. Born bullies, young coho will frequently kill each other in their drive for food and territory. Their legendary gluttony inflicts serious depredation on young sockeye salmon, trout, and charr in rivers. Out at sea, silvers will commonly drive schools of frantic baitfish up to the surface in tightly packed balls, and, with chomping jaws, gorge to the bursting point. And when they gather at summer's end to begin their upstream migrations, they are at absolute peak condition and charged with a frantic sexual energy, which compels them to attack all manner of enticements with vigor, from bait to flashy spoons to spinners to flies.

FISHING ALASKA'S SILVER SALMON

Alaska anglers catch well over a million silver salmon each year, predominantly by saltwater trolling and freshwater spincasting, with most effort concentrated in Southeast (Ketchikan, Juneau, Sitka, and Yakutat) and Southcentral (Kenai Peninsula, Susitna River, and Kodiak). A smaller but significant amount of silver fishing occurs on clear-flowing drainages of the North Gulf Coast east of Cordova, in eastern Prince William Sound, and along the more remote rivers of Southwest (northern Alaska Peninsula to the lower Kuskokwim) and Norton Sound. Popular stocked, landlocked coho fisheries also exist in and around the Anchorage area, Kenai Peninsula, and Interior.

Freshwater Methods & Gear

Spin/Baitcasting: The vast majority of coho caught in the state's rivers and tidewaters are taken on spinning gear and hardware. With their amazing strength and spectacular leaps, they demand sturdy tackle. A medium-weight, medium action salmon rod, matched with a high quality spinning reel with a tight, well-functioning drag and premium quality 8 to 15-pound test line, along with an assortment of popular spinners, plugs, and spoons is the preferred armament from the Northern Gulf to Norton Sound.

More than any other salmon, silvers are suckers for flash, which explains why bright spinners and spoons are the biggest selling salmon lures in Alaska and the Pacific Northwest (over a million Pixees are sold each year to salmon anglers). Silver, gold, nickel/chrome, and brass, with attractor highlights of bright red, orange, pink, yellow, or chartreuse seem to be the most productive color combinations, in sizes ½ to 1 ounce. (Use lures with single hooks only; replace all trebles with super strong #2 to 1/0 siwash hooks.)

Because of their innate aggressiveness, silvers are more prone than other salmon to pursue lures through the water column, even rising to the surface on occasion, especially in tidal water or in the lower sections of rivers. Once in fresh water for any time, however, they tend to avoid extravagant expenditures of energy, so careful casts and slower retrieves generally produce the most strikes. (Remember these fish are not feeding.) When searching for good areas to fish, keep in mind that silvers, like all salmon, are best taken in the lower reaches of rivers and intertidal areas when they are still bright and at the peak of their strength, testiness and eating qualities.

In lower rivers, don't overlook main channel lies, especially in smaller streams, but give special attention to sloughs, cutbanks, eddies, large pools, feeder confluences, behind islands, etc., as silvers will group in these areas to rest and engage in prespawning behavior, making for concentrated fishing opportunities. In clear streams, locating and targeting silvers in these holding zones is greatly simplified but, in turbid or very deep water, the angler must look for showing fish or choose the most likely holding locations and fish blind.

In most stream and river situations, you'll be casting ahead of the lie from a slightly downstream to slightly upstream position. (In very clear or shallow water, use caution when approaching silvers, as they can be spooky.) With a steady but slow retrieve, work the lure deep through the most likely fish holding area, varying the placement and retrieve speed on subsequent casts to thoroughly probe each piece of holding water. If you are sight-fishing a salmon group, work the lure along the upstream or downstream periphery of the school, watching carefully for a response of any kind. Quite often, a "taker" (usually an aggressive male) will burst from the ranks and nab or pursue the lure. If you don't hook one right away, you may be able to with repeated casts, but don't flog the water. Silvers, especially those that have been in fresh water a while, can easily go off/on the bite, and working them too hard can put them down. (Be careful when playing any fish not to spook the rest of the group, especially in shallow, clear water conditions.)

Silvers will generally hit lures with more authority than other salmon, causing an unmistakable bump or tap on the line. (If you feel a hit but not a solid hookup, keep reeling, as quite often a silver will chase a lure and nip at it several times before taking it.) When you do connect, you'll need to bury the barbs with a good hook set, as silvers develop very hard mouths once in fresh water. (Keep your hooks super sharp with frequent honing.) When silvers feel resistance of any kind, they react reflexively with an explosive getaway burst, usually in an upstream direction, that can frequently launch them airborne, if there is enough pressure on the line. A big silver, if it gets in the main channel, can strip your reel with astounding ease if you're not careful, so it's important to have the drag set properly so that you can exert the maximum amount of pressure during those initial runs to keep the fish from getting away from you. (It almost goes without saying that you should check your line frequently for any weakening nicks and cuts, make sure your knots are tied snug and proper, and use high quality terminal connections like ball bearing snap swivels.)

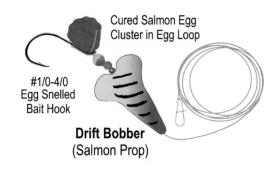

Cured Salmon Egg Cluster in Egg Loop

#1/0-4/0 Egg Snelled Bait Hook

Drift Bobber
(Salmon Prop)

Drift/Troll Fishing: On larger rivers like the Kenai, Naknek, and Alagnak, trolling, drifting, and casting plugs, drift bobbers, spinners, and spoons from boats is standard practice for silver salmon. For drifting and backtrolling, Spin-N-Glos, Lil' Corkies, Cheaters, Teespoons, Hot Shots and Kwikfish are the lures of choice, usually sweetened with bait (salmon roe), where legal. Rigging and techniques are almost identical to those used for king salmon (see the chinook chapter for details), except that the gear is lighter and smaller. A medium to fast action, medium-weight salmon or heavy steelhead casting rod (seven to eight-and-a-half feet long) works fine, mated to a high quality casting reel loaded with 200 yards of 12 to 17-pound line.

On Alaska's larger rivers like Southcentral's Kenai, most of the sportfishing for silvers is done from boats.

Bait Fishing: Fishing bait is still an immensely popular technique on many silver streams (where legal) as, under most conditions, a ball of roe drifted along bottom will outfish anything else, especially in glacial or turbid runoff water. Most egg fishermen use the conventional "egg loop" snell on a #1/0-4/0 bait or steelhead hook, fished with a lead dropper or rubber core sinker. You can dress things up with a piece of colored yarn or, even more deadly, a drift attractor like a #4 Spin-N-Glo. The bait is fished on a drift, keeping a taut line as the rig bounces along bottom. An increasingly common technique is for anglers to use a bobber and split shot for a more drag-free drift and better strike detection. Generally silvers will pick up roe gently and mouth it a bit before either spitting it out or running with it, so this fishing involves a higher level of concentration and finesse, but is potentially more enjoyable.

FLYFISHING ALASKA'S SILVERS

In many ways, the silver salmon is the Pacific Coast's perfect gamefish for flyfishing. More abundant and widespread than chinook or steelhead, they are quick on the take, very sporting, and great jumpers. In the quality and amount of angling they can provide over a wide range of conditions, they are certainly without peer.

You don't need expensive, sophisticated gear or fancy techniques to enjoy Alaska's matchless fishing for the species. A 7 to 8 weight rod, matching heavy duty reel, some floating or short sink tip line, 1X to 3X (8 to 12-pound) tippet, and some basic attractor patterns will work fine for most conditions in Alaska. For trophy fish and/or heavy current you'll want to bump up to possibly a nine-weight rod and some medium to high density (Type II-V, or 200 to 300 grain T-series) sink tip lines if conditions warrant.

A whole genre of Alaska salmon flies has evolved to capitalize on the silver's fondness for bright, gaudy patterns (not to mention the average flyfisher's fetish for colorful, artsy creations). Flash Flies, Sparklers, Maraflash Flies, Krystal Bullets, Flashabous, Silver Comets and the like vie for your attention and dollars at the local fly shop. They're all very effective on Alaska's August salmon, as are the more traditional Northwest patterns like the Skykomish Sunrise, Polar Shrimp, Coho Fly, Leech, and Woolly Bugger (all in sizes #2 to #6). What's more, most of these flies are easy to make and, with very little imagination and some practice, you can come up with original creations that are just as effective and much cheaper, not to mention the satisfaction you'll receive from hooking fish on your own hand-ties.

As with other salmon, the closer to salt water you can intercept the Alaska silver, the better. Bays and estuaries, river mouths, and lower stream sections right above tidewater are ideal. Farther up into fresh water, the silver's behavior, appearance, and gaminess begin to change. The basic approach is similar to that used for chinooks: deep drift presentations and "short strip" streamer swings through holding water—channels, sloughs, pools, confluences, eddies, and current seams—anywhere silvers might be resting or moving through. (Keep in mind that silvers usually move less through deep main channels than kings do.) Sight fishing individual salmon in clear water, with the more precise casting it allows, certainly is ideal, but not always possible—although sighting and working a school of coho is more realistic. More often than not, however, you'll be fishing blind. As in fishing kings, the most important thing is to get your fly down right above bottom, which may entail adding some split shot or switching to a denser line. (For greater effectiveness, you can shorten your leaders to three to four feet when fishing sinking lines, as Alaska silvers are not leader shy.)

As in spinfishing silver salmon, you should work each potential salmon lie thoroughly, especially if you know salmon are there, as silvers that have been in fresh water for a time might need some provoking before they strike a fly. When they do take, quite often you'll feel a bump or two before a solid hookup. As noted, they have hard mouths, so getting a good hook set and keeping your hooks super sharp is vitally important to keep them on the line when they start their sizzling runs and trademark leaps.

A silver caught on a pink Pollywog. Under the right conditions, silvers can be coaxed up to the surface.

Stopping a big silver salmon in moderate to heavy current can be a formidable task, so every effort must be made to keep the fish from getting too far out into the main channel during its initial runs. A high quality reel with a strong drag system is just as critical to your success as your fly rod, which should have a stout butt section to give you the power needed to control the fish. Most anglers fishing from boats use landing nets, but shore fishermen can do an adequate job beaching fish in shallows, especially if they enlist the help of a partner or fishing guide. As with all salmon, stout, large needle-nose pliers are indispensable for releasing the hook quickly and minimizing stress and injury to fish you do not want to keep. (See information in back of book on proper catch and release fishing techniques.)

During the peak of the runs in average streams, silvers can congregate in great numbers in good holding water, which quite often means abundant, exciting fishing for the angler lucky enough to be where the action is. But not always. They can get spooked and otherwise go off the bite for a number of reasons, especially in shallow, clear waters or when they have been in fresh water for some time. If you are fishing these conditions, be extra cautious when approaching and fishing holding areas, so as not to spook salmon, much as you would when stalking feeding trout. To get silvers to take in extreme clear or shallow water conditions, you may have to forego fishing during the brightest time of day (although dark or neutral colors—grey, black, brown, and purple may work very well at times). In contrast, during high, turbid flows, you'll want to tie on patterns with maximum color and flash—things like Wiggletails, Baker Busters, big bright Alaskabous, Zonkers, etc. that have a high degree of visibility. Sometimes with tight-lipped silvers, it can come down to changing patterns, retrieves, or even locations until you find something that works.

In recent years, an increasing number of anglers are targeting fresh-run silvers in clear lakes, primarily in or near outlet or inlet areas where schools of fish have a tendency to congregate. Although a variety of water craft can be used to access the more productive locations, float tubing is an innovative and exciting means of moving in on fish, with the ensuing battles often quite thrilling—especially if a hell-bent, late-run 20-pound buck should happen to get your fly stuck in its kype! Ideal lakes for float tubing are those associated with smaller coastal drainages, but any water body where silvers hold in numbers can be fished this way. Obviously, caution must be exercised on large lakes predisposed to strong winds or those with outlets leading to fast-flowing rivers.

Under certain conditions, silver salmon can be lured up to the surface with dry flies, a fact anglers quite often discover by accident. Shallow, clear waters (four feet or less) close to the sea are generally the most promising for enticing surface action, and the best flies are good floaters like the Irresistible, Bomber, Wulff, Elk Hair Caddis, or Double Humpy, tied large (#2-4) or specialty topwater patterns like Poppers or Pollywogs. (Some anglers even do well with shrew or mouse imitations.) Unlike flyfishing for trout, you'll want to use short, fast strips across the current, to make surface commotion and noise. (Remember, these fish are not feeding.) Techniques and patterns used for summer steelheading (such as skating flies, riffle hitches, etc.) would certainly work for raising Alaska silver salmon.

Bright colors work best to entice Alaska's silver salmon to the fly.

Top Flies for Alaska Silver Salmon

Flash Fly, Coho Fly, Polar Shrimp, Egg Sucking Leech, Woolly Bugger, Maraflash Fly, Krystal Bullet, Alaskabou, Comet, Skykomish Sunrise, Zonker, Wiggletail, Leech, Popsicle, and Everglow.

Top Rivers for Flyfishing Alaska's Silvers

Kanektok (SW), Goodnews (SW), Shaktoolik (NW), Karluk (SC), Talachulitna (SC), Tsiu (SE), Italio (SE)

Top Ten Alaska Trophy Silver Salmon

26 lbs.	Icy Strait (SE)	1976
25 lbs., 6 oz.	Prince William Sound (SC)	2002
25 lbs., 4 oz.	St. Nicholas Creek (SE)	1991
24 lbs.	Grant Cove (SE)	1986
24 lbs.	Uganik River (SC)	1995
23 lbs., 8 oz.	Yakutat (SE)	1981
23 lbs., 2 oz.	North Shelter Island (SE)	1974
23 lbs.	Italio River (SE)	1981
23 lbs.	Handtroller's Cove (SE)	1982
23 lbs.	Ahrnklin River (SE)	2002

Alaska Silver Salmon Trophy Timing

Kenai River (SC)	second half of Sept.
Uganik River (SC)	mid-Sept. – early Oct.
Pasagshak River (SC)	mid-Sept. – early Oct.
Situk River (SE)	early Sept. – early Oct.
Italio River (SE)	early Sept. – early Oct.
Kiklukh River (SE)	early Sept. – early Oct.
Tsiu River (SE)	early Sept. – early Oct.
Kaliakh River (SE)	early Sept. – early Oct.
Icy Strait (SE)	second half of Aug.
Cross Sound (SE)	second half of Aug.
Sitka Sound (SE)	mid-Aug. – early Sept.
West Behm Canal (SE)	late Aug. – late Sept.
Gravina Is./Tongass Narrows (SE)	late Aug. – Sept.

SILVER SALMON
Oncorhynchus kisutch

SPECIES SUMMARY

Alaska common names: Silver, silver salmon, coho, coho salmon.

Description: A medium-sized salmon, similar in appearance to small king salmon, but less robust, with steel-blue/green back, silver sides, and a white belly. Has irregular black markings across back and upper lobe of caudal fin (none on lower lobe) and no dark pigment along gumline of lower jaw. Breeding fish duskier, with green on backs, blackish heads and red/maroon sides. Males have prominent jaw kype. Flesh is orange-red.

Size: Average 6-8 lbs., to 15 lbs. or more.

State Record: 26 lbs., Icy Strait (SE), Andrew Robbins, 1976.

Habits: Reckless feeder, especially fond of baitfish; easily provoked.

Notes: Similar habits and appearance to rainbows when young.

Meristics: Gill rakers 18-25; vertebrae 61-69; pyloric caeca 45-114; lateral line scales 112-148; branchiostegal rays 11-15; dorsal fin 9-13 rays; tail fin 12-17 rays; pectoral fin 13-16 rays; pelvic fin 9-11 rays; anal fin, 12-17 rays.

Range: Coastal Southeast to Point Hope (NW), intermittent in northern end of range; also into Interior via Yukon/Tanana rivers.

Preferred Habitat: Short, gravelly, coastal runoff streams for rearing and spawning; rich offshore habitat for maturing adults.

Best waters: Coastal streams and adjacent salt water, Kodiak Island (SC) to Ketchikan (SSE); also northern AK Peninsula (SW) to Kuskokwim Bay (SW) fresh water.

Run timing: Late July through November; peak August-October most of range.

Best Bait/Lures/Flies: Salmon egg clusters, plug cut, or whole herring; large bright spinners, spoons, plugs, and drift bobbers; attractor pattern flies.

Best Trophy Areas: NSE saltwater (Icy Strait, Stephens Passage, etc.); Kodiak Island (SC)—Pasagshak, Karluk, Uganik and Saltery Rivers; Italio River (NSE); Kenai River (SC).

RECOMMENDED GEAR

Spinfishing: Medium-wt. (rated 8-15 lb. line), medium action salmon/steelhead graphite rod, 7-8 1/2 ft.; high quality, medium-heavy freshwater spinning reel, 175 yds., 12-15 lb. test line.

Baitcasting: Medium-wt. (rated 8-17 lb. line), medium-fast action, salmon/steelhead backbounce/trolling graphite rod, 7-8 ft.; high quality, medium-heavy freshwater casting reel, 175 yds., 12-17 lb. test line.

Flyfishing: High performance, 8 wt., medium-fast action, 9-9 1/2 ft. graphite flyrod; medium salmon class reel, 150 yds. 30 lb. backing. Lines: WF performance taper floating, and Type II-V or 200-300 grain T-series, sink tip; 7-9 ft. leader, 8-12 lb. tippet.

ALASKA'S MAJOR SILVER SALMON LOCATIONS

SOUTHEAST

Angling for silvers here is predominantly by marine trolling. The Haines/Skagway, Prince of Wales, and Yakutat areas receive most of the freshwater sport effort. Runs peak in September and October. Hatchery enhancement accounts for over 20% of region harvest.

Yakutat/N. Gulf Coast: Yakutat Bay; Situk, Italio, Lost, East Alsek, Akwe, Doame, Kiklukh, Tsiu and Kaliakh rivers; Tawah Creek.

Haines/Skagway: Chilkat Islands, Lutak Inlet; Chilkoot and Chilkat rivers.

Juneau: Upper Lynn Canal, Favorite/Saginaw and Gastineau channels, North Stephens Passage, North Chatham and Icy straits, Cross Sound; Montana and Cowee creeks; Mitchell Bay System.

Sitka: Sitka Sound (including Nakwasina Sound and Katlian, Starrigavan, Silver and Redoubt bays), Khaz Bay, Whale Bay (Port Banks), Chatham Strait (all bays and points near salmon streams); Starrigavan and Sitkoh creeks; Plotnikof, Nakwasina, Katlian and Black rivers; Surge, Ford Arm, Salmon, Eva and Klag Bay lakes systems.

Petersburg/Wrangell: Ernest and Frederick sounds; Wrangell Narrows/Duncan Canal, Lower Stephens Passage, Eastern Passage; Stikine, Zimovia, Upper Clarence and Sumner straits; Duncan Saltchuck and Blind Slough; Petersburg, Kadake, Thoms, Ohmer, Anan, Aaron creeks; Kah Sheets, Harding, Kadashan, and Castle rivers; Stikine River system.

Ketchikan: Bushy, Caamano, Cone, Indian, Island, Mountain, Niblack points; Gravina Island (Vallenar Point, Grant, and Nelson coves, Dall Head); Percy, Ship, and Skin islands; Clarence Strait, Behm Canal (Yes Bay, Bell Island, Clover Pass, etc.); Fish, Carroll, Ward, and Ketchikan creeks; McDonald Lake system; Wilson, Blossom, and Naha river systems.

POW: Baker Island (Cape Felix, Port Santa Cruz), Coronation Island, Dall Island (Cape Muzon), Heceta Island (Port Alice), Lulu Island (Point Santa Gertrudis), Noyes Island (Shaft Rock, Roller Bay, Cape Ulitka, East Addington), San Juan Batista Island, San Fernando Island

| #2 Wiggletail | #4 Egg Sucking Leech | #4 Coho Fly | #2 Alaskabou | Rigged Herring |

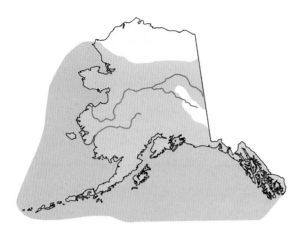

(Point Armagura, Point Cuerbo, Fern Point), St. Ignace Island, St. Joseph Island, Warren Island (Black Rock); Lower Clarence Strait (Kasaan and Thorne bays); Staney and Kegan creeks; Sarkar, Salmon Bay, Sweetwater, Luck, Red Bay, and Saltchuck lakes systems; Klawock, Thorne, Harris, and Karta rivers.

SOUTHCENTRAL

Southcentral has Alaska's most fished salmon streams. Run timing is from late July through October, with peak August and September.

PWS: Johnson Bay, Valdez Arm, Wells Passage, Knight Island/Passage, Montague Strait, Hinchinbrook Entrance, Orca Bay/Inlet (Fleming Spit), Passage Canal; Nellie Martin-Patton, Beach, Robe, and San Juan rivers.

Copper River: Tonsina River system. (Landlocked: Strelna, Jans, and Lou's lakes).

Copper River Delta: Katalla, Martin, Eyak and Bering river systems; Alaganik Slough; Ibek Creek; Controller Bay Stream.

Kenai Peninsula: Kachemak Bay (Homer Spit), Resurrection Bay, English Bay, Cook Inlet; Kenai, Moose, Russian, Anchor, Swanson, Kasilof, Ninilchik and Rocky rivers, Deep and Crooked creeks. (Landlocked: Longmere, Scout, Aurora, Elephant, Loon, Rogue, Centennial lakes.)

Upper Cook Inlet: Little Susitna, Chuitna, Lewis, and Theodore rivers.

Lower Cook Inlet: Kamishak, Chakachatna-McArthur, Crescent, Kustatan, and Beluga rivers; Polly, Silver Salmon, and Amakdedori creeks.

Matanuska Valley: Landlocked: Bear Paw, Carpenter, Diamond, Kalmbach, Echo, Victor, Barley, Finger, Klaire, Knik, Matanuska, Memory, and Prator lakes.

Susitna River: Chulitna, Deshka, Talachulitna, Talkeetna, and Upper Susitna (tributaries) rivers; Alexander, Lake, Willow, Little Willow, Montana, Sunshine,

Peters, Caswell, Greys, and Sheep creeks; Christiansen Lake.

Anchorage/Turnagain: Ship, Campbell, and Bird creeks; Twentymile and Placer river systems.

Knik Arm: Cottonwood, Wasilla (Rabbit Slough), Fish, and Jim creeks; Eklutna tailrace.

Kodiak/Afognak/Shuyak Islands: All bays and straits adjacent to salmon streams (Chiniak, Ugak, Uyak, Olga, Shuyak, Big, Discoverer, Neketa, etc.); Mission and Mayflower beaches (Chiniak Bay); Mill Bay; Portage, Danger, Deadman, Akalura, Olga, Miam, Roslyn, Malina, Marka, Pauls, and Salonie creek systems; Karluk, Afognak, Red (Ayakulik), Saltery, Uganik, Little, Dog Salmon, Terror, Zachar, Pasagshak, and Spiridon rivers; Chiniak Bay streams (Buskin, Sid, Olds, American rivers, etc.).

Shelikof Strait (West): Swuishak and Big rivers.

SOUTHWEST

Southwest has some of Alaska's finest stream-fishing opportunities The run timing is late July into early September, with peak in August.

Bristol Bay: Nushagak-Mulchatna, Wood, Kulukak, Togiak, Alagnak, and Naknek river systems.

North Alaska Peninsula: Egegik and Ugashik river systems (including King Salmon rivers); Nelson Lagoon system; Port Heiden; Cinder, Chignik, Meshik, and Ilnik rivers; Swanson Lagoon.

South Alaska Peninsula: Russell Creek, Mortensen Lagoon, Thin Point Cove (Cold Bay), Lefthand Bay, Beaver River, Volcano River, Belkofski Bay.

Kuskokwim: Goodnews, Arolik, Kanektok, Kisaralik, Kwethluk, Kasigluk, Aniak, and Holitna rivers.

Lower Yukon: Andreafsky and Anvik rivers.

NORTHWEST

Northwest's high quality fishing opportunity is limited to eastern Norton Sound and a few Seward Peninsula drainages. The run timing is from August to mid-September, with a peak in August.

Norton Sound: Unalakleet, Shaktoolik, Ungalik, Inglutalik, Kwiniuk, and Tubutulik rivers.

Seward Peninsula: Fish-Niukluk, Nome, and Sinuk rivers.

INTERIOR

There are a few notable opportunities for late fall-running silver salmon in Interior. Run timing is late August into November, with a peak mid-September to mid-October.

Upper Tanana: Delta Clearwater River. (Landlocked: Quartz, Birch, Chena lakes.)

Nenana: Clear Creek, June Creek, and Seventeenmile Slough.

3/4 oz.
Wiggle Wart

#6 Super Vibrax

7/8 oz. Pixee

#2 Woolly Bugger

#4 Spin-n-glo
and eggs

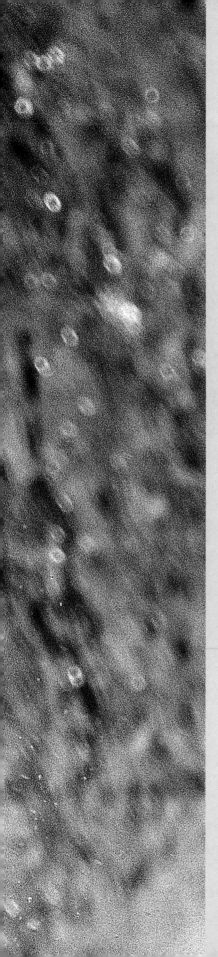

Sockeye
Shy Salmon

All along Alaska's southern coast, from Southeast to Kuskokwim Bay, a familiar scene plays out in early summer as bright hordes of salmon jam up the mouths, sloughs, and lake outlets of the major salmon systems. Far too numerous (and diminutive) to be that glamorous icon of Alaska's salmon—the chinook—these sleek fighters, with their sides of burnt silver and shimmering tails are a sight to behold nonetheless, for they herald the real beginning of Alaska's season of plenty and the start of some of the most challenging, but exciting, fishing to be had in fresh water.

Tyro Alaska anglers, confronted by the sight of so many salmon, will grab rods, tie on sure salmon slayers, and and anxiously heave their offerings into the swarm, confident of sure action. This is, after all, Alaska, land of legendary fishing. But they're in for a rude surprise, as they flail the water with increasing agitation and nary a bite. These fish, it seems, are not the least interested in their offerings, steadfastly refusing every manner of enticement. What gives, they wonder in amazement, as they systematically fling their entire store of lures and flies to no avail.

After a while, many give up in utter frustration, others resort to unsporting (and illegal) methods like snagging. But here and there you'll spot a few characters who seem to be getting all the action. They're using, of all things, strange flies you'll never see on any rivers down south, and rigging and methods that would make traditional flyfishermen blush. But boy, do they hook fish! And what fighters! These salmon catapult instantly when hooked, leaping repeatedly with such astounding vigor, they seem to defy gravity. Their explosive runs strip a reel in seconds, busting knuckles and parting leaders with frightening ease.

What's more, the joy of catching these crazed freedom fighters doesn't end when you drag one ashore. Their rich, flavorful, bright red fillets, grilled over a smoky alder fire, are a feast no king could best, and after a meal of them you'll have even more respect for Alaska's shyest, but fightin'est, salmon.

Sockeye salmon action, lower Togiak River, Southwest Alaska.

SOCKEYE: SHY SALMON

The sockeye or red salmon, *Oncorhynchus nerka,* is in many ways the most challenging and enigmatic of Alaska's five salmon for sportsmen. Prolific almost beyond measure in some parts of the state and extremely coveted for its flesh—the richest of all the salmon—the sockeye has long been the state's most valuable commercial species, contributing millions to Alaska's economy. But because of its steadfast reluctance to take a lure, for the longest time it was not even considered a sportfish.

Since they spend most of their lives grazing plankton, sockeyes are more predisposed to passive behavior than fly-shredding bouts of predatory aggression. But beneath that meek exterior and generic appearance lies an intensity and physical prowess that is truly astounding. Endowed with amazing energy—they are the strongest swimmers of the salmon and can easily leap 15-foot waterfalls—sockeyes move up from the sea into the far reaches of rivers with remarkable speed. More than any other salmon, they are creatures of single-minded purpose, possessing a supreme will to let nothing short of death keep them from their destiny upriver. Anglers who succeed in tempting this normally tight-lipped salmon are in for one of the world's wildest battles on rod and reel. With explosive leaps, mad, reel-smoking dashes up and downriver, and incredible stamina, they are, for their size, the strongest and most demanding of all gamefishes in Alaska, an assessment unanimously confirmed by all who have come away from their first sockeye encounter with bruises, broken gear, and battered nerves.

DESCRIPTION

Sockeyes display a remarkable uniformity of appearance throughout their range in Alaska. Millions come in from the sea averaging around six pounds in weight (8 to 12 pounds or more in large specimens; the state record sport caught fish, 16 pounds, came from Southcentral's Kenai River) and 24 inches in length, with streamlined bodies of metallic blue/gray/green on the back, silver sides and silver-white bellies. Prominent markings on the topsides and tailfins of sockeyes are almost always absent and this, along with the presence of 30 to 40 fine, closely spaced, and serrated rakers on the first gill arch, identifies the species. Sea-bright sockeye can closely resemble chum salmon. As the sockeye is predominantly a plankton feeder, teeth on prespawning fish are usually less developed than those on other salmon.

Spawning sockeye salmon present one of Nature's most striking images. The males develop vivid red bodies, greenish black heads, thick humps, and pronounced hooked jaws, while females are generally more subdued in appearance. Color can vary in intensity and hue in different populations. Juvenile sockeye have short, dark, oval parr marks usually terminating at or shortly below the lateral line. Kokanee, the landlocked form of the sockeye, are very similar in appearance, but much smaller, reaching about 10 inches average length and rarely exceeding one and one-half pounds in weight in Alaska.

Sockeye are the most prized of Alaska salmon for eating, with rich, red flesh of unparalleled flavor, whether grilled, smoked, or canned. Their value as a food fish, uniformity in size, and relative abundance have made them the most desirable and economically significant component of Alaska's commercial, subsistence, and personal use fisheries.

RANGE, ABUNDANCE, & STATUS

Sockeye salmon were originally found coastally from northern California and Oregon to Point Hope, Alaska (with scattered sightings in the Arctic Ocean) and in Asia from Hokkaido, Japan to the Anadyr River in northeastern Siberia. In Alaska, distribution is broadest in the large drainages of Southwest and Southcentral's Susitna and Copper rivers, where runs may be found as far as 250 miles or more from salt water. (Unique runs of the Yukon River system, like the Nenana River tributaries, once occurred as much as 1,200 miles inland, but are now thought to be at or near extinction.) The third most abundant of the Pacific salmon, sockeyes are found now in greatest numbers from the Fraser River in British Columbia to Alaska's Bristol Bay (and in Asia, in the rivers of Kamchatka). In the immense, lake-river habitat of the Alaska Peninsula and Bristol Bay, runs can number in the millions, supporting valuable fisheries and rich, diverse food chains. Important populations also exist in Cook Inlet, the Copper River, and isolated areas of Prince William Sound and Southeast.

Alaska's sockeye runs have fluctuated over the years, rebounding from depressed levels in the 1960s and 1970s to record numbers during the 1980s and 1990s. (Commercial fishermen caught over 63 million fish in 1993 and 1995.) Today's smaller harvests reflect more the economic realities of the changing world salmon market than fish abundance, with overall status very good for the future of this amazing resource and the almost unlimited potential it holds for world-class sportfishing.

LIFE, HISTORY, & HABITS

The remarkable success of sockeye salmon as a species stems from their ability to directly exploit the rich blooms of plankton in the North Pacific as a main food source, and utilize countless lakes found along the coast as nurseries. Because of the economic importance of this fabulous fishery, Alaska's sockeyes have been the most extensively studied of the state's salmon, and quite a bit is known of their life history and movement patterns.

Mature prespawning sockeye salmon begin appearing in rivers across the state in late spring with peak inmigration periods occurring in early to mid-summer. Their local abundance can be staggering, choking the larger river systems in the most productive parts of their range with numbers in the millions. As a general rule, sockeyes are found in rivers that are connected in some way with lakes, but some sockeye are adapted to breeding entirely in rivers or, rarely, in estuaries (these fish will tend to go to sea the first summer after hatching). Residuals—sea-run fish that for some reason spend their entire lives in fresh water

–and true landlocked populations (kokanee) exist in numerous lakes throughout Southeast and a few in Southcentral.

Like the rest of the Pacific salmon, the female sockeye digs the gravel nest, then mates in several bouts of egg-laying that may involve the digging of more than one redd and fertilization by several males. Up to 4,000 or more eggs are deposited and incubate in anywhere from six weeks to five months, depending on water temperature. Breeding is terminal, though fish may linger for weeks after spawning, despite pronounced physical deterioration. Young sockeye fry emerge in early spring (April to May) and usually migrate to the nursery lake by summer. There in the shallows, they feed primarily on insects and crustaceans before moving in schools to deeper waters to consume plankton in the upper water column. Some fry migrate downriver to the sea after their first summer, but most Alaska sockeye will spend two and, in some cases, even three years in freshwater before "smolting up." Smolt outmigration occurs in the spring, usually May to June.

Once at sea, young sockeye grow rapidly on diets of crustaceans, squid, zooplankton, and on rare occasion even small fish such as sandlance, eulachon, herring, and rockfish. Their deep ocean existence takes them considerable distances out into the North Pacific, where they usually complete two or three immense, counterclockwise circuits before returning to inshore areas to begin preparing for spawning. In open water, they generally prefer to be near the surface (less than 45 feet deep) a large percentage of the time. Ocean stay of Alaska sockeyes varies, but it is usually two or three years (rarely four), making the predominant returning age classes four-, five-, and six-year-old fish. Principal predators of sockeye in the ocean are whales, seals and man. In rivers and lakes they are preyed on by charr, trout, coho salmon, sea birds, eagles, bears, and man.

Run Timing

As with other salmon, timing and duration of Alaska's sockeye runs varies, influenced greatly by the temperature regimes of spawning systems. Early runs, found in the cooler drainages of Southcentral and Southwest, can commence as soon as early May, peaking sometime between early June to early July, and ending in early August. Fish size is fairly healthy, averaging six to eight pounds.

Sockeye salmon runs can be phenomenally abundant in the more productive systems, like the Naknek of Katmai (SW), shown here.

The most common strain of sockeye in Alaska runs somewhat later, beginning in early June, with a peak in early July through early August, and diminishing by mid-September. These populations exist in more temperate systems containing one or more lakes, and even some glacial rivers without lakes. Size can vary greatly, from four to eight pounds, with up to twelve pounds or more possible. (These runs produce most of Alaska's trophy fish.)

Late sockeye runs are least common, found in the warmer coastal systems comprised of smaller lakes and ponds or glacial drainages and streams with significant spring and ground seepage, from Southeast to Southwest. Lake spawning is a typical trait of late runs. Fish enter rivers and streams starting in early July, with numbers peaking from early August through early September, and tapering off in late October. Late run fish tend to be on the small side, averaging three to six pounds, seldom exceeding ten pounds.

Anamolous seasonal occurrences of sockeye are reported from time to time. Southcentral's Kenai River sometimes receives fresh-from-the-sea reds in mid-March, while March spawning has been confirmed at Long Lake (a tributary of Chitina River) in the extensive Copper River system.

Favored sockeye spawning locations are in stream outlets directly below lakes, in feeder creeks, and along gravelly lakeshores, with peak activity taking place in late summer and fall (August through October). In a few locations in Alaska, however, spawning may commence as early as June or as late as December (or later).

Spawning sockeye salmon present one of Nature's most striking images, with vivid red coloration, humped backs, and enlarged jaws.

Kokanee

Kokanee, or landlocked sockeye salmon, thrive in large, deep lakes with enough year-round food sources to sustain fish to maturity without warranting sea-run migrations. The fish are universally small in size, averaging six to twelve inches in length (depending on location), with rare individuals up to 20 inches and four pounds. Unlike landlocked or residual populations of king and silver salmon, kokanee are capable of reproduction and undergo seasonal prenuptial changes much like that of their larger, anadromous brethren. Breeding occurs in suitable lake bottoms or inlet streams late in the year (October and November). Although most kokanee populations establish due to a natural blockage of outlet streams preventing juvenile fish from migrating to the ocean, there are exceptions. In Kenai Peninsula's Hidden Lake, both sea-run and pure freshwater forms of sockeye may be found side by side.

Sockeyes have some unique and interesting habits that can be exploited by anglers. Along with pinks, they are the most gregarious of salmon, grouping by the thousands during upstream migrations, where they mill in estuaries, river mouths, lake outlets, sloughs, and pools, to rest from their strenuous journey. They also have a tendency to hug shorelines and utilize side channels and sloughs. Both of these habits make them especially vulnerable to predation (by bears and anglers).

Like the other salmon, sockeyes will show themselves quite frequently in fresh water, breaching and jumping as they engage in prespawning behavior. This is easily mistaken for aggression, and has led many an unknowing angler into futile bouts of casting. Their legendary aloofness is perhaps the most mysterious and exasperating aspect of their nature for anglers to comprehend. Standard hardware and conventional salmon/trout patterns, along with traditional techniques can be, under most conditions, totally ineffective. Until someone comes up with the magic "plankton fly" that somehow sparks a strike response from deep within the primitive sockeye brain, sport angling for the shyest of salmon will continue to be Alaska's most iffy enterprise, involving a special set of conditions, techniques and fly patterns.

FISHING ALASKA'S SOCKEYE SALMON

Alaska sport anglers catch well over a half million sockeye salmon each year. Almost all of these fish are taken in streams and rivers, from areas of greatest abundance, Southeast to Kuskokwim Bay (SW), but especially Prince William Sound, Kenai Peninsula and Bristol Bay. A limited number are taken in saltwater by salmon trollers (sport and commercial), incidentally or with special lures, flies, and techniques developed farther south in the coastal waters of British Columbia and the Pacific Northwest states. Saltwater flyfishing for the species is even more limited. Nearly all the consistent freshwater methods involve specialized techniques with streamer flies, with the exception of fishing for the landlocked kokanee populations, where more conventional gear and tactics are used.

Freshwater Methods & Gear

Despite their general unaggressive nature, sockeyes can, under certain conditions, be coaxed to strike. Commercial trollers and hardcore sport anglers down south experimented during the 1960s with various lures and techniques to come up with a basic methodology that was applicable to many northern waters. They found that certain spoons, hootchies (plastic-skirted jig streamers), streamers, and even bare, colored hooks, when trolled slowly and erratically, will draw strikes from red salmon, albeit usually not in great numbers. In some of the major rivers and estuaries of Washington and southern British Columbia, a thriving sport fishery for the species developed, using gear and techniques refined from some of these original observations.

In Alaska, for various reasons, sockeyes are fished almost exclusively in fresh water, using a variety of enticements/techniques, most of them similar to those used down south, but some unique to Alaska waters. On most rivers, sparsely tied flies of bucktail, yarn, or synthetics in certain colors produce the most results, although in a few areas, spoons, spinners, bait, and even colored sponge balls seem to work at times. Though no one seems to have any rational explanation as to why sockeyes will hit certain things in some areas and not in others, there seems to be a consensus, at least for fresh water, of the conditions that are most favorable for eliciting a response of some kind.

Best Conditions for Fishing Alaska's Sockeye Salmon

Fish Concentration: Dense fish concentration is perhaps the one factor common to all situations, both in salt and fresh water, where sockeyes routinely hit sport gear. For reasons obvious and obscure, sockeyes are more prone to strike when they're jammed up in great numbers, even though they lack a strong predator response. There's an undeniable stress factor at work in crowded waters that may trigger a reflex, whether it be feeding, aggravation, or territoriality. And since your lure passes in front of many mouths in these situations, your chances of a take are obviously much greater than in sparse waters.

Timing your efforts to coincide with the height of the runs, the tides, or commercial fishing closures, along with targeting the more abundant run locations, are the ways to maximize your chances of success by fishing dense fish concentrations. So too is an ability to read water and hone in on better areas. Some of the areas where sockeyes tend to concentrate in running water are lake outlets and inlets, river mouths, confluences, big pools, sloughs, narrows, and below structures like waterfalls, rapids, and islands. Not all the places where sockeyes gather will offer good fishing; only areas that also have the following conditions will generally have some potential.

Current: Almost all good Alaska sockeye water has moderately fast current. Despite what you may be inclined to believe when you see hundreds of fish jumping and showing off lake shores in productive sockeye systems, your chances of enticing them in dead calm water are slim, under most conditions. (Sockeyes will at rare times hit lures on the edge of sloughs, in lake outlets, and river mouths.) Fish that must negotiate current, especially when grouped in large concentrations, seem more apt to respond to strike stimuli, for various reasons (aggravation, oxygen stress, reflexive feeding behavior, etc.).

Water Depth and Clarity: Because of the effect water depth has on fish concentration, visibility, and fly presentation, shallow waters of three feet or less are considered ideal for fishing sockeyes. Water clarity is also important. Clear streams and rivers are preferred, as they allow for sight-fishing and precise presentation. Deep, turbid waters with little visibility are much more difficult to fish, no matter how many sockeye may be jammed up in them.

Techniques

Flyfishing for Sockeyes: Flyfishing for sockeyes in Alaska began in earnest during the 1960s and early 1970s on streams in Katmai and the Kenai Peninsula. The success of fishermen down south prompted Alaska river anglers to search for sporting ways of catching the feisty reds which, up to that point, had been caught almost exclusively by snagging, a practice the Alaska Department of Fish and Game was soon to ban in fresh water. Experimenting anglers had initial luck in certain rivers using sparsely tied streamer flies of select color and pattern, fished with a modified, tight wet fly swing. Over a period of time, some of these patterns like the Russian River Fly, Sportsman Special, Kenai Yarn Fly, and others, developed reputations as surefire sockeye slammers, and a new, exciting Alaska sportfishery was well on its way.

The question of what patterns and colors work best for sockeye salmon (and why) is something no two Alaska anglers can seem to agree on. But if you observe the action on some of the state's more noted sockeye locales, you'll have to conclude that certain patterns seem to take a good share of the fish landed. A lot of this, no doubt, comes from familiarity and reputation—what the local shops and "experts" are pushing and/or what happens to be "hot" at the moment. The important thing to remember is the basic principles that seem to work: simply tied, sparse hackle, yarn, bucktail, or synthetic streamer, or wet flies in colors of yellow, red, chartreuse, green, orange, pink, and white (mostly in sizes #2 to #8). With a little experimenting, it's easy to come up with your own sockeye standards that match or outperform the old "tried and trues."

Let us imagine the ideal freshwater sockeye salmon fishing location: a stream of gin-clear water, two to three feet deep, with moderately fast current. Thick schools of sockeye salmon pass continuously along shore. Here, spin fishermen should rig up with

Sockeye salmon fishing on the lower Kanektok River, Southwest Alaska. Clear, shallow waters, moderately fast current and heavy fish concentrations make for near perfect flyfishing conditions.

a rubber core sinker, split shot, or pencil lead dropper with a short 18-inch leader, experimenting to find the correct amount of weight to bounce along bottom and keep the fly drifting at the proper depth (eye level of the sockeyes). Flyfishermen, for most conditions, should use a floating line and 7 to 9-foot leader with split shot or wrap-around lead above the fly for proper depth control. (Extreme conditions may call for a short sink tip.) Whether spin or fly casting, the technique is the same—a modified, tight wet fly swing through a short arc (usually 90° or less) that puts the fly right by the noses of dozens of salmon adjacent to or slightly downstream of position.

Note: *Check the regulations for the waters you'll be fishing for rules on position of lead above the fly, use of weighted flies, and type of hooks allowed for sockeye salmon fishing.*

Presentation: Direct observation of countless sockeyes during river migrations will reveal that, under most conditions, it is a rare fish (usually one in a thousand, or less) that breaks rank even slightly for a lure moving above it in the water column. Any lure worked at fish eye level has the most chance of a take, but only for the brief moment it passes in front of the fish's mouth, for sockeyes only rarely pursue a lure in freshwater. For this reason, you must use enough weight to keep the fly drifting right above bottom and a short enough line so you have total control (no slack) over the drift.

Fishing only from shore, if possible, keep your casts short (15 feet or less is fine) to work only the water that lies adjacent to, or slightly downstream of, your position. Use a swing or flip technique to lob out the line in one quick motion, thus eliminating back casts and any possible slack in the line. Using your free hand to control the line, follow the fly as it completes its short arc downriver, paying close attention to the drift. If you are using a lead dropper, you should feel it bumping along bottom, otherwise you may need to add weight. When the fly swings to shore, flip it back up to begin the drift again and repeat the whole process over and over. (The entire cast and drift takes but seconds, and you should practice the movements until they become fluid and automatic.)

One of the hardest things for beginners to learn is the often subtle nature of the sockeye take; it can be very similar to that of a finicky winter steelhead—barely perceptible. That is why you must keep a tight

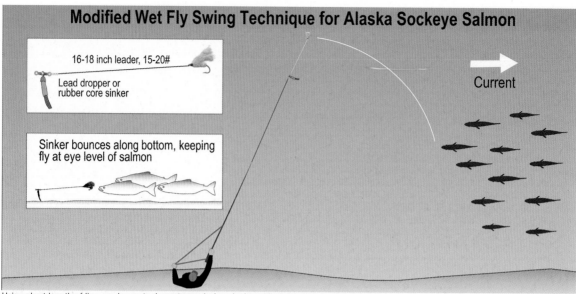

Modified Wet Fly Swing Technique for Alaska Sockeye Salmon

16-18 inch leader, 15-20#

Lead dropper or rubber core sinker

Sinker bounces along bottom, keeping fly at eye level of salmon

Current

Using short length of line, angler casts downstream (using single motion) at approximately 60-45° angle, then follows line as it swings toward shore at proper depth, through ranks of advancing fish. Using one hand on line to take up any slack, angler is ready for any hesitation or bump in drift that signals a possible take.

line at all times and your hooks "sticky sharp." In turbid waters where you cannot see the fish mouthing the fly, any variation in the drift might signal a response from a sockeye, so you should be ready to set the hook the instant you think a fish has taken your fly. (Since these fish are already on the move, they sometimes hook themselves when they feel the resistance from the line and shoot upstream; a quick upward snap of the rod and strip set should be sufficient to set the hook.)

If you're sight fishing in clear, shallow water, you've got a definite advantage in the ability to fine tune your casting and presentation for maximum results. Obviously you will not work any sections of dead water, instead waiting for groups of salmon to move upriver, or finding a more productive location. And since you know more or less where your fly is during the drift and what the fish are doing, you can be more selective in your response, to avoid foul hooking fish or bottom.

Once you hang a sockeye, the fun begins. They are incredibly strong for their size, and will generally do some rod-ripping runs into the main channel, punctuated with astounding leaps. Try to keep the fish out of the strongest currents, if possible, and don't hesitate to break one off if it is foul-hooked or too far into your backing, as a prolonged battle that exhausts the fish (and you) isn't sensible or desirable, given the

number of available salmon in these conditions. Most sockeye anglers use a medium sized salmon landing net to help capture the fish, which makes subduing and unhooking these feistiest of salmon much easier. (Fish you decide to keep should be killed immediately.)

Snagging/Lining

Given the concentrations of fish involved and techniques used, it's inevitable that you'll snag a few sockeyes in the course of a day's fishing, especially if you're fishing blind in turbid waters and/or using heavy lead. When you do, it's important to free your line as soon as possible. To do this, reel in all slack, point your rod at the fish, grab your spool firmly so it can't turn and let out line, then yank sharply while moving away from the fish. If you do this early enough before the hook becomes deeply imbedded, you can usually pull free. (Turn your face away while you do this, and always wear eye protection, as the stretched line can potentially whip back with destructive force, especially when there is some lead attached.)

If you watch the action on a busy summer's day on some of the more popular glacial rivers like the Kenai, Kasilof, Klutina, and others, it's difficult not to conclude that a good percentage of the sockeyes are taken by lining—where the fish are not actually hitting the

The rich, red flesh of sockeye salmon makes them the most desired commercial, subsistence, and sports species.

fly but being hooked in the side of the mouth as the line passes through their gaping and closing jaws. As a technique, it can be very effective and easily mastered, and many anglers have no qualms about "force-feeding" salmon when it comes to filling the freezer. Though these fish are legally hooked, no one would argue that this is sporting.

Other Tactics/Lures & Bait

If you don't have any luck getting sockeyes to hit using the technique just outlined, check your depth (amount of weight) and presentation carefully. Try different patterns or colors, smaller (to size #10) or more sparsely dressed flies if you have them. (Check with local sources on favored patterns for each location.) Sockeyes will mysteriously go on and off the bite or change preferences for no apparent reason, so you must be flexible and prepared to try different things, even changing locations if necessary.

In some waters of the state, usually river mouths, lake outlets or sloughs of semi-glacial streams, lures like Pixee spoons, Mepps or Vibrax spinners, jigs, sponge balls, or even bare hooks dressed with small pieces of yarn, will sometimes prompt takes when conventional tactics with flies fail to produce. In the slower, lower sections of some rivers, sockeyes will sometimes even pick up roe balls bounced along bottom. (A big split shot set about 18 inches in front of a super-sharp, #1/0 egg-looped steelhead hook, and fresh roe if you can get it, works best.)

Fishing Kokanee

To fish Alaska's diminutive, lake-dwelling kokanee, you'll most certainly need a boat, as most kokanee lakes are deep and fish populations are scattered during open water season. In Southeast, home to most all the state's good kokanee water, these fish are taken on a variety of flies, small spoons and spinners, jigs, and even bait. Kokanee rarely reach a pound in weight, so an ultra-light spinning or lightweight fly rod works best. Most are caught incidentally, while angling for more desirable species like cutthroat trout.

As feeders on small aquatic organisms, kokanee will school at various depths and locations through the season. Shorelines, bays, inlets and outlets, drop-offs, and islands are common areas to locate this concentrated activity, with the subdued light of early morning and late evening, or cloudy, breezy days most conducive to surface feeding. Once you locate schools of kokanee, try working a small spoon or spinner (like the Luhr-Jensen #0 Kokanee Special Needlefish, #1 Kokanee King or $\frac{1}{32}$-ounce Panther Martin) in their vicinity, fished right below the surface with an erratic retrieve. Experiment with different color combinations, lures, and retrieves until you connect with a fish (keep in mind that kokanee, unlike their saltwater brethren, have soft mouths, so set the hook gently). Flyfishermen should similarly fish small (size #12 to #16) nymph, midge, shrimp, or scud patterns, in orange, pink, or brown.

If no obvious signs of feeding are present, the best strategy is to troll a spoon or spinner at various depths through likely areas (mentioned above) until fish are located. Begin deep right above bottom and work your way up through the water column until you connect with a feeding kokanee, then stay with that depth and location as long as possible. A fish locator is obviously the way to go for these blind fishing situations. Like saltwater sockeye, kokanee can be extremely finicky and capricious, going off and on the bite without any warning or reason. (They'll sometimes hit only tiny bait-shrimp, maggots, grubs, scuds, etc.) Patience and experimentation are the keys to success.

Top Flies for Alaska Sockeye Salmon
Russian River, Comet, Brassie, Sockeye Orange, Sportsman Special, Yarn Fly, Sockeye Willie, Boss, Flash Fly, Supervisor, Sockeye Charlie, Mickey Finn, Coho Fly.

SOCKEYE SALMON

Oncorhynchus nerka

SPECIES SUMMARY

Alaska common names: Red salmon, red, sockeye salmon, sockeye, kokanee (landlocked form).

Description: A medium-sized, sleek, red-fleshed salmon with steel-blue, green or gray topsides, iridescent silver sides and a whitish belly. No prominent markings on the back or tail fins usually. Spawning fish are bright red with greenish black heads; pronounced jaw kypes and humped backs in males.

Size: Average Alaska weight five to six pounds, length 22-28 inches; up to 12 lbs. or more. Landlocked form (kokanee) much smaller.

State Record: 16 lbs., Kenai River (SC), Chuck Leach, 1974.

Habits: Gregarious plankton grazer; rarely aggressive.

Notes: Bright sea-run specimens may be difficult to distinguish from chum salmon, *O. keta.*

Meristics: Gill rakers 30-40, long, serrated first arch; vertebrae 56-67; pyloric caeca 45-115; lateral line scales 120-150; branchiostegals 11-16; dorsal fin 11-16 rays; anal fin 13-18 rays; pectoral fin 11-21 rays; pelvic fin 9-11 rays.

Range: Southeast to Point Hope (NW) coastal streams; small isolated runs inland via Yukon & Kuskokwim tributaries, with landlocked form (kokanee) sometimes found in lakes (common in SE, rare SC-SW).

Preferred Habitat: Moderately fast, clear, gravel bottom streams with headwater lakes and/or ponds for spawning/rearing; North Pacific high seas for maturation.

Best Waters: Extensive coastal lake and river systems, SSE-SW.

Run timing: June through August throughout most of range.

Best Bait/Lures/Flies: Salmon roe (rare); spoon and spinners (rare); sparse bucktail, yarn, or synthetic attractor pattern flies.

Best Trophy Areas: Kenai River (SC); Nushagak River system (SW); Brooks River (SW); Kvichak River system (SW).

RECOMMENDED GEAR

Spin Casting:
Medium wt., medium action salmon spin rod, 6 1/2-8 ft., with matching high performance reel, 150 yds., 12-20 lb. test monofilament line. Heavier gear/line for large, swift glacial streams.

Flyfishing:
High performance, 7-9 wt., medium fast action fly rod, 9-10 ft., matching salmon class reel with 150 yds., 30 lb. backing and WF floating line, 7-9 ft. leader, 12 lb. tippet. Use short (5-7 ft.) sink tip, Type II-IV lines for extreme conditions.

ALASKA'S MAJOR FISHING LOCATIONS

SOUTHEAST

Southeast has scattered opportunities that exist mostly in the southern Panhandle (Petersburg, Prince of Wales, Ketchikan), with quite a few kokanee lakes. The run timing is from June to September, with a peak in July.

Yakutat/North Gulf Coast: Kiklukh, Situk, Italio, Akwe, East Alsek, and Doame rivers.

Haines: Chilkoot and Chilkat river systems.

Juneau: Mitchell Bay system (Cross-Admiralty Canoe Route); Bartlett and Rusty rivers; Hasselborg, Kanalku, and Sweetheart creeks (Kokanee: Hasselborg, Jims, Turner, and Florence lakes).

Sitka: Eva, Salmon, and Redoubt lakes; Surge, Redfish, Ford Arm, Necker, and Klag bay systems.

Petersburg/Wrangell: Petersburg, Thoms, and Anan creeks; Kah Sheets, Stikine rivers; Virginia Lake and Creek (Kokanee: Marten and Eagle lakes).

Ketchikan: Naha River system; Wolverine, Smugglers, Sockeye (Hugh Smith Lake)and Ward creeks; Yes Bay. (Kokanee: Orchard, Manzanita, Wilson, Reflection, Winstanley, Ella, Bakewell, and Humpback lakes).

POW: Karta and Thorne rivers; Sweetwater, Sarkar, and Red Bay lake systems; Kegan and Salmon Bay creeks (Kokanee: Klawock, Sweetwater, Shipley, Chuck Creek, Sutter, Essowah, St. Nicholas, Hetta, Eek, and Kasook lakes).

SOUTHCENTRAL

Alaska's most heavily utilized fisheries occur here on the Kenai River (and tributaries), Kodiak Island and clearwater tributaries of the Susitna and Copper rivers. The run timing is from June into August, peaking in July.

Kenai Peninsula: Kenai, Russian, Moose, Kasilof rivers. (Kokanee: Hidden and Trapper Joe lakes).

Kachemak Bay: China Poot Lagoon.

#4 Russian River

#6 Yarn Fly

#4 Sportsman
Special

#8 Comet

Sponge Ball

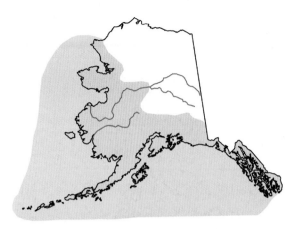

Cook Inlet: Susitna River system (all clear flowing tributaries with lakes—Lake Creek, Talachulitna River, Talkeetna River, and Chulitna River headwater lakes and outlets); Fish Creek (Big Lake), Jim Creek, Cottonwood Creek, Little Sustna River, Big River Lakes; Beluga, Crescent, and Little Kamishak rivers.

Copper River: Gulkana River system, Klutina, Tonsina, Tazlina rivers

Copper River Delta: Eyak River, Alaganik Slough, McKinley Lake, Martin River System (including Tokun Lake), Bering River system (clearwater tributaries).

Prince William Sound: Eshamy Lagoon/Lake, Coghill River.

Kodiak: Karluk, Buskin, Pasagshak, Uganik, Dog Salmon, Afognak, Saltery, Little, and Red rivers; Akalura, Portage, Pauls, and Malina creeks; Olga Lake system. (Kokanee: Pillar and Kotoi lakes).

SOUTHWEST

Southwest has the world's most abundant sockeye salmon runs—numbering in the millions in some rivers—along with the most perfect conditions for flyfishing, in dozens of great locations. The run timing is from June to early August, with a peak in July.

Bristol Bay: Lake Iliamna-Kvichak (including Lake Clark and tributaries), Nushagak-Mulchatna (including lower Tikchik Lakes), Togiak, Igushik, Wood (including Wood River Lakes and tributaries), and Alagnak river systems.

Alaska Peninsula: Many outstanding possibilities, most seldom fished due to remoteness and weather: Naknek (including all locations in Katmai); Egegik (including Becharof and tributaries); Ugashik, Meshik, Chignik, Nelson, Sandy, and Bear river systems.

Kuskokwim: Goodnews, Arolik, and Kanektok river systems.

NORTHWEST

The Northwest's fishing opportunities for sockeye are extremely limited, with only scattered occurrences in Norton Sound, and even rarer sightings in Kotzebue Sound. The run timing is from late June to early August, with a peak in July.

Norton Sound: Sinuk, Snake, and Pilgrim river systems.

Kotzebue Sound: Kelly River (Kelly Lake) of lower Noatak River.

Alaska Sockeye Salmon Trophy Timing	
Kenai River (SC)	mid-July–early August
Gulkana River (SC)	mid-August–early Sept.
Klutina River (SC)	late June–late July
Brooks River (SW)	mid-July–August
Kvichak River (SW)	mid-July–early August
East Alsek River (SE)	late July–early August

Top Ten Alaska Trophy Sockeyes		
16 lbs.	Kenai River (SC)	1974
15 lbs., 11 oz..	Kenai River (SC)	1989
15 lbs., 3 oz.	Kenai River (SC)	1987
15 lbs., 2 oz.	Brooks River (SW)	1993
15 lbs.	Kijik Lake (SW)	1980
14 lbs., 12 oz.	Kenai River (SC)	1979
14 lbs., 12 oz.	Koktuli River (SW)	1993
14 lbs., 8 oz.	Kenai River (SW)	1973
14 lbs., 8 oz.	Lynn Canal (SE)	1974
14 lbs., 8 oz.	Stuyahok River (SW)	1978

Sockeye Tips

- Wear Polarized sunglasses for eye protection and fish spotting.
- Do not wade into the water! Fish from the bank if possible. (Sockeyes normally hug the shore during upstream migrations and are easily spooked into deeper water.)
- Use chemically sharpened hooks and check frequently for wear.
- Use enough weight to get your fly down to the river bottom!
- Avoid blind fishing if possible. Target areas of known fish concentration, if fishing turbid waters.

#4 Sockeye
Orange

#4
Coho Fly

#6 Sockeye
Charlie

#4 Sockeye
Willie

#6 Boss

Chum
Bulldog Battler

Late June on the lower Kanektok River in Southwest Alaska's Kuskokwim Bay is as good a time and place as any to sample some of the state's finest stream fishing. Here, in crystal waters perfect for the fly, you can witness an amazing procession of Pacific salmon in numbers that few rivers this size can match.

Most folks who travel to this world-famous destination this time of year aren't expecting to have their big rods yanked, tweaked, or even snapped by a species that some barely consider a sport fish—the chum salmon. But in Alaska—land of surprises—where the obscure, medium-sized salmon is regarded as mere dog food in many places, these coastal waters hold bright, aggressive chums so full of energy and stamina that they frequently outperform the mighty king of salmon—the chinook—much to the amazement of all. Schooled in sloughs along the lower river, these silvery, husky brutes frequently slam flies meant for the big salmon monarchs, and provide fast-paced, incredibly exciting fishing action that has changed more than one fisher's attitude toward the "lowly" chum. Indeed, after witnessing firsthand the workout a rampaging chum salmon can put a nine or even a ten-weight through, anglers are apt to forget the great king and concentrate their efforts on the more numerous and sporting "bulldog battler."

A hooked chum makes a powerful surge into the main channel and puts gear and skills to the test. These anglers are fishing mixed groups of salmon—chums, sockeyes and kings—that move through the larger coastal systems (SC and SW) in early July.

CHUM SALMON: BULLDOG BATTLER

Many anglers get to know the humble ocean-fresh chum, *Oncorhynchus keta,* by mistake, and never suspect its true identity, thinking it instead to be a sockeye or silver salmon. The most underrated of all salmon species, chums are not highly regarded within the angling community for various reasons, none of which are based on truth. When hooked, a bright chum is capable of matching any battle antics the king salmon can dish out. They are strong and, when encountered in large numbers, tend to be very aggressive. Rarely performing the aerial ballet of a sockeye salmon, the chum instead will employ tactics more in line with that of a bulldog holding on to a bone—a tug-of-war equaled by none.

DESCRIPTION

Ocean-bright chum salmon may be difficult to distinguish from fresh sockeye or red salmon, since both species have dark greenish-blue metallic backs, silvery sides, and similar body shape. However, the chum's belly, in addition to being white, often has an iridescent silvery sheen. Also, some of the fins have whitish tips, and the pupil of the eye may appear larger. The wrist of the tail is typically narrower, proportionally, than on other salmon. Numerous faint, black specks may be present on the dorsal and adipose fins and backs of some specimens in select populations.

Spawning chum salmon develop yellowish-white to olive shading, with distinctive, irregular vertical bands of purplish-red, black, and white along their sides, while the head becomes dark olive with black shading. Males develop ridged backs and hooked jaws with protruding teeth, which partially accounts for their nickname, "dog" salmon. Females have a dark horizontal band along the lateral line and are generally not as colorful. The pectoral, anal, and pelvic fins all feature whitish tips.

Chum salmon fresh from the sea have orange or orange-red flesh. Like pink salmon, they are not especially prized table fare, due to the rapid deterioration of the flesh as the fish close in on their spawning grounds. (The chum salmon's flesh is excellent

A sea bright chum taken from a river, just above tidewater. Fish like this may be difficult, if not impossible, to distinguish from sockeye salmon.

eating on bright fish fresh from the sea, however.) But they are utilized substantially both as a commercial and subsistence species throughout their range in Alaska.

Second largest of the Pacific salmon, chums have been known to reach weights of 30 to 40 pounds and lengths to three feet in certain locations. Averaging 5 to 10 pounds, occasionally more, any fish over 15 pounds is considered very large in most areas of Alaska, with Southeast consistently producing the heaviest specimens (20-plus pounds). Chum salmon of exceptional size are also reported from parts of Northwest.

RANGE, ABUNDANCE, & STATUS

The chum has the widest natural geographic distribution and potentially greatest biomass abundance of all the species of Pacific salmon. Along the Pacific, it is found from South Korea and the island of Kyushu in the Sea of Japan, up along the coast of Siberia and Kamchatka over into Alaska, and then south to Monterey, California. In the Arctic Ocean, chum salmon are present from the Lena River in Russia, east to at least the Mackenzie River in Canada's Northwest Territories. Chums have also been planted in arctic Russia's White Sea, with reports of strays in the North Atlantic of Northern Europe, primarily coastal Norway. Throughout their range in North America, chum salmon are rarely encountered in any abundance south of the Columbia River and are most plentiful in Alaska.

Within Alaska, the chum salmon is known to appear along the entire coastline, being especially abundant from Dixon Entrance below Ketchikan,

north to Point Hope above Kotzebue. Major populations occur in every region of the state except the Arctic. Even the Interior has large runs—the Yukon River historically has runs fluctuating between two and nine million, possibly more in some years, although the last decade has brought dismal returns far below normal. Major commercial and subsistence fisheries exist in areas of Southeast, Prince William Sound, Kodiak Island, Cook Inlet, Bristol Bay, the Kuskokwim and Yukon rivers, and Kotzebue Sound.

Usually spawning within 50 miles of salt water, some populations commit extensive migrations: Chum salmon swim up the Yukon River through the entire state of Alaska into Canada to reach their spawning grounds near the Yukon-British Columbia border—an incredible distance of over 2,000 miles.

Of all the Pacific salmon in Alaska, chums have been the least utilized, except in certain areas of Northwest and Interior where they have traditionally been an important source of food. Though often viewed as nothing more than potential dog food by many users, chums are rapidly gaining recognition for their value as a commercial and sport species. Stocking programs to benefit commercial fishing fleets have become widespread in parts of Southcentral and Southeast.

LIFE HISTORY & HABITS

Beginning in spring and continuing through summer into fall, mature chum salmon begin migrating through the clear, blue waters of the Pacific Ocean and Gulf of Alaska toward the rivers of their birth. Age of the returning fish varies between two and five years (the average is three), with some northern populations as old as six or even seven years. Nearing inshore waters, the fish begin to congregate in schools or runs, according to which river they are bound for.

Once near fresh water, chums begin a period of milling that may last from a few days (if spawning areas are far up inland rivers) to several weeks (when spawning occurs in or above intertidal stretches of streams). The period of milling becomes shorter as the spawning season progresses. Entrance up chosen drainages concurs with high tides and often with rising water levels, such as after a heavy rain.

Runs peak from early July to early September in most of Alaska. The time of entrance, however, extends from early May to mid-December, depending on geographic location (runs generally occur earlier to the north and progressively later to the south). Runs called "early" and "late" locally are usually the "summer" and "fall" runs described by biologists.

Early runs are fairly common along coastal Alaska, being most prevalent in Southwest and Southcentral regions. Cold, run-off rivers and creeks host the majority of these runs. Timing generally lasts from mid-May to early August, peaking mid-June through early July. The interior of the state also receives early run fish, particularly the Yukon River drainage, yet these fish are typically referred to as "summer" chums due to their July arrival (it takes up to six weeks to migrate from the ocean to the upper tributaries).

The most common runs of chums occur somewhat later, from mid-June to early September, with a peak from mid-July through early August. Waters that receive these runs are found all along the coast, from Arctic to Southeast, and inland as well, and include run-off as well as lake-fed drainages. In addition, most intertidal populations fall under the middle run category.

Late runs are usually found in warm drainages of Southcentral, Southeast, and Interior Alaska, but are not very common. They begin in mid-July, peak mid-August through early September, and end in early October. Spring-fed streams and glacial river systems with spring seepages typically support late-run chums. The Yukon River in the Interior hosts late chums through the fall, with abundance peaking as late as November in a few areas.

Reluctant to cross barriers of any significance, chums are predominantly found in shallow rivers and creeks, one to three feet deep, with clean gravel bottoms and moderate current flow. As a rule, glacial or heavily silted waters are not preferred for reproduction, but commonly serve as migration corridors for fish bound for clear-water tributaries. (A few populations of fall-run chums spawn in main stem glacial rivers late in the season, as cooling temperatures halt the flow of silt from melt water.)

Summer-run spawners use mainstems of deep, fast-flowing rivers and streams, where the colder temperatures require longer time for egg incubation and juvenile growth. Fall-run chums commonly spawn in shallower, slower-flowing spring water that has more favorable temperatures through the winter and thus allows shorter incubation time and higher growth rates among offspring. There are also more subtle dif-

A breeding pair of chums prepares to mate on the spawning gravels. Note the distinctive marking of the male (foreground), with the gaping jaws and protruding teeth. The female (background) is less dramatic and displays a characteristic dark stripe down her sides.

ferences between the two races of fish, both physiological and behavioral.

Spawning peaks during periods of falling temperatures, from August to October throughout most of the range in Alaska, but may occur as early as July or as late as February in some locations. Similar to pink salmon, intertidal spawning of chums is widespread in many areas (mostly Southeast and Southcentral). Chum eggs tend to be larger than those of other salmon, and an average female can carry between 2,000 and 4,000. Eggs hatch sometime in winter and early spring; soon after (April to June), the young fry migrate directly to sea, much like pink salmon. Feeding on a variety of small organisms like plankton, crustaceans, and crab larvae, young chums eventually switch to a mixed diet that includes small fish. Size increase is greatest during the first three years of ocean life, slowing after age four. Due to the genetic variability among stocks, and varied habitat, chums from different areas differ in growth rate, age at maturity, and ultimate size.

Since chums are not hardwired to be aggressive piscavores, they are generally of more even temperament than their cousins the king and coho. Extremely social, they will group and mill considerably in bays, estuaries and lower rivers prior to spawning. It is this behavior, along with their great natural abundance and prespawning testiness, that make them such easy and exciting sport in Alaska.

Chums make ample use of Alaska's thousands of short, coastal streams, spawning in many areas just above tidewater.

FISHING ALASKA'S CHUM SALMON

In recent years, sport anglers in Alaska have caught around a quarter million chum salmon annually. Most of these fish are taken from the streams of Southcentral (Susitna and upper Cook Inlet drainages and PWS), Southeast (Juneau and Ketchikan areas), and Southwest (Kuskokwim, Nushagak and Alagnak rivers). A small number of chum salmon are taken in salt water each year (mostly in Southeast), incidentally by sport anglers targeting other salmon, with minor effort directed toward them exclusively. (Consult the Saltwater Salmon chapter for more information on taking chum salmon in salt water.)

Gearing Up for Freshwater Chums

Chums are frequently pursued using gear similar, if not identical, to that used for sockeye, silver, or even king salmon. A stout salmon or heavy steelhead rod and matching salmon class reel with strong drag are essential. Lines used will vary from 8 to 20 pound test, depending on conditions and size of the fish encountered. Because of the prominent, razor-sharp teeth that chums develop once in fresh water, a shock leader of at least 20-pound test is recommended, which

should be inspected frequently for wear. Needlenose pliers or vise grips are requisite for quick hook releases.

Freshwater Techniques

The Right Water: Many an angler who has fished for silver or red salmon during summer and early fall is familiar with the chum in its splendid glory of calico colors. These spawners are usually quite aggressive, and can even be a nuisance when encountered in large numbers—especially when other, more desirable species (like coho or rainbows) are around. But few anglers who have fished around Alaska will argue that the chum, when fresh in on the tide, chrome-flanked and full of sea lice, isn't every bit the equal in sport of his cousins that get all the attention.

The brightest fish and best action for the species occurs in early and mid-summer in the major coastal drainages, the closer to salt the better. As chums like the intertidal zone and lower reaches of rivers, you'll encounter aggressive hordes in holding areas there during the peak of inmigration (usually late June through early August). Kodiak Island, Southcentral's Susitna River drainage, the Alaska Peninsula, Bristol and Kuskokwim bays, and countless areas throughout Southeast all offer some of the best conditions possible for these feisty, early-run river chums. Changing into spawning colors quickly, these chums lose a little of their zip and aggressiveness farther up into fresh water, but they still can provide some abundant and exciting fishing in holding water, often in company with sockeye and king salmon.

The best waters to consistently hook chum salmon will be shallow, two to four feet deep, with moderate to fast current, and clear with perhaps just a slight tint of glacial green or turbidity. Lures and flies should be fished near or along the bottom, and allowed to tumble or drift through pools, runs, and sloughs, or under cut banks—prime holding areas for migrating chum salmon. Although at times chums will strike under nearly any conditions, you should avoid extremely shallow and clear water, or excessively turbid or glacial streams. Like kings, chums show a definite spookiness in bright sunlight, so the best fishing, especially in clearer streams, will be during the low light of early morning, late evening, or inclement weather.

Large, glacial watersheds can provide prime locations to intercept chums destined for clear headwater tributaries. Dime-bright fish can be taken out of the

Alaska's King of the Chums

Rick Thynes of Ketchikan was trolling the outer waters of Behm Canal with several friends, fishing a Little League Salmon Derby early one summer almost 20 years ago, when he hooked and landed a nice fish that everyone assumed was a king salmon. It lay in the hold for four or five hours before they got back to the dock and tossed it on the scales, where the judges recognized it as the biggest chum salmon they'd ever seen. After an initial weighing, they realized it was a potential record and called ADF&G to verify the 32-pounder as the new state (and long time IGFA All-Tackle World) record chum salmon.

Rick Thynes with his 32-pound state record chum salmon, caught off Caamano Point, SSE, 1985.

mouths of streams up to 40 or 50 miles or more from the sea, with a few populations staying reasonably fresh even after several hundred miles. These fish are genetically programmed to stay brighter longer than stocks spawning lower in the river.

The Right Lures: The best chum salmon lures for fresh water are medium to large (half-ounce to one ounce) flashy spoons and spinners (Pixee, Krocodile, Little Cleo, Dardevle, Hot Rod, Syclops, Mepps, Vibrax, Bang Tail, Rooster Tail, etc.) in silver, silver/blue, gold, and brass with bright orange, red, pink, yellow, green, and chartreuse highlights. (Chums show a marked preference for the yellow-green part of the spectrum.) Medium sized drift bobbers (Corkie, Spin-N-Glo, Cheater, etc.) and plugs (Hot Shot, Wiggle Wart, Kwikfish, etc.) in colors of orange, pink, red, yellow, green, chartreuse, and silver are also used.

Quite often in glacial or turbid waters, the use of roe is a common practice for fishing chums, either alone or as a sweetener on drift bobbers. Drifted along the bottom, these scent-emitting enticements are deadly when all else fails.

Whereas kings and silvers and, to some degree, pinks may attack hardware out of a combination of primal feeding and aggravation reflexes, prespawning chums seem to hit more from aggravation alone, and will frequently pursue lures for short distances, nabbing as they go. Spot casting (by sight) can usually be both exciting and very rewarding, as fish can be prompted to strike with repeat casts. Chums rarely hit with the authority of a hungry trout or charr; usually the take is more of a bump than anything. Anglers must be on the alert and ready to respond with a powerful hook set as these fish, like all prespawning salmon, have very hard jaws. Super-sharp hooks are a necessity. Once hooked, chums will react instantly with powerful bulldog runs and even leaps in a remarkable display of strength and will. Fish of full nuptial maturity are prone to strike lures out of territorial aggression—avoid them for obvious reasons.

FLY-FISHING ALASKA'S RIVER CHUMS

Chums provide an increasing share of Alaska's freshwater salmon action on a fly each year. They are widespread and abundant, strong fighters and take readily under most conditions, often providing sport when their more glamorous cousins are scarce or not cooperating. Gear used can be the same or very similar to that used for king, sockeye, or silver salmon, making it easy for anglers to target these "bulldog battlers" when the opportunity arises.

Because of their potential size, strength and the currents you'll encounter them in, a stout eight-weight rod, with matching salmon class or equivalent reel, is the minimum recommended armament for doing battle with Alaska's river chums on a fly. Heavier gear may be required for trophy fishing or extreme conditions.

Lines used for most Alaska river conditions will be either a weight forward, full float or intermediate with seven to nine-foot leader, or a medium-high density sink tip (5 to 15 feet), Type II-VI, with short leader. Longer sinking lines, such as the 200-400 grain T-series or similar are used rarely, except for extreme conditions. Tippets for chums can be as light as eight pounds, but 20-pound is recommended for the measure of abrasion and shock resistance it provides when dealing with these tough, toothy fighters.

The most productive fly patterns for chum salmon are medium to large, bright attractors (in the favored colors of green, yellow, and chartreuse, plus purple, black, orange, and cerise), many of the same used for silvers and king salmon. Oversize egg patterns like the Cluster Fly or forage patterns like the Leech can work

Anglers working the mouth of a slough off the mainstem lower Kanektok River (SW), for a school of chums. This is a common holding area situation, with fish showing frequently in the lower part of the slough.

at times as well. Because of their hard mouths and strength, hooks used for tying chum salmon flies should be super strong and razor sharp, generally sizes 1/0 to 4.

You'll be targeting coastal streams for the best fishing, the closer to salt the better. Clear or slightly turbid waters, not too shallow, deep, or swift are ideal, with holding areas like sloughs, pools, river mouths, confluences, and under cutbanks the best places to find "takers." Sight fishing clear waters with Polaroid glasses is the preferred, but not always possible, scenario. Instead, you'll probably be fishing "blind," which isn't as bad as it sounds, for chums are some of the most likely salmon to show themselves in lower rivers and estuaries, with their frantic sexual energy making them hard to miss, even in turbid rivers.

Chums, when bright from the sea, are easily provoked but, like all Alaska salmon, they are most consistently taken with a fly presented at proper depth, right above bottom. (They will at times aggressively pursue a fly up the water column, however.) Use the proper line for the conditions and additional lead if necessary to get down to the "strike zone." Wet fly swings and short, erratic strips seem to provoke the most strike responses. Aggressive fish may quite often follow and nab at your fly repeatedly out of irritation, so it pays to work lies thoroughly before moving on to new water.

Chums are generally not as subtle takers as other salmon in fresh water, so there's usually no mistaking a fish hitting your fly. They can be hooked with a strip set and sharp lift of the rod but, like sockeyes, they are classic knucklebusters, reacting with explosive fury once they feel resistance from the line, so you must be prepared to react quickly! A big chum in heavy water can strip a reel in seconds, so a properly adjusted drag and willingness to apply pressure can make all the difference.

Chum salmon are quite often encountered in large schools in the lower sections of rivers, providing some of fastest and most enjoyable salmon action you'll ever experience on a fly. (It is possible to hook dozens of fish a day in some of the more productive locations.) They may also mix with other salmon like sockeye and kings in certain systems during early summer, providing additional variety (and excitement!) for anglers pursuing these more coveted species. For this reason, it pays to come prepared with enough gear and patterns to cover the possibility of encountering all three species. A stout eight, plus a 10 or 11-weight, with matching floating, intermediate, and sink tip lines, plus an assortment of large salmon attractor, egg, and sparse bucktail flies should cover all the bases for the productive and varied flyfishing available in many of the larger coastal rivers during early summer.

CHUM SALMON
Oncorhynchus keta

SPECIES SUMMARY

Alaska common names: Chum, chum salmon, dog, calico, silver salmon (INT), silver bright.

Description: A medium to large salmon with dark metallic-blue back, silvery sides and silver-white belly when fresh from the sea. Spawning individuals yellowish-white to olive with wide, irregular vertical bands of reddish-purple, black, and white on sides. Females may have a dark lateral band on the sides. Some fins have whitish tips. Breeding males develop ridge backs, pronounced kyping and protruding canine teeth. Flesh orange.

Size: Average 6 to 10 lbs., 24-27 in.; to 36 in. and 25 lbs. or more.

State Record: 32 lbs., Caamano Point (SSE), Fredrick Thynes, 1985.

Habits: Not a reckless feeder like coho or king salmon, but easy to entice in fresh water.

Notes: Sea-bright specimens easily mistaken for sockeye salmon.

Meristics: Short, smooth gill rakers 16-28; vertebrae 59-71; pyloric caeca 140-249; lateral line scales 124-153; branchiostegal rays 12-16; dorsal fin 10-14 rays; tail fin 13-17 rays; pectoral fin 13-16 rays; pelvic fins 10-11.

Range: Cape Muzon (SE) to Beaufort Sea coast (ARC).

Preferred Habitat: Short, clear coastal streams or spring-fed headwaters for spawning; estuarine or nearshore marine waters for juveniles; offshore waters of Bering Sea or north Pacific for maturing adults.

Run timing: Present near shore May through December; peak river-runs July through September.

Best Bait/Lures/Flies: Salmon roe; flashy spoons, spinners, plugs, drift bobbers & hootchies; bright attractor pattern streamers.

Best waters: Clear, shallow, coastal streams (and adjacent salt water) and glacial tributaries, SSE, NW and INT.

Best Trophy Waters: Behm Canal and Chilkat River (SE); Susitna and Dog Salmon rivers (SC); Nushagak, Alagnak, and Lower Kuskokwim rivers (SW); Unalakleet, Noatak, and Kobuk rivers (NW); Tanana River tributaries—Salcha and Delta rivers (INT).

RECOMMENDED GEAR

Spinning/Casting:
6-7 1/2 ft., medium-action, medium salmon or heavy steelhead graphite rod, with matching heavy duty reel loaded with 150 yds., 8-12-lb. test line (15-20 lb. for extreme conditions). Shock leader (20+ lb. test) recommended.

Flyfishing:
High performance, 8-9 wt., 9-9 1/2 ft., medium-fast action, graphite rod and salmon class reel loaded with 150 yds. 30 lb. backing; performance taper full float, intermediate and medium-heavy density, 5-15 ft. sink tip lines (Type II-VI); or 200-400 grain T-series or equivalent for extreme conditions. Use 7-9 ft. leader for floating lines, 4-5 ft. for sinking; 20 lb. hard mono bite tippet recommended.

ALASKA'S MAJOR CHUM SALMON LOCATIONS

SOUTHEAST
Southeast has outstanding chum fishing (salt and fresh water), with some of Alaska's largest chums taken from select areas. The run timing is from July-October, peaking from late July to early August.

Yakutat: East Alsek River.

Juneau: Cross Sound; Icy Strait; Stephens Passage; Chilkat River; Fish Creek, Mitchell Bay system.

Sitka: Sitka Sound, Katlian River.

Petersburg/Wrangell: Lower Stephens Passage; Castle, Kah Sheets, Eagle, Harding rivers; Kadake, Petersburg, Ohmer, Falls, Irish, North Arm, Thoms creeks.

Ketchikan/Prince of Wales Island: Behm Canal, Gravina Island/Tongass Narrows; Sarkar, Unuk, Klawock, Karta rivers; Fish Creek.

SOUTHCENTRAL
You'll find some outstanding chum fishing in Southcentral, mostly on Kodiak, Prince William Sound, some Susitna tributaries, and select upper Cook Inlet drainages. The run timing is from early July to September, with a peak in mid-July through early August.

Susitna/Upper Cook Inlet: Little Susitna, Deshka, Talachulitna, Chuitna, Talkeetna rivers; Alexander, Willow, Little Willow, Goose, Sheep, Caswell, Montana, Lake, Jim creeks.

Kenai/Cook Inlet: Kachemak Bay; Silver Salmon Creek.

Kodiak Island: American, Olds, Dog Salmon rivers; Roslyn, Salonie, Russian creeks.

Prince William Sound/Gulf Coast: Resurrection Bay, Valdez Arm, Knight Island, and Wells passages, Hinchibrook Island, Ports Gravina and Fidalgo, Hartney Bay.

7/8 oz.
Pixee Spoon

#2 Clouser
Minnow

#6 Lil Corkie/Yarn

1/2 oz. Hotrod
Spoon

1/0 Flash Fly

Yukon River: Nowitna, Chandalar rivers.
Tanana River: Salcha, Chatanika, Delta Clearwater rivers.
Nenana River: Julius, Clear creeks.
Koyukuk River: Gisasa, Hogatza, South Fork, Dakli, Jim rivers.
Porcupine: Sheenjek, Coleen, Black rivers.

Top Flies for Alaska Chum Salmon
Comet, Clouser Minnow, Polar Shrimp, Flash Fly, Mickey Finn, Wiggletail, Coho Fly, Alaskabou, Outrageous, Egg Sucking Leech, Woolly Bugger, Deceiver, Everglow, Bunny Fly.

Alaska Chum Salmon Trophy Timing	
West Behm Canal (SE)	late June–late July
Harding River (SE)	late July–early August
Bradfield Canal (SE)	mid-July–early August
Clarence Strait (SE)	mid-June–late July
Gravina Island/Tongass Narrows (SE)	July

Top Ten Alaska Trophy Chum Salmon		
32 lbs.	Caamano Point (SE)	1985
28 lbs., 2 oz.	Caamano Point (SE)	1985
28 lbs.	Boca de Quadra (SE)	1991
27 lbs., 9 oz.	Jackpot Bay Creek (SE)	1989
27 lbs., 8 oz.	Behm Canal (SE)	1990
27 lbs., 3 oz.	Behm Narrows (SE)	1977
26 lbs., 8 oz.	Ketchikan (SE)	2003
25 lbs., 6 oz.	Island Point (SE)	1985
25 lbs.	Behm Narrows (SE)	1983
25 lbs.	Herring Cove (SE)	1982

Guides' Tips for Chum Salmon

Best chances for chums are in lower river sections, in holding areas like sloughs, confluences, pools, tailouts, along cutbanks, etc.

Best conditions for fishing are slightly turbid waters of moderate depth and flow, and during cloudy days. Clear, shallow waters and bright sun can be challenging, especially for hardware slingers.

Use bright color flies and lures, except when fishing clear shallow waters or bright days, when darker (purple, black, blue) and smaller enticements work best.

Keep your hooks razor sharp and use a sturdy bite tippet or leader (20 lb. test hard mono).

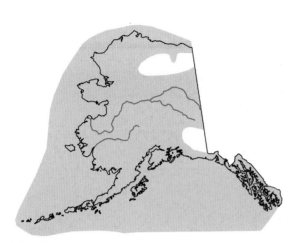

SOUTHWEST

Some of Alaska's most abundant stream fishing can be enjoyed in the Southwest region, with perfect conditions for sight fishing and fly-fishing. Dozens of outstanding locations are here, often with great concurrent action for king and sockeye salmon. The run timing is from late June-Aug., with a peak in the first half of July.

Bristol Bay: Nushagak (includes Mulchatna and Nuyakuk), Wood, Igushik, Togiak, Kvichak rivers.

Alaska Peninsula: Ugashik Lake system; Egegik, Naknek, Alagnak rivers; Izembek-Moffet Bay streams; Russell Creek; Belkofski Bay, Canoe Bay rivers; Stepovak Bay streams.

Kuskokwim: Goodnews, Kanektok, Aniak, Holitna rivers.

Lower Yukon: Andreafsky, Anvik rivers.

NORTHWEST

This region has some outstanding but little-fished rivers, primarily in eastern Norton and Kotzebue sounds. The run timing is July and August, with a peak in the first half of July.

Eastern Norton Sound: Unalakleet, Shaktoolik, Ungalik, Inglutalik, Tubutulik rivers.

Seward Peninsula: Fish-Niukluk, Fox, Kwiniuk rivers.

Kotzebue Sound: Kobuk, Noatak, Wulik rivers.

Lower Yukon: Nulato River.

INTERIOR

Although Interior has abundant fish runs, the fish are in less than prime condition because of their great distance from the sea. The Yukon River is North America's prime producer of chum. Many areas offer potentially good sport fishing, including all river mouths along the Yukon and Tanana rivers. The run timing is from July to November, peaking in July (early run) and September (late run).

#2 Wiggletail

#5-6 Super
Vibrax Spinner

3 1/2" Hoochie

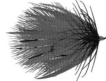

#1/0 Alaskabou

034 Hot Shot
Plug

Pink

Humpback Salmon

The salty aroma of sun-burned kelp fills the cool ocean air as you steer your boat out of the mild chops of Prince William Sound into the protected waters of a small cove on the eastern side of the Kenai Peninsula. The awesome natural beauty is intoxicating. Rugged, spruce-covered mountains drop precipitously a thousand feet or more into the glassy blue waters, with misty waterfalls cascading down their sides. Immense, bluish-green tidewater glaciers spill down valleys right to the edge of the sea.

As you scan the near shoreline in search of a suitable freshwater outlet, a family of sea otters pops into view, while puffins make low overhead passes before diving into the cove in hot pursuit of prey. The boat glides quietly to rest near the head of the cove, where a sizable stream emerges from the thick Alaska rainforest to empty into the brine—a prime location to intercept Alaska's smallest, but most ubiquitous, member of the Pacific salmon clan, the pink.

The tide is rising and fish are moving through the water. First one or two break the surface, then more and more, until the once calm waters are alive with thousands of jumping, splashing, rolling salmon. You waste little time casting a fly into the thick of it, stripping it in short, quick bursts for only a brief moment before the line tightens and your five-weight doubles over. The fight is on as a chrome-bright, six-pound pink salmon slashes through gin clear water with your fly firmly embedded in its kype, tearing out line in quick and powerful sprints like a trout or charr. After several minutes, the salmon comes to the boat—a robust beauty with sea lice clinging to its sides. Other casts bring repeated action, over and over. For the better part of a day you battle this horde of diminutive salmon brawlers, taking full advantage of the peak of the run until your wrists can take no more.

Pink salmon action above tidewater, Kodiak Island, Southcentral Alaska.

PINK SALMON: HUMPBACK SALMON

Pink salmon, *Oncorhynchus gorbuscha*, are one of the most delightful light-tackle game fishes to be had in Alaska's coastal waters. Although hampered by persistent rumors concerning their sporting and eating qualities (or lack thereof), pinks have nonetheless stood the test of time and today enjoy a growing interest among anglers who recognize the many fine attributes of these feisty little salmon. One of the main impediments to their acceptance is the grotesque appearance they develop prior to spawning, especially males with their gnarly jaws and giant humped backs (hence the nickname "humpies"). Few anglers would recognize a sleek, dime-bright specimen full of spunk straight out of the Pacific Ocean. (They're frequently mistaken for other, more glamorous species like jack kings, small silvers, or even Dolly Varden charr.)

Catch them in their prime, at sea or in or above intertidal areas of clear-water streams, and you will experience a fishery of magnitude and intensity never before imagined. Far more prolific than most other salmon, returning pinks often fill waters by the tens of thousands, making them boil with activity and triggering awe and humility in anglers. Surrounded by countless flashy, three to five-pound fish swarming in a seething mass of heads, tails, and fins, one can only begin to comprehend the importance of this species within the coastal ecosystem. Angling for these playful fish can bring you close to the essence of wild Alaska.

DESCRIPTION

When encountered fresh from the sea, the pink is a small, sleek salmon displaying a dark blue or green back, silvery sides, and a white belly. Faint oval-shaped spots cover the back and both lobes of the tail fin. Due to their similar size and appearance, bright pinks can be easily misidentified as jack kings or silver salmon.

Spawning fish turn dirty brown with sides of mottled, yellowish green. Males develop a distinctive humped back and an elongated, hooked snout. Females generally retain more of their seagoing shape. The oval markings on the back and tail lobes become especially prominent, and the belly and lower jaw turn creamy to yellowish-white.

The flesh of bright, sea-run pink salmon has an orange to a slight pink hue and moderately soft texture. When fresh from the sea, it is excellent table fare. Pink salmon are an important species within the commercial fishing industry and comprise the bulk of Alaska's canned salmon.

The smallest of the Pacific salmon, the pink varies little in size from one watershed to another. Typically averaging only three to five pounds in weight (20 to 25 inches in length), it seldom exceeds seven or eight pounds throughout its range. However, a few rivers and streams produce larger specimens that may reach ten pounds or more. (The Alaska state record is 12 pounds, 9 ounces, for a fish taken from the Kenai's Moose River, Southcentral Alaska, in 1974.) Throughout the state, odd-year pinks tend to be slightly heavier than even-year fish, except on the Alaska Peninsula. You can usually take trophy pinks from certain areas of Southeast and Southcentral.

RANGE, ABUNDANCE, & STATUS

The pink is the most abundant Pacific salmon, comprising up to 60% in numbers and 40% in weight of the commercial catch in the North Pacific. It ranges from Sacramento, California, north to the Bering Strait and along the coast of Siberia (including Kamchatka), as far south as northern Japan and North Korea. Transplant efforts have spread the species far and wide to locations such as Scandinavia, parts of South America, and the eastern United States and Canada.

In Alaska, pink salmon are plentiful from Dixon Entrance below Ketchikan, north to Point Hope above Kotzebue, with sporadic occurrences around Point Barrow in the Arctic Ocean, to the Mackenzie River delta in the Northwest Territories of Canada.

Major pink salmon populations are found in the multitude of streams in Southeast, Prince William Sound, coastal Blying Sound, Kodiak Island, Cook Inlet, Bristol Bay, the Alaska Peninsula, along the lower Yukon and Kuskokwim rivers, and Norton Sound. Seldom do pinks move far upriver, usually spawning within 50 miles of the coast. However, they're occasionally found as far inland as Ruby on the Yukon River (about 350 miles from the sea), with unconfirmed reports of fish in Fairbanks area streams. Intense stocking efforts by various private hatcheries have created "terminal" fisheries in many areas, mostly to benefit commercial interests.

LIFE HISTORY & HABITS

Unlike other Pacific salmon, pinks have a fixed life span of around 18 months. One or three-year-olds are rarely found. Some areas of the state have stronger runs of pinks on even-numbered years, while others have stronger returns on odd-numbered years. Even-year and odd-year fish do not mix and are considered two distinct genetic stocks.

Mature adults begin returning from Gulf of Alaska feeding grounds to coastal areas in late spring. They typically peak in number by midsummer in inshore waters and continue to arrive until early fall, concentrating in huge schools near major spawning streams. (Males tend to appear earlier than females, and when pinks are large, run timing is earlier.) During their final homeward migration, the fish feed heavily and significantly increase in size.

Nearing freshwater, a period of "milling" commences, from several days if fish are committed to an extensive upriver migration, to several weeks if spawning takes place in intertidal areas or near salt water. Sharp increases or decreases in stream volume or temperature further regulate inmigration.

Though pinks typically appear in mid to late summer to spawn in fast-flowing coastal rivers and streams, bright fish in Alaska may be present in fresh water anytime between early June and late October. As with other salmon species, the timing of individual runs is influenced by different factors, especially water temperatures. Early runs, common in northern Alaska, occur in cold, coastal runoff streams and in larger glacial systems where the fish face a lengthy upstream migration. They enter fresh water from mid-June to mid-August, peaking during the first half of July. Throughout much of Alaska, somewhat later runs are the norm, with fish inmigration starting in late June, peaking from mid-July to early August, and concluding by early September. Warmer drainages in southern Southcentral and Southwest and most of Southeast support populations of late run pinks. Timing is from mid-July into early October, peaking the latter half of August.

Not adept at leaping waterfalls or negotiating even short stretches of high-velocity current flow, these small salmon are much more prone to spawn in lower areas of rivers and creeks. During abnormally strong runs with high spawner density, pinks tend to migrate farther upstream than in normal years. "Straying" is particularly common among artificial runs of pink salmon, but is otherwise relatively low to almost nonexistent in natural populations.

Actual spawning typically peaks in August and September throughout Alaska, with a few populations beginning as early as July or as late as November. One reason why these salmon are so abundant almost everywhere they're found is that they can spawn in almost any conditions, from mere trickles of water to major rivers. However, their general preference is for shallow (five inches to three feet deep), moderate-flowing, clear-water streams with clean gravel substrate. Waters with mud-covered bottoms, slow or no current, and deep, quiet pools are avoided.

Pinks commonly use intertidal areas for reproduction, especially in parts of Southeast and Southcentral, since pink eggs can withstand a high degree of salinity. (In some coastal streams, as much as 75% or more of spawning takes place there.)

A female pink may deposit 1,100 to 2,300 eggs in several nests, guarding the area from ten days up to three weeks. The eggs hatch in late winter and, after a brief stay in fresh water, the juvenile salmon move out to sea during April and May. For the first couple of months, the pink fry remain within a few miles of the stream mouth and are preyed upon heavily by other fishes, including silver salmon smolts. The growing pinks feed on a variety of small organisms, such as lar-

Pink salmon undergo rapid and dramatic physical changes as they approach sexual maturity.

val fishes, plankton and, occasionally, insects, eventually switching to a diet of small fishes as size increases. High seas pinks are suspended at depths between 30 and 120 feet, may travel vast expanses during their stay (3,000 to 4,000 miles), and suffer a marine mortality of nearly 97%, mostly during the first few months of life.

Intensely social, mature pinks are the easiest salmon for anglers to target, as they mill about in large numbers in bays and river mouths and swim en masse to upriver spawning areas. Their aggressiveness and sheer numbers make them a favorite of tourists and young children, but for anglers intent on other quarry they share waters with—silver salmon, charr, trout, etc.—they can be a nuisance. The little salmon is also noted for undergoing accelerated physical changes as it nears home waters. Quite often fish will show a marked degree of alteration even before entering fresh water. Finding fish that are near the peak of ocean-bright physical condition is quite often the major challenge confronting anglers.

FISHING ALASKA'S PINK SALMON

The sport catch for pink salmon in Alaska has fluctuated from well over half million to almost a million fish annually in recent years. Most of these fish are taken from the waters of Southeast and Southcentral Alaska, particularly around the Ketchikan/Prince of Wales, Juneau, and Sitka areas, and the Kenai Peninsula, Prince William Sound, and the east side drainages of the Susitna River. A small number of pink salmon are taken each year in the state's salt water, mostly incidentally from anglers trolling for salmon in the North Gulf of Alaska (SC) and waters around Southeast.

Freshwater Techniques/Gear

Since these little salmon only average three to four pounds, anglers will enjoy fishing for them more if they gear down to an ultralight, fast action, six to seven-and-a-half-foot graphite rod, with matching reel and four to six-pound test line. (Use heavier tackle in areas with strong current or when surf casting.)

Pinks commonly spawn in the lower reaches of intertidal areas of most coastal drainages, and within a week to ten days reach full nuptial maturity. (The period of availability for bright pinks is relatively short, with the second or third weeks of a four to six-week run producing the freshest fish in the greatest numbers.) Large glacial systems that force pinks to migrate extensive distances to reach spawning beds can yield silvery specimens at the mouths of tributaries some 40 to 50 miles from salt water. In contrast, small and shallow coastal creeks may never see anything other than full-fledged spawners, as the fish usually mill around off stream mouths until ripe and ready.

Ideally, you should choose a location with a fair amount of volume and few feet of depth, with clear or semi-clear water and moderate current flow. Try to avoid using oversized lures. Smaller (1/8 to 1/2 ounce) spoons and spinners (Pixee, Krocodile, Little Cleo, Syclops, Dardevle, Vibrax, Mepps, Rooster Tail, Panther Martin, Bang Tail, etc.) in neutral colors like green, blue, silver, gold, bronze, and copper work better for waters with high visibility, while slightly larger lures in bright fluorescent colors like neon red, orange, pink, yellow, and chartreuse perform better for semi-glacial, turbid, or low-light conditions. Medium-sized chartreuse and silver lures also work well in glacial waters. Much the same goes for flies as for hardware.

Pinks seem to be "on the bite" more often in rivers and creeks with a good flow and at least two to three feet of water. As with most salmon, all lures, including flies, should be fished right above the bottom for best results. Holding areas such as deep holes, runs, and pools are great for finding schools of waiting pinks. Although one may spot a lot of fish in spawning condition in shallower areas, the brighter (and larger) specimens are usually caught from the deeper sections of a stream.

In very slow or still waters, pink salmon can be considerably more difficult to catch, especially under bright, clear conditions. Anglers fishing small, dark lures and flies do best. A slow, erratic retrieve is warranted. However, if the water is a bit on the greenish glacial side, slightly larger lures may be necessary, in colors less neutral, with more accent toward visibility. Fish tend to respond more readily to anglers' offerings in these drainages.

FLYFISHING ALASKA'S RIVER PINKS

When encountered close to their prime in intertidal areas or lower rivers, Alaska's abundant pink salmon can provide exciting sport for flyfishermen who gear down appropriately for them. A five or possibly six weight, fast action graphite rod, eight to nine feet long, with matching reel, and some floating, intermediate, or sink tip line (5 to 15 foot, Type II-IV), with light, 4 to 8 pound tippets, (5X-2X) should be suitable for most conditions encountered in Alaska.

Pink salmon can be taken on a wide range of fly patterns. Bright and flashy attractors, smaller versions of those used for larger salmon, are especially productive, in colors of silver, gold, pink, red, orange, yellow, white, chartreuse, purple, and black, sizes #2 to #8. Leech, smolt, and egg patterns can also used to great effect, as many anglers discover when targeting trout and charr in lower rivers during mid to late summer.

Ideal conditions will be fairly clear waters of shallow to moderate depth and not too swift current, in areas holding fish—river mouths, pools, rapids, sloughs, etc. Dead drift and wet fly swing presentations right above bottom will produce the most responses, as pinks are fairly aggressive takers in and out of salt water.

Since they mill in great numbers in lower rivers during the height of the runs, you can expect all the action you can handle in the more productive locations. You may hook a few fish that are fairly advanced in their spawning phase, and maybe even an occasional stray chum, silver, or sockeye, depending on when and where you are fishing, so bring plenty of flies and extra leaders to allow for "break-offs."

Top Flies for Alaska Pink Salmon

Comet, Boss, Polar Shrimp, Flash Fly, Alaskabou, Everglow, Coho, Egg Sucking Leech, Crazy Charlie, Krystal Bullet, Wiggletail, Blue Smolt, Pink Sparkler, Skykomish Sunrise.

PINK SALMON

Oncorhynchus gorbuscha

SPECIES SUMMARY

Alaska Common Names: Pink, pink salmon, humpy, humpback salmon.

Description: A small, common salmon, with steel blue to blue-green topsides, blending into iridescent silver sides and whitish belly. Oval-shaped black markings on back and entire tail fin. Spawning individuals are dirty brown on back, sides yellowish-green with slight vertical markings. Males develop pronounced humped backs, jaw kypes and prominent teeth. Flesh pink.

Size: Average weight 2-5 lbs., length 16 to 22 in.; up to 10 lbs. or more.

Alaska State Record: 12 lbs., 9 oz., Moose River (SC), Steven Lee, 1974.

Habits: Very social; mill in great numbers in intertidal areas and river mouths.

Notes: Sea-bright specimens can be mistaken for jack king or coho.

Meristics: Gill rakers 24-35; vertebrae 63-72; pyloric caeca 95-224; lateral line scales 145-208; branchiostegal rays 9-15; dorsal fin 10-15 rays; tail fin 13-20 rays; pectoral fin 14-17 rays; anal fin 13-19 rays; pelvic fin 9-11 rays.

Range: Coastal Alaska, Cape Muzon (SE), to Beaufort Sea Coast (ARC).

Preferred Habitat: Clear, gravel bottom coastal streams of moderate gradient and flow for spawning/incubation; rich nearshore habitat for rearing; North Pacific/Bering Sea for maturation.

Best Waters: Lower sections of clearwater rivers and streams, also adjacent saltwater, SSE-NW.

Run timing: Fish present coastally June through October; peak July through August.

Best Bait/Lures/Flies: Salmon roe; small spinners, spoons, jigs, and hootchies in silver, gold, red, orange, pink, green, chartreuse; attractor pattern flies.

Best Trophy Areas: SC—Valdez Arm (PWS), American and Pasagshak rivers (Kodiak), Kenai River; SSE—Yes and Mink Bays (Behm Canal); NSE—Starrigavan Bay (Sitka), Auke Bay (Juneau) and Chilkoot River (Haines).

RECOMMENDED GEAR

Spinning:
Ultralight 6-7 1/2-ft., fast action, graphite trout rod; matching reel with 150 yds. 4-6-lb. test monofilament line. Heavier tackle recommended for rivers with strong current or for surf casting.

Flyfishing:
5-6-wt., medium fast action graphite rod (8-9 1/2 ft.), matching reel with 150 yds. 20-30 lb. backing and WF floating, intermediate or sink-tip line (Type II-IV) with 5X-2X tippet.

MAJOR PINK SALMON LOCATIONS

SOUTHEAST
Tremendous opportunities exist in a multitude of coastal clear-water streams and straits, channels, and bays. The run timing is from July into September, peaking mid-July through mid-August.

Yakutat: Situk River.

Juneau: Cross Sound, Icy Strait, Lynn Canal, Stephens Passage, Favorite/Saginaw channels; Chilkat and Chilkoot rivers; Montana, Turner, and Auke creeks; Mitchell Bay system.

Sitka: Sitka Sound, Chatham, and Peril straits; Nakwasina, Katlian rivers; Eva and Sitkoh creeks.

Petersburg/Wrangell: Wrangell Narrows/Duncan Canal; Stephens, Eastern passages; Ernest, Frederick sounds; Clarence, Sumner, Zimovia straits; Kah Sheets, Eagle, Castle rivers; Hamilton, Gunnuck, Bear (Big), Irish, Andrew, Aaron, Anan, Thoms, Petersburg, Ohmer, Falls, Pat, Fools, Ketili, Government, St. John, Oerns, Marten, North Arm, Snake, Kunk, Porcupine, Kadake creeks.

Ketchikan/POW: Behm Canal; Revillagigedo Channel; Gulf of Esquibel; Bucareli Bay; Gravina Island; Clarence Strait; Sarkar, Klawock, Harris, Thorne, Karta, Naha, Unuk, Wilson, Blossom rivers; Ward, Wolverine, Kegan, Whipple creeks.

SOUTHCENTRAL
Southcentral's Cook Inlet and Kodiak offer top freshwater angling for bright, sea-run pinks, while Prince William Sound has some of Alaska's best ocean fishing for the species. The run timing is from July to September, peaking mid-July into mid-August.

Pixee Spoon
1/4 oz.

#6 Egg Sucking
Leech

#3 Mepps
Aglia

2 1/2"
Hoochie

#6 Flash Fly

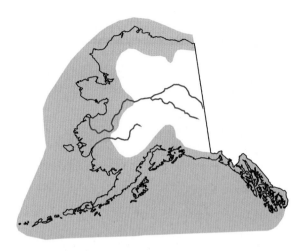

NORTHWEST

The pink salmon is one of the primary species (along with chum salmon) residing in Norton Sound, with many excellent fishing opportunities under utilized because of the area's remoteness. Run strength fluctuates greatly from one year to the next, with general timing from July into August, and peak from mid-July to early August.

Norton Sound: Golsovia, Unalakleet, Shaktoolik, Inglutalik, Ungalik, Tubutulik rivers.

Seward Peninsula: Kwiniuk, Eldorado, Nome, Snake, Fox, Sinuk, Niukluk, Pilgrim, Solomon, Kuzitrin rivers; Safety Lagoon.

Lower Yukon: Nulato River.

Alaska Pink Salmon Trophy Timing	
Kenai River (SC)	late July – late August.
Pasagshak River (SC)	late July – late August.
Wolverine Creek (SE)	mid-August – early September.
West Behm Canal (SE)	mid-July – mid-August.
Chilkoot River (SE)	mid-August – September.

Top Ten Alaska Trophy Pink Salmon		
12 lbs., 9 oz.	Moose River (SC)	1974
12 lbs., 4 oz.	Kenai River (SC)	1974
12 lbs.	American River (SC)	1998
11 lbs., 14 oz.	Shelter Island (SE)	1980
11 lbs., 8 oz.	Montana Creek (SE)	1973
11 lbs., 7 oz.	Chilkoot River (SE)	1983
11 lbs., 6 oz.	Coghill River (SC)	1977
11 lbs., 6 oz.	Biorka Island (SE)	1969
11 lbs., 4 oz.	Chilkoot River (SE)	1981
11 lbs.	Kenai River (SC)	1984

Mat/Su: Talkeetna, Deshka, Talachulitna, Little Susitna, rivers; Willow, Little Willow, Sheep, Montana, Alexander, Goose, Caswell, Lake creeks.

Kenai-Cook Inlet: Lower Cook Inlet and Kachemak Bay; Kenai, Anchor, Ninilchik, Chuitna, Seldovia, Windy Left, Windy Right, Bruin Bay, Kamishak, Little Kamishak, Rocky, Theodore rivers; Deep, Stariski, Amakdedori, Brown's Peak, Humpy, Port Dick, Bird, Sunday, Resurrection creeks.

Kodiak: Shuyak Island; Uyak, Ugak, Uganik, Chiniak bays; Karluk, Ayakulik, Pasagshak, Saltery, Afognak, Buskin, Uganik, Olds, American, Dog Salmon rivers; Pauls, Portage, Salonie, Roslyn, Akalura, Malina, Olga, Russian creeks.

PWS: Resurrection Bay, Valdez Arm, Wells Passage area, Orca Bay, Coghill River, Cow Pen Creek.

SOUTHWEST

The abundant pink fisheries in this region are little utilized, because of their remoteness or the presence of more prized species. The run timing is July and August, peaking the first half of August.

Bristol Bay: Nushagak River system (including Mulchatna, Nuyakuk, and lower Tikchik rivers); Wood, Kvichak, Togiak rivers.

North Alaska Peninsula: Naknek, Alagnak, Ugashik, Egegik river systems; Herendeen-Port Moller Bay streams.

South Alaska Peninsula: Abundant throughout, including Aleutian and Shumagin island streams.

Kuskokwim Bay: Goodnews, Eek, Arolik, Kanektok rivers.

Lower Yukon: Andreafsky River.

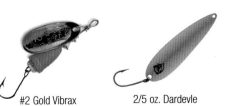

#2 Gold Vibrax   2/5 oz. Dardevle Spoon

#4 Alaskabou

#6 Boss

#6 Krystal Bullet

Rainbow
Fish With a Heart

Southwest Alaska's Nushagak River has provided unforgettable fishing experiences for countless salmon anglers the world over. But for a group of upper Midwest farm boys, the memory of it that most haunts their dreams has little to do with its fabulous chinook fishing.

Some guys from Minnesota were fishing kings one June years ago, out at a camp on the lower river above Portage Creek. The run was late that year; they drifted and pulled all manner of baits, bobbers, plugs, and spoons through the water without the least bit of luck. With each day they grew increasingly sullen, and drank more heavily in camp at night, which brought a load of worry onto their young guide, who wondered how bad things would get before the week was over.

As fate would have it, their dark cloud of misfortune had a silver lining. On the fourth day, one of the guys hooked what appeared to be a nice salmon on an early morning drift about a half-mile above the village. The fish whacked a bright Spin-N-Glo and eggs, sounded briefly, then shot upriver like a lightning bolt and made a spectacular leap, clearing the water by what seemed like three or four feet—very unusual for a king salmon.

Only it wasn't a king. This chinook-sized fish had a blazing red stripe down its midline that positively glowed in the morning sun. Everybody's jaw dropped when they realized they were looking at what had to be the God-darned, biggest rainbow trout in Alaska, or so it seemed!

The giant trout was strong, for sure, but also amazingly quick and agile for its size. It zigged and zagged up and down the river and jumped repeatedly, each time revealing its awesome size and beauty from a different angle before crashing down in a welter of spray. It was the most magnificent fish they had ever seen! Then it bored under and around the boat, jamming that poor boy's rod in an impossible arc as he tried valiantly to hang on. But he was no match for the fish's energy and gyrations and, despite his (and the guide's) best efforts, the line fouled the prop. Before they could work it free, the fish, in a powerful surge, snapped the line like it was thread. It made two more exalted leaps as it tore upriver, giving the group a parting glimpse of a trout unlike any other.

That night in camp, you could have heard a pin drop. No loud carousing, just a bunch of quiet guys staring into the fire, pondering, no doubt, just how big that trout really was and what chance there might be to hook another like it in the days ahead. And, wouldn't you know, the next morning tide brought in so many kings, the river was just boiling, and those boys from Minnesota got what they paid for. But you can bet they'll never forget that rainbow. Their guide sure won't. Its been twenty years since that magic morning and, if I close my eyes, I can still see that fish jumping.

Fall trophy rainbow action, Kvichak River, Southwest Alaska.

RAINBOW TROUT: FISH WITH A HEART

The rainbow trout, *Oncorhynchus mykiss,* certainly needs no introduction to American anglers. Perhaps the most prized of all our coldwater gamefishes, the colorful native trout of the Pacific Coast has been dazzling us for decades with its high-spirited antics and beauty. And few will argue that this glamorous fighter reaches its finest expression in the icy, vast waters of Alaska, where an age-long struggle in a challenging but rich environment has honed it to a robustness seldom seen elsewhere. Alaska rainbows are indeed big! And in the deep, strong currents you'll find them in, they certainly rank as one of the premier challenges in the world of light tackle angling.

The state's immense wild rainbow territory, from the Southeast panhandle to the remote reaches of Kuskokwim Bay, encompasses hundreds of rivers and lakes, in what is undoubtedly the last significant stronghold for the species. For serious trout anglers the world over, visiting this ultimate rainbow mecca is the dream of a lifetime. In terms of dollars and effort anglers put forth to pursue good fishing, no other Alaska species except, perhaps, the great king salmon, elicits the same kind of fanatical esteem from anglers of all persuasions.

DESCRIPTION

Alaska's rainbow trout present an unmistakable but varied appearance. More graceful in form than salmon, their bodies are more elongate, with slightly smaller heads proportionately.

The topsides vary—usually olive green or gray (or steel blue in lake resident fish)—the sides are silver or silver-gray and the belly whitish. A broad pink to crimson stripe or blush along the midline and gill plate is the salient identifying feature. Markings consist of small to moderate-sized black spots that cover the upper body and entire tail fin, which is usually less forked than in the salmon or charrs. Belly fins are generally pinkish to pearly white. Flesh varies from white to pink. Rainbow fry and parr can be hard to distinguish from young coho salmon, which display similar color and markings.

The Alaska rainbow's appearance can vary with time of year, diet, maturity, and location, with each watershed producing its own color variation. Fish from the big lakes, like Iliamna, Naknek, and Kenai, are bright silver and sparsely marked, like steelhead, while rainbows from smaller tributary streams can be exquisitely hued (lilac, rose, or crimson) with pronounced markings that cover their entire bodies (the

RANGE, ABUNDANCE, & STATUS

Rainbow trout were historically distributed along most of the Pacific slope, from northern Mexico to Kamchatka. In Alaska, they occur naturally from streams and lakes in Southeast to tributaries of the lower Kuskokwim River in Southwest, but not continuously along this range, as they are conspicuously absent from parts of the Northern Gulf Coast, Prince William Sound and most of the Alaska Peninsula. Steelhead, the sea-run form of the rainbow trout, have a more extensive but sporadic Alaska distribution. Through propagation and transplanting, numerous new lake fisheries for rainbow trout now exist, particularly in Southcentral and Interior Alaska.

The status of the wild rainbow in Alaska seems remarkably secure, bolstered by the new ethics in sport angling and more conservative management. Though many an old-timer may wistfully recall the bygone days of really stupendous rainbow fishing, Alaska still has some of the world's best fishing for the species in terms of abundance, variety, and trophy potential.

LIFE HISTORY & HABITS

Rainbow trout begin their lives in much the same manner as their larger cousins, the salmon, hatching from eggs laid and fertilized in a gravel stream bed (spawning usually occurs in late April, May or early June in Alaska). Young fry develop quickly, feeding on insect and crustacean life almost exclusively in their first year of life, but opportunistically utilizing any food source that becomes available, especially as they grow older.

As they become larger, rainbows will feed extensively and at times exclusively on minnows (sticklebacks, sculpins, and juvenile salmon) and, when available, they will also prey heavily on leeches, freshwater shrimp, snails, and even small rodents (voles, mice, and shrews). Insect life (nymphs, emergers, and adults) is also utilized to a varying extent. But, more than anything, what distinguishes these fish from their counterparts to the south is their feeding habits during summer and fall. During this period, practically every rainbow in Alaska becomes associated in some way or another with spawning salmon, for a chance at their abundant, rich roe and flesh, choice foods for achieving the prime condition necessary to survive Alaska's long, lean winters. In major systems

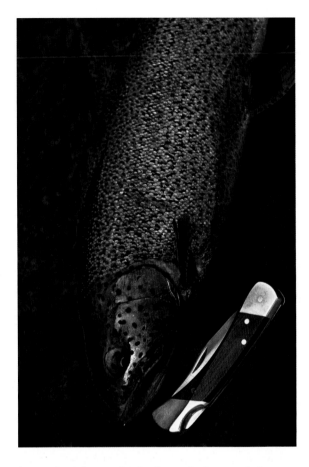

leopard rainbows of Bristol Bay, for instance). Spawning in spring brings physical changes, but not as dramatic as in salmon.

Size is similarly varied, with the largest rainbows coming from the state's big lake and river systems (Naknek, Iliamna, Wood-Tikchik, and Kenai). Fish of four to seven pounds, or more, are caught there with predictable regularity, with rainbows of more than ten pounds not uncommon. On most Alaska rainbow streams, however, the fish run much smaller, averaging somewhere around two to three pounds, with the occasional five-pound or larger fish. The largest sport-caught rainbow ever taken in Alaska was an IGFA world record steelhead, a few ounces over 42 pounds, but freshwater resident fish of more than 20 pounds are rare these days. (See the steelhead chapter for more details on Alaska's sea-run rainbows.) The isolation of most of the state's waters, the short fishing season, and the growing predominance of catch-and-release, undoubtedly contribute to preserving the hefty average size of most Alaska wild rainbows.

that receive annual returns of millions of salmon, the significance of this roe (and flesh) to rainbow, charr and other resident fish species is crucial, for it allows large populations to survive in waters that are otherwise quite unproductive.

Alaska's rainbows usually reach sexual maturity in three to five years, and can live to well over ten, with habitat and available food sources playing a big part in life span and ultimate size. Generally, growth is slow, and occurs mostly during the four to five warm months of the year, when food is most plentiful. A ten-pound rainbow may well be twelve years old. Despite the apparent abundance of large fish, most of Alaska's waters are deceptively low in productivity; all the more reason to use minimum impact, catch-and-release techniques when fishing these beauties in their last wild strongholds.

Rainbows have never had a reputation for being wily or finicky feeders and, in these lean northern waters, where life is feast or famine and the competition keen, they become notoriously voracious and unsophisticated. Knowing what their main food sources are and how to imitate and present them can be the easy part of the angling equation. The real trick is locating fish for, like Alaska's charr, the state's rainbows can have immense and complicated movement patterns, shifting locations and feed throughout the season to exploit different food sources as they become available. (In smaller lakes and other closed systems, the Alaska rainbow will have movements more local and predictable.) An understanding of these important feeding movements (when, where, and why they occur) and familiarity with the appropriate angling strategies, are essential to success.

FISHING ALASKA'S RAINBOW TROUT

Anglers in Alaska catch well over a half million rainbow trout a year. Most of this angling effort takes place in populous Southcentral, and concentrates on the Kenai and Susitna rivers systems and lakes in and around Anchorage. A considerable amount of rainbow fishing also takes place in the immense, clear river and lake systems of Bristol Bay, which offer the state's finest trout fishing experiences. Some promising, but mostly underutilized, rainbow fishing exists in scattered lakes and streams throughout Southeast, the Kenai Peninsula, the Susitna and Copper River valleys, and Kodiak Island.

Catch-and-release: trout fishing's new ethic helps preserve the high quality of fishing in Alaska.

Spring Conditions

As the ice leaves Alaska's lakes and rivers in April and May, rainbow trout become more active, searching for food and (mature fish) preparing for spawning. Like the charr, they'll opportunistically seize any available insects, crustaceans, or small fish. In most of the flowing waters that contain rainbows in Alaska, the alevin, fry, parr, and smolt of salmon will be primary spring food sources. The very best fishing locations at this time will be the lake outlets, inlets, and narrows, river mouths, confluences, and pools of major salmon systems, as these are areas that concentrate juvenile salmon and attract feeding trout and charr. (Young salmon are most active in subdued light. Cloudy, windy days, and early morning and late evening, are the best times to fish these areas.) The most effective lures, obviously, will be those that mimic young salmon or other forage species—small spinners and spoons, plugs, jigs, and smolt, parr, fry, sculpin, and leech patterned streamers.

The biggest factors affecting your success this time of year will be weather and water conditions. Spring outings on most trout waters in North America can be challenging, but especially so in Alaska, with it's notorious climate, big water, and remoteness. Rivers can stay blown out with high flows and turbidity long after the ice goes out if temperatures warm too quickly in years of heavy snowpack, and/or prolonged spring rains occur. Conditions vary from year to year but, as a general rule, most Alaska rivers fish better very early (late March through April) or late (June) in the spring. Check with local sources like air taxis, outfitters, or tackle shops before heading out. (Many of the better trout waters in Alaska are closed in late spring to protect spawners.)

Spin/baitcast fishermen fishing early season rainbows in Alaska have traditionally had the most success working small, bright spinners or spoons (1/8 to 1/2 oz.) in areas of fish concentration or visible feeding. In the deep water of lake outlets or big rivers, larger spinners, spoons, jigs, and plugs can be more effective. The most productive colors are silver, silver mylar/ prism, silver-blue, gold, brass, black, and purple.

The challenge for flyfishers this time of year will be the same: to locate feeding fish, then determine and present the proper prey imitation in a manner most like the real thing. You'll use most of the same techniques here as you would stateside for streamer fishing this time of year—floating lines or short sink tips, quarter casts, and downstream, crosscurrent swings of the fly. Short, fast strips and "jigging" rod twitches will impart lifelike, strike-provoking action to your offerings. Since minnows are the predominant prey, you'll be fishing mostly smolt, fry, parr, and minnow patterns (sizes #2 to #8), in addition to perennial spring rainbow favorites (in the same sizes) like Matukas, Woolly Buggers, Leeches, and Muddlers. Small alevin and nymph patterns (size #8 to #12) can also be quite effective early in the season.

In smaller lakes and streams with few or no juvenile salmon, spring rainbows will be feeding more on insect larvae, crustaceans, leeches, and fish like sculpins or sticklebacks. Various nymph, crustacean, minnow, sculpin, and leech patterns, along with small spoons, spinners, and jigs, can be effective, depending on conditions and local food sources. In lakes with no outlet, good locations to target are shorelines and around prominent structures (islands, reefs, weed beds, and drop-offs), if no signs of feeding are present. Early morning and late evenings will generally be the most active feeding times. Here, a boat, bathymetric map, and an electronic fish finder can improve your chances of success tenfold, but don't underestimate the effectiveness of skillful shore angling on these usually hungry and plentiful lake rainbows. Better lakes for spring fishing are scattered throughout the upper Kenai Peninsula, Mat-Su Valley, Kodiak, Southeast, and parts of the Interior.

Spring rainbow taken on a black Leech.

Spring Rainbow Flies & Lures

Scud

Leech

Spinners

Smolt

Spoons

Muddler

Plugs

Jigs

Summer Conditions

As spring shifts into summer, Alaska's incredible salmon runs pump life into most of the state's waters, and rainbow trout, like charr and other resident species, will shift their activities to key into the movements of their returning cousins. In river mouths, lake outlets, sloughs, confluences, pools, tailouts, along cutbanks, etc., anywhere salmon congregate, you can expect attendant hordes of excitable rainbows "shadowing" the salmon that will later provide vital sustenance through their rich roe and flesh.

Most of these fish can be tempted using many of the same lures that work so well for spring conditions or, for more appeal, they can be spiced up with attractor colors like fluorescent red, orange, pink, and chartreuse. (All the popular Alaska lures come in bright color combinations or you can use stick-on reflective tape, colored paints, markers, or even colored yarn to dress them up.) For flyfishing, attractor patterns like Polar Shrimp, Egg Sucking Leech, Skykomish Sunrise, Mickey Finn, and Zonker can be fished, along with forage patterns, with good results.

The big salmon and trout waters of Bristol Bay (Naknek, Alagnak, Iliamna, Wood-Tikchiks, etc.) and, to a lesser extent, the major salmon systems of Southcentral, along with a few in Southeast, come to mind as offering the very best of Alaska's early summer rainbow fishing. If you time it right, when the first of the major salmon migrations begins entering these systems, you can have some great action with the big, excitable trout that gather there.

Once the first of the salmon reach their home gravel and begin their passion play (usually by mid-July), Alaska's rainbow/charr fishing kicks into high gear. In just about every lesser tributary stream or gravelly midsection of the many major salmon systems spread along the coast, thousands of salmon busily engage in the mating ritual of pairing off, scooping out shallow gravel nests, and laying and fertilizing phenomenal numbers of eggs. These are the areas where Alaska's late summer rainbows (and charr) can be found in greatest concentration.

It is an exciting, high-energy time for all life in these waters. The big salmon get so caught up in their ardor, they can seem almost oblivious to the egg-stealing onslaughts of abundant trout, charr, and grayling. Anything that comes drifting through these spawning areas remotely resembling salmon roe, be it egg pattern fly, fluorescent-bladed spinner, drift bob-

Summer/Fall Rainbow Flies & Lures

Egg Sucking Leech

Glo Bug

Flesh Fly

Mouse

Plugs

Spoons

Drift Bobbers

Spinners

ber, or even a bright yarn-wrapped hook, will usually draw immediate response from the rambunctious hordes.

Spin/baitcast fishermen will have the most success with brightly accented (pink, red, orange, or yellow) spinners, spoons, plugs, jigs, and drift bobbers. For flyfishers, these summer conditions mean egg pattern flies and drift presentations for most waters. The simplest, most popular Alaska egg fly is, of course, the Glo Bug, a puff of orange, pink, peach, or red chenille on a size #4 to #12 egg hook. It's extremely effective fished on a dead drift, just above bottom, in the vicinity of holding or spawning salmon. Other popular egg patterns (or egg-like attractors) include Babine Special, Two-Egg Marabou, Battle Creek, and Cluster Fly.

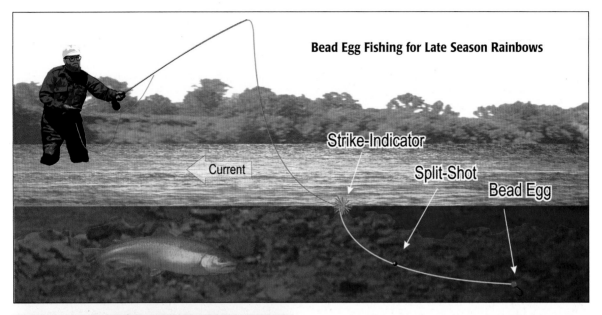

Bead Egg Fishing for Late Season Rainbows

Strike-Indicator

Split-Shot

Bead Egg

Current

It is most important this time of year to fish deep, as these marauders become increasingly focused on the river bottom, looking for drifting roe from redds. Fish lures that are large and bright enough to be seen by your quarry, and use the slowest retrieve possible. Flyfishers may have to use small split shot, wrap lead, or sink tip lines to put their offerings in the "strike zone". Polarized sunglasses will give you an edge in locating holding and spawning salmon and save a lot of time otherwise spent casting to dead water.

Bead Eggs: The "bead egg," a novel and extremely effective variation of the egg pattern fly, has become increasingly popular among flyfishers targeting Alaska's late summer trout and charr. Originally developed by Katmai guides, the bead egg is nothing more than a bright, translucent, orange, pink, or red plastic bead (5 mm to 8 mm) riding above or pressed on (by heat) to a small egg hook (#6 to #10). It is fished using floating line, usually with a strike indicator and a small split shot located about a foot above the bead. (For most situations, a seven to nine-foot tapered leader works fine.)

Many different shades and sizes are used to simulate different species and egg conditions (small, bright red bead for sockeye, larger orange for chum, milky pink for old eggs, etc.). Some guides coat their beads with pearlescent nail polish for even more effect.

The bead egg is most deadly drifted through salmon holding and nesting areas of shallow to moderate depth (less than five feet). Strike indicators, attached near the fly line-leader junction, have become quite popular when fishing bead eggs or glo-bugs, as they definitely make it easier to detect the lightning fast takes of egg-crazed trout and charr. Otherwise, close attention to the line is necessary, with frequent mending, to achieve a drag free drift and maximum hookups.

The real beauty of fishing beads is their economy (only pennies per setup), efficiency, and minimum impact on trout, as you usually only hook the side of the lip, for a quick release with the small egg hooks you'll be using. (Check regulations for restrictions on bead egg setups for the waters you intend to fish. On some rivers like the Kenai, beads must be free sliding or fixed within two inches of the hook.)

The rainbows of summer: Alaska's trout throng salmon spawning areas, July-September, to vie for energy-rich roe and flesh from carcasses.

Dry Fly Fishing & Patterns

Many opportunities for exciting surface fishing go underutilized all across Alaska's rainbow country, for the simple reason that wet presentations work so fabulously well in most waters throughout the season. But you can get in on some of this action if you know what to look for and come prepared with the proper gear and fly selection.

Insect activity in and around Alaska's waters occurs primarily during the warmest part of summer (June and July), but dry fly anglers certainly aren't limited to those times for taking fish. (The Alaska rainbow, if he's hungry enough and the water conditions are right, will whack surface patterns in spring and fall as well.) Your best chances for enticing a surface take will be in the shallow, clear waters of tailouts, riffles, shallow pools, and feeder creeks, especially where there's surface feeding or hatching insects. (Don't overlook Alaska's numerous small lakes either.) Standard floating line presentations and numerous patterns like Elk Hair Caddis, Humpy,

Wulff, Adams, Cahill, Irresistible, even the Gnat or Mosquito, in sizes #8 to #14, will usually produce results. Sometimes a dropper fly rigged behind a dry like a Caddis or Humpy, works when trout are finicky.

No discussion of topwater fishing for Alaska rainbows would be complete without mention of the most notorious "dry fly" of them all, the Mouse. Usually tied with deer or elk hair or rabbit fur, these amazingly lifelike creations imitate the ubiquitous northern vole or lemming, favored items of Alaska's large trout, whenever they can get them. They are best fished (using twitches of the rod to impart lifelike action) around cutbanks, brush piles, sloughs, etc., anywhere hapless rodents might be swept into the river. They are most productive during the low light of evening and morning, and on cloudy, windy days.

Fall Conditions

From September until freeze-up, cooling temperatures, diminishing daylight, and tightening food supplies spark a desperate hunger and wanton recklessness

Rainbow caught on a deerhair Mouse, Alaska's most notorious "dry fly".

among Alaska's trout. With the wane of the salmon runs, they will leave the extreme upper sections of rivers and tributaries and move down into the mainstems, feeding heavily all the while. In the large lake and river systems, big rainbows will cruise the shallows of tributary streams and rivers, scouring the bottom for lingering salmon roe, and even stripping the flesh off carcasses to bolster reserves against the long, dark siege ahead. This is the premier time for the trophy angler, as fish are in prime condition and extremely aggressive. Bristol Bay's Lake Iliamna-Kvichak River system, the rivers of Katmai, the Wood-Tikchiks, and Southcentral's Kenai River are world-famous for their late fall trophy rainbow trout fisheries. If you haven't already done so, you owe it to yourself to make at least one fall outing to fish these waters. With any luck, you can have the kind of trout fishing most folks only dream about. Egg patterns, flesh flies, attractors, along with bright plugs, spoons, spinners, and drift bobbers fished deep are the ticket.

Many of these big waters are best fished from boats, using casting rods to drop lures or drift bobbers down deep where the trout lie. Regardless of your fishing methods, you'll need stout gear to handle the steelhead-sized rainbows and strong currents you'll encounter. (See summary page for recommended gear for trophy fishing.) From mid-September until freeze-up is the traditional peak period for this special trophy season.

Winter Conditions

Once hard winter starts in Alaska (usually sometime in November), rainbows will usually be in the shelter of deep pools, lower river mainstems, and headwater lakes, slowing down with the cold and diminished light to conserve energy for the long haul. Feeding is limited and consists of the occasional minnow, crustacean, or insect larva. Not as exciting to catch this time of year, these winter trout will still put up a tussle, and provide a significant amount of angling opportunity throughout the season, mostly in lakes, where they are taken along with charr and landlocked salmon.

Most winter trout anglers use bait (shrimp, eggs, grubs, etc.) or small jigs, spoons, or flies (attractor and forage patterns) fished off bottom. (Using live fish bait is illegal in Alaska.) Southcentral's Mat-Su Valley, the Anchorage area, Kenai Peninsula, and Kodiak, along with locations around Fairbanks, Delta, and Glennallen see the majority of effort, with the more remote waters of Bristol Bay and Southeast Alaska offering many underutilized opportunities.

Tactics for More Rainbows

Though most of Alaska rainbow fishing isn't rocket science, the art of taking them consistently under the wide range of Alaska conditions can certainly seem to be. High flows and cold temperatures in the spring can hinder fishing considerably, while the height of summer can bring so many spawners (particularly sockeye and pinks) into the state's more productive waters that resident trout and charr become glutted with roe and very selective. Heavy rains at any time can fill rivers with silt and drifting debris, putting fish down as well. And in rare, dry summers, waters can become exceptionally low and clear, making trout spooky and hard to entice. Then there are times when, for no apparent reason, rainbows go totally off feed or disappear altogether.

Anglers who take fish in these and other challenging conditions are, first and foremost, keen observers. They note every possible factor that might be affecting the fishing. Is the water high, low, clear, turbid, warm, or cold? Is the weather cloudy, windy, or sunny and calm? Are there signs of feeding and, if so, what are the trout feeding on? What lures or patterns work best and how are they presented? What condition are the fish in? Where and when are most of them being taken? These are a few of the more important things that keen anglers note every time they fish. (And they are humble enough to seek the observations of other anglers, guides, and air taxis, to augment their own information.) They keep field journals to record data and provide a cumulative reference of their observations and fishing.

When it comes time to put it all together, these anglers, through trial and error and innovation, develop strategies that can take trout when nothing else can. Sometimes it can be a simple matter of creative experimentation with different lures/patterns, presentations, or rigging to turn fish on. For instance, fishing super attractors like Wiggletails, Egg Sucking Zonkers, Alaskabous, or Popsicles, or the gaudiest dressed spinners or brightest spoons can be the ticket in turbid, high water conditions. Similarly, changing to smaller lures and sparse flies can make a difference in bright, low water conditions when fish are spooky. Most anglers are aware of how strike indicators can improve hooking percentages when dead drifting flies late in the season. But much more useful (and artful) is to master advanced line mending and downstream swing techniques to increase your detection and

Angler with rainbow that hit on the edge of a school of spawning sockeye salmon, in a stream in Katmai, Southwest Alaska.

Some of Alaska's most productive and unexploited rainbow trout fishing can be accessed by rafts.

hookups on even the most subtle takes, especially when fishing trout that are glutted with food. (See steelhead chapter for more information on some of these advanced techniques.)

Location and timing are always of the essence. If fish seem scarce, they may be elsewhere, targeting localized food sources. A run of outmigrating smolt, headwater spawning activity, concentrated insect hatches, seasonal lake forage, extreme tides washing prey items into brackish river mouths, etc., can all potentially effect the location of the highly mobile and opportunistic Alaska rainbow. Experience, advice from local sources, and trial and error are the only real ways to determine the right times and right places for a given system.

Successful Alaska rainbow anglers never leave home without a substantial assortment of lures and flies in all colors and sizes. This should always include standard forage imitations like leech, minnow, and sculpin (Muddler) patterns (in drab and dark as well as attractor colors), and the equivalent small, unadorned spinners, jigs, and spoons. Equally important are all manner of attractor and egg/flesh fly patterns and bright spinners, spoons, jigs, plugs, and drift bobbers. Don't forget to bring sufficient gear and terminal tackle for the wide range of fishing tactics you may have to try. And, finally, don't limit yourself by thinking that Alaska rainbows will only hit the standard lures and patterns that people have been fishing for years. When it comes to taking fish when nothing else works, how many anglers would scoff at plastic softbaits, spinnerbaits, and dropper flies? Be versatile and innovative and open to any possibilities; the Alaska rainbow is full of surprises.

Top Flies for Alaska Rainbow Trout

Polar Shrimp, Woolly Bugger, Glo Bug, Bead Egg, Alaska Smolt, Thunder Creek, Parr Fly, Alevin, Egg Sucking Leech, Marabou Muddler, Leech, Zonker, Scud, Hare's Ear Nymph, Caddis Larva, Woolly Worm, Babine Special, Skykomish Sunrise, Pink Sparkler, Battle Creek, Bunny Fly, Mouse, Flesh Fly, Elk Hair Caddis, Humpy, Adams, Maggot.

Alaska Trophy Rainbow Timing

Kenai River (SC)	mid-Sept. – freeze-up
Lk. Iliamna/Kvichak River (SW)	mid-Sept.– freeze-up
Naknek Lake/River System (SW)	mid-Sept. – freeze-up
Nushagak River System (SW)	Sept. – freeze-up
Wood-Tikchiks (SW)	Sept. – freeze-up

Top Ten Alaska Trophy Rainbows

23 lbs.	Naknek Lake (SW)	1991
22 lbs., 7 oz.	Kenai River (SC)	1982
20 lbs., 1 oz.	Kenai River (SC)	1985
20 lbs.	Kenai River (SC)	1992
19 lbs., 12 oz.	Kvichak River (SW)	1981
19 lbs., 8 oz.	Naknek Lake (SW)	1981
19 lbs., 6 oz.	Naknek Lake (SW)	1979
18 lbs., 8 oz.	Naknek River (SW)	1969
18 lbs., 8 oz.	Kvichak River (SW)	1980
18 lbs., 4 oz.	Kenai River (SC)	1987

RAINBOW TROUT

Oncorhynchus mykiss

SPECIES SUMMARY

Alaska common names: Rainbow trout, rainbow, trout, 'bow, 'rainer.

Description: Sleek, small-medium sized, freshwater salmonid, native to coastal streams and lakes of southern Alaska. Has green, greenish-yellow, or gray back, blending with silver on sides, silver-white belly, and trademark pink, scarlet, or lilac band along lateral line and gill plate. Abundant black spot marks on back, sides, and entire tail fin. Flesh pink to white.

Size: Average 1-2 1/2 lbs. (14-20 in.), to 5-7 lbs. (24-30 in.); up to 15 lbs. in large river/ lake systems.

State Record: No separate records kept for rainbow; largest specimen species *O. mykiss*- 42 lbs., 3 oz., Bell Island, SSE, David R. White, 1970.

Habits: Voracious, opportunistic predator, constantly on move for food. Especially fond of small fish and salmon eggs.

Notes: In feeding habits and movements can be very similar to Alaska charr.

Meristics: Gill rakers long 15-22; vertebrae 60-66; pyloric caeca 27-80; lateral line scales 100-155; branchiostegal rays 8-13; dorsal fin 10-12 rays; tail fin 8-12 rays; anal fin 8-2 rays; pectoral fin 11-17 rays.

Range: Coastal Southeast Alaska to Kuskokwim Bay (SW); also transplanted to lakes and ponds in Interior.

Preferred Habitat: Clear, swift flowing, productive coastal streams, and large lake and river systems.

Best waters: Major salmon systems of Southcentral and Southwest, especially those in: Katmai (SW), Lake Iliamna area (SW), Wood-Tikchik State Park (SW), Kuskokwim Bay (SW), Kenai Peninsula (SC), and Susitna Valley (SC); also certain stocked lakes of Tanana Valley (INT).

Best   **Times:**
 Available year-round; best in spring and late summer-fall.

Best Bait/Lures/Flies: Salmon roe; spinners, spoons, plugs, drift bobbers, and jigs; egg, flesh, attractor, and forage pattern flies.

Best Trophy Areas: Naknek River & Lake (SW); Kenai River (SC); Lake Iliamna/Kvichak River (SW); Nushagak River System (SW).

RECOMMENDED GEAR

Flyfishing: 5-6 wt., 8-9 1/2 ft., medium-action flyrod; light-medium trout class reel; 150 yds. 20-30 lb. backing with WF floating, intermediate, or short sink-tip (Type II-IV) line; 7-9 ft. tapered leader, 5X-2X tippet (4-8 lb.).

Trophy fishing/big water: 7-8 weight, 9-9 1/2 ft., medium action flyrod; steelhead or light salmon class reel; 150 yds. 30 lb. backing with WF floating, intermediate or sink tip (Type III-VI or 200-400 grain T-series or equivalent) line; 7-9 ft. tapered leader, 8-12 lb. tippet.

Spinning: Ultralight or light-medium weight, medium-fast action trout rod, 6-7 1/2 ft.; Matching high quality spinning reel; 175 yds. 4-8 lb. nylon monofilament line.

Trophy fishing/big water: Light-medium steelhead trout rod, 7-8 1/2 ft., fast action; matching high-quality spinning reel, 175 yds. 10-15 lb. nylon monofilament.

Bait Casting: Light steelhead, medium action, graphite casting rod, 7-8 1/2 ft., high quality, light-medium weight freshwater casting reel, 200 yds. 6-10 lb. line.

Trophy Fishing/big water: Medium action, 7 1/2-9 ft., steelhead or light salmon drift rod; high quality, medium-heavy freshwater casting reel, 200 yds. 10-15 lb. line.

MAJOR RAINBOW TROUT LOCATIONS

SOUTHEAST
Most of Southeast's waters have steelhead which, in their younger forms, are commonly mistaken for resident rainbows, but there are dozens of lakes containing stocked and native, non-anadromous rainbow populations.

Yakutat: Situk, Mountain lakes.

#4 Marabou
Muddler

1/2 oz.Kastmaster
Spoon

#6 Battle Creek

#10 Bead Egg

#2 Spin-N-Glo

East Fork Chulitna, Kashwitna (especially North Fork), and upper Susitna (Indian River, Portage, and Prairie creeks) rivers; Montana, Little Willow, Willow, Peters (Kahiltna River), Lake, Sheep, and Byers creeks.

Upper Cook Inlet: Chuitna River and Beluga River tributaries.

Upper Copper/Wrangell Mountains: Upper Gulkana and Tebay river systems; Crater, Tex Smith, Tolsona, Van, Silver, Strelna, Gergie, Jans, and Sculpin lakes.

PWS: Blueberry, Ruth lakes.

Kodiak: Many lake and river systems contain small populations of wild rainbow trout, though it may be difficult to distinguish small fish from immature steelhead in some areas. There are also stocked fish in 20 lakes along the road system: Saltery, Buskin, Uganik, Afognak and Ayakulik river systems; Big Kitoi, Olga, Little River, Twin, Cicely, Cascade, Aurel, Malina, and Long lakes.

SOUTHWEST

Alaska's ultimate region for abundant, wild rainbows. Hundreds of rivers, streams, and lakes offer some of the world's best flyfishing, with many trophy opportunities.

Bristol Bay: Lake Iliamna-Kvichak River system (Kvichak, Newhalen, Copper, Gibraltar, and Tazimina rivers; Talarik, Dream, and Belinda creeks); Nushagak/Mulchatna River system (Chilikadrotna, Mulchatna, Little Mulchatna, Koktuli, Stuyahok, Nuyakuk, and upper Nushagak rivers); Wood River lakes and associated tributaries (Wood, Agulowak, Agulukpak, and Peace rivers; Lynx, Grant, and Little Togiak lakes, etc.); Tikchik and Nuyakuk lakes, lower Tikchik River; Togiak River system; Igushik River, Ungalikthluk River.

Alaska Peninsula: Naknek Lake and River system (Brooks River, Grosvenor and Coville lakes, American and Idavain creeks, etc.); Alagnak River system (Nonvianuk-Kukakluk, Kulik, and Battle lakes; Funnel and Moraine creeks, etc.); Egegik River system (King Salmon River—clear tributaries).

Lower Kuskokwim River: Goodnews, Kanektok, Arolik, Kwethluk, Kasigluk, Kisaralik, and Aniak rivers.

INTERIOR

Alaska's Interior does not have naturally occurring populations of rainbows, but it has numerous stocked lakes with good fishing: Quartz, Birch, Chena, Little Harding, Johnson, Robertson, Donna, Little Donna, Koole, Rainbow, Dune, Jan, Lisa, Lost, Craig, Bluff Cabin, Bolio, Coal Mine #5, Tschute, and Geskakmina lakes; Piledriver Slough.

NSE: Hoktaheen and Lost lakes.

Sitka: Sitkoh, Sukoi, Swan, Surge, Salmon, Redoubt, Plotnikof, Davidof, Blue, Sashin, Avoss, Rezanof, Gar, Politofski, Khvostof, Betty, and Deer lakes.

Petersburg/Wrangell: Swan, Thoms, Anan, Boulder, Reflection, Grebe, Goat, Eagle, Marten, and Petersburg lakes.

Ketchikan/POW: Naha River and Lake system; Karta, Klawock, and Thorne rivers; Fish Creek; Harriet Hunt, Connell, Nakat, Filmore, Luck, McDonald, Hugh Smith, Sarkar, Sweetwater, Red Bay, Rainbow, and Kegan lakes.

SOUTHCENTRAL

Kenai Peninsula: Kenai River, Russian River, upper Deep Creek and Anchor River, upper Moose River and associated lakes; Swanson River Lakes; Longmere, Dolly Varden, Vagt, Grant, Upper and Lower Russian, Upper and Lower Ohmer, Upper and Lower Summit, Jean, Kelly, Peterson, Island, Egumen, Watson, Mosquito, Forest, Rainbow, Paddle, Douglas, Cabin, Chugach Estates, Daniels, Sport, Spirit, Swan, Barbara, Cecille, Stormy, Johnson, Quintin, and Encelewski lakes.

Anchorage: Campbell Creek; Otter, Beach, Jewel, Clunie, and Rabbit lakes.

Mat-Su Valley: Matanuska, Echo, Kepler/Bradley, Irene, Long, Ravine, Knik, Reed, Kalmbach, Seymour, Carpenter, Kashwitna, Dawn, Marion, Lynne, Honeybee, Diamond, Walby, Crystal, Finger, and Florence lakes.

Susitna River System: Deshka, Talachulitna, Upper Talkeetna,

| #3 Mepps Black Fury Spinner | #6 Egg Sucking Zonker | #2 Mouse | #8 Fry (Thunder Creek) | #4 Bristol Bay Smolt |

Steelhead
Prince of Sportfish

The early morning fog hangs like a heavy curtain at water's edge and the mercury hasn't yet crested the magic 40° mark, but it's time to don waders and leave the warm security of the 48-footer anchored in the inlet and head into shore on the ebb tide.

Once ashore, a mile-and-a-half hike through alder, spruce, hemlock, cedar, and devil's club brings us to several promising-looking runs below a twelve-foot falls. We waste no time breaking the rods out and getting our lines in the tannin-stained water.

"Fish on!" yells Larry. I turn and see a dark fish of about twelve pounds tear downstream, jumping all the while. After 30 seconds, his line suddenly slacks. Fish off, Larry. Our little group fishes out the remainder of the day and manages to hook 16 steelhead and several Dollies, cutthroats, and rainbows.

The weather on the second day remains drizzly and cold. Thirteen fish are hooked, most of them dark. The troller rocks and rolls that night, as the southeast wind gusts to 60 miles per hour. Forced to "lay on the hook" instead of attempting the trip back across Clarence Strait, the skipper fights a grin as he informs his guests: "Oh well, I guess we'll just have to stay here and make the best of the situation."

Next morning, I begin at one of my favorite holes about a mile up from salt water and quickly hook a hot, bright hen—a "new fish"—with gunmetal blue back, silvery flanks, and sea lice. After hooking three more bright steelhead, I move upstream to join my companions. We are the only ones on the river that day and are thankful for it. Another bright hen leaps for the sky four times and runs off 50 feet of line in a single burst. When the fish is brought in, she turns and streaks like a lightning bolt downstream 75 yards, into a logjam, where the line parts with a twang and the steelhead goes free.

Rain and the southeast wind have given us a special bonus day of fishing. We paddle back to the *Julie Ann*, our floating hotel, having hooked 19 steelhead.

Fall steelheading, Tebay River system, Wrangell Mountains, Southcentral Alaska.

STEELHEAD: PRINCE OF SPORTFISH

The steelhead trout, *Oncorhynchus mykiss*, the sea-roving form of the rainbow, is perhaps the most sought-after and prized of the North Pacific's many fine gamefishes. An elite band of anglers the world over diligently pursues them with a passion that borders on the fanatical, braving all manner of stream conditions, weather, and logistics—not to mention expense—to enjoy some high-quality fishing.

And while the mystique of "steelheading" may be hard to grasp for some, its appeal is infectious and easily understood after a single bout with the super-charged saltwater rainbow. They fight spectacularly, with the same high energy and astounding leaps of their river-bound brothers, only more so, because of their size and the vigor imparted by their life in the sea. As iron is to steel, the rainbow trout's noble qual-

ities of spirit, beauty, and grace are refined and tempered in rare form to produce the steelhead, prince of sportfish.

Steelheading in Alaska has been described in many ways. Of all that has been written and said, however, perhaps the most significant and attractive feature is the opportunity to angle for wild fish in wild environs—a luxury in these days of put-and-take fisheries. Alaska, too, is changing and unfortunately, some places are not as wild as they once were, and some runs have been depleted. Yet overall, the state still offers some of the world's best remaining opportunities to experience a little of "how it used to be" everywhere for this magnificent species.

"Explosive fish are the steelhead and salmon that stalk our memories and dreams," wrote Ernest Schwiebert. We stalk steelhead in Alaska not because

gunmetal blue-back changes to an olive black. A distinct reddish color develops on the flanks above and below the lateral line, and the shiny white undersides become a dusky gray. Upon completion of spawning, the steelhead's colors gradually revert to their ocean phase.

Steelhead in Alaska are not noted for their size relative to races elsewhere, such as the outsized fish of the Skeena River drainage in northern British Columbia. Steelhead throughout much of Southeast generally average eight to nine pounds. The fish of the other regions are slightly smaller, usually averaging six to eight pounds (steelhead from Kodiak's famous Karluk River and Kenai's Anchor River fall into this size class), with some fish no larger than four pounds.

Reports of 20-pound-plus fish run rampant, but most of these accounts are nothing more than good fish stories. (Of all the hooked steelhead logged in my fishing diary, the largest remains a 38-inch buck that was probably slightly less than 20 pounds. I have personally witnessed two fish over 20 pounds landed and released. Will Jones, owner of Prince of Wales Lodge, over many years has seen only five hooked steelhead that reached or exceeded 20 pounds.)

The world record sport-caught steelhead, a fish just over 42 pounds, was taken from Southeast's Behm Canal in 1970. Judging by the extraordinary dimensions of this specimen and current weight and length information for steelhead around the state, it is largely assumed that the fish was of British Columbia origin. Southeast has long been recognized as the cradle of trophy steelhead in Alaska; however, reliable reports of fish measured at over 40 inches have come from Southcentral's Ninilchik and Kasilof rivers (as well as other area streams). Prior to Alaska statehood and the subsequent sharp increase of angling effort associated with roadside access, steelhead weighing in excess of 30 pounds were not unheard of in streams on the Kenai Peninsula.

of their size or numbers, but because of the experience afforded. Through these experiences, one welcomes the stalkers of our memories and dreams.

DESCRIPTION

The steelhead can be identified from the various salmon species by having eight to twelve rays in the anal fin (most salmon have 12 to 17 rays). Usually more streamlined and slender than resident rainbow trout, the steelhead in its ocean phase exhibits a bright silvery sheen that is essential to survival. The topsides are generally a shiny, gunmetal blue, contrasted with silver-white below the lateral line. There are black, regularly spaced spots on the back and sides, as well as on both lobes of the tail.

In preparation for spawning, the steelhead's colors become more similar to resident rainbow trout. The

RANGE, ABUNDANCE & STATUS

The native range of the steelhead closely follows that of the resident river rainbow along the north Pacific rim—from the mountains of northwest Mexico to the rocky coast of the Kamchatka Peninsula. In Alaska they are distributed from Dixon Entrance to the vicinity of Cold Bay on the Alaska Peninsula. They are found most continuously from southern

Southeast to the North Gulf Coast, with sporadic distribution west into Cook Inlet, Kodiak, and the Alaska Peninsula (both sides). Though numerous isolated occurrences suggest otherwise, no documented spawning populations exist north of Chignik on the Alaska Peninsula, or in Bristol Bay or upper Cook Inlet. Officially, the continent's most northern run occurs in the Gulkana River (Copper River drainage) north of Cordova.

There are 350 streams in Southeast now known to receive steelhead. The greatest majority of these occur from south of Frederick Sound to Dixon Entrance. In comparison, Southcentral steelhead populations are mainly found on Kodiak Island with isolated, yet stable, runs occurring in lower Cook Inlet, eastern Prince William Sound, and the vast Copper River system. Little documented information exists on Southwest steelhead streams. Comprehensive data on the great majority of Alaska steelhead systems is, unfortunately, not available at present. There is a great need for further research.

Populations of steelhead in Alaska are, with few exceptions, relatively small. The largest runs in Southeast total only 500 or more fish annually, with far more streams receiving 200 to 300, and the greatest number of runs in the neighborhood of 100 fish. These populations are obviously quite low compared to the size of salmon runs in Alaska, and to many steelhead runs elsewhere, and this is no doubt due to the lower diversity of forage and other limiting factors typical of northern streams. Most, if not all, Alaska steelhead streams are strongly influenced by the presence of salmon and, without the addition of these spent fish to the nutrient cycle, would most likely be almost sterile. Some of the larger steelhead runs in Alaska occur in the Karta River of Prince of Wales Island (500 to 1,000), the Anchor River on the Kenai Peninsula (1,000 to 1,800), the Karluk River on Kodiak Island (4,000), and the fabulous Situk River near Yakutat (5,000 to 9,000 in recent years).

LIFE HISTORY & HABITS

Steelhead are large anadromous rainbow trout that rear in freshwater streams. Most Alaska fish spend three years (occasionally four) in fresh water before they journey to the ocean as six to seven-inch smolts, eventually subsisting on a diet primarily of various fishes, crustaceans, and squid. Roaming the food-rich open sea for two to three years, they attain

Most Alaska steelhead streams are small, shallow, and brushy; only a few systems approach the classic conditions seen in the Pacific Northwest and British Columbia.

large size relative to most resident rainbow trout before returning as mature adults to their natal streams.

Steelhead return to streams in Southwest and Southcentral primarily in the fall, while Southeast receives runs in three seasons (spring, summer, fall). Fall-run fish typically begin returning in September, peak in numbers during October, and continue arriving through November (even into December and early January in Southeast). Depending upon the system's timing and weather conditions, entry may vary several weeks between drainages and even within a location from one year to the next. Runs seem to occur progressively earlier farther north. Populations on the Kenai Peninsula, for example, may begin ascending spawning streams as soon as early August with peak inmigration occurring in mid to late September. Ocean returns are generally complete by late October.

Spring-run steelhead are by far the most widespread race in Southeast. Many streams with low flows are host to spawning steelhead during the spring months. These fish begin returning in March, with April and May being the peak arrival periods. Inmigration is usually over by late May, although a few locations see fish arriving into early July. Spring fish are therefore generally available to the angler for a shorter period of time. Some research has determined

Steelhead, as supercharged rainbows, fight spectacularly, testing an angler's gear and skill to the utmost. Here an angler battles it out on a gravel bar in Southwest Alaska.

that female spring fish also spend less time in fresh water than males. (On occasion I have landed chrome-bright hen fish with sea lice, that had already spawned just a short distance from tidewater.) These short appearances in fresh water are especially common in smaller streams during low water periods, and can present a frustrating challenge to the angler. Beyond Southeast, spring-arriving steelhead are rare, for reasons not known. It is thought that perhaps a small component of the fall-run fish may, in some years, overwinter in the tidal area/estuaries or off the mouth of spawning waters waiting for suitable conditions in the spring. Or they may simply represent anomalies within the population.

There are only a few known runs of summer steelhead in Alaska (Baranof Island, SE). These fish enter streams in July and August, and spend the fall and winter there until commencing reproduction the following spring. Taking into account these fish, it is possible to take steelhead in Alaska every month of the year, though the best fishing times are confined to the few months that coincide with the peak of the spring and fall runs.

Both steelhead run types share many habits. Generally, they hold in the same water, and can be found in the same type of spawning habitat. But there are some key differences. Summer and fall fish return sexually immature and also tend, at times, to be more aggressive toward the fisherman's offerings than spring fish. This is due, in part, to warmer water temperatures and to true feeding tendencies. I have personally landed many early fall fish that were gorged with pink salmon spawn and were dropping small, pale pink eggs from their jaws while I was releasing them. Some of these fish will hold in the upper reaches of holes and runs to opportunistically pick off drifting eggs. Fish under these conditions are easy prey to egg imitations.

Summer and fall-run fish are more limited in their habitat requirements. The majority of fall runs and all summer runs return to river systems with lakes. The exceptions are rivers or large streams with enough deep pools to allow overwinter survival.

All races generally spawn in the spring and early summer (mid-April to mid-June), regardless of when they enter fresh water. However, there are confirmed reports of steelhead in Alaska reproducing as early as December and observations of fish in certain systems spawning as late as July. And, unlike salmon, steelhead are capable of spawning more than once (up to four times). Most runs of spring steelhead are comprised of a significant portion of repeat spawners (research has shown that repeat spawners can account for as high as 45% of a given run, although the average percentage is lower). These repeat spawners usually account for fish that exceed 30 inches.

Steelhead tend to favor relatively short, coastal drainages for spawning (mostly within 25 miles of the ocean). The longest migrations occur on the Copper River system, with steelhead bound for the upper reaches of the Gulkana River—a distance of some 250 miles from the North Gulf Coast. However, as is the case with many smaller creeks (such as those in Southeast), spawning may commence just above the tidal sections. Suitable habitat includes clear, tannic-stained or even glacially tinted waters, of moderate current and shallow depth, with gravel substrate. Water temperatures during the spawning cycle commonly range between 40 and 55°F. The female lays from 100 to 12,000 eggs, which hatch in late summer and fall.

FISHING ALASKA'S STEELHEAD

Sport anglers capture 20-40 thousand steelhead a year from Alaska's waters. The majority of these fish are taken in Southeast, from the Yakutat and Ketchikan/Prince of Wales areas. Populous Southcentral Alaska's significant steelhead effort is focused on the streams of the lower Kenai Peninsula and Kodiak Island. A small amount of fishing is done in Southwest on the remote streams of the Alaska Peninsula.

Finding Fish—Reading the Water

Steelhead are usually found in holding water that has a depth of three feet or more. They usually opt for moderate or fast current, instead of slack water where some Pacific salmon will hold. They are especially fond of secondary currents or seams on the edge of the main current. Anglers should look for these flow characteristics and any obstructions that may cause them, such as boulders and logs. As in steelheading elsewhere, if a fish is hooked in a given spot, chances are good fish will be there again under similar conditions, provided there are no major changes in the stream bed composition.

Most steelhead streams in Alaska are fairly short, small, and brushy compared to the huge mainland streams of the Pacific Northwest states and British Columbia. The structure of the stream beds remains more constant in these smaller Alaska streams, and they also hardly ever "go out" in the sense of being too muddy to fish, though they may be occasionally too high and of less than ideal clarity. The large mainland streams usually experience a great disparity in flow range due to the large areas they drain.

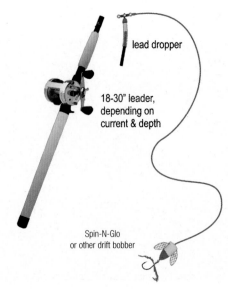

The standard Pacific Northwest steelhead drift setup will work on many of Alaska's streams: a drift bobber fished off a lead dropper that is bounced along the bottom. Most popular colors for Alaska are pink, orange, peach, chartreuse, and purple.

Basic Techniques

Drift Fishing: Under most water conditions and in all seasons, drift fishing is the most effective way of hooking steelhead. When all other methods fail, steelhead can usually be hooked in deep water this way. In Alaska, as elsewhere in the Pacific Northwest, most (but not all) drift fishing is done with an eight to nine-foot graphite, medium-action, steelhead rod, in tandem with a level wind bait casting reel. The rod should have a sensitive tip to detect when fish "mouth" bait and stout butt section for solid hook setting and fighting capabilities. Most accomplished drift fishermen agree that the bait caster affords distinct advantages over the spinning reel for drift fishing. With thumb on the spool of the casting reel mounted on top of the rod, the angler has more feel of the line and stream bottom, plus greater control when setting the hook. Also, the level wind reel, because of its design, is inherently stronger and has a superior drag.

Numerous lures are used effectively for drift fishing steelies, the most effective for Alaska being Li'l Corkies, Spin-N-Glos, Glo Glos, and other egg-simulating attractors, in pink, orange, peach, chartreuse, and purple.

Regardless of the type, color, or size of lure the angler is using, its correct action during the drift is paramount to success. Simply stated, the lure must drift with a natural appearance. It must not hang on the bottom, and should not even "skip" with the weight as some have proposed; rather, it should drift with as near neutral buoyancy as possible. The closer you can come to attaining a natural drift, the better your chances are of getting steelhead to pick up the lure. When determining the amount of weight to attach above the attractor, you should remember that too little weight is always better than too much, as a general rule.

The angler who has become adept at drift fishing before graduating to flyfishing usually becomes a more effective flyfisher, with a greater insight into the steelhead's habits of holding in various lies, and how they take or mouth the attractor.

Jig Fishing: Fishing jigs has become increasingly popular in recent years, because of its ease and efficiency over a wide range of conditions. It's a particularly effective method in slow currents, for the "tanks" and "frog water" encountered on many streams.

An eight to nine-foot, medium-weight spinning rod and matching reel (with 8 to 15-pound test mono) is the preferred setup for jig fishing, as the spinning reel is ideally suited to pay out line freely during the downstream portion of the drift. Terminal tackle consists of small, feathered jigs ranging in weight from 1/16 to 1/4 ounce, with the 1/8 ounce size most popular in Southeast waters. The hottest colors are pink, pink/white, pink/purple, black/pink, black/white, orange, and red/yellow.

Fish the jigs below a large, two-inch-diameter plastic bobber, varying leader length with water depth to ensure a drift right above bottom. Cast the bobber and jig setup upstream and drift it through potential holding water, keeping an eye on the bobber for the slightest bump or sway, indicating a take by a fish.

Spinners: Spinners can be very effective for fishing steelhead. However, you must remember that steelhead in very cold water generally don't move well to take spinners, but more readily mouth an attractor drifted directly to them. Many anglers work around this by using ultra-light gear and smaller spinners for cold water conditions, working the blade ever so slightly as the lure tumbles through steelhead lies and into close striking range of lethargic fish. With the

smaller, more sensitive gear, the often subtle take is more easily felt. These setups can also be very effective in extreme shallow or bright conditions, when steelhead get spooky. Some of the more popular spinners used for steelhead are the Mepps Aglia, Vibrax, and Rooster Tail, in sizes #1 to #5 and colors of silver, gold, fluorescent red, black, chartreuse/yellow, pink, and green. Many of the techniques used in fishing spinners for Alaska steelhead are similar to those used for rainbow. (See chapter on rainbow trout.)

FLYFISHING ALASKA'S STEELHEAD

The experience of stalking and hooking a steelhead in its wild environs using fly gear arguably is the most sporting and satisfying in all of angling, and certainly among the most exciting to be had in Alaska. Under most conditions, the flyfisher knowingly sacrifices some potential hook-ups when choosing fly equipment over drift gear. The exceptions are during low water conditions or in extremely shallow parts of a stream, like riffles, tailouts, and some pocket water.

Equipment

Although most hardcore steelheaders have amassed a large arsenal of tackle, a modest amount of main tackle can suffice. A nine to nine-and-a-half-foot, eight-weight rod is the main stick used. Some choose seven-weights followed by the lesser used nine-weight for extreme conditions. In choosing main tackle it is more practical to invest money in quality rods, rather than reels with expensive disc drag systems. Since most Alaska streams are small relative to the large streams of the Pacific Northwest, expensive disc drag reels are often overkill, as fish do not make the long runs they would in big water down south.

The types of fly lines used for Alaska steelhead are very much the same as those used for rainbow trout—full-floating line, a sink-tip or two, and possibly a high density, 24-foot, T-series sink line or shooting taper for extreme conditions. The interchangeable tip line systems now widely available are very useful, allowing anglers to adapt to different water conditions without changing an entire line and spool. (The individual tip sections attach to the main floating line by a loop to loop connection, with a surprisingly efficient transfer of energy during casting.) Most of these systems have "density compensated" tips, which sink first before the midsection, allowing the angler to remain in much better contact with the terminal end when fishing.

A Lucky Boy's Big Trout

The largest steelhead ever taken on rod and reel was caught by an eleven-year-old boy! David Robert White of Seattle was trolling herring with his dad near Bell Island out of Ketchikan (SE) on June 22, 1970, when he hooked and landed a fish over 42 pounds (43 inches long) that they presumed was a king salmon. The catch was promptly frozen and shipped to a taxidermist, who astutely contacted some fish biologists who examined it and confirmed it as a new world record steelhead.

Fly Patterns: Of all folklore circulated among the steelheading fraternity, none is so great as that which surrounds fly patterns. Most likely this stems from the real need for hundreds of trout patterns to meet the many great variables involved in fishing the variety of species and conditions encountered elsewhere. Though one may respect the rich tradition behind the many local patterns and beliefs, it is possible to isolate some general principles that can apply everywhere.

Lani Waller simplified the discussion in his 3M videos when he classed flies as bright, dull, and dark patterns. The bright patterns include flies of loud color, such as orange, pink and chartreuse. These are most effective on bright fish under normal and high water conditions. Flies such as the Burlap and Muddler are examples of dull patterns, which are especially effective during low-water periods and for fish that have been worked over by other anglers. Dark patterns describe such well-known standbys as the Skunk, Silver Hilton, and Black Bunny Leech. These work in a broad range of conditions and situations; on some systems in the Skeena drainage in British Columbia, they are the main patterns used. They tend to be more effective on long river systems where fish have already journeyed quite a distance from salt water. Dull and especially dark patterns are good choices for fishing a second time through a good piece of water that has shown to be holding steelhead. Seasoned anglers have long known that changing patterns to "give them a new look," is very often the stimulus that induces more strikes.

Fly anglers determined to present something found naturally in streams might try using Glo Bugs.

As the accomplished fly tier and teacher Andre Puyans has often commented, "Why be a snob about it? After all, it is matching the hatch." It is ironic that this pattern that does "match the hatch" is scorned by some as not being a real fly pattern. However you feel about them, Glo Bugs are highly effective and can out-produce all others in some situations. A wide variety of colors and sizes should be carried in your vest.

Basic Techniques

Swing Fishing: The traditional crosscurrent, swing technique or "wet fly swing" is still one of the most widespread methods of working trout water with a fly. This involves a cast across or quartered (at 45° angle) upstream, followed by a series of line mends (repositioning the trailing line with a flip of the rod, which alters the amount of drag) as the fly travels down and across the stream, to achieve a drift and presentation most likely to prompt takes from holding fish.

In the colder waters of late fall or early spring, when the majority of Alaska's steelhead runs occur (races of true summer run fish are rare), many of the traditional techniques find less application because fish tend to be less active. The single most important element in the equation becomes the angler's ability to slow the fly during its crosscurrent swing.

A modified technique known as the "downstream swing" achieves much better line control in slowing the fly across current with the line under tension. It is arguably one of the most enjoyable methods as well, as the "take" or "yank" is always felt and usually comes as a surprise, since the fish are downstream and usually out of sight. It works best in rivers where the bottom structure tends to be somewhat even, not overly deep, and fairly wide from bank to bank.

Usually the cast is made slightly downstream, followed with an upstream mend, or "reach cast" toward

Downstream Swing Technique

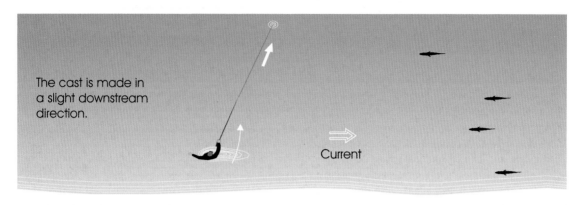

The cast is made in a slight downstream direction.

Current

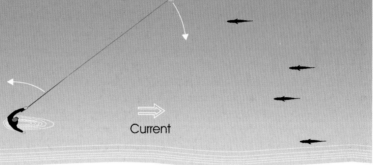

After casting, change the rod to the left hand and move it to a position perpendicular to the bank. Hold the rod up at a 45 degree angle to the water, letting the fly drift inward until the line is parallel to the bank.

Current

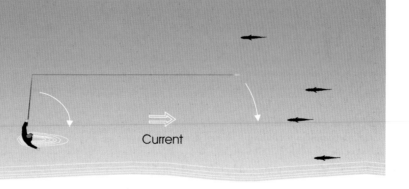

Continue to hold the rod tip up, while swinging it in the direction indicated until the fly line is directly downstream of you.

Current

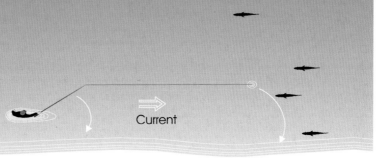

Change the flyrod back to the right hand and continue to swing it toward the bank until the fly reaches near shore, then take a step downstream and cast again in the same manner.

Current

the opposite bank. The reach cast is, in effect, an aerial mend. The rod should then be held perpendicular to the current (this is imperative) with the upstream hand, regardless which hand is used for casting. For instance, if the current is coming from left to right, a right-handed caster should complete the cast and upstream mend, then quickly change hands to fish with the left hand. This technique aids in the main goal of slowing the fly. The rod is maintained at a right angle while the fly swings until it is directly below the angler. (The longer the line, the greater the waiting time for it to completely straighten.) The rod is then slowly swung across current below one's position (after changing hands again), "milking" the drift in slower currents and allowing following steelhead ample time to take the fly.

By learning to fish with both hands, water is fished slowly and covered more effectively, resulting in increased hook-ups. The casts are begun short and lengthened to the necessary distance. The angler then takes one step downstream and continues by again casting that same long length of line until the entire section of stream has been covered. As these steps are followed, anglers will effectively be slowing the fly through the entire drift (including the start near the opposite bank), instead of pulling flies out of these lanes too quickly for steelhead to take them.

Rod tips should also be held fairly high above the water's surface, creating a belly of line from rod tip to the water. This will enable steelhead adequate time to engulf the fly and turn on it, increasing hook-ups. Anglers accustomed to swing fishing with nymphs for trout will find this technique to be awkward at first, as trout anglers have long known that a rod tip held low to the water's surface will result in a greater number of hookups. In this approach to swing fishing, with the line always under tension, it will naturally tend to "buoy up" in current. An adequate sink tip line, in terms of sink rate, must therefore be chosen for the current and depth.

Strike Indicators: The use of strike indicators in trout fly-fishing is centuries old. In her book, *A Treatise on Fishing with an Angle*, Dame Juliana Berners in the 15th century wrote, "For the trout, take a piece of cork no bigger than a garden pea and burn it through with a hot iron, and that shall be your float." The application of indicators to fly-fishing for steelhead is relatively new, becoming popular in the past 25 years. Indicators today are made of various materials including cork, wood, styrofoam, and other synthetic materials that are attached usually below the end of the floating line. After casting upstream, the angler makes a series of mends in order to sink the fly en route to attaining a true drag-free drift. (The fly may be weighted, or the angler may elect to add a microshot a short distance above the fly.) The strike indicator remains at or near the surface throughout the drift and provides a highly visible, sensitive monitor to detect variances that may be fish mouthing or attacking the fly.

Hinged Indicator Fishing System: The hinged indicator system was developed by David Hickson and Dean Shubert in Northern California, and was first employed in trout fishing. It is highly effective, particularly in site-specific locations like pocket water, slots, shoots, depressions etc., which abound in the small, brushy streams of Alaska. Many steelhead that would otherwise not move to strike will engulf a fly drifted naturally in front of them with this technique.

The goal in hinged indicator fishing is to attain a true and natural dead drift. Right-handed casters should practice this technique with the current coming from their right to left. (It is much easier to learn effective mends on this bank.) The angler begins with an upstream "tuck cast." This is an overhead cast which is simply overpowered and stopped short, allowing slack line to pile on the water at the target spot. The indicator is then gently lifted from the water with a roll mend, placing it slightly upstream of the fly. Another roll mend follows, sending slack line above the indicator. (The roll mend is executed by a downward "flick" of the rod while turning the wrist inward toward one's body.) By piling line in this way behind the indicator, the fly is allowed to sink to the desired depth, while drifting naturally without drag caused by the indicator. The fundamental key to this technique is proper line mending. As the indicator passes in front of the angler, downstream mends in front (or downstream) of the indicator are usually necessary to continue a long drag-free drift throughout the potential holding area. As the fly drifts below the angler, he/she can increase the length of the drift by shaking the rod tip briskly from side to side in order to pay out additional slack. When the indicator twitches or submerges, the hook should be set immediately by a brisk upward sweep of the rod and simultaneous haul (line pull) with the non-casting arm.

Hinged Indicator

Fly-Line   Nail Knot

4' - 4 1/2' Butt Section (20-25#)

Clinch Knots   Fluorescent Yarn
for Strike Indicator

0X-3X Tippet, length 1-1/2
times depth of water

Split Shot
8-10 inches above fly

Glo Bug, nymph or traditional
steelhead pattern

Spey fishing has advantages that are especially useful on some Alaska steelhead waters.

Spey Fishing: Spey rods are long and powerful, and are made for two-hand use. They were the original fly rods, though they are relatively new to Alaska fishing, gaining popularity only within the last ten years. Deriving their name from Scotland's River Spey and developed mainly for Atlantic salmon, they are fished using the traditional downstream swing method mainly, but not exclusively, on larger streams or larger sections of streams. The revered Roderick Haig-Brown wrote, "On big waters, I should still use a double-handed rod. Perhaps it is a matter of confidence."

Romance and tradition aside, there are some very practical advantages in the use of the longer, two-handed rods. The first immediately apparent one is increased casting efficiency, with greater distance and much less false casting. Another most important advantage is greater line control. With the added length of rod, the angler is able to make mends with less effort, as well as control the drift more using the rod tip. The added length of these rods also enables anglers to cover water previously inaccessible due to wading hazards or casting obstructions.

Those desiring to learn Spey cast fundamentals can take casting classes and/or avail themselves of numerous publications and videos that cover this growing segment of the flyfishing market. In the excellent instructional video by RIO Products called *International Spey Casting*, Simon Gawesworth explains three principles that are fundamental to effective Spey casting. First, create the biggest belly of line behind the angler in order to load the rod for the forward stroke. Second, attempt to leave as little line lying in the water as possible, to reduce "line stick." And third, create the belly exactly opposite the intended direction of the forward cast in order to load the rod to its maximum potential. Spey casting, like every method of angling, requires much practice in order to become proficient.

Top Flies for Alaska Steelhead

Glo Bug (all colors), Leech (including rabbit fur and articulated versions), Muddler, Bomber, Woolly Bugger, Marabou Fly (Alaskabou, Popsicle, Showgirl, etc.), Polar Shrimp, Sparkle Shrimp, Green Butt Skunk, Purple Peril, Egg Sucking Leech, Mickey Finn, Rajah, Fall Favorite, Silver Hilton, Skykomish Sunrise, Traditional Trout Nymph Patterns (tied on steelhead hooks).

STEELHEAD TROUT
Oncorhynchus mykiss

SPECIES SUMMARY

Alaska Common Names: Steelhead trout, steelhead, steelie.

Description: Large, salmon-like, sea-run rainbow trout. Silver-metallic appearance when fresh from sea, shading and markings generally more subdued than in rainbow trout. Spawning fish darker, with color and markings much like resident rainbow trout. Flesh: pink to orange-red.

Size: Average 6-9 lbs.; to 34 in. or more and 15 lbs.

State/World Record: 42 lbs., 2 oz., Bell Island, SSE, David R. White, 1970.

Habits: Temperamental and elusive.

Notes: In genetics, life history, habits, and sporting qualities, closest of all Pacific salmonids to exalted Atlantic salmon, *Salmo salar*.

Meristics: Gill rakers long 15-22; vertebrae 60-66; pyloric caeca 27-80; lateral line scales 100-155; branchiostegal rays 8-13; dorsal fin 10-12 rays; tail fin 8-12 rays; anal fin 8-12 rays; pectoral fin 11-17 rays.

Range: Coastal streams, SE panhandle to Alaska Peninsula (SW).

Preferred Habitat: Swift, rocky streams with headwater lakes for rearing; spends adult life at sea.

Best Waters: SSE coastal streams—Petersburg to POW.

Best Times: April-June; October-December.

Best Bait/Lures/Flies: Salmon roe; jigs, spinners, drift bobbers; egg pattern and sparse attractor flies.

Best Trophy Areas: Situk River (Yakutat); Sitkoh Creek (SE); Petersburg Creek (SE).

RECOMMENDED GEAR

Drift fishing:
8-9 ft. graphite, medium-action, steelhead casting rod (rated for 8-12 lb. test), matching high quality reel and 150 yds. 8-15 lb. test line.

Jig Fishing:
8-9 ft., medium-fast action, steelhead spinning rod (rated for 8-15 lb. test), matching high quality reel and 150 yds. 8-12 lb. monofilament line.

Flyfishing:
9 to 9 1/2 ft., 8-wt., medium-fast action graphite fly rod with matching reel; or 7-10 wt., 11-15 ft., traditional action Spey rod with matching reel. 150 yds., 30 lb. backing and either WF floating, intermediate, sink tip (Type II-VI or T-series 200-300 grain), or interchangeable tip lines, with 7-9 ft. leader, 3X-0X tippet.

MAJOR STEELHEAD LOCATIONS

SOUTHEAST

Most of Alaska's steelhead streams are located here. There are several hundred documented systems, with small runs (200 fish or less) the general rule. Spring steelhead are dominant, with peaks in May, but some significant late winter and late fall fishing can be had also.

Ketchikan: Fish, Humpback, Ketchikan, and Ward creeks; Naha River; McDonald Lake system.

Prince of Wales: Harris, Karta, Klawock, and Thorne rivers; Staney, Eagle, Kegan, and Salmon Bay creeks.

Wrangell: Anan, Aaron, Eagle, and Thoms creeks.

Petersburg: Petersburg, Hamilton, Kadake, Ohmer, Falls, and Duncan Saltchuck creeks; Kah Sheets and Castle rivers.

Sitka: Sitkoh and Eva creeks; Plotnikof and Ford Arm rivers.

Juneau: Peterson and Hasselborg creeks; Taku River.

Yakutat and Gulf Coast: Situk, Italio, and Tsiu rivers.

SOUTHCENTRAL

Southcentral has some of the state's most heavily fished steelhead streams on the Kenai Peninsula, with considerable high-quality opportunities on Kodiak Island (17 known steelhead systems). These are mostly all fall and winter run fish, with peaks in late September through October.

Kenai: Anchor, Ninilchik, and Kasilof rivers; Deep and Stariski creeks.

#6 'Lil Corky & Yarn   #8 Glo Bug   #4 Egg Sucking Leech   #6 Skykomish Sunrise   #4 Vibrax

Copper River: Tebay (including Hanagita River), Tazlina, and Upper Middle Fork Gulkana, (Dickey, Twelvemile, and Hungry Hollow creeks) rivers.

Kodiak: Karluk, Ayakulik, Afognak, Little, and Uganik rivers; Pauls, Akalura, Malina, Marka, and Saltery creeks.

SOUTHWEST

Southwest has a handful of documented spawning streams that are scattered along the Alaska Peninsula to Cold Bay, with rumors of many more. All indications are that these are fall run fish, September through October being the peak of the run. This is definitely the unexplored frontier of steelheading in North America.

Port Moller: Bear and Sandy rivers.

Nelson Lagoon: Sapsuk and Nelson rivers.

Cold Bay: Russell and Trout creeks.

Alaska Trophy Steelhead Timing	
Situk River (SE)	mid-April–mid-May
Sitkoh Creek (SE)	late April–late May.
Petersburg Cr. (SE)	late April–late May.
Karta River (SE)	late Mar.–early May, late Nov.–late Dec.

Top Ten Alaska Trophy Steelhead		
42 lbs., 2 oz.	Bell Island (SE)	1970
26 lbs.	Douglas Island (SE)	1980
26 pounds	Situk River (SE)	1988
24 lbs., 8 oz.	Waterfall Resort (SE)	1990
23 lbs., 9 oz.	Situk River (SE)	1987
23 lbs., 8 oz.	Situk River (SE)	1982
23 lbs.	Situk River (SE)	1985
22 lbs.	Situk River (SE)	1987
21 lbs., 14 oz.	Situk River (SE)	1974
21 lbs., 8 oz.	Situk River (SE)	1986

Ethics for Wild Steelheaders

1. Preserve wild steelhead.
2. Practice catch-and-release.
3. Don't use bait or treble hooks.
4. Leave spawning fish alone.
5. Respect the privacy of others streamside.
6. Get involved in local chapter Trout Unlimited.

1/8 oz. Marabou Jig

#6 Rajah

#4 Sparkle Shrimp

#5 Mepps Aglia

#6 Woolly Bugger

Cutthroat
Noble Trout

It was the end of my junior year in college, and my '62 VW van was packed for a summer of flyfishing the West, when I received a fateful call from the U.S. Forest Service. They were looking for help on a remote project in Prince William Sound, Alaska, and I listened intently to details of the job offer over piles of maps, insect hatch charts, and astounding estimates of Montana's 2,000 fish per mile. The lure of blue ribbon western trout streams was certainly hard to resist, but Alaska was the chance of a lifetime.

Six weeks later I was in Cordova. An awesome flight in a 1955 DeHavilland Beaver and a 45-minute hike straight up a mountain brought me to base camp, where my supervisor and campmates lost no time briefing me—a total greenhorn—on the finer points of Alaska salmon and halibut fishing. But I had my designs at the moment on some slightly different rewards—casting a fly into some of those delectable ponds and streams I had passed earlier on the trail, to see what mysteries they held.

A light breeze from the ocean spilled over a hill and rippled the surface of the most perfect little lake you could imagine. Nervously, I tied a #16 Mosquito on and rolled it out, letting it drift in the weak current near the outlet where I'd seen a rise. I twitched it ever so slightly and it vanished in a carnivorous vortex, as a bright little package of muscle took off for the sky. This beautiful trout, heavily spotted, with a luster like a newly minted gold coin, had two brilliant scarlet slash marks on its throat—the definitive brand of a fish I knew well from my youth on the coastal streams and rivers of northern California—the cutthroat trout.

I stayed until sunset, hooking fish on just about every cast, then stumbled back to camp, where the guys were finishing a game of cards in the kitchen tent. It was midnight, and I'd been fishing for six hours—this Alaska scene was definitely going to take some getting used to! As I lay collapsed on my bunk, lulled by the haunting cries of loons, I pondered on how many lovely cutthroats had never seen a fly in the countless ponds and streams of this coastal paradise. The Madison River would have to wait.

Fishing cutthroat trout in one of the countless ponds found along Alaska's Southeast coast.

CUTTHROAT: NOBLE TROUT

The cutthroat trout, *Oncorhynchus clarki*, was the first true trout to be documented in the United States of America. Described in early accounts of exploration as far back as the 1500s, specimens sent to England in 1833 from a river in Washington were officially recorded and the species named in honor of Captain William Clark of the famed Lewis and Clark expedition.

Cutthroats are the native trout of the Rocky Mountains—the abundant and at times gullible fish found in small foothill creeks, rivers, and mountain lakes from New Mexico to Alberta. The coastal subspecies, known as "harvest trout" or "bluebacks," are highly admired and sought after in the tidal waters of the Pacific Northwest states and British Columbia. In Alaska, these fish are the jewels of the coastal wilderness; small, brightly-colored trout that liven the fishing and enhance the overall ecology of countless small streams, bogs, and lakes from Prince William Sound to Ketchikan. And though they take a back seat to the state's other sport species when it comes to prestige and glamour, cutthroats have a definite mystique and noble character that, like the small brook trout of the East, endears them to a dedicated following of anglers.

DESCRIPTION

The cutthroat trout of the Pacific Northwest occur in sea-run and resident forms. They are most easily recognized by the two red slash marks under the lower jaw from which they derive their name. An upper jaw line that extends well beyond the eye, heavy spotting on the body and fins, and the presence of small teeth behind the tongue are other recognizable features to look for. Some of these features may not always be present, making the fish sometimes difficult to distinguish from the rainbow trout (rainbows and cutthroats can hybridize, which can further complicate identification). Red slash marks and heavy spotting are often indistinct or nonexistent on sea-run fish. Coloration varies but generally residents have a dark olive-green back with gold or bronze sides that fade to a pale-white belly. Sea-runs usually have a deep metallic blue or green back and bright silver sides and various degrees of spotting. The flesh of Alaska's coastal cutthroat varies from white to pinkish white in color.

Most of the cutthroats caught in Alaska are four and five years old and average eight to ten inches long. Larger, trophy (three pounds plus) resident fish are 9 to 15 years old. Moving between salt and freshwater places added stress on sea-run fish, and they are rarely over eight years old and larger than 20 inches.

RANGE, ABUNDANCE & STATUS

Coastal cutthroat trout range from Eel River in northern California to Prince William Sound, Alaska, and thrive in many watersheds within the coastal temperate rain forests. Individual populations of resident forms average about 3,000 fish (but may be as high as 14,000), and most anadromous populations are several hundred to a thousand (2,000 is large). Resident fish are typically small and stunted, although in some Southeast lakes they grow as large as eight pounds. Populations are fragile and highly susceptible to overfishing and habitat destruction. Even the enhancement of other desirable species, such as coho salmon, can have a negative impact on cutthroat abundance. From the late 1970s to the early 1990s, sport harvests in Southeast Alaska declined while effort increased dramatically. This foreboding trend prompted the Department of Fish and Game and other agencies to take a much more aggressive management approach to expand knowledge of cutthroat ecology and enact more conservative regulations in many areas. Under this new management regimen, harvests of cutthroat since 1994 were substantially lower than in prior years. Hopefully, lower harvests will continue and depressed populations will rebound; however, in popular areas complete closures may be necessary.

LIFE HISTORY & HABITS

Resident Alaska cutthroats spend their entire lives in lakes, streams, sloughs, and small bog ponds. They mature at four to six years of age and spawn primarily in headwaters and small tributaries with gentle gradients. The number of eggs per female depends on size and condition of fish, and can be as few as 200 to as many as 4,000; but the average is between 1,100 and 1,700. Cutthroats bury their eggs in redds like other members of the salmon/trout/charr family. Preferred gravel is pea-sized or slightly larger and fairly clean of sand and fines. Spawning usually takes place in the spring, from late March to early June, depending on latitude and local climate. Hatching occurs in six to seven weeks and fry emerge one to two weeks later. Fry grow quickly, and may be up to three or four inches long by the first fall and five to six inches long by the end of their second growing season.

Anadromous or sea-run cutthroats in Alaska have a life history similar to that of sea-run Dolly Varden. Except for periods in salt water, the life history of the sea-run cutthroat closely parallels that of the resident form. Migration from fresh water overwintering areas to salt water takes place in the spring (from late March to late June). Many of these fish are going out to sea for the first time; some have been out in the previous year but have not yet spawned, and others have just spawned and are anxious to rebuild their energy reserves. Cutthroats going to sea for the first time are usually two or three years of age, but some may go as early as age one or as late as age six. Little is known of their lives in the ocean, but tagging studies have shown that most fish venture no more than 20 to 50 miles from their home stream, many staying within estuaries or the mouths of rivers to feed on smolts. Time at sea is usually short, anywhere from a few weeks to three or four months. They return to freshwater in late summer through fall and, by October, most of Alaska's "cutts" are settled in some lake , river, or stream with suitable habitat for overwintering. Cutthroats can display the same complexity of movement as charr, spawning in different streams than they overwinter in, traveling from stream to stream to feed on salmon spawn, even traveling through salt water from overwintering lakes to reach spawning areas.

Coastal cutthroats are more genetically diverse among populations throughout their range than Pacific salmon and steelhead. Cutthroat form smaller populations that have genetically unique adaptations to their environment. This diversity may reflect their complex life history and migratory behavior. While their ability to adapt has allowed populations to successfully evolve, localized extinctions from factors such as overfishing and habitat destruction are more likely to occur.

Diet

Knowing what cutthroats feed on is certainly important to anglers. Small trout will heavily utilize terrestrial and aquatic insects, especially midge and mosquito larvae. As opportunists, however, their diet will vary with location and time of year. As they get older, "cutts" will still pursue midges, mosquitoes, caddis flies, mayflies, and stone flies, but will prey more heavily on fish, such as sticklebacks, kokanee, juvenile salmon, and sculpins. Leeches also make up a small portion of the cutthroat's diet. In saltwater, "cutts" will feed on small shrimp (euphausids), juvenile herring, capelin, and salmon smolts. Salmon spawn is an extremely important food source to cutthroat trout, as it allows for the rapid weight gain that is essential for winter survival. Availability of salmon eggs may be one of the primary motivations for sea-run cutthroats to return to freshwater. Resident cutthroats often do not have the luxuriant and diverse food sources that sea-runs enjoy, yet the largest cutthroats taken in Alaska (over five pounds) have been from lakes without anadromous salmon. The key to the potential size of these landlocked forms is the availability of kokanee or landlocked sockeye for forage in many Southeast lakes.

FISHING ALASKA'S CUTTHROAT TROUT

In recent years, Alaska anglers have caught over 50,000 cutthroat trout annually, over 90% of them from Southeast Alaska, and the rest from Southcentral's Prince William Sound. Since cutthroat trout are notoriously voracious and will respond to just about any enticement—bait, flies, spinners, spoons, and jigs—locating fish is the key challenge for the Alaska cutthroat angler. Throughout most of their range in the 49th state, they are few in number and have dynamic and, at times, elusive behavior, so understanding their life history and migratory patterns is essential.

Generally, in streams, cutthroats will be found in pools, under cutbanks, in confluences and tailouts, and near logs and boulders. In lakes, they usually

Ultralight spinning and light fly gear give anglers the most enjoyment with Alaska's abundant wild cutthroat fishing.

linger near outlet and inlet streams, shorelines with lily pads, islands, and drop-offs. I prefer to use flies for cutthroat but certainly don't dispute the efficiency of spinning or conventional gear. However, on all lures I recommend using single barbless hooks or replacing the factory treble hook with an appropriate sized fly. This will help prevent mortalities and reduce physical damage to the fish.

Spring Conditions

Access to cutthroats in the early spring (April and May) can be difficult with rotting snow and ice conditions, and some areas are closed to protect spawning populations. But the opportunities for exciting early spring fishing are many and worth going for. Best areas for spring "cutts" are the mouths of inlet and outlet streams in lakes, river mouths, estuaries, and the small tributary confluences of rivers with

Summer Conditions

Sea-run cutthroats can be extremely difficult to locate once out in the ocean, and few anglers have consistent success catching them after the smolt runs are over and they move seaward. (Cutthroats that spend the entire summer in estuaries are the exception.) These fish will begin reentering freshwater along with salmon, in some systems, during early to mid-July. This inward migration can take place rapidly within a week or be spread out through the summer, depending on location. Generally, cutthroat runs occur with either the first pink salmon runs in July or the later coho runs of August and September. The best places to try are estuaries, river mouths, tidal pools, and any holding water in lower rivers and streams, fishing the incoming tides for best results. Sometimes you will be able to spot small schools of cutthroats waiting for salmon eggs in tailouts or pool edges. During salmon runs, Glo Bugs, other egg patterns, and flesh flies are the ticket to "match the hatch." During heavy pink salmon invasions, when fish tend to be glutted with spawn, I've had good luck fishing Egg Sucking Leeches and weighted white Marabou Muddlers (both #8), perhaps because they imitate other prey species making off with something good. You can also expect an exciting, mixed bag of fishing in and around tidewater, especially during the height of the salmon invasions. Pink or silver salmon will be jumping and surfacing everywhere, and hooking them can be difficult to avoid in their prespawning testiness. Dollies, too, will most likely be numerous, providing additional encounters. Interspersed among this rowdy bunch should be some incredibly aggressive cutthroat trout. A deep, slow retrieve of a small spinner or streamer in bright, attractor colors is usually all it takes to bring them in, too.

Resident cutthroats are actively feeding during the early part of summer, and can provide some excellent fly-fishing. In lakes, look for fish feeding along shorelines, and near outlets and inlets. Southeast lakes can stratify dramatically in the latter part of summer, causing fish to avoid their shallower feeding locations and remain in deeper, cooler waters. A small boat or float tube will allow you greater access to prime lake areas. Lily pads can offer some challenging fishing. I use heavier tippets of 8 to 10-pound test line to minimize breakoffs in these snag-filled waters. Aquatic vegetation attracts damselfly and dragonfly nymphs and adults, amphipods (freshwater shrimp), snails

spawning populations. After ice-out, anglers can fly in to some of the better Southeast lakes (see locations at end of this chapter) and enjoy some of Alaska's best fishing (Humpback, Turner, Jims, Wilson, and other lakes have all produced trophy cutthroat during the month of May).

Spring cutthroats in or near salmon systems will congregate in strategic locations for intercepting outmigrating smolt. Salmon smolt outmigrations occur sporadically throughout the day but peak between 10 P.M. and 2 A.M., so fishing during evening hours can be most productive. When fishing river mouths and estuaries, I like to fish around a moderate high tide, the best time being about two to three hours before and after flood. I look for smolts scattering and fleeing, seabird activity, or surface disturbances of any kind that might signal concentrations of cutthroat. This can be exciting fishing for short periods and the angler must be ready to make quick, accurate casts when a feeding binge is in progress. Because Dolly Varden charr are more numerous in Alaska's coastal systems, you'll probably catch much more of them than cutthroat, as well as other surprises (I've caught greenling, juvenile Pacific cod, and starry flounder while fishing these tidal zones for cutthroats).

Imitating forage fish with lure and fly is, of course, your best bet at this time. Small, bright spinners, like the matchless Super Vibrax series in sizes #0 to #2, are hard to beat, as are the 1/8 to 1/6 ounce Pixee, Kastmaster, Swedish Pimple, Krocodile, and Mepps Syclops spoons/jigs. Streamer fishing with smolt and other baitfish patterns and bright attractors can be equally effective, using the standard "wet fly swing" or fast, short strips through likely holding water.

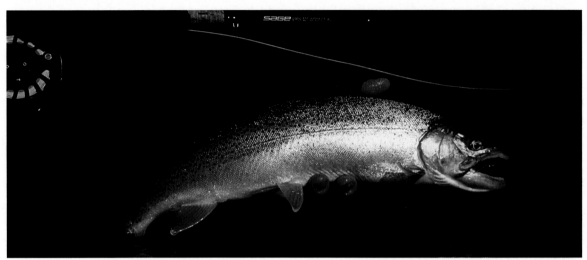

Sea-run cutthroats provide seasonally abundant angling in many locations throughout Southeast Alaska.

and a host of other prey organisms. Cutthroats will cruise the weed borders or remain stationary under cover to employ the "ambush predator" strategy of pike on unsuspecting prey. My favorite flies for these conditions are a Gold-ribbed Hare's Ear and other standard fuzzy type nymphs (size #10 and #12), and an olive, black, or brown Leech (size #8 to #10). I've also had good success with small Woolly Buggers and Matukas. Hardware tends to target larger, more aggressive fish but fewer numbers in the long run. I like to use 1/12 to 1/8-ounce red and yellow Roostertail spinners, 1/8-ounce Pixee and 1/12 to 3/16-ounce silver or gold Kastmaster spoons. Lead head jigs (chartreuse, crawdad, pink, or black) work well, too, and are less susceptible to snags.

In streams, fish the pools and riffles much the same as you would farther south this time of year. Typically, the smaller but more numerous juvenile fish will occupy the shallow riffle areas, whereas the larger adult fish occupy the deeper pools or pocket water among the large woody debris. In moving water, if I am not using flies, I'll stick to small lead head jigs, the 1/8 oz. Pixee spoon, or a (#0 or #1) silver or gold Super Vibrax spinner.

The islands in Prince William Sound and Southeast are full of small, unnamed lakes and muskeg bog ponds, many receiving little, if any, angling pressure. I've found dozens of colorful, feisty "cutts" from waters as small as a quarter acre, with little more than an ephemeral rivulet connecting to the main stream. The presence of juvenile coho rearing along the edges is a good sign to look for when prospecting for cut-throat trout in these rather "unlikely" areas, as the two occur together most frequently. Taking a minute or two to search for surface activity of any kind is another way to find fish. Exploring Alaska's abundant coastal waters for trout can be one of the most satisfying aspects of fishing this species, with rich rewards of abundant, wild fishing, and quiet contemplation in the most inspiring of settings.

Fall Conditions

Fall is a popular time to fish for cutthroat trout, both resident and sea-run, because fish are in prime condition and extremely voracious. Some of the best fishing for sea-run cutthroats can be had in the inlet and outlet waters of lakes with overwintering populations. The cooling temperatures and shortening days prompt fish into reckless feeding binges that can make for some electrifying fishing action. My most memorable experiences with cutthroat have taken place in September and October, when coho are spawning in streams and lake tributaries. In some places I've seen fat sea-run "cutts" concentrated near outlets, in deep pools or river mouths, ravenous for anything that comes their way. Attractor patterns, egg and flesh flies, forage imitation streamers (Sculpins, Muddlers, Leeches), bright spinners, spoons, and jigs all work well for these hungry fall cutthroats.

Winter Conditions

It's common knowledge that cutthroats can be caught through the ice but, because of fluctuating winter conditions, few anglers are willing to risk the

Small lake troll flasher rigs like the Jensen Cowbell, Willow Leaf, Tiny, Jack-O-Diamonds, etc. can be used with trolling spoons for maximum effect when working the deeper trophy cutthroat lakes of southeast Alaska. The flash and movement of the whirling blades simulates feeding kokanee and other forage of large trout.

potentially dangerous ice conditions on Southeast lakes during most winters, regardless of how good fishing could be. It is probably safe to say that all cutthroats in Alaska are in a lake or slow moving river during the winter. Unlike streams in Washington and Oregon, no migrations of cutthroats have been documented in Alaska in the winter, although there are persistent rumors of bright sea-runs being caught in estuaries in February and March. Occasionally, unseasonably warm spells during the winter allow anglers to fish lakes and streams as they would during the normal open water season.

GEARING UP FOR CUTTHROATS

Tackle: Use an ultra-light spinning rod, five to six-foot, medium-action, with 150 yards four to eight-pound test mono on a high-quality, ultra-light spinning reel. Or use a two to six-weight, six to nine-foot flyrod with matching, floating or sinktip line and 2X to 4X tippet. Use a leader of seven to nine feet. For deepwater trophy fishing, use a light to medium-weight spinning or steelhead casting rod, 7 to 8 1/2 feet, medium-action, with 150 yards of 10 to 15-pound line on a high-quality spinning or casting reel.

Lures: Many lures work well for cutthroat. Small, 1/16 to 3/16 ounce spinners like Vibrax, Mepps, and Panther Martin, in silver or gold (also with fluorescent orange or red highlights), or Roostertail in red and yellow; small spoons like 1/8-ounce Pixees (silver or gold) with red or pink inserts, or 1/10 to 1/4-ounce Kastmasters, Krocodiles, Syclops or Swedish Pimples in silver or gold (also with blue or red highlights); and 1/32 to 1/6 ounce, lead or leadhead jigs like Crippled Herring, Beau-Mac, or Foxee, in black, purple, pink, flourescent red, green, silver/blue, and chartreuse.

Flies to use include most standard Northwest wet flies (size #6 to #12) like the Glo Bug, Polar Shrimp, Spruce, and Scud (in orange, pink or brown), Gold-ribbed Hare's ear Nymph (size #10 and #12) and Fall Favorite; Dry Flies (size #10 to #14) like the Humpy, Dark Blue Damsel, Mosquito, Black Gnat, Irresistible, and Elk Hair Caddis; and Streamers (size #6 and #8) like the Muddler Minnow, Woolly Bugger, Sculpin, Bunny Bug, Smolt, Leech (Olive, Brown, or Black), Egg Sucking Leech, and Maribou Muddler.

CATCHING TROPHY CUTTHROAT

If catching a trophy in one of Southeast's premier lakes is your goal, specific strategies should be employed. A boat is almost a necessity to fish the better water. The U.S. Forest Service is kind enough to provide small boats for the fortunate souls able to obtain cabin reservations at some of the more popular locations (check beforehand for availability and condition of craft). If you're not so lucky, an inflatable raft or canoe might be the way to go. A portable fishfinder and bathymetric lake map, if available, will greatly improve your chances of locating fish.

Trophy resident cutthroat trout can be taken shallow during spring near inlet waters but, generally, will disperse and go deep during the summer. The most effective way of catching them is by trolling. Conventional trolling gear—lead weights or planer on 10 to 15-pound test, with a small flasher or lake troll flasher rig and medium-sized spoons/jigs (Crippled Herring, Deep Stinger, Krocodile, Needlefish, Trixee, etc.)—trolled slowly, moderately deep (15 to 30 feet), works best. Also try deep diving plugs like the Rapala Down Deep Husky Jerk, Jensen Power Dive Minnow, and Yo-Zuri Crystal Minnow Deep Diver. Don't use treble hooks with plugs. Use instead a single (or double if legal) barbless hook at the tail end. Downriggers or lead core line can also be employed to maintain a known depth and make proper adjustments when necessary. Keep in mind that the once immensely popular and effective method of trolling bait, such as herring or shrimp, is illegal in these lakes.

When fishing without electronic aids, concentrate trolling along shorelines with steep drop-offs, in deep waters surrounding islands or rocks, bays with inlets, and other areas that might appeal to larger, lazier trout in search of a fish dinner. The lower-light periods of the day are most productive for catching big ones, so time your efforts accordingly.

Cutthroat Trout
Oncorhynchus clarki clarki

SPECIES SUMMARY

Alaska Common Names: "Cutt," cutthroat, harvest trout, blueback.

Description: Sleek, small to medium sized coastal trout, sides bronze to silver; back, olive-green to blue; belly pale white. Usually heavily spotted with two red slash marks under lower jaw and small teeth behind the tongue. Flesh white to pinkish white. Similar in appearance to rainbow; differentiation may be difficult because features not always prominent.

Size: Average 8 to 12 in.; large fish to over 20 in. and up to 6 lbs.

State Record: 8 lbs., 6 oz., Wilson Lake (SSE), Robert Denison, 1977.

Habits: Can be very itinerant within home range. Voracious feeder on insects, other fish, and salmon eggs.

Notes: Very similar in genetics to rainbow trout; may hybridize in certain systems.

Meristics: Gill rakers 15-21; vertebrae 61-64; pyloric caeca 25-55; lateral line scales 140-180; branchiostegal rays 10-12; dorsal fin rays 8-11; anal fin rays 8-12; pectoral fin 12-15 rays; pelvic fin 9-10 rays.

Range: Coastal waters, SSE to Prince William Sound (SC).

Preferred Habitat: Lake shorelines and vegetation, beaver ponds, stream pools.

Best Waters: Lake systems, especially those that also have kokanee; also systems with abundant coho salmon and/or steelhead.

Best Times: Late spring/early summer and fall.

Best Bait/Lures/Flies: Small, bright spinners, spoons, and jigs; attractor, forage, egg, nymph, and dry fly patterns.

Best Trophy Areas: Turner (Juneau); Reflection, and Humpback lakes (Ketchikan); Hasselborg, Distin, Guerin, and Jim's lakes (Admiralty Island); Chilkat Lake (Haines); Martin Lake/River (Cordova).

RECOMMENDED GEAR

Spinning:
Ultralight, medium action spinning rod, 5-7 ft., matching high quality reel and 100 yds. 4-8 lb. test monofilament line.

Deepwater Trophy Fishing:
Light-medium wt., medium action trolling rod (spinning or casting), 6-8 ft., mated with matching reel and 150 yds. 8-15 lb. test line.

Flyfishing:
4-5 wt., medium action, graphite flyrod, 6-8 1/2 ft., with matching small trout reel; Floating, intermediate or short sink tip lines, 7-9 ft. tapered leader, with 2X-6X tippet.

ALASKA'S MAJOR CUTTHROAT LOCATIONS

There are so many systems known to contain cutthroat in Alaska (and many more yet to be cataloged) that it is impossible to list all the best areas. Some locations, like Hasselborg and Turner lakes, are so noteworthy and popular that they barely need mentioning, while others may be local hot spots known to only a few anglers. Successful fishing, even at the best locations, depends highly on timing, especially for sea-runs. Local Fish and Game or Forest Service offices, guides, and air taxis can provide invaluable help on the most up-to-date conditions. Most lakes have resident fish, but some support sea-run cutthroats as well, while some streams have only itinerant sea-run fish.

SOUTHEAST

Most of Alaska's cutthroat trout streams are located here. Anadromous and resident forms are most abundant in lakes and streams that are also used by spawning salmon, whereas only resident forms are found in the land-locked lakes. The U.S Forest Service has cabins and shelters located on many of the prime cutthroat locations.

Yakutat and Gulf Coast: Bering River tributaries; Katalla, Akwe, Situk, Lost, Tsivat, and Kiklukh rivers; Kaliakh River system.

Haines/Skagway: Chilkat Lake and River, Mosquito Lake and Chilkoot Lake.

Juneau (mainland): Windfall Lake, Turner Lake, Auke Lake.

Admiralty Island: Hasselborg Lake and Creek, Lake Alexander, Distin, Guerin, and Jims lakes; Kanalku Creek and Lake.

#6 Woolly
Bugger

1/8 oz. Foxee Jig

#12 Hare's Ear
Nymph

3/16 oz. Kastmaster

#12 Black Gnat

other unnamed creeks and sloughs along the Copper River Hwy. For nearby fly-out or boat-accessible sites try Junction and Hidden lakes and Hawkins Creek (Hawkins Island), Shelter Creek and Boswell Creek and Lake (Hinchinbrook Island), and Martin Lake (east Copper River Delta).

Top Flies for Alaska Cutthroats

Black Gnat, Griffith's Gnat, Hare's Ear Nymph, Scud, Mosquito, Cahill, Irresistible, Adams, Wulff, Midge, Brassie Nymph, Caddis Nymph, Glo Bug, Polar Shrimp, Fall Favorite, Sculpin, Marabou Muddler, Alaska Smolt, Salmon Fry, Parr Fly, Minnow, Leech, Egg Sucking Leech, Babine Special, Woolly Bugger, Bunny Fly, Black Nose Dace, Thunder Creek.

Top Ten Alaska Trophy Cutthroats

8 lbs., 6 oz.	Wilson Lake (SE)	1977
7 lbs., 8 oz.	Wilson Lake (SE)	1981
7 lbs., 6.5 oz.	Turner Lake (SE)	1991
6 lbs., 14 oz.	Reflection Lake (SE)	1977
6 lbs., 12 oz.	Orchard Lake (SE)	1973
6 lbs., 7 oz.	Turner Lake (SE)	1980
6 lbs., 5 oz.	Wilson Lake (SE)	1973
6 lbs., 3 oz.	Ella Lake (SE)	1982
6 lbs., 2 oz.	Humpback Lake (SE)	1969
6 lbs.	Patching Lake (SE)	1980

Cutthroat Trout Ethics

Don't fish bait! Studies have shown up to half of all cutthroat hooked on bait die. Almost all Alaska cutthroat waters are closed seasonally or year-round to use of bait.

Don't use treble hooks on lures. Pinch barbs down on your single hooks or use barbless hooks.

Practice catch and release fishing. It takes many years for Alaska's cutthroat to reach trophy size. A minimum and maximum size limit applies in all trout waters of Southeast (see Regulations for details).

Chichagof/Yakobi: Sitkoh Lake and Creek, Goulding Lakes; Surge and Hoktaheen lakes.

Sitka (Baranof Island): Florence Lake (excellent fishing, but surrounding area was heavily logged), Baranof Lake and River (no other species are available here), and Eva Lake and River. Also numerous lakes on southern part of island have little-fished resident populations.

Petersburg/Wrangell: Kah Sheets, Pat, and Virginia lakes; Eagle Lake and River, Castle River, Thoms Creek and Lake, Petersburg Creek and Lake, Stikine River (various clearwater tributaries and sloughs), Blind Slough, Hamilton Creek.

Ketchikan: Revillagigedo Island and mainland-Naha River drainage (Patching Lake); Humpback, Ella, Wilson, Reflection, Manzanita, Orchard, and Winstanley lakes.

POW: Salmon Bay Lake, Honker Lake, Karta Lake and River, Thorne River and Lake, Sarkar Lake, Neck Lake.

SOUTHCENTRAL

Prince William Sound: Here many named and unnamed ponds and lakes have feisty populations of small resident cutthroats. Many rewards await the angler with the interest and enthusiasm to explore pristine or unknown areas. Try Stump Lake (Montague Island), Green Island Lake (Green Island), Sockeye Lake and Otter Lake (Knight Island), Eshamy Lake and Cowpen Lake (mainland).

Cordova and vicinity: For roadside fishing, try Alaganik Slough, McKinley Lake, Eyak Lake and River, Mile 18 drainage, and various

#2 Silver Vibrax

1/8 oz. Marabou Jig

#6 Marabou Muddler

1/8 oz. Panther Martin

#6 Alaska Smolt

Charr
Fish of the Rainbow

Guiding our rafts down through the heavily braided midsection of Southwest Alaska's Aniak River, my partner and I eagerly scout the water for signs of our quarry. Bill, in the lead boat, gives a shout and we beach the SOTARS on a thin spit of gravel above a giant slough swarming with spawning chum salmon. I motion to our guests not to grab their big rods, but their light trout outfits instead. What we are after here is not the fearsome-looking, deep-bodied salmon, but an altogether different animal that is more sporting and much better looking.

Bill whips out a box of brightly colored plastic beads, some small hooks, and split shot and prepares each rod with an elementary simple rig. We take the fishermen in single file, carefully wading out along the edge of the drop-off to the main channel, and instruct the lead man to toss his line into the seam of current along the edge of the slough. The bead vanishes in the swift water and almost instantly the line straightens with a hard jerk. Fish on! Bill directs the excited angler into the slough shallows to play the fish while I bring the next guest forward. He whips the bead a little farther out than his predecessor and it sinks for only a second or two before it's grabbed and another feisty fighter begins gyrating on the end of a line. Our grinning fisherman moves over and another steps up into the "batter's box." He too dips his line and connects, this time to a fish much larger that runs out in the main channel before it is brought under control. And so it goes, one after another, like some kind of crazy fish factory, until we wonder if we aren't catching the same ones over and over again.

Our pleasant diversion comes not from the legendary Alaska rainbow, but the charr, a colorful salmonid that shares many of the same waters and is every bit the equal of its glamorous cousin on light tackle. What's more, it would be difficult, indeed, to imagine a creature of more exquisite beauty than these fall specimens. *Akalukpik* to the Eskimo, the charr is the "fish of the rainbow." Said to have descended from the sky ages ago, they retain all the colors of the Heavens, in an artistry so sublime it can inspire visions of taxidermy in the most confirmed catch-and-release angler. For now, we're content with taking pictures and slipping these lovely fish back in the river, so they may live and fight another day.

Trophy charr fishing under a midnight sun, lower Noatak River, Northwest Alaska.

CHARR: FISH OF THE RAINBOW

Perhaps more than any other fish, the charr is associated with the mystique of our wildest places and most pristine waters, with a delicate beauty that has inspired poetic admiration from generations of anglers. Part of a worldwide northern fish group (genus *Salvelinus*, distributed latitude 35-82 North), charrs in North America include some of our most well known and beloved sport species—the brook trout of eastern streams, the bull trout of the west, Dolly Varden of the Pacific coast and lake trout and arctic charr of the north.

In Alaska, they are found in a variety of forms, from the creeks and sheltered tidewaters of Southeast to the vast, naked rivers of the Arctic, in numbers that are truly astounding. In preliminary investigations done in Alaska during the late 1800s, the U.S. Fish Commission encountered thick hordes of the feisty "salmon trout" in nearly every stream and bay surveyed. Later, intense efforts by the salmon industry to control their numbers during the 1920s and 1930s barely affected their abundance, despite the eradication of millions annually. This remarkable fishery, for the most part, remains undiminished to this day— which is a good thing, as the Alaska charr is a fine, underrated gamefish, certainly the equal of the more glamorous species it shares waters with. In its various

forms, it is capable of providing exciting fishing action twelve months of the year, in nearly every fishable body of water from Ketchikan to Kotzebue (and beyond).

The different varieties of charr found in the state may be an endless delight to anglers, but they are a perpetual headache for biologists, who are still struggling to make sense of their complex life histories and develop a universal classification for the species. Major problems arise in differentiating the various forms of Dolly Varden (*Salvelinus malma*), the western brook charr, from the arctic charr (*Salvelinus alpinus*), as their ranges overlap in Western and Arctic Alaska, and outward appearance can be almost identical at times. It would certainly simplify matters greatly for sportsmen, guides, and outdoors writers (perhaps scientists as well), if we could begin to think of the various forms of this species complex as simply "charr." With this in mind, we'll use "charr" throughout this book to mean either Dolly Varden and/or arctic charr and, when dealing with areas like Southeast or Southcentral, where almost all the fish are Dolly Varden, we'll refer to them as such. Lake charr, or lake trout as we have come to know them, have long been recognized as a distinct, stable species (*Salvelinus namaycush*), so we'll treat them separately (see lake trout chapter).

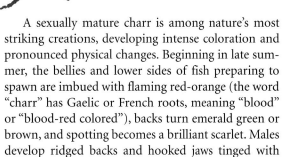

DESCRIPTION

The charrs are built along the same classic lines as the trouts, with powerful, streamlined bodies, slightly forked tails, large mouths, small scales and attractive coloration. What distinguishes them from the true trouts are their more minute scales (100 to 150 along the lateral line), lack of teeth on the upper-middle jaw shaft, and different marking scheme (lighter spots on a dark background, as opposed to the trouts' darker spots on a light background).

Coloration and markings on Alaska's charr vary considerably, according to location, age, life history, and sexual ripeness. Back and upper sides on sea-run fish are generally steel blue to silver or gray, varying to brown or green in river and lake-resident charr. Sides are usually silver-blue or gray in sea-runs, or brown, orange-brown, dusky green, and even gold in lake and river forms; bellies are usually whitish. Markings consist of small to medium-sized concentric red, pink, cream, yellow, or orange spots across the back and sides, not always distinct in bright sea-run fish. Lower fins are dusky yellow, orange, or carmine, with prominent white leading edges; tails are slightly forked. Wormlike markings (vermiculae) on the back and dorsal fins, found on the eastern brook charr (*S. fontinalis*), are missing on most Alaska fish.

A sexually mature charr is among nature's most striking creations, developing intense coloration and pronounced physical changes. Beginning in late summer, the bellies and lower sides of fish preparing to spawn are imbued with flaming red-orange (the word "charr" has Gaelic or French roots, meaning "blood" or "blood-red colored"), backs turn emerald green or brown, and spotting becomes a brilliant scarlet. Males develop ridged backs and hooked jaws tinged with black and orange.

Charr is also one of the finest eating fishes in the world, with firm, pink or orange flesh more delicately flavored than salmon. Its fat content is perfect for all methods of cooking, whether deep-fried, baked, sautéed, broiled or smoked. Lightly seasoned, grilled steaks of charr, or tender fillets dipped in spicy batter and deep fried, certainly rank as some of the finest treats from nature's kitchen.

RANGE, ABUNDANCE & STATUS

Alaska's charrs are part of a northern species complex that dominates the waters of northern Europe, Siberia, Alaska, Canada, and some of our northern states. They are found in nearly all Alaska's coastal drainages, in a continuous band from the Beaufort Sea down to the tip of the Southeast Panhandle (including the Aleutian Islands). They occur mostly as resident and sea-run river forms, with isolated populations of lake-dwelling and even dwarf stream charr scattered throughout the state.

As the state's most widespread and abundant sport species, the charr has shown remarkable resilience, despite a long history of exploitation. Now recognized as a legitimate and desirable sport species, its future in Alaska has never looked so good. Hopefully, with wise management, the state will continue to offer what is undoubtedly some of the world's most prolific and varied angling for the species.

LIFE HISTORY & HABITS

The charrs of Alaska have interesting and, in many ways, little-understood life histories. Sea-run forms begin their lives in much the same way as salmon, spending their initial development in freshwater lakes and streams, feeding on minute aquatic life. At anywhere from one to seven years of age (usually four to six) they "smolt," heading seaward in the spring of the year. Unlike salmon, however, they usually remain close to shore for the duration of their ocean stay (generally less than 120 days), wandering in nearby bays or, in some instances, traveling as far as several hundred miles along the coast. Almost all charrs overwinter in fresh water. Sea-run fish begin their in-migration sometime in summer or fall (late June through September), though not necessarily to their natal streams. They have been found wintering in rivers hundreds of miles from home; tagged fish from Northwest Alaska have been recovered in rivers along the coast of Far East Russia.

Resident or freshwater charrs in Alaska can have complicated and varied movement patterns. Some fish spend their entire lives in streams (stream-resident charr), some overwinter in lakes and move into streams to feed and spawn (lake-resident charr), and others, like the dwarf charr (the "old man fish" of the Inuit), live out their entire existence in small creeks, springs, or headwaters. The presence of different forms of resident and anadromous charr in the same system may be exasperating to biologists, but anglers need only concern themselves with the general habits of the species, which are similar for all forms.

The charr is an opportunistic and voracious predator, utilizing any available food source—insects, leeches, snails, small fish, salmon spawn (and flesh), even rodents and small birds. Growth rate and potential size are variable, but generally Alaska fish are slow-growing and long-lived (up to 20 years), with the most northerly occurring fish reaching maximum size and age for the species. Canada's Northwest Territories has produced some of the largest specimens in the world (25 pounds or more, with the current IGFA world record of 32 pounds, 9 ounces from the Tree River in 1981), and there are reports of even larger fish from eastern Siberia. But, in Alaska, the largest charrs (up to 15 pounds or more) come from the Kotzebue Sound/Chukchi Sea area, in the northwest corner of the state. (The current state record, a whopping 27-pound, 6-ounce fish, was taken there in 2002.) Stream-resident forms are generally much smaller and slower-growing than lake-resident or ocean going fish and, in some systems, residual or dwarf forms might only reach 10 to 12 inches in length.

Alaska's charrs reach sexual maturity at anywhere from four to seven years of age (up to nine in the extreme Arctic) and spawn in late summer and fall (late July through November). In most systems, major spawning activity occurs in September and October (some rivers even have a separate summer and fall run). Charr spawning behavior closely mimics that of

Dwarf stream charr, interior Alaska

the Pacific salmon, except that they do not necessarily die after breeding and can return to repeat the mating ritual two or even three times, in rare cases. In some areas, mature, overwintering sea-run charr will forego their spring exodus and hold over to breed in headwaters in late summer (late July to August).

New research on charr in Arctic Alaska has revealed a major life history variation among certain fish along the North Slope east of the Colville River. Most of the charr there are of above-average size (4 to 10 pounds) and reside in fresh water most of the year, making extensive forays in summer out along the coast far into Canadian waters, before returning to fresh water to spawn in the fall. It is believed that a small contingent may actually spend most of their adult lives in saltwater, residing off river mouths in the Arctic Ocean from early summer through winter until spring, then moving into selected rivers to spawn during the month of May, returning afterwards to salt water. This may help explain why these spring spawners attain a generally larger maximum size (25 to 30 pounds, or more) than other groups of charr, with a near year-round high-protein fish diet to spur growth. More information is still being collected, and current data reveals that still more sub-forms of the northern charr may be found. As yet, only very limited subsistence fisheries target these unique, giant, spring-spawning, ocean charr.

The northern charr's gluttony and lack of feeding sophistication are legend; stories of monster 20 and 30-pound fish hanging around shoreside canneries feeding on fish waste, or of anglers limiting out on bare hooks, are not hard to believe if you've fished around the state much. (One of my early encounters

Alaska's charr can be so abundant they cover the bottom of streams in certain areas and times of year.

with the delicate feeding habits of the species involved a twelve-pound Dolly Varden that tried to swim away with a stringer of rainbows I had tied to a riverbank.) The charr's well-known fondness for salmon smolt and spawn led at one time to a territorial bounty for their eradication, though later studies proved their appetite no more destructive than that of the rapacious rainbow trout or coho they share waters with.

FISHING ALASKA'S CHARR

Anglers in Alaska catch over a half million charr each year. Most of these fish come from northern Southeast, the Kenai Peninsula, Kodiak, and Bristol Bay, with smaller but significant numbers from the Kuskokwim, Northwest Alaska, the Arctic, and Prince William Sound. A good portion of Alaska's charr catch occurs incidentally, while trolling for king and coho salmon, flyfishing for rainbows, and the like. But a significant, growing number of anglers target charr, particularly during spring and fall, or in areas such as Northwest, Arctic, or Southwest that are known for outstanding trophy potential.

Although Alaska's charrs can be caught any time of year, they are best fished in spring and late summer through fall, when the great seasonal changes and movements of salmon bring concentrated feeding patterns. In many of the state's coastal waters, the charr shares many similarities in feeding and habits with resident trout (rainbow and cutthroat) and, consequently, the strategies employed for sportfishing may be very similar, if not identical. (Consult the trout chapters for more information.)

Spring Conditions

After ice-out, all charrs become extremely active, leaving overwintering areas and feeding heavily on emerging food sources (such as fishes, insect larvae, and crustaceans). They'll gather in river mouths, estuaries, confluences, inlets and outlets of lakes, and along shorelines, as these are the first waters to stir with life as winter loosens its grip. Studies have shown charrs to feed extensively and, at times, exclusively on salmon fry, smolt, and alevins when available, and it is the presence and movement of great numbers of these

The inlet/outlet waters of Alaska's salmon-rich lake and river systems are ideal places to target for spring charr.

young salmon, more than anything else, that makes Alaska's spring charr fishing so extraordinary.

On any of the hundreds of salmon-rich streams and lakes across Alaska (particularly those of Bristol Bay, Kodiak, the Alaska Peninsula, and Southeast), during peak periods of young salmon emergence in the spring, waters can actually churn with the frenzy of feeding charr as they slash through schools of fry, smolt, or alevins. If you time it right, you can get in on some of the most exciting, fast-paced fishing action imaginable, using flashy spinners, spoons, flies, jigs, or what have you to easily provoke these ravenous hordes.

The trick is to locate feeding fish or concentrations of young salmon, not always a simple task in Alaska's immense waters and changing conditions. Timing and location are of the essence. May and June are the peak months for spring juvenile salmon movement across most of Alaska, with the most prolific waters—Katmai, Kodiak, Iliamna, Wood-Tikchiks, etc.—the obvious choices for best fishing. Target lake outlets and inlets, bays, shorelines with drop-offs, river mouths and confluences, pool eddies and cutbanks—anywhere young salmon might be concentrated that provides efficient ambush sites for charr. Studies have shown the low-light, late evening and early morning hours to be most conducive to juvenile salmon movement, so time your efforts to fish as close to those hours as possible. (Cloudy, windy, and rainy days are also best.) Look for signs of feeding or shoaling activity—surface disturbances, "shimmering" in the water, or flocks of wheeling and diving seabirds (gulls and terns).

If you don't have the luxury of locating feeding sites from a plane, like some lodges and guides do, you'll have to rely on the whims of nature and your own fish sense to connect with these hungry spring feeders. You may have to fish "blind," casting to likely holding water or trolling from a boat. Small, flashy 1/6 to 1/2 ounce spoons or jigs (like the Krocodile, Crippled Herring, Hot Rod, Kastmaster, Silver Minnow, etc.) or 1/8 to 1/2 ounce plugs (Wiggle Wart, Hot Shot, Tad Polly, Shad Rap, etc.) in nickel, blue/chrome, silver prism, gold, gold scale, or brass are first choices for working deeper waters for spring charr. Vary your retrieve, depth, and location until you find feeding fish, much as you would for lake trout this time of year. In shallower inlet/outlet waters, streams or rivers, the flash and fluttering movements of a small spinner are hard to beat for provoking hungry charr. Leaf bladed, 1/8 to 3/8 ounce (Vibrax, Mepps Aglia, Rooster Tail, Panther Martin, etc.) spinners in colors of silver, nickel, blue/chrome, silver prism, gold, and copper work best.

If you are flyfishing, start with a generic smolt, parr, or fry imitation streamer—say a #2 to #4 Alaska Smolt, Supervisor, or Parr Fly—as a "searching" pattern, fishing a light strip (inches, not feet!) through likely holding areas. A floating line or short sink tip works best, depending on the strength of the current and depth of the water. On flowing water, make crosscurrent, downstream swings, just as you would for spring trout. Use a little rod tip action, if necessary, to imitate the nervous pulses of movement these little fish display as they dart through the water. Some other patterns to include in your spring charr arsenal

DOLLY VARDEN: The delicate, pink spotted charr of the Pacific Northwest is named after a character from a Dickens novel who wore fetching outfits of gray and cherry calico. Young Elda McCloud, whose dad ran a boarding house on California's Sacramento River in the early twentieth century, was so taken by the gaily marked "calico-trout" and its resemblance to the snappy fabric, she bestowed the catchy name, which spread and was eventually recognized by David S. Jordan of the Smithsonian as the official name for *Salvelinus malma*. (A proper noun, it is always capitalized.)

are Marabou and silver Muddlers, Matukas, Woolly Buggers, Leeches, and an assortment of smolt/fry/parr variations (even alevin patterns) and attractor patterns (Polar Shrimp, Skykomish Sunrise, Mickey Finn, etc.), in sizes #2 to #8 (the larger hooks sink better). Don't be afraid to experiment; some of the biggest charr you'll ever see are taken on the most unlikely fly creations.

Sea-Run Charr: Surprisingly, most overwintering sea-run charrs do not linger long in fresh water during the spring dispersal, but instead move quickly down into river mouths. Studies done in Western and Arctic Alaska show that most of these sea-run fish feed hardly, or not, at all during outmigration. Once they reach river mouths and estuaries, however, they begin feeding heavily, like their freshwater counterparts, with diets that consist almost exclusively of fishes and crustaceans. They are caught quite freely at these times (usually late March, April, or early May, depending on location) by fishermen casting from shore or boats, working tide rips, saltchucks, spits, jetties, beaches, bays, and river mouths. Southcentral (Kodiak, Homer, Seward, Prince William Sound), northern Southeast, and Northwest (Norton and Kotzebue sounds) are traditionally the most popular areas for this spring saltwater charr fishing.

Long, silver, "Norwegian-style" casting spoons and jigs (3⁄8 to 3⁄4-ounce) are deadly on these sea-roving spring charrs, as they imitate

Swedish
Pimple

very closely the sandlance, herring, and young salmon they feed on. Spinners, diving minnow plugs, crankbaits, flutter spoons, etc., in silver, gold, green, prism, white, and blue combinations can be worked effectively as well, depending on conditions. At the right time in certain areas, you can find success flyfishing, working river mouths, spits, beaches, and other likely areas with bait fish imitation streamers (smolt, candlefish, sandlance, and small herring patterns).

Look for signs of surface activity just as you would in fresh water, but be aware that saltwater charr will quite often be feeding deep or off bottom. If you're fishing from a boat, a fish locator/depth sounder can certainly save a lot of time putting you where the action is. Most anglers working the salt this time of year have the best luck fishing the tides (from two hours before to two hours after high tide), although you can find good charr fishing around the clock in the more productive areas.

Early Summer Conditions

From June on, Alaska's coastal waters jam up with mind-boggling numbers of salmon. In the major systems, thousands, even millions, of fish swim up from the sea into rivers, lakes, and streams. This creates an absolute manna of abundant angling, not just for salmon but also for the countless charr and trout (rainbow and cutthroat) that gather in anticipation of the feast to come. Most of these egg pirates are primed and anxious, and can be easily provoked into striking.

These fish are keyed in to slightly different stimuli than during their spring smolt bash, with attractor colors the spice that really turns them on. Spinners, spoons, and plugs in silver or gold with fluorescent red, orange, pink, or chartreuse highlights seem to work best. For fly fishermen, best results will be with attractor patterns like the Polar Shrimp, Purple Egg Sucking Leech, Mickey Finn, Black Zonker, and Woolly Bugger, along with proven standby forage imitations like the Muddler Minnow, Leech, Smolt, etc.

The trick now will be to fish deep and not too fast, as charr become less inclined to energetically pursue prey once the salmon arrive. Work river mouths, confluences, pools, and inlet/outlet waters, giving special attention to any areas where you locate salmon (cast around and behind them). Generally that is where the quick, agile charr (and rainbow and cutthroat) hold, as they "shadow" their larger cousins' movements. If

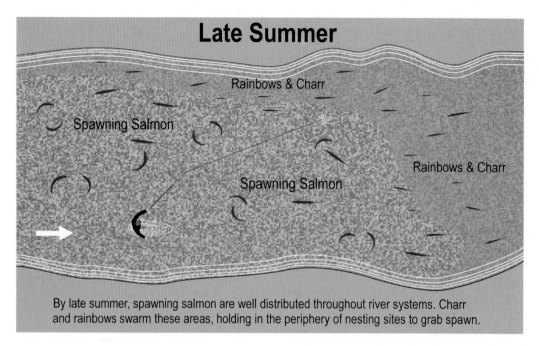

By late summer, spawning salmon are well distributed throughout river systems. Charr and rainbows swarm these areas, holding in the periphery of nesting sites to grab spawn.

you're working deep lake or river water from a boat or raft, you might want to try fishing a drift rig (pencil lead off a three-way swivel) or planer with a plug (3/8 to 5/8-ounce) or fluorescent drift bobber like a Spin-N-Glo (size #4 to 10). Sometimes this will produce results in big water (like that found in Southwest) where spoons and plugs alone aren't very efficient.

Late Summer Conditions

Just when you think fishing can't get any better, August rolls around and the action peaks. By now, most charr and trout will be concentrated in the gravelly middle and upper sections of rivers and in feeders, where considerable salmon spawning is underway. First king salmon, then sockeye and chum, and finally pinks and silvers glut these areas with their profuse spawn and carcasses, spurring hosts of resident species like charr, rainbow trout, cutthroat trout, grayling, and even whitefish into a frantic free-for-all.

In late summer (usually mid-July to early August) in most coastal systems, the great influx of sea-run charrs peaks. They form mass congregations in river mouths and lower holding areas before moving upriver to join their egg-pirating cohorts on the spawning gravels. These sea-run fish are in peak condition—firm, fat, and full of energy—and, with their great abundance and voracious hunger, can provide some of the best sport Alaska has to offer.

Alaska's river scene this time of year is a high-energy, mixed bag of fishing excitement. Schools of charr, along with zippy rainbows (or cutthroat trout in Southeast) and even bold grayling compete for a piece of the action, while waves of fresh salmon arrive daily. Different species can be taken on consecutive casts, and amazing numbers of fish hauled from the better holes. This is the premier time for egg patterns, beads, flesh flies, and bright attractors, all the familiar Alaska standards like the Glo Bug, Two Egg Marabou, Polar Shrimp, Babine Special, Battle Creek, Flesh Fly, Bunny Bug, Egg Sucking Leech, etc. Depending on how much these fish have had to eat, and other factors, you can expect good to excellent results drifting any of the above through holding water—pools, riffles, cutbanks, sloughs, or confluences—anywhere salmon might congregate or spawn. Cast to the periphery of any holding salmon you can locate (avoid disturbing or provoking them when on their redds), and fish a dead drift or light strip above bottom.

Bright spinners are deadly this time of year. Thousands of August charr have succumbed to the potent appeal of whirling blades in shades of black/red, black/yellow, silver/red, chartreuse/orange, gold/orange, and chartreuse/yellow/red, 1/4 to 1/2 ounce.

Fish them deep and with very slow retrieve for best results. In deeper waters, spoons, plugs, and drift bobbers similarly colored will bring the ravenous hordes to your line.

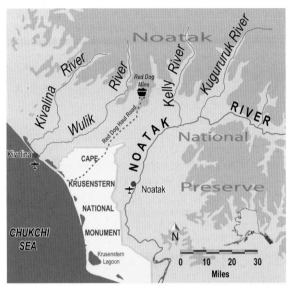

A majority of Alaska's trophy specimens come from the drainages of upper Kotzebue Sound vicinity (Wulik, Kivalina, lower Noatak tributaries).

Fall Conditions

Beginning in August and continuing into October across much of coastal Alaska, vast numbers of charr crowd rivers and streams to spawn and/or overwinter, providing some unique fishing opportunities. Some of the year's best trophy angling can be had, with an abundance of fish in prime condition, many in striking spawning colors. The charr at this time is overly aggressive, and will readily hit spoons, spinners, plugs, and flies in bright attractor colors (spawners may become picky as they begin breeding, but they should be left alone anyway). The big waters of Bristol Bay and the Alaska Peninsula, Southcentral's Kenai River, the lower Kuskokwim tributaries, and the fabulous fisheries of Northwest and Arctic Alaska are some of the more outstanding areas for fall charr fishing, with potential for trophy specimens (to ten pounds or even more). The weather, although changing, is still generally not too extreme. (The Arctic is the exception, as winter can set in as early as the end of August.)

For millennia, native people have harvested great numbers of charr during these fall migrations. At traditional sites along the Arctic coast, before the advent of white man and his nets, schools were herded into stone weirs and speared by the thousands. Quite a bit of fall subsistence harvesting still occurs along the Northwest coast and, to a limited extent, the Arctic as well, where villagers net fat charr in river mouths, pools, confluences, and estuaries.

Winter Conditions

Because the charr is one of the few fishes that can be taken readily and in abundance through the ice all winter long, they sustain an important fishery through Alaska's long dark, cold season. The Inuit used carved ivory jigs, spears, and fur-adorned bone hooks in the old days, but today most anglers take charrs through the ice with small jigs, spoons, and bait. Certain lakes in Southcentral's Kenai Peninsula and Mat-Su Valley, parts of Bristol Bay, a few lakes in the Interior (for stocked fish), and waters along Kotzebue Sound are where most of this effort occurs.

Top Flies for Alaska Charr

Glo Bug, Egg Sucking Leech, Fall Favorite, Copper and Orange, Skykomish Sunrise, Bead Egg, Smolt, Fry, Parr Fly, Alevin, Mickey Finn, Polar Shrimp, Flash Fly, Woolly Bugger, Pink Sparkler, Muddler, Battle Creek, Bunny Fly, Supervisor, Zonker.

Top Ten Alaska Trophy Charr

27 lbs., 6 oz.	Wulik River (NW)	2002
19 lbs., 12.5 oz.	Noatak River (NW)	1991
18 lbs., 15 oz.	Wulik River (NW)	1994
18 lbs., 3 oz.	Wulik River (NW)	1999
17 lbs., 9.5 oz.	Wulik River (NW)	1995
17 lbs., 8 oz.	Wulik River (NW)	1999
17 lbs., 8 oz.	Wulik River (NW)	1968
16 lbs., 14 oz.	Lake Iliamna (SW)	1973
16 lbs., 8 oz.	Wulik River (NW)	1988
16 lbs., 4 oz.	Noatak River (NW)	1994

Alaska Trophy Charr Timing

Kenai River System (SC)	Late August–October
Naknek Lake System (SW)	July–October
Iliamna Lake System (SW)	July–October
Becharof Lake System (SW)	July–mid-September
Noatak River System (NW)	Late July–mid-September
Wulik/Kivalina rivers (NW)	August–mid-September

ARCTIC/DOLLY VARDEN CHARR

Salvelinus alpinus/malma

SPECIES SUMMARY

Alaska common names: Charr, arctic charr, Dolly Varden, Dolly, trout, salmon-trout, blue or golden fin trout, western brook trout/charr.

Description: Abundant, widespread small to medium-sized salmonid. Color and markings vary; generally silver-blue, gray, or brown back and sides, with red, pink, yellow, or orange oval spots; whitish belly. Ventral fins are yellow to carmine with white edges. Sexually mature fish striking, with dark brown or greenish topsides, bright orange-red shading on undersides, and vivid spots. Males have pronounced jaw kypes and back ridges. Pink to orange flesh.

Size: Average 1-2 lbs. and 14-20 in.; to 12 lbs. and 34 in. or more, SW-NW.

State Record: 27 lbs., 6 oz., Wulik River (NW), Mike Curtiss, 2002.

Habits: Voracious, opportunistic predator; especially fond of salmon roe and young.

Notes: In feeding habits and seasonal movements, very similar to rainbow trout.

Meristics: Gill rakers variable 11-32; vertebrae 57-71; pyloric caeca 13-75; lateral line scales 105-152; branchiostegal rays 10-15; dorsal fin 12-16 rays; anal fin 8-15 rays; pelvic fin 8-11 rays.

Range: Coastal statewide; inland along major rivers and isolated lake/stream forms across state. (Also stocked fisheries SC-INT.)

Preferred Habitat: Fast flowing, clear coastal streams and associated lakes.

Best waters: Major coastal salmon streams and adjacent salt water, SE-NW, but especially NSE, Kodiak, Alaska Peninsula, Bristol and Kuskokwim bays, Norton and Kotzebue sounds.

Best Times: Available year-round; best in spring (April-June) and late summer-fall (August-October).

Best Bait/Lures/Flies: Salmon eggs; flashy spinners, spoons, plugs, jigs; flourescent drift bobbers; smolt/fry, egg/flesh, and attractor pattern flies.

Best Trophy Areas: Kotzebue Sound (NW)—Wulik, Noatak, Kivalina rivers, etc.; Northern Alaska Peninsula (SW)—Iliamna, Naknek, Ugashik, Becharof lakes; Kenai River (SC); Wood-Tikchik Lakes (SW).

RECOMMENDED GEAR

Spinning/Casting:
Ultralight-light, medium action, 5-7 1/2 ft. graphite trout rod; matching reel and 150 yds. 4-8 lb. test line.

Trophy or Big water:
Medium-heavy wt., medium-fast action trout rod, 6 1/2-8 ft.; matching reel with 175 yds. 8 to 12-lb. test line. Or:

Medium wt. freshwater, fast action graphite casting rod, 6-7 1/2 ft.; matching high quality reel with 200 yds. 8-12-lb. test line.

Flyfishing:
5-7 wt., 8-9 ft., medium-fast action graphite flyrod; matching reel with 20-30 lb. backing and WF floating, intermediate or short sink-tip (Type II-IV) lines; 7 ft. leader and 4-10 lb. (5X-0X) tippet.

ALASKA'S MAJOR CHARR LOCATIONS

SOUTHEAST
Southeast has some of the state's most abundant Dolly Varden charr, found in nearly every stream that supports fish. Saltwater angling opportunities also abound, beginning in early May, as Dollies cruise beaches feeding on salmon fry, and continuing into July.

Yakutat/North Gulf: Situk, Italio, Akwe, Lost, Tsiu, Kaliakh, East, Doame, and Alsek (clearwater tributaries) river systems.

Juneau: Northern Stephens Passage, Icy Strait, Cross Sound, Gastineau Channel; Auke, Turner, and Windfall lakes; Tenakee Inlet; Cowee, Montana, Admiralty, and Peterson creeks; Bartlett River; Mitchell Bay system.

Haines/Skagway: Chilkat, Chilkoot, and Lutak inlets; Taiya, Chilkat, Chilkoot rivers; Chilkat and Mosquito lakes.

Sitka: Nakwasina, Salisbury, and Sitka sounds; Indian, and Nakwasina rivers; Salmon, Eva, Surge, Goulding, and Klag Bay lake systems; Sitkoh and Starrigavan creeks.

Petersburg/Wrangell: Lower Stephens Passage; Ernest, Frederick sounds; Upper Clarence, Zimovia, and Chatham straits; Wrangell Narrows/Duncan Canal, Bradfield Canal; Blind Slough, Wilson Beach; Falls, Bear, Exchange, Aaron, Thoms, Anan, Kadake, Andrew, Pat, Hamilton, Petersburg, Ohmer, and Saltchuck creeks; Castle, Eagle, Harding, and Kah Sheets rivers.

Ketchikan/POW: Clarence Strait, Behm Canal, Gravina Island, Revillagigedo Channel, San Alberto Bay; Carroll, Ketchikan, Kegan, Fish, Staney, and Whipple creeks; Wilson, Klawock, and Harris rivers; Thorne, Karta, and Naha river systems; Humpback, McDonald, Ward, Sarkar, Sweetwater, Luck, and Orchard lakes systems.

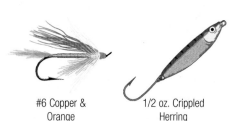

#6 Copper & Orange

1/2 oz. Crippled Herring

#8 Glo Bug

#3 Mepps White Fury

3/8 oz. Hotrod

SOUTHCENTRAL

About 2/3 of the state's sport-caught charr are taken here, mostly from the Kenai Peninsula.

Kenai Peninsula: Kenai, Kasilof, Anchor, Russian, Ninilchik rivers; Deep, Stariski creeks; Grouse, Summit, Jerome, Island, and Swanson River lakes; Rocky River; Kachemak and Resurrection bays.

Copper River: Klutina, Tonsina, Tsaina rivers.

Copper River Delta: Eyak, Bering, Katalla river systems; Power and Clear creeks; Alaganik Slough; Martin, McKinley lake and river systems.

Prince William Sound: Cordova and Valdez Arm; Jackpot Bay, Eshamy Lagoon; Coghill, Beach, Nellie-Martin Patton and San Juan rivers; Boswell and Markarka creeks.

Knik Arm: Big Lake, Little Susitna River, Wasilla Creek, Nancy lakes

Mat-Su Lakes (stocked): Long, Finger, Kepler-Bradley, Carpenter, Matanuska, Seventeenmile, and Benka lakes.

Susitna River: Talkeetna River system; Willow, Lake, and Alexander creeks.

Upper Cook Inlet: Chuitna and Theodore rivers; Crescent Lake system.

Lower Cook Inlet: Kamishak River.

Kodiak: All bays in vicinity of salmon streams, especially Uyak, Ugak, Uganik, Chiniak, Mill, Monashka, Perenosa, Olga, and Seal bays. All salmon-producing streams and associated lakes, especially: Karluk, Buskin, Pasagshak, Saltery, Olds, Thumb, Uganik, Ayakulik, American, Afognak, Spiridon, Dog Salmon, Zachar, and Little rivers; Portage, Pauls, Akalura, Roslyn, Salonie, and Malina creeks; Barabara and Hidden lakes; Shuyak Island salmon streams, bays, and straits.

SOUTHWEST

Southwest Alaska has some of Alaska's finest freshwater charr angling in terms of abundance and size (to 15 lbs.).

Alaska Peninsula: Nearly all streams and lakes, down to and including the Aleutian Islands, with heavy salmon runs generally offer the most outstanding fishing: Naknek Lake and River system (including Brooks River, American Creek, Idavain Creek and Lake, and other associated streams and lakes); Becharof Lake and Egegik River system; Ugashik Lake and River system; Chignik River system; Aniakchak, Meshik and Bear rivers; and Nelson Lagoon system.

Bristol Bay: All major salmon systems also have prolific charr populations, especially: Iliamna-Kvichak system, Nushagak system (mostly Mulchatna, Nuyakuk, upper Nushagak mainstem), Wood River-Tikchik Lakes (mostly outlet and inlet streams);Togiak River system, Igushik River, Kulukak River.

Kuskokwim: Goodnews, Arolik, Kanektok, Eek, Kwethluk, Tuluksak, Kisaralik, Kasigluk, Aniak, and Holitna river systems.

Nunivak Island: Some huge, trophy sea-run specimens have been taken from streams here.

Lower Yukon: Andreafsky and Anvik rivers.

NORTHWEST

Thirty percent of the state's largest trophy charr have been taken from this region.

Eastern Norton Sound: Unalakleet, Shaktoolik, Inglutalik, Ungalik, Tubutulik, and Kwiniuk rivers.

Seward Peninsula: All salmon streams, especially Fish-Niukluk, Nome, and Pilgrim rivers; Salmon Lake; Snake, Sinuk, Solomon, Kuzitrin, Agiapuk, Bonanza, Eldorado, and Buckland rivers.

Kotzebue Sound: All trophy potential: Lower Noatak River and tributaries (Kelly, Kugururok, Nimiuktuk rivers, etc.), Kobuk River drainage (including Walker and Selby lakes), Wulik and Kivalina rivers.

ARCTIC

Arctic has outstanding, barely explored fishing possibilities in its many lakes and streams, quite a few with trophy potential.

Colville River system (especially Anaktuvuk, Chandler, and Killik rivers); Sagavanirktok, Canning, Kongakut, and Hulahula rivers; also Chandler, Karupa-Cascade, Galbraith, Elusive, Schrader-Peters lakes.

INTERIOR

Only small, streams resident charr occur naturally in streams here, but stocked fishing is available in some Tanana Valley lakes.

Tanana and Nenana rivers (clearwater tributaries); Quartz, Birch, Harding, Chena, Four Mile, Donnelly, Manchu, and Polaris lakes.

#6 Battle Creek

3/8 oz. Wiggle Wart

#6 Black Muddler

#2 Silver Vibrax

#6 Fry

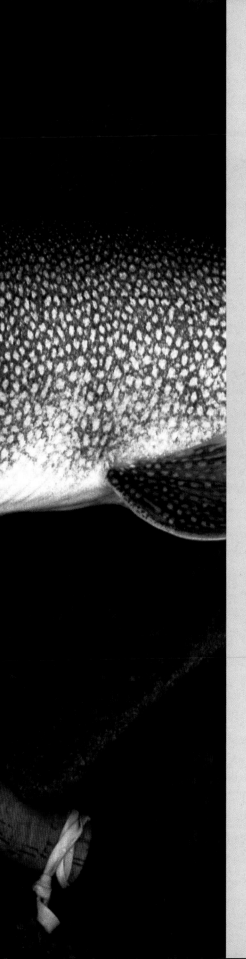

Lake Trout

Old Man of the Lakes

Among the Inupiat of Northwest Alaska, there is an age-old legend of a giant fish they call *Idluk*, found in the deepest, most remote lakes of the Brooks Range. Said to be as old as the hills, this finny will-o'-the-wisp is reputed to reach sizes large enough to swallow a man whole, should he stray too near the water. Fabulous tales like this are easy to dismiss as nothing more than silly folklore, having no basis in the reality that surrounds most of our lives. But perhaps not.

Some years back, two men were fishing the headwaters of the Kobuk River at Walker Lake in the Brooks Range. It was early summer, and they were putzing around in a small raft, enjoying the exquisite weather and 24-hour daylight that time of year brings to northern Alaska. The hour was late, but they had a notion to troll some big plugs before they headed in to camp and called it a night. Fishing with heavy lines and stout baitcasters, they were awestruck when one of the beefy rods doubled, and its reel screamed, only seconds after they had let their lures out. Now, these fellows were experienced Alaska anglers and men of the wilderness, with years of time in some of Alaska's most remote backcountry. But to this day, they swear that whatever it was on the end of their line that night was no ordinary fish. Clamping down on the drag and pumping the big rod for all he was worth, one of them barely brought the beast under control. As it gyrated and spun the light boat around and around, they realized they didn't have a ghost of a chance with the thing. But what really got them was that when the behemoth headed for the lake's far shore, some 15 miles away, it was only slightly fazed by the raft it was dragging behind. They way they tell it, after 20 minutes in tow, with no indication of the fish tiring, and a strong offshore breeze kicking up, they had a very brief discussion and agreed it was best to cut loose, and so they parted ways with this lake monster.

113

Casting for lakers, Aniak Lake, Southwest Alaska.

LAKE TROUT: OLD MAN OF THE LAKES

The lake trout, *Salvelinus namaycush*, is certainly one of our better-known northern fish denizens. Originally found in deep, clear, cold waters from New England to the Arctic, the big, native trout of the northern lakes is actually a charr, closely allied with the familiar eastern brook trout and Dolly Varden of the West. It has the distinction of being our continent's largest and longest-lived freshwater salmonid, reaching potential weights of 100 pounds or more and lifespans of over 50 years.

In Alaska, the lake trout is widely distributed and thriving, with fishing potential in many waters comparable to some of the better fisheries in Northern Canada. But, because anglers in Alaska have a variety of world-class fisheries at hand, few areas in the state receive the intense, systematic effort seen in lake trout waters elsewhere. For that reason, much of the state's good lake trout water remains underutilized.

Not a spectacular gamefish by any stretch of the imagination, the laker's reputation is nonetheless secure. This is the fish of the primitive northern wilderness, inhabiting the crystal depths of the loneliest watersheds, even where no other species will thrive. Draw out a map of Alaska, pick out any lake of size, depth, and elevation who-knows-where, and it's a safe bet you'll find some some of its kind waiting to pick a fight with you there, should you travel and fish those far-flung waters.

DESCRIPTION

Built like a true trout, with a large mouth and protruding belly, the lake trout looks every bit the predator that he is. His basic color scheme involves a darker background of silver gray to brown (sometimes greenish), with a profusion of white, yellow, or gold oval spots, and vermiculations across the back and sides. Bellies are usually cream-colored, with lower fins of the distinct, trademark charr coloration: clear, milky, yellow, or orangish, with narrow white borders. Lake trout have deeply forked tail fins and no red or pink spots on their sides—two distinctive character differences that distinguish them from the other charrs.

The average size of Alaska's lake trout varies, but is generally from three to five pounds in most waters that are not heavily fished. The state's largest lake trout generally come from deep, large lakes with abundant food sources, with fish of 20 pounds or more considered trophy specimens for Alaska (the state record is a 47-pounder from a lake in the central Alaska Range).

The lake trout's appeal is certainly enhanced by its excellent eating qualities. Its firm, white, pink, or orange flesh has a delicate flavor and is superb fried, baked, or smoked. Don't count your outdoor career complete until you've sat on a gravelly shore, indulging your hearty appetite with succulent lake trout fillets, lightly seasoned and grilled over a smoky fire.

RANGE, ABUNDANCE & STATUS

Lake trout occur only in North America, originally in a wide swath of lakes stretching from New England to the Great Lakes, across most of Canada, down into the Rockies and up into Alaska (a range that coincides with the limits of the last major period of glaciation). In Alaska, they are common in the alpine lakes of the Alaska Range, Bristol Bay, the Kenai and Alaska peninsulas, the Brooks Range, and the central and eastern Arctic coastal plain. They are absent from Kodiak, the Seward Peninsula, low-lying lakes of the Yukon and Kuskokwim basins, the northwest Arctic coast, and most of the Alaska Peninsula. Though they are almost always associated with lake systems, some stream-dwelling populations may occur in the Sagavanirktok, Colville, and Canning rivers of the Arctic.

Very little has been done to adequately assess the status of any but the most accessible of the state's lake trout stocks. All indications, however, point to a healthy fishery overall, although many of the state's more heavily fished locations are showing the effects of overharvesting, with a decline in average size and number of trophy specimens. More conservative management and a growing trend toward catch-and-release hopefully mean a bright future for the high quality of angling currently available.

LIFE HISTORY & HABITS

Much of what has been learned about the general life history and habits of lake charr comes from extensive studies done throughout Canada. Lake trout research in Alaska has been very limited, focused mostly on the more accessible lakes of the Alaska Range. We know that, like all charrs, lake trout are voracious, opportunistic predators that spawn in the fall (not necessarily every year), and have movement and feeding patterns that change with the season. There are some key differences, however, between lake trout and their charr cousins that are of prime importance to anglers.

The most obvious characteristic unique to the species is their preference for lake habitat. Almost all of the lake trout you'll encounter in Alaska will be associated with some lake body (except the distinct river-dwelling populations mentioned above). The need for cold, highly oxygenated water determines, to a great extent, their movements and feeding patterns. With the arrival of spring breakup, lakers move into shallows to feed, consuming small fish, molluscs, crustaceans, insect larvae and even rodents. When available, fish is the preferred prey of larger lake trout, and, in many Alaska waters, a rich and varied forage of sculpins, sticklebacks, juvenile grayling, whitefish, suckers, ciscoes, smelt, salmon smolts, etc. is available.

As water temperatures rise, lake trout will go deep, preferring to remain in waters that are in the mid-40 to lower 50°F range. Studies have shown that, even in lakes with abundant food supplies, some lake trout will forgo a meal for an empty stomach if it means they have to leave their preferred band of cooler water for any length of time.

With the arrival of fall and cooler temperatures in Alaska (in late August and September in most of the state) lake trout begin to congregate for spawning in offshore areas of shallow to moderate depth (less than 40 feet), with gravel or rocky bottoms free of sand or mud. Ideal spawning areas are far enough from shore to escape the pounding of wind-induced wave action, but shallow enough to resist sedimentation. Spawning at night, lake trout, unlike salmon, do not use a nest. Instead, they scatter their eggs to settle into the cracks and crevices of the substrate, where they slowly develop and hatch in late winter.

Alaska's lake trout are slow-growing, late-maturing and long-lived; fish older than 25 years are not uncommon, with some specimens from the Arctic exceeding 50 years. (Arctic populations generally mature later and live longer.) Because of their slow growth rates, long lives, and rather low fecundity, trophy lake trout populations are surprisingly easy to overfish, a fact that many fish managers have realized, hopefully in time to save the trophy potential of the more hard-hit locales that have already had most of the worthy specimens gleaned by overharvesting. Many of the better trophy lake trout fisheries in northern Canada nowadays have strict catch-and-release policies, a trend that may soon catch on in some of the more urban-accessible waters of Alaska.

FISHING ALASKA'S LAKE TROUT

The sport catch of lake trout in Alaska varies, but is generally less than 50,000 fish annually. Most of this effort is focused on lakes of the upper Copper and upper Susitna rivers and Kenai Peninsula in Southcentral, and in the Tanana River watershed of the Interior. A significant number of fish also come from lakes of the Southwest region. Because of the similarities in life cycle and habits across their range at high latitudes, many appropriate fishing strategies for Alaska's lakers are similar to those used in lakes of northern Canada, with some key differences, noted in the following discussion of the different seasonal fishing conditions encountered in Alaska.

Downriggers and trolling rods are *de rigueur* for fishing many of Alaska's larger and deeper lake trout waters.

Spring Conditions

Across the North, as the returning sun frees fish from their icy prisons and winter stupor, all charr become very active and begin feeding extensively. Lake trout will cruise shallows and surface waters, aggressively searching for anything that remotely resembles a food item but, especially, small fish, crustaceans, and molluscs. In Alaska waters, their spring recklessness may be heightened by the presence of competitor species—other charr and rainbows, for instance—and/or a richer, more varied forage (juvenile salmon, ciscoes, whitefish, suckers, etc).

Rambunctious feeding and spring conditions make for some of the best fishing of the year. Almost any properly presented lure or fly will have an even chance with spring lakers and, in shallow crystal lake waters, there's no trick to locating them either. Timing, weather, and location will be the most significant factors in your success this time of year. Though many of these lakes don't get fished until they're open enough to allow for floatplane or boat access, if you can somehow get to them just as the leads are opening up, especially around outlet/inlet waters, you can have some amazing action. (Some fish-crazed pilots even land ski planes on the rotten ice of remote lakes in late spring and toss spoons or jigs into the slush water surrounding the edges, with awesome results.)

No matter how early you get to fish these trout lakes, the idea is still the same: work the open water as it becomes available, which generally occurs sooner around outlet and inlet streams, bays, and shorelines

"Alaska Plug," a classic lure for lakers (replaced by today's "J-plug")

that lie on the windward side. Sunny weather can really bring the lakers out into these open areas, much the same as it does for people emerging from a long winter's confinement. Bright spoons, jigs, or spinners (Krocodile, Dardevle, Super Vibrax, Crippled Herring, Mr. Twister, etc.), and bait tossed into these waters will usually do the trick.

Spring is also one of the most opportune times for taking lakers on a fly, as they tend to scatter and go deeper later in the season. Smolt, leech, sculpin, and attractor patterns, size #1/0 to #6, work exceedingly well for Alaska spring lakers, with nymphs and even dry flies eliciting strikes under the right conditions. Look for signs of fish in the shallows of small bays, outlet and inlet waters, and along beaches with drop-offs, especially in the early morning or late evening hours, when they are prone to prowl. (One of the greatest thrills of fishing wild lake trout waters is to be gently stirred from sleep by the slurping of big fish in the shallows, only yards from your lakeside camp.)

After the ice completely disappears and lakes start to warm, fish may not be so easy to find. Work any obvious shallow feeding locations, just as you would for charr this time of year (in many of Alaska's lake systems the two will freely mingle during spring feeding, particularly during smolt outmigrations). If you don't have any luck, you'll need to probe deeper water, from shore or from a boat or raft. Big, bright spoons such as Krocodiles, Dardevles, Silver Minnows, Wablers, Doctors, or Pixees are time-tested favorites for this kind of fishing, as are diving plugs like Wiggle Warts, Tadpollys, Rapalas, Crystal Minnows, or Kwik-fish. They should be worked deep and with a slow retrieve or troll. Quite often during the period between late spring and early summer, lakers will be found moderately deep, to 15 feet or so, in offshore areas like shoals or bays that have concentrations of baitfish. A small boat and fish locator/depth sounder are certainly advantageous for these conditions, especially on big waters.

Summer Conditions

Much has been said and written about the lake trout's preference for cooler, oxygen-rich waters and bottom structure. As northern waters warm from the advancing sun and long days, lakes will stratify into more or less defined layers of temperature and oxygen saturation. This is especially true in big deep lakes of southern Canada, but may not always be the case in Alaska's high latitude waters, where the thermocline may not be so pronounced because of cooler yearly temperatures, prevailing winds, and lake morphology.

As summer advances, lake trout will tend to scatter from their spring haunts to deeper water, but not necessarily to the deepest parts of the lake. Depending on factors like the availability of food, bottom structure, weather, and time of day, you can expect to encounter many of them in water 10 to 40 feet deep in most Alaska lakes during summer (July and August). Most smaller lakers (two to eight pounds) will stay fairly close to shore near lake outlets and inlets, islands, bays with cover, and beaches with drop-offs, even during the hottest part of summer. They can provide some of the more consistent and enjoyable fishing this time of year. The low-light hours and cloudy or windy days are the best times to encounter these shallow holding summer lakers, with spinners, small spoons or baitfish and attractor pattern streamers the most popular and effective enticements.

No matter what kind of stratification or structure a lake has, summer feeding habits and movements of Alaska's lake charr can be greatly influenced by the wide range of food sources available. This is particularly true in the salmon-rich Southwest lake systems of Katmai, Iliamna, the Tikchiks, and Kuskokwim Bay; and, to a lesser extent, certain locations in Northwest and the Arctic slope, where it is not uncommon to encounter lakers feeding heavily in streams, miles from lake sources. Though these fish rarely push the ten-pound mark, they are quite often abundant, fat and feisty—a welcome surprise when angling the standard river fare.

For trophy fishing the big lakes, the summer months of July and August are the prime times for deepwater trolling. This usually means stout rods, downriggers, fish locators, thermistors (temperature reading devices), flashers, and what-have-you, if you're a serious fisherman or guide on the state's more popular big water fisheries. Large (four-inch plus) trolling spoons like the #5 ½ to 7 Canadian Wonder,

Alaska's Monster Laker

Dan Thorsness of Anchorage, with his mounted 47 lb. state record lake trout, taken June, 1970, Clarence Lake (SC).

On a fly-out fishing trip with his dad in early summer 1970, 12-year-old Dan Thorsness cast a #3 Mepps into a deep dropoff near the outlet of Clarence Lake in the Alaska Range and hooked a monster—the largest lake trout ever taken in Alaska! With coaching from his dad, the boy beached the behemoth after a lengthy battle and convinced his father not to cut it up for the frying pan; the fish made it back to Anchorage intact and was certified as the new state record, 47 pounds!

005 Diamond King, #4 Les Thompson, #7 Tom Mack, #4 Williams Wabler, and 550 Apex, along with long plugs (up to nine inches) like the K16 Kwikfish, T55 Flatfish, 005 J-Plug, #14 to #22 Magnum Rapala, and #6 Jensen Power Dive Minnow, in colors of silver, gold, silver/blue, silver/green, green/yellow, or white pearl are the most commonly used lures, producing excellent results. Slow but varied trolling speeds at depths of 15 to 60 feet through areas where baitfish congregate (shoals, reefs, islands, shelves, etc.), seem to produce the most fish. A good knowledge of the lake's bottom structure, thermocline, forage, and areas of fish concentration (along with fish locators/depth sounders) certainly can save a lot of wasted effort this time of year. If you don't have the necessary experience or equipment, it makes good sense to seek the services of a reputable guide.

Fall Conditions

Fall is another favored time for lake trout fishing, though the season in Alaska can be quite short. From late August well into September, lake trout begin their prespawning movements. During this phase, they are more concentrated near gravelly or rocky beaches, shoals or small bays, and other areas conducive to spawning, in water anywhere from a few to fifteen feet deep. If you time it right and know where to go, you can get into some of the year's best fishing, as the trout become territorial and aggressive. The company of a knowledgeable guide or local fisherman can save a lot of guesswork and wasted time in searching out these areas. Bright spinners, spoons, jigs, and baitfish/attractor pattern streamers (Alaska Mary Ann, Mickey Finn, Smolt, Gray Ghost, Marabou Muddler, and Leech) all work well on fall lakers. Since many Alaska fishermen are busy with hunting activities this time of year, many truly outstanding, easily accessible fall fishing opportunities go underutilized.

Winter Conditions

Lake trout, along with northern pike, charr, and burbot, provide the mainstay of Alaska's long winter ice fishing season. Many anglers, lacking the ways and means (or time) to fish the state's better lakes during open water season, can access prime areas in winter by truck and/or snowmachine for outstanding fishing.

Most of this winter effort for lake trout occurs in the more urban-accessible waters of the upper Susitna, Tanana, and Copper rivers, and the Kenai Peninsula, where fishermen quite often take lakers as part of a mixed bag of winter species. Techniques involved are much the same as fishing for northern pike, with a series of holes drilled, and lures (big spoons and jigs) and/or bait (herring usually) worked to entice some response from lethargic predators. Lake maps, personal knowledge of the waters' depth, bottom structure, forage species, etc., and portable fish finders are invaluable for enhancing your success this time of year.

Fishing Bait: The use of live bait, a deadly effective, time-honored tradition elsewhere, is restricted in Alaska by a statewide ban to prevent introduction of non-native species. Though you can't rig a squirming, six-inch grayling to tantalize the big ones like they do in Canada, you can do quite well at certain times trolling rigged deadbaits or lures like spoons with four-to five-inch strips of whitefish, herring, smelt, or cisco added for extra pizazz. Some fishermen have had good results at certain times drifting chunks of whitefish, herring, shrimp, even salmon eggs through weedy bays, channels, and outlet and inlet waters.

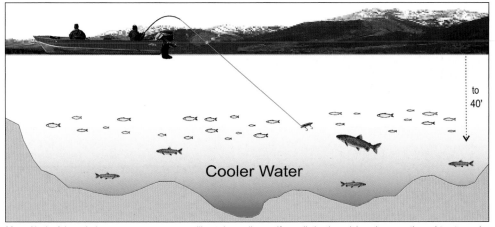

to 40'

Cooler Water

Many Alaska lakes, during open water season, will not thermally stratify as distinctly as lakes down south, and trout may be more scattered. A good strategy when working unfamiliar waters is to locate schools of baitfish (usually whitefish or cisco) with fish finders, and work that depth zone for feeding lakers.

GEARING UP FOR ALASKA'S LAKE TROUT

Spin & Casting Gear

For spinfishing Alaska's lake trout under most conditions, you'll want to rig up with a light to medium-weight (rated 6 to 12-pound test line), 6 to 7 1/2-foot, medium-fast action, freshwater spinning rod, matched with a high quality reel capable of holding at least 150 yards of 8 to 12-pound test nylon monofilament line.

Casting gear fishermen will probably want a medium-weight (rated 8 to 15 pound line), fast-action, (7 to 8 1/2-foot) rod, with a matching, high quality reel spooled with at least 150 yards of 8 to 15-pound test.

For deepwater trolling, a medium-heavy weight (rated 10-25 pound line), fast action, trolling rod, (7 to 8 1/2-foot) is recommended, matched with a high quality heavy casting/trolling reel (Ambassadeur 6000-7000, Shimano Calcutta 400-700, Penn 965-975, Okuma Convector 20-30, etc.), spooled with 200 yards of 15 to 25-pound test line.

Flyfishing Gear

For most fishing conditions, a 7 or 8-weight, medium-fast action rod (8 1/2 to 9 1/2 feet) will serve well, matched with a medium-heavy trout or light salmon class reel, loaded with 100 yards 20 to 30-pound backing, and performance tapered, WF floating, intermediate or sink tip line (Type II-V, or 200-400 grain—depending on depth). Use a seven-foot leader with 8 to 12-pound tippet.

WHERE TO GO

With all the attention lavished on Alaska's world-famous salmon and rainbow fisheries, the state's outstanding lake trout potential is easily overlooked. Well-known and perennially favorite locations like lakes Louise-Susitna, Paxson-Summit, Crosswind, Hidden, and Harding continue to pump out trophy specimens (20-pound-plus fish) each year, thanks to better management and growing numbers of catch-and-release anglers. More remote, higher-quality fishing experiences can always be had a short ways off the road (accessed by foot, snowmachine, or ATV) along many of Alaska's highways (Denali, Dalton, and Alaska highways, and Nabesna Road).

For the very best lake trout fishing in the Last Frontier, you'll need to climb in a small plane and fly beyond the fringes of civilization to the state's more isolated waters. Some of these are not too far or expensive to access. The majestic Wrangell and Talkeetna mountain ranges, north and east of Anchorage, all contain numerous lakes with great fishing that can be reached with relatively short, inexpensive flights from the nearby hubs of Palmer, Talkeetna, and Glennallen. Fabulous Southwest Alaska likewise contains many headwater lakes that are seldom sampled, but have some of the state's best wild lake trout angling. And, for those lucky souls blessed with time and resources to explore Alaska's ultimate wilderness watersheds, there are the remote lakes of the Brooks Range and Arctic North Slope, where one can encounter the "old man of the lakes" in the most pristine surroundings.

LAKE TROUT
Salvelinus namaycush

SPECIES SUMMARY

Alaska common names: Lake trout, laker.

Description: Troutlike, upland lake-dwelling charr, common in Alaska. Has silver-gray or brown back and sides, with numerous gold, yellow, or white oval spots and vermiculations. Mouth large, belly usually cream-colored, with lower fins milky, yellow, or orange with white borders. Tail fin is deeply forked. Flesh white, yellowish-white, or light orange.

Size: Average weight 3-5 lbs., up to 30 lbs. or more.

State record: 47 lbs., Clarence Lake (SC), Daniel Thorsness, 1970.

Habits: Voracious, opportunistic, and omnivorous predator.

Notes: Found only in North America, the lake charr (trout) is our continent's longest lived salmonid.

Meristics: Gill rakers 16-26; vertebrae 61-69; pyloric caeca 92-210; lateral line scales 116-138; branchiostegal rays 10-14; dorsal fin 8-10 rays; anal fin 8-10 rays; pelvic fin 8-11 rays; pectoral fin 12-17 rays.

Range: Highland lakes, Chugach/Wrangell mountains (SC) to Arctic coastal plain, except Seward Peninsula.

Preferred Habitat: Deep alpine lakes with abundant forage.

Best Waters: Large, productive lakes in Alaska and Brooks ranges and northern Alaska Peninsula.

Best Times: Available year-round; best in spring (late May and June) and fall (late August and September).

Best Bait/Lures/Flies: Whitefish, herring; bright spoons, spinners, plugs, and jigs; forage and attractor pattern streamers.

Best Trophy Waters: Lake Louise (SC), Lake Clark (SW), Harding Lake (INT), Paxson Lake (SC), Crosswind Lake (SC).

RECOMMENDED GEAR

Spinning: Medium-wt. (rated 6-12 lb. line), 6 to 7 1/2 ft., medium-fast action trout rod; matching high quality reel with 150 yds. 8 to 12-lb. test monofilament.

Casting: Medium-heavy wt. (rated 10-25 lb. line), fast action trolling rod, 7 to 8 1/2 ft.; heavy freshwater casting/trolling reel with 200 yds. 15-25 lb. test mono or braided line.

Flyfishing: 7-8 wt., medium-fast action, 8 1/2-9 1/2 ft. flyrod, large trout or light salmon class reel with 100 yds. 20-30 lb. backing. Performance taper WF floating, intermediate and sink tip lines (Type II-V, or 200-400 grain T-series, depending on depth), with 7 ft. leader and 8-12 lb. tippet.

ALASKA'S MAJOR LAKE TROUT LOCATIONS

SOUTHCENTRAL

Southcentral holds some of Alaska's most heavily fished but productive lake trout waters, including some outstanding trophy locations.

Susitna River drainage: Susitna, Tyone, Louise, Clarence, Watana, Crater, Big, Deadman, Chelatna, Stephan, Shell, and Butte lakes.

Copper River drainage: Paxson, Summit, Crosswind, Fish, Deep, Shell, Klutina, Tonsina, Tazlina, Tanada, Tebay, and Hanagita lakes.

Copper River Delta: Tokun Lake.

White River drainage: Rock, Ptarmigan, and Beaver lakes.

Kenai Peninsula: Hidden Lake; Kenai River system (including Skilak and Kenai lakes); Swan, Juneau, and Trail lakes; Trail River, Tustumena Lake-Kasilof River.

Cook Inlet: Beluga, Chakachamna, and Crescent lakes.

SOUTHWEST

Southwest has some of the state's best lake trout waters in terms of abundance, though few trophy (20-lbs.-plus) fish are taken.

Kvichak River/Lake Clark: Lakes Clark and Iliamna; Kokhanok, Gibraltar, Lachbuna, Kontrashibuna, and Kijik lakes.

Katmai: Lakes Naknek, Brooks, Kulik, Nonvianuk, Kukaklek, and Coville-Grosvenor.

Alaska Peninsula: Ugashik Lakes.

Nushagak River drainage: Tikchik Lakes (all); Twin, Fishtrap, Snipe, and Turquoise lakes.

Togiak drainage: Nenevok Lake.

Upper Kuskokwim River: Whitefish (Hoholitna), Telaquana, and Two lakes.

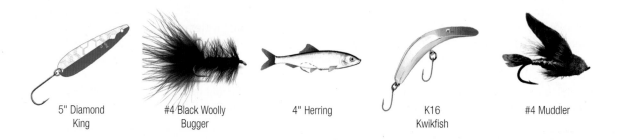

| 5" Diamond King | #4 Black Woolly Bugger | 4" Herring | K16 Kwikfish | #4 Muddler |

Many of Alaska's lakes provide abundant flyfishing opportunities for small to medium-sized lake trout throughout the open water season.

Lower Kuskokwim River: Aniak, Kisaralik, Heart, Kanektok River (Kagati-Pegati, Kanuktik, Klak, Ohnlik, etc.), Goodnews River (Goodnews, Middle Fork, Kukatlim, Canyon, etc.), and Arolik lakes.

INTERIOR

The Interior includes some of the state's most popular fisheries in the Tanana drainage and some excellent remote lakes.

Brooks Range: Ackerman, Squaw, and Chandalar lakes; Big and Twin lakes; Old John Lake.

Tanana: Tangle Lakes; Fielding, Boulder, Glacier, 16.8 Mile, Sevenmile, Harding, Landmark Gap, Monte, Tetlin, and Two-Bit lakes.

NORTHWEST

The Northwest has many outstanding possibilities in numerous, remote Brooks Range mountain lakes. A few of the more well-known ones are listed below.

Kobuk River Valley: Walker, Minakokosa, Selby-Narvak, and Norutak lakes.

Noatak River Valley: Feniak, Matcharak, and Desperation lakes; Kiingyak, Kikitaliorak, and other Howard Pass lakes.

Upper Koyukuk River: Wild, Iniakuk, Helpmejack, and Agiak lakes.

ARCTIC

Arctic has the state's wildest lake trout waters, many receiving little, if any, fishing pressure. Potential for high-quality fishing is tops.

Colville River: Etivluk River Lakes (Etivluk, Nigu, Tukuto, etc.); Karupa and Cascade lakes; Chandler and Amiloyak lakes; Anaktuvuk River Lakes (Irgnyivik, Shainin, Tulugak, Lower Anayak, etc.); Itkillik Lake.

Central Plain Lakes: Teshekpuk and deep lakes east of the Ikpikpuk River.

Dalton Highway Lakes: Galbraith, Elusive, Toolik, Itagaknit, Kuparuk, and Campsite lakes.

Eastern Slope: Porcupine, Schrader, and Peters lakes.

Top Fly Patterns for Alaska Lake Trout
Blue Smolt, Leech, Mickey Finn, Muddler, Grey Ghost, Black Ghost, Zonker, Alaska Mary Ann, Egg Sucking Leech, Supervisor, Black Nosed Dace, Parr, Scud, Deceiver, White Ghost, D's Minnow, Woolly Bugger.

Top Ten Alaska Trophy Lake Trout		
47 lbs.	Clarence Lake (SC)	1970
33 lbs., 8 oz.	Lake Clark (SW)	1980
33 lbs., 4 oz.	Harding Lake (INT)	1993
32 lbs., 4 oz.	Lake Clark (SW)	1983
31 lbs., 13 oz.	Harding Lake (INT)	1997
30 lbs., 15 oz.	Lake Louise (SC)	1973
29 lbs., 8 oz.	Skilak Lake (SC)	1985
29 lbs., 2 oz.	Old John Lake (INT)	1981
28 lbs., 6 oz.	Lake Clark (SW)	1982
28 lbs., 5 oz.	Harding Lake (INT)	1994

1 1/2 oz. Dardevle

#4 Black Ghost

005 "J-Plug"

#2 D's Minnow

#4 Black Nose Dace

Arctic Grayling
Sailfin of the North

During midsummer in Alaska, as fishing wanes with the end of the first salmon runs, some anglers have a hard time drumming up action that can compare in any way with the electrifying excitement of June. Things might slow to a complete crawl if not for an amazing fishery that comes into its own this time of year. In headwaters, lake outlets, and countless swift, rocky streams across this immense state, abundant insect hatches brought on by the warmest, sunniest days of the year spark a frenzy of feeding activity among resident populations of one of the northland's most charming fighters—the Arctic grayling. In some of the more prolific areas, such as the lakes of the northern Alaska Peninsula, the headwaters of Bristol Bay, and the rambling, clear streams of Northwest, you'll find vast armies of "sailfins" dimpling the surface of rivers and lakes like raindrops as they feed voraciously on emerging insect life.

It can be a simple matter of laying a dry fly on these waters to produce some nonstop fishing fun, reminiscent of youthful days and plucky panfish. These grayling, usually not the least bit shy, will rise to the occasion instantly and fight vigorously, running in tight circles and using their broad shape to great advantage. This is Alaska's best and only real dry fly-fishing of the season, and folks here wouldn't consider the summer complete if they didn't break out light, whippy rods at least once and enjoy some of this delightful diversion.

Remote headwater grayling fishing, Southwest Alaska.

ARCTIC GRAYLING: SAILFIN OF THE NORTH

The Arctic grayling, *Thymallus arcticus*, is a most interesting and exotic resident of northern waters. Found in the clear, swift stretches of nearly every river and stream throughout the northland, including Alaska, the grayling is a valued sport species, abundant and eager to the fly as is no other fish in the high latitudes.

With its unfurling dorsal banner decorated in royal colors of purple, crimson, and gold, the grayling has a striking, aristocratic appearance that distinguishes it from all other northern species. A valiant and spirited fighter, it'll surprise you with its top-water antics and subsurface rolls, outmaneuvering other species many times its size. Pursued by a dedicated following of anglers, the grayling is an essential part of the Alaska fishing experience, not to be missed in the rush to sample the state's other species.

DESCRIPTION

The general appearance of the grayling is of a sleek and slender, dark whitefish, with a characteristically large dorsal fin that may extend as far as the adipose fin in some mature males, but is slightly smaller and rounder in females. The mouth is small, with numerous fine teeth on both jaws. Coloration varies considerably between watersheds, and ranges from silvery gray to dirty brown to purplish blue or almost black, spawning individuals generally being darker. Sparse black vermiculations decorate forward sides and scales are large. The dorsal and pelvic fins are especially noteworthy for their unusual color variety—marked with pink to blue dots and stripes, their leading edges being white to pink, increasing in brilliance during spawning. The belly is yellowish white, but may appear gray in some populations.

The flesh is white and flaky and of delicious flavor when eaten fresh but, because of its fragile nature, grayling meat has no commercial value. However, the fish is regarded with high esteem for its food value within the angling community, and often seen as a significant supplement for subsistence in remote areas.

Not particularly known for their size, Alaska grayling average about eight to twelve inches in

length, with some populations producing good numbers of fish in the 15 to 18-inch range. Maximum weight is four to five pounds and 22 to 23 inches, given the right growing conditions, but rarely exceeding three pounds and 20 inches. Most trophy-sized grayling are taken from parts of Southwest and Northwest, but a few specimens from isolated stocks in Southcentral and Interior can also reach significant proportions.

RANGE, ABUNDANCE & STATUS

Arctic grayling are part of a widespread fish genus comprising several species and sub-species distributed throughout the northern latitudes. They are found in varying degrees of abundance, from Hudson Bay in Canada, westward to the Ob River in Russia, and south to the Yalu River in eastern Asia. Other very similar species are present from northern Europe to western Russia and in Mongolia. In western North America, the arctic grayling is present from central Alberta and the headwaters of the Missouri River in Montana north into Alaska, being most abundant in northern Canada and Alaska. Introductions of the species have extended its range into mountainous regions of Colorado, Wyoming, Utah, and Vermont.

In Alaska, grayling are most numerous in cold, clear waters of the subarctic, from the Alaska Peninsula north to the Seward Peninsula, in inland rivers, streams, and lakes, and east through the vast Yukon River drainage into the Interior and down into the clear-water drainages of the Copper and Susitna rivers (with minor populations in large, glacial mainland rivers in Southeast). Successful stockings of this prolific sport fish have been made in several lakes on the Kenai Peninsula, the Anchorage area, Kodiak Island, and parts of Southeast.

LIFE HISTORY & HABITS

Starting in March or April in lowland areas to the south, but not until June in mountainous regions to the north, arctic grayling congregate at the mouths of spawning streams. As soon as the ice breaks, the fish move on up, usually in numbers that may range in the hundreds to thousands or more depending on drainage size. The urge to spawn is so intense at times that some fish proceed upstream through channels cut in the ice by overflow. Most grayling spawn in fairly small bog or marshland streams with sandy gravel substrate, although this is not a strict preference. They avoid spring-fed creeks, however.

Grayling commit quite extensive migrations, up to 100 miles or more in some areas and regions. This is particularly true for populations overwintering in deep channels of large, glacial watersheds with spawning streams at the headwaters. The journey may last from a few days to one or two weeks.

Peak reproductive activity takes place anytime between mid-May and mid-June. There is no redd construction, but a slight depression is often created during the mating rituals. Females deposit from 3,000 to 9,000 eggs, which are adhesive, attaching to bottom structure. The eggs hatch in 11 to 30 days, depending on water temperature.

The young begin feeding almost immediately on minute organisms, shifting to insect life as they grow larger. Small fish, salmon eggs and even small voles and lemmings complete the diet as the fish mature. Growth accelerates each year from birth up to age five, at which time it slows down, the length of the fish being about 8 to 15 inches. After age 10, growth (if any) is minimal. As is common in many resident fish populations, growth rates are higher in regions to the south due to longer open water season and optimal feeding conditions. In the southern part of their range in Alaska, maturity is reached as early as age two or three, but mostly not until age four or five. Maturity is later in the Arctic and colder mountainous regions, usually commencing at age five, but sometimes not until age eight. (Seward Peninsula fish have been aged up to 20 years, which accounts for their larger than average size.)

After spawning, adult grayling, depending on stream habitat, either move to upstream areas within the same drainage or leave it altogether for another watershed more suitable for feeding. It's very common for grayling to use streams full of spring meltwater for spawning and, after the water levels recede in early summer and become too shallow, move back into lakes or larger rivers and creeks until freeze-up.

Summer feeding grounds are often located at the headwaters of large river systems in small, clearwater streams or springs with plenty of riffles, deep pools, and undercut banks. In landlocked lakes, the fish are distributed throughout specific areas with cooler temperature regimes, but tend to avoid deep water, seeking cool, upwelling springs instead. Showing a low tolerance towards warm water, these fish thrive best in colder flows (35 to 50°F) where they actively feed on insects, both aquatic and terrestrial, in addition to small numbers of fish. Night feeding is common.

As temperatures drop in autumn, Arctic grayling begin to prepare for winter by going into a feeding frenzy. Night feeding halts, shifting to midday, and insects are no longer the sole diet. In areas with heavy runs of spawning salmon, grayling will prey heavily on salmon eggs and even flesh from carcasses. Toward the end of September into October, just prior to freeze-up, the fish begin a rapid downstream movement to overwintering areas. By November very few grayling remain in upstream areas, with most spending the winter in the lower stream sections where the water is deep enough to survive. During the coldest months, grayling remain suspended in lakes and hunkered in deep holes and pools of large rivers, moving about and feeding relatively little.

Grayling have many curious habits of interest to anglers. Perhaps their most famous is the bold manner in which they rise to the fly, sometimes leaping out of the water to pounce on insects.

Another well known grayling behavior is the dominance hierarchy they display in pools, lake outlets, river mouths, etc., where the largest fish position themselves at the head of the pack to be first in line for drifting food items, with subordinate individuals arranged according to size farther downstream. In waters that receive little pressure, you'll commonly catch the very largest fish if you cast first to the farthest upstream perimeter of holding areas.

Grayling are notoriously excitable feeders. There are times when a school of grayling will show no interest in anything presented to them, until one fish finally dashes out and mouths an offering out of irritation, inciting the other fish to go bonkers. Conversely, in the middle of a hatch-induced feeding frenzy, they can shut down without any apparent reason and refuse all manner of offerings.

As fighters, they are known for their pluck, with signature strategy to dart this way and that and cut tight circles in the current, using the shape of their bodies and large back fin to create remarkable resistance for fish of their size. On very light tackle in swift current, they can put on quite a show, leaping about and boring down in a valiant effort to win their freedom. No wonder they are so adored by anglers.

FISHING ALASKA'S GRAYLING

Alaska's sport catch of grayling in recent years has varied from a third to well over a half million fish annually. Most of these fish come from the Tanana River drainage in the Interior, streams in Bristol and Kuskokwim bays, (Southwest Alaska), and the Susitna River drainage, north of Anchorage.

Despite their diminutive size compared to most salmon, trout, and charr, grayling are a delight on ultra-light tackle or a light fly rod, attacking a wide variety of flies and hardware with abandon. Unlike salmon and other species, they can be taken throughout the open water season, with good to excellent fishing to be had in countless locations spring through fall, with a only modest amount of skill and gear required.

Spring Conditions

This is one of the best times of the year for grayling fishing. Even before the ice breaks up on large lakes and rivers, grayling gather in masses around opening stream mouths and outlets, looking for food and preparing for their spawning runs (April and May). Anglers lucky enough to find these conditions can quite often enjoy "fish on every cast" action, using small flies, spoons, and spinners. Since small

Fresh grayling makes excellent eating, fried or grilled

fish provide important forage this time of year, sculpin and salmon fry, parr, and smolt imitations (size #6 or smaller) will produce vicious strikes, particularly from larger grayling. Dry flies and nymphs like the Humpy, Caddis, Hare's Ear, and Black Gnat in sizes #12 to #18 work well also. Spinners are the best fish imitators, since they have the most tantalizing combination of flash, vibration, and motion. Sizes #0 to #3 are most popular.

As the spawning streams break up, the fish swarm up by the thousands in many areas and provide continued opportunities for two to three weeks before dropping back into main stem rivers or moving farther up into feeders for the summer.

Summer Conditions

Although a few locations may see a lull in activity during the short summer months (June through August), superb grayling angling can be had in most areas, particularly headwater streams and lakes, as waters warm and Alaska's abundant insect populations peak, prompting the most active feeding of the year. Grayling do not take the summer heat well. They get sluggish in the warm, slower waters associated with lower main stems and will migrate in large numbers up into cooler, shallower headwaters to feed during the warmest part of the year. In this alpine grayling country it's hard to find a trickle of water

deeper than a few inches that does not have a few fish present this time of year. Headwater lakes can be very productive also, especially in the early mornings or late evenings along the shorelines, but also at the inlets, outlets, and springs where cooler water temperatures prevail.

This is the season for Alaska's best dry fly-fishing, with the most productive patterns mimicking the hatch, whether it be mosquitoes, gnats, midges, or caddis flies. Although they usually can be tempted with a variety of enticements during these times of active feeding, grayling can sometimes become very selective, much like trout in still water. They may refuse offerings that normally would elicit a response, even patterns that closely resemble the insects they are feeding on. For finicky summer grayling, anglers should try smaller flies (size #12 or smaller) and tiny (1/6-ounce or less) spinners and spoons in colors of black, brown, or purple, with silver or gold. Forage patterns like Muddlers, Smolt, and Leeches are perennial producers always worth a try. If nothing else works, a simple egg pattern like a Glo Bug, or attractor like the Egg Sucking Leech or small Mepps Black Fury spinner may prompt strikes, especially in late summer, when salmon are spawning all around.

Fall Conditions

From September to October is probably the best time of year to tangle with grayling. After the long summer days and abundant feed, fish are in prime shape—chunky, and full of fight—and, with falling temperatures, very aggressive towards most anything that moves through the water. Nymph, forage, and attractor patterns tend to yield fast-paced action, as do egg and flesh imitations in waters where spawning salmon are present. Silver or gold spinners or small spoons with attractor highlights of red, pink, orange, yellow, or chartreuse are also deadly on these testy fall grayling.

Once the last of the salmon have spawned and temperatures begin their steep decline, grayling will quickly leave their summer feeding stations in feeders and retreat into lower mainstems and lakes. The later part of fall right up to freezup is a prime time to target deep mainstem pools and lake outlets and inlets for big grayling. Larger attractor and forage pattern flies, along with bright spinners and spoons dredged through these areas can often yield the largest grayling of the year.

Alaska's Grandaddy Grayling

Paul Kanitz with his Alaska record grayling, 4 lbs., 13 oz.,
caught at Ugashik Narrows, SW AK, 1981

In the summer of 1981, Paul Kanitz of Anchorage, and his longtime buddy, Ralph Johnson, finished a two month Southwest Alaska fishing odyssey at world famous Ugashik Narrows on the northern Alaska Peninsula, to try for some big charr and grayling. On the last day of vacation, Paul hooked what he thought was a nice charr, but with a giant dorsal turned out to be a humongous grayling. It pulled his pocket scale down to 4 1/2 pounds, a few ounces shy of the state record, but was so ugly, only his buddy Ralph's insistence to keep it for a mount kept Kanitz from releasing it back into Ugashik's vast waters. The fish was weighed in Anchorage at 4 pounds, 13 ounces, and later certified by ADF&G as a new Alaska state record, which has stood now for almost twenty-five years.

Winter Conditions

Without a doubt, this is the most challenging time of year to catch grayling. From November to March, most streams are frozen over, and ice fishing on lakes has never been truly consistent. In these cold, dark, oxygen-depleted waters, fish tend to be deep and inactive, and are hard to stimulate with artificial lures. In parts of remote Northwest and Arctic Alaska, natives do fish quantities of grayling for subsistence, but most of the legitimate sport catch occurs incidentally, when fishing for other species, such as rainbow trout, charr, and landlocked salmon, especially when using small baits like shrimp, worms, maggots, etc. In other parts of the grayling's range (northern Europe and Russia), anglers have good results using tiny jigs called "Mormyshka," but these have not yet been tried to any extent in Alaska waters.

GEARING UP

Spin Tackle and Gear

Ultralight gear (six to seven-and-a-half-foot, fast-action rod) with two to four-pound test line is preferred, but a slightly heavier outfit may be advisable in waters where there is potential interaction with larger species such as salmon, trout, and charr.

Many lures can be used effectively on grayling. Small (1/8 oz. or less) spinners, spoons, jigs, even plugs, in dark, neutral colors like black, purple, brown, blue, green, and copper, work best, especially when mixed with silver or gold or (sometimes) attractor highlights of red, pink, yellow, and chartreuse.

Fly Tackle and Gear

For the most enjoyable fly-fishing for Alaska grayling, most folks use light gear—anything from a two weight, up to a four or five, depending on conditions. Matching single action reels and weight forward floating and short sink tip lines work fine for nearly all the grayling water you'll encounter. When floating dries for grayling, leaders and tippets can be shorter (5 to 7 feet) than those used for dry fly presentations for trout, as grayling are not leader-shy. Shorten up to four feet for sinking presentations. Most common tippets used are 7X to 3X (2 to 6-pound test).

Fly Patterns

Grayling are not known to be finicky when it comes to flies and will devour most any pattern that is presented correctly, even larger patterns meant for trout and salmon. Almost all the flies used effectively for grayling can be grouped into two broad categories: naturals and attractors. Naturals are realistic representations of food sources, while attractors are artificial designs created specifically to stimulate an instinctive strike response from the fish. As with any situation where an angler must observe fishing conditions closely to "match the hatch," it helps to be familiar with the grayling's seasonal movement and feeding behaviors, as explained earlier.

Naturals

Dry Flies: With the phenomenal abundance of flying insects in Alaska, especially within the grayling's range, it is no secret that dry flies are often the most effective enticement, particularly during the warmest months when hatches occur. Popular patterns with proven track records include Black Gnat, Mosquito, Light Cahill, Elk Hair Caddis, Humpy, Wulff, and Adams, in size #10 or smaller.

Forage Patterns: This is a fairly large category encompassing a number of perspectives and represen-

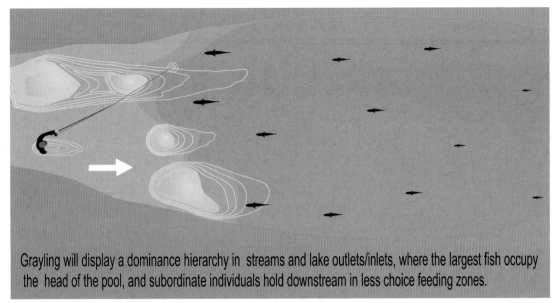

Grayling will display a dominance hierarchy in streams and lake outlets/inlets, where the largest fish occupy the head of the pool, and subordinate individuals hold downstream in less choice feeding zones.

tations of food items other than flying insects and includes aquatic insect (nymph/larva), small fish, fry/smolt, flesh, and egg imitations. If spawning salmon are present in a system containing grayling, the latter three can be very productive, as grayling, like other resident fish species such as trout and charr, will opportunistically binge feed on these rich food items whenever possible. Examples of these most productive patterns include the Glo Bug, Alevin, Salmon Fry, Thunder Creek, Alaska Smolt, Two-Egg Marabou, Iliamna Pinkie, Bead Egg, and Flesh Fly, which are all very effective flies for rainbow trout and charr as well. (For most grayling, use flies tied on #6 hooks or smaller.)

Aquatic insects include the nymphs/larvae of stone, caddis, and damsel flies and mosquitoes and midges, all of which have equivalent fly imitations and can be good producers, even when grayling are finicky. Other popular forage patterns for grayling are the Woolly Worm, Black Ant, Muddler Minnow, Leech, Hare's Ear, and Bitch Creek.

Attractors

Grayling, like other salmonids, can be tempted by the bright color and movement of attractor pattern flies, such as the Egg Sucking Leech, Polar Shrimp, Mickey Finn, Fall Favorite, etc. They are particularly susceptible during early spring and late summer-fall. These patterns should be fished deep and with a lively strip.

Tips for Larger Grayling

Arctic grayling are primarily visual feeders, so anglers must present their offerings in ways that seem both natural and desirable to the bigger, wiser fish.

Fish larger (1/2 ounce or more) spoons, spinners, jigs, even plugs, along with large (#2) attractor streamers and oversize forage patterns to entice heftier grayling in the 16 to 18-inch (or more) class.

Work lures and flies deep and slow (except during surface feeding and spring conditions) to entice bottom-hugging, larger grayling.

Lesser-fished waters always hold the biggest grayling. Seek out areas beyond the zone of easy access, like remote lake inlets/outlets, obscure headwater streams, small tributary ponds, etc., for your best chances at a potential trophy.

Grayling are light sensitive and may be easily spooked in clear waters. Fish early mornings, evenings or during cloudy days for the best chance of encountering older, larger grayling.

When fishing streams, prospect for pools or runs with moderate to strong current flow, since calm stretches lack sufficient amounts of drifting forage (and fooling fish is more difficult).

ARCTIC GRAYLING
Thymallus arcticus

SPECIES SUMMARY

Alaska common names: Grayling, sailfin.

Description: A small, sleek, whitefish-like, freshwater salmonid with huge dorsal fin, especially males. Coloration varies, from silver-grey to dirty brown to purplish blue or black, with spawning individuals darker. Black and purple spots decorate forward sides; belly is yellowish white. Red and pink markings on dorsal fin are common during spawning period. Flesh is white.

Size: Average length 8 -14 in.; up to 23 in. and 5 lbs.

State Record: 5 lbs., 1 oz., Fish River (NW), Peter Cockwill, 2008.

Habits: Itinerant and seasonally abundant; omnivorous, but very fond of insect life.

Notes: Grayling can live to twenty years or more.

Meristics: Gill rakers 16-23; vertebrae 58-62; pyloric caeca 14-21; lateral line scales 75-103; branchiostegal rays 7-9; dorsal fin 17-25 rays; tail fin 11-15 rays; pelvic fin 10-11 rays; Anal fin 10-15 rays; pectoral fin 14-16 rays.

Range: Revillagigedo Island (SSE) to North Slope (ARC).

Preferred Habitat: Clear, cool, rocky streams and lakes.

Best waters: Clearwater highland lakes, streams and tributaries of glacial drainages, SC-NW and INT.

Run timing: Fish present year-round; peak May to September.

Best Bait/Lures/Flies: Salmon eggs; small spinners and spoons in silver, gold, blue, and black (also with red and yellow highlights); small dry flies, attractors, and nymphs.

Best Trophy Areas: Becharof Lake (SW); Sinuk River (NW); Pilgrim River (NW); Goodnews River (SW); Boston Creek (NW); Ugashik Lakes (SW).

RECOMMENDED GEAR

Spinning:
Ultralight, 6-7 1/2-ft., fast-action trout rod; matching reel with 175 yds. 2-6-lb. test monofilament line.

Flyfishing:
2-4 wt., 6-8 ft., medium fast action graphite rod, matching reel and WF floating, intermediate or short (5-7 ft.) sink tip line, Type II-III; 7-9 ft. leader with 7X-3X (2-6 lb. test) tippet.

ALASKA'S MAJOR GRAYLING LOCATIONS

SOUTHEAST
Scattered opportunities exist from stocking done years ago.

Sitka: Beaver Lake.

Juneau: Antler Lake.

Petersburg/Wrangell: Tyee Lake.

Ketchikan/Prince of Wales Island: Naha River system; Manzoni, Marge, Summit lakes; Big Goat, Shinaku creeks.

SOUTHCENTRAL
The region offers some fairly good grayling fishing, but much of the more accessible locations have been well worked over for larger fish; for truly exceptional action, the best bet is to hike or fly in to remote headwater tributaries.

Matanuska/Susitna: Bonnie, Harriet, Long, Seventeenmile lakes; Clear, Lake, Coal, Alexander creeks; Deshka, Talachulitna, Talkeetna, upper Susitna rivers.

Kenai: Crescent, Grayling, Fuller, Twin, Bench, Paradise lakes; Crescent Creek.

Kodiak: Abercombie, Aurel, Cascade, Cicely, Long lakes.

Upper Copper/Susitna: Gulkana, Little Tonsina, Tyone rivers; Mendeltna, Cache, Tolsona, Moose, Gunn, Sourdough, Haggard, Poplar Grove creeks; Mae West, Little Junction, Louise, Connor, Susitna, Gillespie, Tyone, Dick, Kay, Tolsona, Arizona, Twin, Big Swede, Paxson, Summit, Tanada lakes.

SOUTHWEST
Southwest has some of Alaska's best fishing in terms of abundance and average size, with trophy potential possible in many watersheds, particularly those with headwater lakes. Fly-fishing conditions are among the best in Alaska.

Bristol Bay: Lake Iliamna/Lake Clark system, all clear-flowing tributaries; Wood-Tickchik Lakes; Nushagak, Igushik, Togiak river systems.

Alaska Peninsula: Alagnak, Naknek, Becharof, Ugashik lake and river systems.

#14 Black Gnat

#8 Glo Bug

#12 Mosquito

Krocodile Spoon
1/6 oz.

Roostertail
Spinner - 1/8 oz.

The Ugashik Lakes (SW), one of Alaska's most famous hotspots for big grayling. (Note: grayling fishing closed in river; catch-and-release only at Narrows.)

Lower Kuskokwim: Goodnews, Arolik, Kanektok, Kwethluk, Kisaralik, Aniak, Holitna, Hoholitna, Stony rivers.

Lower Yukon: Andreafsky, Anvik rivers.

NORTHWEST

Some of the largest trophy grayling come from this region (Seward Peninsula streams).

Norton Sound: Unalakleet, Shaktoolik, Ungalik rivers.

Seward Peninsula: Fish-Niukluk, Sinuk, Snake, Nome, Kuzitrin, Tubutulik, American-Agiapuk, Pilgrim river systems.

Kotzebue Sound: Noatak, Kobuk, Wulik rivers.

INTERIOR

Alaska's most intensively fished grayling streams, in the Tanana drainage, are located in this region. The most remote drainages will have the largest fish.

Tanana: Goodpaster, Salcha, Chatanika, Chena, Chitanana, Cosna, Zitziana, Tangle rivers; Kantishna, Nenana river systems; Clearwater, Rock, Fish, Crooked creeks; Landmark Gap, Glacier, Boulder, Tangle lakes.

Yukon: Nowitna, Ray, Dall, Hadweenzic, Melozitna, Tozitna, Charley, Black, Kandik, Nation, Seventymile, Hodzana rivers; Birch, Beaver creeks.

Brooks Range: Jim River.

ARCTIC

North Slope: Kuparuk, Sagavanirktok, Kongakut, Canning rivers; Colville River system.

Top Flies for Alaska Grayling

Egg Sucking Leech, Krystal Bullet, Polar Shrimp, Fall Favorite, Boss, Skykomish Sunrise, Mickey Finn, Brassie Nymph, Pheasant Tail Nymph, Teeny Nymph, Hare's Ear Nymph, Bitch Creek, Zug Bug, Mosquito, Black Gnat, Caddis, Cahill, Glo Bug, Babine Special, Fry, Alevin, Leech, Muddler, Midge, Adams, Woolly Worm, Griffith Gnat, Wulff.

Top Ten Alaska Trophy Grayling

5 lbs., 1 oz.	Fish River (NW)	2008
4 lbs., 13 oz.	Ugashik Narrows (SW)	1981
4 lbs., 4 oz.	Ugashik River (SW)	1975
4 lbs., 3 oz.	Ugashik Lake (SW)	1973
4 lbs., 3 oz.	Ugashik River (SW)	1976
4 lbs., 2 oz.	Ugashik Lake (SW)	1972
4 lbs., 2 oz.	Sundial Lake (SW)	1977
4 lbs.	Ugashik Lake (SW)	1972
4 lbs.	Ugashik Lake (SW)	1978
4 lbs.	Sinuk River (NW)	1984

#1 Mepps Black Fury

#12 Hare's Ear Nymph,

#6 Egg Sucking Leech

#8 Fry

#12 Elk Hair Caddis

Sheefish
Tarpon of the North

I'd heard the Eskimos many times tell of the early summer spawning run of smelt in the lower Kobuk, and of the ravenously hungry sheefish that congregated there. But I fished the river for many years before I had the good fortune of being at the right place and time to actually witness this amazing spectacle. It was during the second week of June one year, when I was stirred from sleep by a commotion in the river, scant yards from my tent door. Just as my native friends had said, the water churned with thousands of silvery smelt, driven into a mad frenzy by the savage onslaught of big sheefish that seemed everywhere. A lure tossed into the fray was instantly pounced on by fish weighing anywhere from 3 to 30 pounds, supercharged with an energy and jumping ability like I'd never seen before. My fishing partner brought out his flyrod and, with a white streamer, hung one big shee after another in exhilarating battles that were every bit as spectacular as fishing for tarpon. The action continued as the smelt made their way upriver but, after an hour or two of nonstop arm-yanking excitement, we were too bushed to pursue them any further.

Sheefish action under a midnight sun, Northwest Alaska.

SHEEFISH: TARPON OF THE NORTH

The sheefish, *Stenodus leucichthys*, also called "inconnu" and "Eskimo tarpon," is a large, predatory whitefish related to the salmon and trout. Its long, slender body shape, extended lower jaw (similar to the pike), silvery color, and size distinguish it from the more common whitefish species. The world's largest and only whitefish consistently caught on hook and line, the sheefish is generally freshwater river dwelling, although in the Kuskokwim, lower Yukon and Selawik-Kobuk rivers, certain populations may spend part of their life cycle in the estuarine portions of river mouths. They spawn in the upper reaches of clearwater rivers and are highly migratory. They do not die after spawning, as do salmon, and may return to spawn repeatedly.

The major significance of sheefish in Alaska and elsewhere has been as a subsistence food for rural residents and their dogs. A few small, highly regulated commercial fisheries exist on the more abundant populations. Called "inconnu" for "unknown fish" by early French-Canadian fur traders, the Alaska shee today still remains obscure as a sportfish, mostly because of its remote and limited distribution, seasonal availability, and the presence of more glamorous and desirable sportfish species. Indeed, only in recent years has the International Game Fish Association recognized it as a trophy fish for record-keeping purposes. Many are taken incidentally by anglers fishing for pike, who are surprised by a long, silvery torpedo of a fish exploding from the water.

Despite its lack of notoriety, the sheefish has tremendous sportfish potential, as it readily takes a variety of lures and flies, reaches respectable size, and has outstanding fighting and eating qualities. Its tail-walking, topwater acrobatics have earned it the respectful title, "Eskimo tarpon" or "tarpon of the North," for it indeed compares favorably with the silvery, leaping giant of tropical waters.

DESCRIPTION

Sheefish from all stocks show little variation in shape and color throughout life. They have narrow, tapered bodies, with long heads and pike-like mouths (with lower jaw extending well beyond upper) that can open wide like a tarpon. Their color is silvery, with backs of light blue or pale brown, and whitish bellies. Markings are usually absent. Sheefish inhabiting darker-colored waters in Interior Alaska are slightly darker than fish coming up from the sea. The sheefish body is deepest behind the pectoral fins, with a fleshy adipose fin in front of the tail, which is deeply forked. Eyes are large; scales are silvery and come off easily. During spawning, males maintain their torpedo-like body shape, while the belly of a female becomes flaccid and the vent area enlarges.

Juveniles as small as six inches have the same recognizable pike-like mouth and head as adults. Occasionally they are found with a metallic green sheen on the upper body, which turns to blue or brown as the fish grows. In all populations in Alaska, a sheefish-whitefish hybrid can be encountered. This fish is more brown than a sheefish and has a terminal (trout-like) mouth rather than the extended lower jaw of sheefish. The hybrid fights more like a whitefish, rapidly wiggling its head during capture. It seldom exceeds five pounds in weight.

Sheefish from most Alaska populations reach a weight of 5 pounds at 26 inches, and 10 pounds at 30 inches. At 30 pounds, a sheefish might be 36 to 42 inches. There is much variation in potential size, with sheefish of local populations in the Minto Flats, Nowitna, Porcupine, and upper Yukon River areas seldom exceeding 12 pounds and 32 inches in length, while Kuskokwim and Yukon River anadromous populations reach 30 pounds and 42 inches. Only in the Kobuk-Selawik drainages are fish of 50 pounds or more found (the current Alaska and world record sport-caught fish is a 53-pounder from this area). Females generally grow larger than males.

Sheefish flesh is white in all cases. The small-sized fish are quite bland in taste, while larger-sized fish contain more fat and are very tasty. Sheefish are excellent baked, fried, barbecued, or smoked. Raw frozen sheefish, eaten with seal oil, is an Eskimo delicacy. As with other fish, sheefish lose body fat during spawning and their eating value diminishes.

RANGE, ABUNDANCE & STATUS

In Alaska, sheefish have a limited distribution from the Kuskokwim River to the Kobuk-Selawik drainages in Northwest. Except for feeding and over-wintering fish that appear in Selawik Lake and Hotham Inlet, sheefish are not normally found in lakes. In the Kuskokwim River they are found from tidewater upstream to the vicinity of Telida. In the Yukon River, they reside throughout the entire drainage, from the mouth upstream to the Laird and Bell rivers (Porcupine drainage) in Canada. Sheefish are not found in smaller rivers that empty directly into the ocean, with the possible exception of a small population in the Koyuk River. They are not found on the Seward Peninsula or on Alaska's North Slope. In Asia, they are found in all the large north-flowing rivers of central and eastern Siberia, including the Ob, Irtysh, Lena, Yenesei, and Kolyma. They are absent on North Slope Alaska rivers but are encountered east in Canada's Mackenzie River system as well as in the Anderson River.

Sheefish reach their greatest abundance in the larger, slower-moving waters of Alaska. They do enter first-order tributaries of the Kuskokwim and Yukon rivers, but on the Kobuk and Selawik rivers they are confined to the mainstem and associated sloughs in the lower reaches. In general, anadromous populations are larger both in numbers and in individual size. Population estimates of spawners on the Kobuk River between 1995 and 1997 indicated a healthy 32,000 to 43,000 fish, plus an additional 5000 spawners in the Selawik River. The anadromous Yukon River population probably contains as many fish. The non-anadromous local populations in Minto Flats and the Nowitna, Porcupine, Black, and upper Yukon rivers may contain at most only a few hundred fish each.

Sheefish stocks in Alaska are not as closely monitored as salmon, but all indications show stable, healthy populations. Since sea-run populations do not venture far out into the ocean, they are safe from most marine predators and gill nets. The small, non-anadromous populations are most easily affected by overfishing and habitat alteration. Because of scant biological data available, sheefish management has always been rather conservative. Subsistence fishing harvests declined during the 1970s and 1980s as snow machines replaced dog teams, while commercial harvests have remained stable and sport-take only slightly increased. As more anglers become familiar with the fabulous "Eskimo tarpon," fishing pressure can only rise; hopefully, this will be offset by the growing catch-and-release ethic taking hold among anglers everywhere.

LIFE HISTORY & HABITS

A most important aspect of sheefish behavior in terms of sportfishing is their migratory nature. Since sheefish do not die after spawning, they undertake both upstream and downstream migrations to prime areas for feeding and overwintering. In the major rivers, the upstream spawning movements begin at ice break-up, generally preceding the salmon inmigration. These migrations slow considerably as fish linger at mouths of tributary streams to feed. For instance, in the Kuskokwim River, sheefish reach Aniak by early June, Sleetmute by late June, and the McGrath area by late July. In the Yukon River, the spawning run is spread throughout the lower and middle river in June and July, but the peak of the run reaches the Tanana area by mid-August, and the Rampart area by early September. In the Kobuk and Selawik rivers, the run hits the lower rivers in late spring, then proceeds upriver as summer progresses; it reaches the Kiana and Selawik areas in late June, the Ambler area in mid-July, and the upper Kobuk River area in August and early September. A portion of the lower Yukon River stock continues up the Koyukuk River to spawn near Hughes and Allakaket, while the majority of the population spawn in the main Yukon River between Beaver and above Fort Yukon.

Total distance traveled can be quite impressive. Fish tagged on the Alatna River and in the mainstem Yukon near Fort Yukon have been recovered at the mouth of the Yukon River three to four months after spawning, for a round-trip migration of 2,000 miles. Migrations of freshwater local populations may range from less than 100 miles for fish in the Koyuk River to over 400 miles for Porcupine River sheefish. Sheefish are quite old before their first spawning, with females from the Kobuk-Selawik population spawning at age 12 to 14. Males spawn three to four years earlier. Fish of the faster growing Minto Flats population spawn at younger ages and have shorter life spans.

Sheefish are an important subsistence food for native Alaskans—frequently dried or smoked for later consumption. Here, split fish hung to dry are covered by an early fall snow at a Northwest Alaska fish camp.

The sheefish is an arctic spawner, evidenced by major populations on the Kobuk, Selawik, Koyukuk, Alatna, Yukon, Porcupine, and Black rivers, breeding within a few miles of the Arctic Circle. For egg laying, they require a combination of six to eight feet of water, moderate to fast current and a bottom of small to medium gravel—a condition found only in upper sections of certain rivers within their range, usually quite remote. Spawning occurs in late September and early October, with fish in the mainstem Yukon spawning as late as October 18, when water temperatures are near freezing and the river runs with ice. Sheefish cease feeding for two to three months before spawning (their large reserves of body fat sustain them during migration and spawning). Spawning takes place only during late afternoon and early evening, and frequently occurs on or near the surface,

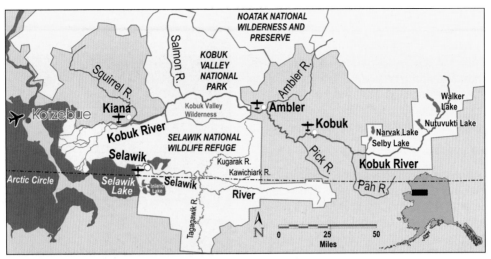

Northwest's eastern Kotzebue Sound's brackish waters, and the Kobuk and Selawik rivers, are the state's premier waters for trophy sheefish, with larger fish than any other sheefish stocks in Alaska. (See Northwest region for more details.)

with eggs often shot into the air. Fertilized eggs sink to the bottom, where they slowly develop in the near-freezing water, and young hatch out in April or May. Spring floods carry fry downstream to suitable slow moving, rearing habitat.

Sheefish in the rearing and feeding portions of their life history are found in association with pike, burbot, suckers, lampreys and five species of white-fish. They grow rapidly and usually weigh three to four pounds at five years of age, initially feeding on plankton and insects, but turning to fish predation by age one. Suckers, lampreys, small pike, and whitefish are the most important forage species. Sheefish must swallow their prey whole since they have no teeth for gripping; consequently, food items tend to be less than eight inches in length. Concentrations of sheefish in Selawik Lake and Hotham Inlet feed actively throughout the winter—as is believed all sheefish in Alaska do.

Sheefish continue to grow throughout life. The impressive size of fish from the Kobuk and Selawik rivers is due to the fact that they live so much longer than other Alaska sheefish. (There, a 40-pound trophy might be 19 to 22 years old, whereas age 13 for Yukon River, and 11 for Minto Flats sheefish is about tops.) They have no significant predators other than man, although adult pike, burbot, and even their own kind prey on the young.

The incredible abundance of sheefish one day, and their total absence in the same area the next, can be extremely frustrating for anglers. Being a schooling species, they are prone to move en masse from areas, for reasons related to food availability and water clarity, depth, and temperature. They exhibit these same schooling tendencies under the ice, while feeding and during migrations. Except for the later stages of the spawning migration, when they no longer feed (but can be enticed with attractor flies and lures), sheefish of all sizes are found in these schooling aggregations.

Shees are not considered strong swimmers. They often utilize large eddies, sloughs, and stream mouths for resting, hugging the shore and staying close to bottom in strong current. In these situations they are vulnerable to a well-placed lure or fly and subsistence gill nets. Their upstream migrations are easily blocked by falls or other impasses that pose no problem for salmon or trout.

Sheefish feeding habits vary. Quite often they will feed deep or off bottom (on lampreys for instance), but under certain conditions (when baitfish are present) they will be active near or on the surface. The frenzy of sheefish smashing bait on top of the water presents, of course, classic conditions for the most exciting angling, as this is when they are at their most reckless and prone to wild leaping.

Unfortunately, not all sheefish fight like the tarpon they resemble and, like any other species, at times they may be as challenging as the proverbial log—especially prespawners or fish in the warm water habitats of Interior Alaska. Unlike salmon or trout, shees generally do not make long runs, and tend to be more acrobatic the larger they get.

FISHING ALASKA'S SHEEFISH

Sheefish sport angling in Alaska is still in its infancy. Recreational fishing pressure has increased only slightly over the last 10 years or so, with a catch varying from around 3,000 to over 7,000 fish annually, mostly from drainages (and brackish waters) of southern Kotzebue Sound, with lesser numbers from tributaries of the Yukon and Kuskokwim rivers.

Methods

For successful sheefish angling, locating your migratory quarry is the primary goal. Once you've found the general area containing fish, you'll need to determine the depth they are holding or feeding in. Surface-feeding shees will be easy to spot. They'll often jump completely out of the water pursuing their prey, or drive "boils" of baitfish to the surface, which often draws gulls and terns to the melee, making it even more obvious. In these situations, a fly or lure fished in the upper three feet of the water column will usually produce bone-jarring strikes. The annual out-migration of chum, king, and silver salmon smolt in northern Alaska rivers during June and early July provides a short but rich feeding bonanza for sheefish and excellent opportunities for the sport angler. That's if he/she can locate feeding concentrations, especially those at the mouths of clear tributary streams.

Occasionally, sheefish in a spawning aggregation can be observed rolling on the surface, especially in early evening. These fish are not feeding, but may be trying to break the eggs loose in the egg skein prior to spawning. They can be enticed to strike a slowly retrieved lure or fly in the upper water column. Pre-spawners generally hold in deeper, swifter water than fish taken earlier in the summer. An angler should fish the "seam" or zone between slower and swifter currents. An anchored boat can position the angler so the lure or fly can be cast slightly upstream and be allowed to sink before retrieving. A slow retrieve works best. The fish will follow a lure or fly from the deep, and sometimes strike close to the boat. Although larger lures and flies are generally used for sheefish, smaller lures and more sparsely dressed flies (like Clouser Minnows or Lefty's Deceivers) work well also. Placement of the lure and fly, and speed of retrieve, are most important in sheefish angling.

Special consideration by anglers should be given to sheefish that spend the entire summer feeding at

Lawrence E. Hudnall's magnificent 53-pound, state and IGFA World Record sheefish taken August 20, 1986, on a tributary of the Kobuk River, Northwest Alaska. The fish was taken on a spoon and 20-pound test line, and fought for 40 minutes, jumping repeatedly.

the mouths of virtually all clearwater streams and sloughs of interior and northern Alaska rivers. A lure or fly cast into the interface of the muddy and clear water usually gets results, as sheefish often feed or rest throughout the entire water column in this zone. The fish in these groups are generally smaller but, quite often, they bite more readily than spawners.

While sheefish and pike often coexist in the same general area of a river, their specific habitat requirements are different. Sheefish are hardly ever found in shallow water, close to willows and brush, or in grassy sloughs. Instead, they prefer the open water of deep

Fishing from an anchored boat is the preferred method of working the lower sections of some of the larger sheefish rivers.

holes and sloughs or tributary mouths. If the angler is catching more pike than sheefish, the water he is fishing is probably too shallow. If he is catching charr, salmon, or grayling, he is probably in the wrong habitat. Sheefish have hard mouths, and the angler must strike with sufficient force to drive the hook home. Those fish that jump will become airborne as soon as they feel the hook and, as with tarpon, present a special challenge to hold, especially energetic fish in the 20 to 40-pound range.

When ice fishing, locating the school of sheefish is ninety percent of the battle. In rivers, deep holes (located during open water) are the best locations to try, but on Selawik Lake, Hotham Inlet, and certain other locations, random testing of a large number of spots by groups of anglers on snow machines is the preferred technique. Once a school is located, many holes are drilled in the vicinity and excellent fishing is usually enjoyed, sometimes for days before the school leaves in search of food. Most anglers use a stout jigging stick with 15 to 25 feet of 75 to 100-pound Dacron line. A three to four-inch lure is tied directly to the line and jigged two to four feet under the surface with an erratic, slow motion. As you can imagine, hauling a big, 30 or 40-pound fighting shee up through the ice can be quite a job, not unlike trying to contain a bucking horse on a short rope.

Gear

Medium or medium-heavy freshwater spinning or casting rods matched to high-quality reels with good drags and 200 yards of 10 to 15-pound line are the accoutrements of most successful sheefish outings in Alaska. When fishing for smaller shees in Interior and the upper Yukon River, lighter tackle (six to eight-pound line) is sufficient and can provide better action. Best lures include Dardevles, Krocodiles, Hot Rods, and Pixees in weights from three-eighths to one ounce. Traditional red and white, bright orange, and silver seem the best colors. (There are situations, like on the upper Kobuk River, when bronze-colored lures work best.) Fish the heavier sizes to get down in deeper, swifter water. Diving plugs and rattling crankbaits (Wiggle Warts, Shad Raps, Hot Shots, Rat-L-Traps, etc.) can also be worked effectively. For ice fishing, large (three-inch) Doktor lures in silver and bronze are dynamite, but other bright spoons and jigs can be used with good results, at times.

Fly rods should be seven to nine-weight with plenty of backbone to coax large fish from the currents. In slower water or for smaller fish, you can get by with lighter gear, down to a five-weight in some instances. Flies used for feeding sheefish should resemble prey items—white Woolly Buggers, Smolt patterns, Leeches (including Egg Sucking Leech), etc., in sizes #4 to #1/0. Large (up to size #3/0) attractor streamer flies work well for fish that aren't feeding, with colorful patterns utilizing some of the newer materials (such as Krystal Flash and Flashabou) most popular.

It is essential to get the fly close to the fish for best results. Use short leaders and tippets of 8 to 20 pounds, depending on conditions and the size of fish pursued. Flies should be weighted, even when sheefish are feeding on the surface. Floating and short sink tip lines are adequate for feeding fish, but for fish holding in deep water or non-feeding prespawners, high density sinking lines like the Teeny Nymph are better. A shock leader or wire leader is not really necessary because sheefish do not have teeth, but sharp hooks are a definite plus for penetrating their hard bony mouths.

Top Flies for Alaska Sheefish

Alaska Mary Ann, Smolt, Deceiver, D's Minnow, Herring, Woolly Bugger, Leech, Supervisor, Bunny Fly, Gray Ghost, White Ghost, Seaducer, Egg Sucking Leech, Zonker, Black Ghost, Clouser Minnow.

SHEEFISH
Stenodus leucichthys

SPECIES SUMMARY

Alaska common names: Sheefish, shee, inconnu, cony, Eskimo tarpon, arctic tarpon.

Description: A large and long, slender, silvery whitefish with a strong projecting lower jaw. Dorsal body surface is a darker color—metallic green, blue, or light brown. Dorsal and tail fins are dusky; other fins are clear. No spots are present. Both sexes identical—no coloration differences or tubercles present during spawning, but larger-sized fish are always female. Mouth is toothless, fin rays spineless, flesh is white.

Size: Up to 12 lbs. (non-anadromous populations); up to 25 lbs. or more (anadromous populations).

State/World record: 53 lbs., Pah River (NW), Lawrence Hudnall, 1986.

Habits: Highly piscavorous and migratory by nature.

Notes: Anadromous sheefish can live over 20 years.

Meristics: Gill rakers 17-24; vertebrae 63-69; lateral line scales 90-115; dorsal fin 11-19 rays; pectoral fin 14-17 rays; anal fin 14-19 rays; pelvic fin 11-12 rays; head length 30% of body length.

Range: Northern Bering Sea (Kuskokwim River) to Southern Kotzebue Sound drainages and adjacent brackish waters (SW-NW); also Interior, via Yukon/Tanana rivers and tributaries, and introduced into some lakes. Not found south of the Alaska Range or 60 degrees north latitude.

Preferred habitat: Large, slow moving mainstem rivers and associated sloughs.

Best waters: Yukon River tributaries (INT)—Rodo, Innoko, Yuki, Melozitna, Nowitna, Koyukuk, Dall, Ray, Porcupine, Kandik, Nation, Seventymile, Chena, Tolovana, and Chatanika rivers (and Hess and Goldstream creeks); Kuskokwim River tributaries (SW)—Aniak, George, Holitna, Tatlawiksuk, Takotna, and Middle Fork rivers; and Kobuk and Selawik rivers, Selawik Lake and Hotham Inlet (NW).

Run timing: Available year-round (especially Kotzebue area and lower Yukon River); peak fishing during open water (May to October).

Best Bait/Lures/Flies: Herring, whitefish, smelt; large, bright spoons, jigs, and plugs; large forage and attractor pattern streamers and tube flies.

Best Trophy Areas: Kobuk and Selawick rivers and Hotham Inlet (NW), Lower Innoko River (SW).

RECOMMENDED GEAR

Spin/Baitcasting: Medium to medium-heavy, medium-fast action, 6-7 1/2 ft., freshwater spin or casting rod, matching high-quality reel with 175 yds. of 10-15-lb., mono or braided line.

Flyfishing: 7-9-wt., 8-9 1/2 ft., medium action, high performance graphite rod with salmon class reel and 150 yds. 30 lb. backing. WF forward, intermediate, sink tip (Type II-V or T-series 200-400 grain) lines, depending on conditions, with 7-ft. leader and 8-20 lb. tippet.

MAJOR SHEEFISH LOCATIONS

Kuskokwim River: Most sheefish taken in the Kuskokwim River are fish feeding during the summer upstream migration. Since the Kuskokwim is muddy, prime angling locations are always at the mouths and lower reaches of clearwater tributaries. Sheefish are found in early June in streams between Bethel and Aniak while, in July, they appear in the Holitna, Tatlawiksuk and clearwater streams between Sleetmute and McGrath. Upstream of McGrath, the spawning migration spreads out and fish are found in the Takotna River, Middle Fork, Big River, and North Fork and in the Telida area. A few non-spawning fish are present all summer in Kuskokwim streams. Since most sheefish in the Kuskokwim overwinter below Bethel, little ice fishing for them occurs.

Yukon River: In the lower Yukon River, sheefish stop at the mouths of tributary rivers to feed while migrating upstream during early summer. Often the water is too muddy early on but, as tributaries clear, sheefish can be taken. The lower Innoko River in the Shageluk and Holikachuk areas is a major feeding zone. In the Ruby area, sheefish are present in the Yuki, Melozitna, and Nowitna rivers from late June to mid-July. During July and August they can be found in the lower reaches of the Ray, Dall, Hodzana, and Chandalar rivers, and Hess, Birch, and Beaver creeks. They are present in the streams between Circle and Eagle, such as the Charley, Kandik, Nation, Seventymile, and Tatonduk rivers and Eagle Creek. The huge migration of spawners reaching the vicinity of the Dalton Highway Bridge in early September remains in the muddy water and thus are inaccessible to anglers.

#1/0 D's Minnow | 3 to 4 1/2" Doctor Spoon | Storm 4 3/8" Thunder Plug | #2 Gray Ghost | #1/0 Alaska Mary Ann

After these sheefish have migrated back to the lower Yukon River area for overwintering, there is an active ice fishery during November, March, and April in the villages from Holy Cross downstream to the mouth of the Yukon. The Koyukuk River has its own spawning migration and, although fish are passing through lower Koyukuk River villages during August, little sportfishing occurs until the run reaches Hughes in late August and September. The main Koyukuk River from Hughes to Allakaket, and the lower 40 miles of the Alatna River, provide good sportfishing during September and early October. Sheefish are found in the Porcupine River during summer in all sloughs and rivers that enter the Porcupine from the mouth at Fort Yukon to the Canadian border. They are found up the Black River beyond Chalkyitsik and up the Sheenjek River to the mouth of the Koness River.

Tanana River: In the Tanana River, most sheefish are found in the Minto Flats, although they can be taken in clearwater streams from the mouth at Tanana upstream to Fairbanks. The Tolovana, Tatalina, and Chatanika rivers and Goldstream Creek in the Minto Flats contain sheefish in the deeper holes from break-up to early August. They are found throughout most of the Chatanika River to milepost 30 on the Steese Highway and in the Tolovana River upstream of Minto village. Other locations where sheefish are found in the lower Tanana River include Fish and Baker creeks and the Chitanana, Zitziana, and Kantishna river systems, while closer to Fairbanks a few are taken at the mouths of clearwater streams such as Rosie and Nelson Clearwater creeks and the Chena River. Most of the Chena River fish are taken soon after break-up near the mouth, while smaller numbers are taken throughout summer in the lower 20 miles of the Chena.

Kobuk and Selawik Rivers: Major sheefish fishing areas include the entire Kobuk River upstream to the Reed River, the Selawik River upstream for about 125 miles and the extensive lake, stream, and slough system of Hotham Inlet and Selawik Lake. In the Selawik area, sheefish are found in the Tuklomarak and Fox rivers, Inland Lake and its tributaries, as well as the man-made channel connecting Inland Lake to the Selawik River. Once sheefish begin moving up the Kobuk and Selawik rivers, they remain in the main river except for resting stops at mouths of sloughs and tributary streams.

As summer progresses, good fishing locations in the Selawik River are the deep holes upstream of Selawik village. In the Kobuk River, prime early summer (June) fishing grounds include all the channels making up the mouth of the Kobuk River, Hotham Inlet, and deep holes and sloughs upstream to Kiana. This run reaches the Ambler area by mid-July. During mid to late summer, the run spreads out, but prime fishing spots include deep holes in the main river, sloughs, and tributary mouths from Ambler upstream to Kobuk village.

The spawning run of fish can be intercepted at various points from Kobuk upstream to the Reed River until the last week of September, when the fish complete spawning and migrate rapidly downstream to feeding and overwintering areas.

Winter ice fishing locations are essentially all of Hotham Inlet and Selawik Lake, as the fish form huge schools and migrate throughout both bodies of water during the winter months.

Top Ten Alaska Trophy Sheefish		
53 lbs.	Pah River (NW)	1986
52 lbs., 8 oz.	Kobuk River (NW)	1968
49 lbs.	Kobuk River (NW)	1995
43 lbs.	Kobuk River (NW)	1993
42 lbs., 4 oz.	Kobuk River (NW)	1994
39 lbs., 8 oz.	Kobuk River (NW)	1967
38 lbs., 12 oz.	Kobuk River (NW)	1987
38 lbs.	Kobuk River (NW)	1979
37 lbs., 11 oz.	George River (NW)	1971
37 lbs., 4 oz.	Kobuk River (NW)	1978

1 oz. Dardevle   #1/0 Deceiver   1 oz. Hotrod   1 oz. Bucktail Jig   #2 Supervisor

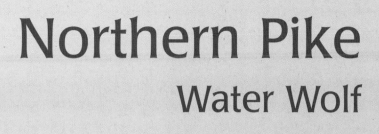

Northern Pike
Water Wolf

The big rivers of western Alaska are full of surprises. In the quest to sample the unmatched fishing they hold, many an angler unwittingly locks horns with Alaska's most unremitting predator, sometimes with spectacular results.

A group of East Coast anglers is fishing salmon along one of the more productive tributaries of the Kuskokwim early one summer, when they notice an evening hatch occurring in a long stretch of river right below camp. The water's surface is dimpled with rises, and thinking, trout—this is, after all, Alaska!—the fishermen scramble for their light flyrods and attempt to "match the hatch" for a welcome break from salmon fishing.

The feeding fish are actually grayling, not slab-sided rainbows, but that's not the only surprise in store this evening. The fishermen whip their lines out and almost instantly draw a response with their wispy imitations. One of the guys connects with a feisty fish that darts into the deep water of the main channel, running in tight circles in the current. It puts on quite a show on the light rod, pulling line toward the deep brushy bank of the river and the mouth of a small, weedy slough.

The frantic gyrations of the grayling draw interest from something with far more sinister intent than catch-and-release fishing, however. Like a streak of lightning, a yellow-green form shoots out from the dark, tannic waters and seizes the grayling in vise-like jaws. The angler senses something as he feels heavy resistance, and reflexively pulls back on the rod. The big fish responds by bolting into the main channel—he will not surrender his meal so easily!

Our hapless fisherman exerts more pressure, which only incites more determination from the primordial predator and, in a matter of seconds, the tug of war escalates into a desperate struggle to save a fly line, as the giant fish flattens the four weight and strips well into the backing. The other anglers shout, "Break the fish off!," and the novice commits the supreme error of trying to part the leader with a savage backward yank of the rod. The brittle graphite cannot stand the strain and shatters; all is lost, save the makings of a great fish story to tell back home!

Pike action, lower Yukon River, Southwest Alaska.

NORTHERN PIKE: WATER WOLF

The northern pike, *Esox lucius*, aka the water wolf, jackfish, snake, or devilfish, is the familiar and notorious toothy glutton of northern waters, known for its supreme savagery when feeding. Lean and mean, with a giant maw and rakish jaws like the barracuda, the pike is the ultimate ambush predator, with body plan and demeanor designed to wreak havoc on a variety of prey—fish, rodents, even waterfowl—with lightning-swift speed. No other fish attacks a lure with such resolve and vigor!

The pike's wantonness lends well to fantastic legends among Alaska's indigenous people. The Athapaskans speak of giant pike that dwell in large lakes and sloughs along the great waterways of the Interior where, should a man be foolish enough to stray by these "devil waters," they can consume him in a single gulp. The Eskimo, similarly, has tales of forbidden waters, wherein lurk evil spirits incarnate in the form of monster northerns the size of trees. White folks also speak of the northern's incredible boldness. One famous old trapper swore a six-footer had gone after him one spring when he fell into a slough in a remote part of the Kuskokwim country.

Legends and spirits aside, the northern pike, in Alaska at least, remains a tremendously underrated and underutilized sport species. Perhaps due to the presence of so many other more notable gamefish, and the prejudice many folks feel toward this maligned fighter, little focused effort occurs for pike in many areas that offer outstanding fishing. But the fact remains—Alaska's better pike potential is every bit the equal of anything Canada has to offer, with the added appeal of almost no angling competition on many waters.

DESCRIPTION

An adult northern pike is not easily confused with any other fish. Its body is elongated and somewhat compressed, the dorsal and anal fins riding far back towards the tail. The head is large and dark green above, and light or pale below; the snout is flattened, and some 700 very sharp teeth line the pike's powerful duckbill jaws. The back and sides are dark green or brown or grayish green, with numerous yellowish oval spots arranged in irregular longitudinal rows. The scales are moderately small and may have a touch of gold to the edges. The belly and lower jaw are

creamy white. Dorsal, anal, and caudal fins are typically greenish yellow, in some populations even appearing almost orange or red with dark blotches. A color variant known as silver pike is also found in Alaska, as well as in the Lower 48.

Pike meat is white and flaky and considered quite flavorful, but it is also very bony, which may contribute to its false reputation of not being a good food fish. However, after mastering how to cut boneless filets, most folks agree that pike are no less than scrumptious.

Northern pike in Alaska are not officially known to achieve the same dimensions as fish in central and northern Europe (65 to 90 pounds), but specimens up to 50 pounds or more are speculated to thrive in certain vast, remote watersheds of the state. Typically averaging between three and ten pounds, depending more or less on location and amount of angling effort, many areas in Alaska yearly yield trophy pike up to 20 pounds or more.

RANGE, ABUNDANCE & STATUS

Northern pike belong to a widespread family of fishes (six species of pike, pickerel, and muskellunge) with circumpolar distribution. They range in Europe from northern Italy and Spain to the Scandinavian countries, and across northern Asia to the Pacific coast of Siberia. In North America, pike are found from New England, Missouri, and Nebraska, up into and across Canada to the Arctic coast of Alaska. They are particularly abundant in Alaska, northern Canada, Russia, and Scandinavia.

Within Alaska, pike are most numerous in sloughs, lowland lakes, and slow-flowing, clearer drainages of the Interior and Southwest, particularly along the Yukon and Tanana River systems, but are also very common in lakes and streams of Northwest and Southcentral. Southeast is the only region in Alaska that does not have populations of northern pike, aside from a small remnant stock from the last Ice Age present in the Ahrnklin River system in the Yakutat area. The species has extended its range recently to include the Susitna River drainage, waters in and around Anchorage, and lakes connected to the Kenai River in Southcentral.

Although the pike's popularity as a sportfish has spread from the Interior to other parts of the state, there remain many ideal waters yet to be discovered and fully recognized. Only a few of the more accessible locations have been tapped to their maximum potential, and conservative management policies now in place guarantee a continuing high quality of fishing for years to come.

LIFE HISTORY & HABITS

In spring, mature northern pike leave the cold depths of over-wintering areas to seek out the warmer shallows of marshy areas to spawn. This significant movement commences right after breakup (usually sometime in April and May or even June, depending on location), with fish often congregating in coves or backwaters prior to spawning. Generally, reproduction takes place during the month of May in most locations, just as the ice melts and recedes from shorelines. Lake populations commonly use shoreline areas, channels, and sloughs with suitable bottom structure, but may at times leave the lake environment and migrate to slow-moving, tributary streams. River populations commit similar migrations, preferring sloughs and lower reaches of tributary rivers and creeks for reproduction. However, spawning migrations are seldom extensive and generally no more than a few miles.

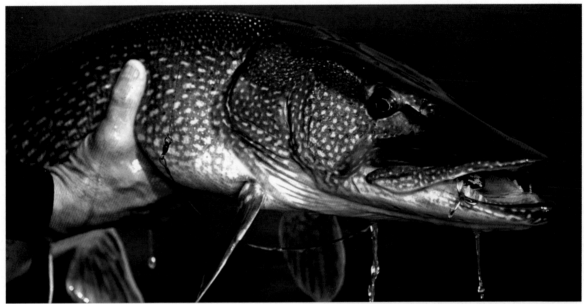

Bright yellow eyes, large, duckbill jaws, and abundant, sharp teeth give the northern pike a formidable countenance; always fish with wire leaders and use extreme caution when handling these brutes.

The most important factors in choice of spawning habitat are shallow and quiet water with emergent vegetation mats. Actual spawning occurs only during daylight in areas no deeper than one or two feet, and ceases at night or during periods of heavy cloud cover, rain, and, in some instances, cold air temperatures. Like other sport fish species, pike may return to spawn in the same exact location every year. Sexual maturity is reached by the age of four or five, at which time the fish is from 16 to 22 inches in length. Generally, females mature later than males and at a larger size.

Northern pike are neither very territorial nor monogamous, and frequently spawn with several members of the opposite gender. The spawning act is repeated often (every few minutes for up to several hours), as only relatively few eggs are released at a time. Depending on the size and age of the mature female, eggs number anywhere between 2,000 and 600,000. A ready-to-spawn female contains both large, ripe eggs and immature eggs that will ripen the following year.

After expulsion, the adhesive eggs settle along the bottom, sticking to vegetation and other materials, where they remain until hatched, a period of time that may range from four or five days up to a month, depending largely on water temperature. The young feed off the yolk sacs until they are old enough to consume zooplankton, later switching to a diet consisting of insect larvae and nymphs. Mortality from egg to fry is very high (99.9%), primarily caused by predation from fish species and birds, competition for food, fluctuating water levels, and even cannibalism by larger pike. Before long, juvenile pike begin to forage on small fish, at which time growth increases dramatically. Young pike reach a size of about four to six inches in length by the end of the first summer. Rate of growth is fast the first few years, and then slows. It is also more rapid in the southern range and progressively slower to the north, and appears largely tied in with water temperature. Maturity is attained as early as age two, but usually not until age three or four. Pike in more northern latitudes live longer.

After spawning, the spent adult pike stay on or near the spawning beds anywhere from one and a half months up to four months, depending on water temperatures and availability of food. Voracious and omnivorous, a big northern will eat just about any food source it can swallow, but fish make up the majority and, in some areas, the entire diet. Burbot, grayling, trout, whitefish, suckers, smelt, ciscoes, and even smaller pike are among the favored species, but in Alaska they prey upon juvenile and adult salmon as well. Pike also consume frogs, mice, shrews, and large insects without hesitation, and are serious predators of young waterfowl in some areas. They are capable of consuming prey up to 40% of body size.

Studies done on pike feeding behavior reveal significant variations according to season and fish size. The vast majority of predation takes place in the early morning or late evening hours (up to 80% of food consumed), with little activity during daylight hours. No feeding was reported to occur at night. Additionally, pike were found to be largely sight feeders and would take advantage of the low-light conditions at dawn and dusk to stage their stalking behavior.

Smaller pike feed most intensely and on a daily basis, while fish larger than 24 inches attain nourishment much less frequently—averaging only twice per week during the warmer months. Very large pike are believed to feed only once a week from spring through fall, and perhaps as infrequently as once every several weeks during the winter months. This finding lends credibility to the reports of ice fishers experiencing poor or inconsistent action for larger pike in waters known to support healthy populations of big pike. It may also explain the behavior of large northerns only "nosing" or closely observing decoys or lures without attacking.

Northern pike have long been both despised and admired for their uncanny ability to infiltrate new drainages, using rivers as well as tiny trickles of water to spread their range. Their hardiness is almost prehistoric. Reports of pike in brackish water in Alaska have been confirmed, with one such specimen caught in a set net in upper Cook Inlet in Southcentral. The fish was purple in color due to its reaction to salt water; more than likely, it was scouting for new watersheds to inhabit. A sub-species, named silver pike for its silvery coloration, thrives in the brackish Baltic Sea of northern Europe. But usually, true northern pike strictly reside in fresh water.

Additional studies done in Alaska and Canada using radio-tracking equipment reveal that pike generally do not commit any lengthy migrations during the summer and winter months, and will seldom move more than a few hundred yards from one day to the next. Also, pike tend to remain within 300 yards of shore. Overall, preferred habitat is lakes containing an abundance of weedy areas with fish suspended at depths of 15 feet or less. During adverse weather, such as heavy rain or wind, and on days with hot, bright sunshine, pike will seek out deep water. Dark or cloudy days tend to bring fish closer to shore and into shallower water.

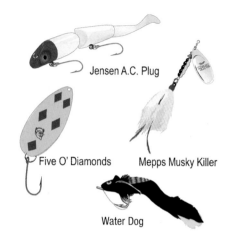

Jensen A.C. Plug

Five O' Diamonds

Mepps Musky Killer

Water Dog

The majority of Alaska's pike are taken on large spoons, spinners, plugs, and flies.

FISHING ALASKA'S NORTHERN PIKE

Alaska sport anglers in recent years have caught over 100,000 pike annually, most of them from Southcentral's Mat-Su valley and drainages associated with the Yukon and Tanana rivers. The state's reputation for high quality wilderness trophy fishing is attracting more and more anglers worldwide, along with an increasing number of urban anglers taking advantage of the growing pike fishery north of Anchorage. Unlike many other of the state's species, pike provide significant opportunity year-round.

Spring Conditions

Some of the fastest and most rewarding action for large pike can be had in the spring. Starting in early April, and continuing through June, big spawners take up positions in the shallows around weed beds near shore in lakes, ponds, sloughs, and streams. Just prior to (a week to ten days) and immediately after reproduction, fishing can be excellent, as pike begin a feeding frenzy to replace energy stores depleted by the long winter. With a careful approach to weed beds so as not to spook any fish, anglers in many locations can actually spot pike suspended right beneath the surface, still and motionless, like driftwood or logs—until a lure is thrown out.

Flashy spoons, plugs, and spinners retrieved with an erratic action through promising water this time of year almost always produce smashing strikes from ravenous pike. But this is also one of the best times to twitch top water plugs and big bushy flies through the weed beds for the exalted thrill of watching a big, toothy monster attack on the surface.

Anglers should be especially selective about the number and gender of the fish they retain this time of year. Since the majority of large pike are female and crucial to the well-being of the local stock, and the total number of fish present on the spawning beds represents a good portion of the adult population, catch-and-release angling is encouraged.

Summer/Fall Conditions

As summer comes on and water temperatures rise, many pike leave spawning areas for more opportune feeding in river mainstems, lakes, and big sloughs. Top-water fishing can still be very effective at times in certain areas, but many anglers switch to traditional sinking/diving hardware for efficiency in working the wider variety of pike water this time of year.

Boaters fare best on large lakes, trolling or casting big spoons or plugs, but angling from shore can be productive, particularly on smaller lakes, ponds, rivers, and streams. On lakes with minimal vegetation, pike tend to migrate more in search of food and rely more on smell than any other sense to catch prey. Oily baits are very effective (herring, hooligan, smelt, etc.), either rigged alone or used as attractors with jigs, spoons, or plugs.

Some of the better locations to find pike in summer are in the backwater sloughs and mouths of slow-flowing, clearer tributaries of large, silty rivers like the Yukon, Tanana, or Kuskokwim. The semi-turbid mix of some of these areas is a favorite hangout for big northerns, many of which succumb to properly presented spoons, plugs, spinners, and even bait. But, as always, avoid open water and concentrate efforts near vegetation and structure, where pike hide.

In lakes, search out structure that provides both access to opportunistic feeding and lies for ambush. The edge of weed beds and steep drop-offs are favored hangouts; even rocky points serve as pike magnets due to the abundance of forage. Retrieve speed should vary with the depth of the water and type of lure, with an erratic action often bringing the best results.

As waters cool in late summer and fall, baitfish migrations into spawning and/or winter holdover areas will prompt northerns to begin leaving many of their summer feeding grounds. This can be one of the best times of year for fishing, as the pike are in prime condition and aggressively on the feed with winter fast looming. Spoons, plugs, and flies that mimic baitfish are top producers this time of year. Sloughs, river

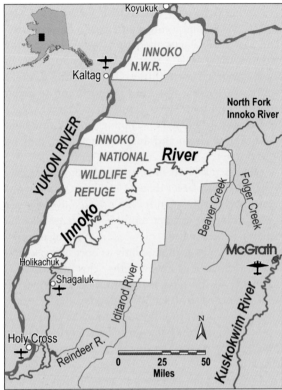

The Innoko River, an immense tributary of the lower Yukon in Southwest Alaska, has emerged in recent years as one of Alaska's premier locales for trophy northern pike.

mouths, lake outlets/inlets, and other bait staging areas will offer the best chances for encountering big, hungry fall pike.

Winter Conditions

The close of the open water season in Alaska signals the start of another dimension of pike angling, as many of the more remote waters that are difficult or expensive to access by floatplane can be reached by snowmachine in winter. Braving daunting conditions, the adequately prepared winter pike angler can often experience some of the state's best fishing without hardship or great expense.

In the early part of the season (November to January), as ice cover develops and lakes and rivers begin to settle into winter dormancy, pike can be taken frequently through the ice in waters from 15 to 30 feet deep, as they follow schools of prey species that are still quite active. Ice conditions, weather and diminishing daylight will be the major limiting factors to the pike angler this time of year, but superb catches are possible in many areas, using jigs, spoons, and bait.

Pike can be taken through the ice all winter long in Alaska, using simple gear and spoons, jigs, and bait.

As winter progresses and waters become increasingly colder, darker, and devoid of oxygen, all fish species, prey and predator alike, become increasingly lethargic. These doldrums, when snow and ice cover (and the negative factors listed above) reach their maximum levels in late winter, affect all ice fishing, and anglers may have a hard time stirring up action in even the best locations this time of year. The general strategy is to open up several scattered holes (using a power auger) and fish oily baits such as herring, smelt, and salmon on the end of bright jigs and spoons to help attract the sluggish predators. Quite frequently, it takes some time working several holes before any action occurs, particularly from larger pike, and it may be necessary to probe different areas to locate excitable fish.

Avoid extremely shallow lakes, sloughs, or backwaters that may be productive in spring, because of oxygen depletion this time of year. Focus instead on areas that have a variety of depth, bottom structure, and/or cover to provide refuge for prey species. Bathymetric maps, if available, can be invaluable, as can some of the new, highly portable fish finding systems. Ice houses or portable, sled-drawn shelters are especially useful in Alaska's often extreme winter weather, especially for extended trips. Aside from the physical shelter they provide, the darkness they create accents the little light emanating from the water, for better visibility.

Wood decoys have traditionally been used for decades for luring winter pike within range of a spear, both in Alaska and abroad, and can add a novel and exciting twist to fishing through the ice. Be warned that it takes sufficient skill and patience (in addition to a very large hole), to successfully fish this way.

Late winter (March-April), when the light returns, days lengthen and weather moderates, is the most popular time for ice fishing pike in Alaska. The fish become emboldened as they sense the onset of spring spawning season and the stirrings of bait species (particularly grayling and salmon smolt) preparing for seasonal migrations. Anglers can enjoy the best conditions and biggest catches of the season.

Weather and Timing

Although pike have never been known to be particularly finicky, most successful anglers target these fish with particular lures and colors to match elements of the weather. Early morning and late evening are the best times to fish, as pike are most aggressive and in the feeding mode, with the best action in relatively shallow or shaded water. As the day progresses, the fish will move into deeper water, on the edge of weed beds and other structure, to avoid bright sunshine and rising temperatures associated with the shallows. Strong winds and wave action will cause the fish to move deep as well.

Best lure colors depend on lighting conditions and water clarity. Bright, sunny days and shallow water command dark (black, brown, purple, etc.) colored enticements, while cloudy ones see gold, yellow, orange, copper, brass, and similar hues work better, both in clear and murky water. However, in very murky, very deep, or very cloudy conditions, white, silver, chartreuse, and light blue are effective colors.

FLYFISHING ALASKA'S NORTHERN PIKE

The pike's reputation for reckless aggression toward all manner of enticement makes it an exciting species to pursue with a fly, particularly for topwater fishing. An increasing number of anglers fish Alaska each summer for this pleasure alone, and wouldn't have their pike any other way.

Although pike will hit just about any fly presented properly, large, bushy attractors and forage imitations work best, length preferably two to four inches. Oversize versions of popular Alaska patterns like the Flash Fly, Alaska Mary Ann, Outrageous, Alaskabou, Sculpin, Bunny Bug, Bunny Leech, etc., are reliable

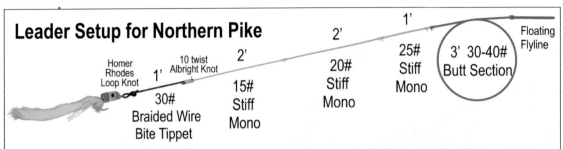

Leader Setup for Northern Pike

Homer Rhodes Loop Knot — 30# Braided Wire Bite Tippet — 1' — 10 twist Albright Knot — 15# Stiff Mono — 2' — 20# Stiff Mono — 2' — 25# Stiff Mono — 1' — 3' 30-40# Butt Section — 1' — Floating Flyline

The pike's abundant, sharp teeth and the large flies used require a stout leader/tippet system with bite resistant terminal section. Several manufacturers offer prefabricated pike leaders or you can rig your own, as shown.

producers. Also excellent are tube flies and saltwater patterns like the Clouser Minnow, Deceiver, Seaducer, Herring, and Tarpon Fly. Large, specialty top-water or diving creations like the rabbit fur Lemming, deer hair Frog, Dahlberg Diver, Water Dog, Pollywog, or even poppers, can be exciting and productive to fish, but expensive, as they seldom survive more than four or five vicious strikes. You can keep it simple and cheap if you tie your own. Aim for flies with a certain amount of bulk, since they help grip pike's teeth. Super sharp, strong hooks (sizes #3/0 to #4) are recommended, with weed guards for topwater patterns in extreme conditions. All flies should be stripped in an erratic manner to simulate wounded prey.

GEARING UP FOR ALASKA'S NORTHERN PIKE

Spin/Bait Casting Gear

For spinning or bait casting, serious pike anglers will use a six to eight-foot, medium-heavy freshwater, medium-action rod with matching high-quality level wind (5000 to 7000 series Ambassadeur, 300 to 700 series Shimano Calcutta, 900 Series Penn International, etc.) or tournament quality spinning (5000 to 7000 series Penn SS, 3500 to 4500 series Daiwa, or 5000 to 6000 series Shimano) reel loaded with 12 to 20-pound line. Wire, plastic-coated wire, or super-heavy mono shock leaders are a requisite for preventing break-offs from the northern's abundant, sharp teeth although, with large spinners and buzz baits, this may not be necessary. Hooks and other terminal tackle should be super strong and of the highest quality. Trophy fish and/or big waters may require heavier gear.

Like elsewhere, pike can be taken in Alaska on just about any kind of lure, as long as it creates a commo-

tion in the water. Large spoons, plugs, jigs, spinners, spinnerbaits, plastic softbaits, and what have you, in silver, gold, yellow, green, orange, brown, white, red, and black, with wobbling, darting, and diving actions, and skirts, legs, and tails to mimic the movement and likeness of forage species (fish, frogs, voles, mice, etc.) are especially alluring.

Some of the more popular lures include: Krocodile, Dardevle, Red Eye, Doctor, Syclops, and Silver Minnow spoons; Rapala, Rebel, Flatfish, Storm, Yo-Zuri, Lucky Strike, Heddon, and Tad-polly plugs; Vibrax Musky Buck and Mepps Giant and Musky Killer spinners; Terminator, Lindy, and Strike King spinnerbaits; and Mister Twister, Culprit, Berkley, and Storm softbaits. For big pike, use as large a lure as you feel comfortable casting with (at least 4 inches).

Silver Minnow with bait strip teaser

Large plugs, along with spoons, are the most widely used lures for northern pike and, in Alaska, all types are used: divers, jointed minnows, topbaits, crankbaits, jerkbaits, etc. Topwater bass plugs, poppers, buzzbaits, and frog and mouse imitations can also be used to great effect. Preferred plug length varies with weather, water conditions, and fish size, but generally falls in the four to eight-inch category.

Bait is extremely effective, particularly on shy or finicky pike. It is usually fished either whole (rigged on one or two hooks) or in chunks or strips as a teaser on the end of a spoon, jig, or spinner. Herring, smelt, sucker, or whitefish are the most commonly used bait species, but they must be fresh or pike will not take them. (Remember, the use of live bait is prohibited in

Taking on Alaska's pike with a flyrod is an exciting challenge that more and more anglers are discovering each year

the state of Alaska; only non-game species can be used whole as bait.) Some anglers fish a rigged baitfish with just a sinker, others fish it with a bobber. The distance between the bait hook and the bobber varies, but usually runs about four to six feet. As the bait is taken, resist the temptation to set the hook until the pike has properly positioned the bait for consumption. (Pike will seize prey in the middle and then shift to swallow head first.)

Fly-fishing Gear

Fly fishers wanting to do battle with pike need at least an eight or nine-weight rod to effectively cast large, bulky pike flies, with stout backbone and matching reel with a strong drag to handle any trophy size fish encountered. Most common lines used are performance taper, weight forward floating, intermediate or sink-tips (Type II-V). Leaders used are usually seven foot, with a 12 to 20-pound tippet and the last six to twelve inches wire or super-heavy mono. (See illustration on previous page.) The new braided, tieable wire leader materials and commercially prepared pike leaders are valuable innovations that save time and increase efficiency.

Pike Slider

Articulated Leech

Seaducer

Pike Popper

Pike flies—from oversize forage imitations to saltwater attractor patterns to specialty topwater/diving creations—keep them bright, big, and bushy.

NORTHERN PIKE
Esox lucius

SPECIES SUMMARY

Alaska common names: Pike, northern pike, jackfish, pickerel.

Description: Easily recognizable, freshwater predatory fish, with duckbill snout, bright yellow eyes, elongate body (with dorsal and anal fins near tail), and large mouth with prominent teeth. Has green to greenish-gray or brown topsides with rows of irregular, oval yellowish-white spots and yellow or creamy white belly. Fins greenish-orange, yellow-orange or red-orange, with dark mottling (except paired fins); flesh white.

Size: Average 4-7 lbs., up to 30 lbs. and 50 in. or more.

State record: 38 lbs., Innoko River (SW), Jack Wagner, 1991.

Habits: A voracious ambush predator and piscavore.

Notes: Can consume prey up to 40% of body size.

Meristics: Vertebrae 57-65; no pyloric caeca; lateral line scales 105-150; branchiostegal rays 14-16 each side; dorsal fin 15-25 rays; anal fin 12-22 rays; pectoral fin 14-17 rays; pelvic fin 10-11 rays.

Range: Northern Southeast to Arctic slope fresh water.

Preferred Habitat: Vegetated lowland sloughs, lakes, and large, slow river mainstems with abundant forage.

Best waters: Sloughs, lakes, and lower reaches of tributaries along Yukon, Tanana, and Kuskokwim rivers (Yukon and Minto flats, Nowitna, Holitna, Innoko, Koyukuk rivers, etc.), INT-SW; Kotzebue Sound (Kobuk, Selawik, and Noatak rivers) and Imuruk basin drainages, NW; Susitna valley lakes, SC.

Run timing: Available year-round; best fishing spring through fall (May to October).

Best Bait/Lures/Flies: Whole or strip whitefish, smelt, and herring; large, flashy spoons, spinners, and plugs; jigs, crankbaits, and soft-baits; big baitfish and attractor pattern streamers and bulky, top water specialty flies.

Best Trophy Areas: Innoko River (SW); Alexander Lake (SC); East Twin Lake (INT); Nowitna River (INT); Trapper Lake (SC).

RECOMMENDED GEAR

Spin/baitcasting:

6 - 7 1/2-ft. medium-heavy, medium-action freshwater rod (rated 8-20 lb. line), high-quality, medium-heavy freshwater or muskie class casting/spinning reel and 175 yds. 12-20-lb. test mono or braided line with braided wire or heavy mono shock leader. Trophy fish and/or big waters may require heavier gear.

Fly-fishing:

8-9 wt., 9-10 ft., medium-fast action, high performance graphite rod, matching high quality reel with 150 yds., 30-lb. backing. Performance taper WF floating, intermediate or sink-tip line (Type II-V), with 7-ft. leader and 12-20 lb. tippet, with the last 6-12 in. braided wire (30 lb.) or super-heavy mono.

ALASKA'S MAJOR PIKE LOCATIONS

SOUTHEAST
Only one relict population is found in entire region, along the North Gulf Coast.

Yakutat: Ahrnklin River Lakes.

SOUTHCENTRAL
Northern pike invaded and spread throughout the Susitna and Matanuska valleys not too long ago, and now provide abundant, year-round opportunities, though large fish have become increasingly scarce in recent years.

Mat/Su: Chelatna, Bulchitna, Red Shirt, Lynx, Vern, Flathorn, Sucker, Alexander, Hewitt, Whiskey, and Trapper lakes.

Kenai: Cisca Lake.

SOUTHWEST
With abundant, widespread opportunities, many of them untapped because of the fantastic salmon and trout fishing available, this region is fast becoming the state's number one destination for the adventure trophy angler.

Bristol Bay: Nushagak River system; Wood-Tikchik, Clark, Telaquana, Chulitna, Long, Whitefish, and Pike lakes.

Alaska Peninsula: Naknek Lake system (portions).

Kuskokwim: Lower Aniak and Holitna rivers.

Lower Yukon: Lower Andreafsky, Anvik, and Innoko rivers.

| 4 1/2" Dardevle | #3/0 Pike Flash Fly | Rigged Whitefish, Smelt, or Herring | #1/0 Weaver Lake Snake | 5 1/2" Red Eye |

Top Flies for Alaska Pike

Alaskabou, Bunny Bug, Flash Fly, Rabbit Lemming, Seaducer, Deceiver, Dahlberg Diver, Reynold's Pike Fly, Bunny Leech, Herring, McNally Magnum, D's Minnow, Clouser Minnow, Pollywog, Deerhair Frog, Water Dog.

Top Ten Alaska Trophy Northern Pike

38 lbs., 8 oz.	Innoko River (SW)	1991
38 lbs.	Fish Creek (INT)	1978
31 lbs., 2 oz.	Donkey Lake (SC)	1992
30 lbs., 4 oz.	Innoko River (SW)	1995
29 lbs., 11 oz.	East Twin Lake (INT)	1988
29 lbs.	Innoko River (SW)	1990
28 lbs., 6 oz.	Innoko River (SW)	1991
28 lbs., 2 oz.	Wilson Lake (INT)	1971
28 lbs.	Lake Clark (SW)	1982
27 lbs., 8 oz.	Alexander Lake (SC)	1992

Recommended Pike Guides

Pike Safaris: P.O. Box 102, Holy Cross, AK 99602, 907-476-7121.

Midnight Sun Trophy Pike Adventures: P.O. Box 542, Columbus, TX 78934; 800-440-7453.

North Country River Charters: 4741 Harvard Circle, Fairbanks, AK 99709; 907-479-7116; *www.ncrc.alaska.com.*

Alaska Yukon Tours: P.O. Box 221, Fort Yukon, AK 99740; 907-662-2727. *www.akyukontours.com.*

NORTHWEST

This region has awesome potential, with minimal or no fishing pressure in most areas. Lots of big fish have been taken here over the years (many never recorded).

Norton Sound: Unalakleet, Shaktoolik, Ungalik and Kwiniuk rivers.

Seward Peninsula: Fish, Kuzitrin, and Pilgrim rivers; Imuruk Basin, Buckland River.

Kotzebue Sound: Lower Kobuk, Selawik, and Noatak rivers.

Lower Koyukuk River: Mainstem and tributaries—Gisasa, Dulbi, Huslia, Dakli, Hogatza, and Kateel rivers.

INTERIOR

Traditionally holding the state's most popular and intensively managed pike fisheries, this vast region still has some of Alaska's best fishing for the species, particularly along the middle Yukon and lower Tanana.

Tanana: Chisana and Nabesna river systems; Chatanika, Tolovana, lower Tatalina, Cosna, Chitanana, Chena, and Zitziana rivers; Swan Neck Slough; Fish, Gardiner, Moose, and lower Goldstream creeks; Jatahmund, Wellesley, Dog, Island, Wien, Wolf, East Twin, West Twin, Deadman, Mucha, Volkmar, Tetlin, Minchumina, Mansfield, George, and Bear lakes.

Yukon: Melozitna, Tozitna, Nowitna, Hodzana, Hadweenzic, Chandalar, Christian, Sheenjek, Ray, Dall, lower Charley, lower Nation, Kandik, Porcupine, and Black rivers; lower Hess, Birch, and Beaver creeks.

Lindy Giant tandem
Spinnerbait

#1/0 Reynolds
Pike Fly

5" Super
Shad Rap

#3/0 Pike
McMurderer

#6 Vibrax
Musky Buck

Alaska Saltwater Salmon

It's a balmy, sunny August morning as we head out on calm seas through the rugged, forest-lined straits separating northern Kodiak from Afognak Island. The boat glides by rocky, driftwood-strewn beaches and secluded coves, where dark little foxes stare at us in bewilderment and eagles wheel and dive for the leftovers of some bear's salmon dinner. Far away on the edge of the strait, plumes of spray rise rhythmically from a pod of minke whales on their way to or from who knows where.

The beautiful weather entices the captain to head out into unsheltered waters, where giant swells loom out of the Gulf of Alaska and threaten our serenity this peaceful morn. The skipper, undaunted, consults his charts and bears north and east a ways to put the *Lady Lize* over a large reef 50 feet below the surface.

In a heartbeat, rods are rigged with bait and jigs, and lines let down in hopes of enticing one of Alaska's homely, but supremely scrumptious, bottom dwellers. I have other designs and grab my eight weight and steal to the bow where, with little grace, I sling a leadcore line that quickly takes my pink sparkle shrimp down into dark depths below.

The rich waters off Kodiak seldom disappoint and, in no time at all, one of the guys working a white plastic-tailed jig hooks what appears to be a giant halibut or lingcod and, soon after, someone else connects with something just as big, as all hell breaks loose on the stern.

I'm having my doubts, as I strip my small fly up from bottom with nary a nibble when, suddenly, my line tightens and rises abruptly, as if tethered to some kind of missile. This is no bottomfish! A flash of silver-white catches my eye in the emerald waters as a magnificent salmon—a giant Kodiak silver, easily 15 pounds—launches twenty yards off the starboard bow, with my fly stuck firmly in its jaw!

My reel screams—the drag is too loose—and the fish is quickly out of control, ripping deep into my backing. I palm the reel and try to tighten the drag, but it's already too late. The fish has pulled so much heavy fly line into the kelp-filled swells that I can't possibly hold it and suddenly, sickeningly, my leader parts. What a fish! But before I have time to feel sorry for myself, the sharp cry of the captain for the harpoon rouses me into action, as another exciting day of fishing unfolds along Alaska's coast.

Trolling for spring feeder kings, Kachemak Bay, lower Cook Inlet, Southcentral Alaska.

ALASKA SALTWATER SALMON

From Ketchikan to Kodiak (and beyond), an almost unlimited amount of inshore fishing adventure beckons, with the excitement of abundant angling and the incomparable beauty of Alaska's magnificent coast. Salmon anglers in particular find it hard to resist the allure of Alaska's salt waters, for once you have sampled the fight (and the taste) of a chrome-bright fish, fresh from the sea, it is difficult to have your salmon any other way.

But locating and enticing salmon in the wide open marine environment is not always a sure thing, even in fish-rich Alaska, and, for freshwater anglers accustomed to stalking their quarry within the confines of river banks, the task can be absolutely daunting.

People who do it for a living—commercial trollers and charter boat captains—have dedicated years to unraveling the mysteries of salmon behavior and their whereabouts in Alaska's nearshore waters. Much of this hard earned savvy is applicable anywhere salmon are found in the North Pacific. But there are some significant differences that make the Alaska saltwater salmon scene unique and especially challenging.

For one, Alaska's southern coastal waters during fishing season contain a broad mix of salmon from different origins and age classes. At any strategic location in the Gulf of Alaska in late spring, for instance, it is possible to encounter immature, wild "feeder" kings from local waters, larger, maturing fish from British Columbia, big, prespawning chinook bound for Cook Inlet or streams as far south as Washington and Oregon, and a good number of mature hatchery fish (kings, chums, pinks, even silvers) returning to terminal release sites up and down the Alaska coast. (Each has unique habits and behavior that respond best to different fishing strategies.)

And Alaska, unlike parts of southern British Columbia and the Pacific Northwest states, does not enjoy a significant nearshore fishery for immature salmon other than kings, as the other species spend their adult existence at considerable distances out in the North Pacific, where food sources are more plentiful. Small coho or silver salmon are taken incidentally during spring and summer in some areas along the coast but, for the most part, the overwhelming majority of Alaska's saltwater sport fishery intercepts

mature fish that have left their deep ocean pasturage for natal waters along the coast. All these salmon have begun, to some degree, the complex changes in physiology and behavior that accompany their return to fresh water and subsequent spawning.

These physical changes, well known to stream anglers, can be seen in some salmon even 20 or more miles out at sea from their final destinations, and include a darkening skin color, development of hook noses or kypes in males, ripening of gonads in both sexes, and an imbedding of scales to adhere better to their bodies.

Most of these prespawning fish early in the season can be pursued and taken with strategies that exploit their aggressive feeding responses, as they binge on baitfish, shrimp, squid, and other food sources to put on weight for the arduous spawning ritual. (Coho salmon, in the final weeks of their ocean existence, can gain a pound a week.) As the season advances, however, their behavior becomes more unpredictable; they feed less and finally cease feeding altogether, though they will, out of instinct, still respond to standard enticements much of the time.

A big part of success with these prespawners comes from learning their typical migration routes, as they stage around the same islands, channels, and points year after year to rest, mill, and feed. The well-known commercial trolling drags, such as the Breadline out of Juneau, Biorka Island out of Sitka, the west side of Gravina Island out of Ketchikan, etc., are examples of areas of historic salmon concentration and potentially productive fishing.

Adding to the complexity of Alaska's saltwater salmon scene are some rather unique hatchery-produced terminal fisheries, which have become significant in certain areas of Southcentral and Southeast Alaska (Resurrection Bay, Valdez Harbor, Homer Spit, Blind Slough, Neets Bay, etc.) and provide substantial opportunities for sport and commercial fishermen. Most of these fish are released as smolts at the heads of bays or along spits, and return as sexually mature adults with no hope of breeding, truly terminal fish in the strictest sense of the word. Their behavior, movements, and the strategies used to take them are decidedly different than those of their wild brethren.

FINDING THE FISH

Regardless of where, when, and what you fish, locating your quarry is priority one in the challenging saltwater salmon game. Aside from knowing the traditional feeding hotspots, gathering points, or migration routes along the coast, the successful saltwater salmon hunter uses his familiarity with basic salmon feeding habits, plus a battery of well known tactics, to locate salmon in the often mysterious and diffuse ocean environment.

Since adult king and coho salmon—the two most commonly sought-after species in Alaska—are primarily fish eaters, a good general plan for locating them is to seek out areas where baitfish (herring, sandlance, smelt, capelins, etc.) concentrate. This is a surefire strategy for feeder kings and works for most prespawners (all species except sockeye) as well. Some of the traditional inshore areas where baitfish (and feeding salmon) may be concentrated include: bays, straits, channels, and passes; around kelp beds, islands, jutting points, rock outcroppings, reefs, and deepwater dropoffs; and along beaches, cliffs, bars, tide rips, and spits.

Veteran salmon anglers have a keen understanding of the many factors—tides, ocean currents, weather, species habits, time of day, etc.—that can influence salmon feeding behavior. When in waters less familiar, they rely on this experience, plus information from nautical charts, instrumentation (fish finder/ depth sounder), local fish reports and visual cues (flocking and diving seabirds, jumping or rolling salmon, the shimmering waters of milling baitfish, or the presence of other boats) to home in on the best areas to fish. And a really good skipper who freely shares his success with others frequently monitors the VHF/CB radio to see how other boats in the area are doing.

Tides, Water Depth, Time of Day, and Other Factors

To understand how baitfish and salmon are drawn to certain areas within the vast marine environment, it is useful to think of the ocean as having the qualities of both river and lake.

As in a river, the tide and ocean currents work on the many irregularities of shore and bottom to stir up and concentrate marine life. And, much like in a lake, the dramatically varied ocean bottom, with its reefs, dropoffs, seamounts, etc., creates cover for sea life concentration and good fishing.

The effect of tides is extremely significant. The ebb and flow of these great currents flushes all manner of marine life in and out of cover, creating, in some areas, concentrations of forage (some described in the previous section) that are most conducive to good fishing. When you look at a nautical chart of a section of the north Pacific coast, try to visualize how a big change (high or low tide) will act on the various physical features (keeping in mind the river analogy), where this action will be most intense, and how it will concentrate baitfish and salmon. These areas of concentration will fish differently throughout the day, with best times usually, but not always, in the flood right after a slack (low tide) and the period right before (approximately one hour) and during a high tide.

Much has been said and written about salmon depth preference in the ocean, with the general consensus being that prespawners are usually found shallower than nonspawning feeders, and that coho or silver salmon (and pink, chum, and sockeye) prefer shallower water than chinook. This is generally true most of the time for Alaska, but not always. When baitfish schools are not gathered inshore, salmon are quite often found very deep, up to 200 feet or more. In some areas along the coast, like Southeast during July and August, these deep-feeding fish can often be

Downriggers and rigged herring account for a large majority of salmon caught in Alaska's marine waters.

located by watching the location of commercial trollers. In these situations, mooching and motor mooching may be the most effective methods, allowing anglers to reach depths which are difficult to fish effectively with downriggers.

Most salmon, particularly chinook, are light sensitive, and are found shallower and strike better early and late in the day (and on windy, overcast days), especially feeders and terminal salmon. As a rule, when the optimum tide periods coincide with the low-light times of day, fishermen can expect the most productive fishing. Needless to say, a tide book and fishing log (to record pertinent information, dates, tides, time of day, lures/bait used, depth fished, etc.) are important to fishing smart and improving your skill as a saltwater salmon angler.

COMMON METHODS FOR ALASKA'S SALTWATER SALMON

Trolling

As the easiest method of taking salmon over a wide range of conditions, saltwater sport trolling borrows considerably from decades of experience hard won by commercial salmon trollers throughout Southeast and elsewhere, who have refined the art of attracting and hooking salmon to a high level of efficiency.

For sport trolling, usually two to six lines are employed off the back and sides of the boat, using downriggers (see illustration), diving sinkers (i.e., Pink Lady) or keel weights to pull the terminal rigging down to the desired depth. Fish dodgers or flashers (see illustration) in combination with herring (whole, plug-cut, or strips), hoochies (plastic squid imitations), plugs, spoons, or streamer flies are commonly

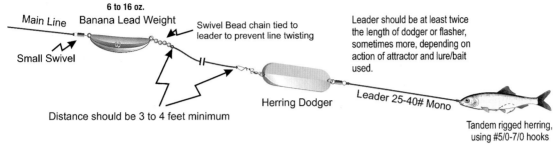

6 to 16 oz.
Main Line · Banana Lead Weight · Swivel Bead chain tied to leader to prevent line twisting

Small Swivel

Leader should be at least twice the length of dodger or flasher, sometimes more, depending on action of attractor and lure/bait used.

Distance should be 3 to 4 feet minimum

Herring Dodger

Leader 25-40# Mono

Tandem rigged herring, using #5/0-7/0 hooks

Simple Trolling Rig

used. With downriggers, it is possible to troll lines at different depths without the cumbersome drag of heavy weights or planers, allowing lighter tackle and greater sport. Two or even three lines can be run or "stacked" off clips set at various points along each cable, for greater efficiency.

Dodgers & Flashers: The use of metal fish attractors has been a standard trolling practice for years. The most commonly used types are "flashers" and "dodgers"—long, thin rectangular blades that spin or sway when trolled, adding considerable, strike-inducing stimuli (flash, vibration, and erratic action) to trailed baits or lures. Dodgers are usually four to ten inches long, with a slightly concave shape to develop a side-to-side motion best suited to complement the action of spoons, plugs, and bait at a slow to medium trolling speed. Flashers are generally larger (up to 14 inches or more) and spin around in full 360° rotations. They are generally used with lures like hoochies and flies that have no action of their own, and in deep water trolling situations where maximum attractor stimuli is desired. Both kinds come in a variety of sizes, colors, and finishes—chrome, chrome/silver scale, green, chartreuse, pearl pink, mylar, white, and orange being some of the most popular used in Alaska.

The rigging of the attractor and lure/bait setup can vary considerably but, generally, dodgers (with their lesser action) are used with much less line connecting them to the depth device and the lure/bait. For best action, the attractor is generally rigged a minimum of three to four feet behind the sinker or diver, and at least six feet (commonly 20 feet or more) from a downrigger cable. A stout leader (30-pound test, usually) at least twice as long as the flasher or dodger connects to the terminal end. (This length varies with

Trolling Tips

1. Check your terminal rigging (lures, bait, flasher/dodger) alongside the boat, at speed, before sending any line down into the water, to ensure proper action.

2. Always check your bait after any interaction with salmon.

3. Periodically check your lines (every 15 minutes) for fouling with kelp/seaweed.

4. Watch your turns when fishing multiple lines off the back and sides of the boat.

5. If you don't have any luck, try varying your speed, depth, and course, and experiment with different bait rigging or other lures and/or lure colors and sizes.

the species targeted and lure/bait used; generally silvers like a faster action from a shorter leader, kings like the slower action from a longer leader; lures like spoons are usually fished with a short leader resulting in a fast, tight wobble.) For light tackle fishing, the attractor can be run alone off the downrigger, with the lure/bait run off a separate line stacked above or below (see trolling illustration on next page).

Trolling Techniques

Successful trolling techniques used for Alaska's saltwater salmon vary, depending on location, time of year, species pursued, kind of lures/bait used, etc. A general all-around strategy is to troll likely fish holding areas (around bait patches, kelp beds, points, islands, bays, etc.) using lines at various depths, until a taker is encountered, then work the zone/area intensively until the action stops. Generally, kings are found deeper than coho (60 to 120 feet for feeders, usually less for prespawners) and take a slower trolled lure or bait. Silvers are predominantly top water feed-

Continued on page 161

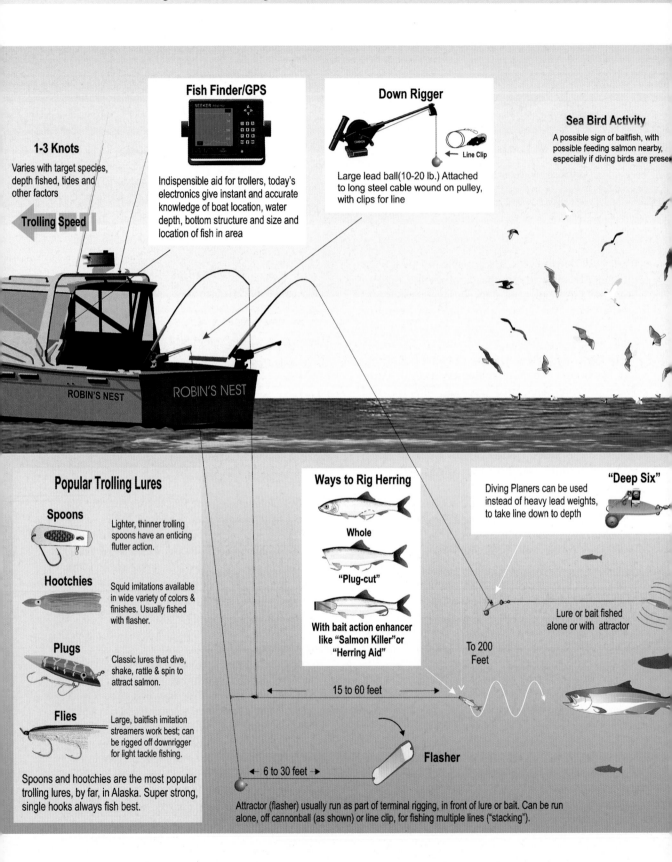

Fish Finder/GPS

Indispensible aid for trollers, today's electronics give instant and accurate knowledge of boat location, water depth, bottom structure and size and location of fish in area

Down Rigger

← Line Clip

Large lead ball(10-20 lb.) Attached to long steel cable wound on pulley, with clips for line

Sea Bird Activity

A possible sign of baitfish, with possible feeding salmon nearby, especially if diving birds are present

1-3 Knots

Varies with target species, depth fished, tides and other factors

Trolling Speed

ROBIN'S NEST

ROBIN'S NEST

Popular Trolling Lures

Spoons

Lighter, thinner trolling spoons have an enticing flutter action.

Hootchies

Squid imitations available in wide variety of colors & finishes. Usually fished with flasher.

Plugs

Classic lures that dive, shake, rattle & spin to attract salmon.

Flies

Large, baitfish imitation streamers work best; can be rigged off downrigger for light tackle fishing.

Spoons and hootchies are the most popular trolling lures, by far, in Alaska. Super strong, single hooks always fish best.

Ways to Rig Herring

Whole

"Plug-cut"

With bait action enhancer like "Salmon Killer"or "Herring Aid"

Diving Planers can be used instead of heavy lead weights, to take line down to depth

"Deep Six"

Lure or bait fished alone or with attractor

To 200 Feet

← 15 to 60 feet →

← 6 to 30 feet →

Flasher

Attractor (flasher) usually run as part of terminal rigging, in front of lure or bait. Can be run alone, off cannonball (as shown) or line clip, for fishing multiple lines ("stacking").

Continued from page 159

The Art of Trolling

For the wide range of conditions encountered in Alaska's waters, trolling remains the single most productive method of saltwater salmon angling, from Ketchikan to Kodiak.

Borrowing heavily from the hard won wisdom of the commercial fleet, sport trollers' refined rigging and techniques vary with location, time of year, and species sought after, but the basics remain the same: presenting bait or lures at proper depth and speed and with the right action to elicit response from salmon.

Specialized gear for trolling (downriggers and diving planers) allows for multiple lines to be fished at various depths off the back and sides of the boat, greatly increasing chances for success.

Using visual cues and electronic aids, plus a knowledge of local waters, to locate salmon is essential, as fish concentrate in certain areas for feeding and migrating. The successful troller must also find the right combination of speed and depth to put his enticements in the "strike zone."

But the real art of trolling is in the rigging and presentation, how the captain uses a variety of well known, novel, and even arcane tactics to play on the fishes' instincts for arousal. The use of attractors (flashers and dodgers), bright finishes/colors, and scent are common ways of bringing fish in from distances. But many experienced fishermen believe that having the proper movement of the lure or bait is critical and use specially cut or rigged herring or secret lures that have just the right spin or wobble when pulled through the water. Some even maintain that electromagnetic charge influences fish behavior and have special devices hooked to the hull or downrigger to alter the charge surrounding the boat and rigging.

ers (usually within the first 40 feet) and are attracted to a faster pulled enticement. A typical three-line array for kings might include a lure/bait run deep, say 60-90 feet (or more); one at medium depth, 30-50 feet; and one shallow line somewhere around 20 feet, run at a trolling speed of 2-3 knots (or less). Coho can be effectively prospected using medium (30 feet) and shallow (15 feet) depth lines, with a faster troll speed (up to 5 knots). To mix up the array with bait and lures is a common and very effective practice.

Diligence is required to keep the lines from fouling and the downrigger from hanging up on any underwater hazards. When a fish of any size hits one of the baits/lures, the resistance will usually pop the line from the downrigger clip, or spring the diving planer open. (On lures/baits trolled with weights, the fish will usually bury the rod tip and hook itself.) The alert angler must grab the rod and reel quickly, to take up any slack, before setting the hook firmly. By varying the speed and direction of the troll, a skipper can greatly affect the action and depth of the baits/lures, sometimes prompting strikes from salmon. (Most skippers will troll either with or across the direction of the tide, since salmon usually face into the current.)

Mooching

Mooching is a popular, enjoyable, and very effective saltwater technique for fishing bait in areas where fish tend to be deeper and/or concentrated by currents or structure. Because the bait can move through the water column, it is a more efficient and intensive way of working water when fish are not actively feeding near the surface. In contrast to trolling, where the boat operator controls the action of all baits, each moocher (in the same boat) controls his or her own bait, imparting action to elicit a strike response or, sometimes, coaxing salmon to engulf a bait that they might otherwise just play with. In Southeast, most of what is referred to as "mooching" is "motor mooching," or "power mooching," rather than drift mooching with live bait, as is commonly practiced in British Colombia. In certain areas of the state, like Prince of Wales Island (SE), it is the main method employed by the charter fleet.

The preferred bait for mooching in Alaska is frozen, cut herring. Most anglers remove the heads with a combination angle and bevel cut. This cut provides the spin or roll that attracts salmon. As a general rule, a greater angled cut is made when targeting

Bait For Alaska's Saltwater Salmon

Despite all the advances in gear and lures, trolling or "mooching" bait remains far and away the most productive way of taking Alaska's saltwater king and silver salmon, if you believe the fishing derby records and salty old charter boat captains. And a properly handled and rigged herring will generally outfish anything else over a broad range of conditions. Using fresh, if possible (or flash frozen if not), small to medium-sized fish (three to five inches) for coho, larger (to seven inches) for king salmon, the herring is rigged whole, "plug cut" or in a bait harness (like the "Herring Aid" or "Salmon Killer"—see trolling illustration), according to preference, to impart a tantalizing spin (either a tight fast roll, favored by coho anglers, or big lazy spirals, preferred by king salmon fishermen) that mimics a stunned or maimed baitfish when dragged or drifted behind the boat. Most trollers fish their herring behind an attractor (flasher or dodger), with weights, diving planers, or downriggers used to reach proper depth.

A very effective way of rigging whole herring is "choking." Choked herring retain their shapes better than "cut plug" herring at speeds required in trolling. Anglers use a double hook, slip tie leader, to place a bend in the herring, again attaining a roll that imitates wounded or stunned bait. Some anglers use a toothpick to aid in keeping the bend. Also employed, at times, are small clips placed on the nose to keep the herring's mouth closed.

silvers than when targeting kings, since silvers prefer a faster spin. (However, many times, both are caught on the same baits in mixed stock situations.)

Attractors are not used, with the leader running straight off the banana lead (one to six ounces) five to nine feet to the bait. Fishing with the tides, line is stripped or slowly free-spooled from the reel until the rig hits the desired depth (usually above bottom). The bait is then worked by the action of the drift, by retrieving line, or with a slight troll (motor mooching), the most efficient way being determined by the tides, concentration of fish, prevailing winds, and/or personal preference.

Motor Mooching

In motor mooching, the motor is used to alter the speed of the drift. The boat operator will generally attempt to track true with the drift in order to keep the lines parallel with the boat. (This is especially important when fishing in heavy currents, or when there are several anglers fishing out of the same boat.) As a general rule, the lines are kept at a 45° angle from the rod. This will vary according to the situation. The angle is necessary in order to maintain a constant roll and spin of the bait.

The bait is "worked" by anglers as they reel at a slow to moderate speed. When the angler pauses, the bait continues to roll and spin because of the drift. This alteration of speeds is a factor in eliciting strike responses. By alternately "free spooling" line out and subsequently reeling, the angler more effectively covers a desired portion of the water column. (Recent fishing reports, presence of salmon and/or baitfish on the depth sounder/fish finder screen, or recent personal experience will determine the desired depth.) A reel with a level wind guide (or feet counter) is strongly recommended, as is it imperative to know the approximate depth that is being fished. The Penn 109 and Penn Mag 10 are time tested and reliable. They are durable, have a fairly high gear ratio, and are lightweight. There are other good reels for mooching including the Shimano, models Bantam-50, G-100, and Charter Special.

Of virtues required for mooching, patience is paramount. Though professional guides are divided on how to specifically respond to the bite (some encourage paying out line, while others support reeling), all agree that one MUST NOT set the hook while the salmon is biting as, often times, they play with and

The presence of seabirds, especially diving species, is a very good indicator of baitfish below and the possibility of feeding salmon nearby.

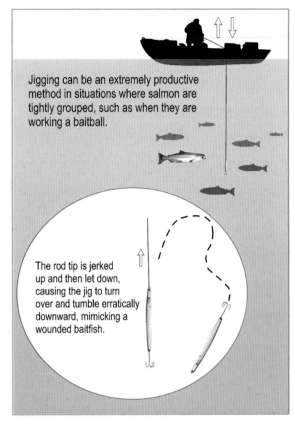

Jigging can be an extremely productive method in situations where salmon are tightly grouped, such as when they are working a baitball.

The rod tip is jerked up and then let down, causing the jig to turn over and tumble erratically downward, mimicking a wounded baitfish.

mouth the bait before engulfing. Experienced guides, therefore, continually preach not to set the hook until the rod loads.

Rods for motor mooching should be sensitive (usually graphite) and fairly long (8 to 10 feet), in order to detect bites and play large fish well. Good mooching rods are medium action to moderate action when compared to salmon jigging rods. The Kenai Special and Kenai King by Lamiglas are good rods for silvers and kings respectively. Lamiglas and G. Loomis are among companies that produce a number of fine rods suitable for motor mooching.

Jigging

Jigging is another extremely effective method; in fact, it can be the most effective in situations where salmon are concentrated around structure or bait patches. Salmon anglers in the Pacific Northwest have known this for years, as jigging is very popular there. Jigs are, in fact, the oldest used fishing lures in history. Although in Alaska it is still a somewhat obscure technique compared to trolling or mooching, it is practiced with a high level of success by a small cadre of anglers and charter captains, mostly in Southeast.

Of all techniques used for salmon, jigging is the most demanding. The success of the angler is dependent upon locating the salmon and also upon manipulating the jig properly to elicit the strike response. Jigging is much more like hunting than other methods. Anglers are advised to not even begin fishing

until signs of fish are present. This may involve moving from location to location until baitfish or salmon are observed on one's depth sounder/fish finder screen, or other obvious signs of fish are present (milling, diving seabirds).

Most serious jiggers fish around the tide change, as jigs should be fished only vertically. The lures are lowered to the desired depth based upon information from the fish finder. The angler briskly works the rod up, then down to the water's surface, causing the jig to turn over and flutter erratically downward, mimicking the action of a stunned and wounded baitfish.

The boat skipper, as in fishing other techniques, has a great deal of control over everyone's lines. When fishing in tidal currents and windy conditions the boat must be kept in position by shifting the motor in and out of reverse, "backing down" against the drift. This is imperative to keep the lines fishing vertically, and the boat in the area where baitfish and salmon have been observed on the fish finder screen. Attention to boat control is often the difference between success and failure between two boats fishing the same area, using the same jigs.

Lures for Alaska's Saltwater Salmon

When salmon are concentrated and actively feeding, trolling, casting, or jigging lures can be the most exciting and efficient way to fish.

Some of the more famous spoons that have proven themselves over the years for both commercial and sport trolling are the Coyote, Manistee, Point Defiance, Canadian Wonder, Superior, McMahon, Diamond King, Krocodile, Clendon Stewart, Tom Mack, Lou Pac, and Katchmac, in sizes #5 to #8, and colors of chrome, nickel, brass, bronze, gold, mother-of-pearl, blue, green, yellow, chartreuse, white, pink, black, and red. The most popular casting spoons in Alaska are the Pixee, Krocodile, Hotrod, Syclops, Dardevle, Kastmaster, and Cast Champ, sizes ½ to 2-ounce, in colors of silver, nickel, brass, green, blue, red, white, and pink.

Plugs have also been traditional favorites for trolling, with the Tomic, J-Plug, Apex, Hot Shot, Kwikfish, Flatfish, Magnum Rapala, and Yo-Zuri Crystal Minnow, in sizes 4 to 7 inch, and colors of silver, pearl, blue, green, yellow, and red being most popular in Alaska. For jigging, Alaska anglers use mostly the Teazer, Chinook Special, Swedish Pimple, Dart, Stinger, Nordic, and Buzz Bomb, ranging in size from one to six ounces, with three to four ounce and colors of nickel, gold, opaque green, blue, and white being the most popular. Medium-large spinners like the Super Vibrax, Mepps Aglia, Bolo, Teespoon, and Clearwater Flash are also used, mostly for casting, in colors of silver, gold, brass, red, yellow, white, and green.

Most strikes come as the jig is falling. (Reel drags should be tightened down completely, as even very little slippage can keep a salmon from being hooked.) Hook sets should be fast and brutal. Effective jiggers set once, immediately reel down to the water, set and reel down again, before backing off on the drag to fight the fish. Jig-hooked salmon are fought with care in an attempt to keep the fishes' heads under water, as salmon can easily throw a jig that is flailing in the air. (Hooks should be kept extremely sharp, and knots—the Palomar is recommended—retied often, as jigging is more abusive to fishing line than other methods.)

Jigging rods differ greatly from those for trolling or mooching, as they are selected more for their hook-setting capabilities than for their fighting capabilities. A fast taper, medium-heavy to heavy action, in lengths from 7 to 8 ½ feet is ideal. Lamiglas, St.Croix, G. Loomis, and GX Custom each produce fine salmon jigging rods. Lightweight reels with high gear ratios are generally used. (See reel recommendations for mooching. These reels serve the dual purposes of mooching and jigging.)

Using the right line is very important in jigging. Monofilament lines that don't stretch much are preferred, to insure a solid hook set. Brand names such as Ande, Berkley Big Game, and Inshore work well, as do copolymers such as Bagley's AN 40. The newer braided multiple strand lines, such as Tough Line and Cabela's Ripcord, are extremely strong, are half the diameter of conventional monofilament, and stretch hardly at all. Yet anglers need to exhibit some restraint when hook setting in shallow water with these "unforgiving lines," as rods can easily be broken.

Casting

Casting lures from shore or boats can be extremely effective when salmon are concentrated and relatively shallow. Late season coho, in particular, are usually aggressive, near the surface, and easily spotted working bait patches or marauding around bays and along beaches. If an angler can get within range from shore or with a boat, a well placed, bright spoon, jig, or even spinner can often result in hookups and some of Alaska's most enjoyable sport, particularly on the lighter tackle used for this kind of fishing. Chums, pinks and, in some areas, terminal hatchery kings can be taken in the same manner at the appropriate time of year, using many lures that are the same as those used in freshwater (see sidebar for details), with the

Shore casting for salmon along the road system at Valdez, Southcentral Alaska.

Fishing prespawning salmon in their final bay and estuary destinations can sometimes be very productive

addition of small keel sinkers, one to three ounces, to get the lure down, if needed.

Shore casting opportunities abound in nearly every community along Alaska's southern coast. Some, like those found around Valdez, Homer, Seward, or Kodiak, are among the most popular marine fisheries in Alaska. Check with locals for information on the best spots. (Many are listed in this book.)

TERMINAL/TIDEWATER SALMON

The search for salmon in the marine environment becomes greatly simplified when they reach their inshore destinations and congregate in straits and bays, along beaches, and around estuaries and river mouths, waiting for the right conditions (high stream water levels, high tides, physiological changes, etc.) to enter fresh water. Indeed, the majority of effort along the more accessible stretches of Alaska's southern coast targets terminal and tidewater salmon, as they most often can be pursued without benefit of fancy boats or specialized gear.

But since most of these fish are pretty far along in the prespawning changes described earlier, the fishing can be anything but a sure thing, as the salmon stop feeding and become very unpredictable in their response to traditional techniques. Nowhere is this more true than in tidewater, when salmon make their push into the mouths of rivers and streams.

Anglers targeting wild salmon in estuaries and river mouths have traditionally worked the tides, favoring the period of flood right after the slack, when fish make the surge up through brackish shallows and are concentrated and easily targeted. Using mostly freshwater casting spoons, jigs, and spinners in colors of silver, gold, blue, green, yellow, and pink, they are frequently able to elicit strike responses from the more testy fish. Flyfishermen using attractor patterns (both fresh and salt water) can do just as well, sometimes even better, than hardware slingers.

But, just as common, these fish may show total indifference to a conventionally presented lure or fly, though they may be jumping and milling about in great excitement. Frustrated anglers experimenting with erratic retrieves, dark colored or smaller lures, or novel patterns/presentations will sometimes be able to rouse a bite from these salmon that are locked into their inmigration mode. Though the various species behave differently in these conditions (pinks and silvers seem more prone to hit than kings and chums; sockeyes always are most elusive), the overall success rate with these fish is much lower than with salmon out in the salt.

Terminal hatchery fisheries create a new class of fishing, as the salmon undergo their total spawning metamorphosis in salt or brackish waters. Depending on how far along these fish may be, on a whole, they tend to range shallower and be more aggressive and less temperamental than wild salmon. They also show more light sensitivity and are more prone to bite early and late in the day (in a trolling study done on a terminal king fishery in southern Southeast, 45% of the catch occurred before 7:30 A.M.). With liberal bag limits and often easy access, these fisheries are extremely productive and growing in popularity.

Surf casting for silvers, southern Afognak Island, southcentral Alaska

SPECIALIZED TECHNIQUES FOR OCEAN SOCKEYE, CHUM, & PINK

Compared to the nearshore fishing situations described in the two previous sections, very little sport fishing effort occurs offshore for Alaska's pink, chum, and sockeye salmon. Most are taken incidentally while trolling or mooching king or silver salmon, but they can be successfully targeted in some areas, using specialized techniques.

Sockeyes, for various reasons, have always been fished minimally, mostly in areas of Southeast by commercial trollers. Using flashers or dodgers rigged in front of small, sparse hoochies, spoons, streamers, and even bare, colored hooks (red Gamakatsu), they are able to interest the notoriously reticent salmon into striking, though not with the consistency seen in waters farther south. The most productive colors seem to be pink, fluorescent red/orange, blue, green, white, and purple. Downriggers, diving planers (Pink Lady), or salmon sinkers (up to 16 ounces) are used to reach proper depth, which can vary considerably and is usually determined by trial or with fish locators. A very slow trolling speed and frequent direction changes are used to induce strike responses. Inlets, bays, straits, and points along major sockeye migration routes are the best areas to concentrate on.

Chums are similarly pursued by a relatively small number of sport and charter boats, mostly in Southeast and in Southcentral's Prince William Sound. This is especially paradoxical when one considers the great numbers in which they exist relative to kings and silvers. Some captains, like Eddie Lucas of Sweet Success Charters in Ketchikan, have been very successful targeting chums, and are able to consistently produce boat limits on their charters. Like others, Eddie trolls very slowly, and stresses that speed is the number one factor in producing consistent catches. He finds the majority of chums at depths of 70 to 180 feet and recommends using baited and unbaited hoochies behind flashers, with leaders of 36 to 42 inches. The colors of hoochies that have produced best are green/pink, blue/pink, and pink variables in general.

Pink salmon are encountered frequently in great numbers during mid to late summer while trolling or mooching for other species like silvers, and can be a nuisance when more desirable quarry is the goal. They can be targeted using small, sparse (plucked) pink or red hoochies; bright, medium-sized spoons, jigs, or small herring trolled behind flashers or dodgers at slow speeds, working bait patches and tide rips at relatively shallow depths.

SALTWATER FLYFISHING

Compared to other parts of the Pacific Northwest, saltwater flyfishing in Alaska remains in its infancy, presently confined to waters in Southeast and select areas along Southcentral's North Gulf coast (Prince William Sound, Seward, Kodiak, and Lower Cook Inlet/Kachemak Bay).

Aside from the concentrated and more easily fished opportunities presented by prespawning salmon staged in salt chucks and bays, along beaches, and around river mouths, Alaska's ocean environment for the most part presents a daunting challenge to the fly angler.

With its rugged coast, frequent bad weather and rough seas, it can overwhelm and threaten the safety of anglers, particularly in the unsheltered, but potentially very productive outside waters. Quite often the salmon, especially chinook, are located too deep for practical fishing with conventional methods or they may be totally uninterested in flies. Many of the best areas are remote and difficult and expensive to access. And the number of charter boat captains familiar with and prepared to deal with the special needs of flyfishermen is pitifully small at present.

Here, as elsewhere, the challenge is in locating concentrations of shallow feeding salmon. Anglers traditionally work the same areas that they would with bait or hardware—around points, islands, reefs, kelp beds, bait patches, tide rips, etc.—using the same fish locating strategies outlined earlier, but more selectively, in hopes of finding conditions ideal to fly casting. Working the tides (and the time of day) becomes much more critical, from the standpoint of the bite, depth of the fish, and getting a good drift, so careful planning is important.

Since conditions favorable to flyfishing cannot be counted on with any consistency, many anglers take a more practical approach and bring conventional trolling or mooching gear along, so the day is not wasted if the opportunity does not arise for flycasting. This philosophy can be very useful on charters, with an amenable captain and group of like-minded anglers, who may want to fish hard for limits early and devote the latter part of the day to the challenge of raising some fish on a fly and releasing them.

Alaska chinook present a special challenge. Aside from some very limited wild tidewater opportunities and a few well-known (and heavily fished) terminal hatchery fisheries, much of the state's better fishing will be had tracking down prespawners that are still migrating, staging, or feeding at depths shallow enough for the fly. The most promising areas will be those that lie along major migration routes (particularly those outside), with an abundance and variety of features (islands, points, inlets, reefs, rocks, kelp beds, dropoffs, etc.) that attract fish and provide maximum opportunities for finding shallow-feeding kings. Some of the best areas to explore with these conditions are in Southeast: the west coast of Prince of Wales Island (accessed from Craig and Klawock); lower Chatham and Keku straits and Kuiu Island (accessed from Kake); Stephans Passage and Upper Chatham Strait (accessed from Juneau or Angoon); Sitka/Salisbury sounds and the west side of Chichagof and Baranof Islands (accessed from Sitka); and lower Clarence Strait and Behm Canal (accessed from Ketchikan). Shallow water king opportunities are much more rare and sporadic in Southcentral, occurring mostly in certain areas of lower Cook Inlet, Kachemak Bay and Kodiak.

Unless you can locate some shallow-feeding salmon, you'll be called to use high-density (500 to 1150 grain, Type V-IX), sinking lines and tungsten core shooting heads. Large baitfish patterns and attractors, fished with an erratic, (but not too fast) strip are usually most productive. Some of the specialized techniques used for improving the odds with these ocean chinook include running snubbed flashers off downriggers to lure them within range, fishing alongside bait moochers (occasionally chinook will follow a trolled or mooched herring up to the boat) and trolling flies off downriggers (see below).

Coho are much more amenable to the limitations of flyfishing in Alaska's saltwaters. They are abundant, rambunctious, and encountered quite frequently shallow or on the surface, especially late in the season when they school up and work bait patches or cruise shorelines. They are notoriously cooperative when presented with a lively stripped baitfish streamer at the proper depth. With a little luck, you can encounter good conditions for flyfishing them in quite a few locations along the North Gulf Coast (PWS, Seward and Kodiak) and countless waters in Southeast, from mid-July into September.

Trolling and "bucktailing" streamer flies, common practices for coho (and pink salmon) in British Columbia and other waters down south, are done only infrequently in Alaska, but can be very productive. To do this, it is best to use a mooching reel spooled with 15 to 20-pound test monofilament and large, bushy, single or tandem hook streamer or tube flies (and keel weights up to six ounces or more if trolling without downriggers). Several rods are usually employed at the same time, pulling flies on the surface and at different depths below using downriggers, to increase the chances of a strike. The flies are trolled 25 to 75 feet behind the boat, usually fast, from three to five knots (or more), with frequent direction changes to incite strikes from following salmon.

Alaska's ubiquitous pink salmon are a blessing or a curse to fly anglers, depending on point of view, as they can literally clog waters with their numbers during late summer in many coastal areas. The best sport is with bright fish, early in the season (July to early August), when they are feeding (along with coho) in bait patches, tide rips, and around kelp beds. They can be taken on just about any small to medium-sized (size #2 to #6) baitfish, forage, or bright attractor pattern, fished with a lively, erratic strip. Southeast Alaska, and Southcentral's Prince William Sound and Kodiak, have the best flyfishing conditions.

Ocean chums usually run too deep for flycasters, except in tidewater or terminal fisheries. They will sometimes succumb to a lively stripped attractor or baitfish imitation in color combinations of green, white, blue, and silver. Sockeyes are perennially tight-lipped, whether fished in rivers or the sea, and rarely does the saltwater angler encounter them, other than in tidewater situations, in conditions favorable to fly-casting. They can sometimes be tempted with sparse bucktail, rabbit fur or yarn attractor, or shrimp patterns, size #2 to #6, in colors of pink, orange, green, or red, in areas where they concentrate during their (prespawning) migrations. Kachemak Bay, Kodiak, parts of Prince William Sound, and southern Southeast are the best places to try.

Fly Patterns/Lines

Productive flies for Alaska's saltwater salmon fishing include: traditional Northwest bucktail baitfish streamers; classic saltwater attractors; shrimp, euphasid, and other forage patterns; some standard, Alaska saltwater patterns; and local creations sold in shops and tackle stores along the coast. Hook sizes range anywhere from #8 to #5/0, and the most productive colors seem to be combinations of silver, white, yellow, green, pink, blue, purple, red, and

Flies for Alaska's saltwater salmon include many familiar Northwest baitfish, attractor, and forage patterns, plus some Alaska standards.

orange. A remarkable variety of new synthetic materials available today add a great measure of flash, durability, and fish appeal to many traditional patterns.

Fly lines for Alaska's saltwater salmon run the gamut from floaters to the deepest dredgers, and everything in between, to match the many different conditions encountered. Many new, specialty saltwater lines, in addition to versatile, interchangeable tips and ultra high density shooting heads, are available to increase performance and efficiency in ways never before imagined. For most fishing, you can narrow your line selection to a medium to heavy density sink tip or two (15 to 24 feet), a full sink saltwater line, 400-850 grain or heavier (depending on rod weight), plus maybe a super high density shooting head or two (30 feet, Type V-IX, depending on conditions/rod size), if you desire. Tippets used for Alaska's saltwater salmon vary from 8 to 20 pounds.

Top Fly Patterns for Alaska Saltwater Salmon

Herring Fly, Clouser Minnow, Deceiver, Lambuth Candlefish, Alaska Candlefish, Smolt, Sandlance, Needlefish, Seaducer, Baitfish, Whistler, Tarpon Fly, Coronation, Pollywog, Shrimp, Euphausid, Coho, Crazy Charlie, Egg Sucking Leech, Comet, Bunny Fly, Salmon Trolling Fly, Squid, Crab.

Fly-caught, tidewater king, northern Southeast Alaska.

"Matching the Hatch" for Alaska's saltwater salmon.

GEARING UP FOR SALTWATER SALMON

For general saltwater trolling, most Alaska anglers opt for a medium-fast action, medium-heavy to heavy weight trolling or downrigger rod (rated 12 to 30-pound line), seven to nine-and-a-half feet long, to handle the increased resistance from weights, flashers, planers, etc. A high quality, levelwind inshore trolling reel (Shimano TLD or Tekota, Daiwa Sealine, Ambassadeur 7000, etc.) capable of holding at least 250 yards of 25-pound test is used. Lighter gear can be employed when fishing from downriggers: a medium-fast action, medium-weight (rated 12 to 20-pound line), seven to eight-and-a-half feet trolling or downrigger rod, with a heavy freshwater or light saltwater trolling reel (Ambassadeur 6000 to 7000, Shimano Calcutta, Okuma Convector, etc.) loaded with 250 yards 12 to 20-pound line.

For spin or bait casting saltwater salmon, a medium-heavy to heavy-weight (8 to 25-pound line range) medium-fast action, seven to eight-and-a-half feet long, steelhead or salmon rod is generally used, with a matching high quality reel loaded with 200 yards of 8 to 20 pound test line.

For mooching in Alaska, most anglers use a special, long (eight to ten feet), limber, medium-fast action, medium to heavy-weight (10 to 30-pound line range) mooching rod, mated with a high quality bait-casting or mooching reel (see mooching sections for details) capable of holding several hundred yards of 12 to 20-pound test line.

Jigging rods are generally seven to eight-and-a-half-feet, fast action, with a cuestick taper for working lures vertically and producing a strong hookset. Reels are generally the same size as those used for trolling or mooching, with strong drags, and spooled with 25 to 40-pound mono on braided line.

Flyfishermen will need to use either: a 6-7 weight, medium-fast action, eight to nine-foot, high performance flyrod for pink salmon; an 8 to 9 weight, medium-fast action, nine to ten-foot, high performance flyrod for silver, chum, and sockeye salmon; or a 10 to 12 weight, medium-fast action, nine to ten-foot, high performance flyrod for king salmon. Matching reels should be high quality, light to heavy salmon class, spooled with at least 200 yards of 20 to 30-pound backing.

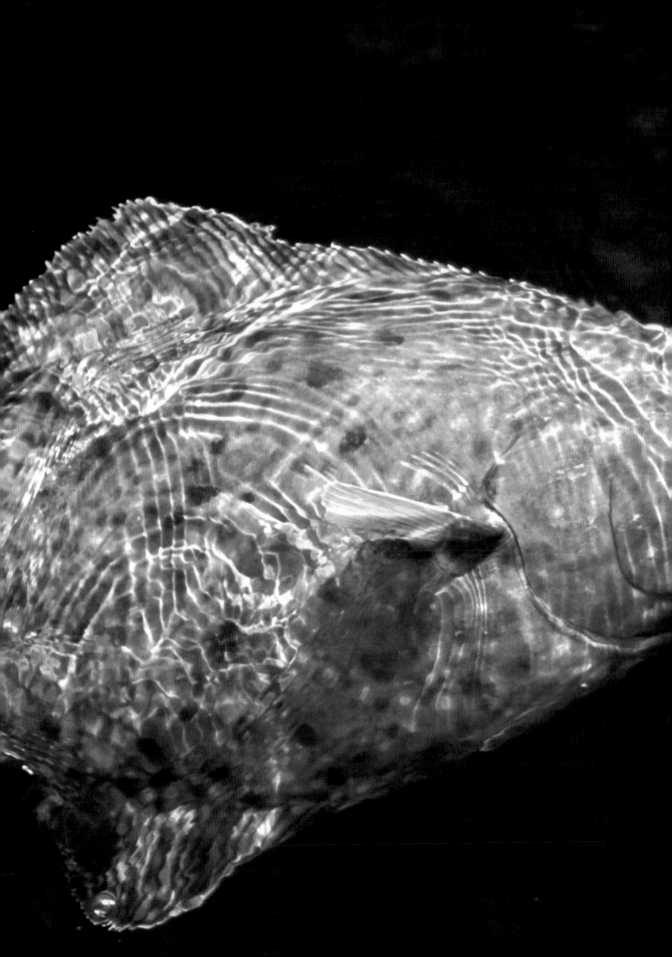

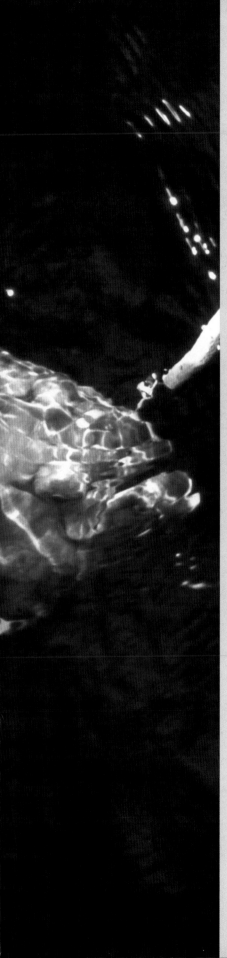

Halibut
Denizen of the Deep

A taste of the excitement that sportfishing for halibut can provide came on a picture-perfect day early one August in Southcentral Alaska. A three-hour run on calm seas south from the port of Homer took the charter boat *Sourdough* past sea otters, puffins, and porpoises to the rugged Barren Islands of lower Cook Inlet. Shirtsleeve weather, no wind, and a miniscule three-foot tide change promised pleasant sun tanning, if nothing else.

Hopes were high when I lowered a whole herring 150 feet to the bottom. It undulated slowly as I gently raised and lowered the 20-ounce sinker, occasionally tapping bottom to keep the bait in the prime strike zone. Soon the easy tugs of a characteristic halibut bite gave way to a solid pull as a large one inhaled the bait. A ten-minute fight brought the 146-pounder on deck. Impressed with such early success, I opted to help the crew as the other anglers fought bending rods to land impressive prizes of their own. By early afternoon the stern was awash with the white undersides of big halibut.

With only a half-hour left to fish, I rebaited and immediately hooked another big one. Weighing 102 pounds back at the dock, it bookended my first double 100-pounder day and pushed the boat's total for the trip to eleven fish of more than 100 pounds. What a fantastic rack of fish from a glorious day on the water!

Halibut action, Dutch Harbor/Unalaska, Alaska Peninsula, Southwest Alaska.

PACIFIC HALIBUT: DENIZENS OF THE DEEP

The Pacific halibut, *Hippoglossus stenolepis,* is renowned as a premium eating fish, but has only recently come into its own as a sport fish, with the development of light, strong gear and the techniques to match. Although halibut are available as far north as Norton Sound, present sport effort is concentrated along the Gulf of Alaska from Ketchikan through Southcentral's Prince William Sound, Cook Inlet, and Kodiak Island. From there, it ranges out to virgin territory near Dutch Harbor/Unalaska in the Aleutian Islands.

With a charter fleet of more than 150 boats, Homer in Southcentral Alaska has been justifiably proud of its ranking as the world capital of halibut sportfishing. It has been eclipsed in recent years, however, by the 270-boat fleet that launches into Cook Inlet about 30 miles north at Deep Creek. Once available to small boats only, 28-foot, six-passenger vessels access this water from the beach using tractors or skidders. The high volume commercial port of Dutch Harbor/Unalaska is the rising star of halibut sportfishing with the current IGFA All Tackle World Record fish of 459 pounds taken there in June 1996. A 439-pounder in 1995 hinted at what was to come, as did commercial catches in recent years of giants weighing more than 500 pounds.

Fishing for halibut is enjoyable on many levels. Alaska's marine environment entices with seals, whales, and myriad sea birds. The big flatfish share waters with other edible species such as rockfish, lingcod, and salmon, all of which take baits meant for halibut. It's a fish that almost any angler with patience, who can tolerate a day on the ocean, has a chance to hook and, with care, has a good chance to boat. Noted outdoorsman Jay Massey likened halibut fishing to big game hunting in that a trophy may appear at any time, often when least expected.

A halibut's bite is rarely like a freight train's plummet out of nowhere. Usually it's just nibbles and tugs that eventually culminate in a rod-yanking pull. The pull is your cue to drive home the hook with a short,

DESCRIPTION

As a member of the right eye flounder family and the largest flatfish of the Pacific Coast, the halibut can reach immense proportions. Commercial catches to 550 pounds and nine-and-a-half feet in length have been reported. Fish in excess of 100 pounds are common in many areas of the state, particularly in off-shore locations that receive little or no pressure. However, the average halibut taken by sport anglers is much more modest and falls in the 10 to 40-pound range, with the yearly heaviest 'but weighing in at 400 pounds or so. It's interesting to note that all very large halibut are females; males rarely exceed 50 pounds. (And, a blessing to anglers, females far outnumber the males of the species.)

Aside from their occasional "barn door" size, halibut are fairly easily recognized. The body shape is more elongated than other species of flounders, the width being approximately one-third the length. Scales are small and smooth, with the lateral line forming a high arc over the pectoral fin. The mouth is quite small, not extending past the middle of the lower eye, and contains well-developed teeth on both sides of the jaw. Coloration tends to vary with the bottom environment of its habitat, but is usually dark brown or green to gray on the topside, with the bottom uniformly white. This allows halibut to avoid detection by both prey and predator.

RANGE, ABUNDANCE & STATUS

Pacific halibut range along the North Pacific from central California to northern Japan. In Alaska, they are found in varying abundance from Cape Muzon in Southeast up through the Gulf of Alaska to the Bering Sea, and on to Point Hope along the Arctic. The most important fisheries occur in British Columbia, Southeast and Southcentral Alaska, and the Bering Sea.

For centuries, the halibut has been a key source of subsistence for indigenous Pacific coast peoples. Much of their folklore mythologizes the fish. Native Americans carved immaculate designs on their ivory fish hooks to ensure good luck and large fish. Today, anglers of all backgrounds hunt this white-fleshed monster, with the majority of sport effort originating in major coastal ports such as Ketchikan, Sitka, Petersburg, and Juneau in the Southeast region, and Valdez, Homer, Seward, and Kodiak in Southcentral. More than 65% of the statewide harvest (about 1.5 million

sharp strike. Depending on its size, and other factors, the fish may make a determined run, struggle vainly close to the boat, or just lay there. The first and last actions indicate good size. The battle may go back and forth for five minutes to two hours as the angler tries to pump the fish up to the boat. Larger fish may come up with little fuss, only to see the surface and dive all the way to the bottom.

Immediately after a hookup, and often during the fight, a good-sized halibut gives a characteristic head-shake as it attempts to shed the hook. The strength of that shake and the sheer mass against which the angler pulls can be enough to give goose bumps of anticipation until the behemoth finally materializes out of the depths. Then the cry, "I've got color!" as the fish sideslips, flashing its white belly, triggers rapid action on deck to prepare gaff, harpoon, and firearm to safely subdue and land the beast. The best finally comes once the chef is done in the kitchen and serves this delectable white fish for dinner.

pounds) comes from Southcentral Alaska (primarily lower Cook Inlet and Kodiak Island). Due to the fish's popularity, this number increases steadily, despite current regulations for a two fish of any size daily limit.

LIFE HISTORY & HABITS

Male halibut become sexually mature at age seven or eight, females slightly later at 8 to 12 years. Concentrations of spawning fish are found in deep water along the continental shelf during winter months (November through March), with peak activity occurring from December to February. Females may produce 2 to 3-million eggs that hatch after two weeks and become free-floating larvae, drifting hundreds of miles with ocean currents. After six months, the larvae's fish-like forms begin to flatten and their left eyes migrate to their right side. Juvenile halibut spend their first few years on the bottom of shallow, inshore waters (the Bering Sea is a major nursery ground for growing flatties). Young halibut move to deeper water at around age five and eventually commit extensive migrations that may range 2,000 miles or more, moving in a clockwise direction east and south throughout the Gulf of Alaska.

Occupying depths between 60 and 3,600 feet, halibut thrive on flat-bottomed structure such as sand, fine gravel, mud, and clay. Adult diet consists of fish (mainly cod, turbot, and pollock, but also sand lance and herring), squid, crab, shrimp, clams, and marine worms. Females grow faster, reach greater weight, and live longer (up to 45 years) than males. The growth rate depends largely on location, food availability, and other factors. For example, in recent years fish in Cook Inlet have declined in their weight-to-age ratio while those in the Aleutians seem particularly fat.

FISHING FOR ALASKA'S HALIBUT

Alaska sport anglers catch well over a half million halibut every year, most of them from the waters surrounding Southcentral's Kenai Peninsula. A significant number are taken from Southeast, in the waters off Prince of Wales Island, Sitka, Juneau, and Glacier Bay. Since halibut are highly migratory and move inshore and offshore according to the seasons, anglers do best in late spring, summer, and fall when fish feed in fairly shallow coastal areas. In winter, the fish are situated too deep and far from shore to be accessible to most sport anglers. However, in some trenches near

the Gulf, anglers can catch smaller fish fairly regularly throughout the cold months.

Tidal-influenced depressions, major channels, tidal rips, reefs, and shelves bordering steep drop-offs are prime areas since these attract bait fish and, subsequently, voracious halibut. Also, stream mouths can be seasonally productive, since 'buts often gather there in late summer and fall in anticipation of salmon carcasses washing out to sea. The best catches there are made in 30 to 60 feet of water, with some locations producing good catches down to 300 feet— especially early and late in the season, as the fish are in transition between offshore spawning and inshore feeding grounds. In summer, depths of 100 to 250 feet can produce decent catches. Many successful anglers and, especially, guides, use sonar recorders and hydrographic charts in identifying likely areas.

GEARING UP

Rods

Thanks to new materials, rods are shorter and lighter, yet stronger than ever. Gone are the days of the six-and-a-half-foot, solid fiberglass, "pool cue" action trolling rod. It has been replaced by a five-and-a-half-foot, fast taper, high-strength fiberglass or graphite composite stand-up rod. Metal guides now have competition from high-tech metallic oxide guides that reduce friction and dissipate heat while resisting line wear. Long foam foregrips and foot-long butt sections allow anglers to tuck rods closely to their bodies, giving leverage for battling big fish. Gimbal fittings keep rods from rolling laterally as fish are fought to the surface. Light to medium line test-rated rods are 30 to 80 pounds or 40/50 to 100 pounds. Heavy rods rate at 80 to 130 pounds. These are highly arbitrary designations determined by each manufacturer. Bend the tip and test the action for yourself. The heaviest rods handle large sinkers when tides run high, such as in Cook Inlet's 26-footers.

Many rods are equipped with a roller tip, which acts like a pulley to ease taking in line under stress. Look for ones with close tolerances, since the thinner lines can wedge between the roller and the frame, causing fraying and breakage. Also, the rod must be kept upright, so that the tip is perpendicular to the horizon, for the roller to work properly. Many rod builders avoid this problem by using complete sets of

30-50 lb. class, graphite, high-speed, lever-drag reels, like the Penn Formula two-speed series (shown), make excellent choices for the new synthetic line halibut angler.

metallic oxide guides. With full circle eyelets, the rod can even be fished upside down if necessary! These rods work well in a holder or in the hands of any easily distracted anglers. They're nice for jigging, too. If you buy only one rod, get this kind.

An excellent all-around rod length is five-and-a-half-feet. Those fishing exclusively with bait might enjoy a five-footer, where a jigger would appreciate a six-foot model. Those in small boats fishing close to the water should use shorter rods to make hook setting easier. In general, use shorter rods for greater lifting power and ease of handling. Light tips increase sensitivity and the enjoyment of fighting smaller fish, yet sturdy butt sections give the backbone needed to control and land big ones.

Regarding materials, uniform diameter, solid fiberglass blanks have given way to hollow, high-strength fiberglass (S or E glass) which is lighter, more flexible, and more sensitive. However, Penn has led a resurgence in solid fiberglass by offering tapered blanks that approximate the feel of hollow glass, but which are much more durable under rough handling and cost less. G. Loomis offers hybrid rods that blend graphite and fiberglass. You'll find many quality hollow glass rods of standard guide configuration.

Reels

Your reel must be sturdy and saltwater resistant with a good drag system. The latest reels feature technological advances such as graphite components for lightness and strength, improved drag washers for smoothness, and a viable level wind capability. Lever drags with pre-set strike settings and larger drag surfaces than the old style star drags give instant, smooth control of line release that makes light line fishing a practical reality.

In the days of Dacron lines, a 4/0 reel was the smallest that an angler could use to hold the minimum of 200 yards of 80-pound test line required in most waters. Now, with the advent of the thinner Spectra fiber lines, that's the large end of the spectrum. Penn, Shimano, and Daiwa all make quality products, most of which require using your thumb to level the line on the spool when retrieving. However, Penn has introduced the 345 GTI, a graphite level wind that works fine for the angler who uses 50 or 80 pound Dacron. Novices and children like it as it eliminates the sometimes-vexing task of manually leveling the line while trying to fight a fish. It's not recommended for the daily rigors of charter boat fishing, nor can I recommend it for the Spectra lines since it can't cross-lay the line.

A gear ratio of 3:1 or higher is critical for fishing the depths that halibut occupy. Some expensive reels now have two-speed gearing with a low gear for big fish. This helpful technology is worth investigating, although good basic gear is available for a lot less money.

Line

For years the standard line was braided Dacron in 80-pound test. Its virtues include high strength, limited stretch, low memory, freedom from rot, abrasion resistance, and ease of knotting and handling. Its disadvantage is that its relatively large diameter causes it to balloon when pushed by strong currents, which necessitates using heavy sinkers to hold the baited hook on the bottom. In areas with smaller tide changes, 50-pound Dacron can be used by light tackle anglers.

Hard finish, low stretch monofilament in 40 to 60-pound test has proven itself capable of handling big fish in depths of less than 150 feet and light tide changes using bait or with jigs of two to 12 ounces. Brands such as Ande, Maxima, Berkley Big Game, or

Stren High Impact are suitable for this fishing. Mono's inherent stretch acts as a shock absorber to help beat the biggest fish. The usual injunction to constantly check your line for wear doubly applies here.

New lines made of Spectra fibers solve most of these problems. Incredibly thin, yet strong, 80-pound Spectra is the diameter of 20-pound Dacron, and 130-pound Spectra is the size of 30-pound Dacron. Its slick finish combines with the smaller diameter to allow very little water resistance. Anglers can fish at greater depths with less lead than ever before. Abrasion resistance has increased with new generation lines using varied numbers and types of fibers and new line coatings. The lowest stretch of any line means that there is little forgiveness, even with the most limber rods. I've learned to watch for damage as I do with monofilament.

With these lines, you must use special knots like the Palomar knot or Uni knot. Doubling the line to keep it from cutting itself also helps. Use quick setting glue to reinforce and protect your knots. This new technology isn't cheap. Plan to spend 12 to 16 cents per yard for Spectra lines versus four to six cents per yard for braided Dacron. Use care when handling it under pressure since it can act like wire and cut a finger quickly. Lay the line on your reel in a crisscross pattern so that it won't dig into itself, causing the drag to work in a jerky manner that might lose a fish. You may be able to use a lighter drag setting and a short, sharp hook set with this product. These caveats notwithstanding, Spectra is a great step forward in line technology if used properly.

Hooks

The standard hook for years was the O'Shaughnessy in size #10/0 or #12/0. It's been replaced in recent years by the circle hook in size #16/0, #18/0, or #20/0. The O'Shaughnessy is also called the "J" hook for its traditional design. Available in plain or stainless steel, the plain steel is easier to sharpen but requires more care (freshwater rinsing and air-drying) after use than the stainless. This style hook is used in lead head jigs (see the lure illustrations this chapter).

Only light line anglers who want the easy hook setting that a needle sharp, open design model provides should use the O'Shaughnessy. Its defects are major. One is that the angler must maintain constant pressure while reeling up a fish in order to prevent the hook from working free. The second flaw is that it is a

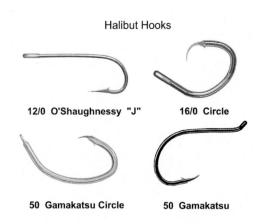

Halibut Hooks

12/0 O'Shaughnessy "J"   16/0 Circle

50 Gamakatsu Circle   50 Gamakatsu

killing hook. Fish swallow it easily, hooking themselves in the gills or in the throat where unhooking leads to serious bleeding. With a daily limit of only two halibut, the urge to release smaller, uninjured fish in order to continue legal fishing for a larger fish creates an ethical dilemma for the conscientious angler. Fortunately, it needn't reach that point, thanks to a second option: the circle hook.

Modern circle hooks were developed by the Japanese commercial fishing industry from an ancient Polynesian design. Long liners needed a self-acting hook that was difficult for fish to dislodge, since their gear often lay on the bottom for a day or longer. Its shape is like a capital "G". The shank is half the length of the J hook's, reducing the fish's leverage to pry it loose. Also, the tip is longer and is bent at a right angle toward the shank, creating the effect of a second barb. It firmly hooks most fish in the lip or in the corner of the mouth. Any pressure imbeds the point deeper, much like the action of a simple corkscrew. In field tests, commercial fishers caught 35% more halibut with this type of hook, yet left fish largely unharmed. Sport fishers eager to practice catch-and-release fishing have taken note and the hook has grown in popularity.

The Mustad model 39965 in size #16/0 is readily available, as is a similar model from Eagle Claw. VMC produces the excellent model 9788 PS in size #3, which has an anodized finish and a round point that is sharp out of the box. Gamakatsu makes an expensive ($7) forged hook in size #45 or #50 that is very sharp and is known for its ability to hook solidly. They all work, especially with the angler's attention to keeping sharp points and tying good knots.

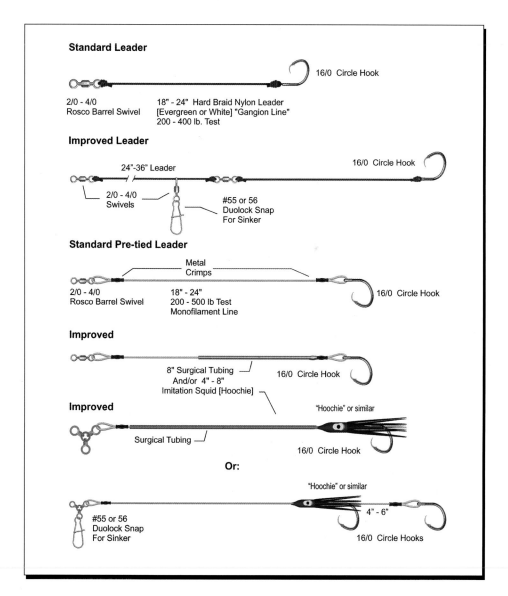

Standard Leader

16/0 Circle Hook

2/0 - 4/0
Rosco Barrel Swivel

18" - 24" Hard Braid Nylon Leader
[Evergreen or White] "Gangion Line"
200 - 400 lb. Test

Improved Leader

24"-36" Leader

16/0 Circle Hook

2/0 - 4/0
Swivels

#55 or 56
Duolock Snap
For Sinker

Standard Pre-tied Leader

Metal
Crimps

2/0 - 4/0
Rosco Barrel Swivel

18" - 24"
200 - 500 lb Test
Monofilament Line

16/0 Circle Hook

Improved

8" Surgical Tubing
And/or 4" - 8"
Imitation Squid [Hoochie]

16/0 Circle Hook

Improved

"Hoochie" or similar

Surgical Tubing

16/0 Circle Hook

Or:

"Hoochie" or similar

4" - 6"

#55 or 56
Duolock Snap
For Sinker

16/0 Circle Hooks

Leaders

Sportfishing leaders are usually 18 to 24 inches long. Green, braided nylon leader line (such as Neptune by Sunset) of 200 to 400-pound test makes superb leaders. Commercial fishing supply stores carry half-pound spools for under $15, which can make more than 100 leaders. Only a cutting tool is required to start, and a flame to singe each end once the tying is done. New leaders can be made on a moment's notice and they're easy on the hand when grabbed to control or boat a fish. This material resists abrasion and stays strong after many uses. You'll find countless other uses for this line on a boat, not least of which is to truss a halibut so that it can't thrash. The standard leader has a hook on one end and a large swivel on the other. My improved version adds 24 to 36 inches of leader on which I thread a large snap swivel and then tie another swivel. This creates a leader to which only bait and a sinker need be added. It allows light biting fish to take line a short distance before they feel the sinker's weight. It handles even the biggest sinkers with minimal wear, and it makes deck hands happy since they don't have to risk main line hand cuts when hauling aboard small halibut for release.

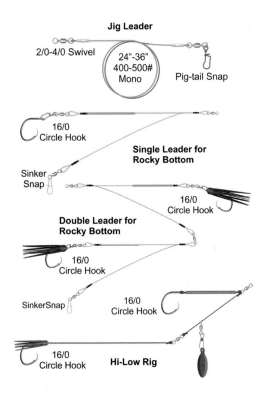

Jig Leader

2/0-4/0 Swivel

24"-36"
400-500#
Mono

Pig-tail Snap

16/0
Circle Hook

**Single Leader for
Rocky Bottom**

Sinker
Snap

16/0
Circle Hook

**Double Leader for
Rocky Bottom**

16/0
Circle Hook

SinkerSnap

16/0
Circle Hook

16/0
Circle Hook   **Hi-Low Rig**

Pre-tied nylon monofilament leaders are available in 100 to 500 pound test. A casual angler can last an entire season with a half dozen unless he fishes in gear-stealing territory. Serious bait and jig fishers should plan to spend at least $100 for crimps, a crimping tool, and leader material to make their own. Practice is important in order to make uniform crimps that won't slip and won't cut or weaken the leader. Once fishing, check mono leaders often for nicks and plan on replacing them after landing big fish. Reuse the hook and swivel later. Most anglers in Alaska don't use wire leaders. Custom leaders designed for fishing over rocks put the sinker at the bottom on a breakaway snap so that a snag takes only the weight. Since two hooks are legal, some use one above and one below the sinker over a smooth bottom or three feet above rocks.

Many leader makers add plastic squid imitations (hoochies) and/or five to ten inches of glow-in-the-dark surgical tubing above the hook. These serve to attract fish, help hold scent, and act as a sheath to protect the mono from damage. When used over braided nylon, the tubing acts as a stiffener to help the angler keep the bait from tangling his main line when lowering it to the bottom.

Swivels

Use the best that you can afford. That means quality ball bearing swivels and coast-lock or cross-lock style snaps. If using Crane or Rosco swivels, use #3/0 (approximately 300-pound test) or larger. I tend to stay away from three-way swivels after an offshore brand came apart on one of the biggest halibut catches of my life. A captain showed me that the heaviest American-made ones can take trophy fish. For those who still have doubts, there's a 600-pound test-rated three-way barrel swivel. Add a snap to the non in-line lobe of the swivel to attach the sinker.

Sinkers

Bank   Cannonball   Rock Cod

Sinkers

Halibut fishers will be interested in four types of sinkers. The cheapest and easiest to obtain is the bank variety. All lead, it's cast in an elongated figure-eight shape and is usually available in 2 to 20-ounce sizes. It has flattened sides that help prevent it from rolling.

Cannonball sinkers are round with a brass wire loop or an imbedded swivel for attachment to the terminal gear. Their compact shape makes them excellent for bottom bouncing, although they do roll easily on deck. Slightly more expensive than bank sinkers, they're made in sizes to four pounds.

Rock cod sinkers (charter boat specials) are rectangular, like a sash weight with a wire loop; sometimes they have a rounded bottom. They come in whole sizes from one to five pounds and don't roll.

The fourth type is a pyramid sinker, which is designed to dig into the bottom. Surf casters developed it to anchor their bait as far out from shore as could be cast. Shore-bound halibut anglers may find it useful, but it's rarely suitable for boat fishing.

Plastic sliders are available that work fine for sinkers to 20 ounces. Heavier sinkers may break the slide, which limits their use in some waters. Thread the main line through the slide and tie to the leader swivel. The snap on the slider lets the angler increase or decrease the size of the sinker in order to stay on the bottom with minimum weight as the tide rises or falls, while maintaining maximum sensitivity to biting fish.

Lures

Jigs commonly used for halibut are plain chromed metal or with paint schemes that resemble baitfish. Another variety is the lead head jig, either plain or painted (sometimes in luminescent off-white), which has a rubber sea worm or shrimp tail (Scampi). Many colors are available, but white or "glow" have proven effective for visibility to 200 feet, while black, purple, or dark blue work best at the greatest depths. Add a piece of bait such as an octopus tentacle, herring strip, or squid to enhance effectiveness.

Jigs as light as four to six ounces can catch big fish when tide and currents permit, though 8 to 24-ouncers are more the norm. They often induce strikes when bait won't. Since motion is essential, continuous jigging while prospecting for fish can become tiring but, once you hit a concentration of fish, they work wonderfully. Where bites on bait are usually tentative, there's no doubt when a fish hits a jig. It's an exciting way to fish and, unless the tail gets chewed off, you know that you still have a viable lure even if the fish strikes but misses getting hooked. Drop it back and hook the fish the second time it tries, since halibut are aggressive and rarely hook shy.

Examples of popular metal jigs for halibut are: the Vike, a Norwegian-style cod jig; the Teezer, a needle-fish imitator; and the Metzler Mooch-A-Jig, which resembles a herring. The lead heads with their tails and skirts resemble fish, crab, or octopus, depending on how they're dressed and fished.

Accessories

Fighting belts are a worthwhile investment since they protect the abdomen from bruising whenever the rod is rested against the angler's body. The simplest are leather or plastic triangles with a molded cup for the rod butt and a sturdy belt strap to circle the waist. Fancier models have a metal bar designed to lock into the matching gimbal fitting on rod butts. This keeps the rod from rolling with the torque created by cranking the reel. Larger models rest on the tops of the thighs or completely encircle the hips with two neoprene-padded arms. These are extremely comfortable to wear and effectively distribute the force of a fighting fish. Shoulder harnesses, vests, or kidney belts, with two quick-release snaps for attachment to the reel, take stress off the arms and the hands. This is particularly important in an extended battle, since the angler is standing rather than using a fighting chair.

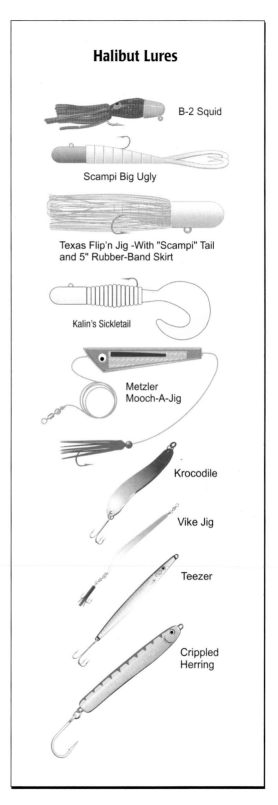

Halibut Lures

B-2 Squid

Scampi Big Ugly

Texas Flip'n Jig -With "Scampi" Tail and 5" Rubber-Band Skirt

Kalin's Sickletail

Metzler Mooch-A-Jig

Krocodile

Vike Jig

Teezer

Crippled Herring

Bait

Halibut are voracious feeders on other fish and shellfish. (I once caught a 50-pounder that had 14 half-dollar-size king crab in its stomach.) Herring, salmon, needlefish, eulachon (hooligan), sculpins, octopus, and crab comprise much of their diet. Herring is a popular bait because it's readily available and exudes an excellent scent. Fresh or fresh frozen is best. A whole fish is particularly good, given the "bigger bait, bigger catch" theory. Charters use a half or a third of a large herring, but this isn't a problem since they have 6 to 16 baits in the water creating a significant scent trail.

One of the halibut's favorite foods, octopus, is a superb bait because it's durable. Squid is similar, but it has only a fraction of the durability of octopus. It's found in most supermarkets as well as in bait shops. Either may be used with herring on the same hook. Put a two or three-inch diameter chunk of octopus on the hook, sliding it past the eye and onto the leader knot, or ribbon fold and hook a squid in the same way. Then impale a half herring below it as usual. This combination is deadly, because even if the herring is stolen, the mollusc remains. The deeper the angler is fishing, the more he or she appreciates that quality.

Fresh gray cod, cut in steaks or fillets, is a tough, toothsome bait. Salmon heads or strips work well also. Whole, frozen pinks or chums are reasonable to use even at grocery store prices. A 2 x 10-inch strip of salmon split six inches from one end and hooked at the other makes a superb bait. Even when tattered by numerous strikes, it retains its appeal. Leave it on when adding a new one and spice the bait with a piece of herring. Scents such as herring or shrimp oil, or even a garlic spray, can help attract fish; some anglers even add rattles and/or green light sticks to the leader to increase the appeal of baits.

TECHNIQUES

When using bait, free spool the sinker to the bottom with a thumb-controlled fall. This prevents leader/line tangles and a backlash on the reel when the weight stops. Also, occasional stops during the fall reduce the belly in the line, especially in a strong current. When you reach bottom, engage the gear mechanism and crank two or three turns. Set the drag at two-thirds tension so that line will barely release. Hold the rod horizontally and gently undulate the bait by raising and lowering the rod tip. Keep the bait

Some of the largest halibut from the state come from the Dutch Harbor area and surrounding Aleutians, where halibut in excess of 200 pounds are frequently taken.

within three feet of the ocean floor. During slack tide, big fish can be caught 5 to 15 feet up (or higher), and some times they can be at any depth in the water column (visible on your fish finder/depth sounder).

Remember that most bites start as gentle tugs or nibbles. Give slack line by dropping the rod tip to a 45° down angle. Wait a count of ten. If the fish puts immediate heavy pressure or runs with the bait, you needn't wait the full count. If the fish doesn't tighten the line, lift the rod gently with your thumb locked against the reel spool until you feel solid weight and/or a headshake. Set the hook with a short, hard strike. Don't lift the rod up past 45° on the set, or while pumping the fish, since this can create stress that could break it. As soon as the fish is hooked, remove your thumb.

Hang on! The fish may run. If it does, lower the rod tip and lighten the drag so that the line doesn't break, while still maintaining pressure on the fish. Sometimes the captain may have to maneuver the boat to follow the fish. Only when the fish stops should you retighten the drag and begin to bring it in with a pumping action. Lift the rod without reeling, then drop the tip and crank on the way down. Try to keep tension against the fish at all times. Use your thumb to level the line while reeling it in. Take your time to enjoy the fish. It's less wear on you and your gear, making it easier to boat the fish when it's tired.

Two main fishing techniques are used with jigs. With lead heads, allow the jig to hit bottom. Raise the rod to lift the lure two to four feet, then allow it to drop while keeping constant line tension, since bites usually come on the fall. Grand, sweeping lifts are not necessary. Gentle lifts and drops, punctuated by an occasional dramatic upsweep, are more effective and less tiring. If your boat is anchored and the bottom is smooth, rest the jig on it for a moment, then snap it up. This can produce a savage strike. Otherwise, maintain intermittent contact with the bottom until you strike a fish. The upturned hook design of lead heads snags the ocean floor less than other styles.

Jigs with single or treble hooks at the bottom end require a modified technique. Once the lure touches bottom, reel one to three turns before beginning to jig.

Both methods demand keeping constant tension on the line once a fish is hooked, in order to prevent the counter-weighted hook from working free (and releasing the fish). Some serious anglers slip a second hook (sizes #10/0 to #12/0 O'Shaughnessy) over the point of the jig's hook after installing the rubber tail. This stinger hook settles to the bottom of the jig hook's bend, where it nabs short striking fish, though it makes catch-and-release difficult.

Let the crew know as soon as you see the fish. Do not lift its head out of the water, as that usually will send it diving back to the bottom. Loosen the drag

and hold the fish suspended, with your thumb on the reel spool. On the crew's order lift the fish the rest of the way to the top, making every effort to have it lay flat. Then it can be harpooned or gaffed. It may be shot and/or it may be bled with a cut to the gills. When the fish is pulled over the railing, it's your job to grab and hold the sinker, releasing it only after the fish is pacified and unhooked. This saves the crew from injury by a flying sinker caused by a thrashing fish. Have the line, leader, and hook checked for damage before baiting again.

Drifting is used to prospect for fish concentrations, to fish when tides and currents are too strong for safe anchoring, or to fish well-known holes where it's important to be able to stay with a big fish (and keep it from taking all of your line). This method is tough on gear because of snags. It requires a deft touch to keep that from happening. Hooks require more frequent sharpening.

Anchoring can be a very productive waiting game. Anglers' baits alone establish a scent trail that leads fish to the hook, but a scent bag of ground fish and oils tied on the anchor chain can draw fish even better. While on anchor you soon learn the contour of the bottom beneath the boat, preventing loss of gear.

HALIBUT ON A FLY

Taking halibut on a fly rod presents one of angling's extreme challenges. Presenting a suitable pattern to these bottom dwellers, and manipulating line and fly to entice strikes in depths that often far exceed 40 feet—not to mention the prospect of hauling a monster flatfish up from those depths—pushes the limits of current technologies and the innovative skills of the very best fly anglers.

But, for some, the thrill of being on the absolute cutting edge of a new and exciting dimension of fishing, where it's possible to take giant halibut of several hundred pounds or more on a fly rod, can be intoxicating. And the accomplishment of dealing successfully with conditions that most anglers would deem impossible can be reward enough.

Gear

For fly anglers wishing to take on the challenge, today's technology provides an array of highly refined products that can put the odds more in your favor. There's a whole new class of bluewater, mega-taper fly rods specially designed for the unique conditions of deepwater pelagic fishing. Available in sizes up to 15 to 17 weight (you'll need a minimum of 12 to 13 weight for halibut), these rods are not built like typical casting rods. They are shorter, with fast tapers and greater wall thickness in the butt and mid-section, plus foregrips to give anglers maximum leverage when pulling up big fish from the depths.

Saltwater reels have likewise evolved. These reels feature no fade drag systems and super large capacity spools for holding the ample backing you'll need to tussle with the big boys down deep—at least 300 yards of 50 to 80 pound backing. (I use 300 to 400 yards of 80 lb. Spectra Gel spun backing).

Lines have also come a long way in recent years, with new designs, materials, and coatings that will help you fish deeper, faster, and with less effort. The special conditions of Alaska's halibut waters require super high density sink lines or heads, 500 to 600 grain minimum for shallow water, minimum tide situations, and 850 to 1100 plus grain for deepwater, extreme tide situations. For interchangeable heads, I recommend starting with Amnesia or Cobra backing, then a short section (20 to 30 feet) of .029 level (floating) line. (This is used as a strike indicator, which also buoys the back of line so it descends properly without collapsing or tangling on itself.) Then finish with a super density (850 to 1100 grain or more) 30 to 40-foot head. I like to mark my line with marking pens or paint every 20 feet to aid in depth control. This system allows you complete depth control, as the indicator or floating line, in combination with the depth markers, gives you a visual on the depth you are fishing.

Like much sinking line fishing in Alaska, you'll do best with short leaders, never longer than 50 to 54 inches. When rigging for halibut and lingcod, I recommend a hard, stiff mono like Mason for the butt section, usually 40 to 50-pound (60 to 70% of the diameter of the end of the fly line is the rule for determining the size of the butt section), looped to a 20-pound double bimini class leader (of course you can use any of the current line class leaders). I recommend that you join the IGFA and research the proper saltwater fly rod rules for world record fishing. The bite tippet or connection into the fly is constructed with knotable wire (40 to 50-pound test) that is joined to the class tippet with an Albright knot. Use a Homer Rhode loop knot at the end connection to the fly so it can swing on the leader. The setup should be less than five feet long. (Constantly check for abrasions.)

Crab, baitfish, giant flesh flies, and squid pattern flies all are very effective on Alaska halibut, as they mimic major food items. A stripping basket is essential when fishing from a boat, to avoid fouling on the clutter on deck. Anglers should be positioned fore and aft, and on the side of the boat appropriate for their most efficient and comfortable casting, which should be coordinated among the group to avoid colliding and fouling lines. Unless you're on a really big boat, you'll find it extremely difficult, if not impossible, to cast with gear fishermen on board, so it's best to go with a group of flyfishermen with similar objectives.

The importance of finding a skipper experienced with the needs of the saltwater flyfisherman is 90% of the game. You'll want one who can put you in areas conducive to flyfishing, with shallower and calmer water than normally fished with conventional gear. A good flyfishing captain will have his boat set up to make your job easier, and will position the craft so that you can make effective drifts over promising water. Very seldom will you be able to flyfish effectively off anchor, due to the depths and amount of tidal current involved. The only real advantage to fishing off anchor is when you use a chum bag.

Tippet Class Leader for Halibut

Homer Rhodes Loop Knot
Hufnagle Knot
29-30 Turn Bimini Knot
29-30 Turn Bimini Knot
Fly Line
12" Bite Tippet
15" Class Tippet
Four Turn Surgeons Loops
1 - 2' 50 lb. Butt Section
20 Turn Albright Knot

Techniques

The basic technique is cast and drift, similar to that used when "swing fishing" (casting downstream with flies and swinging them in the current). The difference is you are now fishing vertically instead of horizontally. The line is cast into the tidal current and drops and sweeps down into the target zone as the boat drifts above. When it is directly beneath, in the "hang down" phase, you should be drifting right above bottom, using short strips (about one-and-a-half-feet long—too much pulls the fly up into the water column) to work the fly through this most productive zone (90% of strikes will occur here). The fly should be dead drifted for the rest of the drift.

In some situations, you can pay out line at depth to prolong the drift. But you risk losing control, as the dense head sinks to the bottom, and the buoyant section continues to drift, often tangling the line and confusing your sense of where the fly is. Line management is crucial. You should be aware of the depth and position of your fly at all times, managing the line to avoid fouling and excessive scope in the line.

Unlike in bait fishing, a hungry halibut's response to a fly is a hard take as the offering quickly swings through the fish's range, tempting it to react instantly, slamming the fly.

When fighting the fish, the specialty rods are designed for a much different technique than traditional longer rods. The rod is pumped with tip well below deck level, in an upward motion that utilizes the powerful muscles of the back and legs for more efficient, less tiring reeling. The motion is pull up with hips and legs, reel back down quickly, pull up with hips and legs, reel down quickly, etc. Keep arm-pumping to a minimum. Keep the rod close to your body, use a fighting belt if you need it, and don't raise the rod higher than 45°, instead dip it very low, using short, very fast upward strokes (6 to 8 inches) to prevent the fish's head from dropping. Boats with high rails will interfere with this technique and thwart you from using the full power of the rod; avoid fishing from them.

TIDES, TIMING, LOCATION & OTHER FACTORS

As in fishing other saltwater species, tides are the number one factor in your success. Tides bring food to the fish, and extreme tide change areas (5 to 8 knots) have some of the best fishing because higher tides bring the most food into the fish. Unfortunately, these areas are also the most difficult for fly anglers to fish. To make it easiest, try to pick dates that have moderate tides—preferably on the new moon cycle—and concentrate your effort on the periods on either side of the slack tide.

As far as locations, not all areas that offer good bait fishing are suitable for flyfishing. The challenge is to find the right structure or terrain in not-too-deep water (less than 100 feet), and with moderate tides. A good charter boat skipper or experienced local saltwater flyfisherman can save a lot of time and effort in locating these most productive zones.

When is the best time for flyfishing halibut? My favorite month for halibut fishing is June, when weather is ideal and fish are starting to come out of their winter deep water. Fall is another productive season, as halibut follow salmon runs so they can feed on flesh, and are concentrated in areas around major river mouths. But the weather typically presents different and more challenging scenarios.

Ideal conditions are 40 to 80 feet of water, with a tide differential of less than ten feet and lots of big fish within a couple of miles from shore. The Aleutians (Dutch Harbor), where quite a few record halibut have already been taken, come to mind as one of those ideal locations where it can all come together for the halibut fly angler.

Top Flies For Alaska Halibut
Squid, Calamari, Crab, Herring, Baitfish, Halibut Flesh Fly, Deceiver, Sea Snake, Sandlance, Seaducer, Tarpon Fly, Whistler.

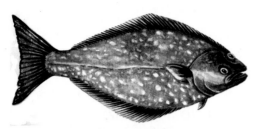

PACIFIC HALIBUT
Hippoglossus stenolepis

SPECIES SUMMARY

Alaska common names: Halibut, 'but, flatfish, flattie.

Description: Large flatfish, with somewhat elongated body. Topsides dark gray or dirty brown, with irregular cream or white blotches; bottom is white or yellowish-white. Scales small, with lateral line extending from head to tail, curving over the pectoral fin. Teeth on both sides of jaw. Flesh white.

Size: Average 15-60 lbs., up to 550 lbs. and 100 inches.

State/World Record: 459 lbs., Unalaska Bay (SW), Jack Tragis, 1996.

Habits: Bottom dwelling, opportunistic feeder, eats a wide range of live and dead prey.

Notes: Can be taken shallow and throughout water column at certain times of year.

Meristics: Vertebrae 49-51; scales cycloid, about 150 along lateral line; dorsal fin 90-106 rays; anal fin 69-80 rays; pectoral fin 19 rays; pelvic fin 6 rays.

Range: Cape Muzon (SE) to Bering Strait (NW).

Preferred Habitat: Gravel or sand bottom structure off beaches, around points and islands, and shoals in 30-150 ft. of water.

Best waters: Outer coast and adjacent waters, SSE to Alaska Peninsula/Aleutians (SW).

Best Times: Fish present year-round; peak May to September.

Best Bait/Lures/Flies: Herring, squid, octopus, salmon head; large jigs (Krocodile, Sebastes, Vi-Ke, etc.); large flesh flies and prey imitation saltwater flies.

Best Trophy Areas: North Gulf Coast—Yakutat Bay to Kodiak (includes Lower Cook Inlet, NE Kodiak coast, Resurrection Bay, PWS); NSE (Icy Strait/Cross Sound to Chatham Strait); Dutch Harbor/Unalaska (SW); West coast POW—and Behm Canal (SSE).

RECOMMENDED GEAR

Bait/Lure Fishing: 5-6 ft., fast taper, medium-heavy (50-130 lb. class), fiberglass or composite standup rod with powerful butt section, foam foregrip, high quality guides and metallic oxide tip. Matching (30-50 lb. class for Spectra or 4/0-6/0 for Dacron), high-speed, lever (or multi disc star) drag reel with minimum of 300 yds. braided, 50-130 lb. test line.

Fly Fishing: 11-13 wt., megataper saltwater rod, with matching big game saltwater reel capable of holding 300 yds. 50-80 lb. backing. Super high density (600-1100+ grain) sink line or shooting head with short (4-5 ft.) leader, including wire (40-50 lb.) or heavy mono (60-80 lb.) bite tippet, and 20-30 lb. (or class) tippet.

ALASKA'S MAJOR HALIBUT LOCATIONS

SOUTHEAST

Ketchikan/POW: Revillagigedo Channel (Foggy Bay, White Reef, Snail Rock, and Point Alava); East Behm Canal (Alava and Princess bays and Short Pass); Clarence Strait (Doctor, Caamano, and Clover points; Twenty-Fathom Bank; Grindall Passage; Vallenar and Kasaan bays; Bucareli Bay (Ports Caldera, Saint Nicholas, and Estrella; San Alberto Bay; Baker, Cabras, San Juan Bautista, and San Fernando islands; San Cristobal Channel and Point Providence); West Behm Canal (Behm Narrows, Helm Bay, Betton, and Back islands); Gulf of Esquibel (Maurelle, St. Joseph, and Noyes islands; Warm Chuck Inlet and San Cristoval Channel).

Petersburg/Wrangell: Sumner Strait (Point Baker; Port Protection; the Eye Opener; McArthur Reef; Kah Sheets Bay; Vank, Sokolof, Greys, Rynda, Liesnoi, and Kadin islands; lower Duncan Canal); Upper Clarence Strait (Blashke and Rose islands; Seal Rock; Key Reef; upper Kashevarof Passage); Ernest Sound (Point Warde and Blake Island); Zimovia Strait (Young Rock and Woronkofski Island); Frederick Sound (Thomas and Portage bays; Sukoi Islets; Frederick, Boulder, North Passage, and West points; upper Wrangell Narrows; Finta Rocks; Turnabout Island; Cape Fanshaw; Gedney Harbor; Keku Strait).

Sitka: Sitka Sound (Vitskari Rocks; St. Lazaria Island; Starrigavan Bay; Olga and Hayward straits; Nakwasina Sound/ Passage, Midway and Whitney islands); Baranof Island (Khaz, Whale, and Branch bays; Necker Islands, Salisbury Sound); Chatham Strait (Tebenkof, Sitkoh, Florence, Kelp, Funter, and Hood bays; Peril Strait; Tenakee Inlet; Port Malmesbury; Point Gardner).

Juneau/NSE: Upper Stephens Passage (Taku Harbor; Grand, Colt, Horse, and Shelter islands; Gastineau, Saginaw, and Favorite channels; Young and Auke bays; Outer, Middle, and Inner points); Lynn Canal (Vanderbilt Reef; St. James Bay; Poundstone Reef); Icy Strait

Large, Whole Herring

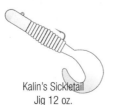

Kalin's Sickletail Jig 12 oz.

#5/0 Halibut Flesh Fly

#3/0 Squid Fly

10 oz. Crippled Herring Jig

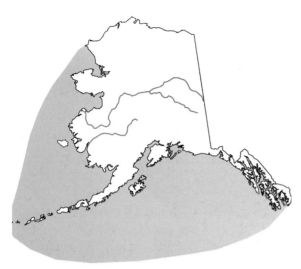

(Point Couverden; Couverden, Sisters, Spasski, Hoonah, Pleasant, and Lemesurier islands; Sisters Reef; Port Frederick; Halibut Rock; Icy and South passages; Mud Bay; outer Idaho Inlet; Glacier Bay); Cross Sound (North and South Inian Pass; Lisianski Inlet; George and Yakobi islands; Cape Spencer); Lower Stephens Passage (Pybus, Gambier and Holkham bays).

Yakutat: Yakutat Bay; Point Mamby; Icy Bay.

SOUTHCENTRAL

Seward/Prince William Sound: Resurrection Bay/Blying Sound (Capes Junken, Fairfield, and Cleare; Chiswell Islands; Nootka Bay); Latouche and Knight Island passages; Montague Strait; Hinchinbrook Entrance; Jack, Galena, Anderson, and outer Orca bays; Potato Point; Knight, Naked, and Montague islands.

Cook Inlet: Ninilchik; Deep Creek; Happy Valley; Anchor Point; Compass Rose; Point Pogibshi; Flat, Elizabeth, and Barren Islands; the Sand Waves; Magic Mountain; the Deep.

Kodiak/Afognak/Shuyak: Chiniak Bay (Williams Reef, Buoy Four, Long Island, Humpback Rock); Whale Pass; Marmot, Uganik, Ugak, Uyak, and Alitak bays; Shelikof, Sitkalidak and Shuyak straits.

SOUTHWEST

Unalaska/Dutch Harbor: Hog Island; Devilfish Point; Unalga Pass; Capes Cheerful and Winslow; Driftwood Bay.

Umnak Island: Nikolski Bay, Cape Udak.

Guides' Tips for Halibut Fishing

1. Use the best gear you can afford and then take care of it. Don't scrimp on terminal tackle.
2. Avoid big minus or plus tides, when water movement will limit your time to fish. A mid-morning and a mid-afternoon change would be ideal, since action is often best on either side of slack tide.
3. Learn good knots. Practice and use them, particularly for the new Spectra fiber lines.
4. Keep your bait or lure near the bottom.
5. Be patient. Give the fish time to take the bait well into its mouth before striking. Big baits for big fish demand even more time.
6. Respect the power of the fish. Kill it cleanly, then immobilize it in case it thrashes reflexively. (Tie a rope around the tail and then run it through the gills and mouth before cinching it tight like a bowstring.)
7. Respect the meat. Bleed the fish, keep its dark side down, and keep it cool. Do not put it back in the water.
8. Match your gear to the situation. If taking your own rod and reel on a charter where the boat uses 130-pound test line, don't take your 50 or 80-pound. Don't use Dacron if the boat has Spectra. Try to match the style of their leaders and their sinker weights. Single hook rigs are quicker, easier, and safer for the crew to unhook when you want to release a fish. (Ask what your boat uses as some have changed to two hook rigs.)
9. Remember that for IGFA certification, a fish may not be harpooned or shot. Be sure to let your skipper know of your intentions beforehand to plan for alternate methods of subduing.

Top Ten Alaska Trophy Halibut

459 lbs.	Unalaska Bay (SW)	1996
450 lbs.	Cook Inlet (SC)	1995
440 lbs.	Point Adolphus (SE)	1978
439 lbs.	Dutch Harbor (SW)	1995
422 lbs.	Ugak Bay (SC)	1992
419 lbs., 12 oz.	Cook Inlet (SC)	1997
414 lbs.	Kodiak (SC)	2002
411 lbs.	Barlow Cove (SE)	2003
404 lbs., 9 oz.	Icy Strait (SE)	1981
404 lbs.	Point Carolus (SE)	1980

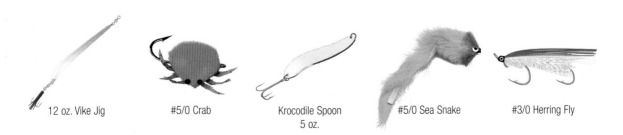

12 oz. Vike Jig   #5/0 Crab   Krocodile Spoon 5 oz.   #5/0 Sea Snake   #3/0 Herring Fly

Lingcod
Rock Dweller

I'm sitting with my colleagues in the galley of the 50-foot *Legacy*, en route to a secret sea pinnacle nearly two hours travel from Seward, Alaska. We are after one of the most beastly, but desirable, Pacific coast fishes—the toothy, serpentine lingcod. We fish, not for sport or food, but to poke, prod, and examine for data to increase our knowledge of the esoteric life of these deepwater dragons. Our bodies sway around the galley table as we head into the large swells of the Gulf of Alaska and, under the somnolent grind of the ship's diesel engines, my mind drifts back two decades, to the special day when these strange fish first entered my life.

I was twelve, with quite a few fish species already taken from the shores, piers, and charter boats of southern California. On a half day party charter, working a deep reef where everyone was jigging up rockfish, I lowered my rock cod rig to bottom and snagged something substantial. After quite a battle, I subdued a monstrous, dark greenish-blue mottled, prehistoric-looking fish that hissed at me when we got it aboard. I had never seen anything like it: my first ling.

My head thumps against the window, daydreams instantly cleared as the *Legacy's* throttle suddenly backs down. We exit the galley, grab rods, and take positions along the rails. Captain Bob Candopoulos maneuvers the boat in circles, eyes glued to the bottom chart and Loran, pinpointing his secret location. Then he pulls the boat out of gear and nods to the anxious anglers on deck.

Before I can get my jig to the bottom, someone already has a giant ling to the surface. I race my gear back up and secure my rod, while the behemoth is placed on a padded board. I record data—length, sex, tag number, etc.—then the fish is slipped back into the brine. By this time three more lings are holding in a tote full of saltwater. They are measured and tagged, but no new recruits take their place on deck. A lull has occurred as we drift away from the submerged reef. Captain Bob remanuevers and I take up arms and position, anticipating the moment to release my lure 120 feet down to a swarm of hungry, black serpents. As soon as it hits bottom I feel my jig get stuck; I pull hard and it comes free-rocks? Suddenly my rod tip is yanked clear to water level. I solidly connect to set the hook; surely this is no rock! With 80-pound test, a Penn Senator 6/0, and a tuna stick, I battle a swimming dragon from its lair to the surface. After an intense struggle, I land by far the largest lingcod of my life, a fish I estimate at 45 to 50 pounds. We work hard that day, catching, netting, measuring, tagging, then releasing fish. All told, 112 lingcod, with 23 from a mere speck of uncharted rock amid Alaska's vast and rugged coastline.

Working prime lingcod water along Alaska's rocky North Gulf Coast.

LINGCOD: ROCK DWELLER

The lingcod, *Ophiodon elongatus*, is a well-known marine species that has been sought for decades by Pacific coast anglers from northern California to Washington. However, only in the last 15 years has there been focused lingcod effort by sport and commercial fishermen here in Alaska, as they have gone from an incidental catch by anglers fishing for halibut or trolling for salmon, to a primary target species. Formerly released unrecognized, or feared for its intimidating sea-monster appearance (like something out of a Jules Verne novel) this voracious, unsightly bottom dweller is now celebrated as both a prized sport species and choice table fare (it is delicious to eat, with firm flesh and delicate flavor).

Anglers who set aside their fears and brave the tumultuous personality of Alaska's marine environment will be greatly rewarded. The state's growing reputation as a destination for world-record lingcod has lured increasing numbers of anglers away from exclusive pursuit of halibut or salmon. Rumored to reach weights over 100 pounds (the Alaska state record is over 81 pounds), with most ranging in weight from 10 to 30 pounds, lings can be challenging. Living in the rockiest habitats, they are notorious for sudden grabs and explosive dashes to protective cover. Because gear requirements are similar to those for halibut or salmon, anglers can make an easy transition when opting to fish for lingcod, adding another exciting element to the diverse fishing opportunities found in the stunning marine settings along Alaska's coast.

DESCRIPTION

With a common name that is misleading, being neither ling nor cod (and not to be confused with the burbot, a freshwater cod also called lingcod or ling), lingcod are the largest members of the *Hexagrammidae* family which includes several species of green-

relatively small mouths with small teeth, and three separate dorsal fin sections. Wolf fish look more eel-like, have big raised foreheads, a solid brown color, and long, continuous dorsal and anal fins, with no notch on the dorsal fin.) Sculpins, another group of fish you will no doubt encounter, have some resemblance to lingcod but are rarely over 24 inches, with broad toad-like heads, eyes fairly close together and situated more on the top of their heads, and most species with preopercal spines resembling rose thorns near the edge of the gill covers.

RANGE, ABUNDANCE & STATUS

Lingcod are found only along the Pacific coast of North America, from northern Baja California to the Shumagin Islands near Sand Point, Alaska. They are most abundant from central California to Cape Spencer (northern Southeast Alaska). In Alaska they are abundant along the outer coasts of the Alexander Archipelago (Southeast Alaska), Prince William Sound, Kenai Peninsula, and around the Kodiak Archipelago. The largest lingcod are generally taken from the British Columbia coast to Kodiak Island. They are found in rocky areas at depths ranging from intertidal to over 1,000 feet, but most occur at depths from 30 to 300 feet.

Abundance or biomass estimates of lingcod in Alaska are nonexistent. Stock status is assessed by monitoring sport and commercial catches, and length and age information. Since 1991, annual sport harvests in Alaska have ranged from 20,000 to a little over 30,000 lingcod, decreasing in some areas due to declining abundance and more restrictive regulations, while increasing in others because of growing interest in lingcod and a burgeoning charter boat industry.

Prior to 1990, presumably healthy stocks existed throughout Alaska, and there were few restrictions on commercial and sport fisheries. Widespread declines and localized depletions have been noticed since the late 1980s, particularly in Resurrection Bay, the Chiswell Islands, and Sitka Sound, making it necessary for anglers to travel farther to find good numbers of large lingcod. Alaska Department of Fish and Game (ADFG) began to formally monitor sport harvests via their postal angler survey in 1991. Lingcod harvests are also counted and sampled at many ports. ADFG has since enacted seasonal closures to protect spawning females and nest-guarding males (which are essential to egg survival; see life history below),

lings, often called sea trout in the Pacific Northwest, or pogie in the Aleutian Islands. Their scientific name comes from the Greek words *ophis,* or snake, and *odons,* meaning tooth, and the Latin word *elongatus,* meaning elongate. Hence, lingcod have an elongate body, large head, and a large mouth full of needle sharp, prey-snatching teeth. Body color can be a gray, brown, or greenish color with varying degrees of darker mottling or spotting along the sides and back. Another characteristic is a long continuous dorsal fin with a notch separating the spiny rays from the softer rays. They have large, rounded pectoral fins, sometimes exceeding the size of their head. Their white flesh may have a greenish or bluish hue; unusual, but perfectly edible.

Lingcod are sometimes confused with several unrelated species, such as the Pacific cod or the rarely caught wolf fish. (Pacific cod, or gray cod, are generally brown mottled with light or white bellies, have reduced bag limits, and added minimum size limits. The Pinnacles, an area off Cape Edgcombe near Sitka, was established as a preserve and closed to all bottom fishing, and lingcod fishing is also prohibited in Resurrection Bay, near Seward. Regulations have been increasingly restrictive throughout Alaska, especially for non-resident and charter boat anglers in northern Southeast. (Lingcod fishing could be curtailed or closed by emergency order at any time, so anglers should check with Fish and Game before heading out.) Lingcod abundance, at least in Southcentral, appears to have stabilized under the tighter regulations, but the cause of the declines remains unknown. Overfishing, natural variations in abundance, climatic changes, or a combination of factors could be to blame. Sudden increases in sport and commercial harvests on perceivably pristine stocks probably had some negative impacts. Surprisingly, no studies were done on the possible injury to lingcod from the Exxon Valdez oil spill in 1989.

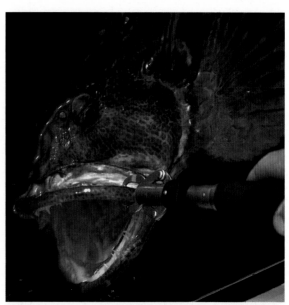

Lingcod have numerous sharp teeth capable of inflicting severe wounds; great care should be taken when bringing fish in, particularly if you are planning on releasing them.

LIFE HISTORY & HABITS

Lingcod can reach an age of 20 to 25 years, grow to five feet or more, and exceed 70 pounds. (The Alaska state record is 81 pounds, six ounces.) Males and females differ in potential size and length at age, with females the larger. Growth rates and average size also vary throughout Alaska. Most of the lingcod harvested in Alaska are between five and eleven years old, weigh from 10 to 30 pounds, and measure 30 to 40 inches.

Most males become sexually mature when two years old and about 20 inches in length, and females mature when three to five years old, at 24 to 30 inches in length. Spawning occurs from December to as late as May in Alaska. Males make the first move to find suitable nest sites in areas that offer both protective rocky cover and good current flow. Deeper water tends to attract the larger males and females. A female will join the male and begin the process of extruding eggs along with a gelatinous substance that serves to cement the eggs to the substrate. The male fertilizes the eggs as they are extruded. This process is repeated several times in the same nest site until the female is done and leaves the nest site. The male remains to protect the eggs until they hatch. Depending on her size, a female may deposit from 50,000 to 500,000 eggs. Egg survival depends highly on the ability of the male to protect the eggs from predators (rockfishes, sculpins, greenlings, starfish, sea urchins, etc.), and

adequate current to ensure the egg mass will receive sufficient oxygen. Studies have shown that unguarded nests were entirely consumed by predators in a short time. Occasionally, however, when a male is removed from a nest, another male will move in.

Depending on location and nest site quality, hatching begins after one to three months, peaking from March to April and continuing until June in some areas. All the eggs from one nest will hatch within one to seven days. Nest guarding males leave the site soon after hatching is complete; some may leave sooner. Newly hatched lingcod are about 1/4 to 1/2 inch long, and basically weak swimmers that float around with the water current. For several months they swim up and down the water column, straying near the surface during day and hugging bottom at night. As they get larger and better at swimming they seek nursery areas on the sea bottom and near shorelines with kelp or eelgrass beds. After their first or second year they move off these nursery areas seeking similar habitat as older lingcod, but in generally shallower depths and closer to shorelines. Once lingcod reach adulthood, they tend to be homebodies, remaining at or near the area where they first spawned. Tagging studies in British Columbia showed that 95% of the fish recovered stayed within six miles of home.

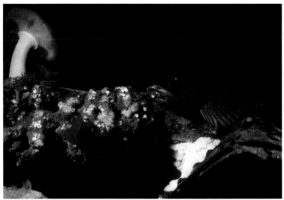
Male lingcod guarding nest with white egg mass. Egg survival and brood success depend highly on the male's ability to defend nest site from predation.

Lingcod are opportunistic predators throughout their lives, eating a wide variety of locally available prey. Immediately after hatching, their large mouths enable them to eat much larger organisms than other fish their size. Prior to becoming bottom dwellers, juvenile lingcod feed on large copepods, amphipods, euphausids, and larval herring. After they make their transition to bottom life, juvenile herring become a priority food item. As they grow they continue to depend on herring, but also feed on juvenile cod, sandlance, various species of smelt and flatfish (sole and flounder), and shrimp. Adults will eat herring, smelt, sandlance, rockfish, greenling, pollock, Pacific cod, salmon, crab, squid, shrimp, octopus, and each other at times. Predators of juvenile and adult lingcod include salmon, rockfish, greenling, seals, sea lions, and other lingcod.

FISHING ALASKA'S LINGCOD

Alaska anglers catch between 50 and 70 thousand lingcod every year, mostly from Southcentral's North Gulf Coast (Prince William Sound, eastern Kenai Peninsula and Kodiak), and Sitka and Prince of Wales Island in Southeast. Gear and techniques used for lingcod are very similar to those used for halibut, rockfish, and saltwater salmon, with bait, jigs, and lures—either mooched, jigged or trolled—being very effective. (Read those chapters for a review of appropriate tackle and techniques.) The main difference between halibut and lingcod fishing is the type of habitat targeted. Like halibut, lingcod feed voraciously from a bottom lair, but reside in rocky areas that provide the kind of cover they require—underwater reefs, pinnacles, sea mounts, etc. Successful anglers use nav-

igational charts, electronic aids, and visual cues to locate these natural concentration zones. Underwater observations of lingcod in Alaska have found that lingcod like to be "kings of the hill." They concentrate on the flattened tops of sea mounts, with rockfish keeping their distance along the slopes and base. Lingcod don't migrate as halibut do, so anchoring up in one spot and baitfishing through the tidal changes is not effective.

Besides Alaska's often wicked marine weather, there is another obstacle to enjoying the state's great lingcod waters that serious fishermen need to be aware of. Rockfish are abundant and voracious and reside just about everywhere lingcod do, which can bring potential legal and ethical complications for the Alaska lingcod angler. All marine waters in Alaska have low bag limits for rockfish, particularly the bottom dwelling or non-pelagic type, the most well-known being the yelloweye or red snapper. In nearly all cases when a non-pelagic rockfish is brought up from the depths, its air bladder irreversibly expands. The fish is unable to dive back home and inevitably dies. Rockfish are slow growing and potentially very old fish (some may reach 100 years) and highly vulnerable to overfishing. In Prince William Sound, the first two (the daily bag limit) non-pelagic rockfish must be retained, and in some areas, this includes only one yelloweye. Once an angler has caught his/her bag limit, any additional non-pelagic rockfish caught must be released, with most facing sure death. Therefore, an angler with a bag limit of rockfish is obligated to stop bottomfishing entirely.

Hiring a charter boat that can access Alaska's outer coast, or staying at a lodge/resort that specializes in marine fishing, will maximize your opportunities for good lingcod fishing. Discuss your intentions with the charter operator before signing up. Much of the lingcod fishing done by charter boats is secondary to halibut and salmon. Lingcod are normally targeted after bag limits for the other species have been achieved, or when weather prevents access to the best fishing grounds for these primary species. Some operators do not fish for lingcod, or may not be willing to, if limits of rockfish are aboard. Charter boat captains who do fish for lingcod will know the best locations, and most will have the nautical expertise to ensure a safe and rewarding trip. When shopping for a charter keep in mind that the outer coasts and open waters have the best fishing, but are more susceptible to poor sea and weather conditions. Larger (greater than 36 feet), faster boats and multiple-day trips will increase your chances for success. When planning a trip date make sure the lingcod season is open and remember that neap tides (when the difference between high and low is minimum) will give you more time for effective and easier bottom fishing in deeper waters.

Fishing from your own or a friend's boat offers the advantage and flexibility to explore numerous and possibly lesser fished niches. Boat size and speed, along with weather conditions, will normally dictate where you can fish and may restrict you from accessing more open waters. Smaller boats can get closer to shallow-water reefs and rocky shorelines, but such risks depend on the knowledge, experience, and comfort range of the boat owner. When fishing an unknown area, begin your search for lingcod habitat with nautical charts. Nautical charts are not only navigation aids, but show bottom type, depth, kelp beds, exposed rocks, and a host of other features useful to anglers. Although you will find great places to fish with the charts, other people can just as easily find these places too, and charts certainly do not show every potential lingcod hideout. Secret hotspots, the ones that often result in numerous monster fish, are found by refining your search with a good fish finder. Get a feel for the general lay of the shoreline and underwater features. A prominent rocky point in line with a small offshore island or rock may indicate a ridge or mountaintop in between, or beyond, that eluded the chart makers. Tidal changes can unlock some clues for finding great lingcod lairs. Underwater topography will reveal itself at the water's surface in the forms of boils, swirls, unusual chops, or confused seas, especially when currents are strong. Not every house-sized pinnacle or sea mount is charted, so keying in on certain oceanic signatures and geology, combined with steadfast exploration, will help you dial in a hotspot.

Gearing Up

Rods and Reels: Typical halibut bottom fishing setups are fine for lingcod, not so much for the size of the fish, but because the depths and currents sometimes require up to 20-ounce weights to stay on the bottom. (Large barndoor halibut are certainly a possibility when fishing lingcod, though.)

Having some lighter tackle aboard will enable the angler to fish a greater variety of conditions with more

Quite often lingcod and rockfish are found in the same areas. The larger and slower lings will utilize advantageous sites to hide and ambush small rockfish. The trick for anglers is to avoid hooking the more numerous, aggressive rockfish.

ease and pleasure. Depending on your preference, such a lighter setup could fall in the range of a 6 1/2 to 8 foot, heavyweight freshwater or medium weight saltwater spinning or casting rod, with matching sturdy saltwater reel spooled with 17 to 30-pound test monofilament. Some anglers like to go even lighter. Rods should have sufficient backbone and moderate to fast action to allow you to cast or jig one to four-ounce lures, or mooch with bait and sinkers. Most salmon mooching or king salmon drift-fishing or even muskie rods will suffice. I like using lighter tackle for fishing close to shorelines, kelp beds, and water less than about 50 feet deep. Being able to cast is advantageous for fishing around rocks with surging surf when keeping the boat a safe distance away is a priority.

Terminal Tackle: Many lingcod enthusiasts prefer using large lead-head jigs up to 20 ounces, with rubber Scampi or sickle tails in colors glow-in-dark white, green, red, yellow, and black. These jigs are inexpensive, snag less, and catch few rockfish. Their main disadvantage is that the rubber tails get chewed up, but replacements are relatively cheap. The heavy all-metal jigs such as Crippled Herring, Kandlefish, Stinger, Teezer, Vike, Gibbs Cod, Zingama Codfish, Diamond, and Norwegian work great too. They are more expensive but will hold up to more fish, provided you don't get them snagged. Colors are some-

Bringing in a big ling along the southern coast. Standard halibut bottomfishing gear will work fine for most Alaska lingcod fishing. Note: gaffs cannot be used to land lingcod in some areas (SC) of Alaska.

what more limited, with chrome or chrome/blue the most common and popular, but white, orange/red, and yellow/chartreuse are good colors too. Replacing the treble hooks with appropriately sized single O'Shaugnessy or Siwash hooks will help prevent snags and be less damaging to the fish. You should also have some lightweight, relatively large sized lures commonly used for tuna or yellowtail, such as the Iron-man and Salas jigs. These lures are great because their size/weight ratio allows them to be used with medium weight rods, while being selective for lingcod (and halibut) rather than rockfish. Regardless of the type of jig used, you should have it attached to a heavy duty leader similar to that described in the halibut chapter. (Use 200 to 400 pound test monofilament and a high quality locking snap or corkscrew swivel, 4/0 to 6/0, at the terminus, and a barrel swivel on the other end for tying the main line to.) This leader will resist abrasions caused by rocks and sharp teeth. You can further combat abrasion, with added attractiveness, by placing several inches of surgical or glow tube on the leader.

Softail, lead-head jigs are ideal for lingcod.

Techniques

Jigging: Fish large lead-head jigs or lures just off, or only occasionally on, the bottom. It is good practice to be aware of where your lure is in relation to the bottom by frequently letting out line until the bottom is felt, then reeling in a few feet. This will help you distinguish a bite from the bottom and decrease snags. Follow the lure down with your rod tip, maintaining line control. Common to jigging for many species, strikes are indicated by your line suddenly going slack as the lure is falling, or by a sudden and strong resistance when pulling up. If fishing a sloping shoreline or bottom pinnacle, start at the shallowest point first and drift toward deeper water to help prevent snags. Strong sweeping and repetitive sets, especially in deeper water, are often required to set the hook. Lingcod will often clamp down hard, even allowing themselves to be dragged to the surface, without being hooked.

"Pipe Jig" for lingcod. Keep it simple and durable.

Trolling/Mooching: Trolling is another method for targeting lingcod, as many are incidentally caught while trolling for salmon. (Please review the saltwater salmon chapter for descriptions of trolling rigs and use of a downrigger.) One of the most effective ways of commercial fishing for lingcod is slow trolling with a dinglebar setup. A dinglebar rig is a horizontal or trailing gangion of up to a dozen lead-head jigs attached on a mainline or wire about three to four feet above a 30 to 75-pound iron bar. Commercial fishermen like this method because it results in virtually no bycatch. Sport salmon trollers can make a simple transition to targeting lingcod with use of a downrigger. Instead of spoons, hoochies, or bait, try lead-head jigs in bright colors. Flashers are optional, and I believe the only difference they make is in the cost of a lost rig. Diving planers will suffice if you don't have a downrigger, but depth is difficult to ascertain, and you can easily lose your rigging or waste your time. Work the gear slowly through lingcod territory near rocky bottoms, around sea mounts, pinnacles, and reefs. Savvy use of a GPS and good graphic fish finder will greatly enhance your ability to learn and fish an area. A certain amount of finesse and experience certainly helps to fish this way without numerous hang-ups; but, if done right, decent catch rates are possible in areas with moderate or even low lingcod densities because more area is covered in a shorter time. Another advantage of trolling, especially if a large lead-head jig is used, is that non-pelagic rockfish (such as yelloweye) are rarely hooked.

Mooching (as you would for salmon) or simply baitfishing (as for halibut) with herring, octopus, or squid, will also work for lingcod. These methods have a tendency to catch a wide variety of species—salmon, various flatfishes, rockfishes, cod, sharks, sculpins, etc., adding an element of mystery to the excitement. (Some of the rigging for these methods is described in the saltwater salmon and halibut chapters.) Large lingcod are notorious for latching on to another smaller lingcod or rockfish. The use of whole fish is tempting, but the intentional use of sport-caught fish (except head, tail, fins, viscera) for bait is illegal, with the exception of species for which bag limits, seasons, or other regulatory methods haven't been established. (This may include sculpin, greenling, true cod. Check regulations for the area you intend to fish to determine what species you can keep for bait.)

FLYFISHING ALASKA'S LINGCOD

Saltwater flyfishing for lingcod offers an intriguing challenge. With spawning and nest guarding seasons (when lingcod move to shallower waters) closed to sportfishing in Alaska, the trick is finding appropriate habitat at suitable depth (less than 50 to 60 feet of water) and using the right gear and presentation to get down to and provoke these bottom dwellers, while avoiding any interaction with the usually abundant and super-aggressive rockfish. As in conventional angling, ideally you'll be working rock structures along the deeper, open waters of the Gulf of Alaska/North Pacific, where the chances of hooking a big ling are greatest.

Fly lines can be marked at regular intervals to show depth when fishing lingcod or other bottomfish.

Gear

Gear for the lingcod fly angler is much less specialized than that used for halibut. Generally a 10 to 12-weight rod, with matching high-quality anodized reel, loaded with 200 yards of 30-pound test backing, is required to handle the heavy lines and big fish (this includes the possibility of hooking a monster halibut). High density (up to 750 grain, or more) sink lines are used, either long sink section (24-foot), full sink, or sinking shooting heads. Your leader/tippet setup should be short, 4 to 6 feet, tapered down to 15 to 20-pound (or less if you're seeking line class records) hard nylon or fluorocarbon with a 6 to 12-inch piece of 60 to 80-pound monofilament, fluorocarbon, or flexible multistrand wire for a shock tippet.

Bringing a ling to the surface. Note the stripping basket to avoid fouling the line on the deck or railing.

Flies: Large attractor and bait pattern streamers tied on #3/0 to #5/0 straight eye, big game saltwater hooks are the standards for flyfishing lingcod, in colors of white, green, yellow, blue, brown, black, red, and orange, with lots of flash. The larger flies tend to discourage interest from rockfish, but also increase the possibility of encounters with giant halibut, for which anglers must be prepared. Tandem and tube fly patterns work well, and synthetic materials are increasingly popular for fly tying because of their ability to hold up to extreme abuse.

Techniques

When chartering a boat, it is imperative you discuss your flyfishing desires with the operator. Few captains will tolerate someone backcasting a #5/0 fly when other people are dropping heavy weights down to the bottom. Without access to a personal boat, your best option is to get a group of anglers with similar interests together for an exclusive charter. As with halibut or rockfish fishing, it is most advantageous to go out with a skipper experienced in the special requirements of fly anglers, who is set up and prepared to give you the best chance at accessing and fishing them with your specialized gear. (See the rockfish chapter.)

By fishing as early as possible in the season (early July in SC; mid-May in SE), you may still find some larger fish in shallow enough water. The Holy Grail is to get some good weather and find a virgin pinnacle, rock pile, or sea mount, with lots of crevasses and ledges, but little cover for rockfish, and at a depth of less than 50 feet. It is here you will find your best flyfishing opportunities for lingcod over 30 pounds.

In waters too deep for a fly, different tactics are employed to bring lingcod closer to the surface within casting range. Large, flashy jigs or spoons with the hooks removed can be banged on the rocks and used to coax big lings from the depths. Likewise, the frantic movement stirred up by fishing and hooking small rockfish or greenling in the area will frequently incite bigger lings to come out of their lairs to inspect the commotion. (Remember it is illegal to use game species like rockfish for bait; greenling, however, are not restricted from use.)

Presentation for lingcod is similar, if not identical, to that used for rockfish—doing deep sweeps of the fly past likely holding areas, positioning your boat, and casting/working lines to accommodate tidal current, depth, and drift. Lingcod are usually decisive takers, but you'll still need firm, repeated hook sets to ensure penetration of their hard mouths. When hooked, they'll usually instantly bolt for cover, so it's very important to use enough pressure to keep their heads up and prevent them from diving down into the rocks. (They may jam your line if they do, with the only recourse being to let them have slack and hope they will back out.) It is best to use a soft net or mouth gripper to minimize stress/damage to fish you release.

Lingcod
Ophiodon elongatus

SPECIES SUMMARY

Alaska Common Names: Ling, ling cod.

Description: Elongate, scorpaeniform marine bottomfish with large head, mouth (with prominent teeth) and pectoral fins, and long dorsal fin. Body mottled bluish-green, to black or brown, lighter towards belly; sometimes with darker spotting. Flesh white or greenish to bluish-white.

Size: Average 30-40 in. and 10-30 lbs.; may attain lengths greater than 5 ft. and wts. to 100 lbs.

State/World Record: 82 lbs., 6 oz., 2007, Cook Inlet, SC

Habits: Mostly sedentary, but sometimes migratory, found on or near bottom from intertidal zone to 1,000 ft. deep. Voracious and indiscriminant piscavore.

Notes: One of few fish species in which male guards nest.

Meristics: Gill rakers 16-19; vertebrae 55-57; dorsal fin 24-27 spiny rays, 21-24 soft rays; anal fin 3 spiny, 21-24 soft rays.

Range: Coastal and outer waters from Southeast Alaska to Kodiak Island and Alaska Peninsula to Shumagin Islands.

Preferred Habitat: Rocky areas on outer/coastal waters with high tidal and wave action.

Best Waters: Outer coastal reefs, sea mounts, and pinnacles, SSE-Kodiak; especially POW, NSE, PWS, Kenai Gulf Coast, and Kodiak.

Best Times: July to September, usually whenever weather allows longest boating range.

Best Bait/Lures/Flies: Greenling, herring, squid; large lead-head and metal jigs and spoons (all colors); large baitfish/attractor flies.

Best Trophy Areas: Outer coasts and islets of Kruzof, Chichagof, Baranof, and Prince of Wales islands (SE); Outer Prince William Sound-Danger Island, Seal Rocks (SC); Cross Sound/Icy Straight (SE); Pye Islands/Reef (SC).

RECOMMENDED GEAR

Baitcasting:
Halibut bottomfishing setup (5-6 ft. medium-heavy standup rod, 50-130 lb. class with matching reel) or lighter, as conditions allow.

Spinning:
Medium-heavy (rated 15-30 lb. test), fast action inshore spinning rod, 7-8 ft. Matching high quality reel, 200 yds. 17-30 lb. test line. May go lighter or heavier depending on depth and other conditions.

Flyfishing:
9-12 wt. saltwater flyrod, 9 - 9 1/2 ft., with matching, high-quality anodized reel and 200 yds. of 30 lb. backing. High density (up to 750 grain or more) full sink lines or sink shooting heads, with 5 ft. of hard mono leader, tapered to 15-20 lb. test with 6-12 in., 60-80 lb. fluorocarbon, mono or multistrand wire shock tippet.

MAJOR LINGCOD LOCATIONS

Many of Alaska's lingcod hotspots are unnamed, submerged mountains, pinnacles, reefs, rock piles, and rocky dropoffs. The following locations are the major ports where lingcod are landed, followed by general geographic features and directions to help you locate the best areas for the most abundant and largest lingcod. Pay particular attention to "high energy" areas. These are the capes, isolated rocks, and islands subject to strong tidal flows and open waters. No doubt you will find lingcod, sometimes in good numbers, in protected straits and bays, but they will be less than average size.

SOUTHEAST

Ketchikan: Gravina Island (southwest side to Dall Head), Duke Island, Tree Point, Cape Fox.

Prince of Wales*: Craig and Klawock are the major ports, comprise the largest sport fishery for lingcod in Alaska.

Outer coasts and capes of Noyes (Cape Addington), Baker (Cape Chirikof), Suemez (Cape Felix), and Dall islands.

Sitka*: One of Alaska's best lingcod destinations, with some of the largest lingcod ever caught on sport tackle, and the largest commercial lingcod fishery in the state. Seemingly uncountable islands, reefs, and underwater pinnacles offer anglers more than a lifetime's worth of fishing exploration.

Outer coasts and islets of Kruzof, Chichagof, and Baranof Islands (Biorka Island, Necker islands).

#5/0 Rockfish Fly

10 oz. Diamond Jig

Sea Serpent
#3/0

12 Oz. Kalin's
Sickletail Jig

#3/0 Herring Fly

Homer/Kachemak Bay: Lingcod opportunities are very limited. The best fishing occurs on the gulf side of the Kenai Mountains, an area best accessed by larger boats during cooperative weather. Chugach and Barren Islands, outer shores and rocks of Port Dick, Gore Point.

Kodiak Island: This archipelago offers a vast, unexplored arena for lingcod fisherman.

Outer points, small islands and rocks around Chiniak, Marmot Bays and Shuyak, Afognak, Ugak, Sitkalidak, and Sea Otter islands.

Top Flies for Alaska Lingcod

Herring, Squid, Rockfish, Greenling, Candlefish, Baitfish, Anchovy, Deceiver, Clouser Minnow, Seaducer, Flashtail Whistler, Sea Serpent.

Juneau: A jump-off point for Hoonah, Gustavus, and Elfin Cove where charters can access Icy Strait, Cross Sound, and Glacier Bay. The saltwater fishing opportunities are extraordinary.

Icy Strait (Sisters Reef, Pleasant Island Reef, Point Couverden); Cross Sound, Cape Spencer, Yakobi Island.

Yakutat: A sleeper lingcod destination that also offers fantastic halibut and rockfish fishing (plus steelhead, salmon, and cutthroat trout in streams fairly close to town).

The submerged reefs and remnant glacial moraines in Yakutat and Icy bays.

SOUTHCENTRAL

Prince William Sound (Valdez/Cordova/Whittier)*: The best lingcod fishing accessible from Valdez and Cordova occurs along the Gulf coast of Prince William Sound, such as at Seal Rocks near the Hinchinbrook Entrance. Such a trip is not for the faint of heart, but a good number of charter boats have the size and speed to take you there, weather dependent. The largest lingcod caught in Alaska have come from this area in recent years.

Bligh Island and Reef, Goose Island, Knight Island, Seal Rocks (Hinchinbrook Entrance), south Elrington Island, Montague Island, and Danger Island (also accessible from Seward).

Seward*: The most popular road accessible port on the mainland for lingcod. (Resurrection Bay itself is closed to lingcod; consult regulations.)

Chiswell Islands, Cape Aialik, Seal Rocks, Granite Cape, Pye Islands, Pye Reef, Cape Fairfield, Cape Junken.

Top Ten Alaska Trophy Lingcod		
82 lbs., 6 oz.	Cook Inlet (SC)	2007
81 lbs., 6 oz.	Monty Island (SC)	2002
81 lbs.	Pearl Island (SC)	2003
78 lbs.	Elizabeth Island (SC)	2007
77 lbs., 2 oz.	Elizabeth Island (SC)	2006
76 lbs., 10 oz.	Prince William Sound (SC)	2001
76 lbs., 2 oz.	Homer (SC)	2007
76 lbs.	Homer (SC)	2004
75 lbs., 8 oz.	East Chugach Island (SC)	2001
74 lbs., 8 oz.	Gulf of Alaska (SC)	2008

* Denotes Trophy Hot Spot

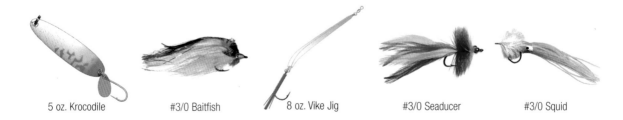

5 oz. Krocodile   #3/0 Baitfish   8 oz. Vike Jig   #3/0 Seaducer   #3/0 Squid

Rockfish
Old Reliable

Grizz, the half-crazed wolf-husky, wasn't buying the meal of deer bone soup and rice I laid before his feet that cold morning in January. For what seemed like the tenth time in a row, he and I were reduced to a meal of the barest essentials, as caretakers of a cabin on a remote island in Prince William Sound. We had all the comforts—hydropower, satellite TV, running water, etc.—but no good grub, as we had long exhausted our meager provisions and exceeded the good will of the folks back at the Cordova General Store with a long overdue bill. Now, late in the season, we had to make do with what was left of a deer I had shot, plus an occasional spruce grouse, and things were getting a little dicey.

A couple of halibut rods lay collecting dust in a corner of the shed. Maybe I could dredge up a small halibut? Not an easy task in winter in these parts, especially when fishing from a small 13-foot Boston Whaler.

I decided to make a go for it and try a rocky pass between two small islands, not too far from the cabin. With Grizz by my side, we shot across the bay into the calmer waters of the strait. I cut up a couple stinky salmon heads we had saved, and lowered big chunks on a tandem rig into some tidal eddies. I fished around but nothing was biting and, with darkness coming on, began to dread yet another meal of bone stock gruel.

Desperate to try something different, I found some faded, rusty flies lying under the seat—remnants of some ancient fishing adventure, no doubt. I dressed up the hooks, carefully clipped the leader on, and made one more final position of the boat. On the outside of one of the islands was a rock wall that steeply sloped down to a 70-fathom trench. Even fishing right up beside the island it seemed bottomless. I got as close to the rock face as I dared with the powerful surge. Old Grizz gave me doubtful looks as I crammed on about two pounds of lead and let out nearly all my line for what seemed an eternity.

I felt the line hit bottom—or a least some part of the wall on the way down—and began working my rig up and down, not really feeling what was going on. I drifted around and pumped those flies for nearly twenty minutes with no response so, finally admitting defeat, I began winding back in. There was only the dead weight of the sinkers at first, but then something else, perhaps some kelp or coral, I thought. The more I reeled, the more I was certain it was a fish, as there was considerable resistance now. Determined not to let dinner get away, I bullied the line up to find two lovely quillback rockfish immobilized by the drastic pressure change. They definitely weren't trophies, but would make one hell of a meal. Lightly sautéed in olive oil, dried parsley, celery seed, and garlic, served with a side of rice, those delicate white fillets were quite a feast, especially for a half-starved young biologist (and his dog) living on the edge of the world. I realized that night that there are certainly more glamorous prizes in Alaska's seas, but none more willing (and appreciated at times) than the eager rockfish.

199

Hot rockfish action, North Gulf Coast, Southcentral Alaska.

ROCKFISH: OLD RELIABLE

Rockfish are the bread and butter of the Pacific coast charter boat industry. As a kid I remember the eye-candy assortment of rockfish with names like chucklehead, flag, cowcod, salmon grouper, widow, chilipeppers, barberpole, gopher, etc., that were taken on boats I fished in California. They can be caught all year, and almost always counted on to fill the gunny-sack when the glamorous species—halibut, salmon, bonito, white seabass, and calico bass are seasonally unavailable or not cooperating.

Rockfish (genus *Sebastes*, from the Greek word *Sebastos*, meaning magnificent) are truly a fish lover's fish. Their beauty, intrigue, edibility, and year-round availability more than make up for any perceived lack of fighting qualities as a gamefish. Alaska is not usually thought of as a rockfish destination, but very well should be, as local and visiting anglers plying Alaska's expansive coastline find when they routinely encounter one or more of roughly 30 species of this profuse group of marine fishes. As their name implies, many of the rockfish species live near or on rocky bottoms as well as in shoreline kelp forests. Some species may attain weights of nearly 40 pounds and live over 150 years, being among the longest-living animals on the planet. Quite easy to catch and fairly ubiquitous, they can be counted on when fishing is tough for the host of saltwater fishes higher on the rung of sport value. And, delightfully, they are good to eat, and no significant investment in gear or terminal tackle is needed for catching them.

DESCRIPTION

Rockfish are often confused with other bottom-dwelling species such as sculpin (irishlords) and greenling. All rockfishes, however, share a few distinguishing characteristics. They are generally perch or bass-like in shape. Originally they were classed as

There are over 30 species of rockfish in Alaska's marine waters, many quite common, others seldom encountered by anglers. All rockfishes have sharp, venomous spines and should be handled with care. This is a tiger rockfish, found in waters from Prince William Sound south.

"rosefishes" due to the numerous spines and thorns on fins and head. Nearly all have 13 sharp, spiny rays on the dorsal fin, three spiny rays on the anal fin, as well as a variable number of spines on the head, gill covers (operculi), and eye orbit.

Sculpins, on the other hand, have large, somewhat flattened heads and large mouths. Overall, sculpins are more catfish or bullhead in shape, with eyes placed towards the top of the head. Most sculpins are only partly scaled, with some having no discernible scales (rockfish are very scaly), and they have no spines on the anal fin. Some sculpins have spines on the dorsal fin but fewer than ten. Greenling (closely related to lingcod) have no spiny fins, and most have multiple lateral lines (usually up to five are noticeable), relatively small mouths, and relatively long based anal fins.

Although basically easy to identify as a group, individual rockfish species can be difficult to distinguish. The number and position of spines can often be used to determine the more difficult species. Color is also a useful key for narrowing down identification to two or three species, generally varying from bright orange or light red to completely dark blue or nearly black, with pattern solid, mottled, or striped.

Rockfish are divided into three groups, based on their habitat preference and behavior: pelagic shelf, demersal shelf, and slope, or deepwater. Pelagic rockfishes occur mostly in schools and live mainly in midwater, but can occur throughout the water column, and are usually associated with rocky structures and kelp beds. Pelagic species are usually more common in areas near open water rather than in protected areas. Demersal rockfishes occur at or near rocky bottoms in small groups or individuals. The third group, slope, or deepwater, includes species that live in deep waters (usually more than 100 fathoms) near the edge of the continental shelf. With few exceptions, they are rarely encountered by sport anglers. The latter two groups are lumped into one group called non-pelagic. The following species are caught regularly by Alaska anglers:

PELAGIC:
black rockfish (*S. melanops*)
dusky rockfish (*S. ciliatus*)
yellowtail rockfish (*S. flavidus*)
widow rockfish (*S. entomelas*)
blue rockfish (*S. mystinus*)

DEMERSEL SHELF:
yelloweye (*S. ruberimus*)
copper rockfish (*S. caurinus*)
quillback rockfish (*S. maliger*)
canary rockfish (*S. pinniger*)
China rockfish (*S. nebulosus*)
tiger rockfish (*S. nigrocinctus*)
rosethorn rockfish (*S. helvomaculatus*)

DEEPWATER:
shortraker rockfish (*S. borealis*)
rougheye rockfish (*S. aleutianus*)
silvergray rockfish (*S. brevispinis*)
Pacific Ocean perch (*S. alutus*)
bocaccio rockfish (*S. paucispinis*)
redstripe rockfish (*S. proriger*)
vermilion rockfish (*S. miniatus*)

Three to four of the above species comprise 99% of the sport rockfish harvest in Alaska. The dominant species vary from port to port and from year to year but, in general, the most common in Southcentral is the black rockfish, which comprises approximately 30% to 80% of the harvest, followed by yelloweye 5% to 40%, dusky 1% to 35%, and quillback 0% to 12%. In southeast Alaska, the dominant species harvested also varies from port to port but generally they are yelloweye 5% to 48%, quillback 5% to 40%, and black 4% to 35%. Low relative proportions of dusky, copper, China, tiger, yellowtail, and silvergray are harvested throughout Alaska.

Knowing how to distinguish pelagic from non-pelagic species is extremely important because bag limits are usually different for each group, with limits more restrictive for non-pelagics in most of Alaska due to their longevity and lower reproductive rates. In contrast, pelagic rockfish are more numerous, have higher reproductive rates, and may tolerate higher harvests. Another reason non-pelagics are more protected is the high rate of mortality they suffer when brought up from the depths. All rockfish have air or swim bladders that exchange air gradually through the circulatory system (termed physoclistic) and cannot accommodate rapid pressure changes. The air bladders in fish pulled up from deep water will over-expand, often forcing their stomachs out of their mouths. The eyes will bulge and other organs will lethally embolize, similar to a diver getting the "bends." This lethal phenomenon is assured when they are pulled from depths greater than 60 feet (10 fathoms). Although pelagic rockfish can suffer the same consequences, most are caught in benignly shallow depths.

The pelagic species as a group can be recognized by their color, which is generally uniform or only slightly mottled shades of gray, green/brown, or black/dark blue, with lighter bellies. The non-pelagic species come in various color schemes but usually have brighter colors, such as red or orange, and are often expressively mottled or distinctly two-toned. All rockfish have spines that are mildly poisonous, and are best released without being handled by using long-nosed pliers or similar tools. If you must handle them, use extreme caution or a pair of thick leather gloves. Following are some basic descriptions and photos of the most common rockfish caught in Alaska.

Black & Dusky: These rockfishes are popular because they are often found near the surface in large schools, offering the greatest sport opportunities for anglers, particularly for flyfishermen. These two fish are very similar in appearance. Both are mostly solid or only lightly mottled or blotched black to dark blue and gray. Duskies have two pores on each lower jaw, and have darker bellies than blacks. Duskies also have a dark peritoneum, or inner body cavity, whereas blacks are light, but you have to kill the fish to see this. Duskies also come in a light brown form that is not usually encountered by anglers. Black rockfish grow to about 24 inches, duskies to about 20 inches. Most of the black rockfish caught are from eight to 20 years old but may reach ages of 50 years. Duskies may reach ages of nearly 70 years.

Yelloweye (also commonly called red snapper): These are the largest, oldest, and most desirable for trophies and table fare of all rockfishes. They are recognized by their orange/yellow or orange/red color and bright yellow eye (iris). Some young adults and most juveniles will have a light or white stripe along the lateral line, with juveniles often showing two such bands, one on and one below the lateral line. Some may also have darkened fin edges. They can be easily confused with a few other but uncommonly caught non-pelagic rockfish such as shortraker, rougheye,

Pacific Ocean perch, vermilion, and canary rockfish. They grow to lengths up to 36 inches and reach ages of 100 years or slightly more. Most yelloweye caught average five to ten pounds and are from 15 to 45 years old. Yelloweye prefer depths greater than 60 feet and are often found in areas also inhabited by lingcod.

Quillback and Copper: Quillback and copper rockfish look similar, but usually display enough distinguishing characteristics to help tell them apart. Both fish have relatively long and sharp dorsal fin spines, but the quillback's are slightly longer and less "webbed." Quillbacks are brown/dark brown with mottled, subdued shades of yellow, orange, or tan. The mottling, however, is concentrated on the forward half of the fish, with the rear half being mostly solid in color. Coppers are variable in color, but usually olive brown to copper, with pale pink to almost white and/or yellow blotches. Usually on coppers the lateral line is partially highlighted with a pale streak. Blotches or mottling on the copper are much more extensive and brighter than on the quillback. These two fish, copper in particular, might be confused with the rarer China rockfish, which has strikingly contrasting black and yellow mottling—quite a beautiful fish, usually less than 14 inches. Quillbacks reach up to 24 inches and live to more than 70 years old. Coppers grow to 22 inches and may live to at least 50 years old.

RANGE, ABUNDANCE & STATUS

Rockfishes inhabit rocky inshore and open offshore environs from Southeast Alaska to the Bering Sea, along the Alaska Peninsula and Aleutian Islands. The number of species and composition varies throughout their range and, generally, the number of species diminishes northward. Most of the Alaska species are also found along the northwest Pacific coast, some as far south as Baja California.

There are some good references for rockfish identification that I recommend. I'm sure you will at least enjoy looking at the pictures of the myriad rockfish species:

Guide to Northeast Pacific Rockfishes, by Donald E. Kramer and Victoria M. O'Connell. Alaska Sea Grant Marine Advisory Bulletin #25. University of Alaska, (2003), *www.uaf.edu/seagrant/Pubs_Videos /pubs/MAB-25.html.*

Coastal Fish Identification: California to Alaska, by Paul Humann. New World Publications, Inc., Jacksonville, FL, 1996.

The **National Marine Fisheries Service—Alaska Marine Science Center** has an excellent website on rockfish identification: *www.afsc.noaa.gov/ groundfish/RockfishGuide/rockfishtoc.htm.*

The Alaska Department of Fish and Game and Alaska Sea Grant have a color brochure, *Angler's Guide to the Rockfishes of Alaska,* that is available at offices throughout coastal Alaska.

According to the Alaska Department of Fish and Game's annual postal survey, anglers harvest an average of approximately 120,000 rockfish annually in Alaska. Many more are released than are reported harvested; sadly, most of these returned fish die. Currently, stock status of near-shore species is unknown due to the difficulty and costs of conducting adequate studies. According to the Alaska Department of Fish and Game, populations of some species appear depressed in some areas as indicated by harvest information, age composition (relative decrease of older fish or lack of young fish coming into population), and angler reports. Because rockfish are easy to find and catch, are slow growing, mature at a late age, and have low reproduction rates, they are highly susceptible to overfishing. It takes many years for them to replenish and some species, once down, may not recover within a single human lifetime. Management of Alaska rockfish is now more conservative, with increased restrictions on sport and commercial harvests.

The deepwater, non-pelagic rockfishes include some of Alaska's longest-lived and largest species, such as the short-raker rockfish, shown here. This specimen is the largest rockfish ever caught in Alaska (38 lbs., 11 oz., with angler Rosemary Roberts of Iowa) and was taken in over 600 feet of water from South-central's Prince William Sound.

LIFE HISTORY & HABITS

Most rockfish species have similar life histories, with main differences occurring in age at maturity, growth, and adult habitat preferences. Sexual maturity is reached at 4 to 23 years of age, depending on species. Mating takes place in the fall and fertilization of eggs is internal but delayed. The female carries viable sperm through the winter. The eggs are fertilized when the time is right, and from spring through the summer they give birth to live young. Fecundity ranges from several thousand to several million; large rockfish such as the yelloweye can have as many as three million young. The young are planktonic larvae, hardly resembling fish for several months, before settling in shallow waters near kelp beds, piers, and other structures. Juvenile rockfishes feed on plankton and, as they grow, they work their way up the food chain, switching to copepods, shrimp, small fish, etc. As they develop, they also move off to deeper waters. Success of broods is quite variable, and rockfish populations are characteristically comprised of several strong (successful) year classes interspersed with many weak ones. Most rockfish species stay within a specific area their entire adult lives, while some migrate to deeper water for the winter. Adult rockfishes are opportunists and feed on sand lance, herring, juvenile fish of any species, crabs, shrimp, squid, and octopus.

FISHING ALASKA'S ROCKFISH

Anglers in Alaska catch over a quarter million rockfish every year. Most of the effort occurs in the Sitka and Ketchikan/Prince of Wales areas in Southeast, and Prince William Sound, Kenai's Gulf Coast, and Kodiak Island in Southcentral. Many of these rockfish are caught incidentally while fishing for halibut, lingcod, or salmon.

Because the non-pelagic species are easily overfished, and quite often die once brought to the surface, I recommend you concentrate on fishing the pelagic species, mainly black and dusky rockfish. These fish are often numerous, most likely to be found within 10 to 40 feet of the surface, and are great sport on light tackle, especially flyfishing gear. Anglers used to fishing for freshwater bass or walleyes will feel right at home fishing for these species.

The best areas to find pelagics are around points, capes, and small islands and rocks, particularly those areas with kelp beds in close proximity to deeper water. The closer to the tumultuous waters of the Gulf of Alaska/North Pacific the better. It is often not possible or even desirable to anchor up in these areas; better to simply drift and reposition when necessary. When conditions allow, some anglers find success anchoring on a shallow shelf adjacent to deep water.

When scoping out areas and probing for rockfish, try casting towards or along kelp lines or rocky outcrops, and work the lure or fly through various depths. Often schools of pelagic rockfish will be about mid-depth but can be encouraged or teased to the surface. Offshore pinnacles or reefs can also provide hot fishing for pelagic rockfish. Be wary too of any surface feeding and bird activity.

Location is the primary factor for catching rockfish and, if you feel you have worked a promising location through various depths with no luck, move on. In some cases you may want to try trolling to efficiently search more area, especially if you are already rigged up to catch salmon.

Although rockfish have small home ranges, they do move around; some places will be good most of the time while others may be hit or miss. Often they will simply move according to the tide, finding tidal lees or eddies where food will be brought to them. Usually, though, rockfish are voracious feeders, so when you do find them action will be hot. If they seem to have gone off the bite, try different lures; if that doesn't work, relocate.

Fishing for the non-pelagic or bottom-dwelling rockfishes is very easy. Among non-pelagics are the prized yelloweye or "red snapper," and the enormous (up to 40 pounds or more) shortraker. Both of these ancient sages are found in waters deeper than 60 feet and, in the case of shortrakers, as deep as 600 feet. Again, because they are rockfish, search for deep rocky ridges, shelves, pinnacles, and plain rocky substrate, and fish near or on the bottom with jigs or bait. Areas that have good food-bringing tidal action will often be the best. You should have no problem finding the smaller non-pelagic rockfish too, such as coppers, quillbacks, and Chinas, in just about any rocky habitat in bays, passes, outer reefs, and islands at a wide range of depths. Due to legal and ethical issues, fishing for non-pelagic rockfish has constraints. In most areas of Alaska the bag limit is one or two yelloweye, and no more than five non-pelagics in combination. If the water depth is greater than 50 or 60 feet, bringing one to the surface is almost certain death unless you can reel one in slowly enough for it to "decompress"—highly unlikely. Although some fish can be released unharmed, it can be tough to judge their survival chances until you throw them back, when many will float back up to the surface. If you've been halibut or, especially, lingcod fishing, chances are you also have some non-pelagic or trophy yelloweye to take home.

The most commonly used artificials for Alaska rockfish are small to medium sized flashy/bright spoons, jigs and flies.

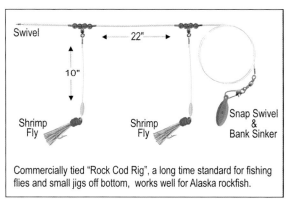

Commercially tied "Rock Cod Rig", a long time standard for fishing flies and small jigs off bottom, works well for Alaska rockfish.

Gearing Up

Conventional Tackle: An appropriate set-up for Alaska's rockfish is a light to medium weight, 6 1/2 to 8-foot spin or casting setup with 6 to 15-pound test line. Some people prefer using a lightweight fiberglass live bait type rod, such as those made by Calstar or Seeker. I like these set-ups, popular for calico bass fishing on the California kelp beds, because of their stout butt section, fast taper, and durability. They are also handy to have for other lighter tackle duties such as fishing for small halibut. "Muskie sticks", especially those on the lighter side, are good too; they are stout enough to work a wide range of lure weights, yet are light enough to enjoy. A stiff tip is desired for hook setting and working jigs. Of course, any ultra-light outfit will serve an essential role for intrepid anglers fishing for shallow-water rockfish. Heftier conventional or typical halibut gear is used for deepwater fishing for non-pelagic rockfish.

For terminal tackle, Crippled Herring, Nordic, and Stinger jigs, Krocodile, Kastmaster, and Mepps Syclops spoons, or other similar lures such as the offshore standbys like Diamond, Gibbs, YoYo, and Salas jigs all work well. Lead-head jigs with bucktail or rubber scampi-type tails work great too. The upturned hook is advantageous for avoiding snags in rocks and kelp. Best colors are chrome or chrome/metallic blue, white, red, yellow, orange, green/chartreuse, or combinations of these colors. Best size and weight will depend on your set-up and the type of fishing.

For most pelagic (and, in some cases, non-pelagic) rockfish, lure weights from 3/8 to 2 or 3 ounces will cover most situations. If you intend to fish for yellow-eye or other deepwater non-pelagics, you will want to use lure weights of 6 to 20 ounces or more, depending on depth, current, wind, etc. When using lighter outfits requiring smaller lures, stick to the denser types such as the Crippled Herring, Nordic, etc., for maximum sinking and casting efficiency. There is no need to use barbed hooks or trebles on lures for rockfish, so you should replace any factory-supplied trebles with barbless siwash hooks.

ROCKFISH ON A FLY

Rockfish can provide exciting and abundant angling on a fly throughout much of their range in Alaska, if you look for the right conditions and gear up properly. You can enjoy good rockfishing without lengthy, expensive charters or a lot of specialized equipment. Some of the best areas are within reach of major coastal hubs, and good rockfish tackle can easily be fashioned from some of the basic saltwater setups used for other species.

The ideal conditions for taking rockfish on a fly in Alaska's nearshore environment are the pinnacles, rock piles, and other structure they favor, in depths of 40 feet or less, that can be easily reached with lines up to 400 grains. One of the problems with areas that offer abundant rockfishing at depths of 80 to 100 feet or more is the work (and time required) to sink a line down that far, and the fact that it's hard and often dangerous to anchor on a rock pile.

Gearing Up

The ideal gear combination will be a fast action, 9 to 10-weight rod with a 400-grain line. This system is fast sinking, strong enough to handle the big lingcod that are always a possibility when fishing rockfish areas, and still will allow you to have fun with a good seven to eight-pound rockfish. You can fish lighter, say with a 6, 7, or 8-weight, and it certainly makes catching the fish a lot more fun, but the problem you'll have is fishing the heavier lines above 300 grains. They're

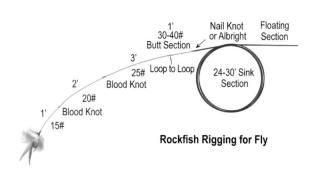

Rockfish Rigging for Fly

too cumbersome with the lighter rods, and you won't get the fly down as quickly as you need to. (Plus, you'll have a heck of a job dealing with a big ling on the lighter tackle.)

You'll need a matching, sturdy reel capable of holding your line plus about 150 yards of backing, one built with a reliable drag system, either sealed graphite or high quality cork. Saltwater is rough on all the gear, especially reels, so regular maintenance is essential, including liberal freshwater rinsing and wiping down after each use, plus periodic disassembly, cleaning, and lubrication.

To meet the challenge of the different conditions encountered on a typical Alaska rockfish safari, you'll want to bring an assortment of sinking line weights; say, for instance, the T-series from 200 to 750 grain, or the Deepwater Express saltwater lines, or even some shooting heads. (You can manufacture your own heads using sections of high density, 550-860 grain line.) The problem with fishing heavier lines is the fun they take out of catching small fish, plus the big rods you need to cast them, so it goes without saying that the shallower you can fish, the better.

For leaders, any type of hard monofilament (like Mason or Maxima Chameleon) will do. You can use straight monofilament, but you'll find that a tapered leader works much better in turning the fly over. Keep your leader short, no longer than five feet. Start with a butt section that's about 60% of the width of the fly line, usually 30 to 40-pound, and taper it down to 25 and then 20-pound, and finally 15. (You can use 8 to 12-pound tippet, but it doesn't seem to make that much difference as rockfish are not leader shy, and the heavier line will allow you to hoist up many of the fish.)

For flies, the number one thing is durability, as rockfish are not super selective and, on a good piece of water, you'll catch 20 to 60 fish a day, so all the gear takes quite a beating. Original rockfish patterns were developed to mimic a lot of their natural food sources—krill, shrimp, squid, crab, small bait fish, etc.—found throughout their environment. But it was soon realized that attractor patterns work just as well as the natural food imitations.

Rockfish flies should be simple, rugged creations tied tarpon, jig, or streamer style. Rabbit fur and synthetics hold up much better than feathers, and the best colors seem to be Mylar (silver and pearl), yellow, chartreuse, orange, red, green, and white. (Keep in mind that colors change drastically with depth—at 20 feet most color is very muted, and at greater depths the only real prominent color is green to black.) Fluorescent and even phosphorescent materials that you charge with a portable flash can be used with great effect in extreme conditions. Use high quality, saltwater, straight eye baitfish hooks, size #2 to #2/0, and wrap with heavy thread and epoxy the heads for maximum durability.

Typically, in most of the nearshore areas you can effectively flyfish, you'll be targeting black rockfish, a species which varies in size from a pound and a half to seven or eight pounds or, in the case of trophies, around ten. One of the problems you have with rockfish, in areas that are within major concentrations of people, is that they're usually overfished, with consequent populations of smaller fish. Ideally, then, you should focus on waters beyond the zones of high use by pleasure and charter boats.

Technique

The technique is very similar to that for used for flyfishing halibut—you're doing a vertical sink with your fly line, only usually at less depth. A stripping basket is handy, but not essential if you have good line control, as you're fishing with short lines. A long line for rockfishing is 60 feet. After you make a roll cast, normally you add two or three slack line mends on top of that to get the fly down deep, and then let it sink before stripping the fly. You want the straightest line into the fish as possible, with the least amount of slack. The rod tip should never be high, but instead pointed down at the water, with your stripping hand on the line. When the fish grabs the fly, come tight on the line at the same time you lift the rod up.

Rockfish grabs are normally hard. Most of the time you can set the hook with a firm strip. You might want to try using circle hooks on your flies, as the rockfish will grab the fly, turn, and set the hooks themselves. The fish will rarely swallow them deep, and mortality is greatly reduced. They are more difficult to remove, however, as you've got to back them out carefully a full turn to avoid tweaking the fish's jaw. If you do fish circle hooks, be sure to pinch the barbs, as it will make the removal process much easier and less destructive.

The boat captain can make or break your rockfish adventure. If he/she has a sound knowledge of local waters and is aware of all the factors that can affect successful presentation—tide, wind, water depth, currents, etc.—he/she can maneuver the boat to keep you in the "strike zone." If the captain doesn't take the time or really care to learn the ropes of flyfishing rockfish, he/she can be a hindrance or even a liability to your enjoyment and safety on the water.

Many charter boat captains do not like to fish rockfish because they're gear intensive—clients get tangled up and hung on bottom frequently so, if you have a lot of people on the boat, it can be a real mess. Plus, rockfish are not generally looked upon as a prize species, as they're a lot of work to clean for the amount of meat they provide. Also, boats and rocks do not mix well, so many charter boat captains do not like fishing areas that can potentially damage their vessels.

A skipper who fishes a large boat with many gear-fishing passengers is not going to have the latitude to handle the special needs of flyfishermen, so it's a good idea to stick with exclusive, small group charters of four people or less. That way there are no conflicts with gear slingers and never too many people fishing at once. It's a good idea to coordinate everyone's casting to keep lines from tangling, and allow for fishing different positions on the boat. (This will be absolutely necessary if you don't have a deckhand; you'll need to rotate and keep one angler free to help with the fish landing/releasing.)

The prevailing winds and tide will have a great effect on casting and drifts, so everyone should pay attention to the conditions and adjust their casting strategy accordingly. If the tide's running right to left, for example, the first fisherman on the left side of the boat would cast "upstream" and, as the fly drifts, the next person to the right would cast "upstream," and then drift, and then the next angler and so on, in an orchestrated effort not unlike fishing from a crowded riverbank. Normally, when you hit a pinnacle or other structure, you can be into hundreds of eager rockfish, so a well-rehearsed group casting effort will go a long way in keeping things under control.

TIDES, TIMING, LOCATIONS & OTHER FACTORS

Tides are not as crucial when flyfishing rockfish as they are with halibut, but moderate tides certainly help. The main problem with large tide differentials is that your drifts become very fast, which may, depending on where you are, make for some tough fishing. If, for instance, you find a location that doesn't have any landmarks within range that you can use to triangulate your position on the water, you'll have to rely on your GPS unit. If there's, lets say, a five or seven-knot tide running, and all you've got is a latitude/longitude position where you know the fish are, it can be almost impossible to predict and control your drift—you may be ten feet or 20 yards off that pinnacle as you pass through, with a very short time for your flies to be within the "strike zone."

When you're fishing a piece of structure, it helps to visualize the rock pile or pinnacle being just like a rock in a river, in the way fish will hold around it. If you're fishing the front side of that rock on an incoming tide, the rockfish aren't going to be there, they're going to be on the backside, where they don't have to swim as much. When nothing is happening over a good structure, you can change position (sometimes 50 yards or less) and suddenly everyone's catching fish. And, if you stay for the tide change, the fish will start to move back to the other side. So the fish are moving constantly around that rock in some formation. Where you find them sometimes requires trial and error until you have the structure figured out regarding the way it fishes with the tide.

Another important factor to consider about tide changes is the way they affect the captain's willingness to approach and steady (or idle) the boat "upstream" from rock structures, so that anglers can flyfish and sink their flies down properly. The majority of charter boat captains are reluctant to put a 30-foot boat within 50 feet of a shallow rock pile, especially with a big tide change running. Now, if you have more subdued tides, you're might find some skippers willing to put you in a position where you're going to be on the fish. (This is the reason that many local rockfish

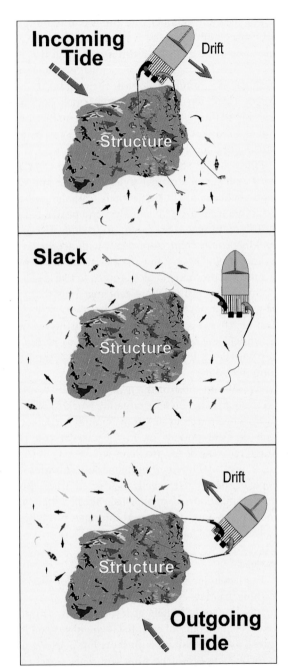

Rockfish concentrated around reefs, seamounts, rock piles, etc., will change their location with the tides, seeking shelter from the current, much like fish in a river. Successful anglers will use charts, fish finders, common sense, and trial and error to fish these areas safely and productively.

populations have survived. Long liners have a hard time dropping gear on rocky outcroppings without losing it, and the big charter boats stay away from the rock zones for the reasons described above.)

Some fishermen will use marker buoys to help get a visual reference on the location of reefs, pinnacles, and other structure, much the same as trollers in the Great Lakes. This can work well, but their accuracy is limited in areas of greater depth and/or when dealing with fast tidal currents. New navigational aids that extrapolate bathymetric data into 3D representations allow anglers to read the bottom like never before, to pinpoint fish locations and enjoy more productive fishing.

Time of day does not seem a critical factor; however, direct sunlight and the brighter hours around noon seem to produce the best rockfishing, perhaps because the flies are more visible in the water, partic-

ularly the synthetics that are activated with light. Under the right conditions, you may even be able to coax rockfish to the surface and catch them on floating flies dabbled off the back of the boat.

Yearly timing isn't as much a factor as with fishing other species. Rockfish can be taken year-round in Alaska's waters, though they are found deeper in the winter months with colder water temperatures. During the warmer, brighter months (April through October), of course, the weather and length of the days are more conducive to making offshore trips in search of good areas for flyfishing.

WHERE TO GO

Alaska has many outstanding locations for flyfishing rockfish. The best, like those for fishing with conventional gear, are located in the rock strewn outer waters along the Gulf of Alaska and North Pacific. The ideal are shallow locations with lots of structure within close range of shore, to make it easier to keep the boat on top of fish. (Locations in the open ocean can be very productive but difficult to get good drifts over.) Great scenery is always a plus, and many of the better rockfish areas are located in beautiful surroundings.

Southcentral's North Gulf Coast, which includes Kodiak Island, the rugged Kenai Fjords, and Prince William Sound, has an abundance of areas that fit these ideal criteria for great flyfishing locations. Southwest's sprawling Alaska Peninsula/Aleutians likewise hold a world of barely touched, ideal waters for abundant rockfishing on a fly. And, of course, Southeast, with its abundant locations (from Icy Straits to POW) and ideal coastal physiography, is the mecca for the rockfish fly angler, offering an unmatched variety of fishing, including many trophy opportunities.

Top Flies for Alaska Rockfish
Weaver's Deep Six, Calamari, Squid, Crazy (Rockfish) Charlie, Shrimp, Seaducer, Crab, Herring, Candlefish, Clouser Minnow, Deceiver, Needlefish, Sandlance, Whistler.

ROCKFISH
Sebastes spp.

SPECIES SUMMARY

Alaska Common Names: Rock cod, sea bass, bass, red snapper, snapper.

Description: Common small to large perch or bass-like ocean fish, with spiny fins and gill covers. Color varies by species, from dark blue to brown or red; mottled, striped, or solid. Flesh white.

Size: Varies; most rockfish, small to medium sized, 2-5 lbs. average, but some species to 40 lbs.

State/World Record: 39 lbs., 4 oz., Whalers Cove (SE). David Mundhenke, 2000.

Habits: Bottom dwelling individuals and groups to schooling pelagic (throughout water column). Sedentary and migratory. Feed on shrimp, small fish, squid.

Notes: Rockfish are among the longest lived fish in the sea.

Meristics: (general, varies by species) gill rakers 25- 41, vertebrae 25-27; dorsal 11-14 spiny rays, 11-17 soft rays; anal fin usually 3 spiny, 6-9 soft rays.

Range: Coastal and outer waters from Southeast Alaska to Aleutian Islands, some species in outer and coastal waters of Bering Sea.

Preferred Habitat: Rocky areas, kelp beds, underwater reefs, and sea mounts.

Best Waters: Rocky shorelines/points, submerged reefs, kelp beds, deepwater shelves, and pinnacles, SSE-Aleutians.

Best Times: Spring through fall.

Best Bait/Lures/Flies: Squid, small herring, octopus; small, flashy/bright, metal, and lead-head jigs and spoons; forage and attractor pattern flies.

Best Trophy Areas: Unexploited, rocky waters along Gulf of Alaska/North Pacific: the outer coasts of Kruzof, Chichagof, and Baranof Islands (Sitka); outer coast, Prince of Wales Island; Cross Sound/Icy Straight (Juneau or remote town/lodge); Prince William Sound (Wells and Knight Island passages and outer coastal points); (Seward) Resurrection Bay/Kenai Fjords coastline and outer islands; Kodiak Archipelago; Aleutian Islands.

RECOMMENDED GEAR

Baitcasting:
Halibut type set-ups typically used for deepwater fishing. May go to medium-heavy steelhead or muskie type set-ups (rated for 10 to 25 lb. test) when fishing pelagic rockfish.

Spinning:
Light to medium-heavy, 6 1/2 to 7 1/2-ft., medium-fast action, inshore rod. High quality anodized reel, 8-17 lb. test line. May go lighter or heavier depending on depth of fish.

Flyfishing:
8-10 wt., fast action, 9 1/2 ft. graphite rod; matching high quality anodized reel with 150 yds. 30 lb.backing. T-series, 200-400 grain full sink or shooting heads (Type III-VI), with short (less than 5 ft.) leader and 15 lb. tippet.

ALASKA'S MAJOR ROCKFISH LOCATIONS

SOUTHEAST

Ketchikan: Anglers can find non-pelagic and a few pelagic species in likely habitat around Gravina Island (such as Vallenar Point and Rock, Blank Island), Breton Island (Tatoosh and the smaller islands along Clover Passage), and Hog Rocks. Good locations for pelagic rockfish are fairly limited and require larger boats, places like Percy Island and other habitats around Duke Island. For adventurous anglers with the wherewithal, resorts such as Waterfall (Prince of Wales Island), usually accessed by plane from Ketchikan, offer outstanding fishing for pelagic rockfish and trophy yelloweye.

Craig (Prince of Wales Island): Because of its proximity to the outer waters of the Gulf of Alaska, Craig offers some of the best rockfish opportunities in Alaska (it's hard to find a place where you won't encounter any rockfish). You will find pelagics around many of the small rocks and islands in San Alberto Bay and beyond. You can even catch some from shoreline areas accessible by road. As with most major port towns, local stocks of non-pelagics have been depleted. The outer water areas, however, will still produce, but require larger boats and good weather.

Sitka: The outer waters adjacent to Sitka Sound are a rockfish mecca. Many enormous yelloweye have been pulled from these

#2 Deep Six

Strata Spoon
2 oz.

Crystal Mino Jig
2 oz.

#2 Silly Legs
Seaducer

Syclops Spoon
1 oz.

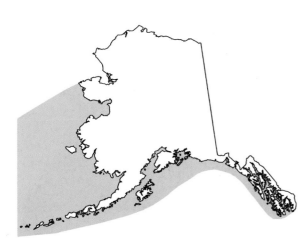

depths. The numerous rocky shorelines, capes, and points, and small islands, such as Vitskari Island, harbor abundant pelagic rockfish.

Juneau/NSE: Rockfish opportunities are limited near Juneau. Head to Hoonah, Gustavus, and Elfin Cove where charters can access Icy Straight, Cross Sound, and Glacier Bay. The saltwater fishing in these areas is extraordinary. A few of many places where rockfish are found include Sisters Reef, Pleasant Island/Reef, Point Couverden, Lemesurier Island, Inian Islands, George Islands, Cape Spencer, and Yakobi Island.

Yakutat: Pelagic rockfish are prolific, while there is only limited fishing for non-pelagics. Use a nautical chart and good sonar fishfinder to find old glacial moraines and rocky areas around Yakutat Bay, or utilize the services of a reputable charter.

SOUTHCENTRAL

Prince William Sound (Valdez/Cordova/Whittier): Best places to find pelagics are the points, capes, and bays of Green Island, Montague and Hinchinbrook islands, the shorelines bordering Hinchinbrook Entrance, and southern ends of Elrington, Latouche, and Montague islands. Non-pelagic rockfish are found just about anywhere in the Sound with a rocky bottom. Trophy-sized shortraker and some nice yelloweye can be caught out of Whittier and Valdez, however, the best fishing locations are closer to Gulf of Alaska waters, such as Hinchinbrook Entrance, Seal Rocks, and Danger Island. Other good places to check for non-pelagics are rocky areas and shelves near deep water in Wells Passage and Knight Island Passage in the western sound, and Port Fidalgo and Port Gravina in the eastern sound.

Seward/Kenai Gulf Coast: The farther away from the port of Seward, the better the fishing for rockfish. Places to try for pelagics include Aialik Cape, Chiswell Islands, Natoa Island, Granite Island, Rugged Island, and Cape Resurrection. For non-pelagics, including trophy yelloweye, look for submerged rocky bottoms, seamounts, and reefs such as Pye Reef (see chapter on lingcod).

Homer: Kachemak Bay, mainly the south/southwest shoreline, offers some limited rockfish opportunities. Pelagic rockfish, mainly blacks, are frequently caught by anglers trolling for salmon along the shoreline near Bluff Point. For good pelagic rockfish fishing and yelloweye your best chances are the outside waters from English Bay on to the Chugach Islands and beyond. Such trips are best done with a fairly good-sized boat, or during extended calm weather conditions.

Kodiak: Anglers will find that there's a rockfish "hole" on every corner among the Kodiak Archipelago, most of which remain virtually untapped. The rocky points on the outer edges of Chiniak Bay are your best bets close to town for pelagics. Good areas can also be accessed by boat from Anton Larsen Bay, such as Spruce Island, and the points, capes, and rocky areas of Afognak Island bordering Marmot Bay and Shelikof Strait.

SOUTHWEST

Most of the Alaska Peninsula/Aleutians offer virtually untapped rockfish angling, with excellent trophy possibilities for species like yelloweye, rougheye, shortraker, black, and dusky. Access is expensive and facilities/services very limited; anglers would do best working from established hubs like Chignik, Sand Point, Dutch Harbor/Unalaska, and Nikolski/Umnak Island.

Alaska's Top Ten Trophy Rockfish		
39 lbs., 4 oz.	Whalers Cove (SE)	2000
38 lbs., 11 oz.	Prince William Sound (SC)	2001
37 lbs., 12 oz.	Unakwik Inlet (SC)	2008
37 lbs., 2 oz.	Passage Canal (SC)	1995
35 lbs., 13 oz.	Clarence Strait (SE)	1994
35 lbs., 8 oz.	Wells Passage (SC)	2001
35 lbs., 6 oz.	Cook Inlet (SC)	2008
33 lbs., 9 oz.	Gulf of Alaska (SC)	2010
33 lbs., 3 oz.	Cape Addington (SE)	1996
33 lbs., 3 oz.	Dall Island (SE)	1995

| #4 Shrimp | #2 Crazy Charlie | Diamond Jig 3 oz. | #25 Nordic Jig | Soft Tail Jig 1 1/2 oz. |

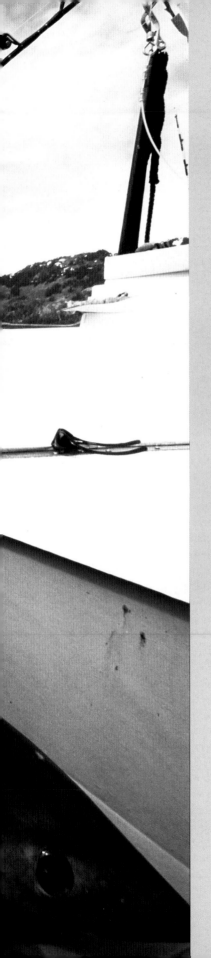

Salmon Shark
Alaska's Big Game Fish

Doug Green and I had wanted to fish the Gulf of Alaska, and we had tried. But the seas had been too rough, even for his 34-foot cabin cruiser. So we had turned and run to a protected bay, where we anchored and waited for better weather.

While Doug made sandwiches, I rigged halibut outfits. We had caught halibut in bays such as this before. Doug free-spooled a herring 200 feet to the bottom and stuck his rod in a rod holder. I jigged for a while, but caught only a small Pacific cod. Tired of jigging, I decided to fish with the cod, which I had kept alive in a bucket of water. The only suitable hook I could find for a live-bait rig happened to be on several feet of steel cable. I hooked the cod through the back, lowered it to the bottom, and sat down to eat my sandwich.

A few minutes later, something took my bait and swam off with it. When I tightened the drag and set the hook, it was as if I had lassoed a passing truck. Cranking down the drag, I bent the tuna stick into a severe arc and eventually stopped the run. It took everything I had to regain a few yards of line.

"If this is a halibut, it's a real barn door," I said.

When Doug reeled in the other line, he found that the 300-pound monofilament leader had been bitten off as cleanly as if it had been cut with a knife. Doug put a fighting belt on me and readied the harpoon, gaff, and gun. The fish went wherever it wanted to go. Twice I had it to within 50 feet or so of the surface. Twice it returned to the bottom. Against this monster, my 50-pound halibut gear felt like an eight-weight fly rod.

Neither of us had ever hooked a salmon shark but, after ten minutes of fighting this fish, we figured this must be one. Rather than coming up near the boat as big halibut usually do, it came up some distance away, swimming hard, just out of sight beneath the surface.

Twenty minutes into the fight, we were certain it was a big shark. Having had all the fun I wanted, I handed the rod to Doug. We decided to release the fish as soon as we got a look at it. With only the two of us aboard, it would have been impossible to boat a fish heavier than about 300 pounds, and this one was definitely heavier than that.

Doug applied steady pressure. After a few minutes of this, the shark looked as if it would surface. Instead, it swam in a circle around the boat. With the anchor down, we had no way of maneuvering. The line caught on a prop or rudder, and the fish was free. Usually, when a big fish gets away, there's some disappointment and a sense of loss. Not this time. When the line broke, the only emotion we felt was relief. We didn't have that shark. It had us.

213

The streamlined *Lamna ditropis* is one of the fastest fish in the sea, capable of catching all but the swiftest prey.

SALMON SHARK: ALASKA'S BIG-GAME FISH

For the longest time, anglers who wanted to pit themselves against big fish in Alaska had to settle for halibut, but no longer. In recent years, salmon sharks have invaded Alaska's waters in unprecedented numbers, creating new and exciting big-game fishing opportunities. While conducting aerial salmon surveys in Southcentral's Prince William Sound not too long ago, Jeff Milton, a production manager for the Prince William Sound Aquaculture Corporation, witnessed an astonishing sight:

"There were several thousand salmon sharks in about a three-mile radius off Chenega Island," Milton said. "It looked like the water was just full of them."

Similarly, in other areas of the state, much larger than normal aggregations of these big fish-eaters are being reported. Scientists suspect that the shark population explosion may be partially due to ocean warming and increases in prey populations, particularly the immense number of hatchery salmon now being released along the southern coast. Whatever the cause, many charter boat captains in this fledgling fishery are claiming upwards of 15 hook-ups per trip, and nearly 100% hook-ups by anglers specifically targeting salmon sharks. As if that weren't enough to make an angler drool, salmon shark meat is highly edible. Often likened to swordfish, it can be prepared in a variety of ways, including baking, broiling, and poaching.

The salmon shark, *Lamna ditropis*, is a member of the family Lamnidae—the mackerel sharks. Its closest relative is the porbeagle (*Lamna nasus*), of the North Atlantic. Other relatives include the mako and the great white, the fish that prompted Brody, in the epic adventure "Jaws," to turn to the grizzled shark hunter Quint and say, "You're gonna need a bigger boat."

Lamna ditropis is a true big-game fish, one that can pin a strong man to the rail and hold him there. This large, fast-swimming predator is not a known man-eater, but it has the size and equipment to eat pretty much anything it wants. Much about the salmon shark remains a mystery, but one thing is clear: in the North Pacific, this powerful fish dominates the top of the food chain.

Commercial interest in shark fishing, coupled with an increase in charter boat fishing for sharks, prompted the Alaska Board of Fisheries in 1997 to regulate shark fishing in state waters. The board closed all commercial fishing and adopted conservative sport-fishing limits. Regulation in federal waters is under consideration.

Salmon sharks are long-lived and reproduce slowly, traits that make them vulnerable to overfishing. Because so little is known about this species,

Salmon sharks quite often prove to be more sport than most folks can handle; many anglers trade off with partners during a prolonged battle.

fisheries managers can be expected to continue to "err on the side of conservation" and to continue studies begun in recent years.

A plague to commercial salmon fishermen, the salmon shark rolls up in gillnets, steals salmon off lines, and carries away trolling gear. A joy to anglers, this aggressive fish offers a chance to do battle with a gamefish capable of reel-trashing runs and heart-stopping leaps. That it is such a mysterious creature only adds to its allure.

DESCRIPTION

Like other sharks, the salmon shark has a streamlined body that sports a prominent dorsal fin. Its caudal (tail) fin provides forward movement, and its large, rigid pectoral fins provide the necessary lift to keep it swimming level. Its head and snout are conical, somewhat round-tipped. It has five gill slits. Its skeleton is cartilage. Its color can vary from dark blue to slate-gray on the top and upper sides; the bottom has distinct gray blotches on a white background. Its mouth is relatively large, with awl-like teeth that are identical in both jaws. One or two series of functional teeth are common, and sometimes a third, immature series is present.

Lamna ditropis is well equipped to detect and home in on prey. For long-range detection, it employs olfactory organs that can smell chemical "odors" at dilutions as low as one part per billion, allowing it to detect prey from several hundred yards away. Its nostrils, functioning independently, guide it left and right, pointing it toward its prey. At medium ranges, other organs sense pressure and sound waves. At short distances and attack range, visual and electromagnetic receptors come into play.

The salmon shark is able to pursue prey throughout the water column because it has no swim bladder. Of neutral buoyancy, it must swim continuously to keep from sinking. This forward motion also forces water through its gills.

Studies have shown that the salmon shark has a higher body temperature than any other shark. Large specimens have been found to be as much as 13.6°C warmer than ambient water temperature. Being warm-bodied gives the salmon shark improved muscular efficiency, faster digestion, and a more efficient nervous system, all of which tend to make it more of a threat to prey fish.

Salmon sharks encountered by most anglers will probably be about seven feet long and weigh about 400 pounds, but much larger specimens have been reported. At Seward and Valdez, more than a few nine-footers have been brought ashore. Of the Valdez fish, which were bled and gutted before being weighed, one nine-footer weighed 400 pounds, and a nine-and-a-half-footer weighed 500 pounds. A fair number of charter boat captains and commercial fishermen swear they have caught and released 14-footers. A salmon shark that long would probably weigh around 1,000 pounds.

RANGE, ABUNDANCE & STATUS

Salmon sharks inhabit the coastal and offshore waters of the North Pacific, from the Sea of Japan to the Gulf of Alaska. In the eastern Pacific, their range may extend as far south as Baja California, Mexico. Usually found in deep water (130 to 350 feet), they become locally abundant in certain areas along the coast in summer, during the peaks of pink and chum salmon spawning migrations. Studies are being conducted on these shark aggregations in Prince William Sound and elsewhere. The overall abundance and status of these northern sharks, along with many aspects of their biology, remain unclear.

High numbers of such large, voracious predators can take a large bite out of salmon runs. In an aerial survey conducted in the fall of 2000 by the National Marine Fisheries Service, 2,000 salmon sharks were counted in one ten-square-mile section of Port Gravina, in north Prince William Sound. Biologist Bruce Wright estimated that those sharks would eat about two million pounds of salmon during the three months they were expected to remain there. Scientists wonder what those thousands of sharks are eating when they aren't eating salmon.

LIFE HISTORY & HABITS

Like all sharks, the salmon exhibits slow growth, late age of maturity, long lifespan, and low fecundity. Male salmon sharks mature typically at four to five feet length and five years of age; females at 5 1/2 to 6-foot length and 6 to 10 years age. Their life span has been estimated at 25 years or more and they have no major predators other than man.

Salmon sharks fertilize their eggs internally. Females often bear scars or marks on their pectoral fins, "love bites" from males that are trying to hold on while mating. Gestation time, based upon mating in late summer and birth in the spring, is thought to be about nine months. The young, called "pups," can weigh as much as 20 pounds at birth, and up to five may be born annually. They are born fully formed, free-swimming, and ready to fend for themselves.

The major prey of the adult salmon shark is salmon, but this opportunistic feeder will feed on cod, pollock, rockfish, sablefish, spiny dogfish, herring, capelin, squid, crab, and other crustaceans.

Little is known about their migration patterns. Biologists say there appears to be some annual movement north and south in both the eastern and western Pacific populations. In the spring, females in Alaska waters apparently migrate to the waters off Oregon and California to pup. Some research has indicated a north-south segregation by size, with the largest fish found in waters off Alaska, and a preponderance of smaller juvenile fish off the California coast.

Very few males are caught by sport anglers in Alaska, another mystery. Cordova charter boat skipper Luke Borer, one of the pioneers of salmon shark angling, claims that of the hundreds of sharks brought to boat each season, only a few are males. (The reverse seems to be true in the northwest Pacific, where populations are comprised mostly of males.)

Salmon sharks are supremely adapted for their roles as high speed apex predators, as this rare underwater photo shows.

These "tigers of the North Pacific" have been seen leaping clear of the water while pursuing salmon. They may be the fastest shark in the sea, according to some scientists. This would put them in the 40-mph-plus category, capable of running down all but the swiftest ocean prey.

FISHING ALASKA'S SALMON SHARKS

Salmon shark angling in Alaska is still very much a pioneer fishery, though it relies heavily on proven techniques and gear developed from shark fishing down south. Presently, almost all the focused effort on this species occurs along the North Gulf of Alaska, from Yakutat to Kodiak.

Though anglers will frequently hook salmon sharks while targeting other species, they seldom succeed in landing them unless they are rigged quite heavily. A big shark's teeth and sandpapery hide make short work of anything but steel leader, and its awesome runs can smoke all but the largest reels. On the rare occasion when one is brought to the boat, few anglers are prepared to handle 400 pounds of sharp-toothed aggression.

The first time you see a salmon shark thrashing the water to foam an arm's length away, Brody's remark about needing a bigger boat will take on real meaning. Bringing a large shark aboard anything less than a 30-footer is a risky undertaking. Even releasing one is hazardous. For these reasons, and others, virtually all salmon shark fishing in Alaska is done from charter boats specifically set up to handle these formidable fighters. These boats provide proper tackle, the right tools for releasing and harvesting sharks, and a safe, stable, and comfortable fishing

Super strong (2-3X), sharp 10/0- 14/0 circle or J-style tuna or shark hooks

14-20 feet multistrand, stainless cable leader, 400 lb. test minimum, with super heavy duty (600 lb.) swivels

Big Game reel (50-80 Class) spooled with several hundred yards 80-150 lb. line

Heavyweight, 5'6"-6', offshore, "stand-up" rod (rated 50-130 lb. line) with gimbal butt

platform. The good ones have a captain and crew with years of shark-fishing experience. Day-long charters with these professional salmon shark hunters range from $200 to $350 per person.

Gearing Up

Successful salmon shark fishing requires heavy offshore tackle. A typical setup would be a 5 1/2 to 6-foot tuna-stick rod (50 to 130 pounds) mated with a big game reel like the 50 series Penn International (or 50 series Shimano or Okuma), loaded with several hundred yards of 130-pound test superbraid line. A suitable leader is about 14-20 feet of one-sixteenth-inch steel aircraft cable. (500 to 600 pound clear mono can be used for catch and release fishing.) Bait is usually a whole pink or small chum salmon or cod fillet. (Note: sport-caught salmon cannot be used for bait.) Giant, strong hooks like the #16/0 circle, #12/0 Mustad Stainless Tuna, or #10/0 Owner Gorilla BG are usually employed.

Salmon sharks are located by watching for them on the surface and on the screen of a fish-finder. Sometimes they can be seen finning on the surface, alone or in groups. A large, boil-like disturbance on the surface is a good indication sharks are present. In

bays, where most shark fishing occurs, the fish are often found in shallower water of less than 100 feet.

Upon locating sharks, the bait is either mooched or trolled. Some skippers like to mooch while at anchor, free-spooling the bait to the bottom, then reeling it back up. A shark (or two) will sometimes follow the bait to the surface. Trolling can be done freestyle or from downriggers, depending on the depth of the fish, and is usually at fast speed. There's no mistaking the bite, although it's probably more subtle than most anglers would expect from so large a fish. Setting the hook is often more a matter of just hanging on and trying to stay in the boat.

When sharks are concentrated and shallow, some captains have had success with lures, using giant off-shore trolling plugs or large profile softbaits. A few daring anglers have even tried rousing them with large bluewater flies, with mixed results.

This is stand-up fishing. Some captains equip their clients with gimbal fighting belts and fighting harnesses that clip onto the reel. Others give anglers only a fighting belt, preferring not to harness clients to a fish that can pull them overboard. The typical fight consists of two or three runs and can last anywhere from 15 minutes to two hours. The trick is to keep the shark from tangling and rolling in the line, as its sandpaper-like hide can easily cut anything above the leader. One or two salmon sharks is all most anglers want to fight in a day of fishing.

The decision of whether to release or harvest a salmon shark deserves serious consideration and should be determined prior to fishing. First, processing and shipping 150 pounds or more of meat can cost several hundred dollars. Second, it's not easy to eat that much fish, even with the help of friends. Third, killing and butchering such a large animal is hard work that consumes time that could be spent fishing.

Another factor has a bearing on whether to release or harvest. Salmon shark meat contains high levels of urea and other metabolic constituents. To avoid "off" flavors and odors, the fish must be properly bled and processed. Because they are warm-bodied, the meat should be quickly cooled by surrounding it with ice. Unless this is done, spoilage will result.

The sport-fishing bag limit is one shark of any species per day and one in possession. The annual limit is two sharks. Anglers are required to record harvested sharks on a harvest report.

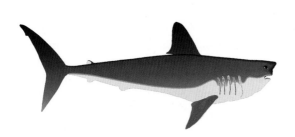

SALMON SHARK
Lamna ditropis

Best Times: June-September.

Best Bait/Lures: Whole or halved salmon or cod; large whole herring, squid; can also be enticed at times with large plugs, spoons, flies, and softbaits.

Best Trophy Areas: Salmon-rich areas, Northern Gulf-Aleutians; especially PWS, Kodiak, eastern Aleutians.

RECOMMENDED GEAR

5 1/2 ft. to 6 ft., stand-up, offshore tuna class rod, rated 50-130 lbs., with matching big game reel (Penn International 50-80 series or equivalent) loaded with 80-150 lb. braided line; terminal shock/bite leader of 16 ft. stainless cable (400-lb. test minimum) or 500-lb. clear mono leader with 2X-3X, #10/0-#14/0 circle or tuna/shark hooks.

SPECIES SUMMARY

Alaska Common Names: Salmon shark, porbeagle shark, mackerel shark, bottlenose shark, bonito shark.

Description: A large, warm-blooded, pelagic shark common in north Pacific. Streamlined, with conical snout, large mouth with smooth, dagger-like teeth, and robust body with blue-gray topsides, gray or white bottom, and grayish blotch marks. Flesh grayish to pinkish white.

Size: 6-8 ft., 250-400 lbs. average; to 10 ft. and 700 lbs. or more.

State Record: Currently not recognized as gamefish by ADF&G; IGFA All Tackle World Record fish 230 lbs., Port Gravina, PWS (SC), Ken Higginbotham, 2002.

Habits: Migratory, feeds opportunistically on a variety of fishes and invertebrates, especially fond of Pacific salmon. Forms dense schools around concentrated prey.

Notes: A large and formidable game fish; not to be pursued casually by sport anglers.

Range: Southern coastal waters, Dixon Entrance (SE) to Bering Sea (SW), to approximately 60° North latitude.

Preferred Habitat: Inshore/offshore areas containing large aggregations of prey.

Best Waters: Varies seasonally; locally abundant in summer in nearshore areas that concentrate prey, SSE-Aleutians: PWS (SC); Cross Sound/Icy Strait (NSE); lower Stephens Passage and Chatham Strait (CSE); Behm Canal (SSE); also can be taken in deepwater refuge areas during winter.

MAJOR SALMON SHARK LOCATIONS

Shark fishing is rapidly changing due to the explosive increase in shark numbers in some locations. Also, this is a relatively new fishery, one which even experienced charter boat skippers are still pioneering.

As with fishing for any migratory species, timing is all-important. Because the main diet of salmon sharks is salmon, the best time to fish for sharks is when salmon are milling around in bays, just prior to entering spawning streams. This means early July until mid-September for the peak fishing in most areas, though sharks can be taken as early as late May. The size of salmon runs can vary dramatically from year to year, which has an affect on where salmon sharks will be found. Check local sources before making arrangements.

SOUTHCENTRAL

Salmon sharks can be encountered in just about any salmon-rich bay during summer, but especially in areas that receive exceptionally heavy returns of pinks.

PWS: Bays with major salmon concentrations in Eastern Sound, like Port Gravina and Port Fidalgo accessed from Cordova and Valdez; also bays and other concentration areas in Southwest Sound (Montague Strait), accessed from Whittier or Seward.

Seward: Outer Resurrection Bay; salmon-rich bays along Kenai Coast (Aialik Bay, McCarty Fjord, etc.), and southwest Prince William Sound.

Kodiak: Chiniak, Ugak, Uyak bays.

Small Chum Salmon

Small Pink Salmon

Large "Horse" Herring

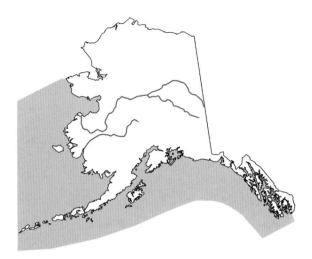

The Alaska Department of Fish and Game currently does not include salmon sharks in its Sport Fish Trophy Program. Anglers or organizations interested in getting this fish listed should write to: ADF&G Division of Sport Fish, P.O. Box 25526, Juneau, AK 99802-5526. The trophy program and a trophy fish affidavit are included in the Sport Fishing Regulations.

Salmon Shark Ethics

Unless you have the specialized gear, boat, and skills necessary to safely subdue fish as large and potentially dangerous as salmon sharks, hire the services of a competent shark charter.

Do not attempt to land a salmon shark hooked incidentally on lighter tackle. If you are fishing other species and hook a salmon shark, cut the line immediately.

If you fish with a charter, seriously consider whether you really want to kill any sharks and let the captain know your wishes before you begin fishing, so the appropriate gear and procedures can be used.

Take care of the meat. Make sure the shark is properly dressed and bled immediately once it is landed. Keep the carcass cool and process it as soon as possible to avoid off flavors and spoilage.

SOUTHEAST

Even more than Southcentral, this region has widespread salmon shark fishing potential beyond these historical hotspots.

Yakutat: Yakutat Bay.

Juneau: Cross Sound/Icy Strait.

Ketchikan: Behm Canal.

Sitka: Chatham Strait.

Petersburg/Wrangell: Lower Stephans Passage.

Recommended Salmon Shark Charters

Saltwater Safari Company: P.O. Box 241225, Anchorage, AK 99524-1225, 800-382-1564, (907) 224-5232, *www.saltwater safari.com*

Orion Charters: P.O. Box 3577, Valdez, AK 99686, (907) 835-8610, *www.orioncharters.com*

Sea Sound Charters: P.O. Box 422, Cordova, AK 99574, (907) 424-5488. *www.seasoundcharters.com*

Whittier Marine Charters: P. O. Box 2693, Soldotna, AK 99669, (907) 440-9510, *www.fishwhittier.com*

Mann's 11" Menhaden Soft Bait with scent oil

11" Yo-Zuri Bonita Plug with Blue Mackerel Finish

Large (10"), #7/0 tandem hook, baitfish/attractor streamer

Arctic

Extreme climate creates short open water season, with limited diversity of game fish species. Remoteness and lack of infrastructure make for challenging logistics and the most expensive and limited services of any region of state.
Main species: LT, GR, CHR
Climate: Arctic maritime to transitional arctic continental.

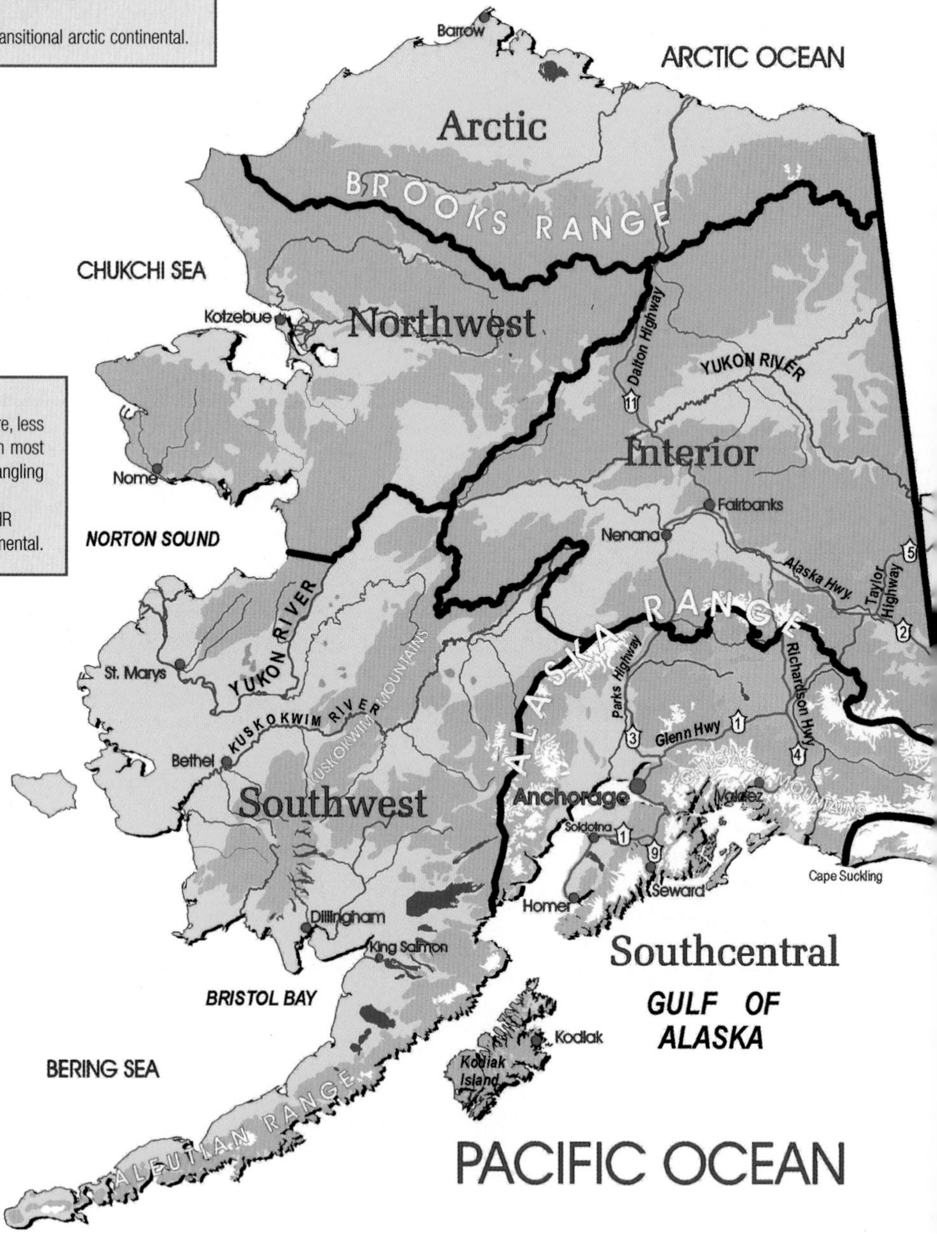

Interior

Well-developed infrastructure with wide range of guided and unguided options for anglers, at comparable prices to other regions. Consistently offers the state's best weather and fishing conditions, June to mid-September.
Main species: SF, NP, GR, LT, SS, KS
Climate: Extreme continental.

Northwest

More remote, with limited infrastructure, less visitor services and higher prices than most Alaska regions (but with unique angling potential).
Main Species: GR, LT, NP, SF, SS, CHR
Climate: Sub-arctic maritime to continental.

Southwest

Remote, roadless, fly-in fishing exclusively, with services geared to multi-day, guided fishing experiences—lodge, remote outpost, and float trips. Costs higher than comparable services in SC, SE, INT.
Main Species: KS, SS, RS, CS, RT, GR, CHR, LT, NP
Climate: Northern maritime to transitional continental.

Southcentral

Centrally located with very well developed infrastructure (including good roads) and abundant visitor services; prices among the lowest anywhere in Alaska.
Main Species: KS, SS, RS, PS, RT, HT, LC, DV, LT
Climate: North Temperate Maritime-Transitional Continental.

Barrow

ARCTIC OCEAN

Arctic

BROOKS RANGE

CHUKCHI SEA

Kotzebue

Northwest

Dalton Highway

YUKON RIVER

11

Interior

Nome

Fairbanks

NORTON SOUND

Nenana

Alaska Hwy

Taylor Highway

5

A L A S K A   R A N G E

2

St. Marys

YUKON RIVER

KUSKOKWIM RIVER

KUSKOKWIM MOUNTAINS

Parks Highway

Richardson Hwy

Bethel

3

Glenn Hwy

1

4

Southwest

Anchorage

Valdez

MOUNTAINS

Soldotna

1

6

9

Cape Suckling

Homer

Seward

Dillingham

Southcentral

King Salmon

GULF OF ALASKA

BRISTOL BAY

Kodiak

Kodiak Island

BERING SEA

ALEUTIAN RANGE

PACIFIC OCEAN

Regions Overview

Southwest

Maritime region, from Alaska Peninsula to Norton Sound. Fabulously endowed with prolific salmon and trout fisheries and the state's best stream fishing. Known for trophy rainbow trout, king, silver and red salmon, charr, and grayling. Country mostly rolling upland tundra with forested lowlands, clear flowing rivers, and Alaska's largest lakes.

Northwest

The coastal drainages from Norton Sound to Point Hope, including western Brooks Range. The country varies from broken boreal forests to arctic tundra, coastal lowlands to expansive mountain valleys and peaks. A lesser inhabited and visited region, with diversity of fine lake, river, and stream fishing opportunities, especially for trophy sheefish, charr, and grayling.

Interior

Alaska's heartland, province of giant rivers and countless associated lowland lakes and sloughs, vast birch and spruce forests and extremes of heat and cold. Fishing lacks the diversity of coastal regions, but offers perhaps Alaska's most abundant opportunities for northern pike, sheefish, and graying.

Southcentral

The mainland along the north Gulf, Alaska's most populous region. Offers greatest diversity of fishing, with marine, stream, and upland lake opportunities that are very representative of the broad range of fishing experiences Alaska has to offer. Country varied, from coastal rainforest to alpine tundra, lowland valleys to rugged mountains.

Arctic

The state's most northerly, remote, and uninhabited region. Known for its superlative wilderness, wildlife, and extreme climate. Country is treeless arctic tundra, from lake-dotted coastal plain to foothills and rugged mountain peaks and valleys. With exemplary wild rivers and lakes—among Alaska's most pristine—this region has potential for high quality angling experiences.

Southeast

Alaska's "panhandle," known for its outstanding saltwater fishing—Alaska's best—and abundant stream fishing for cutthroat and steelhead trout. This region is comprised of rugged, densely forested coastline, with countless islands and protected waters; almost all streams and lakes are small compared to mainland.

Southeast
Very well developed infrastructure, but no connecting roads to mainland. Abundant visitor services offering unmatched range of options for fishing vacations. Prices comparable or lower than elsewhere in Alaska. Has extended open water season, to twelve months in some areas.
Main Species: KS, SS, CS, PS, HT, RF, LC, ST, CT, DV

Southwest Alaska

It's five A.M. on an early August morning, and my East Coast buddy is waiting to greet me in the lobby of Anchorage's International Inn. Dave is one of those rare, lucky guys who can fish anywhere he wants in the world, yet every summer he returns for another adventure in a place that I'm convinced is more a state of mind than a region on the map—Southwest Alaska.

Land of prodigious salmon runs, giant brown bears, and the timeless Yupik Eskimo culture, this area of the state has potent mystique for anglers, with some of the sweetest stream fishing this side of Heaven in the countless sparkling tributaries of its major lake and river systems.

We make it to the airport on time and board a 737 jet that takes us several hundred miles west to one of the major fishing villages along the Bering Sea coast. From there, a small floatplane whisks us across broad tundra valleys and through mist shrouded mountains to the extreme headlands of Bristol Bay, where a lonely little stream awaits. We inflate our small raft and begin floating and fishing our way through some of the prettiest wild country we've ever seen.

Giant-finned grayling pounce on our flies in the shallow, rock-strewn headwaters and fight valiantly in the swift current. In crystal blue pools below long canyons, bright charr chase our streamers, along with dark salmon much too large to contemplate hooking on our light four-weights. We break up the fishing with short hikes up into the hills (to scout for caribou, wolf, and bear), berry picking, and long naps on the raft.

As it leaves the mountains, our river breaks up into gravelly braids and sloughs. Dave pulls one of the lifelike mouse imitation flies from his hatband and uses it to prompt explosive surface strikes from chunky, gorgeously marked rainbows. I stick with the notorious Egg Sucking Leech and do pretty well coaxing greedy charr and trout from under cutbanks. And so it goes for the next few days—rainbows, charr, grayling, and even some fairly bright silver salmon, in numbers that wouldn't make any sense anywhere but Alaska.

We lose all track of time exploring this stream fishing nirvana. But all too soon our time is up and we grudgingly put the rods away and bid farewell to our special river, secure in the knowledge that somewhere, at least, there are rivers that can deliver fishing adventures to haunt your dreams.

Headwater grayling and charr fishing,
Kilbuck Mountains

Floatfishing the upper Kisaralik River.

Stretching from the Alaska Peninsula to Norton Sound (an area the size of Montana), Alaska's vast Southwest corner is so rich and varied in natural wonders, it truly defies adequate description. It has the world's largest runs of Pacific salmon, and Alaska's most fabulous freshwater sportfishing locations in and around Bristol Bay, along with the state's most scenic mountain lake country (Lake Clark and the Wood-Tikchiks). There are unique volcanic landscapes (and fishing bears) in Katmai and the northern Alaska Peninsula, and an incredible, seldom-explored arc of rugged islands, the Aleutians, that sprawls across the North Pacific almost to the rocky shores of Asia. A haven for wildlife, with special marine mammal sanctuaries and immense waterfowl habitat, much of Southwest has been set aside in some of the largest parks, refuges, and preserves in America.

Most important to anglers are the abundant rivers and giant lakes found there. Unlike the glacial drainages that predominate along much of the Gulf coast, most of Southwest's waters run sparkling clear, providing perfect habitat for a profusion of salmon and an unrivaled variety of resident sport species—charr, grayling, rainbow trout, pike, lake trout, and even sheefish in some waters. No area better represents Alaska's extraordinary freshwater fishing opportunities than amazing Southwest.

COUNTRY, CLIMATE & FISHING CONDITIONS

Southwest Alaska is the area of the state that lies west of the Gulf of Alaska and south of the great Interior. It is predominantly a maritime province, heavily influenced by the nearby icy, stormy Bering Sea. (The 1,600-mile arc of the Alaska Peninsula/Aleutian Islands effectively isolates most of the region from the moderating influences of the Gulf.) The climate is definitely raw, with summers typically cool, cloudy, foggy, and breezy, broken by brief sunny interludes, more prevalent in locations away from the coast. Winters are long, moderately cold, and snowy. Dramatic shifts of weather are possible any time of year, and the region is notorious for having some of the most unforgiving conditions in Alaska.

Brown bears and salmon—Southwest has
more than any other region of the state.

The landscape is dominated by great expanses of naked, rolling tundra, broken by patches of forests (mostly in the lowlands), long winding rivers, deep, glacial lakes, and ice-sculpted highlands. There are also more than 50 active volcanoes, most of them scattered along the Aleutians and Alaska Peninsula. The intense glaciation of the last Ice Age gouged many deep bedrock basins that now cradle enormous lakes that are the rearing grounds for the largest concentrations of salmon, trout, and charr in the world. Lakes Iliamna, Becharof, Ugashik, Naknek, Nonvianuk and, to a lesser extent, the interconnected Wood-Tikchiks all support phenomenal fisheries and provide, in their outlets and associated river systems, some of the greatest angling to be had anywhere.

Southwest fishing conditions are varied and often quite challenging. Much of the more productive salmon and trout angling takes place in big water, best worked from boats using stout casting or spinning gear. Shore angling is limited and difficult in many of these areas. Flyfishermen and light tackle anglers will

have the best luck working headwater streams, confluences, or smaller rivers. Because of their size and volatile weather, most of the big lakes are seldom fished, except at outlet and inlet waters. Water levels influence the fishing greatly, with high river flows typically expected from late spring to early summer (sometimes longer) and sometimes in fall during particularly wet, rainy seasons (August-October). In an average year, most Southwest rivers will fish well from late June into September. Weather, always the limiting factor, can be especially bad in certain locations (Alaska Peninsula) and times of year (late August to October). Anglers with little or no experience dealing with the volatile conditions of the region are strongly advised to seek out the services of a reputable lodge or experienced Southwest wilderness fishing guide.

ACCESS, SERVICES & COSTS

With no connecting surface transportation, access to most of Southwest Alaska is by plane, through the main hubs of Dillingham, King Salmon, Bethel, Iliamna, Aniak, etc. (Limited ferry and barge service from the mainland is available to some of the Alaska Peninsula.) All the major towns are serviced by regularly scheduled commercial flights from Anchorage. From these hubs, local air taxis and riverboats provide additional access to villages and fishing locations within the region.

This is Alaska's definitive fly-in fishing country, with a world-famous coterie of lodges, guides, and outfitters offering a wide range of exciting options for that ultimate fishing vacation. (Because of its remoteness, Southwest has higher prices than Southcentral and Southeast.) You can rent gear, then fly to remote headwaters and raft and fish wild rivers where brown bears far outnumber any folks you might happen to see. Or stay at Alaska's finest (and most expensive) lodges and be pampered with gourmet meals and plush accommodations, while you enjoy daily fly-outs to world-class fishing locales. If your tastes run somewhere in between, you can even visit rustic outpost camps on far-flung rivers with unpronounceable names, where you'll get a cot in a wall tent, three square meals a day, and all the fishing action your arms can handle. No matter how you decide to go, Southwest Alaska can consistently deliver a quality of angling that few areas in the world can match, a place where the truly serious can put their fishing passion to the ultimate test.

WHAT TO EXPECT

Maritime conditions: cool, cloudy, windy weather much of the year, without the extremes of the continental climate. Summer temperatures generally range from the mid-50s to mid-70s (Fahrenheit); winters are long, snowy, but not too cold. Yearly precipitation is locally variable, 20 to 40 inches, with April through June generally the sunniest, driest months, and August through October the wettest. Rivers and lakes usually begin freezing sometime in late October to early November, and break-up occurs sometime in May (later in some of the mountain lakes). Fog is quite common in summer. The weather is extremely unpredictable, with intense storms bringing prolonged wet and windy periods at any time of year. Biting insects, abundant and aggressive during warmer months (June through August), generally taper off by late summer and early fall. Travelers planning to venture into any part of this country should equip with expedition-quality gear and ample provisions for any contingency.

SW Costs

RT Airfare: Anchorage to Dillingham, King Salmon, or Aniak: $338-384.
Lodging: $75-250/night.
Family Style Fishing Lodge: $450-700/day/person.
Deluxe Fishing Lodge: $700-850/day/person.
Outpost Camp Fishing: $400-500/day/person.
Cabin Rentals: $200-400/day.
Guided Float Trips: $340-470/day/person.
Unguided Float Trips: $150-250/day/person.
Boat Rentals: $100-300/day.
Guide/Boat: $150-225/day/person.
Air Taxi: Cessna Supercub: $200/hr; Cessna 172-185: $200-250/hr; Cessna 206/207: $275-375/hr; DeHavilland Beaver: $450-500/hr; Grumman Goose: $850/hr.

SOUTHWEST RUN TIMING

SPECIES	JAN	FEB	MAR	APR	MAY	JUN	JUL	AUG	SEP	OCT	NOV	DEC
King Salmon	Saltwater									Saltwater		
Red Salmon			Saltwater					Saltwater				
Chum Salmon			Saltwater					Saltwater				
Silver Salmon				Saltwater					Saltwater			
Pink Salmon				Saltwater				Saltwater				
Charr												
Rainbow Trout												
Steelhead												
Grayling												
Northern Pike												
Lake Trout												
Sheefish												
Halibut												
Rockfish												
Salmon Shark												

▬ Available   ▬ Peak

Note: Time periods shown in blue are for bright fish in the case of salmon entering rivers, or for general availability in saltwater or resident species (freshwater). Peak sportfishing periods are shown in red. Run timing can vary among different areas within the region. Always check local contacts for run timing specifics for locations you intend to fish.

Alaska's definitive fly-in fishing country.

	Jan	Feb	Mar	Apr	May	Jun	Jul	Aug	Sep	Oct	Nov	Dec
DAYLIGHT HOURS (monthly average)	7	9 ¼	11 ¾	14 ½	17	18 ½	18	15 ½	13	10 ¼	7 ¾	6 ¼
°F Ave. (TEMPS. High/Low)	24/12	25/12	31/17	38/25	49/35	56/43	61/48	60/48	53/41	41/30	27/20	26/14
	1.19	1.10	1.00	.92	1.22	1.71	2.34	3.5	3.29	2.23	1.87	1.86

P R E C I P I T A T I O N (inches)

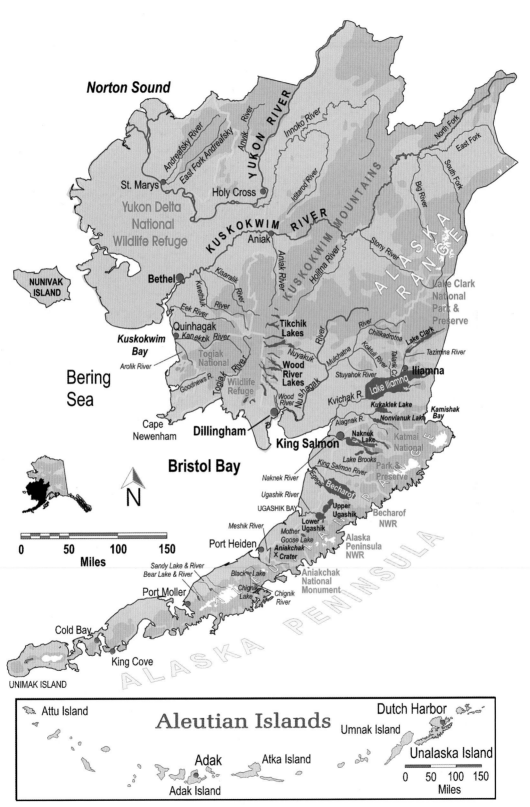

Norton Sound

Andreafsky River
East Fork Andreafsky
Anvik River
YUKON RIVER
Innoko River
North Fork
East Fork
South Fork
St. Marys
Holy Cross
Idliad River
Iditarod River
Big River
KUSKOKWIM MOUNTAINS
Stony River
Yukon Delta National Wildlife Refuge
KUSKOKWIM RIVER
Aniak
Aniak River
Holitna River
ALASKA RANGE
Lake Clark National Park & Preserve
NUNIVAK ISLAND
Bethel
Kisaralik River
Kwethluk River
Eek River
River
Tikchik Lakes
River
Chilikadrotna
Lake Clark
Tazimina River
Quinhagak
Kanektok River
Nuyakuk River
Mulchatna
Koktuli River
Talarik Cr.
Kuskokwim Bay
Arolik River
Togiak National
Wood River Lakes
Stuyahok River
Iliamna
Goodnews R.
Togiak River
Wildlife Refuge
Nushagak River
Kvichak R.
Lake Iliamna
Kamishak Bay
Bering Sea
Wood River
Kukaklek Lake
Nonvianuk Lake
Cape Newenham
Dillingham
Alagnak R.
Naknek Lake
Katmai National
King Salmon
Lake Brooks
Park & Preserve
Bristol Bay
King Salmon River
Naknek River
Egegik
Becharof
Ugashik River
Becharof NWR
N
UGASHIK BAY
Upper Ugashik
Meshik River
Lower Ugashik
Alaska Peninsula NWR
Mother Goose Lake
Port Heiden
Aniakchak X Crater
Sandy Lake & River
Bear Lake & River
Black Lake
Aniakchak National Monument
Chignik Lake
Chignik River
Port Moller
Cold Bay
ALASKA PENINSULA
King Cove
UNIMAK ISLAND

| 0 | 50 | 100 | 150 |

Miles

Aleutian Islands

Attu Island
Dutch Harbor
Umnak Island
Adak
Atka Island
Unalaska Island
Adak Island

| 0 | 50 | 100 | 150 |

Miles

Alaska's best streamfishing opportunities for salmon occur on Southwest's major producing rivers, such as the Alagnak, shown here.

SOUTHWEST FISHING HIGHLIGHTS

A list of the region's outstanding angling locations reads more like a roster of North America's dream waters, so blessed is this region with extraordinary fishing. In fact, there is so much good water it is difficult, if not impossible, for newcomers to select a vacation destination there, as the fishing on practically any Southwest river or lake will easily eclipse the best angling most folks have experienced elsewhere.

Some of the more notable highlights are the fantastic streamfishing opportunities for salmon, particularly king, silver, and sockeye, as most of Alaska's major producing rivers for these species are located there (Kvichak, Naknek, Egegik, Nushagak, Togiak, and lower Kuskokwim rivers). Flyfishing possibilities in the countless clear streams and lakes are almost endless. So, too, are the numbers of feisty, fat charr and grayling you'll encounter in nearly every body of water, with trophy potential in some waters exceeded only by a few locations in Alaska's remote Northwest. And, of course, there are those fabulous rainbows. Can enough be said of the peerless Southwest rivers and their armies of hungry, husky, wild Alaska rain-

bow trout? Nearly every drainage from Katmai to the Kuskokwim is amply endowed with them, with many waters holding fish of mythical proportions. And the flyfishing conditions couldn't be better, especially in spring and fall.

Those fabulous rainbows—Southwest has Alaska's most abundant fishing for the species, with unequaled trophy opportunities.

BRISTOL BAY

World famous Bristol Bay forms the heart of Alaska's Southwest region, encompassing all the coastal drainages from the neck of the Alaska Peninsula to Cape Newenham on the mainland. Known for incredibly rich salmon fisheries, particularly sockeye, its rivers and lakes are unequaled for their abundance and variety of fishing, not just for salmon, but for trout, charr, and grayling as well. The main hubs are the towns of Dillingham (pop. 2466), King Salmon (pop. 442) and Iliamna (pop. 110), connected by daily scheduled flights to and from Anchorage, and offering a wide range of visitor services. Aside from a few short roads leading out of these major communities, this is real Alaska bush country, with access limited to small planes and boats.

Lake Iliamna ★★★★

Location: Eastern Bristol Bay, 175 miles SW of Anchorage.

Access: By floatplane and boat to various points along the lake.

Facilities: No developed public facilities; various services available in towns/villages along lake.

Highlights: Alaska's most productive lake system for rainbow trout and sockeye salmon.

Main Species: RT, RS, LT, CHR

Ocean-sized Iliamna, at the head of Bristol Bay, is the largest lake in Alaska (over 1,000 square miles) and the world's most productive sockeye salmon system. Along with the associated Lake Clark drainage, it supports runs of millions of returning fish. (In 1965, an estimated 42 million sockeyes returned to spawn.) The vast, rich lake environs also produce bumper yields of some of the largest rainbow trout in the state. Studies done over the years show these fish to be a late-maturing, larger-growing strain, with an average size around 20 inches, reaching weights to 15 pounds or more. Along with the fabulous locations of Katmai, Iliamna's immense, productive fisheries have long been synonymous with the finest trophy trout angling in Alaska, if not the world.

Because of Iliamna's size and unpredictable weather, very little fishing is done in the lake itself. Anglers instead target the numerous creeks and rivers associated with this behemoth drainage. Some of the more popular have become legends on their own, places like Talarik Creek or the Copper, Gibraltar, Tazimina, or Kvichak rivers, all with a history of consistent and remarkable fishing over the years. For trophy rainbows, these streams are best hit in late spring or fall when the big, lake resident fish are present for abundant feeding.

Most of the smaller streams are flyfished, with the larger, deeper rivers like the Newhalen or Kvichak worked most efficiently by boat, pulling lures or drifting bobbers steelhead-style along the bottom. Sockeye salmon fishing is best done in early summer (first half of July), in the large lake outlets like the Newhalen and Kvichak rivers. The drainage is also noted for seasonally abundant grayling, charr, and lake trout.

Though almost all the lake's streams offer some kind of fishing for trout and salmon, access can be a problem. Fishermen take daily commercial flights from Anchorage to Iliamna, the main hub, from which a limited road system, boat travel, and floatplanes provide access to quite a few excellent area locations, but weather is always a limiting factor. There are quite a few reputable local lodges, guides, outfitters, and air taxis, with developed public facilities nonexistent, and much of the land privately owned by natives. Careful planning and preparation are essential for any anglers venturing into the Lake Iliamna area.

Note: *Iliamna Lake-Kvichak River and tributaries are closed to trout fishing in the spring (early April to early June); check current Sport Fishing Regulations Summary for Bristol Bay, or contact Dillingham ADF&G office, 907-842-2427, for information on regulations/orders affecting sportfishing in the drainage.*

Kvichak River ★★★★

Location: Iliamna Lake outlet, 250 miles southwest of Anchorage.

Access: By small plane or boat from Iliamna or other nearby hubs.

Facilities: No developed public facilities; limited services available in nearby Igiugik.

Highlights: One of Alaska's premier rainbow trout and sockeye salmon fisheries.

Main Species: RT, RS

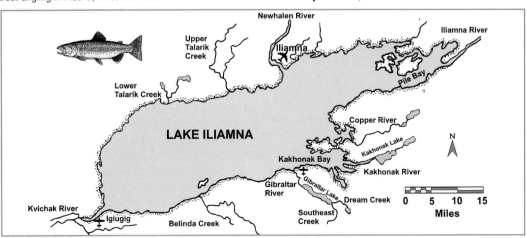

As the giant lake's primary outlet, the Kvichak River is arguably Alaska's foremost locale for jumbo rainbows (to 15 pounds). In spring and fall, hordes of the big, lake-resident trout converge on the river to spawn and feed, providing some of Alaska's most exciting trophy fishing possibilities.

From its outlet at the village of Igiugik, the Kvichak winds through flat, coastal tundra for 60 miles before spilling its jewel-like waters into muddy Kvichak Bay. It's a big river—wide, deep and fast, not easy to fish from shore except at the outlet and mouths of the tributary creeks (such as Peck's, Kaskanak, and Ole). Most of the fishing is done from boats, from the outlet down through the extensive braided section (Kaskanak Flats) that begins five miles below the lake, using Spin-N-Glos, plugs, spoons, and Okie Drifters fished right above bottom. Flyfishing is challenging and best done at the lake outlet, from the cutbanks of Kaskanak Flats, or in the mouths and lower sections of the tributaries. (Bright attractors, egg/flesh patterns, sculpins, or smolt imitations work best.)

Newhalen River ★★★

Location: North shore Lake Iliamna, 200 miles southwest of Anchorage.

Access: By plane from Anchorage to Iliamna, then by car or foot to the river; boat access also possible.

Facilities: No developed public facilities; limited camping available nearby, with lodging and guide services in Iliamna.

Highlights: Outstanding, easily accessed sockeye salmon and rainbow trout fishing.

Main Species: RT, RS

A half-mile hike from the end of the airstrip at Iliamna lies one of Alaska's best salmon fishing holes, the "Falls" on the Newhalen River. In July, you'll find bright, frantic sockeye salmon stacked thick as cordwood and, in the pools and rapids below (especially in spring and fall), maybe some of those famous jumbo Iliamna rainbow trout.

A big, transparent-blue, whitewater river, the 25-mile Newhalen, connects Six Mile Lake and adjoining Lake Clark with immense Lake Iliamna. It is the major pathway for a mind-boggling migration of sockeye salmon that make their way up into the far reaches of this drainage in early summer. Most of the fishing effort for these salmon occurs right below a series of impenetrable Class IV and V rapids (the Falls) on the lower river a couple of miles up from the mouth, but some productive water upriver can be accessed by road at a place called Upper Landing. Below the falls, a limited amount of river can be accessed wading from shore, but better to drift by boat down to the lake for big rainbows in June, or late September through October.

Talarik Creek ★★★

Location: NW shore Lake Iliamna, 220 miles southwest of Anchorage.

Access: By floatplane from Anchorage, Iliamna, or Port Alsworth to the lagoon at the mouth of the river; boat access also possible.

Facilities: No public facilities available.

Highlights: One of the most famous Lake Iliamna flyfishing streams.

Main Species: RT, RS

Perhaps the most famous little trout stream in all of Alaska, Talarik Creek enters Lake Iliamna from the north about 25 miles west of the Newhalen River. Barely a dribble as Alaska rivers go, Talarik's giant reputation comes from its relatively easy access (a short floatplane hop from Iliamna to the lagoon at the mouth of the river) and concentrated fishing for abundant, big rainbows late in the season. One of the most studied trout streams in Alaska, Talarik's fish have been measured and tagged for decades, yielding revealing statistics on this unique fishery. For a river this small, the average size of Talarik's rainbows compares favorably with the best Lake Iliamna locations (the Kvichak and Newhalen rivers), especially during late fall (October), when a large percentage of trophy fish are taken.

Most fishermen land on the lagoon at the mouth, then hike upriver, fishing either fork for good results. You can also put in at one of the headwater lakes, then fish and wade down to Iliamna—a good tactic in late fall. Upper Talarik Creek nearby has some good fishing also, but it lacks the lower creek's convenient access, and is more shallow and difficult to fish.

Copper River ★★★

Location: Eastern Lake Iliamna drainage, 190 miles southwest of Anchorage.

Access: By small plane from Anchorage, Iliamna, or Port Alsworth to headwater lakes or lower river.

Facilities: No public facilities: private lodge on river.

Highlights: One of Lake Iliamna's most famous flyfishing streams.

Main Species: RT, GR, RS

The Copper River, along with Talarik Creek, is perhaps the best known of Lake Iliamna's fabulous trout streams, particularly for its superb flyfishing. In its glory days, it was visited routinely by just about every fly-out lodge in the area; for years, it was one of the lake's most floated streams.

The clear Copper originates in a series of lakes in the Chigmit Mountains east of Iliamna, flowing swiftly for some 15 miles before emptying into Intricate Bay. A 36-foot waterfall below Lower Copper Lake, twelve miles up from the mouth, serves as an effective barrier for most fish and fishermen; several lakes adjoining the river below the falls are the best points of access. (The river can be run by raft or kayak from up above, as long as you take great care not to miss the short portage on the left side.)

The Copper's reputation comes from its near perfect flyfishing conditions and ample supply of husky rainbows, though the fish here generally don't run as large as those taken in some of the other tributaries. It's particularly noted for its dry fly fishing opportunities, best in early season (June & July), and its outstanding grayling and sockeye salmon fishing.

The preferred way of fishing the Copper is by raft (put in at headwater lakes such as Copper, Meadows and Pike Lake), fishing as you go, with a pick-up at Lower Pike Lake or down below in the bay, for a trip of one to three days duration. There is also a fancy lodge on the river (Rainbow River Lodge).

Gibraltar River

Location: SE shore Lake Iliamna drainage, 215 miles SW of Anchorage.

Access: By floatplane from Anchorage or Iliamna to Gibraltar Lake or (sometimes) the river mouth area.

Facilities: None.

Highlights: A popular Lake Iliamna rainbow trout location.

Main Species: RT, RS, GR

Only about four miles long, this well-known area trout fishing stream drains Gibraltar Lake, flowing north into Iliamna near Kakhonak Bay. Most of the fishing occurs from floatplane anglers who target the lake outlet and tributary streams like Dream and Southeast creeks (both of which are outstanding trout locales on their own). The entire river offers good fishing, however, and can be floated from the lake in rafts (a one to two day trip). A two-mile section of swift water in the middle section of the river is the only possible hazard. (Floatplanes may not be able to land by the mouth for a pick-up if it's too windy; be prepared to lay over or hike about three miles to the nearby village of Kakhonak for a wheelplane ride back to Iliamna.)

Lake Clark ★★★★

Location: Lake Clark National Park, 180 miles southwest of Anchorage.

Access: By wheelplane to Port Alsworth, then boat or floatplane to various points around the lake or associated tributaries.

Facilities: No developed public facilities; limited visitor services available at Port Alsworth.

Highlights: One of Alaska's most scenic lake areas, with good fishing for a variety of species.

Main Species: LT, RS, GR, NP, CHR

Gorgeous, turquoise Lake Clark is the gateway attraction for a 3.6-million-acre national park and preserve located west of the Chigmit Mountains, a short hop from Anchorage by float or wheel planes. Said by many to contain Alaska's most spectacular lake and alpine scenery, this area also has some noteworthy fishing opportunities, though the predominantly glacial waters and isolation from the coast limit its potential somewhat.

The outstanding mountain lakes—Clark, Twin, Telaquana, Tazimina, Kijik, Kontrashibuna, etc., are the prime attraction here. These waters are perhaps best known for their superb lake trout (up to 30 pounds), charr, and sockeye salmon fishing, with some excellent grayling opportunities in the clearer tributary streams, and northern pike to 25 pounds in shallower associated lakes, ponds, and sloughs. Rainbow trout are scarce north of the Six Mile Lake drainage. Because of its relative proximity to Anchorage and outstanding mountain scenery, the Lake Clark area is seeing more use every year, with a developing variety of visitor services available. There are several plush lodges that offer weekly stays with daily fly-outs, or more modest, family-style inns that can provide meals and lodging, along with boat excursions and guides to fish the lake and nearby streams. You can even rent remote tent camps and cabins on the area's best fishing lakes and rivers.

For the true adventure fisherman, the park has two Wild and Scenic Rivers, the Mulchatna and Chilikadrotna, which can provide unforgettable float angling experiences. (See the listings in the Nushagak River section for detailed descriptions.) All in all, the Lake Clark area has great possibilities for anyone seeking affordable alternatives to the more humdrum fishing along Alaska's road system.

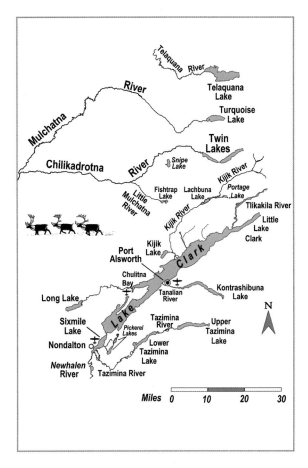

Tazimina River ★★★

Location: Six Mile Lake drainage, 180 miles SW of Anchorage.

Access: By floatplane to headwater lakes or the lower river. Jet boat access also possible.

Facilities: None.

Highlights: One of the more classic Iliamna-Lake Clark stream locations.

Main Species: RT, GR, RS

The Tazimina River has been one of the most popular and productive fishing locations of the Lake Iliamna-Lake Clark region for years, visited regularly for its consistent rainbow trout, sockeye salmon, and grayling fishing. It also is one of the few area fishing rivers, along with the Gibraltar and Copper, that can be floated (one to four-day trips).

Located within Lake Clark National Park, the 54-mile, clear Tazimina drains a series of lakes of the same name before emptying into Six Mile Lake and the Newhalen River. Because of some waterfalls and portages (the most serious located nine miles from the mouth), most fishermen usually access only the lower river (from the mouth to Alexcy Lake) via jet boat or floatplane. Rafters put in at Lower Tazimina, Alexcy, or Hudson lakes (with short portages) and vary the length of their float. Flyfishing conditions on the Tazimina are excellent.

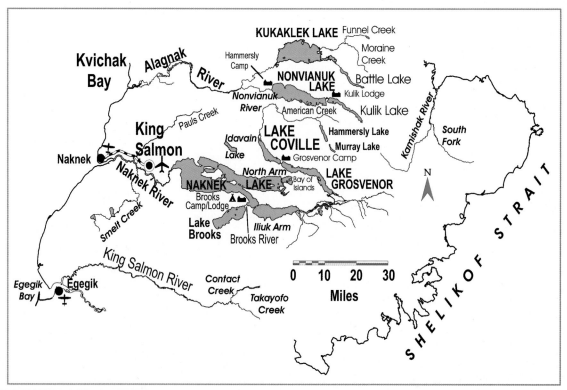

KATMAI

Few places in the world offer the visitor such diverse and superlative wonders as magnificent Katmai National Park and Preserve. Located on the neck of the Alaska Peninsula, 300 miles southwest of Anchorage, Katmai has fantastic landscapes shaped by intense volcanic action, unique wildlife attractions (the famous fishing brown bears), glaciers, and scenic lakes and streams holding some of Alaska's most fabulous trout, charr, and salmon fishing.

It was Katmai's jumbo rainbow trout—some of Alaska's largest—that established the region as a world-class fishing destination back in the 1950s. Although the Park has been in existence since 1918, it wasn't until after World War II, when military personnel from the newly established Naknek Air Base at nearby King Salmon "discovered" the amazing trout fishing nearby, that word got out about the area's fabulous sportfish potential. Ray Peterson, a Bristol Bay bush pilot and entrepreneur, established some of the first sportfish camps to cater to the growing public demand for facilities in this fishing nirvana. These rustic camps—Brooks, Kulik, and Grosvenor—have changed little over the years, offering folks a chance to savor some of the world's best fishing and awesome surroundings in the relaxed atmosphere and comfort of family-style lodges.

Most of the region is accessed by floatplanes from the nearby hub of King Salmon, which is serviced by daily scheduled flights from Anchorage. A number of lodges, guides, outfitters, and air taxis operate in and around the Park, catering to the demand of anglers worldwide for that quintessential Alaska wilderness fishing experience. The National Park Service also maintains a limited number of developed facilities for the public; other than that, Katmai country is totally wild, definitely not for the unprepared or casual sportsman.

Naknek Lake & River ★★★★
Location: Eastern Bristol Bay, 300 miles southwest of Anchorage.

Access: By boat or floatplane from King Salmon to various lake locations; river can be accessed in spots by car.

Facilities: No developed public facilities; full visitor services available in nearby town of King Salmon.

Highlights: One of Southwest's most popular lake and stream fishing locations.

Main Species: KS, SS, RS, RT, CHR, GR

The Naknek Lake system forms the heart of Katmai. The second most productive system in Alaska, its myriad waters run thick with salmon (predominantly sockeye) each summer. This abundant forage supports a trout population that rivals that of famed Iliamna for numbers and average size, in addition to some of Southwest's finest trophy charr and lake trout. Its relatively easy access and varied world class fishing have made it one of the most popular river and lake areas in Southwest Alaska. (Up to a fifth of the region's total angling effort takes place there.)

The lake outlet and river down to the Rapids Camp (about nine miles) are very popular areas to fish rainbow trout, grayling, and sockeye. Flyfishing opportunities abound in the crystal blue waters. King and coho salmon are mostly drift fished from boats on the lower river, from the mouth of Big Creek to Pauls Creek. The most productive times for jumbo trout are spring (as early as March or April in certain years), early summer (season opens second week in June), and late fall (September and October). Salmon fishing heats up in early summer, with kings and sockeyes in late June and early July, then silvers in August.

Over the years, the deep emerald waters of Naknek Lake have provided some remarkable and consistent trophy fishing: big rainbows to 15 pounds or more (a 23-pounder was taken from the Bay of Islands in 1991), giant charr to 20 pounds, and lake trout to 30 pounds. It's immense, very deep, and subject to wild weather, so the services of a seasoned area guide are highly recommended. The most popular areas to fish are the Naknek River outlet, the Bay of Islands in the North Arm, and the coves and bays along the northwest shore. Trolling with big spoons and plugs, or drift jigging, is the ticket (Krocodiles in chrome, silver prism, blue prism; Hot Shots in silver, silver-blue, or fluorescent red; and Crippled Herrings in chrome, nickel/neon blue, fluorescent red/yellow).

Anglers jet into King Salmon, then usually rent boats and/or hire guides there or fly over to Brooks Camp for some reasonably priced daily guided fishing in the nearby Bay of Islands. If you're planning a vacation in Katmai, leave a day open to fish the lake; Naknek has been known to yield exciting treasure when the fishing in the streams has cooled down.

Brooks River ★★★★

Location: Katmai National Park, 275 miles SW of Anchorage.

Access: By floatplane or boat from King Salmon.

Facilities: A NPS campground and private concessionaire lodge/cabins are available.

Highlights: Katmai's most famous fishing location and best bear viewing area.

Main Species: RS, RT

A short hop by floatplane from King Salmon to the southeast end of Naknek Lake takes you to one of Alaska's most famous fishing camps, Brooks Lodge. For over 40 years, it has been the quintessential Katmai attraction, with big rainbow trout, nearby smoldering volcanic valleys, giant bears that fish for salmon, and a rustic "real Alaska" lodge situated in one of the world's prettiest lake and mountain settings.

The camp sits at the mouth of the short outlet stream connecting Brooks Lake with Naknek that serves as a major migration and spawning area for a healthy share of the prolific run of sockeye salmon that swarm the Naknek system each summer. Originally known for its outstanding rainbow trout fishing (in the early days, 30-inchers were quite common), Brooks has also achieved notoriety as one of Alaska's great sockeye salmon fishing locales.

This area is also well known for its brown bears, too, with some of Alaska's highest densities during the salmon season. (On a typical day in July, a dozen or more of Katmai's famous cinnamon grizzlies can be seen from the observation platform at Brooks Falls, as they

try their fishing skills on the milling, leaping salmon.)

You can rent one of the lodge cabins or stay in the National Park Service campground, then get supplies, meals, canoes, and even daily guide service through the concessionaire. Though crowded at times, Brooks Camp is still one of the best places for folks wanting to sample some "real Alaska" country, fishing and wildlife.

Alagnak River System ★★★★

Location: Eastern Bristol Bay, 250 miles SW of Anchorage.

Access: By floatplane from King Salmon to headwater lakes, or boat to lower river; can be floated by raft or kayak.

Facilities: No developed public facilities; private concessionaire lodge at headwaters.

Highlights: One of Southwest Alaska's best trout and salmon rivers.

Main Species: KS, RS, SS, CS, RT, GR

North of the Naknek drainage lies the Alagnak River system, one of the most productive and popular salmon and trout fishing destinations in all of Southwest Alaska. With twin lake sources (Nonvianuk and Kukaklek) feeding separate forks, the Alagnak (sometimes called the Branch River) flows spiritedly some 70 miles or so before emptying into Kvichak Bay. Crystal clear, rocky, and swift, the upper river sections (both branches) offer perfect conditions for flyfishing, and are particularly noted for abundant rainbows, grayling, and prolific sockeye salmon in season (perhaps Alaska's best conditions for flyfishing occur there in early July). King, silver and chum salmon fishing, usually quite good in most years, is concentrated along the slower, deeper, lower river sections.

The Alagnak is world-famous for its trophy rainbows (to 10+ lb.), which are best pursued in the outlet and inlet waters (Nonvianuk, Kukaklek, and Kulik rivers; and Moraine, Funnel, Battle, and Nanuktuk creeks) of its twin lake sources. Early June (right after season opening) and September through October are the prime times to encounter the big, bright, lake-dwelling trout. (The lakes and associated tributaries also offer good lake trout, grayling, and charr.)

One of the best ways of sampling the fishing and the country is to float and fish the Alagnak down from the headwaters, with a put-in at either lake making for a four to six-day float trip down to several pick-up points along the lower river. The best times are early July for sockeyes and kings, and late August through September for silvers and rainbows. There are sections of whitewater (mostly Class I and II, and one Class III rapid twelve miles below Kukaklek), but overall the Alagnak presents no great technical challenge to floaters. Private lodges and camps along the river and on the lakes round out the variety of fishing options available. The river is also known for its abundant bear population, especially during the height of the sockeye run in July; caution and common sense are required that time of year for safe fishing along the river corridor. Caribou, moose, and wolves are also commonly seen.

American Creek ★★★

Location: Katmai National Park, 250 miles SW of Anchorage.

Access: By floatplane or jetboat from King Salmon.

Facilities: None.

Highlights: A popular and productive Katmai rainbow trout and charr location.

Main Species: RT, CHR, GR, RS

American Creek, along with Brooks and Kulik rivers, has some of Katmai's best streamfishing for rainbows and charr. It is a short (40 miles long), relatively small stream (about 15 yards wide average) that flows swiftly from alpine Hammersly and Murray lakes down into Coville Lake, about 45 miles east of King Salmon. Because of its rocky rapids and size, access to most of American Creek is restricted to the outlet and lower few miles of river above Coville Lake. It can be floated by raft or kayak, but has demanding whitewater. (The average gradient is 30 to 60 feet per mile, with two canyons and continuous rapids over much of the river—certainly not recommended for anyone who is not an expert wilderness boater.)

Flyfishing conditions are excellent, some of Katmai's best, particularly in early spring and fall when abundant lake resident charr and rainbows feed heavily on the young and eggs of salmon. (Smolt and egg patterns and small spinners are deadly.) The creek is especially noted for its dry fly fishing opportunities (in June and July) and heavy sockeye salmon runs (in July and August). Be prepared to share the river with an abundant bear population, however, particularly in mid to late summer.

You can fly in from King Salmon to Hammersly Lake, camp and fish the outlet and few miles of stream below for rainbows, charr, and lake trout. (The upper creek can also be accessed via a small pothole lake and trail about five miles down from Hammersly.) Or hire the services of a guide to fish the lower creek for rainbows and charr. If you want, you can even stay at the rustic Grosvenor Lodge nearby and boat over for daily fishing. However you decide to fish it, American Creek is certainly a location you'll want to include in your itinerary if you're planning a trip to Katmai. The best times to fish the American are in June and from August through early September.

Coville-Grosvenor Lakes

Location: Katmai National Park, 250 miles SW of Anchorage.

Access: By floatplane from King Salmon.

Facilities: No developed public facilities; private concessionaire lodge at lake narrows.

Highlights: One of Katmai's best lake fishing locations.

Main Species: LT, GR, RT, RS, CHR

Of the more noteworthy lake locations within Katmai, Coville-Grosvenor, the site of the original Peterson fish camp, receives a substantial portion of the multitude of salmon migrating through the Naknek system. With such a rich forage base, the two lakes are well known for their productive rainbow trout, charr, grayling, and lake trout fishing.

Rustic Grosvenor Lodge is situated at the narrows between the two lakes, a most advantageous fishing location. Rainbows and charr are taken there in abundance, especially in spring, along with some of Katmai's best lake trout fishing, with trophy fish (20+ pounds) taken almost every season. Nearby American Creek and the outlet to Savonoski provide additional opportunities for rainbows and charr. The Bay of Islands (Naknek Lake) can also be accessed by a one-mile trail from the southwest shore of Grosvenor.

In many ways, Grosvenor is the best of the three Katmai camps, as it is ignored by the crowds that flock to Brooks and is more laid back than Kulik. (It also has more fishing variety.) If you're planning a Katmai trip, you might want to consider it over the others. The best times for fishing are in late spring (June), and late summer through early fall (mid-August through September).

King Salmon River

Location: North Alaska Peninsula, 350 miles SW of Anchorage.

Access: By small plane from King Salmon to headwaters; lower river access by boat from Egegik village.

Facilities: None.

Highlights: An out-of-the-way Katmai location with good rainbow trout stream potential.

Main Species: RT, GR, CHR

Rainbow trout get scarce beyond the southern fringes of Katmai, with the headwaters of the King Salmon River, a tributary of the Egegik River system (draining Becharof Lake), being one of the last areas they are found in down along the northern Alaska Peninsula. This seldom-visited river offers an out-of-the-way alternative for trout anglers wanting to explore new water. Charr, grayling, and fair fishing for salmon in season (KS, CS, SS) round out the possibilities for fishing adventure.

Usually accessed by floatplane to the headwaters of Gertrude Creek (Gertrude Lake), or wheelplane to gravel bars on upper Contact Creek, the 60-mile King Salmon for the most part is a silty, predominantly glacial river with good fishing only in its headwaters and some of the clear south side tributaries. It can be floated (about five days down to the Egegik River and village), but the weather is real iffy and navigation along the flat lower sections can be complicated by strong headwinds and tidal action. Wildlife, especially bears, is abundant, so precautions must be taken. It is an interesting area, with some promising rainbow fishing possibilities, definitely worth checking out.

NUSHAGAK RIVER SYSTEM

West of Lake Iliamna lies the heart of Bristol Bay, an area synonymous with world class stream fishing and fancy, fly-out lodges catering to the most discriminating anglers. One of Alaska's largest and most productive clear water drainages, the Nushagak provides most of the superlative fishing opportunities there. With vast headwaters that stretch from the scenic Tikchik Lakes to the rugged highlands surrounding Lake Clark, the Nushagak, with its hundreds of miles of pristine tributaries, encompasses a remarkable variety of water, enhanced by the presence of major runs of all five species of salmon and abundant populations of rainbow trout, charr (including lake trout), grayling, and northern pike (10 sport species in all). A river of rare character and uncommonly high fishing potential, it offers a diversity of world class fishing experiences that few rivers anywhere can match.

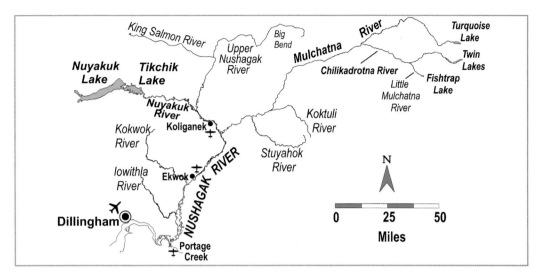

The Nushagak's world-famous headwaters—two of them Wild and Scenic Rivers—can provide some of Alaska's best floatfishing experiences. Most are accessed through Iliamna or Port Alsworth. The rest of the watershed is reached by wheel and floatplane or boat from the coastal hub of Dillingham, which is serviced by regular commercial flights from Anchorage.

With nearly every lodge in Southwest Alaska visiting the river at some time during the season, and dozens of area guides and outfitters providing a wide range of services, finding a Nushagak fishing adventure to suit your tastes and budget should be no problem.

Lower Nushagak River ★★★★

Location: Central Bristol Bay, 275 miles SW of Anchorage.

Access: By small plane from Dillingham or Iliamna; or boat access from Dillingham or villages along lower river.

Facilities: No developed public facilities; limited visitor services available in villages along lower river.

Highlights: One of Southwest's hottest king salmon locales.

Main Species of Interest: KS, SS, CS, RS, RT

Along with the Naknek River, the lower Nushagak, from the village of Ekwok down to tidewater, is one of the most popular locations in Bristol Bay for fishing kings. In late June and the first half of July, a staggering number of chrome-bright chinook make their way into this river system (Alaska's third largest king run, exceeding 100,000 fish in good years).

Dozens of spike camps and fly-out lodges drift the river with boats, but substantial numbers of folks do well (depending on river conditions) camping and fishing along shore. Great numbers of chum and sockeye salmon also enter the Nushagak in early summer, making for a good mix of abundant salmon fishing opportunities.

The action shifts upriver as summer progresses, following the runs up the mainstem and into the major tributaries (Mulchatna, Nuyakuk, Koktuli, Stuyahok, etc.—see listings that follow), where abundant charr, rainbow, and grayling populations spice up the fishing. Silvers enter the Nushagak in late July-early August, providing great fishing through the fall.

Upper Nushagak Mainstem ★★★

Location: Central Bristol Bay, 240 miles west of Anchorage.

Access: By small plane from Dillingham or Iliamna.

Facilities: No developed public facilities; several spike camps along river.

Highlights: Great streamfishing possibilities.

Main Species: RT, CHR, GR

The upper mainstem Nushagak rises in the rambling, crystal clear runoff streams and springs of the rugged hills east of the Tikchik Lakes. Though access can be difficult and expensive, this remote area can provide outstanding small stream fishing for rainbow trout, charr, grayling, and salmon later in the season (July-September).

Several outfitters run spike camps on the river proper and along some of the better tributaries like the King Salmon, but the best way to fish these headwaters is by floating in rafts or kayaks, putting in by small plane. (Check with local air taxis for access options and conditions.) Fast water and sweepers are the only technical obstacles to an otherwise easy float through pleasing mountain scenery. Depending on put-in, figure on 5-7 days to a takeout lower down on the river.

Mulchatna River ★★★

Location: NE Bristol Bay, Nushagak drainage, 175 miles SW of Anchorage.

Access: By floatplane to the upper river via Lake Clark or Lake Iliamna; lower and middle river accessible by boat from villages along the Nushagak.

Facilities: Outpost camps along river and tributaries.

Highlights: A Wild and Scenic River with good fishing.

Main Species of Interest: KS, SS, GR, CHR, RT

The Mulchatna River, as the main, first-order tributary of the immense, fish-rich Nushagak, is one of Bristol Bay's most popular fly-in fishing destinations. A Wild and Scenic River with headwaters in the majestic Lake Clark country, the Mulchatna (and its main tributary, the Chilikadrotna) is also one of Southwest Alaska's most popular rivers for floatfishing.

In its 250 miles, the Mulchatna changes character considerably, from a small, rocky alpine stream to a broad, braided river coursing through lowland forest. Along the way, it is joined by numerous lesser tributaries, some of them well-known and popular fishing streams (Chilikadrotna, Stuyahok, Koktuli rivers, etc.). Most floaters access the headwaters at the Half Cabin Lakes area about 30 miles down from Turquoise Lake. (The headwaters from Turquoise down are not commonly floated because of rocky, shallow conditions.) From there, it's an easy float, with fast water, some minor rapids (all Class I, one short Class II), but no major challenge to anyone possessing basic boating skills and a high-quality raft or kayak. (There are abundant sweepers, especially below the Chilikadrotna confluence.) Most folks end their trip somewhere below the Mulchatna-Chilchitna confluence (a five to seven-day float), but longer trips are certainly possible.

Fishing on the Mulchatna is generally good to excellent, depending on water conditions and the time of year. (The lower river tends to muddy easily during heavy rains.) The mouths of the larger tributaries and mainstem up to the Koktuli have traditionally been some of Bristol Bay's most productive and popular fly-in areas for king and silver salmon, rainbow, grayling, and charr. Also, the river's abundant wildlife, particularly caribou and moose, attracts quite a bit of use from hunters each fall, who float in rafts or stay in outpost camps and enjoy good fishing as a bonus. For folks wanting to sample some of Alaska's better outpost tent camp fishing or an outstanding floatfishing trip, the Mulchatna is pretty hard to beat.

Chilikadrotna River ★★★

Location: NE Bristol Bay, Nushagak drainage, 160 miles west of Anchorage.

Access: By floatplane via Clark or Iliamna lakes.

Facilities: None.

Highlights: A very pretty Wild and Scenic River with exciting floatfishing.

Main Species: SS, GR, CHR, RT, LT

The Chilikadrotna Wild and Scenic River is one of southwest Alaska's premier float trips, with outstanding wilderness values and good fishing. It begins in the rugged alpine reaches of the Alaska Range in Lake Clark National Park. A whitewater river, the 62-mile Chili is swift, with rocky flows, rapids (Class I to Class III), logjams, and plenty of sweepers—not a river for inexperienced boaters.

Fishing is good from July into September for charr, grayling, rainbows, and some salmon (mostly chum, silvers, and a few kings), with excellent conditions for flyfishing. The beautiful Twin Lakes area at the headwaters has some very good lake trout populations, and there are even some pike to be had in the sloughs along the river. Magnificent scenery, wildlife, and numerous hiking opportunities are a definite bonus along the way.

Most rafters put in at Twin Lakes or at several small lakes down below, and generally take a seven-day journey down to the

Mulchatna, putting out on long, flat stretches of river 12 to 13 miles below the confluence. Longer voyages continuing down the Mulchatna can be easily done—check with air taxi service for details.

Koktuli River ★★★

Location: NE Bristol Bay, Nushagak drainage, 220 miles SW of Anchorage.

Access: Floatplane to lakes along the upper river or to the Koktuli-Mulchatna confluence; boat access also possible to lower river.

Facilities: None.

Highlights: A longtime favorite upper Nushagak tributary for fishing, and an excellent floatfishing trip.

Main Species: RS, SS, KS, GR, RT, CHR

The Koktuli River, which is similar in size and character to the Stuyahok, has been one of the more popular upper Nushagak tributaries for some time, fished by lodges from nearby Lake Iliamna. It is noted for good wade and cast flyfishing for salmon, rainbow trout, charr, and grayling. The majority of folks fly in and work the mouth and lower river, but it is best fished by floating in rafts or kayaks from the headwaters.

Floaters usually put in on small lakes along the upper river or in the vicinity of the Swan River confluence. (Short portages are sometimes necessary.) From there, the river is an easy float (one to two days to mouth from the Swan River, four to six days from upper river), with no major hazards except sweepers and logjams. Floaters can take out at the mouth or continue down the Mulchatna. Wildlife is abundant and includes bear, caribou, wolf, moose, and waterfowl.

Stuyahok River ★★★

Location: NE Bristol Bay, Nushagak drainage, 250 miles SW of Anchorage.

Access: By floatplane from Lake Iliamna to lakes along the upper river or the Mulchatna confluence; boat access possible to mouth.

Facilities: None.

Highlights: A delightful headwater of the Nushagak and a well-known floatfishing trip.

Main Species: KS, SS, GR, RT, CHR

The Stuyahok is one of several small Nushagak headwaters that drains the highlands west of Lake Iliamna. It is short, only about 50 miles in length, and is fished mostly from rafts or from camps at its confluence with the Mulchatna. With no real whitewater, it is an easy, enjoyable floatfishing trip (from three to five days duration) for people of average wilderness boating skills. It offers pleasant scenery and good to excellent fishing for rainbow trout, charr, grayling, and king and silver salmon.

The upper river is usually accessed using one of several pothole lakes for a put-in. (Some may require short portages to reach the river.) Below this area, there is no floatplane access until the confluence. The upper "Stu" winds through pretty alpine foothills before entering the forested lowlands surrounding the Mulchatna. While it has no rapids to speak of, sweepers are abundant. There is plenty of good flyfishing water. The lower five miles or so of river, including the mouth, have the Stuyahok's best salmon fishing (and its most concentrated angling effort, too). All in all, the Stu makes for a sweet little fishing trip, highly recommended for newcomers as a great introduction to the fabulous streams of Bristol Bay.

Nuyakuk River ★★★

Location: Northcentral Bristol Bay, 300 miles SW of Anchorage.

Access: By floatplane from Dillingham to various points along river; limited boat access also possible.

Facilities: Private lodge along upper river.

Highlights: One of the Nushagak River's most outstanding tributaries, with good fishing.

Main Species: RT, CHR, GR, SS, KS, LT

One of the more beautiful Nushagak tributaries, the crystal-blue Nuyakuk flows swiftly from Tikchik Lake, 60 miles north of Dillingham, for 45 miles to its confluence with the mainstem above the village of Koliganek. As the sole connection and fish pathway linking the Tikchik lakes with the ocean, it receives a sizable influx of migrating salmon and supports abundant populations of rainbow trout, charr, and grayling. Sportfishing, especially along the upper river, can be some of the best in all of Bristol Bay.

The Nuyakuk makes an especially nice floatfishing trip down from Tikchik Lake (four to six days duration, with two stretches of rapids below the lake, Class II to Class III, and one Class IV several miles farther down).

The outlet and first few miles of river below the lake are prime water for big rainbows, lake trout, and charr. (The rapids should be scouted beforehand from the ridge along the right side of the river.) The deep holes right below the rapids have yielded some of the biggest rainbows to come out of the Nushagak system.

If you're not up to a white-knuckle challenge, you can fly downriver a short way and put in below Nuyakuk Falls, at one of the prettiest campsites in all of Bristol Bay. (For those running down from the lake, a landing and portage trail on the right side of the river will allow safe passage.) Below the falls, you'll find mostly smooth sailing (fast water and one stretch of Class I rapids) all the way down to the Nushagak, where you can end your trip at the village of Koliganek, with a wheelplane flight back to Dillingham. The best salmon fishing occurs from the falls down.

Wood-Tikchik Lakes ★★★★

Location: Head of Bristol Bay, 325 miles SW of Anchorage.

Access: By plane, boat or car (limited access) from Dillingham; kayak, canoe, raft, or sport boat travel possible throughout area.

Facilities: No public facilities; several private lodges within park.

Highlights: A scenic lake wonderland with superlative possibilities for fishing adventure.

Main Species: RT, CHR, GR, LT, NP, RS

Legend has it that a giant bear flattened the western end of the Alaska Range and carved the Tikchik Lakes with swoops of its great paws. Like long, deep gouges from colossal claws, the twelve lakes that make up the Wood River-Tikchik chain at the head of Bristol Bay run more or less parallel, varying in length from 15 to 45 miles and to depths of up to 900 feet. Hemmed in by steep, pinnacled slopes that still show evidence of the intense glacial action that actually created this area, the lakes bear a striking resemblance to

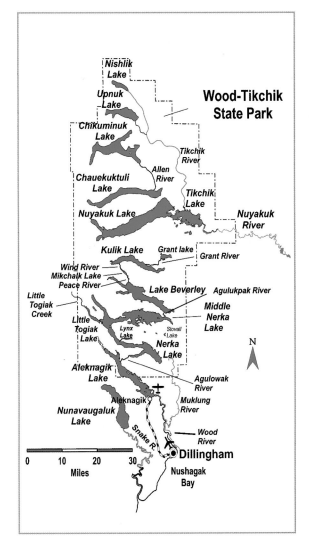

the deep blue fjords of northern Europe. Even more alluring is the fishing in the lakes and numerous streams and outlets; the abundant, pristine habitat supports significant numbers of salmon (mostly sockeye) and a diverse assemblage of resident fighters—rainbow trout, charr, grayling, lake trout, and even big northern pike.

To preserve the scenic wonder and diverse resources of this amazing area, the state of Alaska in 1978 designated 1.6 million acres of this region as Wood-Tikchik State Park. At 2,500 square miles, it is the largest State Park in the nation, and is managed as a total wilderness, with no public facilities.

The many possibilities for adventure angling in Bristol Bay's fabulous lake country have made this one of the most coveted recreation destinations in all of Alaska. You can fly in to any of the lakes and camp, fish, and explore on foot or by boat for days, even weeks if you desire. (Interconnected by short rivers, the lakes can be traversed almost entirely with a few short portages.) Or take a raft or kayak down one of the swift outlet rivers (such as Tikchik or

Nuyakuk) and enjoy good fishing as you drift through magnificent wild country. On the tamer end of things, there are several world-class fishing lodges that will pamper you with all the comforts of home (and more) while you enjoy great fishing action out the front door. If your tastes run somewhere in between, the scores of reputable guides and outfitters who service the area can accommodate just about any adventure whim.

The lakes are noted for having some of Bristol Bay's most abundant spring and late season fishing for rainbow trout and charr (including lake trout), which is concentrated in the major connecting streams and outlets (big grayling can be taken in many of these locations as well): Wood and Agulowak rivers (Aleknagik Lake); Agulukpak River (Lakes Beverley-Nerka); Little Togiak River and Lynx Creek (Lake Nerka); the Goldenhorn and Peace River (Lake Beverley); Grant and Wind rivers (Lake Kulik); the narrows connecting Tikchik and Nuyakuk lakes; the mouth of the Tikchik River and Nuyakuk River outlet (Tikchik Lake); the short stream connecting Nuyakuk and Chauekuktuli lakes; and the mouth of the Allen River (Lake Chauekuktuli). Some of the largest northern pike in Bristol Bay can be encountered in the lakes' weedy, shallow bays.

Tikchik River

Location: Northcentral Bristol Bay, 330 miles SW of Anchorage.

Access: By float plane from Dillingham; boat access to mouth and lower river possible from Tikchik Lake.

Facilities: None.

Highlights: Outstanding wilderness float river with decent fishing.

Main Species: GR, CHR, LT, RS

The Tikchik is one of Southwest Alaska's more notable wild rivers. It drains the uppermost reaches of the Wood-Tikchik chain, emptying into Tikchik Lake some 65 miles or so below. Clear, fast, and gravelly, it makes an exciting float through some of Bristol Bay's more remote and scenic backcountry, with some potentially good fishing (grayling, charr, salmon, and some rainbows) along the way.

The river begins at remote Nishlik Lake, where most folks put in. From there, it's a serene cruise (fast water, with some Class I) through a broad, mountain-ringed tundra valley, where you can expect to see caribou, wolf, moose, ptarmigan, and waterfowl and enjoy good flyfishing for grayling and charr. Farther down, the river gets braided and wider as it takes on more tributaries and enters lowland forest. (Watch the sweepers!) The fishing gets more interesting, too, with some rainbows, brighter salmon, and more charr in the sections above Tikchik Lake. But be mindful of the bears, as there will be plenty along the river during salmon season.

Figure on at least five days down to Tikchik Lake, where most folks take out. You should allow some time to enjoy both lakes, with their scenic views, wildlife, and good fishing for grayling, charr, and lake trout (Tikchik even has monster pike in some of its shallower, weedy bays). Some folks continue down the Nuyakuk River for an additional four to five days of rafting and great fishing, ending the trip at the village of Koliganek on the Nushagak River. (See the Nuyakuk listing.) August through mid-September is the recommended window for the best floatfishing. Check with local air taxis for latest conditions beforehand, as water levels and fishing can vary considerably during late summer and fall.

Kulukak River

Location: Bristol Bay, 50 miles west of Dillingham.

Access: By floatplane from Dillingham; lower river can be reached by boat from Togiak.

Facilities: None.

Highlights: A lesser-visited stream with good coho and king salmon possibilities.

Main Species: KS, SS

This relatively small Bristol Bay drainage is worthy of mention for a high quality, slightly off-the-beaten-path fishing experience for salmon in a small stream setting. Though it supports runs of all five salmon, its coho and chinook draw the most attention from anglers.

The Kulukak begins in a valley east of Pungokepuk Lake, drawing its water from numerous small runoff streams and several lakes in the Wood River Mountains. It flows about 37 miles south and slightly west before emptying into Kulukak Bay, east of Togiak. It is accessed by floatplane, using small headwater lakes or landing in certain areas along the lower river. Most of the angling effort occurs in the pools and other holding water of the lower four to five miles of river, where a couple of lodges do daily fly-out camps, but the Kulukak can be floated and fished from the headwaters, with good flyfishing conditions along much of the way. Present use, relative to other salmon streams in the area, remains light.

Togiak River System ★★★★

Location: Western Bristol Bay, 350 miles SW of Anchorage.

Access: By floatplane or boat from Dillingham or village of Togiak.

Facilities: No public facilities; private lodges along lower river.

Highlights: A very scenic Southwest river with a history of great fishing.

Main Species: KS, SS, CHR, GR, RT

Between the drainages of the lower Kuskokwim and the Tikchik Lakes lies some noteworthy fishing water, most of it in the Togiak River drainage, within Togiak National Wildlife Refuge. The Togiak is a 60-mile, crystal-clear waterway connecting the Togiak Lakes with Bristol Bay, west of the Nushagak. A tundra river, it has been fished for years, at times offering outstanding silver and king salmon angling, in addition to superb charr and fair to good rainbow trout and grayling. It flows through some of the most scenic mountain country in all of Southwest Alaska.

Fair-sized, deep and wide, with considerable current but virtually no whitewater, the Togiak is an easy float, but it can be difficult to fish with anything but spin and casting gear. Flyfishing is challenging and best done in the lakes, mouths of tributary streams, and shallow riffle sections and sloughs. Most of the angling effort has traditionally been along the lower river from fly-out camps, but the best way to fish the Togiak is by raft, from Togiak Lake down to the lower river. (Figure on a trip of four to six days, with a take-out right below the Togiak Wilderness boundary at the mouth of Pungokepuk Creek or along gravel bars farther down.) Upper Togiak and other headwater lakes and tributaries (including Trail, Ongivinuk, Gechiak, Nenevok, Kashiak, and Pungokepuk) are less visited, but offer outstanding possibilities for salmon, grayling, and charr. A few even have rainbows. (Check with local sources for river conditions before attempting a float down Togiak headwaters.)

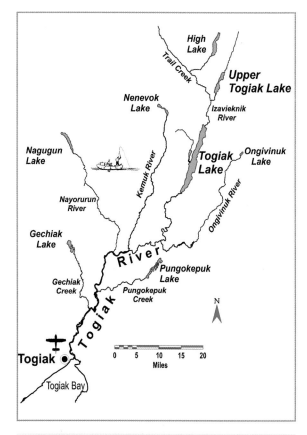

Recommended Guides/Lodges/Outfitters/Air Taxis

Rainbow River Lodge: (505) 429-0511. *www.alaskarain bowriverlodge.com* Custom flyfishing lodge, Copper River.

Iliaska Lodge: 6160 Fairpoint Drive, Anchorage, AK 99507, (907) 337-9844, *www.iliaska.com* Custom flyfishing lodge, Lake Iliamna.

Alaska's Wilderness Lodge: P.O. Box 700, Sumner, WA 98390, (800) 835-8032 or (907) 781-2223, *www.alaskaswilderness lodge.com* Custom fishing lodge, Lake Clark.

Dan Salmon: P.O. Box 4003, Igiugik, AK 99613, (907) 533-3219. Guide service, boat rentals and lodging, Kvichak River.

Roadhouse Inn: Box 206, Iliamna, AK 99606, (907) 571-1272. Lodging, guide service, car rentals, Iliamna area.

Iliamna Air Taxi: Box 109, Iliamna, AK 99606, (907) 571-1248. Areawide floatplane service with daily connections to Anchorage; gear rentals.

Lake and Peninsula Airlines: 3323 Dry Creek, Port Alsworth, AK 99653, (907) 781-2228. Air Taxi service, Lake Clark area.

Skiff Fishing: Jack Ross, General Delivery, Port Alsworth, AK 99653, (907) 781-2255. Lake trout charters, Lake Clark.

Alagnak Lodge: (800) 877-9903. *www.alagnaklodge.com* Full service fly-out lodge, Alagnak River.

Katmailand, Inc.: 4125 Aircraft Drive, Anchorage, AK 99502, (800) 544-0551. *www.katmailand.com* Lodging, cabin, boat rentals, guided fishing, Katmai National Park.

Rainbow Bend: (888) 575-4249. *www.bristolbayfishing.com* Cabin and boat rentals, guided fishing, Naknek River.

Katmai Fishing Adventures: (907) 246-8322. *www.katmaifishing.com* Flyfishing guides, Katmai area.

Branch River Air Service: 4540 Edinburgh Drive, Anchorage, AK 99502, (907) 248-3539 (winter), (907) 246-3437 (summer). *www.branchriverair.com* Air taxi, gear rentals, Katmai area.

Eruk's Wilderness Floats: 12720 Lupine Road, Anchorage, AK 99516; (888) 212-2203. Floatfishing tours, Bristol Bay.

Royal Coachman Lodge: (888) 347-4286. *www.royalcoachman lodge.com* Custom fly-out lodge, Nuyakuk River.

Bristol Bay Lodge: 2422 Hunter Road, Ellensburg, WA 98926 (509) 964-2094. *www.bristolbaylodge.com*

Ultimate Rivers: Box 670534, Chugiak, AK 99567. (907) 688-6535, *www.ultimaterivers.com* Custom floatfishing trips, Bristol Bay.

Portage Creek General Store/Lodge: Portage Creek, AK 99576, (907) 842-7191. *www.akbushguides.com/salmon.htm* Lodging, boat rentals, guided fishing, lower Nushagak River.

Freshwater Adventures: Box 62, Dillingham, AK 99576, (907) 842-5060. *www.fresh-h2o.com* Air taxi, equipment rentals, Nushagak drainage.

Tikchik Air: Box 71, Dillingham, AK 99576, (907) 842-5841. Air taxi service, Nushagak drainage.

USGS Maps References

Lake Iliamna: Iliamna B-5, B-6, B-7, B-8, C-3, C-4, C-5, C-6, C-7, C-8, D-3, D-4, D-5.

Kvichak River: Iliamna B-8; Dillingham A-1, A2, A-3, B-1; Naknek D-3.

Newhalen River: Iliamna C-6, D-5, D-6.

Talarik Creek: Iliamna C-7.

Copper River: Iliamna C-4, C-5.

Gibraltar River: Iliamna B-5, B-6.

Lake Clark: Lake Clark A-4, A-5, B-2, B-3, B-4.

Tazimina River: Lake Clark A-2, A- 3, A-4; Iliamna D-5.

Brooks River: Mount Katmai C-6.

Naknek Lake & River: Naknek C-1, C-2, C-3; Mt Katmai C-5, C-6.

Alagnak River System: Iliamna A-6, A-7, A-8; Mt. Katmai D-3, D-4, D-5; Dillingham A-1, A-2, A-3.

American Creek: Mount Katmai D-4, D-5, D-6.

King Salmon River: Mount Katmai A-6; Naknek A-1, A-2, A-4, A-5, B-2, B-3, B-4.

Coville-Grosvenor Lakes: Mount Katmai C-4, C-5, D-5, D-6.

Nushagak River: Dillingham A-5, B-4, B-5, C-3, C-4, D-4; Taylor Mountains A-4, B-2, B-3, B-4, B-5, B-6, B-7, C-1, C-2, C-4, C-5.

Mulchatna River: Lake Clark B-7, B-8, C-6, C-7, C- 8, D-3, D-4, D-5, D-6; Taylor Mountains A-1, A-2, B-1; Dillingham C-3, D-1, D-2, D-3.

Chilikadrotna River: Lake Clark C-2, C-3, C-4, C-5, C-6, C-7.

American Creek, Katmai

Koktuli River: Iliamna D-7, D-8; Dillingham D-1, D-2.

Stuyahok River: Iliamna C-8, D-8; Dillingham C-1.

Nuyakuk River: Dillingham D-4, D-5, D-6.

Wood-Tikchik Lakes: Bethel A-1, B-1; Dillingham A-8, B-7, B-8, C-7, C-8, D-6, D-7, D-8; Goodnews Bay B-1, C-1, D-1; Taylor Mountains A-7, A-8, B-8.

Tikchik River: Dillingham D-7; Taylor Mtns A-7, A-8, B-7, B-8.

Kulukak River: Nushagak Bay D-6; Goodnews Bay A-3, B-2.

Togiak River: Goodnews A-4, B-3, B-4, C-2, C-3, D-2.

General Information:

Alaska Department of Fish & Game: Division of Sportfish, 546 Kenny Wren Road, Box 230, Dillingham, AK 99576-0230, (907) 842-2427.

Wood-Tikchik State Park: Alaska Department of Natural Resources, 550 W. 7th Avenue, Anchorage, AK 99501-3557, (907) 269-8698, *www.dnr.state.ak.us/parks/units/woodtik.htm*

Lake Clark National Park and Preserve: 4230 University Drive, #311, Anchorage, AK 99508; (907) 271-3751. *www.nps.gov/lacl*

Katmai National Park & Preserve: P.O. Box 7, King Salmon, AK 99613; (907) 246-3305. *www.nps.gov/katm*

Alaska Peninsula/Becharof National Wildlife Refuge: P.O. Box 277, King Salmon, AK 99613, (907) 246-3339, *http://alaskapeninsula.fws.gov/*

Togiak National Wildlife Refuge: P.O. Box 270, Dillingham, AK 99576, (907) 842-1063. *http://togiak.fws.gov/*

For information on the location of private land holdings and leases, easements, and public lands within Bristol Bay:

Bureau of Land Management: Alaska State Office, 222 West Seventh Avenue, #13, Anchorage, AK 99513. (907) 271-5960. *www.ak.blm.gov/blmaso.htm*

Alaska Dept. of Natural Resources: Public Information Center, 550 W. 7th Avenue, #1260, Anchorage, AK 99501-3557, (907) 269-8400, *www.dnr.state.ak.us*

Regulations/Information

Much of Bristol Bay is closed to trout fishing from early April until early June. Additional seasonal restrictions apply for king salmon (see Regs.). Some waters are restricted to catch-and-release fishing, single hook artificial lures or fly-fishing only. Check latest ADF&G Regulations Summary for Bristol Bay or call the Dillingham Sportfish Office, (907) 842-2427 for complete information when planning a trip to the area.

Bristol Bay Fishery Hotline: (907) 267-2506

Online info: *www.sf.adfg.state.ak.us/ statewide/regulations/ bbregs.cfm*

Bristol Bay Species

LOCATION	King Salmon	Red Salmon	Pink Salmon	Chum Salmon	Silver Salmon	Steelhead	Rainbow	Cutthroat	Char	Grayling	Lake Trout	Northern Pike	Sheefish	Halibut	Lingcod	Rockfish	Salmon Shark	Fishing Pressure
Lake Iliamna	R	✪	✓	✓	R		✪		✪	☺	☺	R						M
Kvichak River	✓	✪	☺	✓	✓		✪		☺	☺	R	✓						M
Newhalen River	R	✪	✓	R	R		✪		✓	✓	✓							☹
Talarik Creek	R	☺	✓	R	R		✪		✓	☺	R	R						☹
Copper River	R	✪	✓	R	R		✪		☺	✪	R	☺						M
Gibralter River	R	✪	✓	R	R		✪		✓	✓	R							M
Lake Clark		✪	R						☺	✪	✪	✪						M
Tazimina River		✪	R				✪		☺	✪								M
Naknek Lake & River	✪	✪	☺	☺	☺		✪		✪	☺	✪	✓						M
Brooks River	R	✪	☺	☺	R		✪		☺	☺	✓							☹
Alagnak River System	✪	✪	✪	✪	☺		✪		☺	✪	✓	✓						☹
American Creek		✪	R	R	R		✪		✪	☺	✓	R						✓
Coville-Grosvenor Lakes		☺	R	R	R		✪		✪	☺	✪							✓
King Salmon River	✓	✓	✓	✓	✓		☺		☺	☺								R
Nushagak River	✪	☺	✪	✪	✪		✪		✪	☺		☺						M
Mulchatna River	✪	☺	✓	☺	☺		✪		✪	✪	R	☺						M
Chilikadrotna River	✓	✓	R	☺	✓		☺		☺	☺	R	✓						✓
Koktuli River	☺	✓	✓	✓	☺		☺		☺	☺		✓						☹
Stuyahok River	☺	✓	✓	✓	☺		☺		☺	☺		✓						M
Nuyakuk River	✓	☺	✓	✓			✪		✪	✪	R	✓						✓
Wood-Tikchik Lakes	R	☺	☺	✓	R		✪		✪	✪	✪	✪						✓
Tikchik River	R	✓	☺	✓	R		✓		✓	☺	R	✓						✓
Kulukak River	☺	✓	☺	☺	☺		R		☺									✓
Togiak River System	✪	✓	✪	☺	✪		✓		✪	☺	✓							✓

Legend:

- Species Not present
- R — Rare
- ✓ — Fishable numbers (or light pressure)
- ☺ — Good fishing
- ✪ — Excellent fishing
- LL — Landlocked species
- C — Present, but fishing closed
- M — Moderate pressure
- ☹ — Heavy pressure

Alaska's Largest Lakes
Southwest's immense and productive systems in northern Alaska Peninsula and Bristol Bay (Iliamna,
Becharof, Naknek, Wood-Tickchiks, etc.) provide the state's most abundant lake angling opportunities.

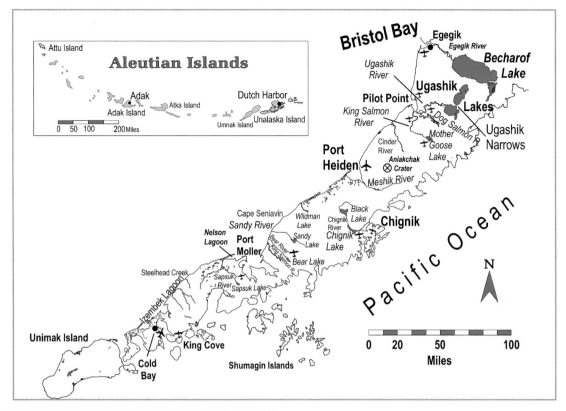

ALASKA PENINSULA/ALEUTIANS

For years the exclusive domain of commercial fishermen and intrepid hunters, the Alaska Peninsula, with it's extreme isolation and inhospitable terrain, has always been the true "no-man's land" of Southwest Alaska. But the enormous, storm-raked arc of tundra-clad islands, volcanic peaks, glaciers, and rugged coastline has always held a certain mystique for sport anglers, with its unexplored streams and lakes, and promise of great fishing.

Salmon and charr throng in nearly every drainage, including those in the Aleutians; and new, exciting nearshore fisheries are developing for halibut, rockfish, and saltwater salmon. There are even steelhead trout streams that go virtually unfished for want of anglers willing to brave harsh conditions and difficult logistics.

To meet the inevitable demand of anglers searching for new and uncrowded fishing destinations, new lodges, outpost camps, and air taxis are opening up areas that not too long ago were just points on the map of fishing dreams. Access to this remote expanse is through the regional hubs of King Salmon (for north Alaska Peninsula locations), Cold Bay, Unalaska/Dutch Harbor, and Adak, which are all serviced by frequent jet flights from Anchorage. Visitor services are scarce and expensive—particularly as you venture farther out from the mainland—and the weather is notoriously limiting at times. Still, the appeal of virgin water and potential record catches for halibut and other species is hard to deny.

Becharof Lake ★★★

Location: North Alaska Peninsula, 325 miles SW of Anchorage.

Access: By floatplane from King Salmon or boat from village of Egegik.

Facilities: No developed public facilities.

Highlights: An underutilized giant fishery, with trophy potential for charr and grayling.

Main Species: GR, CHR, RS, SS

Becharof Lake on the north Alaska Peninsula is an isolated, monstrous body of water—the second largest in Alaska—best known for its abundant salmon and wildlife (brown bears, caribou, and waterfowl) and unforgiving weather. It is a sleeping giant as far as fishing goes, and nearly all who have sunk lines in its vast waters have come away impressed with its awesome potential. This lake and river system receives one of the most significant sockeye salmon runs in Alaska, with smaller numbers of silver, pink, chum, and even a few king salmon. Stories of monstrous charr and giant grayling are substantiated now and then by some remarkable catches from the few anglers intrepid enough to challenge these waters. (Some of the state's largest specimens for these species have been caught there.) When you consider the size, remoteness and productivity of this drainage, there's no telling what this lake might hold.

But here's the catch: this part of the state is known as the "wind tunnel of Alaska" and, on a lake of this size with no cover, it can make for some scary conditions. But if you can duck in on a nice day, all the guides, fishermen, and biologists familiar with Becharof say the outlet waters and numerous creek mouths around the lake offer some truly remarkable fishing. Some of these drainages are even rumored to have rainbows, though you'll have a hard time prying any details from the folks who would know these things. For the adventuresome angler with time and money to burn, Becharof Lake is definitely on the list of Alaska's most promising untapped waters.

Ugashik Lakes/Bay ★★★

Location: North Alaska Peninsula, approximately 350 miles SW of Anchorage.

Access: By floatplane from King Salmon or boat from Pilot Point or Ugashik.

Facilities: Private lodges on lake.

Highlights: A legendary SW location for charr, grayling, and salmon.

Main Species: GR, CHR, SS, RS, KS, CS

The Ugashik area south of Becharof has several notable salmon streams and a famous lake destination where fishermen have traditionally journeyed for trophy grayling and charr. The state record grayling, a whopping, 4-pound, 13-ounce fish, was caught at Ugashik Lake in 1981 (see grayling chapter for details), with the windblown, barren "narrows" between the upper and lower lakes having yielded countless other wall-hanging sailfins and charr during its heyday in the 60s and 70s.

But, over the years, the heavy fishing pressure and other factors brought a noticeable decline in the quality of angling, so much so that in 1990 the entire Ugashik drainage was closed to grayling fishing. A rebound in grayling numbers recently has brought a partial lifting of restrictions (be sure to check latest Regulations Summary for details). Grayling and charr fishing, according to local sources, is as good as ever.

Most of the fishing effort at Ugashik Lakes targets the short but extremely productive narrows, the lake outlet, and mouths of the numerous inlet creeks. Salmon are seasonally plentiful, notably silver and sockeye, and are fished mostly in the lower lake outlet and lagoon or in Ugashik River. There is also very good lake trout fishing. Best times are early summer (June through mid-July) and fall (late August through early September).

Beyond the lakes, the better streams emptying into Ugashik Bay are visited regularly by area guides and lodges for their fine runs of all five species of salmon and abundant charr. The **King Salmon River** is perhaps the most popular of these, as it is easily accessed by floatplane at Mother Goose Lake and offers good fishing for (what else?) chinook salmon, as well as sockeye, coho, and charr in the river below the lake and in adjoining tributaries. (The well-known, private Painter Creek Lodge is in the area, along the creek

of the same name.) **Dog Salmon River**, a few miles away, is turbid, with fishing limited to its clear feeders. (Both streams have glacial sources, but the King Salmon benefits from the settling effect of Mother Goose Lake.) Like its neighbor, it has all five species of salmon, plus northern pike and grayling (one of the southernmost spots to fish grayling on the peninsula).

Cinder River, twelve miles south, is a small but productive runoff stream originating from the cinder beds of nearby Aniakchak. Braided and clear, this black sand drainage is fished only infrequently for its abundant silver salmon. A small hunting camp is located there, with access limited to small wheelplane landings on the beach or on cinder beds along the upper river.

Chignik River

Location: Alaska Peninsula, Pacific side, 175 miles SW of Kodiak.

Access: By small plane from King Salmon; also from Kodiak by state ferry.

Facilities: No developed public facilities; limited services available in nearby villages.

Highlights: A remote, highly productive, unexploited river system.

Main Species: KS, RS, SS

Chignik River, 175 miles southwest of Kodiak, is one of the most important salmon systems of the entire Alaska Peninsula, supporting extensive runs of sockeye, coho, pink, and chum salmon and the south side peninsula's only significant population of chinook. Because of its remoteness, it receives virtually no outside angling pressure. Keep it in mind for future angling adventures, as more and more of the state's accessible waters become well visited.

This short river system connects two very productive sockeye salmon nurseries, Black and Chignik lakes, to the Pacific coast. Most of the present sportfishing effort occurs from Chignik Lake to the lagoon, where boat anglers target the river's chinook, silver salmon, and abundant charr populations. The Chignik's substantial sockeye salmon runs (two separate: one in June, the other from July into September) receive little sportfishing pressure, and there are even some rumors of steelhead spawning there. Access is by small plane to two gravel airstrips or by floatplane to the lake or lagoon. Chignik has regularly scheduled flights from King Salmon and state ferry service from Kodiak. At present, visitor facilities are minimal, but there are definite plans for the construction of a lodge by the village native corporation. If you're looking for something different and have the time and resources to explore this unique fishery, give local guide Johnny Lind a call at Chignik Lake, (907) 845-2228.

Meshik River

Location: Central Alaska Peninsula, 400 miles SW of Anchorage.

Access: By floatplane from King Salmon or Port Heiden; also by boat from Port Heiden.

Facilities: No public facilities; limited services at Port Heiden.

Highlights: A more out-of-the-way Alaska Peninsula location with high potential.

Main Species: KS, RS, SS, CHR

Very little serious sportfishing effort occurs south of the Ugashik Lakes area, because of the expense of transportation, lack of services, weather, and other factors. Most of the better streams—there are quite a few with good salmon and charr fishing—receive only light pressure from locals or the occasional hunter. The Meshik River of the Port Heiden area is worth mentioning because of its high potential, relatively easy access, and location (the upper river) within Aniakchak National Preserve. With more and more folks discovering the outstanding adventure recreation potential of this area, it's only a matter of time before the Meshik becomes well known and utilized for its exciting fishing and floating possibilities.

Originating on steep mountain slopes southeast of Aniakchak Peak, the Meshik flows west for about 50 miles before emptying into Port Heiden. It's known for strong runs of chinook and coho salmon, along with sockeyes, chums, and abundant charr. A headwater lake 40 miles up from the mouth, and numerous smaller lakes along the lower river, provide access for floatplanes. The best way to fish the Meshik is to float down from the upper river by raft or kayak, or to access the lower river and tributaries (where the best silver, king, and charr fishing is) by boat or floatplane from Port Heiden (which is linked to King Salmon by daily air service). Several area lodges provide still more fishing options.

With its many clear, shallow tributaries and shallow runs, the Meshik has considerable flyfishing potential. Aside from the abundant bear population and unpredictable weather, there is nothing here to preclude some very productive and enjoyable fishing explorations along this remote and utterly pristine drainage.

Peninsula Steelhead Streams ★★★
Location: Lower Alaska Peninsula, Cape Seniavin to Cold Bay.

Access: By small plane from Port Heiden or other local hubs; access to some streams by road, boat, or small plane from Cold Bay.

Facilities: No public; a few outpost camps and lodges service area.

Highlights: North America's last frontier for wild steelhead.

Main Species: ST, SS, CHR

On the lower arc of the Alaska Peninsula lie the continent's last unexplored steelhead streams. At least a dozen small drainages from Chignik to Cold Bay have spawning populations of the coveted sea-run rainbows, with the best occurring along Cape Seniavin, the Nelson Lagoon area, and Cold Bay (Sandy, Bear, and Nelson rivers; and Russell, Steelhead, and Trout creeks). The presence of steelhead undoubtedly goes beyond these documented systems, judging from accounts of locals, hunters, commercial fishermen, and others who have had the rare opportunity to sample the far-flung waters of Unimak and the rugged Pacific side of the lower peninsula.

These peninsula steelhead runs are all very small, most numbering in the hundreds. They occur predominantly during fall, with peaks from late September through October. (A few bright spring fish show up in certain drainages during April and May, however.) The average size of the fish is about the same or slightly more than those on Kodiak, with occasional outsized specimens in the teens and even larger on some streams. Untouched salmon and charr populations are an added bonus.

These streams are very remote and most are difficult to get to. Primitive airstrips from old hunting camps allow wheel plane access to some, while floatplanes, boats, and primitive trails and roads can be used to reach others (from Port Heiden, Chignik, and Cold Bay). Most of these streams have only been worked sporadically by hunt-

ing guides during the fall season, with focused sportfishing effort occurring only recently on a few of the better ones, mostly from a few local fishing camps and lodges. All reports indicate some outstanding possibilities for high quality fishing. Drawbacks are the notorious peninsula weather and the expense of getting in, factors that shouldn't stop hard-core steelheaders from exploring the last unfished runs in North America.

Dutch Harbor/Unalaska ★★★★
Location: Eastern Aleutians, 800 miles SW of Anchorage.

Access: By boat (or road for stream and shore fishing) from Dutch Harbor, reached by scheduled air from Anchorage.

Facilities: No public facilities; expanding visitor services available in Dutch Harbor/Unalaska.

Highlights: New world-class halibut location.

Main Species: HT, RF, RS, SS

Out past the end of the Alaska Peninsula, on the edge of the Aleutians, lies the deep harbor of America's number one fishing port, the city of Dutch Harbor. Surrounded by some of the world's richest fishing grounds, it has only recently been explored by sport anglers, but with spectacular results. Giant halibut of record proportions have been taken in Unalaska Bay and surrounding waters in the last decade, and it's no longer a secret that Alaska's top commercial fishing locale is also the new mecca for trophy halibut hunting.

Even by Alaska standards, the fishing is stupendous. Halibut exceeding two hundred, even three hundred, pounds are remarkably common, with new records being set almost continuously. (Since 1995, the IGFA All Tackle World record has been broken twice in Unalaska waters; the latest by an incredible 459-pound fish taken by Fairbanks resident Jack Tragis in June of 1996.)

The season for the best halibut fishing generally runs from June to September. (Don't miss the opportunity to enter the annual World Record Derby held during this time, with a $100,000 prize for anyone who breaks the world record.) In addition to halibut, the Unalaska/Dutch Harbor area boasts unexploited nearshore fisheries for rockfish and cod, as well as notable fresh and saltwater fishing for abundant sockeye (mid June-August) and silver salmon (August and September), with rumors even of some exciting trolling possibilities for saltwater kings.

Recommended Lodges/Guides/Outfitters/Air taxis

Ugashik Lakes Camp: P.O. Box 90444, Anchorage, AK 99509, (907) 248-3230, *www.alaskafishandhunt.com/fish*

Painter Creek Lodge: P.O. Box 190109, Anchorage, AK 99519, (907) 248-1303, *www.paintercreeklodge.com*

Johnny Lind: P.O. Box 4, Chignik Lake, AK 99548, (907) 845-2228. Lodging and guide service, Chignik River.

Alaska Trophy Hunting & Fishing: P.O. Box 220247, Anchorage AK 99522, (907) 344-8589, *www.alaska-trphy-hunt-fish.com* Lodge-based, guided fishing for Peninsula steelhead.

Far West Outfitters: John Lucking, P.O. Box 42, Unalaska, AK 99685, (907) 581-1647 Trophy halibut charters, Dutch Harbor.

Ugladax Lodge: c/o MUM, P.O. Box 669, Los Molinos, CA 96055,

(800) 557-7087, *www.mumwildlife.com/nikolski.shtml* Lodge-based guided fishing, Unmak Island, Aleutians.

Peninsula Airways, Inc.: 6100 Boeing Avenue, Anchorage, AK 99502, (907) 243-2323, (800) 448-4226.

USGS Maps References

Ugashik Area: Ugashik A-3, A-4, A-5, A-6, B-3, B-4, B-5, B-6, C-2, C-3, C-4, C-5, D-2; Bristol Bay B-1.

Becharof Lake: Naknek A-2, A-3; Karluk C-6, D-6; Ugashik C-1, D-1, D-3.

Chignik River: Chignik A-3, B-3.

Meshik River: Sutwik Island D-6; Chignik C-1, C-2, D-1, D-2.

Peninsula Steelhead Streams: Chignik A-5, A-6, A-7, A-8; Port Moller C-4, C-5, C-6, D-4, D-5, D-6; Cold Bay A-2, A-3, B-2, B-3.

Dutch Harbor/Unalaska: Unalaska A-2, A-3, A-4, B-1, B-2, B-4, C-1, C-2, C-4, D-1, D-2, D-3.

General Information

Alaska Peninsula/Becharof National Wildlife Refuge: P.O. Box 277, King Salmon, AK 99613, (907) 246-3339, *http://alaskapeninsula.fws.gov/*

Aniakchak National Monument & Preserve: P.O. Box 7, King Salmon, AK 99613, (907) 246-3305, *www.nps.gov/ania/index.htm*

Izembeck National Wildlife Refuge: Box 127, Cold Bay, AK 99571, (907) 532-2445, *http://izembek.fws.gov/*

Regulations/Information

Most Alaska Peninsula waters are open year-round for all species (except halibut—see regs.), with some seasonal restrictions and area closures. Consult current ADF&G Fishing Regulations Summary for Bristol Bay and Alaska Peninsula, or contact ADF&G Dillingham office, (907) 842-2427, or Kodiak, (907) 486-1880, for complete information when planning a trip to area.

Online info: *www.sf.adfg.state.ak.us/ statewide/regulations/ kodregs.cfm*

Alaska Peninsula/Aleutians Species

LOCATION	KING SALMON	RED SALMON	PINK SALMON	CHUM SALMON	SILVER SALMON	STEELHEAD	RAINBOW	CUTTHROAT	CHAR	GRAYLING	LAKE TROUT	SHEEFISH	NORTHERN PIKE	HALIBUT	LING COD	ROCK FISH	SALMON SHARK	FSHG. PRESSURE
Becharof Lake System	R	★	☺	☺	☺			R		★	★	R		R				✓
Ugashik Lakes System	✓	★	☺	☺	★					★	★	✓		☺				M
Ugashik Bay Streams	☺	✓	☺	☺	★		R			☺	✓			R				✓
Chignik River	★	★	☺	☺	★	R				★								✓
Meshik River	✓	☺	✓	☺	☺					☺								R
Peninsula Steelhead Streams	✓	✓	☺	☺	☺	★				☺								R
Dutch Harbor / Unalaska	R	☺	✓	✓	☺					☺					★	★	✓	✓

Species not present

R   Rare

✓   Fishable numbers (or light pressure)

☺   Good fishing

★   Excellent fishing

LL   Landlocked species

C   Present, but fishing closed

M   Moderate pressure

☹   Heavy pressure

LOWER YUKON-KUSKOKWIM

Alaska's two greatest rivers, the Yukon and Kuskok-wim, spill their waters within 200 miles of each other in a broad, fan-shaped delta that is one of the world's great wetland habitats. Ideally suited for water-fowl, this area is too flat and marshy to support any high-quality sportfishing. However, the surrounding uplands give rise to quite a few notable drainages, some of world class distinction. Since both the 800-mile Kuskokwim and 1500-mile Yukon are too turbid to fish in the main-stem, these clear-flowing tributaries represent perhaps the best opportunities for sampling the remarkable and varied fishing of these giant drainages. Major hubs for the area are the towns of Dillingham, Bethel, and Aniak, all serviced by daily scheduled flights from Anchorage and local air taxis, with limited visitor services available.

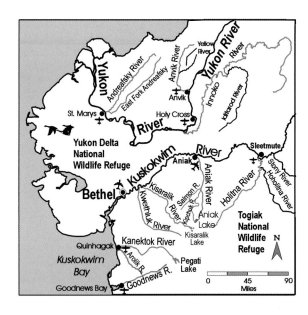

Goodnews River ★★★★

Location: Lower Kuskokwim Bay, 375 miles SW of Anchorage.

Access: By floatplane from Dillingham or Bethel to headwaters; boat or floatplane access to lower river.

Facilities: No public facilities; private tent camps and local guides on river.

Highlights: One of Alaska's premier floatfishing rivers, with out-standing flyfishing possibilities.

Main Species: KS, SS, RS, RT, CHR, GR

The Goodnews River system is one of the best known of the fabu-lously productive streams of Kuskokwim Bay. Like its sister drainage, the Kanektok, it has some of Southwest Alaska's most productive and varied stream fishing (for all species of salmon, trout, grayling, and sea-run charr). It is also a world-renowned float trip destination.

Like other neighboring drainages, the Goodnews is a tundra river. Short (only 60 miles) and sparkling clear, it is comprised of three forks that drain the most southern valley in Kuskokwim Bay. The Middle Fork and mainstem are the most commonly fished sections. A private outpost camp and a few local guides fish the lower river; otherwise, floatfishing in rafts or kayaks is the preferred way of sampling this drainage. Floatplanes from Dillingham or Bethel pro-vide access to numerous headwater lakes (including Goodnews, Canyon, Awayak, Nimgun, Middle Fork, and Kukatlim), and the lower river can be reached by boat from the village of Goodnews for take-outs (highly recommended because the tidal action in the mouth and bay make for hazardous floatplane landings and rafting). None of the forks contains any major hazards to boaters, except for swift water, sweepers, and some minor rapids between Canyon and Arayak creeks in the upper mainstem. (Low-water conditions can be a real "drag" in the shallow sections below the lakes, however, especially on the Middle Fork—check with air taxi beforehand.) They can be floated in anywhere from four to seven days.

With its varied forks, miles of tributaries and numerous headwater

lakes, the Goodnews certainly has a wealth of good fishing possi-bilities. It is noted for its abundant, beautifully marked rainbow trout (the famous leopard rainbows, to 10 pounds), big grayling (to three pounds), sea-run charr (to eight pounds), and outstanding flyfishing opportunities, particularly for king and silver salmon. Nearly all of the deep headwater lakes contain lake trout and other charr, in addition to supporting good runs of sockeye salmon. July and August are the prime months for fishing.

Special note: Portions of the lower river are privately owned; for land-use information, contact Village of Goodnews Bay, Goodnews Bay, AK 99589, (907) 967-8929.

Arolik River ★★★

Location: Kuskokwim Bay, 400 miles SW of Anchorage.

Access: By floatplane from Dillingham or Bethel to headwaters; lower river accessed by jet boat and road.

Facilities: No public facilities.

Highlights: An outstanding, lesser-fished Kuskokwim Bay stream.

Main Species: KS, SS, RT, CHR, GR

While the Arolik is among the outstanding streams of Kuskokwim Bay, it receives just a fraction of the attention lavished on the more glamorous rivers it is situated between, the Kanektok and Good-news. It flows northwest for about 70 miles from headwaters in the ridge of mountains above the Goodnews, with two main forks and numerous tributaries. The lower mainstem braids heavily, then splits into separate mouths that empty into Kuskokwim Bay just south of the village of Quinhagak.

With abundant rainbows, charr, grayling, and salmon, fishing on the Arolik can be every bit as good as the Kanektok or Goodnews, but access and logistics are a problem. For floatfishing trips, the upper river below the Arolik Lake put-in is rocky and shallow in spots and, during low-water times, passage may be difficult, if not impossible. You can float early in the season and take your chances, using a lightly equipped raft, inflatable canoe, or kayak. Figure on a six to seven-day float from the lake down to a prearranged pick-up on the lower river. (Tidal influence makes rafting, as well as floatplane landings, tricky and dangerous near the mouth of the river. Limited road access is now available from Quinhagak to the lower Arolik; check with your air taxi for details.) Lodge-based fishing and locally run spike camps provide additional options for fishing the lower river.

Kanektok River ★★★★

Location: Kuskokwim Bay, 350 miles SW of Anchorage.

Access: By floatplane from Dillingham or Bethel to headwaters; wheelplane or boat access to lower river.

Facilities: No public; tent camps and lodges along lower river.

Highlights: One of Alaska's most celebrated salmon and trout streams; a classic floatfishing destination.

Main Species: KS, SS, CS, RS, RT, CHR, GR

The Kanektok is one of several sparkling tundra rivers that drain the fringe of mountains in mainland Alaska's extreme southwest corner. An abundance and variety of species—"leopard" rainbow trout, sea-run charr, grayling, and all five species of salmon—along with beautiful scenery and perfect wade and cast stream conditions have given it quite a reputation over the years.

The river rambles for 90 miles from mountain headwaters at Kagati Lake to the flat coastal plain and silty waters of Kuskokwim Bay. Gravel bottomed, moderately swift (three to four miles per hour), and crystal clear, with lots of shallow braids and pools containing amazing numbers of fish, the Kanektok is a flyfisher's dream.

The best way to fish it is, without a doubt, from rafts, floating down from Kagati Lake to the village of Quinhagak along the coast (seven to eight-day trip), which has a gravel airstrip. There are no serious hazards except abundant sweepers and fast water. On the upper river, you'll find great scenic views and good grayling and charr fishing, while the best rainbow trout habitat is the heavily braided middle and lower sections as the river emerges from the mountains. The lower 20 miles of river is the preferred location for intercepting the Kanektok's abundant runs of salmon and sea-run charr. If you're not into rafting, you can stay at an outpost tent camp, or have someone run you in a boat upriver from the village, and camp and fish along one of the numerous gravel bars.

Early July is prime time for intercepting the Kanektok's bright king, chum, and sockeye salmon, while August and September offer great fishing for silver salmon, rainbow trout, and charr. All the headwater lakes offer good lake trout fishing.

Guides' tip: *The Kanektok is one of the rivers where the Alaska "Mouse" got its start. They are fished under cutbanks and along slough and pool margins for explosive surface strikes from hungry rainbow trout and charr.*

Special Note: *The lower 17 miles of the river are owned by Quinhagak Village Corporation; for land use information, contact Quanirtuuq Inc., 100 Quanirtuuq Drive, P.O. Box 69, Quinhagak, AK 99655, (907) 556-8289.*

Kwethluk River ★★★

Location: Lower Kuskokwim River, 350 miles west of Anchorage.

Access: By floatplane from Dillingham or Bethel to headwaters; jetboat pick-up along lower river.

Facilities: No public facilities; private tent camps along river.

Highlights: Lesser-fished salmon and trout stream of high potential.

Main Species: RT, CHR, GR, SS, KS, CS

Similar in size, character, and fishing potential to its neighbor, the Kisaralik, the Kwethluk River has only recently received attention from outside sportfishermen. Like its neighbor, its best water is reached by raft from the headwaters, though most of the fishing effort occurs from boats and tent camps along the lower river.

Not as alpine as the Kisaralik, the 130-mile long Kwethluk draws its headwaters from numerous run-off creeks draining the remote reaches of the Eek Mountains. From there it meanders west and north through a broad valley, gaining size and speed as it carves its way down into the lowlands that surround the marshy delta.

Fishing is quite good in most years. The extensive, braided habitat of the middle river section can provide noteworthy fishing for husky rainbows and salmon in late summer, with the alpine upper stretches populated by grayling and charr. Salmon—silvers, chums, and kings mostly—can provide good fishing in season, but are generally not in prime condition like farther down along the Bay.

For rafting, the river is usually accessed by floatplane from Bethel, Dillingham (or Aniak), using pothole lakes adjacent to the upper river (from the Crooked Creek confluence to Breast Mountain and beyond) for put-ins. Floaters usually take out somewhere below Three Step Mountain to avoid the endless meanders and dead water farther down, using jet boat service from Bethel, Kwethluk or other neighboring villages. Figure on a seven to eight-day trip from the headwaters, depending on where you put in, with August and early September the prime time.

Kisaralik River ★★★

Location: Lower Kuskokwim River, 350 miles west of Anchorage.

Access: By floatplane from Dillingham, Bethel, or Aniak to headwaters; jetboat pick-up along lower river.

Facilities: No public; rustic fishing lodge along lower river.

Highlights: An area salmon/trout stream of high adventure recreation potential.

Main Species: RT, CHR, GR, SS, KS

A very pretty and remote mountain river, the topaz-blue Kisaralik has outstanding wilderness values, along with potentially good salmon and rainbow trout fishing. With its whitewater canyons, portages, and abundant sweepers, it makes for a challenging but rewarding floatfishing adventure.

The Kisaralik rises in the rugged and remote headlands (Kilbuck Mountains) between the upper Aniak and Kanektok rivers. From its source at high Kisaralik Lake, it flows spiritedly over bedrock through gorgeous mountain country, with two incised, whitewater canyons that culminate in an impenetrable waterfalls (Class IV-V) about a three-days float down from the lake. Below that there are stretches of whitewater (Class II mostly and one Class III-IV "S-turn" rapid, which should definitely be inspected before running). Below Golden Gate, the river slows and braids as it emerges from the mountains and enters the lowlands surrounding the Kuskokwim River. The lower 15-mile portion of the Kisaralik, above the confluence with the Kuskokwim River, is extremely meandered and silty, with little to offer anglers. Most floaters opt to end their trip there with a jetboat pickup from Bethel. With its length and challenges, allow eight days for a float trip down from the headwaters.

Fishing is a mixed bag. The lake and upper river offer classic fly-fishing conditions for grayling, lake trout, and charr, while most of the rainbows are concentrated in the gravelly braids below Golden Gate. Salmon fishing is challenging because of the swift current and scarcity of holding water. Locals and a few area guides (including a native-owned lodge) do quite well fishing the lower river and adjoining Kasigluk drainages by boat from Bethel or nearby villages along the Kuskokwim. From mid-July until early September is usually the optimum period for good water conditions and abundant fishing. Overall, the Kisaralik has much to offer adventuresome souls seeking a more out-of-the-way wilderness fishing experience.

Aniak River ★★★★
Location: Lower Kuskokwim drainage, 300 miles west of Anchorage.

Access: By small plane from Aniak or Bethel to headwaters; boat access to lower river from Kuskokwim villages.

Facilities: No public facilities; private lodge on lower river.

Highlights: One of Southwest Alaska's better mountain rivers for varied fishing and float trips.

Main Species: KS, SS, CS, RT, CHR, GR

The Aniak River system is a fair sized, remote, mountain river drainage of the lower Kuskokwim, with great potential for fishing adventure. It flows clear and fast (with some whitewater in the upper tributaries) for much of its length, as it comes off the western edge of the Kuskokwim Mountains in three main headwaters: the mainstem issuing from Aniak Lake, and the Kipchuk and Salmon rivers. These three all begin as swift, rocky alpine streams having outstanding grayling and charr fishing (including lake trout in Aniak Lake), superb scenery, and quite a bit of wildlife (bears, moose, wolves, and caribou). As they descend into the heavily forested lowlands, they become a maze of channels, sweepers, and logjams that can be a nightmare to boaters in high water, but make great cover for potbellied rainbows and throngs of charr and salmon. Fishing for these species is best from right above the Kipchuk-Aniak-Salmon River confluence down to about nine miles above the mouth at Doestock Creek, where the river becomes silty and meandering. (The lower Aniak does have good pike fishing, and sheefish are even taken from the river's mouth in spring.)

There are a few area lodges and outpost camps that work the lower river, which can be easily accessed by boat from the village of Aniak or other villages along the Kuskokwim. For float trips (seven to ten days), most folks put in on either the upper Salmon or Kipchuk rivers by wheelplane (primitive airstrip access) via Aniak or Bethel. The trip down from Aniak Lake (floatplane access only) is extremely arduous and dangerous, best done by kayak, inflatable canoe, or small, light raft, as heavy logjams, snags, sweepers, and vegetation make for difficult passage and frequent portages. Overall the Aniak has much to offer, but is definitely not the river to float on your own, unless you are an experienced wilderness rafter. A much better and safer way is to seek the services of an experience wilderness guide.

Holitna River
Location: Middle Kuskokwim River, 225 miles SW of Anchorage.

Access: By small plane from Iliamna, Bethel, Aniak, or Lake Clark to headwaters or points along middle and lower river sections; much of river also accessed by jetboat from Kuskokwim villages.

Facilities: None.

Highlights: A remote, lesser-visited wilderness river system with good fishing possibilities.

Main Species: KS, CS, SS, CHR, GR, NP, SF

The Holitna River system is comprised of some of the more significant tributaries of the Kuskokwim that drain the western edge of the Taylor Mountains and Alaska Range before joining near the village of Sleetmute. These include the mainstem Holitna, Hoholitna, Kogrukluk, and Chukowan rivers. Although they receive limited attention from sport anglers (mostly locals), collectively they support one of the most productive fisheries in the entire region, known for good king, silver, chum, grayling, pike, and charr fishing. Sheefish are also taken in early summer on the lower river.

Access to the headwaters is by floatplane or small wheelplane to the upper Holitna (from Kashegelok up) or Whitefish Lake on the Hoholitna (for extended float trips of 10 days or more, access from lakes Iliamna-Clark). Fishing in the clearer, faster upper sections is generally quite good for grayling, charr, and salmon, with abundant sheefish and pike taken seasonally in the sloughs and backwaters along the lower river. There are even rumors of rainbow trout occurring in certain clear tributary streams. (Some are caught now and then from the river's mouth at Sleetmute.) The scenery and wild animal populations in the primitive backcountry of this system are outstanding, which explains the Holitna's popularity with hunters, who have traditionally been the river's only major users.

A few area guides and lodges, along with locals, work the lower river by boat, and some air taxis have been flying small groups in to camp and fish salmon, charr, pike, or sheefish. But, for the most part, this system doesn't get anywhere near the attention it deserves, considering what it has to offer. Like other similar drainages, the Holitna is greatly affected by runoff, with periods of even moderate rain raising river levels quickly and clouding the water, so fishing is very weather dependent. Other than that, and the logistics involved in getting there, there is nothing major to prevent this drainage from becoming the "next big thing" for anglers in search of uncrowded, productive water.

Andreafsky River
Location: Lower Yukon River, 400 miles NW of Anchorage.

Access: By small plane or boat from St. Marys or other Yukon River villages.

Facilities: None.

Highlights: A lesser-visited, western Alaska Wild and Scenic River with good fishing potential.

Main Species: KS, SS, CHR, GR

The Andreafsky Wild and Scenic River of the lower Yukon has two parallel forks that flow southwest out of the Nulato Hills for 100 miles or so before joining on the coastal flatlands five miles north of the village of St. Marys. Although remote and difficult to access, this lovely, crystal-clear mountain stream has great potential for high-quality wilderness fishing excursions, with good salmon runs (kings, silvers and chums), abundant charr and grayling, even some pike, along with outstanding scenery and abundant wildlife.

Getting up into the headwaters is difficult. You can usually find locals in St. Marys to run you upriver by boat. (Limited guide service and even tent camps have also been available in the past. Contact the folks at Roz's B & B, Box 379, St. Marys, AK 99658, (907) 438-2217, for current availability.) It's also possible at times to land on headwater gravel bars (mostly on the upper North Fork) with small wheelplanes equipped with tundra tires, depending on water levels. Check with local air taxis for latest conditions.

The Andreafsky can be rafted in a week or less, depending on put-in location. Other than fast water, sweepers, and grizzly bears, there are no real major hazards. Due to the cost and difficult logistics in getting here, not too many folks get to visit this lovely, pristine drainage, but everyone who has considers the experience well worth the extra effort and expense.

Anvik River

Location: Lower Yukon River, 375 miles NW of Anchorage.

Access: By boat from Anvik mostly; wheel and floatplane access also possible to points along the river.

Facilities: No public facilities; private lodge located on river.

Highlights: One of the Yukon River's major fish producers, with underutilized sportfishing potential.

Main Species: CS, KS, SS, SF, NP, CHR

Not too many folks know of the Anvik River of western Alaska; fewer have fished it. But it is one of the most important fish producing tributaries of the entire Yukon, and can offer a high-quality angling adventure for a variety of species, with virtually no fishing pressure.

The river heads in the Nulato Hills and flows south 120 miles or so before joining the Yukon at Anvik village, 318 miles up from the mouth. Like many Yukon and Kuskokwim drainages, it has a slow, wide, meandering lower section (with good pike and sometimes even sheefish available), with the best conditions for salmon, charr, and grayling angling in the clearer, swifter upper sections above the Yellow River confluence, 60 miles from the mouth.

Most people fish the Anvik by boat, but it can be floated down from the headwaters, although access is difficult and generally limited to gravel bar landings with a small wheelplane. Anvik River Lodge, 60 miles up from the mouth, is the area's only visitor establishment, offering local fishing plus fly-outs to neighboring drainages like the Andreafsky and Innoko rivers for salmon, sheefish, and pike.

Innoko River ★★★★

Location: Lower Yukon River, 330 miles NW of Anchorage.

Access: By floatplane or boat from area hubs to points along lower/middle river.

Facilities: No public facilities; private lodges and outpost camps along river.

Highlights: An enormous, remote Yukon tributary with world-class trophy northern pike potential.

Main Species: NP, SF

Like a sleeping giant, the Innoko River sprawls lazily across the Yukon flatlands west of McGrath, its vast potential known to only a few anglers. Not the kind of river to excite trout and salmon fishermen, much of it is big, slow water better suited for Alaska's "other" sport species—the wolfish northern pike and leaping sheefish. But fishing for these unsung fighters in the Innoko's abundant backwater is so good that it has been proclaimed one of the best pike and sheefish locations in all of North America by the few sportsmen lucky enough to have tested its waters.

This is an immense river system. The mainstem flows over 500 miles before emptying into the Yukon at Red Wind Slough near the village of Holy Cross. (The Innoko's major tributary, the Iditarod, is over 350 miles long.) For most of this length, it is a slow, wide, lowland river, with meandering and interconnected sloughs and lakes, especially in the lower section (downstream of the abandoned village of Holikachuk, about 90 miles). The water quality is turbid from the mud and swamp water. It is only in the extreme upper reaches (above the North Fork) that the Innoko's character changes noticeably toward that of a mountain stream, with swifter flows, gravel bottom, and clear water. This is really the only part of the river suited for salmon (coho, chum, and some king), grayling and (occasionally) charr fishing, with several adjoining swift and clear mountain creeks (such as Beaver and Folger) offering some of the better angling conditions for these species.

Access is usually by floatplane to points all along the river, or by wheelplane to airstrips at Holy Cross, Shageluk, Cripple, or Ophir. The upper river can be floated by raft, with a put-in at Ophir (or further upriver, from a trail accessed from Takotna) and take-out at Cripple, or at points below by floatplane. Locals use boats extensively to access the lower river.

The lower Innoko is an important feeding area for the migratory Yukon River sheefish population. In spring, it can offer some of Alaska's finest fishing for the species. Pike are especially plentiful, with the lower river's perfect habitat and abundant food sources (whitefish and cisco) producing some really big fish. Opportunities to tempt monster pike with large surface lures and flies are particularly noteworthy. Area lodges and guides working the river have routinely taken fish in excess of 30 pounds, including the current state record of 38 1/2 pounds. It's only a matter of time before someone pulls a new record fish from these prolific waters.

Recommended Lodges/Guides/Outfitters/Air taxis

Anvik River Lodge: Box 353255, Palm Coast, FL 32135 (888) 362-6845, *www.anviklodge.com* Guided fishing, Anvik River.

Kanektok River Safaris: P.O. Box 9, Quinhagak, AK 99655, (907) 556-8211. Outpost camp and guided fishing, lower Kanektok River.

TK Adventures: 555 S. Main, Colville, WA 99114; (509) 684-5937. Multi-species guided sportfishing, Holitna River.

Ultimate Rivers: Box 670534, Chugiak, AK 99567 (907) 688-6535, *www.ultimaterivers.com* Guided float trips, Aniak River.

Camp Kisaralik: Box 147, Akiak, AK 99552, (907) 765-7228. Lodge-based guided fishing, Kisaralik River.

Grant Aviation: Box 1978, Bethel, AK 99559, (800) 764-7607, *www.flygrant.com* Wheelplane taxi service, lower Yukon-Kuskokwim.

Haagland Air: P.O. Box 211, Aniak, AK 99577, (907) 675-4272; or P.O. Box 195, St. Marys, AK 99658, (907) 438-2246. Wheelplane air taxi service, lower Yukon-Kuskokwim.

Aniak Air Guides: (907) 299-3503, *www.aniakairguides.com* Air taxi service, lower Yukon-Kuskokwim.

Freshwater Adventures, Inc.: P.O. Box 62, Dillingham, AK 99576, (907) 842-5060, *www.fresh-h2o.com* Air taxi & equipment rentals, lower Kuskokwim.

Pike Safaris: Box 102, Holy Cross, AK 99602, (907) 476-7121. Trophy pike fishing, Innoko River.

USGS Maps Reference

Goodnews River: Goodnews Bay A-6, A-7, B-4, B-5, B-6, B-7, C-4, C-5.

Arolik River: Goodnews Bay B-6, C-7, C-8.

Kanektok River: Goodnews Bay C-4, C-5, C-6, D-3, D-4, D-5, D-6, D-7, D-8.

Aniak River: Bethel B-1, C-1, C-2, D-1, D-2; Russian Mission A-1, A-2, B-1, C-2.

Kisaralik River: Bethel B-1, 2, 3, 4; C-4, 5, 6, 7, 8.

Kwethluk River: Bethel A-3, 4 ; B-4, 5, 6; C-6; D-7.

Holitna River: Taylor Mountains B-7, C-5, C-6, C-7, C-8, D-1, D-2, D-5, D-6, D-7; Sleetmute A-2, A-4, A-5, B-2, B-3, B-4, C-3, C-4; Lake Clark D-6, D-7, D-8.

Andreafsky River: Kwiguk A-2, A-3, B-1, B-2, C-1, C-2, D-1; St. Michael A-1; Unalakleet A-6; Holy Cross C-6, D-6.

Anvik River: Holy Cross C-3, C-4, D-4; Unalakleet A-4.

Innoko River: Ophir A-4, A-5, A-6, B-5, C-1, C-2, C-3, C-4, C-5, A-1, A-2, B-2; Unalakleet A-1; Holy Cross A-2, B-2, C-2, D-1, D-2; Iditarod D-3.

General Information

Togiak National Wildlife Refuge: P.O. Box 270, Dillingham, AK 99576, (907) 842-1063 *http://togiak.fws.gov*

Yukon Delta National Wildlife Refuge: P.O. Box 346, Bethel, AK 99559, (907) 543-3151 *http://yukondelta.fws.gov*

Innoko National Wildlife Refuge: P.O. Box 69, McGrath, AK 99627, 907-524-3251 *http://innoko.fws.gov*

Regulations/Information

Most lower Yukon-Kuskokwim waters are open year-round to fishing all species (see Regs. for exceptions). Certain waters are restricted to single hook artificial or catch-and-release fishing or closed seasonally. Always check the current Regulations Summary for Region III-Arctic-Yukon-Kuskokwim, or call ADF&G Sportfish offices, Bethel (907) 543-2433, or Fairbanks 907-459-7207 for complete information when planning a fishing trip to the area.

Online info: *www.sf.adfg.state.ak.us/statewide/ regulations/ aykregs.cfm*

Lower Yukon/Kuskokwim Species

Location	King Salmon	Red Salmon	Pink Salmon	Chum Salmon	Silver Salmon	Steelhead	Rainbow	Cutthroat	Charr	Grayling	Lake Trout	Northern Pike	Sheefish	Halibut	Ling Cod	Rock Fish	Salmon Shark	Fshg. Pressure
Goodnews River	✪	☺	☺	✪	✪		✪		✪	✪	☺							M
Arolik River	✪	✓	☺	☺	✪		✪		✪	✪	☺							✓
Kanektok River	✪	☺	☺	✪	✪		✪		✪	✪	☺							M
Aniak River	✪	✓	✓	☺	✪		✪		✪	✪	☺	✓	✓					M
Kisaralik River	✓	✓	✓	☺	✓		☺		☺	☺	☺	R	R					✓
Kwethluk River	✓	✓	✓	☺	✓		☺		☺	☺			R					✓
Holitna River	☺	R	✓	☺	☺		R		☺	☺	R	✓	☺					✓
Andreafsky River	☺		✓	☺	☺				☺	☺		✓	☺					✓
Anvik River	✓		☺	✪	☺				☺	☺		☺	✪					✓
Innoko River	✓		R	✓	✓				✓	☺		☺	✪					✓

Species not present
- **R** Rare
- **✓** Fishable numbers (or light pressure)
- **☺** Good fishing
- **✪** Excellent fishing
- **LL** Landlocked species
- **C** Present, but fishing closed
- **M** Moderate pressure
- **☹** Heavy pressure

Northwest Alaska

Far beyond the crowds of Alaska's roadside fisheries, out past the celebrated locales of Bristol and Kuskokwim bays, lie the fringes of one of the last true frontiers of fishing adventure—Northwest Alaska. Land of the Inupiat Eskimo, giant caribou herds, and Nanook the polar bear, this vast region remains, for the most part, a trackless wilderness with a treasure of untouched fishing opportunity. While other Alaska fisheries bear the brunt of catch-and-release or combat fishing, Northwest's pike, charr, sheefish, and grayling grow to giant sizes and succumb to old age or native stew pots with nary an encounter with a sport angler's lure.

Lifelong Alaskan and sportsman Robert Farmer knows well of the Northwest mystique. He worked and explored the more remote parts of Alaska as a young man, and his recollection of a pike encounter, while doing helicopter surveys in the lower Noatak valley years ago, amply illustrates the awesome fishing potential of the region. He and his survey crew were marking a monument on the edge of a slough one hot August afternoon, when he dropped a piece of bright red survey flagging into the dark tannic waters. In an instant it vanished in a swirl of water and shifting, dark shadows. Curious, he set another piece of tape adrift and was astounded when the water erupted in a welter of spray and flailing jaws, not three feet from shore. More chunks of tape brought similar onslaughts, as the waters churned with the frantic movements of these maniacally hungry beasts.

Impressed by the size, number and outright boldness of the aggressors, Farmer and his crewmates returned the next morning to "finish their work," armed with stout rods, garish lures, and strong wire leaders. In no time they were hooking northern pike on nearly every cast, huge fish with gaping jaws and bellies extended to the bursting point with ducks, lemmings, and large whitefish they had been feeding on. Of the 30 or so caught that morning, according to Farmer, four exceeded the 40-pound mark. But most interesting, perhaps, was the reaction of the locals when they returned to the Eskimo village of Noatak to show off some of their catch. Nonplussed, the elders produced an old "Avgas" box—the 10 by 20 by 18-inch wooden fuel crates once used everywhere in Alaska—that barely contained the gnarlish remains of a cured pike head so huge and grotesque it could have passed for some species of Arctic crocodile!

Flyfishing at Wild Lake,
western Brooks Range

Caribou on the Kobuk River

COUNTRY, CLIMATE & FISHING CONDITIONS

Alaska's Northwest corner is the vast region lying above the lower Yukon, which includes the lands along Norton and Kotzebue sounds, the Seward Peninsula, and the southern slope of the Brooks Range, west of the middle fork of the Koyukok River. (For our purposes, all north-flowing Arctic Ocean drainages are grouped in the Arctic region.)

It encompasses a diverse and vast terrain, from the marshy Yukon flatlands and slight uplands along the coast to the expansive valleys and massive peaks of the Brooks Range, with the general character of the land marking the transition from sparse, broken boreal forests to the extreme tundra regimes of the Arctic. (The maritime influence from the nearby Chukchi and northern Bering seas moderates the climate along the coast much of the year.)

Most Northwest rivers are swift, clear runoff streams that drain coastal mountains or the extensive fan of highlands associated with the western Brooks Range. The more significant drainages, like the Noatak, Kobuk, and Koyukuk comprise some of Alaska's largest clearwater systems, with considerable potential for high quality wilderness fishing adventure.

Anglers will find near perfect stream conditions in the sparkling headwaters of these and other systems throughout the region. Northwest's lakes vary from numerous, shallow thaw ponds and sloughs (some holding fish populations) along the major river lowlands, to the deeper, glacially carved basins of the Brooks Range and upper Seward Peninsula, which are noted for their spectacular, scenic angling possibilities.

Northwest fishing is a mixed bag. Pacific salmon extend into the limits of their natural range, with king and coho thinning out as you move up the coast (fishable runs are found only as far as Norton Sound), and sockeye occurring only sporadically north of the Yukon, leaving chum and pink salmon as the predominant species for most drainages of the region. Too far north to support rainbow trout, Northwest Alaska's waters nonetheless support surprising numbers of charr, grayling, lake trout, northern pike, and sheefish as resident species.

ACCESS, SERVICES & COSTS

Beyond a few short roads linking Nome to surrounding towns on the Seward Peninsula, travel in Alaska's Northwest region is by airplanes and boats (supplemented by snowmachines and dog sleds in winter). Daily scheduled air carriers link the main hubs—Nome, Kotzebue and Unalakleet—to Anchorage, with local air taxis providing connections to the more remote areas.

Northwest anglers will find much more limited (and higher priced) services and facilities than in more accessible parts of the state. There are a few full-service lodges, guides or outfitters, mostly operating from the major hubs and villages scattered along the coast and major rivers. The available guided/unguided fishing options include daily fly-out or boat excursions, float trips, stays at remote outpost tents and cabins, and gear rentals. Air taxis are expensive and the distances involved in reaching some of the better locales considerable; anglers planning remote fly-in adventures should expect to pay more than they would anywhere else in the state, except the Arctic. (Riverboat transportation, where available, provides a more affordable alternative to small plane travel.)

Meticulous planning, well in advance, is of the essence for a safe, enjoyable and productive Northwest Alaska fishing vacation. Anyone contemplating a do-it-yourself adventure should have realistic goals, solid wilderness skills, expedition-quality gear, and the company of others equally qualified. The services of an experienced guide or lodge are highly recommended for anyone not up to that challenge.

COSTS

RT Airfare: Anchorage to Nome/Kotzebue: $387-560.
Lodging: $125-150/day.
Outpost Tent & Cabin Rentals: $150/day/person.
Guided Fishing: $150-155/day/person.
Family-Style Lodge, Guided Fishing: $300-400/day/person.
Deluxe Lodge, Guided Fishing: $400-600/day/person.
Unguided Float Trip: $150-280/day/person (may include air taxi).
Guided Float Trip: $300-400/day/person.
Air Taxi: Supercub: $175-225/hr; Cessna 180-185: $250-300/hr.; Cessna 206-207: $300-350/hr; Beaver: $500-600/hr.; Navaho: $650/hr; R-44 helicopter: $550/hr.

Northwest Fishing Highlights

Trophy sheefish on the Kobuk River

Hefty Northwest charr

Of the many outstanding attractions awaiting sportfishermen here, perhaps the best known are the trophy grayling fishing opportunities on the Seward Peninsula and lunker charr of Kotzebue Sound. These two species run larger on average in these waters than elsewhere in the state. Trophy sheefish are another, unique possibility, with waters of the Kobuk-Selawik area routinely yielding fish that far outclass specimens from other Alaska locations. Similarly, the remote and pristine lakes of the upper Noatak, Kobuk, and Koyukuk valleys can offer quality wild lake trout fishing that is hard to match anywhere else.

Anglers wanting to explore some of Alaska's more out-of-the-way, but productive, stream fisheries for salmon can target the rivers of eastern Norton Sound (Unalakleet to Kwiniuk rivers), difficult to access, but full of promise for virtually unexploited king and coho runs (and charr and grayling populations).

WHAT TO EXPECT

Sub-arctic maritime to transitional continental climate: summer days are usually cool, often overcast or foggy, with temperatures averaging in the low 50s (°F), though they can be much warmer—into the 70°s and 80°s—and drier farther inland. Winters are long and cold, frequently with terrifying wind-chills, but generally without the extreme low temperatures experienced in the Interior region. Annual precipitation is surprisingly sparse—15 inches or less for much of the region, with most of it falling during the warm months. Ice break-up usually occurs in late May or early June (later in mountain locations), with freeze-up sometime in October. Be prepared for abundant biting insects anytime during the open water season.

NORTHWEST RUN TIMING

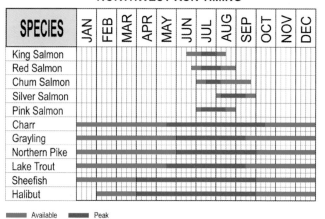

SPECIES	JAN	FEB	MAR	APR	MAY	JUN	JUL	AUG	SEP	OCT	NOV	DEC
King Salmon							▬	▬				
Red Salmon							▬	▬				
Chum Salmon							▬	▬				
Silver Salmon								▬	▬			
Pink Salmon							▬	▬				
Charr	▬	▬	▬	▬	▬	▬	▬	▬	▬	▬	▬	▬
Grayling	▬	▬	▬	▬	▬	▬	▬	▬	▬	▬	▬	▬
Northern Pike	▬	▬	▬	▬	▬	▬	▬	▬	▬	▬	▬	▬
Lake Trout	▬	▬	▬	▬	▬	▬	▬	▬	▬	▬	▬	▬
Sheefish	▬	▬	▬	▬	▬	▬	▬	▬	▬	▬	▬	▬
Halibut	▬	▬	▬	▬	▬	▬	▬	▬	▬	▬	▬	▬

▬ Available   ▬ Peak

Note: Time periods shown in blue are for bright fish in the case of salmon entering rivers, or for general availability in saltwater or resident species (freshwater). Peak sportfishing periods are shown in red. Run timing can vary among different areas within the region. Always check local contacts for run timing specifics for locations you intend to fish.

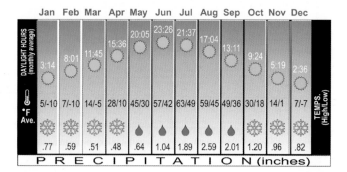

	Jan	Feb	Mar	Apr	May	Jun	Jul	Aug	Sep	Oct	Nov	Dec
DAYLIGHT HOURS (monthly average)	3:14	8:01	11:45	15:36	20:05	23:26	21:37	17:04	13:11	9:24	5:19	2:36
°F Ave.	5/-10	7/-10	14/-5	28/10	45/30	57/42	63/49	59/45	49/36	30/18	14/1	7/-7
PRECIPITATION (inches)	.77	.59	.51	.48	.64	1.04	1.89	2.59	2.01	1.20	.96	.82

Big grayling on Northwest rivers

The Northwest region has some of the largest clear-flowing rivers in Alaska, many with significant fishing potential, like the vast Noatak (shown here).

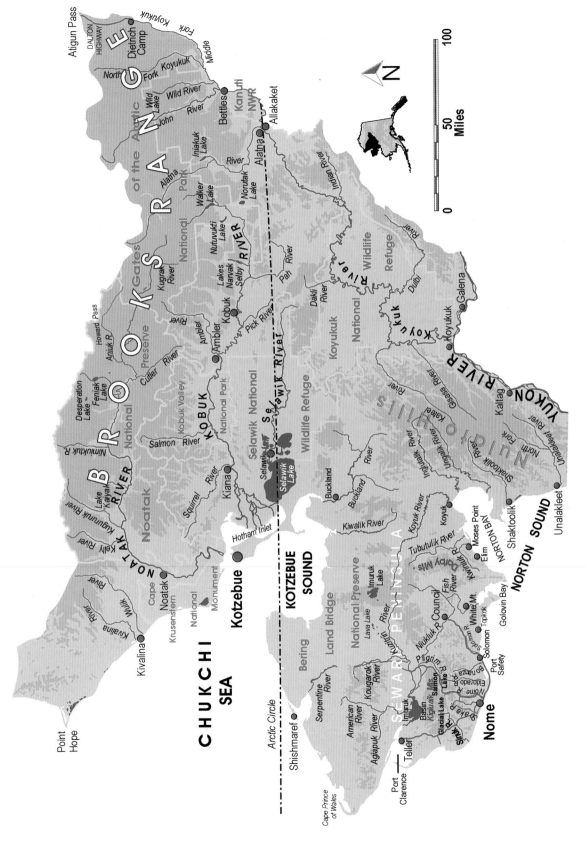

CHUKCHI
SEA

Point
Hope

Kivalina

Kivalina River
Wulik River

Cape
Krusenstern
National
Monument

Noatak

NOATAK

Kelly River

Kugururok River

Nimiukluk R.

Kayak Lake

Lake

RIVER

Squirrel River

Noatak River

Kiana

Salmon River

Kobuk Valley
National Park

Desperation
Lake

Fenjak
Lake

Aniuk R.

Cutler River

National

Ambler River

Ambler

Kobuk

Ambler River

KOBUK

RIVER

River

Howard Pass

Preserve

Gates of the Arctic

BROOKS RANGE

Atigun Pass

DALTON HIGHWAY

Dietrich
Camp

Koyukuk
Fork

North Fork

Koyukuk

Middle

Wild
Lake

Wild River

John River

Alatna River

Iniakuk
Lake

Walker
Lake

Nutuvukti
Lake

Lakes
Narvak
Selby

Bettles

Kanuti
NWR

Allakaket

Alatna

National Park

Pick River

Kugrak
River

Pah River

Dakli River

Indian River

RIVER

Selawik

SELAWIK RIVER

Selawik National
Wildlife Refuge

Selawik
Lake

Hotham Inlet

Kotzebue

KOTZEBUE
SOUND

Buckland

Buckland
River

River

Kiwalik River

Koyukuk
National
Wildlife
Refuge

River

Dulbi River

Galena

Koyukuk

Kaltag

Nulato Hills

Gisasa River

Kateel River

North Fork

Shaktoolik River

Unalakleet River

YUKON RIVER

KOYUKUK

Unalakleet

Shaktoolik

NORTON SOUND

NORTON BAY

Moses Point
Elim

Koyuk

Koyuk River

Tubutulik River

Ungalik River

Inglutalik River

Kwiniuk R.

Kwik R.

Darby Mts.

Fish River

Niukluk R.

Council
White Mt.

Golovin Bay

Solomon

Bonanza R.
Eldorado R.

Tubuk R.

Imuruk
Lake

Imuruk
River

Kuzitrin
River

Bering Land Bridge
National Preserve

Lava Lake

SEWARD PENINSULA

Serpentine River

Kougarok River

American River

Agiapuk River

Shishmaref

Arctic Circle

Cape Prince
of Wales

Port
Clarence

Teller

Pilgrim R.

Port Safety

Salmon Lake

Grand Central R.

Sinuk R.

Snake R.

Glacial Lake

Kigluaik Mts.

Nome R.

Salmon

Basin

Nome

CHUKCHI
SEA

N

0   50   100
Miles

EASTERN NORTON SOUND

The arc of eastern Norton Sound, from Stebbins to Cape Darby, includes several rivers of significant sportfishing potential and the last major runs of silver and king salmon along the coast. These are all runoff streams draining the highlands west of the lower Yukon, with water conditions that vary considerably through the season. Access is the limiting factor, as most of them can be reached safely only by boat or (sometimes) by small plane. Facilities and services are scarce to nonexistent.

Unalakleet River ★★★★
Location: Eastern Norton Sound, 375 miles NW of Anchorage.
Access: By boat from village of Unalakleet to various river sites.
Facilities: Private lodge on lower river, several outfitter tent camps.
Highlights: One of western Alaska's most promising rivers for salmon fishing.
Main Species: KS, SS, CHR, GR

The Unalakleet is the most significant river in Norton Sound, supporting substantial commercial and subsistence fisheries with its consistent runs of salmon (all species except sockeye). It is recognized as potentially one of the finest streams in all of western Alaska for sportfishing, but has enjoyed relatively light angling pressure due to its remoteness.

A Wild and Scenic River, the Unalakleet rises in the Nulato Hills and flows southwest approximately 105 miles through uplands and rolling tundra before emptying into Norton Sound below the village of Unalakleet. Access to the upper river is almost impossible by any means other than boat from the village. Most anglers enlist the services of local guides or outfitters (there are two private lodges on the lower river and several outfitter tent camps in the area) to fish the river's most productive water (the lower 15 miles of the main stem and five miles of the tributary North River). Locals will also take you upriver by boat for drop-offs. (A raft voyage down from the confluence of Old Woman River or Ten Mile Creek to the village makes a nice float and fish trip, with no major hazards except sweepers.)

This clear-flowing stream has always been noted for its outstanding king and silver salmon fishing, but it also has prodigious runs of chum and pink salmon, as well as abundant charr and arctic grayling. There are plenty of deep pools and shallower, not-too-fast runs, so it's easy water to fish. Wildlife—moose, bear, occasional caribou, and numerous waterfowl—are commonly seen. The Unalakleet is a prime choice for anyone wanting to expand their repertoire of great western Alaska fishing rivers.

Shaktoolik River ★★★
Location: Eastern Norton Sound, 410 miles NW of Anchorage.
Access: By boat from village of Shaktoolik; limited small wheelplane access also possible along gravel bars upriver.
Facilities: No developed public facilities.
Highlights: A remote Norton Sound drainage with high sportfishing potential.
Main Species: KS, SS, CHR, GR

The Shaktoolik River, along with the Unalakleet, is one of Norton Sound's most significant fish producers. With solid runs of salmon (all species except sockeye), plentiful charr and grayling, and excellent stream conditions, the Shaktoolik has considerable promise that, up to now, has been underutilized because of its remoteness and difficult access.

It is a medium-sized (100 miles long), clear, swift runoff stream that flows to the coast from uplands surrounding Norton Sound, about 125 miles east of Nome. Gravel-bottomed, with some rapids (Class I & II), and abundant pools, long runs, and shallow riffles, the river forks about 60 miles up from the mouth, at Kingmetolik Creek. Most of the fishing for salmon, grayling, and charr occurs in the stretch of river from this confluence down to the coastal flats 40 miles below.

Access is the trick. For starters, it's perhaps best to hop a flight from Unalakleet or Nome to Shaktoolik, run upriver by boat with someone from the village, then camp and fish (with a guide, if you want). It's also possible at times to land a small wheelplane on gravel bars in the foothills halfway up the river (check with the air taxi folks in Unalakleet), then float down to the village in rafts (about three to four days). The fishing is really good. In fact, there are some who rate the Shaktoolik among western Alaska's finest "undiscovered" streams for flyfishing, particularly for king and silver salmon, sea-run charr, and big grayling (fish up to 20 inches are common). It's definitely a river to add to the "dream list" of promising, unexplored western Alaska fishing possibilities. The first part of July or the second half of August are the best times for a fishing safari to these far-flung waters.

Kwiniuk/Tubutulik Rivers
Location: Norton Bay, Seward Peninsula, 440 mi. NW of Anchorage.
Access: By boat from Moses Point to lower rivers; upper Kwiniuk can be reached by road from Elim.
Facilities: None; limited services in Moses Point and Elim.
Highlights: Promising out-of-the-way Norton Sound drainages.
Main Species: KS, SS, CHR, GR

Farther up the coast lie the adjacent Kwiniuk and Tubutulik rivers of Norton Bay, both with potential for high quality fishing adventure, in one of the prettiest areas of the western Alaska coast. These streams run swift and clear off the Darby Mountains just east of Elim and Moses Point, some 90 miles or so from Nome.

Though seldom fished by anyone but locals, the Kwiniuk and Tubutulik are very productive, with some of the last really significant runs of silver and king salmon this far north and west, and abundant charr and grayling populations as well. Stream conditions are perfect for flyfishing.

Access to the lower reaches of these two drainages is by boat from Moses Point (wheelplanes can get you to Moses Point or Elim from Nome or Unalakleet). The upper Kwiniuk can be reached via a primitive road leading out from the village of Elim to hot springs on the river, about 25 miles up from the mouth. From here, it is possible to float down by raft/canoe/kayak, to a take-out at the mouth near Moses Point.

The upper Tubutulik has hot springs, lava rock formations, and boulder-strewn rapids, along with great fishing, but access by anything other than helicopter out of Nome is unlikely. (There is a primitive airstrip on Clear Creek, a major tributary that joins the river in its midsection, but no places to land a plane above.) Float trips are a tantalizing possibility, as the river can be safely navigated from

Admiral Creek down to the mouth (check water levels before attempting a headwater float). With abundant bird and animal life and some interesting history (there are abandoned Gold Rush mining camps along the upper Tubutulik and a WWII plane wreckage site on upper Kwiniuk), these rivers have much to offer adventure anglers with a yen for exploration.

SEWARD PENINSULA

The Seward Peninsula, the mainland's westernmost extension, nearly touches Siberia and separates the icy Bering Sea from the even colder Chukchi. A remote expanse of slight mountains, hills, tundra, sparse forests, and windswept coast, it boasts some fabulous history and unique fisheries. Remnants of its Gold Rush glory days are found everywhere. Even the names of some of its better rivers—spread from Teller to Koyuk—speak of a colorful past: the Bonanza, Eldorado, Pilgrim, Snake, Fish, Solomon, and Nome. These rivers and their numerous tributaries—almost all clear, rambling streams with great flyfishing potential—still hold a treasure of fine angling for salmon, pike, charr, and some of Alaska's biggest Arctic grayling. (A good portion of the state's record grayling have come from Seward Peninsula streams. Fish up to three pounds are not uncommon). What's more, road access via three gravel highways (350 miles total; call (907) 443-3444 for latest road conditions) links many of these great waters with Nome, which is serviced by three jet flights daily from Anchorage in summer, making it easy for visiting anglers to sample by car some of the area's best fishing.

Aside from the roads and a few primitive public facilities, most of this area is virtually undeveloped, with many of the more remote waters seeing little or no visitation. (Boats and hiking are the main ways of getting off the beaten path; none of the local air taxis have planes equipped for float or remote airstrip landings.) Newly available helicopter service in Nome promises to open up many new areas for fishing exploration.

Fish-Niukluk Rivers ★★★★
Location: Seward Peninsula, 60 miles east of Nome.
Access: By car (via Council Hwy) or small plane from Nome; boat access from villages along river.
Facilities: Private lodges/outpost camps located in area.
Highlights: The Seward Peninsula's premier fishing location.
Main Species: SS, CHR, GR, NP

The Fish-Niukluk River system has historically been one of the most popular and productive fisheries in Northwest Alaska. It is widely used by villagers from two communities along the river, as well as by residents of Nome, who travel the 73-mile Council Highway to access its recreational and subsistence fishing. A local lodge and several outfitters service the growing number of visiting anglers.

Flowing from the Darby and Bendeleben Mountains, the Fish and Niukluk rivers (and tributaries) flow south toward Golovin Lagoon in Norton Sound. The rivers' character changes from clear, gravelly upper stretches (both Fish and Niukluk)—which harbor grayling, salmon and charr—to slow, braided, dark water in the lower sections (from Steamboat Slough down to the mouth—about 20 miles), where pike lurk.

The Fish-Niukluk system is noted for its fast-growing, big grayling (up to three pounds or more) and good silver salmon and charr fishing (also pink and chum salmon). It is also one of the few Seward Peninsula streams with a consistent spawning population of king salmon, and the lower river also has fairly abundant pike.

Popular fishing areas include: the upper Fish River and its tributaries—Boston Creek (salmon, including KS, and CHR); the Rathlatulik River (big GR) and the Etchepuk River (salmon, including KS and GR); Steamboat Slough (NP); the Fox River (salmon and GR; access from the adjacent Council Road); Ophir Creek (GR); and the mouth of the Niukluk (all species in the river). Roads from Council provide access to many tributary creeks, and there are gravel bars and a few scattered airstrips for small plane landings, allowing for many different ways of exploring this drainage, including float trips.

Solomon River
Location: Seward Peninsula, 30 miles east of Nome.
Access: From Nome, east on Council Highway to Miles 40-50; boat access possible from Safety Sound.
Facilities: No developed public facilities.
Highlights: Popular roadside stream for charr and salmon.
Main Species: SS, CHR, PS

The Solomon River empties into the extreme east end of Safety Sound, 32 miles from Nome, near the old mining town of Solomon. It is accessed from the Council Highway, which parallels the river for about ten miles (between Mile 40 and 50), and provides many good spots along the upper river where you can pull off the road and fish. Along with the mouth and adjacent Safety Sound, it's worth checking out for charr, salmon (pinks and silvers), and grayling, especially if you're on the way out to the more prestigious Fish-Niukluk River.

Safety Sound
Location: Seward Peninsula, 30 miles east of Nome.
Access: From Nome, east on Council Highway to Mile 22, where the road crosses the lagoon outlet, then continues eleven miles along spit. Boat access also possible.
Facilities: No developed public facilities.
Highlights: Potentially good, road-accessible beach fishing.
Main Species: SS, CHR

Safety Sound east of Nome, crossed completely by the highway beginning at about Mile 17, is another location definitely worth stopping for, on the way out to Council and the Fish-Niukluk River. Salmon (mostly pinks) are fished with some success at the lagoon outlet and along the inshore side of the spit. Look for feeding charr in early summer around the bridge, as they ambush outmigrating salmon smolt. The action is usually much better at the mouths of the several notable fishing streams emptying into the other side (the Bonanza, Eldorado, and Flambeau rivers). Access to these rivers is limited to helicopter or boat, and negotiating the tides and mudflats can be tricky. June and August are the best times to fish there.

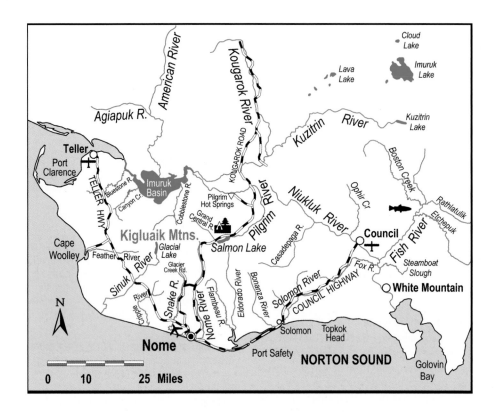

Nome River

Location: Seward Peninsula, 515 miles NW of Anchorage.

Access: By road, four miles east on Main Street to the river mouth; Kougarok Road provides upriver access.

Facilities: No developed public facilities.

Highlights: The Seward Peninsula's most popular, easily accessed river.

Main Species: SS, PS, CHR

The Nome River's close proximity to the Seward Peninsula's main hub has always made it an extremely popular and heavily fished drainage, especially since all 44 miles of its length can be easily accessed by road. Fished for years by locals for its salmon (pink, chum and silver), grayling, and charr, it is worth checking out if you are planning a trip to Nome, even though the fishing in recent years has been severely curtailed due to depressed populations.

With headwaters in the Kigluaik Mountains, the river flows swiftly south through tundra and empties into Norton Sound about three-and-a-half miles east of Nome. It has numerous tributaries, all of them swift and clear runoff streams like the Nome itself. The most popular areas to fish are the mouth, and the section between Mile 8 and the bridge at Mile 13 of the Kougarok Road. The river is usually fished for charr in late May and June down at the mouth, and in August and September from Mile 13 bridge down.

Pink and chum have been the Nome's main salmon highlights (usually from July through September) but, in recent years, weak runs have forced closures on chum salmon fishing. A strong even-year pink run is the river's main attraction for salmon anglers these days,

with some silvers also taken from late August through September. Grayling, not as abundant in the Nome as in other prime Seward Peninsula streams, have been overharvested and the river has been closed to grayling fishing since 1992.

Since the Nome lies just a stone's throw from town, you can inquire with the Nome office of the Alaska Department of Fish and Game, at (907) 443-5796, for the latest sportfish updates. If conditions warrant, hit the river on the way to some of the Seward Peninsula's more glamorous fishing locales.

Snake River

Location: Seward Peninsula, eight miles west of Nome.

Access: By car, via Teller Road to lower river bridge or via Glacier Creek Road to upper river; boat travel possible from the bridge or mouth.

Facilities: No developed public facilities.

Highlights: One of the Seward Peninsula's more popular and productive streams.

Main Species: SS, CHR, GR

The Snake is a popular road fishery located only eight miles west of Nome on the Teller Road. Best known for its good grayling fishing, the river also provides considerable opportunities for salmon (silvers and pink mostly) and charr in season.

Most people fish the Snake by foot, working the river from trails that lead from the Teller Road bridge or Glacier Creek Road. Boat access is also possible along the lower river via the launch at the Nome Port. Fish it in July and August for salmon and grayling, or in June or late August through September for charr.

Sinuk River ★★★
Location: Seward Peninsula, 30 miles west of Nome.
Access: By car from Nome, 26 miles west on Teller Highway; jet boat access also possible.
Facilities: No developed public facilities.
Highlights: One of the Seward Peninsula's finest fishing streams for trophy grayling.
Main Species: GR, SS, CHR

One of the Seward Peninsula's best road-accessible fishing streams, and the largest drainage along the Teller Highway, the Sinuk River offers outstanding trophy grayling potential. More than half of all record Seward Peninsula graying have come from the Sinuk. It also has excellent fishing for charr and good angling for pink and silver salmon, as well as one of the Seward Peninsula's only significant spawning populations of red salmon, although few anglers have figured how to get them to bite.

From headwaters in the Kigluaik Mountains and Glacial Lake, northwest of Nome, this scenic river flows southwest some 46 miles before emptying into Norton Sound. For much of its length, the Sinuk is wide, rocky, and shallow, with small pools and riffles—perfect for flyfishing.

It is reached by a short drive west from town to a bridge crossing at Mile 26.7. From there, further access is had by foot trails or jet boat.

IMURUK BASIN DRAINAGES

North of Nome lie the drainages of the Imuruk Salt Basin, which include some of the Seward Peninsula's most important and promising sportfishing rivers. With scenic mountains, extensive, interconnected wetlands, and a wealth of clear-flowing, cobbly headwaters, this area offers high quality fishing for abundant, large grayling and pike, charr, and salmon.

The drainages of the Imuruk are accessed from either the Teller Highway or Kougoruk Road or by boat from the village of Teller. Small plane or helicopter fly-outs from Nome open up even more possibilities for angling adventure. Some of the more promising Imuruk locations to check out include: Canyon Creek and the Bluestone, Cobblestone, Kuzitrin-Kougarok, Agiapuk-American, and Pilgrim rivers.

Pilgrim River
Location: Seward Peninsula, 33 miles NE of Nome.
Access: By car from Nome via Kougarok Road; lower river also reached by boat from Teller via Imuruk.
Facilities: There is a free BLM campground at the Salmon Lake outlet; camping available on a first come, first served basis.
Highlights: A very famous Seward Peninsula drainage for its trophy grayling and pike fishing.
Main Species: SS, CHR, GR, NP

The Pilgrim River is perhaps the best known of the Seward Penin-

sula's famous trophy grayling fisheries, with a reputation for large sailfins (to three pounds) that few rivers its size can match, along with good salmon and pike fishing. (The Pilgrim is one of Nome's most popular road-accessible fisheries, especially during salmon season.) Originating at the outlet of Salmon Lake north of Nome, it flows northeast then northwest for some 71 miles before joining the Kuzitrin River at New Igloo above Imuruk Basin.

Nineteen miles down from the lake, the bridge for the Kougarok Road at Mile 65 provides the most popular put-in for boats (or rafts for a great float trip), to fish the productive middle and lower stretches of river. Anglers target big grayling, salmon, and charr in the next 15-mile stretch down to historic Pilgrim Hot Springs, and from there to the mouth, 30 miles of slower-moving, slough-filled water, where most of the river's pike (up to 20 pounds) are taken. Chums and pinks are the Pilgrim's main salmon species, with a few coho taken. Salmon Lake and its main tributary, the Grand Central River, are important spawning areas for a rare run of sockeye salmon, but you can't fish them or any other salmon there. (Both the lake and Grand Central River do have good Dolly Varden fishing.) The most popular areas to fish on the Pilgrim system are the lake outlet, the section of river below the bridge, and Iron Creek; the best time is in July and August.

Kuzitrin-Kougarok Rivers
Location: Seward Peninsula, 55 miles NE of Nome.
Access: From Nome via the Kougarok Road; boat and limited small plane access also possible.
Facilities: No public facilities.
Highlights: A fine, abundant grayling and pike fishery.
Main Species: GR, NP, CHR, SS

The Kuzitrin River is the largest drainage on the Seward Peninsula, and one of its most significant fisheries. The river originates at Kuzitrin Lake on the north side of the Bendeleben Mountains, and flows some 85 miles before emptying into Imuruk Basin. It is noted mostly for its fabulous pike, which thrive in the weedy, meandering reaches of the middle and lower river above Imuruk Basin. Grayling are abundant in the tributaries and upper river, but generally run smaller than those in other area streams. It has salmon (mostly chum, pink, and coho) and good charr fishing as well.

The Kuzutrin is accessed by road from Nome (the Kougarok Road crosses the river at Mile 68), or by boat from the bridge put-in, or from Teller via the Imuruk Basin. (Jet boats can travel up to the Noxapaga confluence.) A primitive airstrip along the lower Noxapaga at Rainbow Camp provides the river's only real access by small plane other than helicopter. The headwaters, rocky and shallow, can be floated when water levels permit.

The Kougarok is a major tributary that joins the Kuzitrin about 25 miles up from the mouth. It is reached by the Kougarok Road that follows the river for most of its length a ways beyond the Kuzitrin Bridge, Mile 68. (The road becomes a rough four wheel-drive trail beyond the river crossing at the 86 Mile Bridge.) The Kougarok is fished mostly for grayling and charr. A popular option is to put in with a boat or raft from the road and float the lower river down to the Kuzitrin bridge. (Check local sources for latest water conditions, as the Kougarok's shallow stretches may be difficult floating during dry periods in late summer and fall.)

American-Agiapuk Rivers ★★★
Location: Imuruk Basin drainage, 65 miles northwest of Nome.
Access: By boat from Teller or Kuzitrin River.
Facilities: No developed public facilities.
Highlights: Remote, high potential Seward Peninsula location.
Main Species: SS, CHR, GR, NP

The American-Agiapuk, second largest Imuruk basin drainage, is one of the more outstanding prospects for anyone looking for a truly out-of-the-way, high-quality Seward Peninsula fishing experience. This isolated, lovely river is visited almost exclusively by locals for hunting and subsistence fishing, and receives little pressure at that. It has abundant grayling and charr, and is a major spawning system for chum, pink, and silver salmon.

The American runs swift and clear for most of its length, while the tributary Agiapuk is wider, brownish-colored, and with less gradient. Both rivers have pike in their lower reaches. Access is traditionally by boat from Teller, via the Imuruk Basin, as the river can usually be navigated up to the Agiapuk confluence by jet boat in normal conditions. Another, lesser-taken option is to fly in by small wheelplane from Nome to gravel strips along the upper American (above Budd Creek) and float down to the lower river. The upper Agiapuk could be done with helicopter access.

KOTZEBUE SOUND

Within a space of 150 miles, some of the most significant sportfishing drainages in all of Northwest Alaska empty into Kotzebue Sound and the Chuchi Sea coast, north of the Arctic Circle. These include the Kobuk, Selawik, Noatak, Wulik, and Kivalina rivers, which are known the world over for their abundant trophy fishing (charr and/or sheefish). Very pristine and highly regarded recreational waters, the largest and most fish-endowed of these—the Noatak and Kobuk—are considered among the premier rivers in Alaska for wilderness float adventures. Area angling highlights also include excellent grayling fishing and some fabulous, but virtually unexploited, northern pike opportunities.

Noatak River ★★★★
Location: Kotzebue Sound, 550 miles northwest of Anchorage.
Access: Small plane from Bettles or Kotzebue to headwater lakes or gravel bars; boat travel possible along lower river.
Facilities: No developed public facilities.
Highlights: Premier wild river with world famous trophy charr.
Main Species: CHR, GR, CS

By anyone's estimation, the 425-mile giant Noatak is Alaska's most superlative backcountry river. (It was designated a UNESCO World Heritage Site in 1976, and later incorporated into Noatak National Preserve as a Wild River in 1978.) Along with several other area drainages (such as the Wulik, Kobuk, and Kivalina rivers), it has a world reputation for abundant, trophy sea-run charr fishing (up to 15 pounds and more), as thousands of these robust fish traditionally jam the mainstem and tributaries in late summer through fall

(late July through September), to prepare for spawning and over-wintering.

Lying totally above the Arctic Circle, the Noatak rises on the slopes of the Schwatka Mountains in the western Brooks Range and flows southwest to Kotzebue Sound. Clear and fast for most of its length, with only minor rapids (Class I and II), the Noatak presents no major technical obstacles for floating, other than its size and remoteness (a trip down its entire length is a major, three-week undertaking). A far better option for anglers is to put in on gravel bars or small tributaries at mid-river (the Aniuk and Cutler rivers are popular put-in areas), then float, fish and camp down to the village of Noatak or other points. This cuts travel time considerably and allows more enjoyment of the lower river's abundant fishing. (Most of the Noatak's big charr are intercepted at the mouths of the Kelly, Kugururok, Kugrak, Kaluktavik, and Nimiuktuk rivers.)

In addition to the river's great charr fishing, grayling and big chum salmon are abundant. Fishing the Noatak for ravenous spring charr and grayling right after break-up (June) is also an exciting possibility, and there are countless unnamed lakes and sloughs in the Noatak Flats (between the Eli and Agashashok rivers) that have pike of legendary proportions.

Kobuk River ★★★★
Location: Kotzebue Sound, 475 miles NW of Anchorage.
Access: Floatplane from Bettles, Kotzebue, or Ambler to headwater lakes; boat travel to many points along the lower river.
Facilities: No developed public facilities.
Highlights: A giant of river fishing adventure opportunities.
Main Species: SF, CHR, GR, LT, NP

The Kobuk River, like the Noatak, rises in the western Brooks Range and flows through some of the finest wild country in Alaska before emptying into Kotzebue Sound. Almost 350 miles long, and one of Alaska's largest clear rivers, the Kobuk's size and features make it suited for a variety of high-quality wilderness fishing adventures, particularly float trips. This area has so much to offer. Many folks begin with an exploration of the upper river, flying in from Kotzebue, Bettles, or Ambler to one of several beautiful headwater lakes such as Walker, Selby, and Nutuvukti (see next section), then camping and fishing for lake trout, charr, pike, and grayling for a few days before continuing downriver by raft or kayak. There are two stretches of major rapids (Class III and III-IV) in the canyons of the upper river below Walker Lake. Other than that, the Kobuk is fairly wide and serene as it winds its way through immense scenic valleys, where caribou, bear, wolves, moose, and migratory birds can frequently be seen.

The trip downriver to the village of Kobuk (where you can take out by wheelplane), a journey of at least eight days, will take you through some astounding fishing holes, especially the mouths of the countless tributary creeks that empty into this 125-mile stretch of river. If you're interested in some of the Kobuk's world-famous giant sheefish, you'll need to float down sometime in August or early September, when the big shees make their way upriver to spawn. The best fishing for these silvery brutes seems to be in the vicinity of the notorious Pah River, where fish of 30 pounds or more can be taken. Most people pull out at Kobuk, but there are some unique attractions downriver that make continuing worthwhile.

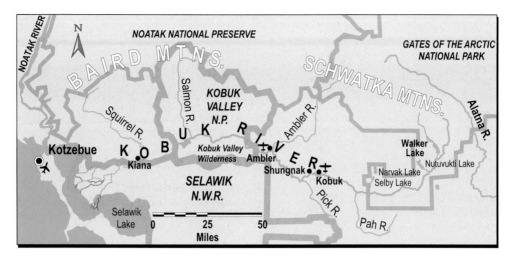

Some of the river's best fishing can be had in the north adjoining tributaries, from Ambler down to Kiana (some make outstanding float trips on their own—sparkling, pristine mountain streams like the Salmon, Ambler, or Squirrel rivers, with superb fishing for grayling, charr, and chum salmon), while the biggest northern pike cruise the lower river's slow-moving pools and sloughs. There are some amazing sights as well, like the incredible Kobuk Sand Dunes, or Onion Portage—the timeless caribou crossing halfway down the river, and the site of numerous archeological digs. The float to Kiana will add an additional six days minimum to the overall trip time; kayaks or motor-assisted rafts are highly recommended, as the wide lower sections of river can slow to a crawl in headwinds. Put in at Kobuk and float down, if you don't have two weeks to burn.

Selawik River

Location: Kotzebue Sound, 475 miles NW of Anchorage.
Access: By small plane to headwater lakes or gravel bars, or boat or foot from Selawik village.
Facilities: Limited supplies/services available in Selawik village.
Highlights: A significant NW river for trophy sheefish, northern pike.
Main Species: SF, NP

In early spring, some of Northwest Alaska's most exciting fishing action takes place on the ice of the giant estuary (called Kobuk Lake by locals) at the mouths of the Kobuk and Selawik rivers, southeast of Kotzebue. Here locals, using bright jigs and spoons, stir the giant sheefish of Kotzebue Sound from their winter lethargy with electrifying results. These semi-anadromous stocks attain the largest size of any sheefish in Alaska, and catches of 20 to 30-pound fish are not uncommon at this time. As break-up proceeds in May, the action shifts inland, following the sheefish as they gorge on whitefish and spring smolt. Later in summer many of these same fish will be found upriver, feeding heavily and preparing for their fall spawning.

The Selawik takes it name, most aptly, from the Inupiat for "place of sheefish." Along with the Kobuk River, it shares a reputation for Alaska's finest trophy angling for the species. The majority of visiting anglers come in summer and fall for a chance at these silvery giants. Most fish upriver from Selawik village, targeting the mouths of the tributary creeks and mainstem up to about 20 miles beyond

Ingruksukruk Creek. The countless sloughs and lakes in the immense flatlands surrounding the lower Selawik also make perfect habitat for monster northern pike, so don't miss the opportunity for some outstanding trophy fishing if you plan on visiting this drainage.

There are several ways to access this river. Small planes can land on headwater lakes (in the Shiniliaok Creek vicinity) or gravel bars along the river, with a float option down to the village. There are also fishing opportunities via foot or boat travel just out of Selawik, with limited guide service available.

Wulik River ★★★★

Location: Chukchi Sea Coast, 70 miles north of Kotzebue.
Access: By small wheelplane from Kotzebue to gravel bars along river; also by boat from Kivalina.
Facilities: A private lodge is located on the river.
Highlights: Alaska's most famous location for trophy charr.
Main Species: CHR, CS, GR

For many years the Wulik River has had the reputation as "the place" for trophy charr in Alaska. In an average year, the Wulik receives tens of thousands of robust (on average five to seven pounds, and up to 15 pounds or more), sea-run Dolly Varden that enter the river in late summer through fall to spawn and overwinter. A good portion of Alaska's record fish for the species have come from the Wulik.

Draining the westernmost slopes of the Brooks Range (the De Long Mountains) and emptying into the Chukchi Sea, for much of its length the 89-mile Wulik is perfect for wade-and-cast fishing: clear, gravel-bottomed, with pools, runs, and braided sections interspersed with plenty of bars for camping. Most of the fishing on the Wulik takes place from above Kivalina Lagoon to where the river branches into east and west forks (42 miles above the mouth), with the greatest concentration of fall charr located above and below Ikalukrok Creek. Other popular areas for fishing are the channels above Kivalina Lagoon (CS), the West Fork, below the falls and 16 miles up from the East-West confluence (CHR), Sheep Creek (CHR), Ikalukrok Creek (CS, CHR), and upper Tutak Creek (GR, CHR).

For a fall trophy charr safari (from August through mid-September), the Wulik is hard to beat. There's also exciting fishing during the spring outmigration in June, and in late July for an early run of spawners. Besides charr, the Wulik also has abundant grayling and chum salmon, along with some rare coho. Animal encounters—bears, caribou, wolves, and moose—are possible, and extreme weather, especially in September, is highly likely. It can be floated, with a wheel plane or boat pick-up along the lower river.

Kivalina River ★★★

Location: Chukchi Sea coast, 90 miles north of Kotzebue.
Access: By small wheelplane from Kotzebue to gravel bars along the river, or boat from Kivalina village.
Facilities: No public facilities; limited supplies/services available in Kivalina village.
Highlights: One of Alaska's best trophy charr fisheries.
Main Species: CS, CHR, GR

The Kivalina is the lesser-known sister river of the fabulous Wulik, Northwest Alaska's best trophy charr stream. Of similar origins, size, and character, the clear-flowing, 64-mile Kivalina is also blessed with abundant runs of big sea-run charr that overwinter and spawn in its spring-fed tributaries and mainstem. Slightly more remote and difficult to fish than the Wulik, the Kivalina doesn't quite receive the attention it deserves, considering the quality of fishing it offers.

The river has three main forks that converge about 27 miles above the mouth. Most of the sportfishing for fall charr and salmon takes place from there down to the lagoon. The lower sections of Grayling Creek (east fork) and the middle fork of the Kivalina are important upper river spawning areas. The best time to fish there is mid-August through early September. Spring charr are fished heavily by natives in the lower river and lagoon in early June.

You can access the Kivalina from Kotzebue by wheelplane, putting down on gravel bars upriver or at the strip in the village near the mouth. A boat ride upriver can be negotiated from locals there; call Caleb Wesley, (907) 645-2150. The river can be floated by raft or kayak to its mouth at Kivalina Lagoon, with a return via scheduled or chartered wheelplane to Kotzebue.

NORTHWEST MOUNTAIN LAKES

In the upper Kobuk, Noatak, and Koyukuk valleys lie scattered small, deep glacial lakes, many unnamed and seldom visited. Some of the more outstanding, listed below, are among Alaska's most pristine mountain lakes, offering solitude, impressive scenery, and fine fishing for lake trout, grayling, pike, and even landlocked charr. Access is from Kotzebue, Ambler, or Bettles, with early summer (June through early July) or fall (mid-August through early September) the best times for fishing. Check with local air taxi services for latest conditions.

Feniak Lake ★★★

Location: Upper Noatak Valley, 150 miles NE of Kotzebue.
Access: By small plane from Kotzebue or Ambler.
Facilities: None.
Highlights: A beautiful western Brooks Range lake with excellent fishing for lake trout and grayling.

Main Species: LT, GR

Feniak Lake is perhaps the finest glacial lake in the upper Noatak Valley. Set in awesome mountain country, its deep (75 feet) blue waters hold some superb lake trout fishing, with abundant catches and large fish (15 pounds or more) not uncommon. There is a major inlet stream on the north side, while the outlet, Makpik Creek, exits due south. Fishing for grayling is good in both streams. It is accessed by float or wheelplane (there is a gravel strip nearby) from Kotzebue or Ambler. Try Feniak when the ice is going out (or soon after) in early summer (June to early July) for the most exciting fishing.

Matcharak & Isiak Lakes

Location: Upper Noatak Valley, 200 miles NE of Kotzebue.
Access: By small plane from Kotzebue, Ambler, or Bettles.
Facilities: None.
Highlights: Beautiful, remote mountain lakes with good fishing for lake trout and grayling.
Main Species: GR, CHR, LT

Matcharak is one of many small but fairly deep lakes situated along the upper Noatak River. It is commonly used as a floatplane put-in for float trips on the Noatak (with a small portage). It is very scenic, and known for its good lake trout and grayling fishing, with a few pike thrown in. Still, it can be inconsistent. Late spring and early summer are probably the best times to try.

Isiak Lake lies less than two miles from Matcharak, on a small plateau above the Noatak. A gravel strip next to the lake provides access. A lovely little lake, it too has lake trout, grayling, and pike. Isiak makes for a nice lake fishing side trip when you put in at Matcharak to float the Noatak.

Walker Lake ★★★★

Location: Upper Kobuk Valley, 220 miles east of Kotzebue.
Access: By floatplane from Bettles or Ambler.
Facilities: None.
Highlights: One of the most outstanding western Brooks Range lakes for fishing.
Main Species: CHR, LT, GR, NP

Walker Lake is one of the most well-known and popular fly-in destinations in the entire Brooks Range. Located about 45 minutes by small plane west of Bettles, at the head of the Kobuk River (in Gates of the Arctic National Park), this scenic, narrow but deep, 14-mile long waterbody is a popular put-in spot for floaters setting out for the long haul down the Kobuk River headwaters to the village of Kobuk.

The lake has outstanding fishing for lake trout (up to 30 pounds) and landlocked charr (up to 15 pounds), with good grayling fishing in the outlet and mouths of the nine tributary creeks, and even some pike to be had in the weedy shallows. Late spring and early summer (June through early July) are probably the best times to fish it, but it does offer fairly consistent opportunities throughout the season, especially to boat anglers who can work the lake's steep dropoffs and access the many tributary creeks. A trip down the Kobuk, allowing a few days to sample these productive headwaters, makes a highly recommended Northwest Alaska fishing adventure.

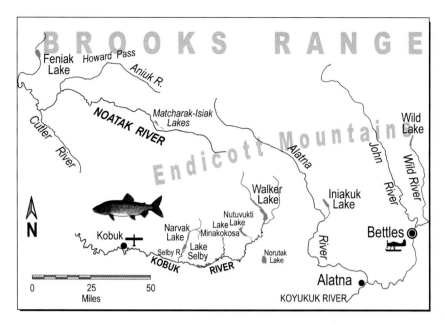

Selby-Narvak & Minakokosa Lakes

Location: Upper Kobuk Valley, 185 miles east of Kotzebue.
Access: By floatplane from Bettles or Ambler.
Facilities: A private lodge, cabins, and camps are available.
Highlights: High quality western Brooks Range lake fishing.
Main Species: GR, LT, NP

Located only about 40 miles southwest of Walker Lake, these two beautiful, connected lakes are worth a visit by themselves, but especially so if you're making a trip to the Kobuk or Pah rivers, as the Selby-Narvak lakes lie but a short distance off the river, midway down. (You can fish the lakes for a few days, then float down the outlet stream to join with the Kobuk right above the Pah. Check with local sources for latest outlet stream conditions beforehand.) Fishing is very good for lake trout, pike, and grayling, in a lovely, most secluded setting.

Minakokosa lies in between Selby and Walker lakes. It's small, but very pretty and private, with decent lake trout fishing. Like the Selby-Narvak lakes, it connects to the Kobuk, so it can be included in an itinerary for an extended float trip. Peace of Selby keeps a tent camp there, as well as cabins and camps on Selby-Narvak and other nearby lakes. They can provide everything needed; such as lodging, canoes, provisions, and guides for outpost-based fishing adventures of the highest order.

Iniakuk Lake

Location: Upper Koyukuk Valley, 45 miles west of Bettles.
Access: By floatplane from Bettles.
Facilities: A private lodge is located on the lake.
Highlights: An easily accessed, very pretty Brooks Range lake with good fishing.
Main Species: GR, LT, NP

A short flight northwest from Bettles takes you to lovely Iniakuk Lake in the Alatna drainage. Small (five miles long and only one mile wide), clear, and very deep (200 feet), Iniakuk is in a spectacular setting, with abrupt, tall mountains on its west and east sides. Fishing is good for lake trout, grayling, and pike, especially in the spring after ice-out. There's a lodge on the north end of the lake. A short stay there, with a float down the outlet (Malemute Fork) to the Alatna, a Wild and Scenic River, is highly recommended. (Note: water levels vary through the summer. Check with the folks at the lodge or Bettles for latest river conditions before attempting a float down to the Alatna drainage.)

Wild Lake

Location: Upper Koyukuk valley, 40 miles north of Bettles.
Access: By floatplane from Bettles.
Facilities: No public facilities.
Highlights: An easily-accessed, scenic Brooks Range lake destination with good fishing.
Main Species: GR, LT, NP

Wild Lake is located at the head of its namesake river, a short distance north of Bettles. One of the deepest lakes of its size (up to 250 feet) in the Brooks Range, the five-mile-long Wild offers good seasonal fishing for lake trout, pike, and grayling, especially around the inlet and outlet waters. It's best right after break-up in early June, or in the fall (late August through early September). A raft or other inflatable craft will greatly improve your chances of success on these deep waters. You can combine a stay at the lake with a short, four-day float down the Wild River, ending your trip at Bettles, for a fairly inexpensive but outstanding Brooks Range experience. Because of easy access and some private land development, however, at times this fly-in lake may be tamer than its name suggests.

Lower Koyukuk River

Location: Middle Yukon River tributary, 370 miles northwest of Anchorage.
Access: By floatplane or boat. The main boat access points are from Galena, Huslia, and Hughes.
Facilities: Limited services, supplies, and lodging are available in

villages of Hughes and Huslia.

Highlights: An unexplored fishing frontier with high potential for sheefish, grayling, and trophy pike.

Main Species: GR, SF, NP

The 320-mile Koyukuk River, one the Yukon's largest tributaries, dominates north central Alaska with its vast network of sprawling streams, which provide major habitat for a wide variety of fish species. In the extensive flatlands downstream of Hughes, the Koyukuk usually runs turbid from sediment and tannic water, but still has considerable sportfish potential for large pike (up to 48 inches) and sheefish in its countless, meandering sloughs, tributary lakes, and adjoining streams.

Grayling (some of trophy size) and some salmon (chums mostly, and a few kings) can be taken from the clearer waters of the Gisasa, Kateel, Dakli, and Alatna rivers and Hensaw Creek. Some Dolly Varden charr are even reported in the Gisasa. Aside from locals, these areas receive very little fishing pressure. They are definitely worth investigating by the angler with time, resources, and a yen for truly wild fishing adventure. Main boat access points are from Galena, Huslia, and Hughes, though floatplanes are also used to explore this river.

Recommended Lodges/Guides/Outfitters/Air taxis

Unalakleet River Lodge, P.O. Box 99, Unalakleet, AK 99684, (907) 624-3031, (808) 883-2660, *www.unalakleet.com* Lodge-based guided fishing, Unalakleet River.

Camp Bendeleben, 12110 Woodward Drive, Anchorage, AK 99516, (907) 522-6663, *www.campbendeleben.com* Lodge & camp-based guided/unguided fishing, Fish-Niukluk River.

Peace of Selby, 90 Polar Road, P.O. Box 86, Manley Hot Springs, AK 99756, (907) 672-3206, *www.alaskawilderness.net* Lodge, cabin, or tent camp-based guided/unguided fishing, Upper Kobuk River lakes.

Nome Convention and Visitors Bureau: P.O. Box 240, Nome, AK 99762, (907) 443-6624, *www.nomealaska.org*

Vance Grishkowsky: P.O. Box 38, Unalakleet, AK 99684, (907) 624-3352. Outpost camp fishing (guided/unguided), Unalakleet River.

Paul's Sportfish Guide Service: 3231 E. 42nd Ave., Apt. A, Anchorage, AK 99508, (907) 955-3471, (907) 279-0126 (winter). Outpost camp guided/unguided fishing, Shaktoolik River.

Stampede Car Rentals: P.O. Box 633, Nome, AK 99762, (800) 354-4606, (907) 443-3838.

Nome Outfitters: 120 West 1st Avenue, Nome, AK 99762, (907) 443-2880. Sporting goods, equipment rentals.

Sourdough Outfitters: P.O. Box 26066, Bettles, AK 99726, (907) 692-5252, *www.sourdough.com* Guided/unguided fishing, outfitting, western Brooks Range.

Bettles Lodge/Air: P.O. Box 27, Bettles, AK 99726, (800) 770-5111, *www.bettleslodge.com* Lodging, air taxi, guided/unguided fishing, outfitting, western Brooks Range.

Bering Air: P.O. Box 1650, Nome, AK 99762, (907) 443-5464, (800) 478-5422, *www.beringair.com* Air taxi service, plane and helicopter, Seward Peninsula.

Hageland Aviation: P.O. Box 207, Unalakleet, AK 99684, (907) 624-3595, *http://www.hageland.com*

Northwestern Aviation: P.O. Box 741, Kotzebue, AK 99752, (907) 442-3525, *www.alaskaonyourown.com* Air taxi service, Kotzebue/western Brooks Range area.

Arctic Air Guides Flying Service: Box 94, Kotzebue, AK 99752, (907) 442-3030. Air taxi service, western Brooks Range.

Ambler Air Service: P.O. Box 7, Ambler, AK 99786, (907) 445-2121. Western Brooks Range air taxi.

General information

Alaska Department of Fish & Game: Sport Fish Division, 1300 College Road, Fairbanks, AK 99701, (907) 459-7207.

Bureau of Land Management: Nome Field Station, P.O. Box 952, Nome, AK 99672, (907) 443-2177.

Koyukuk National Wildlife Refuge: P.O. Box 287, Galena, AK 99741, (907) 656-1231, *http://koyukuk.fws.gov*

Kobuk Valley National Park: P.O. Box 1029, Kotzebue, AK 99752, (907) 442-3890. *www.nps.gov/kova/*

Selawik National Wildlife Refuge: Box 270, Kotzebue, AK 99752, (907) 442-3799. *http://selawik.fws.gov*

Gates of the Arctic National Park & Preserve: 201 First Ave., Fairbanks, AK 99701, (907) 457-5752; *www.nps.gov/gaar/*

Noatak National Preserve: P.O. Box 1029, Kotzebue, AK 99752, (907) 442-3890 (headquarters), (907) 442-3760 (summer visitor info.), *www.nps.gov/noat/*

USGS Maps Reference

Unalakleet River: Norton Sound A-1-2; Unalakleet D-2, D-3, D-4.

Shaktoolik River: Norton Bay B-4, B-5, C-2, C-3.

Kwiniuk/Tubutulik Rivers: Solomon C-1, C-2, D-1; Norton Bay D-6; Bendeleben A-1.

Fish-Niukluk Rivers: Solomon C-3, D-3, D-4; Bendeleben A-5.

Nome River: Nome B-1, C-1, D-1.

Pilgrim River: Nome D-1; Solomon D-6; Bendeleben A-6; Teller A-1.

Kuzitrin-Kougarok Rivers: Teller A-1; Bendeleben A-6, B-3, B-4, B-5, B-6, C-6.

Sinuk River: Nome C-2, C-3, D-2.

Snake River: Nome C-1, C-2, D-1.

Solomon River: Solomon C-5.

Safety Sound: Solomon B-6, C-5, C-6.

American-Agiapuk Rivers: Teller A-2, B-2, B-3, C-2, D-2.

Noatak River: Survey Pass C-5, C-6; Ambler River C-1, D-1, D-2, D-3, D-4, D-5, D-6; Howard Pass A-5; Misheguk Mountain A-1, A-2; Baird Mountains D-3, D-4, D-5, D-6; Noatak A-1, A-2, B-2, B-3, C-2, C-3, D-1, D-2.

Kobuk River: Survey Pass A-3; Hughes D-3, D-4, D-5, D-6; Shungnak D-1, D-2, D-3, D-4; Ambler River A-4, A-5, A-6; Baird Mountains A-1, A-2, A-3; Selawik C-5, C-6, D-3, D-4, D-5, D-6.

Selawik River: Shungnak B-2, B-3, B-4, B-5, B-6, C-3, C-5; Selawik B-1, B-2, B-3, B-4, B-5, C-1, C-2, C-3, C-4, C-5.

Wulik River: Noatak C-5, D-3, D-4, D-5; De Long Mountains A-2, A-3, B-2.

Kivalina River: Noatak D-5, D-6; De Long Mountains A-3, A-4, B-3.

Feniak Lake: Howard Pass A-4, B-4.

Matcharak & Isiak Lakes: Ambler River C-1, D-1.

Walker Lake: Survey Pass A-3, A-4.

Selby-Narvak & Minakokosa Lakes: Hughes D-5, D-6.

Iniakuk Lake: Survey Pass A-1.

Wild Lake: Wiseman B-4, C-4.

Lower Koyukuk River: Kateel River A-3, A-4, B-1, B-2, B-3, B-4, C-1, C-2, C-3, D-1, D-2; Nulato D-3, D-4, D-5, D-6; Melozitna D-3; Hughes A-3, B-1, B-2, B-3.

Regulations/Information

Most Northwest waters are open to fishing year-round. Nome area waters (Sinuk River to Topkok) are closed to chum salmon fishing, with Nome and Solomon rivers also closed to grayling. Always consult current Regulations Summary for Region III, or contact Region or field office, ADF&G, when planning a fishing trip to the region.

Nome: (907) 443-5796   **Fairbanks:** (907) 459-7207

Online info: *www.sf.adfg.state.ak.us/statewide/regulations/aykregs.cfm*

Northwest Species

LOCATION	KING SALMON	RED SALMON	PINK SALMON	CHUM SALMON	SILVER SALMON	STEELHEAD	RAINBOW	CUTTHROAT	CHARR	LAKE TROUT	GRAYLING	SHEEFISH	NORTHERN PIKE	HALIBUT	LING COD	ROCK FISH	SALMON SHARK	FSHNG PRESSURE
Unalakleet River	☆	R	☺	☺	☆				☺		☺							✓
Shaktoolik River	☺	R	☺	☺	☆				☺		☆							✓
Kwiniuk/Tubutulik Rivers	☺	R	☺	☺	☺				☺		☆							✓
Fish-Niukluk Rivers	✓		☺	☺	☺				☺		☆		☺					✓
Nome River	✓		☺	C			✓		☺		C							M
Pilgrim River	R	R	☺	☺			✓		☺		☺		☆					✓
Kuzitrin-Kougarok River	R	R	☺	☺			✓		☺		☺		☆					✓
Sinuk River	R	✓	☺	C	☺				☺		☆							✓
Snake River	R		☺	C	☺				☺		☺							✓
Solomon River	R		☺	C	☺				☺		C							✓
Safety Sound	R		☺	C	✓				☺									M
American-Agiapuk Rivers	R		☺	☺	☺				☺		☺		✓					✓
Noatak River	R	R	☺	☺	R				☆		☺	R	☺					✓
Kobuk River				✓	☺				☺		☺	R	☆	☺				✓
Selawik River			R	R					✓		✓	☆	☆					✓
Wulik River	R		R	☺	R				☆		☺							✓
Kivalina River	R		✓	☺	R				☆		☺							✓
Feniak Lake									☺	☆								R
Matcharak-Isiak Lakes									R	☺	☺		✓					✓
Walker Lake									☆	☺	☆		☺					✓
Selby-Narvak-Minakokosa Lakes									☺	☺	☺		☺					✓
Iniakuk Lake									☺	☺	☺							✓
Wild Lake									☺	☺	☺							✓
Lower Koyukuk River	✓			☺					R		☺	☺	☺					✓

(blank) Species not present
R Rare
✓ Fishable numbers (or light pressure)
☺ Good fishing
☆ Excellent fishing

LL Landlocked species
C Present, but fishing closed
M Moderate pressure
☹ Heavy pressure

2005 Kevin G. Smith/AlaskaStock.com

Interior Alaska

In March, when winter releases its icy grasp on Alaska's immense hinterlands with the first warm, bright, sunny days, a man who has spent the long Interior winter cabin-bound is ripe for outdoor adventure, especially when it's fishing.

About this time, leads open up along the great rivers there—the Tanana, Nenana, and others, and the waters run the lowest and clearest they'll be all year, free of the silty meltwater that clouds them during the warmer months. Resident fish species feel the stirrings of spring and go on the feed, creating opportunity for some delightful diversion for the man who knows where to find it.

Back when I lived on a remote creek in the foothills of the Alaska Range, my native friend and closest neighbor, Tommie, would show up at my cabin door sometime during the first of these warm breaks, suited up on his little relic Ski-doo, small sled in tow, with an invitation I couldn't resist.

I'd quickly throw some gear together and follow him on my machine, down the trail several miles to the immense, willow-thicketed braids of the Nenana, where we'd head upriver along the flows and ridges, about five miles, to a little spring creek that came down from the hills and joined the mighty river.

There, in the icy, swirling waters of the creek mouth, we dangled small flies and spinners, which were grabbed instantly by savagely hungry grayling and charr. Tommie cooked them on sticks over a smoky willow fire and we'd sit in the glorious spring sun and devour them between gulps of scalding black tea. No feast ever tasted so good! And, though I've been on many grander outings, for much more glamorous quarry, no catch was ever more appreciated than those beautiful early spring fish from Alaska's Interior!

Flyfishing the central Brooks Range, Koyukuk River drainage

269

Heading out to fish camp, middle Yukon River

laska's vast heartland, the Interior region, encompasses a major part of the state, in a gigantic area bound by formidable mountains—the Alaska and Brooks ranges—and the Canadian border. (For our purposes, the middle fork of the Koyukuk River is the western boundary.) The immense Yukon River system, fifth largest on the continent, is the dominant feature of this region, shaping the character of the land and its people. Along this great waterway and its tributaries—the Koyukuk, Porcupine, Tanana, and others—you can still catch a glimpse of the "real Alaska," with its native villages and fish wheels, old trapper's cabins, birch forests, and country that, for the most part, is still the sparsely settled wilderness it always was.

Although it can't match the southern coastal regions' diversity of sportfishing, the Interior still has quite a bit to offer anglers, with thousands of miles of scenic, winding rivers, clear headwater streams, and countless lakes, ponds, and sloughs, where some of Alaska's most abundant fishing opportunities for pike, sheefish, and grayling are found.

COUNTRY, CLIMATE & FISHING CONDITIONS

Interior's terrain is varied and impressive, from the extensive foothills, peaks, and valleys of two major mountain ranges (along with the rolling hills, plateaus and modest mountains of the Yukon-Tanana uplands), to the immense lowlands surrounding the state's largest sprawling rivers. Great stands of paper birch, aspen, and spruce cover much of the region, thinning out at timberline—which occurs this far north at 2,000 to 3,000 feet elevation. To the north and west, expanses of tundra take over, in country that greatly resembles that along the coast.

Numerous lakes and ponds (over 40,000 in Yukon Flats alone) provide significant wildlife habitat, including refuge for important sportfish species. Spring-fed aquifers in the eastern Alaska and Brooks ranges provide constant flows for spawning/rearing of Alaska's most inland stocks of king, coho, and chum salmon (along with extended angling opportunities).

Due to its isolation from the coast, Interior's climate is strongly continental, with harsh seasonal extremes. Here are found some of the coldest and

Robin Brandt/Accent Alaska

Flyfishing the Chena River for grayling

ACCESS, SERVICES & COSTS

Access to Interior fishing locations is by road, rail, trail, plane, boat, and snowmachine. Fairbanks, the major hub (pop. 32,000), is serviced daily by jetliners from Anchorage and the outside world, with air taxi services providing access to numerous fly-in locations from there or from smaller outlying hubs like Fort Yukon or Arctic Village. A limited highway network crosses the region, linking the major communities to the rest of the state and Canada (via the Alaska Highway), and providing anglers with road access to quite a few good fishing locations. On the big waterways like the Tanana, Yukon, and Porcupine rivers, boats are the best (and sometimes only) travel option.

The wide variety of available visitor services leans heavily toward rustic accommodations, family-style lodges and do-it-yourself adventures. There are half-day guided fishing charters along local rivers, week-long or more wilderness float expeditions, remote outpost camps and rental cabins, wilderness lodges, even extended horseback trips to remote rivers and lakes, with many prices comparable to services in Southcentral or Southeast Alaska. (Fees are considerably more for remote areas of the Brooks Range or upper Yukon). Public facilities, available mainly along the road network, include state and federal maintained recreation sites, waysides, campgrounds, boat launches, and a few cabins.

Good trip planning is just as important for a safe and successful fishing vacation here as elsewhere in Alaska, for—aside from the major hubs and the few towns and villages scattered along its rivers and sparse roads—the Interior is total wilderness. Only the Arctic and Northwest have country more remote and unforgiving.

hottest places in Alaska. (Fort Yukon has recorded temperatures from 100 to –75°F.) Precipitation is scant—12 inches or so annually—with the region having considerably more calm, sunny, dry weather than anywhere else in Alaska. With the long summer days at these high latitudes, the Interior's climate makes for some of finest fishing conditions in the state from June to September.

Almost all the region's stream fishing occurs in clear-flowing tributaries of the turbid Tanana and Yukon rivers. With the light snow loads and abundant spring sunshine, most of these streams are in good shape by early June in average years, and fish well into the summer, with the runoff from the wet season (July through October) augmenting flows into fall. Because of the region's topography and size of most of the drainages, however, extreme and rapid changes in water conditions can occur anytime during spring and summer, with heavy flooding always possible during periods of heavy localized precipitation. As such, care should be taken when selecting campsites and planning trip itineraries.

COSTS

Custom Wilderness Lodges: $500-600/day/person.
Family Style Lodges: $250-375/day/person.
Guided Float Trips: $250-385/day/person.
Guided Fishing: $50-125/person/half-day; $100-350/person/full day.
B&B Lodging: $50-195/night.
Hotel/Motel Lodging: $50-499/night.
Remote Fishing Cabins: $100-175/day.
Boat Rentals: $100-150/day.
Raft Rentals: $575-630/wk.
Canoe/Kayak Rentals: $150-250/wk.
Air Taxi: Supercub: $145-$225/hr.; Cessna 185: $275-350/hr.; Cessna 206/7: $260-350/hr.; DeHavilland Beaver: $550/hr.; Cessna Caravan: $645/hr.; Heliocourier: $280/hr.; Navaho: $560-650/hr.; R22 helicopter: $300/hr.

WHAT TO EXPECT

Extreme continental climate, with summer high temperatures averaging in low 70s, but frequently climbing into the 80s or even 90s (°F), while winter days average below zero (frequently to -20 to -30°F and -40 to -50°F during intense cold snaps). Ice thickness on Interior lakes and rivers by late winter can reach three feet. Generally, high winds and extended periods of cyclonic activity are rare for the Interior, except for locations near the Alaska Range. Precipitation is sparse, occurring mostly during late summer and early fall.

Freeze-up generally occurs by late October, earlier in elevated locations in the Brooks Range; break-up is usually from late April to early May (into June in the mountains). Because of the preponderance of water, and warmer temperatures during summer, biting insects can be a problem from June to September.

INTERIOR RUN TIMING

SPECIES	JAN	FEB	MAR	APR	MAY	JUN	JUL	AUG	SEP	OCT	NOV	DEC
King Salmon							■	■				
Silver Salmon								■	■	■		
Chum Salmon							■	■				
Rainbow Trout	■	■	■	■	■	■	■	■	■	■	■	■
Charr	■	■	■	■	■	■	■	■	■	■	■	■
Lake Trout	■	■	■	■	■	■	■	■	■	■	■	■
Sheefish	■	■	■	■	■	■	■	■	■	■	■	■
Northern Pike	■	■	■	■	■	■	■	■	■	■	■	■
Grayling	■	■	■	■	■	■	■	■	■	■	■	■

■ Available   ■ Peak

Note: Time periods shown in blue are for bright fish in the case of salmon entering rivers, or for general availability for resident species. Peak sportfishing periods are shown in red. Run timing can vary somewhat from drainage to drainage within the region. Always check with local contacts for run timing specifics for locations you intend to fish.

	Jan	Feb	Mar	Apr	May	Jun	Jul	Aug	Sep	Oct	Nov	Dec
DAYLIGHT HOURS (monthly average)	5 ½	8 ½	11 ¾	15 ¼	18 ¾	21 ¼	20	16 ½	13	9 ¼	6 ½	4 ¼
°F Ave. TEMPS. (High/Low)	1/-19	8/-16	21/-7	37/11	54/30	67/42	69/46	62/41	50/30	29/12	10/-8	5/-14
PRECIPITATION (inches)	.63	.44	.37	.26	.63	1.45	2	2.17	1.63	.91	.61	.71

The Interior has some of Alaska's best easily-accessed lake fishing, with outstanding year-round opportunities for lake trout, charr, and pike.

Yukon Flats—with its countless braids, sloughs, ponds, and lakes—part of Interior's extensive lowland river habitat.

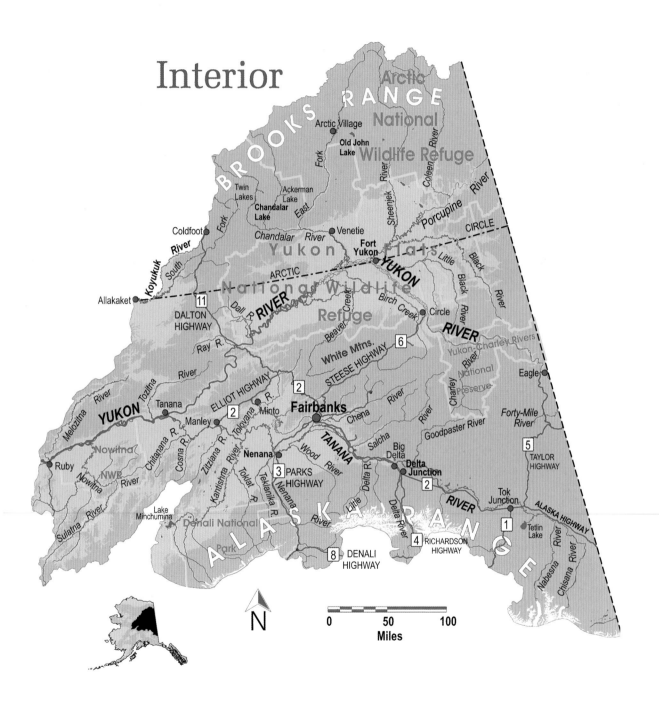

Interior

Lake trout fishing, Old John Lake, Brooks Range

INTERIOR FISHING HIGHLIGHTS

The abundance of large mainstem, lowland river terrain—with its preponderance of sloughs, lakes, and marshy ponds—is the perfect habitat for a variety of still-water baitfish like whitefish, cisco, and suckers, which in turn provide ample forage for predatory game species like northern pike and sheefish. The Interior is well known for its outstanding fisheries for these two fighters (such as in the Tanana and Yukon Flats).

Because of the great distances from the coast, salmon here are fewer in number and species—mostly chum, with some kings and coho. High-quality fishing for these species is limited, occurring mostly in the mouths and lower sections of clearwater rivers, particularly those in the Tanana River drainage. (Alaska's most significant fall runs of chum salmon occur all along the middle Yukon River and its tributaries, but are used primarily for subsistence.) Grayling opportunities abound, however, in nearly every clear stream and headwater, with even some Dolly Varden charr found in a few swift streams (mostly Tanana, Nenana, and Koyukuk river tributaries). Some outstanding opportunities for lake trout in the upper Tanana River drainage and Brooks Range round out the fishing highlights of the Interior region.

The Interior has the state's most abundant northern pike habitat, with many waters of trophy potential.

TANANA RIVER SYSTEM

The Tanana, second largest tributary of the Yukon, originates primarily from meltwater draining off the immense Nabesna and Chisana glaciers high in the Wrangell Mountains near the Yukon border. It flows northwest more than 500 miles before joining the mighty Yukon just west of the town of Manley. The most accessible and popular Interior watershed for recreation, the Tanana River drainage offers a wide variety of water and fishing, with abundant grayling, northern pike, lake trout, some sheefish, and the best of Interior's limited fishing for chinook and coho salmon. Since the Tanana is a braided, glacial river system, sportfishing potential is concentrated in clear, upland tributaries—the Salcha, Chena, Chatanika, and Delta Clearwater rivers—and in sloughs, lakes, ponds, and slower streams along the Tanana Flats (the Minto Lakes, Tolovana and Kantishna rivers, and Fish Creek).

Tangle Lakes System ★★★★

Location: Upper Tanana River drainage, 125 miles SE of Fairbanks.

Access: By foot or watercraft via Denali Highway.

Facilities: Lodging, campgrounds, and canoe rentals available.

Highlights: Some of Interior's best road-accessed fishing for grayling and lake trout in an area of great scenic beauty.

Main Species: LT, GR

Situated in the Amphitheater Mountains on the south slope of the Alaska Range, near milepost 22.5 of the Denali Highway (just west of Paxson), the Tangle Lakes system is a 24-mile long complex of lakes and interconnecting streams that head the Delta River. The surrounding landscape is breathtaking—rugged peaks to 6,000 feet and abundant wildlife (including grizzly bears) are present throughout this nationally designated Wild and Scenic River system. Even more appealing is the fact that this watershed has some of the best road-accessible grayling fishing in Interior Alaska, if not the entire state. The system includes all waters upstream of the "Falls" on the upper Delta River. Generally crystal-clear, this extensive drainage has major fish-producing lakes and streams that receive little angling pressure, except for those parts near the highway.

Starting in early summer and continuing through most of fall, anglers have outstanding success fishing abundant sailfins with dry and wet flies and small spinners. They average 8 to 15 inches, with occasional lunkers reaching the magic 20-inch mark. Though the action can be very good in lakes and streams near the Denali Highway, locations accessible only by trail or canoe offer the best opportunities. Inlet and outlet streams in the lakes, and the shallow runs of the connecting streams and rivers, are prime hot spots. The Delta River, from the outlet down to Eureka Creek, has excellent fishing, and can be floated down to a take-out point adjacent to the Richard-

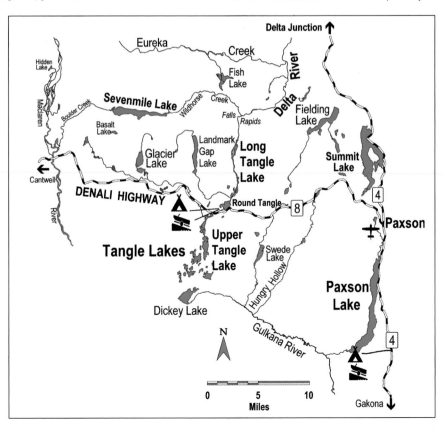

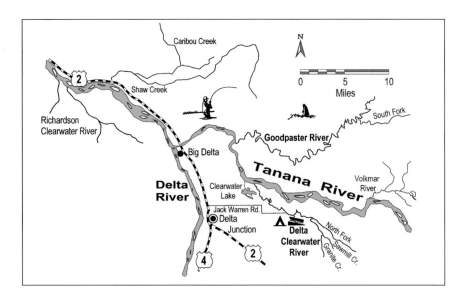

son Highway at milepost 212, a trip of around 35 miles. (A waterfall and series of rapids below the outlet require a portage and careful navigation.)

Lake trout are fairly abundant in the deep-water lakes of the system and are best sought during late spring through early summer, and in fall. Most of the fish taken are not very large as lakers go (averaging three to four pounds), but occasionally some reach trophy size (20 pounds). Landlocked Tangle, about four miles south of the highway, is probably the best to try. An inflatable craft of some kind is recommended for fishing the big ones.

The following are some of the better fishing locales within the Tangle Lakes/Upper Delta River drainage for grayling and lake trout: Upper Tangle, Middle Tangle, Round Tangle, Long Tangle, Landlocked Tangle, Landmark Gap, Glacier, and Fielding lakes (GR, LT); Sevenmile and Two-Bit lakes (LT); Rock Creek (GR); and Upper Delta, Upper Tangle, and Tangle rivers (GR).

Tetlin Lakes

Location: Upper Tanana River drainage, between Nabesna and Chisana rivers, 175 miles SE of Fairbanks.

Access: By car (to locations along the Alaska highway) or by plane or boat from nearby towns of Northway, Tetlin, or Tok. Winter ice fishing access by snowmachine from the Alaska Highway.

Facilities: Rental cabins maintained by the wildlife refuge.

Highlights: A vast expanse of little-fished lakes and streams with good potential for pike and grayling.

Main Species: LT, GR, NP

Located in the remote Tetlin National Wildlife Refuge near the Alaska-Yukon border, the Tetlin Lakes area is an expansive wetland comprised of hundreds of lakes, ponds, and sloughs lying along the lower Chisana and upper Tanana rivers. Significant habitat for nesting waterfowl and other migratory birds, much of the Tetlin Lakes, for gamefish, are too shallow to support overwintering populations or only marginally productive. But some of the deeper, more fertile waters have consistently provided good fishing for northern pike up

to 20 pounds, with grayling in the faster streams and outlet waters. A few of the deepest outlying lakes support lake trout. Because of its remoteness, fishing pressure for most of the area remains light, mostly from nearby villages, local air taxis, and tourists working the more accessible locations near the Alaska Highway.

Forty-mile Air out of Tok offers daily guided fishing and drop-offs in the area. Early summer or fall are the prime times for a high quality fishing adventure there.

Some of the more notable locations worth checking out are: Tetlin Lake (NP); Big Lake (NP, GR); Wellesley Lakes (NP); Jatahmund Lake (NP, LT); Takomahto Lake (NP); Dog Lake (NP); Braye Lakes (LT, GR); Deadman Lake (NP); Scottie Creek (GR); Bitters Creek (GR).

Delta Clearwater River ★★★★

Location: Upper Tanana River drainage, Delta Junction area, 85 miles SE of Fairbanks.

Access: By car from the Alaska Highway via Clearwater and Remington roads, or from the Richardson Highway via Jack Warren and Remington roads. Boat access from campground near Clearwater Ranch (10-mile run) or Clearwater Lake off Jake Warren Road (run up Tanana to mouth).

Facilities: Campground, boat launch, and lodging are available in the Clearwater Ranch area.

Highlights: One of the best silver salmon streams in Interior Alaska.

Main Species: SS, GR

Located in the upper Tanana River drainage, the Delta Clearwater rises from runoff from Granite Mountain and upwellings and seepages in the Tanana Valley just east of the Gerstle River. Its crystal-clear water is lined with dense vegetation as it meanders a short distance (20 miles) to join the glacial Tanana River, twenty miles upstream of the Richardson Highway bridge. With constant flow from its spring sources and abundant spawning habitat, it supports the Interior's largest runs of silver salmon, with outstanding sportfishing possible.

The mainstem Delta Clearwater River is known to have as many as 20,000 or more coho invade its waters in some years. Nearly all the fishing is catch-and-release, as the salmon are generally too far advanced in prespawning to eat. Still, the fishery is extremely popular with boat and shore anglers seeking a taste of some of the finest salmon action available in the Interior.

Usually beginning in early September and peaking in mid-October, the run here is extended, lasting through the fall, until the snow piles up in November. Although fish are present in great numbers throughout the river, the lower section and confluence area are recommended for catching brighter, scrappier coho.

Another popular sport species you'll find in abundance here is the Arctic grayling. The cool, spring-fed waters provide perfect habitat for a substantial number of the plucky, lightweight fighters, from early summer through fall. They succumb to a variety of dry and wet flies and small spinners. Grayling anglers usually do best in the upper sections of the Delta Clearwater around the forks where tributary streams join, but fishing can be productive in all parts of the river during certain times of the year (like the fall outmigration). Around the confluence with the Tanana River, you can expect to encounter fair numbers of late-running chum salmon in September and early October. (The fishery has done well in recent years under more restrictive management, with more and more trophy-sized specimens available.) Even when temperatures slide down into the minus range, the water remains partially ice-free, though few anglers have the moxie to challenge the conditions beyond the normal season (from June through November).

Goodpaster River System

Location: Upper Tanana River drainage, Delta Junction area, 75 miles SE of Fairbanks.

Access: By boat from Big Delta, launching at the Richardson Highway bridge on Tanana River and running upstream to mouth of Goodpaster. Floatplanes can land at Volkmar Lake, a tributary of the Goodpaster. Snowmachine access in winter via frozen Tanana River.

Facilities: None.

Highlights: A traditional local hot spot with excellent fishing for northern pike and Arctic grayling.

Main Species: GR, NP

Originating from Shawnee Peak and the Black Mountain area just north of Tanana Valley State Forest, the clear-flowing Goodpaster meanders through mountainous terrain and flatlands before reaching the glacial Tanana River. The drainage has a long history as one of the better sportfishing waters of the upper Tanana, with a fair amount of angling for pike and grayling from late spring into fall.

The lower river, around Goodpaster Flats, has plenty of slow-moving water with oxbow lakes and sloughs, creating perfect habitat for large, hungry northerns. These toothy, aggressive fighters are abundant from the mouth upstream into the foothills beyond South Fork. In addition, Volkmar Lake, which connects to the river via a very small creek, also offers some consistent pike action, with the best occurring in early summer and fall. Generally not very large (ranging from 3 to 10 pounds), there are a few oldsters there that may weigh as much as 25 pounds or more.

The Goodpaster is also known for its superb fly-fishing for fat Arctic grayling. These fine light-tackle scrappers are available throughout the system, from the mouth upstream to the headwaters, and are at their best from early summer into fall. King salmon also inhabit the river, but fishing for them is currently closed. For a remote river experience within a reasonable distance from the road, but far enough to escape the crowds, the Goodpaster River is highly recommended. Make sure to pack your sleeping bag, though, because there are no developed public facilities in the area.

Quartz Lake

Location: Middle Tanana River drainage, 70 miles SE of Fairbanks.

Access: By car via Richardson Highway (milepost 277) outside Delta Junction.

Facilities: Campground and boat launch.

Highlights: Excellent angling opportunities for the weekend angler.

Main Species: RT, SS, KS, CHR

Located just off the Richardson Highway outside Delta, Quartz Lake offers some good opportunities for the weekend angler.

Stocked by Alaska Department of Fish & Game, species include land-locked silver and king salmon, Arctic charr, and rainbow trout. (Some of the largest rainbows caught in the Interior—up to ten pounds—have come from Quartz.)

While Quartz yields moderate angling opportunity year-round, the best time to fish this lake is during break-up in mid to late May. As the lake's giant ice-sheet begins to melt, beautiful rainbows measuring 16 inches and up are plentiful near shore, and these fish are not shy (contact Alaska Department of Fish & Game in Fairbanks or Delta Junction for current lake conditions). Quartz also is a local favorite ice fishing hot spot during the long winter months.

Salcha River ★★★

Location: Middle Tanana River drainage, 40 miles SE of Fairbanks.

Access: By boat or foot via Richardson Highway (crosses the river at MP 323). A well-developed trail begins at Munson Slough (MP 324) and heads west a half mile to the mouth of the Salcha and its confluence with the Tanana River.

Facilities: State-maintained campground and boat launch.

Highlights: A unique, road-accessible fishery for Interior king salmon and Arctic grayling.

Main Species: KS, GR

One of the larger clearwater drainages of the Tanana accessible from the road system, Salcha River is wide and very deep in places, with a slow, steady current. Originating in the mountains just east of Fort Wainwright Military Reservation, the Salcha meanders west about 120 miles to join the glacial Tanana River, near Aurora Lodge on the Richardson Highway. It is a very popular river for recreation among Interior residents and receives a good amount of angling pressure during the midsummer salmon runs.

The Salcha River has the largest run of king salmon in the Tanana Valley and offers good opportunities for catch-and-release fishing for chinook averaging 20 to 25 pounds, with lunkers to 50 pounds possible. The mouth of the river has the best fishing, with heavy concentrations of kings staging in the area in July, but deep holes and runs upstream may also yield good results. Fair numbers of summer-run chums are present in July as well and, come fall, some acrobatic coho show up. The silvers are destined for the Delta Clearwater River farther up the Tanana, and are intercepted at the mouth of the Salcha in September and October, along with a few fall-run chums.

Although retention of salmon is legal, it is not recommended, since the majority of fish will be very close to spawning and certainly not prime table fare. Occasionally, however, a few semi-bright fish are taken in the early part of the run.

Arctic grayling are also available throughout summer and fall, with the best action on the middle and upper river, accessible only by boat. Flies are the favored lure, but spinners work well here, too. Northern pike are not abundant, but a few are landed now and then in sloughs or quiet stretches of the lower and middle river, or at the mouth. For anyone planning to cruise the road system of Interior Alaska during the middle of summer, the Salcha River is worth checking out for its opportunities for salmon and other sportfish species.

Birch Lake

Location: Middle Tanana River drainage, 50 miles SE of Fairbanks.

Access: By car from milepost 306, Richardson Highway. In addition to the highway pullout bordering the lake, there is a military recreation area access road at milepost 305 of the Richardson Highway.

Facilities: Campground.

Highlights: One of the more popular angling hot spots in Interior Alaska, with a variety of species.

Main Species: SS, RT, GR, CHR

Located just north of the confluence of the Tanana and the Little Delta, Birch Lake offers some good opportunities for roadside angling. Stocked by Alaska Department of Fish & Game, species include landlocked king and silver salmon, Arctic grayling, charr, and rainbow trout.

Though isolated from the Tanana River, two small creeks drain into the lake: Gunnysack Creek from the north, and a small, unnamed creek from the east. Fishing near these stream inlets will generally yield a bite or two to begin the day. While there are trails along the shore from the primitive State Campground on the east end of the lake, an inflatable canoe or small boat will allow access to much more water and greater angling opportunity. Birch also offers some decent ice-fishing opportunities during winter. (If you prefer the comfort of a shelter, contact Alaska State Parks for information on renting public-use ice shacks.)

Harding Lake ★★★

Location: Middle Tanana River drainage, 45 miles SE of Fairbanks.

Access: By car to the north side of the Richardson Highway near milepost 321. Little Harding Lake reached from milepost 318, Richardson Highway, via Salcha Drive (Perimeter Road).

Facilities: State-maintained campground and boat launch.

Highlights: Easily accessed lake with good fishing opportunities for lake trout and charr.

Main Species: LT, CHR

At 2,500 acres, Harding is the largest, deepest, and most productive of the roadside lakes in the central Tanana Valley, and is a pop-

ular recreation spot for locals. Introduced/enhanced populations of charr and lake trout are targeted with fairly consistent success. During open water season, shore anglers can do well at times, particularly at ice-out, but the deeper water of Harding, and the lunkers (lake trout to 30 pounds, charr to 20 pounds) it holds, are best worked from boats, trolling spoons, and plugs. In winter months, Harding offers a roadside ice-fishery that is hard to beat in the Interior, with the added opportunity of catching a burbot (a species of freshwater cod). While northern pike once flourished in the lake, dropping water levels have exposed essential habitat and impacted survival and reproduction. Current restrictions on the pike fishery, in addition to positive water conditions, will hopefully lead to a recovery of this voracious sportfish.

Little Harding Lake, nestled between Harding and the Richardson Highway, is quite small but offers some decent catch-and-release angling for stocked rainbow trout. A small paddling craft is recommended for a morning or evening outing on this lake, but anglers can also do well from shore.

Chena River System ★★★

Location: Middle Tanana River drainage, Fairbanks area.

Access: By boat and foot via Chena Hot Springs Road for upper river, with road access to the lower river via Badger Road, Ft. Wainwright, or Fairbanks.

Facilities: State recreation area/site, campgrounds, boat launch, and a cabin along the river.

Highlights: Diverse, year-round fishing in a river that flows through the heart of Fairbanks.

Main Species: KS, GR

Chena River originates in the uplands south of the Steese National Conservation Area, east of Fairbanks. Five major tributaries enter the river along its course, with at least one sizeable lake annexed to the drainage. While the upper sections are fairly narrow and fast-flowing, the lower Chena is wide and smooth with little current. Because of its proximity to Fairbanks and easy access, local angling interest is high, with a great deal of other recreational opportunities available, such as canoeing, kayaking, camping, etc.

Once the most popular Arctic grayling fishery in the state, Chena River has seen its ups and downs. After a crash in fish populations from overharvesting in the late 80s, restrictive management brought a rebound in grayling numbers and fish size, thus resurrecting the quality of fishing. Today the Chena offers some of the best road-accessible, catch-and-release grayling fishing in Alaska, particularly the upper river, with its pools, cutbanks, and shallow riffles providing some of the most classic conditions for dry fly fishing large grayling (18-inch class), according to local guides and anglers.

The lower and middle Chena are productive locations for salmon, with sporadic catches of sheefish and northern pike also reported. Summer runs of king and chum are present, with good catch-and-release fishing for kings possible in late July in various holding areas throughout the lower river (such as the confluence of the Chena and Tanana rivers, confluence of Chena and Little Chena rivers, and right below the Flood Control Dam, river mile 45). A few "Tarpon of the North," sheefish, are caught occasionally during the summer months when they come in from the Tanana River to feed.

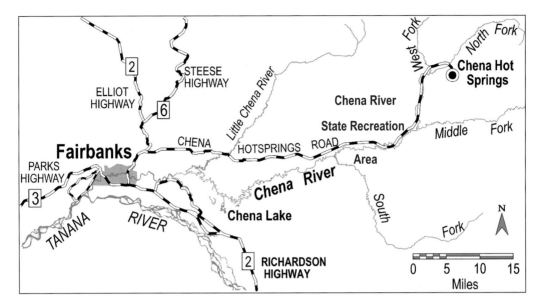

Pike, however, are slightly more common and there are fair chances of hooking one in sloughs and side channels (Badger Slough, among others). Ice fishers do well in the winter and early spring months for burbot in the far lower section of the river and at the confluence with the Tanana.

Nearby Chena Lake, located on Eielson Air Force Base, is stocked with species such as landlocked silver and king salmon, Arctic grayling, charr, and rainbow trout. It is a very popular and well-known Interior fishing location that provides locals with fair to good action twelve months a year. If a visit to Fairbanks is on the itinerary, plan a few hours of pleasant diversion checking out the Chena. Though the lower river is quite urban, the upper sections along Chena Hot Springs Road will surprise you with their solitude. While accommodations are plentiful in and around Fairbanks, the modern Chena Hot Springs Resort at the end of the road offers a relaxing end to a great day on the river.

Chatanika River System

Location: Middle Tanana River drainage, 20 miles NW of Fairbanks.

Access: By boat from Elliott Highway (crosses middle section of the river), Steese Highway (crosses and parallels upper 50 miles of river), or Murphy Dome Road (to fish lower river upstream from Minto Flats).

Facilities: Campground and boat launch off Elliott Highway (MP 10.6) at Olnes Pond.

Highlights: One of the Interior's most popular fishing rivers.

Main Species: KS, GR, NP

This mostly clear, 170-mile river flows through a very scenic valley, surrounded by the Tanana Hills to the south and the White Mountains to the north and west, before joining the Tolovana River near Minto Flats, 50 miles west of Fairbanks. The lower river meanders considerably, with deep holes and quiet sloughs, while the upper Chatanika is shallower and faster, with many riffles and runs. Situated so close to Fairbanks, the river serves as a recreational hub for many outdoor activities, including some varied and abundant fishing.

Starting in late spring or early summer, a number of fine sportfish can be taken on the Chatanika. Arctic grayling invade the river, bound for summer feeding areas near headwaters, and voracious northern pike settle into slower sections on the middle and lower river. Later on (mid and late July), summer runs of king and chum salmon arrive and draw a fair amount of angling interest around the Elliott Highway road crossing. (By the time they have gotten this far, they are usually well advanced into prespawning, so catch-and-release fishing is the general rule.) Towards fall, anglers can intercept migrating grayling and even some small spawning runs of sheefish (September through October).

Major tributaries of the Chatanika, like the Tatalina, Washington, and Goldstream creeks, are all good for grayling during the summer months, while pike fishing is usually hot in the deeper holes and pools around confluence areas. Lower Goldstream Creek and Minto Lakes have both been long known as top pike locations in the Interior, with trophy specimens up to 20 pounds or more. Other areas to try for big pike are the mainstem Chatanika and the sloughs and holes of nearby Tolovana River.

Despite fairly high use over the years, the Chatanika River still holds up as a very productive drainage, with a variety of good fishing opportunities. It's well worth the time if you're planning a trip to the Fairbanks area.

Minto Flats

Location: Middle Tanana River drainage, 30 miles west of Fairbanks.

Access: By floatplane or boat (via Elliot Highway to village of Minto; Murphy Dome Road to Chatanika River, then Goldstream Creek; and Parks Highway to Tanana River at town of Nenana, then to Tolovana River).

Facilities: None.

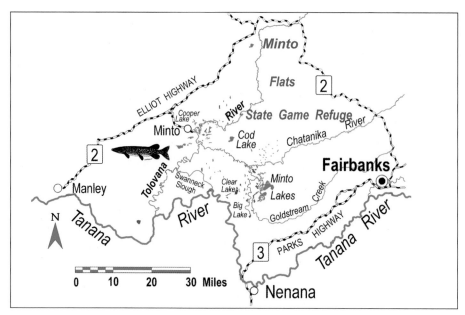

Highlights: Historically productive area for fast-paced pike action.

Main Species: NP

Long a popular local hunting and fishing destination, the Minto Flats area is a sizeable conglomeration of low-lying lakes, ponds, marshes, and sloughs surrounding the sluggish, meandering lower sections of several Tanana tributaries—the Tolovana, Tatalina, and Chatanika rivers and associated creeks.

Most of it is encompassed by the 1,000-square-mile Minto Flats State Game Refuge, a critically important waterfowl habitat. But the slow water and abundance of prey (whitefish and cisco) also make the Minto Flats a most productive locale for pike that lie in ambush throughout the vast, weedy backwaters. Of these, the Minto Lakes, a group of interconnected waters on the east end of the Flats, tributary to Goldstream Creek, are perhaps the best known and most popular for fishing.

The larger Minto Lakes (Big Minto, Upper Minto, etc.), and their network of interconnecting sloughs and channels, have historically received the majority of effort from pike anglers, but there is plenty of productive water (with the added bonus of some chances for sheefish, grayling, and possibly salmon in season) in the windy lower Tolovana or the lower Chatanika River. The deeper, slower sections of Goldstream Creek, Swanneck Slough, and the Chatanika-Tolovana confluence can also be good areas for pike. If you are putting in at Minto, don't overlook the ample waters on the west side (Whitefish Lakes, Rock Island Lake, etc.); though some of them get hit hard by locals, quite a few of the bigger fish taken from the Flats every year come out of there.

Note: *The Flats' constantly fluctuating water levels have a pronounced effect on the access and fishing. Check with local sources for current conditions before heading out.*

Nenana River System

Location: Middle Tanana River drainage, 50 miles SW of Fairbanks.

Access: By foot or boat via the Parks Highway, which follows river

for many miles. The Denali Highway from Cantwell provides access to headwater streams.

Facilities: Campgrounds available in several places along both highways, and a boat launch, lodging, and limited services/supplies are available in Nenana.

Highlights: A variety of road-accessible fishing opportunities, from salmon to grayling.

Main Species: SS, LT, GR, NP

Nenana River originates from the Nenana Glacier high in the Alaska Range east of Denali, and flows north to its confluence with the larger Tanana River near the town of Nenana. It is a fairly large, silty system encompassing small lakes, numerous clearwater streams, and even glacial rivers like the Teklanika of Denali National Park. Numerous roadside fishing spots offer fishing that ranges from poor to good, but some of the best fishing takes some legwork or a boat ride to reach.

Arctic grayling are the most abundant sport species in the Nenana River system. They are available anytime between March and October, but are at a peak during the warmer months. Nearly all the clear tributary streams, from the headwaters above Cantwell down, offer some measure of fishing for them, but the more accessible locations have been worked over, with predictable effects on size and abundance. Some of the more out-of-the-way locations to try, for bigger and better grayling, are: streams along the Denali Highway (Upper Jack River, Monahan, and Brushkana creeks); streams off the Stampede Trail north of Healy (Fish Creek, Eightmile Lake, Upper Savage, and Teklanika rivers); clear tributaries of the Yanert (Moose and Ravine creeks); eastside tributary streams (Moose and Walker creeks); and the less-accessible sections of streams along the highway (Panguingue, Clear, and Julius creeks). Spring and fall are the best times to fish, but the mainstem has some exciting fishing as well in late winter, when the water clears. Open leads by the mouths of tributary streams and beaver ponds are good places to try with flies and small spinners, as you might even run into a few small Dolly Varden. (Some of the more remote clearwater creeks are also good places to encounter this increasingly rare Nenana species.) Use extreme caution on the river ice, however.

Broad Pass Lakes, along the Parks Highway, have populations of lake trout as well as grayling. Summit and Edes lakes produced fish in the 10 to 15-pound range during their heyday. State efforts to stock these waters with lake trout are paying off, with abundance and opportunity once again on the rebound. Small lake trout are rumored to be in Slate Lake and other small lakes at the head of tributary streams.

In mid-summer (late July), small runs of king and chum salmon make their way up the Nenana, followed by a much heavier showing of silvers in the fall. Since most of these salmon are well into their prespawning changes, catch-and-release fishing is the only way to go. Several streams receive salmon, but the more outstanding ones are Seventeenmile Slough, the lower sections of Julius and Clear creeks, June Creek, and an unnamed creek that used to be an old channel of the Nenana near Anderson. The best time for silvers is late August through September. Sloughs off the lower river also offer decent pike fishing for anglers looking for a good time.

Kantishna River System ★★★

Location: Lower Tanana River drainage, 65 miles SW of Fairbanks.

Access: By small plane from Fairbanks via several lakes adjoining the system, or quiet sloughs and straight stretches of the main river. (Wheelplane access limited to a landing strip at Lake Minchumina.)

Facilities: None.

Highlights: A remote and significant tributary of the Tanana offering excellent fishing opportunities.

Main Species: SS, GR, NP

With headwaters in the heart of the Alaska Range, this system is quite extensive, with an amazing number of tributary streams, lakes, and sloughs, many of which are within Denali National Park. Some truly great fishing on this system is largely ignored, save for a few main lakes and other locations.

Northern pike and Arctic grayling are the two main species of interest around the Kantishna drainage, with some of the finest pike opportunities in the state available there, particularly for trophy specimens. Lakes and sloughs of the Lake Minchumina area are particularly noteworthy, as are drainages farther down along the mainstem. Mucha, Wein, and West and East Twin lakes are relatively well-known hot spots for large northerns up to 30 pounds, with many smaller lakes, such as Alma, John Hansen, Sandless, and dozens of others with no names in the Bearpaw River area offering abundant fishing. (These lakes are great ice fishing spots, too, and can be accessed by snowmachine via a trail from the Parks Highway.) Arctic grayling are abundant in all clearwater streams, with the more alpine, faster, and clear-flowing sections being especially productive. Look for suitable locations near the headwaters of the Kantishna or clear tributaries of the glacial Toklat River.

The Kantishna River system also receives a fair number of salmon, (including king, silver, and chum) during the summer and fall months. Although found throughout the drainage, some of the more concentrated areas are the mouths of clearwater streams and

creeks that drain into the Toklat River. (A portion of the mainstem Toklat is also home to a major run of fall chum salmon.)

The lower river has two small lakes, Geskakmina and Triangle, that have been stocked with fish. Geskakmina contains landlocked silvers and rainbow trout, while Triangle has some lake trout and grayling.

Zitziana River System

Location: Lower Tanana River drainage, 85 miles west of Fairbanks.

Access: By boat via Manley Hot Springs Slough to mainstem Tanana River, then upstream several miles to mouth.

Facilities: None.

Highlights: A lightly fished Interior location with good potential.

Main Species: SF, GR, NP

A small, remote Interior river system, the Zitziana meanders from the southwest Kuskokwim Mountains down to the Tanana River just west of the Kantistina drainage. A fair amount of swamp and bog water gives it a brown, tannic-stained color. Its lower reaches, however, are ideal habitat for northern pike. Because of its remoteness, it receives very little angling pressure. A local favorite among residents of Manley Hot Springs, the "Zit" has a history of producing good angling for at least three important sportfish species. Northern pike, the obvious favorite, are taken at the Tanana confluence and upstream for several miles. Typically weighing six to eight pounds, they are aggressive and plentiful, and best fished during summer and early fall. Sheefish are also present on the lower Zitziana, and yield good catches where the off-colored water of the drainage mixes with the silty Tanana River. Generally not very large (four to six pounds average, up to about 12 pounds) the Zitziana shees are quite numerous. Arctic grayling are also encountered in spring and fall during the annual migrations to and from summer feeding grounds in the headwaters. The surrounding country is totally wild, enhancing the experience for anyone taking the time to explore this underutilized location.

Cosna River System

Location: Lower Tanana River drainage, 110 miles west of Fairbanks.

Access: By floatplane from Fairbanks or by boat from Manley Hot Springs (launch from the Hot Springs Slough to reach the mouth of the Cosna via the Tanana River).

Facilities: None.

Highlights: A remote Interior river with great angling potential for northern pike.

Main Species: NP

Like the Zitziana River to the east, the Cosna originates from a highland region of the Kuskokwim Mountains in central Alaska. Meandering considerably during its northward course to a confluence with the glacial Tanana, the Cosna is a true wilderness drainage, with a reputation for good northern pike fishing. Receiving very little angling effort, mostly at the mouth where its slightly tannic waters hit the silty Tanana, the Cosna drainage has miles of highly productive water, as it is an active feeding ground for hungry northerns and even a few sheefish.

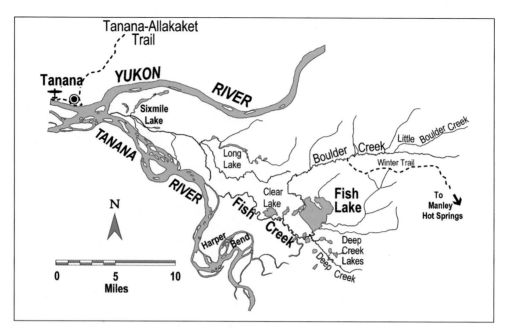

The summer and early fall months are without a doubt the best times to hit its waters. Try the slow, deep stretches where pike between four and ten pounds (even larger) have a habit of lurking for prey. Sheefish are less common and, for the most part, are only caught incidentally. Fair numbers of Arctic grayling are also available in spring and fall.

Chitanana River System

Location: Lower Tanana River drainage, 115 miles west of Fairbanks.

Access: Experienced floatplane pilots may land near the mouth of Chitanana on the mainstem Tanana; wheelplanes can land on the large gravel bar southeast of the confluence.

Facilities: None.

Highlights: A very remote drainage, with outstanding potential for northern pike fishing.

Main Species: NP

The Chitanana River, also known as Redlands Creek, originates from the northwest slopes of Chitanatala Mountains, west of the Kantishna drainage, where it flows north and east towards the glacial Tanana. Not a particularly broad river, it is nonetheless quite vast, with considerable meandering, slow-moving water—perfect conditions for large numbers of toothy pike. Rarely fished, the Chitanana seldom disappoints the few anglers who make the effort to try its waters during the peak of pike season.

This tannic-stained river, with its classic northern pike water, has an abundance of fish in the 4 to 10-pound range, and ample numbers much larger. (This area of the Tanana is known for its monster pike, up to 30 pounds and more.) Casting flashy spoons into the dark waters can result in an occasional sheefish as well, especially when fishing deep near the confluence where the clearer waters of the Chitanana mix with the silty Tanana. You can also expect fair numbers of Arctic grayling during the spring and fall months. Along with

the Cosna River, the Chitanana has yet to be "discovered" and can still offer some fabulous fishing before the masses work it over.

Fish Creek System

Location: Lower Tanana River drainage, 115 miles NW of Fairbanks.

Access: By floatplane, using the mainstem Tanana near the mouth of Fish Creek, or by wheelplanes, landing at Fish Creek Island (anglers use canoes or inflatable rafts to ferry over to the fishing area).

Facilities: None.

Highlights: A small but famous stream known for its healthy pike population.

Main Species: NP

This meandering system begins at Fish Lake, a fair-sized body of water about 20 miles southeast of the town of Tanana. Known for its high productivity, Fish Creek receives a fair amount of angling pressure for northern pike, with a reputation for trophy specimens. (The old state record fish of 38 pounds was taken from the mouth back in 1978.) Fishing in this drainage continues true to its reputation, with many fine pike still reported.

Considerably smaller in size and length than many other rivers along the Tanana, Fish Creek manages to hold its own because it has all the necessary ingredients for a healthy population of large northerns—plenty of sloughs, braided channels, ponds, and still backwaters, with abundant forage in the form of whitefish and suckers. The water is tannic-stained from heavy bog and tundra infiltration.

Most anglers concentrate their attention on the lower stream area and do very well there all through summer into fall, for pike in the four to ten-pound class, with occasional catches up to 20 pounds or more. Spoons, top water plugs, and big, bushy flies are the ticket, according to locals, who insist the new state record is lurking somewhere within the area's deep, dark waters.

MIDDLE YUKON RIVER

With its many meandering tributaries and associated lakes and sloughs, the winding, expansive Middle Yukon dominates the Interior region and provides major habitat for a variety of important sportfish, including chum and king salmon, northern pike, sheefish, and grayling. Carrying a substantial silt load, the river's sportfish potential is concentrated in clear tributary lakes, sloughs, and streams, some well known for outstanding angling, such as the Nowitna, Tozitna, Ray, Dall, Hodzana, and Melozitna rivers and others. Access is usually by riverboat from Fairbanks, the Dalton Highway bridge, or major communities along the Yukon (Galena, Ruby, Tanana, or Manley).

Melozitna River System

Location: Central Yukon River drainage, 230 miles west of Fairbanks.

Access: By floatplane from Fairbanks and other hubs (to mainstem Yukon near the confluence or straighter sections of the middle river). Boat access from Yukon River villages possible.

Facilities: None.

Highlights: A vast, remote river system with significant adventure fishing potential.

Main Species: NP, GR, SF

The Melozitna River originates in the Slokhenjikh Hills of the Ray Mountains in central Alaska, and flows southwest over 200 miles to join the Yukon River near Ruby. It is a slow-moving river in the upper reaches, draining a significant area with many small ponds and muskeg swamps, which greatly influence the water clarity. The river picks up speed as it moves through scenic Melozitna Canyon (Class II and III) until the last few miles, where it slows down just prior to reaching the Yukon. Fairly remote but productive, the Melozitna offers good angling opportunities throughout for several popular sportfish species.

Northern pike are abundant in the middle section of the Melozitna as this area is ideal habitat—slow, deep water with numerous sloughs. While the action can be fast and furious for anglers in spots, the fish are seldom very large. (A typical Melozitna pike weighs four to ten pounds, but larger specimens are frequently taken.) The lower river section is generally too swift for pike, though a few fish may be taken at the confluence.

During the summer months, anglers whipping flies and tossing small spinners may connect with feisty Arctic grayling up to 18 inches or more in any of the many clear tributaries from the headwaters to the mouth. Selecting swift, clear streams to feed in during the warmer months, the grayling move back into the mainstem in fall when temperatures cool. Hot Springs Creek is one popular spot for great flyfishing for this species.

Salmon are also present in the Melozitna. Chums are the most abundant, but a few kings may be encountered spawning in some of the tributaries. In July, large numbers of summer-run chum ascend the river destined for suitable clearwater spawning areas,

yet they do not support any extensive fishery and are only caught incidentally. In midsummer, it is possible to hook sheefish in the four to twelve-pound range at the mouth, with fair action to be expected. These fish will be feeding and are intercepted here on their way upstream to fall spawning grounds. Charr are also taken now and then from the lower mainstem and a few fast flowing tributaries (Fox and Grayling creeks).

The Melozitna River does not receive a great amount of angling effort and is mostly fished by folks from nearby Ruby and Galena, who access the lower river by boat. It is also possible to raft/kayak from floatplane put-in locations along the mainstem down to the Yukon (there are three sets of rapids, including some impassable falls, 14 to 16 miles from the mouth in Melozitna Canyon). Given the size, character, and productivity of this system, the Melozitna will continue to attract more and more adventure anglers in search of new rivers.

Nowitna River System ★★★

Location: Central Yukon River drainage, 190 miles west of Fairbanks.

Access: By boat from the nearby town of Ruby on the Yukon, or by plane from Fairbanks or Galena, landing on the mainstem Nowitna, sloughs, lakes, or the larger Yukon River.

Facilities: None.

Highlights: A significant, remote clearwater Interior drainage with excellent fishing for big northern pike.

Main Species: SF, GR, NP

Designated a Wild and Scenic River, the Nowitna rises from the northwest slopes of the Kuskokwim Mountains and flows 283 miles to its confluence with the Yukon. With a drainage of over 7,000 square miles, it is one of the larger, more productive clearwater systems in the Interior (over 14,000 lakes and ponds lie within the national wildlife refuge that encompasses the lower and middle portions of the Nowitna River), with considerable habitat for slow-water species which, up to now, have received scant attention from anglers.

Over the past few years, more and more interest has been directed toward the Nowitna's abundant and potentially large northern pike. These greedy water wolves are found throughout much of the river and reach weights of up to 32 pounds (sometimes larger), with specimens over 20 pounds not uncommon. Due to prime habitat, particularly on the middle and lower mainstem and adjoining lakes, the fish are year-round residents, with phenomenal catch rates reported among anglers fishing during the summer months. The lower portions of major tributaries also yield good numbers of pike, including the Sulatna, Little Mud, Lost, and Big Mud rivers, and Grand Creek.

Resident sheefish are found throughout most of the system with the greatest concentrations occurring in the middle and lower mainstem Nowitna, sloughs, and lower portions of major tributaries. Lakes in this area only contain small numbers of sheefish. Good action can be expected along the Nowitna River in summer and fall, and Sulatna River in September and October, for large spawners typically weighing between 6 and 15 pounds. Arctic grayling are also found in fishable numbers in the mainstem during spring and fall, while fairly swift headwater tributaries are generally better in summer.

Other species like salmon and charr are available, but in lesser numbers. Both summer and fall runs of chum salmon ascend the Nowitna, spawning in various locations throughout the drainage. Silver salmon have also been reported but are far less numerous, while a small population of stunted, resident charr are present in a few tributaries, such as California Creek and the Sulukna River.

The Nowitna is becoming increasingly popular for floating, which is a great way for anglers to discover the superb fishing and wildlife on one of the more remote rivers of Alaska's great Interior. Put-in is via small plane at the Meadow Creek confluence, with take-out at the Yukon River, after about 250 miles of mostly Class I water.

Tozitna River

Location: Central Yukon River drainage, 140 miles west of Fairbanks.

Access: By boat from the community of Tanana (via the Yukon River), or by floatplane from Fairbanks or Galena, landing on the mainstem Yukon River near the Tozitna River confluence.

Facilities: None.

Highlights: A largely remote and unexplored river system with good sheefish and pike fishing potential.

Main Species: SF, NP

Draining the south slopes of the Ray Mountains, the tannic-stained Tozitna meanders southward to the Yukon some 135 miles. Not quite the size of the nearby Melozitna and Nowitna rivers, it is nonetheless a significant system consisting of numerous small lakes, ponds, and clearwater streams offering good sportfishing opportunities for anyone willing to take the time to explore its isolated waters.

Except for some of the creeks at the headwaters, the mainstem Tozitna is slow-flowing, with many sloughs and oxbow lakes, particularly on the lower section near the mouth. The little angling pressure that does take place occurs where the Tozitna empties into the silty waters of the Yukon. Fishing is good overall, with sheefish and northern pike being the more sought-after gamefish species. (During the summer months, look for feeding sheefish at the mouth where the two drainages mix.) Flashy spoons tossed into the glacial Yukon and retrieved deep into the clearer Tozitna often produce vicious strikes. Northern pike are spread throughout the lower and middle river. The best action occurs in areas with characteristic pike habitat, such as sloughs, oxbow lakes, and outlets of tributaries, including the mouth of the Tozitna. There is plenty of prey in the river, as evidenced by the huge numbers of whitefish in the system (the state record whitefish came from the Tozitna, at nine pounds). Arctic grayling are sometimes taken in the spring and fall during their migrations between the summer feeding grounds at the headwaters and their overwintering areas in the Yukon River. A few charr are taken in tributaries along the upper river.

Salmon are present in mid-summer and may be caught incidentally when fishing for other species. Kings and chums both spawn in the river, but are usually quite dark when entering the fishery. However, an occasional semi-bright specimen may be hooked at the mouth of the Tozitna.

Generally only subsistence-fished by residents of Tanana Village, there is ample opportunity for high quality sport angling to warrant a visit during the summer months.

Ray River

Location: Central Yukon River drainage, 90 miles NW of Fairbanks.

Access: By boat from the Dalton Highway bridge on the Yukon River, three-and-a-half miles from mouth of Ray. Also by floatplane from Fairbanks, to mainstem Yukon River near the Ray confluence.

Facilities: None.

Highlights: A popular Interior location for boaters, with easy access and good fishing for northern pike.

Main Species: NP

Smaller than most popular drainages on the Yukon, the Ray nonetheless holds substantial angling opportunities. Originating from the north slope of the Ray Mountains, the river meanders southward to the silty Yukon. The lower river is fairly wide, and is navigable to boaters for at least six to eight miles up the mainstem. For many years it has been a local hot spot, and continues to produce great pike fishing even today.

Although a few incidental sheefish may be taken from the mouth of the Ray in early fall, the main fishery is for northern pike. Generally not known to produce very large fish (three to ten pounds), the river does hold some good, consistent action for these scrappy fighters, with occasional catches into the teens. The last mile or so of the river is sometimes a hot spot, but pike may be encountered in numbers throughout much of the drainage, except around the headwaters. Deep, slow holes and pools often yield a few fish, as do sloughs and still-water areas. Arctic grayling are present in fair numbers in the spring and fall during their annual migrations to and from summer feeding grounds farther upstream. They may be effectively taken using flies and small spinners. For easy access, and a pretty decent shot at pike action on a semi-remote river, the Ray is hard to beat.

YUKON FLATS/UPPER YUKON

The Yukon Flats, a vast (over six-and-a-half million acres) wetland lying between Circle and Stevens Village, is particularly noteworthy for its tens of thousands of lakes, ponds, marshy backwaters, and slow-moving streams—a paradise for big toothy pike and sheefish, as all reports seem to verify. Though this area, like much of the rest, lies well off the beaten path, its potential for high quality wilderness fishing shouldn't be overlooked. Access is by boat or small plane from Fort Yukon, Circle, or other hubs along the Yukon. Some of the better fishing within the Yukon Flats occurs in the lower sections of the major rivers that comprise the upper Yukon headwaters: Hadweenzic, Christian, Chandalar, Sheenjek, Porcupine, and Black rivers.

Dall River System

Location: Upper Yukon River drainage, 95 miles NW of Fairbanks.

Access: By boat from the Yukon River-Dalton Highway bridge, then 20-miles upstream to the Dall River; floatplanes can land on the mainstem Yukon River near the confluence area.

Facilities: None.

Highlights: A noted upper Yukon fishery with trophy pike potential and good grayling fishing.

Main Species: NP, GR

The mainstem Dall originates just south of Dall Mountain near the Arctic Circle, while the west and east forks flow out of the surrounding uplands within the Yukon Flats National Wildlife Refuge. It is a very extensive drainage, comprised of numerous clearwater streams, lakes of varying size, and stillwater sloughs—the ideal habitat for pike, sheefish, and other "slow-water" species. The Dall is especially known for its hefty northerns. (A typical pike weighs anywhere between four and twelve pounds, with larger pike not uncommon—some old northerns up to 25 and 30 pounds have been taken.)

Most angling activity in this system occurs at or near the confluence of the Dall and Yukon rivers, but fishing is noteworthy in the lower sections of many adjoining streams and lakes, such as the area around the East Fork. Although infrequently caught, sheefish there sometimes attack flashy spoons meant for pike. These silvery, aerial fighters are usually hooked where the clear waters of the Dall mix with the silty Yukon. Sometimes Arctic grayling are encountered in good numbers on the lower river, especially in the spring and fall, though good action can be found during the brief summer months near the headwaters in small streams, lakes and ponds. This river is one of the better bets for a do-it-yourself trip, as the fish are abundant and aggressive and the access relatively easy.

Birch-Beaver Creek System

Location: Upper Yukon River drainage, 50 to 125 miles north of Fairbanks.

Access: By boat from Steese Highway. For Beaver Creek, put in just north of Fairbanks on Nome Creek; for Birch Creek, access at Mile 94.5 and town of Circle.

Facilities: None.

Highlights: A vast watershed with good angling and great float trip possibilities.

Main Species: NP, GR

Birch Creek originates within the Steese National Conservation Area on the east side of the White Mountains, then flows mostly through upland plateaus, forested valleys, and heavy marshland northward to the Yukon River. Beaver Creek, on the other hand, begins in the midst of the White Mountains National Recreation Area and runs through an area with rolling hills, jagged mountain peaks and, finally, the marshy Yukon Flats to the glacial Yukon River. Both systems are designated Wild and Scenic Rivers and are popular with floaters wanting to experience a remote yet accessible part of Alaska.

Birch and Beaver creeks are connected through a long channel towards the lower end of the drainages, but in reality they are two separate systems. The fishing in both can be outstanding, with northern pike and Arctic grayling being the dominant species. Pike are most abundant in the lower areas of the systems where ideal habitat can be found, such as sloughs, ponds, oxbow lakes, and a lot of deep, slow-flowing water. Although small pike may be found up near the headwaters, the larger fish are generally found on the lower end. The drainages are not heavily fished due to their remoteness, but anglers who do fish here are able to find northerns that may weigh as much as 20 pounds or more.

Arctic grayling thrive in the headwaters where the current is swift and deep pools and riffles are present. Action can be very good at times during the summer months using flies and spinners. Feeding sheefish are taken incidentally in the fall while pike fishing at the mouths of Birch and Beaver creeks, though they seldom ascend the systems for more than a few miles.

Floating the headwaters allows fishermen the enjoyment of the very scenic upper sections around White Mountains. A trip down Beaver Creek (approx. 127 miles from highway to Victoria Creek take-out by floatplane) consists of Class I water. For the most part, Birch Creek (126 miles from put-in to take-out at Circle) is Class I also, except for a few Class III rapids that must be negotiated. Keep in mind that after long dry spells the water can be very low, making for difficult passage. Kayaks and canoes are best suited for these trips. The mouths of these two drainages, and surrounding lakes, can also be reached by floatplane from Fairbanks or nearby hubs.

Charley River

Location: Upper Yukon River drainage, 125 miles east of Fairbanks.

Access: By small plane from Fairbanks or other hubs.

Facilities: None.

Highlights: A superb wilderness float trip with great scenery, whitewater, and potentially good fishing.

Main Species: NP, GR

Originating at the 4,000-foot level of the Mertie Mountains within Yukon-Charley Rivers National Preserve, the clearwater Charley flows north 100 miles or so before emptying into the Yukon above Circle. The upper river is swift and rocky, with some braided sections. Arctic grayling are abundant in the mainstem there and in headwater tributaries. The middle section, from Crescent Creek down, has fewer rocky stretches and deeper pools.

The river slows, widens, and deepens as it winds out of the bluffs onto the lowlands surrounding the Yukon, and the last 16 miles or so below Dewey Creek hold northern pike, with the best chances for angling located near the Yukon River confluence. (The river runs clear to the Bonanza Creek confluence, below which it has a tannic stain.) Expect fair action using flashy spoons and wobblers in sloughs and deep holes with slow current.

If you are spending some time at the mouth of the Charley where it meets the silty Yukon, you may hook sheefish in June and July. Don't be surprised to find a salmon (KS, SS, and CS) on the end of the line, either, as they congregate there en route to spawning destinations upriver, beginning in midsummer.

Charley River is rated Class II with some stretches of Class III rapids. Usually running low and clear in the summer (particularly up near the headwaters), the river has a habit of rising several feet in mere hours after rainstorms, which may create a hazard for floaters. Put-in is either at Gelvin strip near Hosford Creek, or farther up near the headwaters at the Three-finger Charley strip (about 20 miles north of Joseph on the Middle Fork of the Forty-Mile River). Takeout is either at the confluence with the Yukon (up to a ten-day trip from the headwaters), or farther down the Yukon at Circle (another two-day float).

EASTERN BROOKS RANGE

This large area—from the south fork of the Koyukuk River to the Canadian border—contains some very significant waters, like the Chandalar River and the northern tributaries of the vast Porcupine. Principal highlights in this remote and seldom-visited area include untold miles of pristine grayling streams, virgin pike populations (especially the Chandalar River drainage), a few deep-water lakes with trophy lake trout potential, occasional sheefish, and even some rare opportunities for salmon (the lower Porcupine drainage). Aside from locations reached from the Dalton Highway, access can be expensive, and services scarce—mostly locals operating from Bettles, Coldfoot, Fort Yukon, or Arctic Village. But the potential for high-quality wilderness adventure angling is certainly there.

Old John Lake

Location: Central Brooks Range, Sheenjek River drainage, 230 miles north of Fairbanks.

Access: By floatplane from Fairbanks or Fort Yukon.

Facilities: None.

Highlights: A well-known and beautifully situated Brooks Range lake, famous for lake trout fishing.

Main Species: LT, NP

Located in the upper Sheenjek drainage (tributary to the Porcupine) about ten miles southeast of Arctic Village, Old John Lake has long been known for trophy lake trout and large northern pike fishing. A deep, mountain-basin lake of fairly good size (five miles long), it has produced two of the largest lake trout caught in Alaska.

Natives from Arctic Village, who access it by snowmachine or four-wheeler, fish the lake year-round. Most visiting anglers fly in during spring at break-up (late May to early June) or in fall (September), and enjoy outstanding fishing. The lake and outlet stream also have an abundant Arctic grayling population, and some big northerns have come out of Old John and nearby lakes of the upper Sheenjek and East Fork Chandalar as well.

Upper Chandalar River System ★★★

Location: Eastern Brooks Range, Yukon River drainage, 170 miles north of Fairbanks.

Access: By plane out of Fairbanks, Bettles, Coldfoot, or Fort Yukon to headwater lakes, river bars, or gravel strips (the east side of Chandalar Lake); winter snowmachine access from the Dalton Highway.

Facilities: No public facilities; there is a fishing lodge on the east side of Chandalar Lake.

Highlights: A remote river system with high wilderness sportfishing potential in a pristine setting.

Main Species: LT, NP, GR, CHR

Draining a sizeable portion of the Brooks Range in its journey from headwaters in the Philip Smith Mountains down to the Yukon (it joins the big river near the village of Venetie), the Chandalar is an extensive, multi-forked system with historical significance for gold mining and subsistence hunting and fishing.

There are northern pike, sheefish, and even some salmon in its lower reaches above the Yukon Flats, but it is the upper river, with

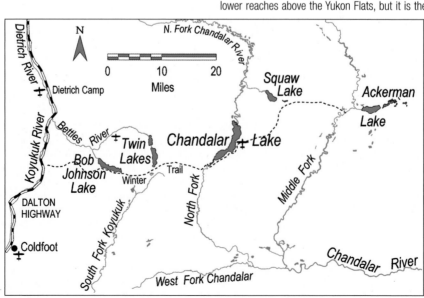

its many swift and pristine headwaters and numerous associated lakes, that has the most exciting fishing possibilities. The larger headwater lakes of the middle and north forks—Chandalar, Squaw and Ackerman—are scenic, deep mountain basins with good lake trout populations. Chandalar probably has the best fishing, with definite trophy potential and good pike action as a bonus. All the lakes have abundant Arctic grayling in their outlet and inlet streams. Chandalar Lake can get turbid from runoff from the North Fork; therefore, fishing is best right at break-up (mid-May to early June) and in fall (late August through September). The three main forks (especially the East Fork) of the Chandalar all have a proliferation of foothill lakes in their upper reaches—many with untouched pike and grayling populations—and all very scenic, with an abundance of wildlife.

Though fly-ins to Chandalar, Ackerman, or Squaw lakes in spring or fall (perhaps combined with hunting) are the most common way of fishing the system, a raft/kayak trip down from the headwaters to points along the lower river (Venetie) can be done by experienced boaters, and combines some exciting sportfish exploration with pristine whitewater. (Stretches of rocky shallows and rapids can be a problem, depending on water levels; check with local air taxis for conditions before making final arrangements.)

Jim River-Prospect Creek

Location: Eastern Brooks Range, Koyukuk River drainage, 165 miles north of Fairbanks.

Access: By car via the Dalton Highway to bridge crossings (Milepost 135, 140, 141, and 144). A winter road from Bettles provides additional access.

Facilities: None.

Highlights: A great roadside fishery with ample opportunities for exploration by raft or on foot.

Main Species: NP, GR

Jim River and Prospect Creek are known as two of the better fishing locations along the Dalton Highway/Haul Road. Tributaries of the South Fork Koyukuk, these clear, shallow streams, in their reaches beyond the immediate area of the highway, can provide some decent Arctic grayling fishing, with some chances for northern pike and a few salmon (see below) as added bonuses.

If you're fishing the Haul Road, you'll probably want to stop at one of the Jim River or Prospect Creek crossings. Most folks stop and fish by the road, but it's best to float and fish by canoe or raft from the highway put-ins, then take out at the Bettles Winter Road that crosses at several points below (either ten miles down on the Jim River or a few miles farther on the Koyukuk). The idea is to get beyond the frequently fished stretches of the river to more virgin water. Spring and early fall are the best times for grayling, while mid-summer brings opportunities for catch-and-release salmon fishing.

Note: Salmon fishing is prohibited within a five mile corridor of the highway on either side.

Bob Johnson (Big) and Twin Lakes

Location: Central Brooks Range, 195 miles north of Fairbanks.

Access: By small plane from Fairbanks, Bettles, or Coldfoot, or by trail from the Dalton Highway.

Facilities: None.

Highlights: Remote, beautiful clearwater lakes with good fishing.

Main Species: LT, NP, GR

No discussion of Brooks Range fishing locations would be complete without mention of these two well-known, neighboring mountain lakes: Bob Johnson (Big) and Twin. Very scenic, deep-basin lakes that lie in the upper Koyukuk drainage east of Wiseman and just west of Chandalar Lake, Bob Johnson and Twin have been traditional sites for hunting camps, as well as popular Brooks Range recreation spots for vacationers out of Fairbanks. Scattered private cabins exist along the lakes and in the vicinity.

These clear lakes have good fishing for lake trout and Arctic grayling, with pike present in Bob Johnson. Twin is deeper and generally has bigger lake trout on average, although both lakes have seen a decline in larger fish over the years due to increasing angling pressure. The outlet and inlet streams (and connecting stream on Twin) right at break-up (late May usually) are probably the best bet for fishing these two.

Recommended Lodges/Guides/Outfitters/Air taxis

Denali West Lodge: P.O. Box 40, Lake Minchumina, AK 99757, (907) 674-3112, 888-607-5566, *www.denaliwest.com* Lodging, guided fishing, Kantishna drainage.

Tangle River Inn: P.O. Box 783, Delta Junction, AK 99737, (907) 895-4022, *www.tangleriverinn.com* Full service lodge, rental cabins, guided fishing, Tangle Lakes.

Lanigan's Retreat: 353 Irish Lane, Fairbanks, AK 99712, (907) 490-5977, *www.alaska.net/~lanigans/* Lodge-based guided fishing, Chandalar Lake area.

Alaska Fishing & Raft Adventures: 269 Topside Rd., Fairbanks, AK 99712, (800) 890-3229, (907) 455-RAFT, *www.aktours.net* Guided float fishing, Chena and Nowitna rivers, Beaver Creek.

Arctic Grayling Adventures: P.O. Box 83707, Fairbanks, AK 99708, (907) 479-0479, *www.wildernessfishing.com* Guided fishing, rental cabins, Tanana, Nenana, Teklanika rivers.

North Country River Charters: 4741 Harvard Circle, Fairbanks, Alaska 99709, (907) 479-7116, *www.ncrc.alaska.com* Trophy northern pike expeditions, Yukon River.

Salcha River Guest Camp: 2376 Nugget Loop, Fairbanks AK 99709, (888) 355-8060, *www.salchariver.com* Guided outpost camp fishing, Salcha River.

Bettles Lodge/Bettles Air: P.O. Box 27, Bettles, AK 99726, (800) 770-5111, *www.bettleslodge.com* Lodging and air taxi service/outfitting, central Brooks Range.

Alaska Outdoor Rentals: P.O. Box 82388, Fairbanks AK 99708, (907) 457-2453, *www.akbike.com* Canoe, kayak rentals and transportation, Interior Alaska.

Alaska Yukon Tours: P.O. Box 221, Fort Yukon, AK 99740, (907) 662-2727, *www.akyukontours.com* Guided trophy northern pike, sheefish, grayling fishing, Yukon Flats.

Chena River Aviation/Alaskan Helicopter Charters: 735 Lowood Road, North Pole, AK 99705, (907) 488-4439, *www.chenariveraviation.or1.com*

Marina Air: 1195 Shypoke Drive, Fairbanks, AK 99709, (907) 479-5684. Fly-in fishing trips, cabin rentals, Minto Flats and other Interior locations.

Forty-Mile Air: P.O. Box 539, Mile 1313 Alaska Highway, Tok, AK 99780, (907) 883-5191, *www.40-mileair.com* Air taxi and drop-off fishing, upper Tanana area.

Yukon Air Service: P.O. Box 84107, Fairbanks, AK 99708, (907) 479-3993 (winter), (907) 662-2445 (summer). Air taxi, upper Yukon drainages.

Wright Air Service: P.O. Box 60142, Fairbanks, AK 99706, (907) 474-0502, (800) 478-0502.

General information

Alaska Department of Natural Resources: Division of Parks and Outdoor Recreation, 3700 Airport Way, Fairbanks, AK 99709, (907) 451-2705, *www.dnr.state.ak.us/parks/index.htm* For information on state campgrounds, recreation sites, cabins, ice fishing huts.

Alaska Department of Fish & Game: Sport Fish Division, 1300 College Road, Fairbanks, AK 99701, (907) 459-7207, *www.sf.adfg.state.ak.us/region3/sf_r3home.cfm*

Bureau of Land Management: Northern Field Office, 1150 University Avenue, Fairbanks, AK 99709, (907) 474-2200, *http://aurora.ak.blm.gov/*

Kanuti National Wildlife Refuge: 101 12th Ave., Box 11, Fairbanks, AK 99701, (907) 456-0329, *http://kanuti.fws.gov/*

Nowitna National Wildlife Refuge: P.O. Box 287, Galena, AK 99741, (907) 656-1231, *http://nowitna.fws.gov/*

Tetlin National Wildlife Refuge: P.O. Box 779, Tok, AK 99780, (907) 883-5312, *http://tetlin.fws.gov/*

Yukon Flats National Wildlife Refuge: 101 12 Avenue, Box 14, Fairbanks, AK 99701, (907) 456-0440, *http://yukonflats.fws.gov/*

USGS Maps Reference

Tetlin Lakes: Tanacross A-4, A-3, A-2; Nabesna D-1, D-2, D-3, C-1, C-2.

Tangle Lakes System: Gulkana D-5; Mount Hayes A-4, A-5.

Delta Clearwater River: Mount Hayes D-3; Big Delta A-3, A-4.

Goodpaster River System: Eagle B-6, C-6; Big Delta A-1, A-2, A-3, A-4, B-1, B-2, B-3, C-1, C-2.

Quartz Lake: Big Delta A-4.

Salcha River: Circle A-1, A-2; Big Delta B-5, B-6, C-2, C-3, C-4, C-5, C-6.

Birch Lake: Big Delta B-6.

Harding Lake: Big Delta B-6.

Chena River System: Circle A-1, A-2, A-3, A-4, A-5, A-6; Livengood A-1; Big Delta C-4, C-5, C-6, D-4, D-5, D-6; Fairbanks D-1, D-2.

Minto Lakes System: Fairbanks D-4.

Chatanika River System: Circle A-6, B-4, B-5, B-6; Livengood A-1, A-2, A-3, A-4, A-5, B-2, B-3; Fairbanks D-2, D-3, D-4.

Nenana River System: Healy A-2, A-3, A-4, B-2, B-3, B-4, B-5, B-6, C-2, C-3, C-4, C-5, C-6, D-3, D-4, D-5, D-6; Fairbanks A-4, A-5, A-6, B-4, B-5, B-6, C-5.

Kantishna River System: Mount McKinley A-2, A-3, A-4, A-5, B-1, B-2, B-3, B-4, B-5, C-1, C-2, C-3, C-4, C-5, C-6, D-1, D-2, D-3, D-4, D-5; Healy B-6, C-6, D-6; Fairbanks A-6, B-6, C-6, D-6; Kantishna River A-1, A-2, A-3, A-4, B-1, B-2, B-3, C-1, C-2, D-1.

Zitziana River System: Kantishna River B-3, C-2, C-3, D-1, D-2.

Cosna River System: Kantishna B-4, B-5, C-4, C-5, D-3, D-4.

Chitanana River System: Kantishna River C-5, C-6, D-4, D-5.

Fish Creek System: Tanana A-3, A-4.

Melozitna River System: Melozitna A-4, A-5, B-4, C-1, C-2, C-3; Ruby D-5, D-6.

Nowitna River System: Ruby A-1, A-2, A-3, A-4, B-1, B-2, B-3, C-2, C-3, C-4, D-3; Kantishna River A-6, B-6; Medfra B-6, C-4, C-5, C-6, D-4, D-5.

Tozitna River: Tanana A-5, A-6, B-5, B-6, C-2, C-3, C-4, C-5, C-6, D-5.

Ray River: Livengood D-6; Tanana C-2, D-1, D-2; Bettles A-1.

Dall River System: Beaver A-5, A-6, B-6.

Birch-Beaver Creek Systems: Livengood B-1, B-2, C-1, C-2, D-1, D-2; Circle B-1, B-2, B-3, B-4, C-1, C-2, C-3, C-4, C-5, C-6, D-1, D-2, D-3, D-4, D-5, D-6; Fort Yukon A-2, A-3, A-4, A-5, A-6, B-3, B-4, B-5, B-6, C-5; Beaver A-1, A-2, B-1.

Charley River: Charley River A-4, A-5, B-4; Eagle C-6, D-4, D-5, D-6.

Old John Lake: Arctic A-2.

Upper Chandalar River: Chandalar A-1, A-2, A-3, A-4, A-5, B-1, B-2, B-3, B-4, C-1, C-2, C-3, C-4, D-1, D-2, D-3, D-4, D-5; Christian A-6, B-5, B-6, C-5, C-6, D-4, D-5, D-6; Fort Yukon C-4, C-5, D-5; Philip Smith Mountains A-2, A-3, A-4.

Jim River-Prospect Creek: Bettles D-1, D-2, D-3; Beaver D-6.

Bob Johnson (Big) and Twin Lakes: Chandalar B-5, C-5.

Regulations/Information

Most remote waters in the Interior have unrestricted fishing seasons, and very liberal bag limits. Certain waters within Tanana drainage (and Yukon drainages along Trans-Alaska Pipeline) have seasonal restrictions or are closed year-round to fishing salmon and/or pike and/or taking grayling. Miscellaneous restrictions apply on use of bait and treble hooks in certain waters, with some size restrictions on northern pike as well. Always check current Regulations Summary for Region III (Arctic-Yukon-Kuskokwim Regulatory Areas) or contact regional/field offices, ADF&G for information when planning a fishing trip to this region.

Delta Junction: (907) 895-4632   **Fairbanks:** (907) 459-7207

Recorded information: (907) 459-7385

Online info: *www.sf.adfg.state.ak.us/statewide/regulations/aykregs.cfm*

Interior Species

LOCATION	KING SALMON	RED SALMON	PINK SALMON	CHUM SALMON	SILVER SALMON	STEELHEAD	RAINBOW	CUTTHROAT	CHARR	GRAYLING	LAKE TROUT	NORTHERN PIKE	SHEEFISH	HALIBUT	LINGCOD	SALMON SHARK	ROCKFISH	FSHG. PRESSURE
Tetlin Lakes Area										☺	☺	★						✓
Tangle Lakes System										★	☺							M
Delta Clearwater River				R	★					☺								☹
Goodpaster River System	C			C						☺		★						M
Quartz Lake	LL				LL		☺		✓									☹
Salcha River	☺			✓	R					☺			✓					☹
Birch Lake	LL				LL		✓		✓	✓								☹
Harding Lake									✓		✓							☹
Chena River System	☺			☺						★		R	✓					☹
Chena Lakes	LL				LL		✓		✓	✓								☹
Minto Flats	R			R						R		✓	★					M
Chatanika River System	✓			✓						☺		✓	☺					☹
Nenana River System	✓			✓	☺				✓	☺	✓	R	✓					M
Kantishna River System	R			✓	✓					☺	R	R	★					✓
Zitziana River System										✓		✓	★					R
Cosna River System										✓		✓	★					R
Chitanana River System										✓		✓	★					R
Fish Creek System										R			★					M
Melozitna River System	R			✓					✓	★		☺	☺					R
Nowitna River System				✓	R					R		☺	★					✓
Tozitna River	R			R						✓		☺	☺					R
Ray River										☺		R	✓					✓
Dall River System										☺		R	✓					✓
Birch-Beaver Creek System	R			R	R					☺		R	☺					✓
Charley River	R			R	R					☺		R	✓					✓
Old John Lake										☺	★		☺					✓
Upper Chandalar River	R			R						☺	☺	R	☺					R
Jim River-Prospect Creek	R			✓						☺			✓					✓
Bob Johnson (Big) and Twin Lakes										☺	☺	✓						✓

Legend:

- Not present
- **R** Rare
- ✓ Fishable numbers (or light pressure)
- ☺ Good fishing
- ★ Excellent fishing
- **LL** Landlocked species
- **C** Present, but fishing closed
- **M** Moderate pressure
- ☹ Heavy pressure

Southcentral Alaska

On a clear creek above the silty tidewaters of Turnagain Arm, an interesting assortment of anglers shares a stretch of water and some warm August sunshine. Some retired folks, a young couple with two small children, a woman who looks like a school teacher, a few business types, and others crowd a piece of riverbank no bigger than your driveway, flipping lines and lures nonstop in all directions. The intensity and anticipation grow unbearable as the tide surges in, and suddenly a commotion erupts as someone connects with a big, bright fish that catapults instantly toward the ocean. Seconds later, a lad in a designer sweatshirt screams as another salmon bursts through the rapids and threatens to pull his rod from his hands. The silvers are in! Pandemonium ensues. Like a chain reaction, the surge of salmon spreads up the creek and wreaks havoc on rods and limbs everywhere. For the next hour, a wild melee of leaping salmon and screaming reels, mad downriver dashes and muddy smiles takes over, as every man, woman, and child gets a taste of salmon fishing the way it was meant to be.

This scene would be remarkable enough just for its level of fishing excitement but, when you consider that these folks are less than a 30-minute drive from Alaska's largest city, Anchorage (260,000 people), in the heart of the state's most populous region, it's no less than astounding. Most states can't match this kind of angling in their wildest backcountry, yet Alaska's most "developed" region—Southcentral—can provide an abundance of similar opportunities no more than a short distance by car, plane, boat, or foot from any of its major (and modern) towns and cities. And while it's true that most of the more popular and accessible of these locations see quite a bit of use by Alaska standards, Southcentral still has plenty of quality fishing that is light years beyond anything available in the Lower 48.

Heading out, upper Susitna Valley

291

Homer Spit, Kachemak Bay, lower Cook Inlet

Southcentral Alaska is the region of the mainland that fronts the north Gulf. It includes the vast Susitna and Copper valleys, Prince William Sound, the Kenai Peninsula, Cook Inlet, and the Kodiak Island complex, in an area of great diversity, scenic beauty, and rich opportunities for the sport angler. With its benign weather, vibrant economy, and roads connecting to the rest of the mainland and Canada, it's small wonder that the majority of Alaskans choose to live and play here.

In many ways the most well-endowed of the state's six physiographic regions, Southcentral offers a range of stream, lake, and marine fishing experiences that is unmatched anywhere else in Alaska. Everything, from saltwater salmon and halibut, to trophy rainbows to big lake trout and grayling, is possible within a short drive, hike or fly-in to Southcentral's coast or mountains.

Indeed, as the one destination that seems to have it all, including the proximity and easy access to many other famous Alaska attractions like Denali National Park, Lake Clark, Fairbanks, and the great Interior, Southcentral is the gateway for a major share of the state's summer tourist trade, including many anglers.

COUNTRY, CLIMATE & FISHING CONDITIONS

Dominated by the massive arc of the Alaska Range and associated coastal mountains, Southcentral has a varied and impressive physiography that includes the state's tallest peaks and largest icefields, immense, silty glacial rivers, extensive tundra uplands, dense coastal rain forests, and some of the world's richest (and most scenic) marine environments.

The weather is surprisingly mild, shielded from Arctic blasts by the high and wide Alaska Range and greatly influenced by the temperate Gulf and warm, moist airflows from the north Pacific. Some of the rainiest and snowiest places in the world are found here, but most of the region is surprisingly dry compared to Alaska's Southeast panhandle. (This is especially true of locations farther in from the coast, which enjoy a more continental climate.) Anchorage, on the north end of Cook Inlet, is shielded by mountains on all sides and receives only about 20 inches of precipitation a year, with winters much milder than in many cities on the U.S. mainland.

After the period of ice break-up in spring, maximum stream runoff usually occurs in May and early June for most non-glacial systems, which usually settle down by early summer. Because of the preponderance of glaciers, however, many Southcentral lakes and streams run tinted, or even turbid, with suspended sediment for much of the year (running clearest from late winter to late spring), making fishing challenging or even impossible in extreme cases. However, as many a visitor has come to learn, some of the most lucrative angling in the region can be found in the multitude of clearwater tributaries draining into these glacial waters. Additionally, experienced guides and local anglers, through years of trial and error, have discovered techniques and lures that consistently produce results—even under the most difficult conditions. (See the species chapters and the various locations descriptions that follow this section for more information on fishing glacial or high water conditions.)

Lacking the abundance of sheltered waters that characterizes most of the Southeast region, Southcentral's significant marine fishing frequently involves forays into waters along the notorious North Gulf Coast, with volatile weather and tempestuous seas always a possibility. Smaller boat, recreational sport-fishing (and some excellent roadside opportunity) is confined mostly to Prince William Sound, Lower Cook Inlet, Resurrection Bay, and parts of Kodiak/Afognak Island.

ACCESS, SERVICES & COSTS

Perhaps Southcentral's most attractive feature is the well-developed network of access, services, and facilities that allows visitors of any age, physical condition, or economic status to enjoy a generous measure of the unbeatable fishing. There are four major highway systems, a state ferry, millions of acres of national forests, and scores of parks, campgrounds, and public use cabins, not to mention the hundreds of private lodges, guides, and outfitters eager to help make that dream vacation come true. From lonely lakes tucked high and far in some of North America's most rugged mountain country, to hatchery-enhanced creeks and ponds in the middle of Alaska's largest city, there is an angling adventure for everyone in Southcentral Alaska. Nowhere else in the world will you find the splendors of wilderness so seamlessly matched with the easy comfort and convenience of civilization.

Four major highways—the Glenn, Parks, Seward, and Sterling—connect the major communities of

Ship Creek, downtown Anchorage: salmon fishing in the heart of Alaska's largest city

Southcentral with each other and the outside world (via the Alaska Highway). A state-run railroad and ferry system provide additional access to parts of the region. Commercial airlines service the major hubs of Anchorage, Kenai, Cordova, and Kodiak with daily flights (some connecting from the West Coast and points beyond), while numerous air taxis provide regular connections to the more remote areas. Access to the best Southcentral fishing locations generally involves floatplane or jet boat travel. Costs vary with distance and size of party, but are typically less than in most other parts of the state.

WHAT TO EXPECT

Temperate maritime or maritime/continental climate for most of the region. Summers are very pleasant with average highs ranging from 60s to low 70s (°F) (80s possible), lows in the 50s. Winters vary with location, but are generally mild, with moderate to heavy snow loads (five to ten feet total on average). Along the coast, winter highs can reach 40°F or more and lows seldom dip below zero. Inland, conditions are drier and colder. Break-up comes in mid-April to early May, later at elevation, while the rivers and lakes usually freeze over by late October. The sunniest, driest time of year is from April through July; the wettest time is from August through October. Biting insects are a problem usually during the warmest time of year (June to August)only, although they can be quite a nuisance along some coastal rivers well into September.

COSTS:

Guided Fishing Lodges: $450-700/day/person.

Marine Charters: $165-225/day/person.

Riverboat charters: $125-150/half day/person.

Guided Float trips: $239-450/day/person (may include air taxi).

Boat Rentals: $125-150/day.

Remote Cabin Rentals: $95-315/day/person (may include air taxi).

B&B Lodging: $55-120/double.

Hotel Rooms: $139-299/double (Anchorage); $70-197/double (elsewhere).

Car Rentals: $37-70/day.

Mini-Van Rentals: $99-119/day.

RV Rentals: $165-240/day (depending on size).

Air taxi: Supercub: $130-175/hr.; Cessna 180/85: $240-265/hr.; Cessna 206/7: $300-355/hr.; DeHavilland Beaver: $375-465/hr; Turbine Otter: $900-950/hr.

SOUTHCENTRAL SALTWATER RUN TIMING

SPECIES	JAN	FEB	MAR	APR	MAY	JUN	JUL	AUG	SEP	OCT	NOV	DEC
King Salmon												
Silver Salmon												
Red Salmon												
Chum Salmon												
Pink Salmon												
Rockfish												
Halibut												
Salmon Shark												
Lingcod												

▬▬ Available   ▬▬ Peak

Time periods shown for salmon are for nearshore presence. Run timing can vary considerably within region. Always check local contacts for run timing specifics of locations you intend to fish.

SOUTHCENTRAL FRESHWATER RUN TIMING

SPECIES	JAN	FEB	MAR	APR	MAY	JUN	JUL	AUG	SEP	OCT	NOV	DEC
King Salmon												
Silver Salmon												
Red Salmon												
Chum Salmon												
Pink Salmon												
Steelhead												
Rainbow Trout												
Cutthroat Trout												
Charr												
Northern Pike												
Grayling												
Lake Trout												

▬▬ Available   ▬▬ Peak

Note: Time periods shown in blue are for bright fish in the case of salmon entering rivers, or for general availability for resident species. Peak sportfishing periods are shown in red. Run timing can vary somewhat from drainage to drainage within the region. Always check with local contacts for run timing specifics for locations you intend to fish.

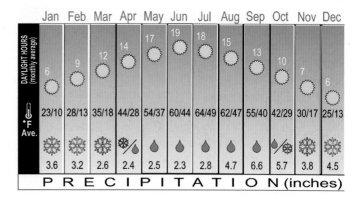

	Jan	Feb	Mar	Apr	May	Jun	Jul	Aug	Sep	Oct	Nov	Dec
DAYLIGHT HOURS (monthly average)	6	9	12	14	17	19	18	15	13	10	7	6
°F Ave.	23/10	28/13	35/18	44/28	54/37	60/44	64/49	62/47	55/40	42/29	30/17	25/13
PRECIPITATION (inches)	3.6	3.2	2.6	2.4	2.5	2.3	2.8	4.7	6.6	5.7	3.8	4.5

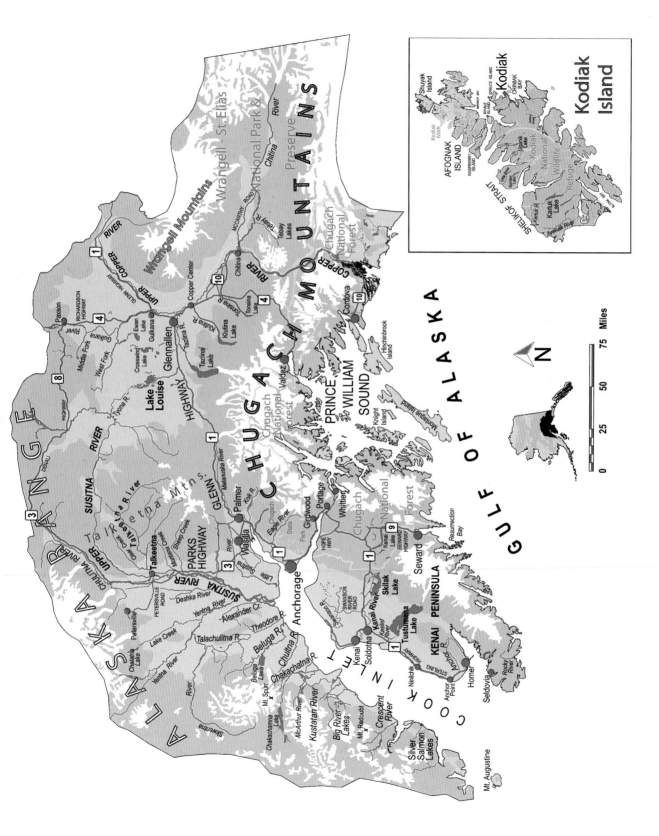

Fall steelhead fishing, Wrangell Mountains

Ken Graham/Accent Alaska

The late, legendary Harry Gaines hefts a trophy king from the emerald waters of the Kenai River. Almost all of the largest chinook taken from Alaska's waters each year come from the Kenai River and lower Cook Inlet.

SOUTHCENTRAL FISHING HIGHLIGHTS

The region's fishing is as varied and impressive as its geography. Abundant runs of all five salmon species occur in numerous coastal streams and lakes, as well as in immense glacial systems like the Susitna and Copper. (These are major producers, even though their fishing potential is confined to clearwater tributaries.)

Southcentral boasts some of Alaska's most accessible and productive marine fishing locations, particularly for salmon and bottomfish. The fabulous fisheries of lower Cook Inlet continue to pump out world-class trophy king salmon and halibut, along with some of Alaska's best rainbow trout, steelhead, and silver salmon fishing on the Kenai Peninsula (and nearby Kodiak Island). These and other northern Gulf waters along the road system are tremendously popular tourist destinations.

If your dream vacation is casting flies in some remote mountain stream or lake, Southcentral's expansive Alaska Range and coastal mountains hold dozens of locations with solitude, gorgeous surroundings, and good fishing for grayling, trout, and charr. Cutthroat trout in the short coastal streams of Prince William Sound, and even some fine northern pike fishing in the lakes of the Matanuska-Susitna valleys, round out the delightful variety of angling possible in the Southcentral region.

60 07 N
149 26 W

CAUGHT AT
SEWARD ALASKA

A good day's fishing along Southcentral's North Gulf Coast

ANCHORAGE AREA

Though most die-hard Alaskan anglers pass by the fishing opportunities in and around Alaska's largest metropolitan area, the fact remains that Anchorage still has the best freshwater fishing of any city its size in America. Where else can you check in to a hotel in the heart of downtown and within a ten-minute walk hook into a bright king or silver salmon? And how many places can boast of at least a dozen or more lakes containing fishable populations of rainbow trout, arctic charr, and landlocked salmon within city limits?

Most of the drainages in the Anchorage area are small, runoff streams that flow swiftly from the abrupt rise of mountains surrounding town. They all hold native populations of charr, trout, and salmon that have been augmented through the years with hatchery plants to meet growing demand for decent local fishing. Almost all of Anchorage's lakes rely totally on seasonal stocking, with landlocked salmon, rainbow trout, charr, and grayling planted.

Though no one would suggest forgoing the more productive and potentially less crowded fishing locales of the Susitna Valley to the north, or the Kenai Peninsula to the south, the streams and lakes of Anchorage can offer some delightful diversion to the traveler with an afternoon to kill, or locals wanting to dip a line after work.

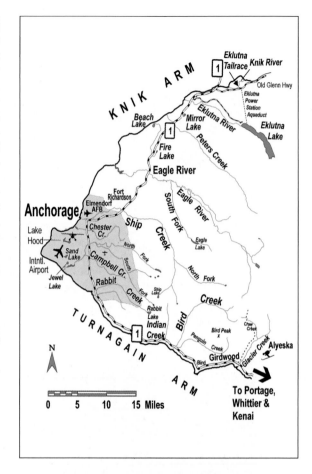

Ship Creek

Location: North Cook Inlet, downtown Anchorage.

Access: By car, off First Avenue and Loop Road near the Port of Anchorage. Both sides of the stream offer parking with foot access throughout. Respect private property.

Facilities: Full services available in Anchorage.

Highlights: Good salmon fishing in the heart of Alaska's largest city.

Main Species: KS, SS, RT

Ship Creek originates high in the Chugach Mountains and flows west through the greater Anchorage area to Knik Arm. It typically runs clear, but may turn quite turbid during periods of heavy rain or hot weather. The upper stream sections are wooded with little development; however, surroundings change drastically as the stream nears it terminus in downtown Anchorage. Salmon fishing takes place in the tidal area of the stream below the Chugach Electric power plant. Although completely lacking the wilderness that is associated with Alaska, angling with the tide can be surprisingly good during the height of salmon season, particularly in deep holes and runs near the road crossings, and Ship Creek is recognized as one of Alaska's top fisheries in terms of angler participation and catch rates. (In some years, the action heats up to provide even better angling success than in the better streams of the Kenai or Susitna.)

Starting in late spring and continuing into midsummer, a run of wild and (mostly) hatchery king salmon returns in good numbers to Ship Creek, drawing huge crowds. Less attention, however, is paid to an equally productive run of silver salmon, which peaks in late summer and continues through most of fall. A fair run of pink salmon is also present during even-numbered years, in addition to a few chums and Dolly Varden charr. The portion of stream between the lower dam near the mouth, and the ADF&G hatchery facility near Elmendorf AFB, has fair rainbow trout fishing.

Warning: *The area open to salmon fishing is heavily influenced by tidal activity; water may rise 10-12 feet or more near the mouth. Use extreme caution in and around mud, and come prepared with good boots/waders.*

Campbell Creek

Location: North Cook Inlet, city of Anchorage.

Access: By car to a multitude of access points from secondary roads, with developed trails leading to and along the stream.

Facilities: Numerous parking areas at or near the water; full visitor services available in Anchorage.

Highlights: A little taste of wilderness, with good salmon and trout fishing, right in Anchorage.

Main Species: SS, RT, DV

Campbell Creek begins in the Chugach Mountains, flowing west through east Anchorage, then south to its terminus in outer Turnagain Arm. It is a clear, fairly swift, gravel bottom stream, with some good holding water scattered throughout, heavily vegetated, and protected for the most part by Campbell Creek Greenbelt. (Several city parks align the banks of the stream.)

It has historically provided Anchorage residents with some fairly productive in-city stream fishing for salmon and trout in a semi-wilderness setting. Today it is open for fishing only above Dimond Boulevard, for silver salmon, rainbow trout, and Dolly Varden charr.

The best salmon fishing occurs during the second half of August in the lower stream area between C St. and Dimond Boulevard, particularly following a good downpour. Most of the charr and trout are found in the upper reaches above Lake Otis Parkway, though the Alaska Department of Fish & Game stocks the middle section of the stream with rainbows every June. Bears are a common sight in upper areas (above the forks at Folker Street), so caution is advised.

Eklutna Tailrace

Location: North Cook Inlet, Knik River, 40 miles NE of Anchorage.

Access: By car to Mile 4.1 on the Old Glenn Highway.

Facilities: Roadside parking.

Highlights: Easily accessed, good salmon fishing, 45 minutes by car from Anchorage.

Main Species: SS, RS, CS, KS

Eklutna tailrace is the terminus for spill water from the Eklutna Hydropower Project, brought down through a tunnel in solid rock from Eklutna Lake in the Chugach Mountains. This greenish-gray glacial outlet runs very slow and deep a few hundred yards from the aqueduct before emptying into the Knik River. Like its headwaters, it has limited natural productivity, but has been augmented through the years by ADF&G stocking (silver and red salmon) to provide decent roadside sport for urban anglers. (There has been renewed stocking effort for king salmon for near-future runs.)

Most of the salmon (silvers, predominantly, in August; reds in July are hard to catch in slow, deep water; a fair number of chums in late summer) are caught at the Knik River confluence, along with a few Dolly Varden charr. Expect good fishing at the peak of the runs; use bait for best results.

Bird Creek

Location: North Cook Inlet, Turnagain Arm, 20 miles SE of Anchorage.

Access: By car to Mile 101.2, Seward Highway.

Facilities: Parking, restrooms on site. Limited services available in nearby communities of Bird and Indian.

Highlights: One of the best Anchorage-area salmon streams.

Main Species: SS, CS, PS

Just past the edge of Anchorage, along Turnagain Arm, lies Bird Creek, one of the most popular (and crowded) roadside stream fishing locations in Southcentral Alaska. Short, rocky, and swift, this semi-glacial to clear Chugach Mountain drainage offers seasonally good fishing for salmon (silvers and pinks mostly; some chum) and Dolly Varden charr.

The lower river (from the mouth approximately one-quarter mile upstream), the only stretch of water open to salmon fishing (all species but kings) is influenced by extreme tidal action. Anglers crowd the muddy banks during the height of the runs and fish the tides with good results, especially when the river runs clear and fish can be seen. Expect shoulder-to-shoulder conditions when the silvers are in (the creek is stocked with early-run fish that come in thick the first half of August), lesser crowding for pinks and chums during the month of July. Upstream of the boundary cables, a quarter of a mile from the highway, there is fair fishing for charr, but be aware of and respect private property along the river.

Portage Area River Systems

Location: Northeast Cook Inlet, Turnagain Arm, 45 miles SE of Anchorage.

Access: By car via the Seward Highway, which crosses all three of the rivers near tidewater. Additional access by jet boats, canoes, or rafts. Hiking is difficult due to dense vegetation.

Facilities: Primitive boat launch at Twentymile and Placer rivers.

Highlights: Semi-remote wilderness streams with good silver salmon and Dolly Varden fishing.

Main Species: SS, DV

The Portage area at the head of Turnagain Arm has three drainages of glacial origin, the Twentymile and Placer rivers and Portage Creek, all within Chugach National Forest. The lower river sections are in open country, with stark reminders of the 1964 earthquake evidenced in the abundant gray stems of dead spruce trees everywhere. (Once a flourishing forest, the whole area subsided during the quake and flooded with saltwater, killing much of the vegetation.) The setting is spectacular, especially on sunny days, as surrounding mountain peaks display an abundance of greenish-blue glaciers, while the slopes are covered with thick forest.

The **Twentymile River** is the larger of the three systems, and originates from ice fields around Twentymile Glacier in the Chugach Mountains, running southward to Turnagain Arm. The lower section near the Seward Highway is wide and slow, but becomes quite swift, shallow, and braided six to seven miles upstream. The most abundant species in the Twentymile are silver, red, and chum salmon and Dolly Varden charr.

Draining out of Portage Lake at the base of world-famous Portage Glacier, **Portage Creek** flows east to silty Turnagain Arm, fairly fast through most of its length, but particularly so on the upper end. Fair to good runs of silver, red, chum, and pink salmon occur in this drainage, along with some Dolly Varden.

Flowing north, the **Placer River** originates from the Spencer Glacier. The lower river is smooth and slow, yet becomes shallow, fast, and braided about two-and-a-half miles upstream from the highway bridge. Placer is known for its strong late run of silver salmon, some specimens of which may weigh up to 18 pounds. Other species of interest include red salmon and Dolly Varden.

Look for clearwater sloughs and stream mouths to target schools of migrating salmon and hungry charr. Keep in mind that many of these hot spots do not have names, but are nonetheless very productive. From mid-August through mid-September is the best time for the peak of the silvers.

ANCHORAGE AREA LAKES

Jewel Lake: One of the most popular angling lakes in Anchorage, located in the south part of town, off Dimond Boulevard. It offers good fishing for stocked rainbow trout, arctic charr, and landlocked salmon, with quite a bit of shore access, along with a ramp (handicap accessible). It is best in late spring and from fall to mid-winter.

DeLong Lake: Accessed off Jewel Lake Road in southwest Anchorage near the airport (at DeLong Lake Park), the lake has good shore access and fair to good fishing for stocked rainbow trout, Arctic charr, and landlocked salmon. It's best in late spring, and from fall to mid-winter.

Campbell Point Lake: A small lake set in a secluded, quiet, wooded part of town (reached from Dimond Boulevard and Jewel Lake Road to Kincaid Park), Campbell Point is stocked with landlocked salmon, rainbow trout, and Arctic charr. Fish it right after ice-out, and in the fall and early winter.

Mirror Lake: Located in Peters Creek, right beside the Glenn Highway at Mile 23.6, Mirror Lake is relatively large compared to other Anchorage area still waters. It has a fair amount of shore access, but is heavily wooded and is best fished during open water with small watercraft. Stocked with landlocked salmon, rainbow trout, and Arctic charr, it offers the best action during spring, and from fall to mid-winter. Respect private property around the lakeshore.

Recommended Guides/Lodges/Air Taxis/Outfitters

6th Avenue Outfitters, 524 W. 6th Avenue, Anchorage, AK 99501, 907-276-0233. Outdoor clothing & fishing gear rentals, Ship Creek

Alyeska Adventures, P.O. Box 561, Girdwood, AK 99587, 907-754-2400, *www.alyeskaadventures.com*. Guided salmon fishing, Portage Area streams

2RAlaska, 3911 Winchester Loop, Anchorage, AK 99507, 907-830-8687, *www.2ralaska.com*. Shuttle service, Bird Creek and Portage area streams

USGS Maps Reference

Ship, Campbell creeks; Jewel, DeLong, Campbell Point lakes: Anchorage A-8.

Bird Creek: Seward D-7; Anchorage A-7.

Mirror Lake: Anchorage B-7.

Eklutna Tailrace: Anchorage B-6.

Portage Area River Systems: Seward D-6

Regulations/Information

Most Anchorage-area streams are open all year for all species, except king salmon over 20 inches and other salmon over 16 inches (except portions of Eagle River and Ship and Campbell creeks), but special regulations/restrictions apply on many streams. Consult current Regulations Summary for Southcentral Alaska or contact Anchorage office, ADF&G at (907) 267-2218 for information and updates before fishing area.

Online info: *www.sf.adfg.state.ak.us/statewide/regulations/scregs.cfm*

Anchorage Area Species

LOCATION	King Salmon	Red Salmon	Pink Salmon	Chum Salmon	Silver Salmon	Steelhead	Rainbow	Cutthroat	Charr	Grayling	Lake Trout	Northern Pike	Sheefish	Halibut	Ling Cod	Rock Fish	Salmon Shark	Fishing Pressure
Ship Creek	★	R	✓	R	★		✓		✓									☹
Campbell Creek	C	C	C	C	☺		☺		☺									☹
Eklutna Tailrace	✓	✓	✓	✓	✓				✓									☹
Bird Creek	C	R	★	✓	★				✓									☹
Jewel Lake	LL								☺			R						☹
Taku-Campbell Lake	LL								☺									☹
DeLong Lake	LL								☺									☹
Campbell Pt. Lake	LL								☺	✓								☹
Mirror Lake	LL								☺	✓		R						☹
Portage Area River Systems	C	✓	☺	✓	★				☺									M

Species not present
R   Rare
✓   Fishable numbers (or light pressure)
☺   Good fishing
★   Excellent fishing
LL   Landlocked species
C   Present, but fishing closed
M   Moderate pressure
☹   Heavy pressure

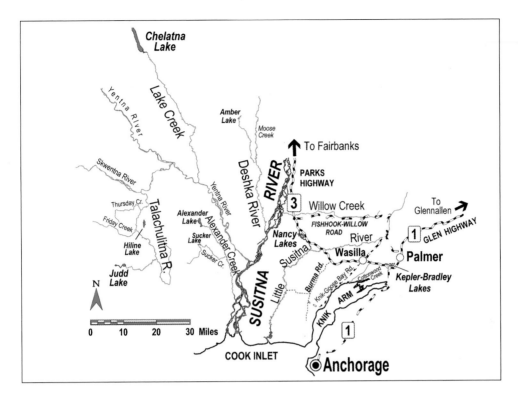

MATANUSKA VALLEY-SUSITNA RIVER

The glacial Susitna River is Southcentral Alaska's most significant drainage in terms of size and recreational use, offering a world of extremely popular, quality sportfishing opportunities for salmon, trout, and grayling in its many outstanding clearwater tributaries. Important adjacent drainages along Upper Cook Inlet enhance the area's great sportfish potential. Access is almost entirely by boat, floatplane, or car via the George Parks Highway.

Kepler/Bradley Lakes

Location: Lower Matanuska valley, 35 miles NE of Anchorage.

Access: By car, boat, and foot via Glenn Highway, Mile 36.4.

Facilities: Day use picnic areas and walk-in boat launches; state and private campgrounds nearby.

Highlights: A popular fishing lake area close to Anchorage.

Main Species: RT, CHR, GR, KS (landlocked)

The Kepler/Bradley State Recreation Area comprises nine clear, landlocked lakes of moderate to shallow depth. ADF&G currently stocks the lakes with three species of sport fish. Most lakes are stocked with at least two species. Fishing is generally best in spring after ice-out (May) and again in fall prior to freeze-up (September-October). Ice fishing is also popular on these lakes. Long Lake, which is catch-and-release only for rainbow trout (the only species present), has some larger fish up to 25 inches or more.

A few of the lakes are next to or near the road, some require a short hike of less than one mile. Casting from the shore is possible on all lakes, but the best fishing is from a canoe or any other watercraft. Consult a map showing detailed features for exact access information.

Nancy Lakes

Location: Lower Susitna River valley, 35 miles north of Anchorage.

Access: By car, canoe, and foot via Nancy Lake Parkway, Mile 67.3 Parks Highway.

Facilities: State campgrounds, boat ramp, and public use cabins.

Highlights: A popular local canoe/trail/lake system with some fishing possibilities.

Main Species: RT, DV, NP

The Nancy Lake State Recreation Area south of Willow consists of a multitude of clear ponds and lakes—some landlocked, others draining into the Susitna or Little Susitna rivers. Most of the lakes are accessed by foot or marked canoe trails. Both natural and stocked populations of rainbow trout are present, in addition to Dolly Varden and salmon in some of the lakes. Northern pike, illegally planted back in the 70s, have spread throughout the system, to the detriment of native fish populations.

The Nancy Lake Canoe Trail System provides access to some good rainbow trout and northern pike fishing away from the more readily accessible waters near the road. Signs mark short portages between the lakes. As is the case for most Alaska lakes, the best fishing is in spring and fall. Ice fishing is good as well. Consult a map showing detailed features of area for exact access information.

The major lake areas include: Nancy Lake (RT, DV); Red Shirt Lake (NP); Lynx Lake (NP); Butterfly Lakes (NP); South Rolly Lake (RT, NP); Big No Luck Lake (RT).

Little Susitna River ★★★

Location: Upper Cook Inlet, Susitna Flats, 15 miles west of Anchorage.

Access: By car, boat, and raft, via Parks Highway at town of Houston, or Knik-Goose Bay Road (off Parks Highway) and Burma Road. Boat access to mouth via a twelve-mile trip across upper Cook Inlet from Port of Anchorage.

Facilities: Full services (including boat launch) available in Houston. Camping and boat launch also available on lower river.

Highlights: A very popular Mat-Su day trip destination with a variety of good fishing.

Main Species: KS, SS, RS, CS

The Little "Su" is a popular road-fishing stream that meanders through spruce and birch from its origins on the south slopes of the Talkeetna Mountains. It is a moody river. During summer hot spells or rainy periods, its clear waters can easily become high, muddy, and difficult to fish, especially on the upper and middle sections of the river where the current is swift. (Beginning and intermediate boaters should stay on the lower river, with its wider water and slower current.) While the lower river has many sharp bends and twists with some sweepers, most of the Little "Su" is fairly tame. However, its upper reaches are rated Class II to Class III. Rafters can spend two or three days floating the river from the upper or middle access points (Houston) down to the lower river and Burma Road.

All five species of salmon migrate up the Little Susitna in good numbers and are encountered from Houston downstream, where they hold in the river's many holes, pools, and runs. The lower river is worked mostly by boaters fishing the tides, although bankfishing is also possible. Salmon hit the lower access points about two to three weeks earlier than the upper points. Shore fishers prefer the middle and upper parts of the Little Su, which are narrower and concentrate the fishing. The kings may exceed 50 pounds, with occasional catches surpassing 70 pounds. Most of the effort for kings is on the lower river (the fish are brighter), with boaters usually anchoring up and still fishing plugs or casting spinners. The confluence with Lake Creek is a popular site with many salmon anglers, providing opportunity for both reds and silvers. Although the reds can be difficult to catch at times, salmon roe and properly presented flies do get fish. The silver runs have been exceptionally strong the last few years, with fish numbering in the tens of thousands, making the river the top producer in the entire northern Cook Inlet area. Ocean fresh chum and pink salmon invade the river every summer in great numbers, making fish-on-every-cast action a distinct possibility. The middle and upper river systems also have fairly good rainbow trout, Dolly Varden, and grayling action during the summer and fall months when spawning salmon are present.

Alexander Creek

Location: Lower Susitna River drainage, 25 miles NW of Anchorage.

Access: By floatplane from Anchorage to calm waters near mouth or Alexander Lake; or boat via Deshka Landing off Parks Highway (navigating downstream on the Susitna River) or Port of Anchorage.

Facilities: Lodging, fuel, water, and guide services available on creek.

Highlights: A great fishing destination with a variety of species, especially suited for float trips.

Main Species: KS, SS, RT, NP

Alexander Creek is one of the most popular, easily accessed, and productive waters of its size in Southcentral Alaska, holding large runs of salmon throughout much of the summer and into fall. The creek drains a fairly significant area between the Yentna River and Mount Susitna in the 40 miles from origin at Alexander Lake to terminus at the glacial Susitna River right above tidewater. Much of the surrounding area is marshland, contributing significantly to the iron-colored tint of this slow, meandering stream. Although fishing from the bank is popular on the upper and middle river, most angling on lower Alexander Creek is done from boats. Jet boats can run from the mouth upstream about 18 miles to the confluence with Sucker Creek, a major clearwater tributary, fishing an abundance of good water along the way. One of the best ways to enjoy the Alexander is to float and fish down from the lake in rafts or canoes (an easy four to five-day trip), with take-out at the mouth.

The creek mouth is the most productive fishing spot. Its confluence with the large glacial Susitna serves as a major holding area for a tremendous number of salmon heading upstream to spawn in the Susitna's other clearwater tributaries. As a matter of fact, the mouth of Alexander has often been referred to as one of the best silver spots in this part of the state. But the Alexander itself has significant runs of king (June) and silver salmon (August), along with good numbers of red, chum, and pink salmon, rainbow trout, Dolly Varden, and grayling. Northern pike are very abundant in Alexander Lake, making it highly productive for spin-casters and fly fishers alike. Though many of the fish are of moderate size, a few monsters are known to inhabit the lake (30 pounds. or more). Some anglers even claim that the new state record may come from here.

Deshka River ★★★

Location: Lower Susitna River drainage, 35 miles NW of Anchorage.

Access: By floatplane to mouth or midsection. (The river can also be floated from Petersville Road down, mainly via Moose Creek, with take-out at the Susitna River confluence.) Jet boat access up to fork of Kroto and Moose creeks, 30 miles upstream from mouth.

Facilities: Boat launch at Deshka Landing, off Parks Highway. Lodging, fuel, water, and guide services available at mouth of river.

Highlights: One of Southcentral Alaska's top salmon producers, a short distance from Anchorage.

Main Species: KS, SS, RT

The Deshka River, also known as Kroto Creek, is a major clearwater tributary of the Susitna, and a highly productive and popular fishing stream. Flowing approximately 90 miles from its origin south of the Alaska Range near Talkeetna, the slow-moving Deshka empties into the west side of the Susitna about eight miles southwest of Willow.

The Deshka River has long been heralded as the premier king salmon hot spot in the Susitna drainage, with average annual runs of 30 to 40 thousand fish, making it one of the most productive king streams in Alaska for its size. Abundant numbers of other salmon, along with a healthy population of resident rainbow trout and grayling, contribute to its perennial popularity. It can be accessed and fished in several ways.

The confluence of the Deshka and Susitna rivers serves as a resting area for vast schools of salmon migrating farther up the Susitna. Anglers can expect to tangle with all five species of salmon there, in season, with action being especially noteworthy for king and silver salmon. (Almost all effort is done fishing from boats.) Other hot spots on the Deshka include the confluences of Trappers, No-Name, and Chijuk creeks. Good numbers of rainbow trout and grayling can be found in the upper Deshka River late in the summer and early fall, where conditions are perfect for flyfishing and ultra-light spin-casting. Growing numbers of northern pike are also present in parts of the river.

Lake Creek ★★★

Location: Yentna River drainage, 65 miles NW of Anchorage.

Access: By floatplane from Anchorage to Chelatna Lake headwaters, small adjoining lakes (such as Bulchatna Lake) downstream or river mouth; wheelplanes can utilize gravel bars. Boat access to mouth from the community of Skwentna.

Facilities: Lodging, guide services available on creek.

Highlights: One of Susitna River's most scenic and productive sportfishing streams.

Main Species: KS, SS, RT, GR

Lake Creek begins at Chelatna Lake, near Kahiltna Glacier, at the base of the Alaska Range. It is a fast, clearwater stream that flows south through rocky rapids and canyons some 50 miles to its confluence with the glacial Yentna River. It offers good to excellent angling for a variety of species, including five species of salmon, rainbow trout, grayling, and even northern pike. With its whitewater and boulders, Lake Creek is not the easiest water to fish, however, and has its best angling opportunities concentrated in the deep holes, slower runs, and mouths of tributary creeks (above and below the canyon in the middle section of the river).

Early in the season, the best fishing is at the confluence of Lake Creek and the Yentna, for bright king salmon holding from their journey upriver (to both Lake Creek and other clear tributaries of the Yentna), and resident rainbow trout and grayling. Later in the season, in the middle and upper sections, salmon fishing continues to be very good. (Lake Creek kings are quite large, some exceeding 60 pounds.) August brings a good run of silvers, and some lively rainbow trout and grayling fishing. Chelatna Lake at the headwaters even has a population of northern pike.

The most exciting way to fish Lake Creek is to put in at Chelatna Lake (or several other lakes along river) and float the entire length by raft, down to the mouth at the Yentna. (With whitewater varying from Class I to Class III, this is not a river that novice floaters should attempt.)

Talachulitna River ★★★★

Location: Yentna River drainage, 60 miles west of Anchorage.

Access: By floatplane to Judd Lake headwaters, Hiline Lake at mid-river or river mouth; boat access from community of Skwentna. Can be entirely floated by raft, kayak, or canoe.

Facilities: Private lodges and guide services along lower river.

Highlights: One of Alaska's premier stream fishing locations, with classic fly fishing conditions.

Main Species: KS, RS, SS, RT, GR

The clearwater "Tal" rises from several sources in the highlands above the lower Skwentna, then winds through birch and spruce forests and scenic gorges for some 50 miles before emptying into the swift, glacial tributary of the Susitna.

The Talachulitna has great fishing, seclusion, scenery, and exciting floating; it's one of the state's choicest rivers to enjoy by raft, kayak, or canoe. The upper section is fairly slow and quite shallow in spots (mostly Class I and II water). There is an abrupt series of Class II and III rapids just below the Hiline Lake put-in at mid-river, and the lower river plunges through several high-walled canyons (Class II and III) before reaching the Skwentna. Overall, the Tal is definitely not a trip for the novice boater.

Despite the fishing pressure of recent years, the Talachulitna is holding up remarkably well, with strong runs of king and silver salmon, and fairly abundant rainbow trout fishing. In its heyday back in the 50s and 60s, the river was notorious for trophy trout, but nowadays you'll have to work the water pretty hard to turn up a fish of any size. (Rainbows average 12 to 16 inches, and are among the prettiest strains found in Alaska.) The best chances for bigger trout are in the middle and upper river during late summer and fall, where you'll find some decent grayling fishing as well.

For salmon, the mouth of the river and confluences of the tributary creeks (such as Friday and Thursday creeks) have traditionally been the best bets, but the river has an abundance of holding water—pools, riffles, and sloughs—for good fishing all the way down. The trip from Judd Lake to the Skwentna makes a perfect seven-day float with plenty of time to fish all the good water. For those not interested in taking on the entire river on, there are several area lodges that can provide guided fishing along the lower river. (You can also access the mouth by boat from Skwentna.)

Willow Creek ★★★

Location: Susitna River tributary, 40 miles north of Anchorage.

Access: By car via four-mile paved road from the town of Willow to Willow Creek-Susitna River confluence. Additional access via Parks Highway (intersects middle river) and Hatcher Pass Road (middle and upper river).

Facilities: Full visitor services available at highway crossing and town of Willow.

Highlights: One of the most productive salmon/trout streams in northern Cook Inlet.

Main Species: KS, SS, CS, PS, RT

Willow Creek is a rocky, clearwater stream that flows swiftly west off the edge of the southern Talkeetna Mountains, onto the flatlands of the lower Susitna near the town of Willow. It is one of the most popular fishing streams in the area, especially for bank anglers, with an abundance of road-accessible holes, runs, and pools that offer decent salmon and trout fishing in season.

Salmon fishing is the top draw here, with four runs providing substantial action from early summer into fall. Kings are the most sought-after species and can reach a respectable size in the Willow. Most fish caught are between 15 and 30 pounds, but anglers have a decent chance of hooking fish weighing as much as 60 pounds. (Kings nudging the 80-pound mark have been taken.) The mouth of the Willow is without a doubt the most popular spot for fishing, and draws considerable crowds during the height of the runs. With a little hiking, more adventuresome anglers can find some good fishing for salmon, trout, and grayling on the river's middle and upper sections. The river is also noted for its outstanding rainbow trout fishing in spring and fall.

Floating is a popular way of accessing and fishing the creek. Rafts, kayaks, and canoes can be launched for short trips from any of the road access points on the upper or middle river. As the Willow is a rapid runoff stream with sweepers, logjams, and a high gradient in its upper reaches, floaters should use caution and stay within the middle and lower river sections.

Sheep Creek

Location: Susitna River drainage, 50 miles north of Anchorage.

Access: By car via Parks Highway to bridge crossing lower creek north of Willow (or gravel road one mile south of bridge to confluence with Susitna River). Trails lead up and downstream.

Facilities: Primitive campground with limited visitor services available nearby on highway. Boat launch just downstream of mouth.

Highlights: A small but highly productive salmon/trout fishery in a semi-wilderness setting.

Main Species: KS, SS, CS, PS, RT

Sheep Creek is a small clearwater tributary of the Susitna that issues from the western edge of the Talkeetna Mountains and flows west some 50 miles before joining the big glacial stream at midriver. It is a well-used highway angling destination, with good salmon fishing, especially for kings (from mid-June to early July).

The creek has an abundance of easily fished water, especially suited for bank fishing, which is the only real way to work the middle and upper river, but the mouth can also be fished from a boat. Small rafts can also put in at the highway bridge for an easy half-day trip down to the mouth (logjams and sweepers are plentiful, however).

Although fishing is good for four salmon species in season, kings draw the most anglers to the banks of Sheep Creek, as they tend to be slightly above average (up to 40 or 50 pounds, with rare specimens up to 80 pounds a possibility). Chum salmon numbers may be very large in some years. In spring or late summer and fall, rainbow trout and grayling are best fished in the lower or upper river. Sheep does have a tendency to become silty and run high during prolonged periods of hot weather or heavy rain.

Montana Creek

Location: Susitna River drainage, 60 miles north of Anchorage.

Access: By car via Parks Highway to bridge on lower creek, or gravel road off Talkeetna Spur Highway to upper creek. Foot trails along creek provide additional access.

Facilities: Campground and sporting goods available at bridge site; gas, groceries, and food located nearby along highway.

Highlights: One of the top road-accessible salmon/trout streams in Southcentral.

Main Species: KS, SS, CS, PS, RT

Montana Creek is a clear, gravel-bottomed, east-side Susitna tributary that comes off the western fan of the Talkeetnas north of Sheep Creek. With headwaters considerably less alpine and glacial than its neighbor (it has three forks that join about ten miles east of the highway), Montana generally runs very clear. This, along with its ample productivity as a salmon stream, makes it one of the more popular of all Susitna road-fishing streams.

Most angling takes place at the mouth, which is within easy walking distance from the state campground beside the Parks Highway bridge. The confluence provides a sanctuary for fish of all species migrating up Montana Creek or continuing up the Susitna to other spawning areas. Anglers concentrating on salmon can also do well in the multitude of runs and holes upstream.

King salmon to 60 or 70 pounds, sometimes even more, are possible, with a good number of fish in the 40-pound range. Silvers, chums, and pinks are also abundant from the late summer into fall. And rainbows of 8 to 10 pounds have been taken, mostly from the lower river in spring and fall. Grayling fishing is not too bad on the upper river. Because of its small size, the Montana is strictly a bank-fishing stream, but small rafts can be launched from the upper access point and floated to the mouth. (Some portions of the creek are shallow and there is an abundance of sweepers, however.)

Talkeetna River System ★★★

Location: Susitna River drainage, 80 miles north of Anchorage.

Access: By car via Talkeetna Spur Highway (from the Parks Highway) to town of Talkeetna and river mouth. Riverboat or raft to mouths of clear tributary streams, or float and wheelplanes to headwaters.

Facilities: Full visitor services including air taxi available in Talkeetna.

Highlights: One of the more accessible and superlative remote fisheries in Southcentral.

Main Species: KS, SS, RS, CS, RT, DV, GR

The Talkeetna is a major tributary of the Susitna and one of the most significant fishing rivers in Southcentral Alaska. Since it is a large, glacial, swift wilderness river, the better fishing potential is concentrated in its clear tributary streams. The mainstem is fishable, however, barring hot weather and heavy rains. (In spring and fall months, the water usually becomes moderately clear with a greenish tint.)

Due to the size and productivity of this system, the Talkeetna offers superb and varied fishing. All five salmon species fill the river from midsummer into fall, along with rainbow trout, charr and grayling. The best way to sample the hot salmon action—some of the best in the region for kings, chums, silvers, and reds—is by boat from the town of Talkeetna, accessing the mouths of some of the clear spawning tributaries upstream. This is definitely not a river for novice boaters, however, with its swift currents, rocky shoals, and hidden boulders. Jet boats can run way up some of the tributaries (Clear and Prairie creeks, for example) for some truly notable fishing for rainbow trout, charr, and grayling. Travel by boat on the mainstem above Iron Creek is not advised.

The Talkeetna is also one of the premier whitewater rivers of Alaska. Two long canyons of rapids (Class III and IV) begin below Prairie Creek, to challenge even experienced river runners. For floating, most folks put in by floatplane at Murder Lake (below Stephan Lake), or by wheelplane on gravel bars along the upper river near Yellowjacket Creek (a five to seven-day trip down to the mouth).

Some of the Talkeetna's many hot spots to consider include: Clear Creek (KS, SS, RS, CS, PS, DV, GR), Larson Creek (SS, RS), Disappointment Creek (KS, CS, RT, DV, GR), and Prairie Creek (KS, SS, RS, RT, DV, GR).

Fish it in late June and early July for kings; late July for reds; and mid to late August for silver salmon. Rainbow and grayling fishing in the mainstem Talkeetna can be very productive in late September and early October, with trout in the two to three-pound category very common.

Upper Susitna River System
Location: Northwest Talkeetna Mountains, 80 miles north of Anchorage.

Access: By boat via Parks Highway bridge or town of Talkeetna, or by plane or train (the Alaska Railroad can make prearranged stops at Gold Creek or Chulitna, where a small gravel road leads to the upper Indian River and lower Portage Creek). Some rafters put in at tributary streams and float down to Talkeetna or the Parks Highway bridge. Planes can access certain sections, with careful scouting.

Facilities: No developed public facilities. Guide services are available in Talkeetna.

Highlights: A remote and little-fished portion of the Susitna River, with good salmon and trout potential.

Main Species: KS, SS, RT, GR

The Susitna River, Southcentral Alaska's most significant fish producer, has its beginnings in the runoff from a series of enormous glaciers in the Alaska Range. From there it flows swiftly south, then west as it cuts through the edge of the Talkeetnas, and south again as it meanders down into the forested lowlands of upper Cook Inlet. Although the upper part of this amazing system is seldom fished, it does have some worthwhile opportunities. Because of the heavy silt load, sportfishing is mostly limited to clear-flowing tributaries and sloughs. The most commonly visited part of the upper Susitna is the section between Devils Canyon—an unrunnable stretch of Class VI whitewater just north of the Talkeetna Mountains—and the confluence of the Chulitna and Talkeetna rivers near the town of Talkeetna. North of Devils Canyon, the upper Susitna is a remote wilderness river with whitewater, limited access, and few sportfishing opportunities. The river below the canyon is much tamer (mostly Class I), heavily braided water with logjams and submerged hazards, but it can be boated, with caution. The scenery is outstanding (great views of Mount McKinley), there are no crowds, and the fishing can be quite good, so it's worth exploring.

Most anglers who visit the upper Susitna do so by powerful jet boats, as the upper Susitna has a multitude of small tributary streams and sloughs, with plenty of opportunities for exploring and locating holding salmon and hungry rainbows and grayling.

Fishing for king and silver salmon can be quite good, with the brighter fish available early in the season. Two major clearwater tributaries, Indian River and Portage Creek, are the top bets and sustain the largest fish populations. Locations and species available include Portage Creek and Whiskers Creek (KS, SS, GR); and Lane Creek, Fourth of July Creek, and Indian River (all KS, SS, RT). For those with the yearning (and resources) for some real wilderness angling adventure, there are remote fly-in lakes off the upper river, such as Watana, Clarence, Deadman, and Big Lake, that see little pressure and have potential for good fishing for lake trout and grayling. The best times are late spring through early summer and fall. Check with local air taxi services for latest conditions.

Chulitna River System
Location: Northeast Alaska Range, 75 miles north of Anchorage.

Access: By car or boat via the Parks Highway, which follows the river and crosses the lower mainstem (at milepost 135) as well as a handful of its clear tributaries. Small wheelplanes can land on gravel bars along river.

Facilities: Food and lodging available along the Parks Highway.

Highlights: A remote and readily-accessible fishery offering dramatic scenery and good fishing.

Main Species: SS, RS, RT, GR

The Chulitna River headwaters drain off the towering slopes of the Alaska Range near Denali National Park. Heavily silted from melting glaciers, the mainstem has good fishing conditions only in its clear-flowing tributaries. (The Middle and East forks both run clear.) The surrounding scenery, with North America's tallest peaks nearby, is quite stirring. Although a major highway bisects the area, the wilderness and some great fishing are only a short hike (or a float) away.

Road anglers would do best by starting from the Parks Highway access points at the major tributary creeks and hiking up- and down-stream to find good fishing. The mouths and lower reaches usually have the best salmon fishing, with trout and grayling more concentrated in the upstream stretches during the summer months. The Chulitna is ideally fished from rafts or by boat, putting in and taking out at the highway bridges (either the Middle or East forks, the Chulitna River Bridge, or Talkeetna). The upper Chulitna above the bridge should not be attempted by novices, however, as it is very fast, with some serious rapids and other hazards.

Some Chulitna hot spots to try include the Middle Fork (RT) and East Fork (KS, SS, GR), Honolulu Creek (SS, RT, GR), Coal Creek (SS, RT, GR), Little Coal Creek (SS, RT, GR), Byers Creek (SS, RS, RT, GR), Spink Creek (SS, RS, RT, GR), Troublesome Creek (SS, RS, RT, GR), Horseshoe Creek (SS, RS, RT, GR), and Sunny Creek (SS, RS, RT, GR). King, silver, and red salmon are the most sought-after species of summer, while rainbow trout are the primary fish in the fall. Lake trout are taken from Summit and Miami lakes at the headwaters in Broad Pass.

Tyone River System
Location: Upper Susitna River drainage, 140 mi. NE of Anchorage.

Access: By boat via Lake Louise Road (from Glenn Highway), or floatplane to lakes or Tyone-Susitna rivers confluence.

Facilities: Full visitor services, including campground and boat launch, available in Lake Louise area.

Highlights: Long-time favorite lake chain for trophy lake trout and abundant grayling.

Main Species: LT, GR

The Tyone River system consists of an extensive complex of lakes and streams in the high plateau country of the upper Susitna, east of the Talkeetna Mountains. Sportfishing opportunities, mostly for grayling and lake trout, are significant, especially in the three largest and deepest associated lakes: Louise, Susitna, and Tyone. These waters are fairly close to the Glenn Highway, a major road between Anchorage and Glennallen. Because of their location and relatively easy access, they see a major share of the state's urban lake fishing effort, but still hold a lot of fine fishing.

The Tyone itself is a slow, meandering river that connects the outlet of Tyone Lake to the silty Susitna River, a distance of about 30 miles. For boaters and fishermen, the clear lakes and associated streams—dozens of them—are of primary interest.

Lakes Louise and Susitna are well known for their trophy lake trout potential, and still boot out a fair share of "lakers" up to 20 pounds or more each year, despite growing pressure from the nearby urban populations. Like many deep, large lakes, they are best fished right after ice-out in the spring (usually late May or early June in most years), or later, in the fall. Trolling big spoons, bait, and plugs is standard practice on these deep waters, but you can do well casting from shore or a skiff at certain times (especially before freeze-up). Grayling are found in most of the system's lakes and streams, and there are even a few good pike lakes and some spots for rainbow trout fishing, according to locals.

Local air taxi services and lodges will be glad to help you find the kind of fishing you're looking for. Since this is wild, big water country with rapidly changing weather and tricky conditions, it's probably best to enlist their services, at least to start. They can fly or boat you to the best areas of the season, for some truly outstanding fishing at reasonable prices.

Recommended Lodges/Guides/Outfitters/Air Taxis

3 Rivers Fly and Tackle, 390 Railroad Avenue, Wasilla, AK, 99654, 907-373-5434, *www.3riversflyandtackle.com*. Matanuska-Susitna Valley's complete tackle/fly shop

Fishtale River Guides, Box 155, Palmer, AK 99645, (907) 376-3687, 800-376-3625, *www.fish4salmon.com*. Guided salmon fishing, Little Susitna River

Deshka Silver King Lodge, Box 870910, Wasilla, AK 99687, (907) 733-2055; 800-928-2055, *www.deshkalodge.com*. Lodge, guided fishing, Deshka River

Talaview Lodge, Box 190088, Anchorage, AK 99519, 907-733-3447, *www.talaview.com*. Lodge and guided fishing, Talachulitna River

Willow Creek Resort, P.O. Box 85, Willow, AK 99688, (907) 495-6343, *www.willowcreekresort.com*. Lodging, guided fishing

Camp Caswell Food & Tackle, Mile 87.5 Parks Hwy, Willow, AK 99688, 907-495-7829. Groceries, RV Park, fishing tackle, Sheep/Montana Creeks area

Sheep Creek Lodge, Mile 88 Parks Hwy, HC 89, Box 406S, Willow, AK 99688, (907) 495-6227, *www.sheepcreeklodge.com*. Restaurant, lodging, guided fishing, Sheep Creek

Montana Creek Campground, Mile 96.5 Parks Hwy, HC 89 Box 543 Willow, AK 99688, 907-733-5268, *www.montanacreekcampground.com*. Groceries, Camping, Fishing, Montana Creek

Lake Louise Lodge, HC01 Box 1716, Glennallen, Alaska 99588, 877-878-3311, *www.lakelouiselodge.com*. Food, Lodging, fishing, Lake Louise area

Alaska Bush Float Plane Service, PO Box 264, Talkeetna, AK 99676, 866-733-1693. Floatplane Air taxi, upper Susitna area

Lee's Air Taxi, P.O.Box 148, Glennallen, AK 99588, (907) 822-5030, *www.leesairtaxi.com*. Air taxi, Susitna headwaters/Wrangell St. Elias

Rusts Flying Service, P.O. Box 190325, Anchorage, AK 99519, (907) 243-1595 or (800) 544-2299, *www.flyrusts.com*. Air taxi, Susitna Valley

USGS Maps Reference

Kepler-Bradley Lakes: Anchorage C-6.

Nancy Lakes: Anchorage C-8; Tyonek C-1.

Little Susitna River System: Anchorage C-6, C-7, C-8, D-6; Tyonek B-1, C-1.

Alexander Creek: Tyonek B-2, C-2, C-3, D-3.

Deshka River: Talkeetna A-1, A-2, B-1, B-2; Tyonek C-1, D-1, D-2.

Lake Creek: Talkeetna A-2, A-3, B-3, B-4, C-3, C-4; Tyonek D-3.

Talachulitna River: Tyonek B-4, C-3, C-4, C-5, D-4, D-5.

Willow Creek: Anchorage C-7, C-8, D-6, D-7, D-8; Tyonek D-1.

Sheep Creek: Talkeetna Mtns A-5, A-6; Talkeetna A-1; Tyonek D-1.

Montana Creek: Talkeetna Mtns A-5, A-6, B-6; Talkeetna A-1.

Talkeetna River: Talkeetna Mountains A-3, A-4, A-5, B-3, B-4, B-5, B-6, C-4, C-5, C-6.

Upper Susitna River: Talkeetna B-1, C-1; Talkeetna Mountains C-1, C-6, D-1, D-2, D-3, D-4, D-5, D-6; Healy A-1, A-2, B-1; Mount Hayes B-6.

Chulitna River System: Talkeetna B-1, C-1, D-1; Talkeetna Mountains D-6; Healy A-5, A-6, B-5, B-6.

Tyone River System: Gulkana B-6, C-6.

General Information

Alaska State Parks: Mat-Su Superintendent, HC 32 Box 6706, Wasilla, AK 99654, (907) 745-3975. Information on state public facilities within area.

Regulations/Information

Sporfishing in the Mat-Su area is open year-round for all species except king salmon and rainbow trout. (Restrictions on the use of bait and keeping of trout, along with many special regulations limiting fishing periods for king salmon apply—check regulations for details). Always consult latest Regulations Summary for Southcentral Alaska and/or call region or field offices of ADF&G when planning a fishing trip to area.

Anchorage: (907) 267-2218   **Palmer:** (907) 746-6300
Glennallen: (907) 822-3309

Online info: *www.sf.adfg.state.ak.us/statewide/regulations/scregs.cfm*

Matanuska/Susitna Species

LOCATION	King Salmon	Red Salmon	Pink Salmon	Chum Salmon	Silver Salmon	Steelhead	Rainbow	Cutthroat	Charr	Grayling	Lake Trout	Sheefish	Northern Pike	Halibut	Ling Cod	Rock Fish	Salmon Shark	Fshg. Pressure
Little Susitna River System	☺	✓	★	★	★		✓		✓	✓			R					☹
Kepler-Bradley Lakes	LL								☺	✓	✓							☹
Alexander Creek	★	✓	★	✓	★		✓		☺	✓			☺					☹
Deshka River	★	✓	★	✓	★		☺		☺	☺			✓					☹
Lake Creek	★	✓	★	☺	★		★		☺	☺								☹
Talachulitna River	★	☺	★	☺	★		★		✓	★								M
Nancy Lakes		R			R		R		☺	✓		R	★					☹
Willow Creek	★	R	★	☺	★		☺		R	☺								☹
Sheep Creek	☺	R	★	★	☺		☺		R	☺			R					☹
Montana Creek	★	R	★	☺	★		☺		R	☺								☹
Talkeetna River System	★	☺	★	★	★		★		☺	☺								M
Upper Susitna River System	★	R	R	R	☺		★		R		★	★						☹
Chulitna River System	☺	☺		✓	✓		☺		★	R	☺	✓		R				☹
Tyone River System							✓				★	★	☺					☹

Species not present
R — Rare
✓ — Fishable numbers (or light pressure)
☺ — Good fishing
★ — Excellent fishing

LL — Landlocked species
C — Present, but fishing closed
M — Moderate pressure
☹ — Heavy pressure

King salmon action on the lower Deshka River

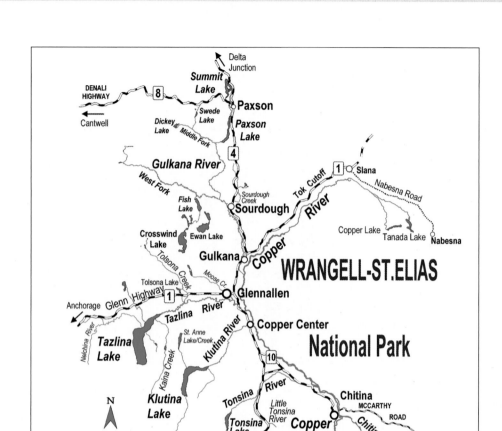

COPPER RIVER/WRANGELL MOUNTAINS

In the early 1980s, reports of giant rainbow trout over 20 pounds, from a remote location in the rugged Wrangell Mountains, focused attention on the vastly underrated sportfishing potential of this scenic corner of the state. Dominated by the huge, glacial Copper River (a 287-mile-long, 24,000 square-mile drainage—one of Alaska's major salmon producers) and towering, icy coastal ranges, this area has much to offer fishermen in its many clearer-flowing tributary streams and associated lakes: world-famous king and red salmon, grayling, lake trout, some rainbow and steelhead and, in the myriad streams and sloughs of its broad delta, silver salmon and even cutthroat trout.

Copper/Tanada Lakes
Location: Copper River drainage, 210 miles NE of Anchorage.

Access: By floatplane or hiking; a primitive ATV trail leads from the Nabesna Road (Mile 24.3) into Tanada Lake (you'll need a permit from Park Service to go in this way), with a short trail running along the west shore to Copper Lake, but the going is tough. Snowmachine access possible from highway in late winter/early spring.

Facilities: None.

Highlights: Magnificent views of surrounding Wrangell-St. Elias National Park, world class hiking/camping opportunities, and good angling.

Main Species: LT, GR

These extreme headwater lakes of the Copper River, lying on the north side of the Wrangells near Nabesna, are worthy of mention for the high quality fishing experience they offer. Remote, adjacent glacial lakes of modest size in a scenic setting, they have consistent fishing for lake trout, grayling, and burbot.

Headwaters for Tanada Creek and the upper Copper above Slana, these lakes receive modest numbers of red salmon which make the long journey upriver each fall to spawn in the farthest reaches of the Copper River system. Tanada is the larger and more productive of the two, but both lakes have fished well over the years, turning out lakers to 25 pounds, along with nice grayling, burbot, and even some kokanee in Copper Lake. Trails leading to neighboring lakes (Sheep and Grizzly) and creeks offer additional opportunities for hiking, camping, and fishing exploration.

Gulkana River System ★★★
Location: Copper River drainage, 165 miles NE of Anchorage.

Access: By car, plane, boat, and foot. The Richardson Highway parallels most of river, offering access at various locations. Several cross-country trails allow hikers access to strategic points along the river system.

Facilities: Full range of visitor services available along the road.

Highlights: One of Alaska's premier recreational waters, and the most significant sportfishing tributary of the Copper River.

Main Species: KS, RS, RT, LT, GR

The Gulkana River system is an immense clearwater drainage of lakes and streams, rising at the base of the Alaska Range near the headwaters of the Susitna, then flowing south and east approximately 100 miles to join the Copper River below Gakona Junction. It has two major tributaries, the Middle Fork and the West Fork, short streams that begin in a series of lakes and uplands west of the mainstem river.

The Gulkana, designated a National Wild and Scenic River, has one of Alaska's most productive and popular grayling fisheries, particularly on the mainstem between Paxson Lake and the West Fork confluence, but also in tributary lakes and streams of the Middle & West Fork drainages. Although their average size has suffered from the fishing pressure of recent years, grayling are still abundant and easy to catch. The Gulkana is also known for its good king salmon fishing (from the Middle Fork confluence down) in early summer, and a prolonged run of red salmon (late June through mid-August; they can be hard to catch, however). Lake trout are found in the large, deep headwater lakes, such as Summit, Paxson, Crosswind, and Swede, and fishing can be quite good to outstanding, with catches up to 30 pounds (best times after ice-out in early June and later in fall prior to freeze-up). The Gulkana also has a fair population of rainbows, and the northernmost confirmed runs of steelhead trout in North America. The best times to fish these battlers are in spring and fall in tributaries of the upper Middle Fork and in the mainstem above the West Fork confluence.

There are many ways to fish the Gulkana. Perhaps the most popular and exciting is by raft, canoe, or kayak, putting in at either Paxson Lake, Tangle River at milepost 22 of the Denali Highway (with a portage into Dickey Lake), or flying into one of the headwater lakes of the West Fork. The most popular take-out point is Sourdough Campground, at milepost 147.5 of the Richardson Highway. (Almost all powerboat users put in here and fish the stretch upriver to the West Fork confluence.) You can fish farther down and take out where the Richardson Highway intersects the river near Gakona Junction, if you like. The only serious hazards to boaters and floaters are boulders, sweepers, and swift currents (mostly Class II, with some short stretches of Class III in the Canyon Rapids 18 miles below the lake on the mainstem, and one Class III six miles below Dickey Lake on the Middle Fork). The Swede Lake Trail, beginning at milepost 16 of the Denali Highway, the Meiers Lake Trail, beginning at milepost 169 of the Richardson Highway, and the Haggard Creek Trail, beginning at milepost 161 of the Richardson Highway, are popular for accessing the Gulkana by foot.

Tazlina River System
Location: Copper River drainage, 110 miles east of Anchorage.

Access: By car via Richardson Highway, which intersects lower river (Glenn Highway provides access to clearwater tributaries). Launch boats and rafts from highway crossings. Floatplane access (via Tolsona and Anchorage) to more remote areas.

Facilities: Full range of visitor services available in nearby Glennallen.

Highlights: A little-visited river system with good fishing and wilderness.

Main Species: KS, RS, RT, GR

The Tazlina Glacier spills down the northeast slope of the central Chugaches, and forms a large, deep body of water at its terminus, Tazlina Lake. From its outlet, the Tazlina River flows east about 60 miles to join the huge Copper River. Although the river and lake are for the most part too silty for sport fishing, the clear tributary lakes and streams offer good fishing for grayling, rainbow trout, Dolly Varden charr, and fair opportunities for two species (king and red) of salmon. The stream mouths are best for salmon in summer. In spring and fall, try for trout, charr, and grayling. Some of these streams are major grayling producers and can be phenomenal during the annual spawning migrations in May; use flies and small spinners. A small population of steelhead is reported to spawn in the Tazlina River and a few tributaries.

There are several ways to sample the Tazlina's fishing. Floatplanes offer the quickest and easiest way to reach various choice locations. Rafts can be put in at the Little Nelchina River on the Glenn Highway, with a float down to Tazlina Lake. You can camp and fish at the inlet and fly back, or cross the lake and continue down the Tazlina River to the Richardson Highway bridge. (Be aware of strong winds that can blow off the glacier and make for hazardous conditions. Take a small outboard along, just in case, and take all necessary precautions.) It is also possible to launch jet boats from the Richardson Highway bridge and run up the Tazlina River. Since the Nelchina and Tazlina rivers are fast, whitewater rivers (possible Class III to Class IV rapids during high-water conditions) and very cold, they definitely should not be attempted by anyone except experienced river runners, and only during low water conditions.

Some of the hot spots to try in the Tazlina System include: Tazlina Lake (RS, LT), Kaina Lake (RT), High Lake (RT, LT, GR), Moose Lake (RT, GR), and Tolsona Lake (RT, GR); Mendeltna Creek (GR), Moose Creek (GR), Tolsona Creek (GR), and Kaina Creek (KS, RS, DV, RT).

Klutina River System ★★★
Location: Copper River drainage, 140 miles east of Anchorage.

Access: By car, boat and plane. Richardson Highway crosses lower river near the town of Copper Center. Limited trail system along the river, with an unimproved, four-wheeler road from the highway to the outlet of Klutina Lake. Floatplanes and jet boats provide access to more remote fishing areas.

Facilities: Full range of visitor services available in Copper Center.

Highlights: A major Copper River sockeye and trophy king fishery.

Main Species: KS, RS, DV, GR

The Klutina, a popular road-accessible river system, originates at Klutina Lake at the base of the Chugach Range. This greenish semi-glacial river flows northeast 30 miles, through rugged and scenic highlands, to its confluence with the Copper River at Copper Center. Swift (Class III) and cold, the Klutina offers challenging, but good to excellent, fishing for king and red salmon, Dolly Varden, and Arctic grayling.

The swift, glacial nature of the Klutina complicates the fishing. With a limited amount of holding water, shore anglers do best intercepting red salmon along the banks (they run continuously, June through September, with a prolonged peak of about four to five weeks), with an occasional king (if water levels are right and luck is with them) taken using very heavy line and tackle. Boaters fishing the lower eight miles of river have the most success (drift fishing plugs/bobbers and bait) for kings, as the choicest locations lie beyond the reaches of the road angler. The Klutina is not recommended for novice or intermediate boaters—the current is very strong, and there are numerous hidden rocks and boulders.

The Klutina kings are the largest in the Copper drainage, with fish over 50 pounds not uncommon, and catches to nearly 90 pounds reported. There are two runs of these monarchs, one in June and July, another in July and August, but not always distinct. The best Dolly Varden fishing is on the upper river and in the outlet of Klutina Lake in late summer and fall, with large specimens up to six or seven pounds possible.

Other less-significant species, such as grayling and lake trout, are taken near the mouths of clear headwater streams, at times. Spots to try for these, as well as the more abundant species, include Manker and St. Anne creeks and the Mahlo River.

Tonsina River System

Location: Copper River drainage, 150 miles east of Anchorage.

Access: By car or boat from the Richardson and Edgerton highways that cross the middle and lower river, respectively. A few faint trails exist for hiking in to the river and tributaries. Floatplanes access to Tonsina Lake, with raft trips possible, but potentially dangerous (Class III and IV rapids) during high water.

Facilities: Guides and lodging available along the road system.

Highlights: A seldom fished glacial system that offers excellent salmon fishing.

Main Species: KS, RS, SS, DV, GR

The Tonsina drainage is a fairly small system that heads in Tonsina Glacier on the north slope of the Chugach Mountains, and flows north and east some 60 miles before emptying into the lower Copper River. A challenging whitewater river for boating, the greenish-gray Tonsina offers some good fishing for salmon, charr, and grayling in the slower upper section below the lake, and mouths of its clearwater tributary streams.

Although not fished much except by locals, the Tonsina shouldn't be overlooked, as it can offer some quiet and productive fishing. Anglers would be wise to search for slower water or places where clearwater tributaries join the milky river; it is here that schools of salmon, along with charr and grayling, tend to congregate and can be enticed with flies, spoons, and spinners.

Some of the Tonsina's best fishing can be found in the mouths of streams draining into Tonsina Lake, and the first few miles of river below the outlet. Here in midsummer anglers can vie for red salmon, grayling, charr, a few rainbows, and even an occasional laker. Farther down, the Little Tonsina River offers productive, roadside angling for a small fall (September) run of silver salmon, as well as Dolly Varden and grayling. King salmon also run the river in mid-summer, rewarding anglers in the know with good sport and the chance of hooking a fish up to 50 pounds or more. Another good spot for salmon is at the mouth of the Tonsina, which may be reached by boat or raft from the Edgerton Highway. Here, the river is slower and wider, ideal holding water for migrating fish. A few steelhead trout are rumored to spawn in the Tonsina system.

Tebay River System ★★★

Location: Copper River drainage, Wrangell Mountains, 200 miles east of Anchorage.

Access: By floatplane from nearby hubs of Tolsona, Glennallen, or Cordova, landing at Hanagita, Tebay, and Summit lakes.

Facilities: No developed public facilities.

Highlights: Remote, wild watershed with high-quality trout, charr, and grayling fishing, and spectacular scenery and abundant wildlife.

Main Species: RT, GR, LT

The remote Tebay River system, in the heart of the rugged Wrangell-St. Elias Wilderness is a seldom-visited but esteemed drainage comprised of several high mountain lakes and streams that empty into the silty Chitina River, a major tributary of the Copper. With the area's isolation, magnificent surroundings, and wild populations of rainbows, grayling, and lake trout, it offers the potential for some of the finest wilderness angling experiences to be had in Southcentral Alaska.

The river heads at Tebay Lakes, a fine spot for a fly-in fish camp, with abundant fishing (especially at the connecting outlets) for small to medium-sized rainbows. Six miles below the lower lake outlet, the Tebay is joined by its major tributary, the Hanagita River, which drains a series of small lakes to the east. There are rainbows and grayling in the Hanagita and its tributaries, as well as a few lake trout in the lakes. (A small, fall run of steelhead also spawns in the river below the lakes, but they can be elusive.) The Summit Lake and Bridge Creek drainage, which joins the Tebay from the west about a mile above the Hanagita, also has rainbows and a very interesting history.

Though native to the Tebay River System, rainbow trout were absent from Summit Lake until sometime in the mid-60s when, somehow, these feisty fish were introduced to the invertebrate-rich watershed. By the 1980s, Summit Lake was producing phenomenal trophy trout, many in the 20-pound plus class. The lake was plundered in subsequent years by crowds of fly-in fishermen. Since that time, the population has rebounded but, unfortunately, the prey base is not sufficient to support the large-bodied trout that once flourished there.

The best time to fish Summit and the rest of Tebay is in early July, or from late August into September (check conditions with air taxis before any late season fly-in trips).

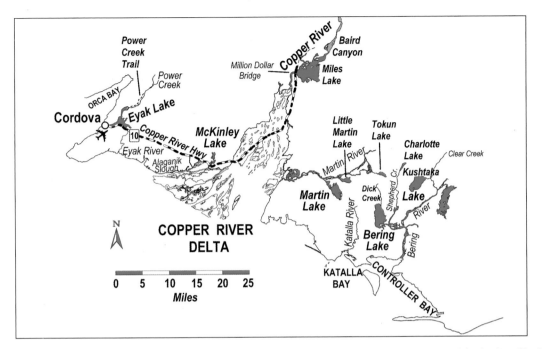

COPPER RIVER DELTA

B elow Miles Glacier, the mighty Copper braids out into an enormous 75-mile-wide delta that is one of the world's great wetland habitats. Abundant runoff and upwellings augment the silty flow of water with clear-flowing streams that support good numbers of salmon and some trout. Sportfishing opportunities there are further enhanced by a 50-mile gravel highway that traverses the delta from the town of Cordova, providing easy access to many prime locations.

Streams along the Copper River Delta were reopened to sportfishing in 1988 after closures in the early 70s for conservation reasons. The fishery that has developed since has made the Copper River delta one of the major freshwater sporfishing destinations along the coast, particularly for coho and red salmon, and Dolly Varden charr.

Eyak River/Lake ★★★

Location: Copper River Delta, 150 miles SE of Anchorage.

Access: By car and foot from Cordova. A well-developed trail system provides foot access to the middle river section as well as to Power Creek, a major tributary emptying into the north arm of Eyak Lake. Remote reaches of lake system can be fished by small boat.

Facilities: Full services available in Cordova. A Forest Service cabin is located on Power Creek.

Highlights: One of the more popular, easily accessed and productive locations in the entire Copper River system.

Main Species: SS, RS, DV, CT

The Eyak River is a semi-glacial stream, originating from Shephard Glacier in the Chugach Mountains above Cordova. Power Creek drains the valleys of the Heney Range before emptying into Eyak Lake, from which the smooth-flowing river begins. The Eyak flows wide and deep for a short distance before fanning out onto the flats of the muddy Copper River Delta and then into the Gulf of Alaska.

Since it's fairly glacial, anglers do best working the river with extremely bright lures or bait. Although red salmon are present in large numbers in early summer (late June through early July), they can be finicky about lure selection, with best results occurring in areas with large fish concentrations and currents. (For more details, see the sockeye salmon chapter). Silvers are much more responsive and provide good action in late summer and fall, while trout and charr make themselves known during their annual migrations to and from the sea.

The lake itself offers limited fishing possibilities for cutthroat and Dolly Varden (salmon fishing is closed in lake). The outlet is perhaps the best location for fishing (flyfishing only from below the bridge to above the dam, June through September—see regulations), with the remainder of the lake being fairly shallow, with deeper channels toward the middle, following the pattern of the Eyak River.

Power Creek (accessed by Power Creek Road, which heads north out of Cordova and ends at a trailhead on the lower creek) is also semi-glacial, and salmon fishing is prohibited there, but anglers do very well with Dolly Varden, with individual catches of up to four or five pounds. The best stretch of stream is from the road downstream to Eyak Lake. Cascading falls prevent migration of salmon, and upstream there are only small, resident Dollies. Some cutthroat trout are also taken. The area is very thick with brown bears, and extreme caution should be used when hiking/fishing the creek. There is a Forest Service public use cabin four miles upstream from the trailhead. The best time to fish is from late August to late October, when salmon are on the spawning beds and cooler temperatures start clearing up the creek

Alaganik River/Slough System ★★★

Location: Copper River Delta, 165 miles SE of Anchorage.

Access: By car from Cordova via the Copper River Highway, which follows the slough for a few miles, crossing some tributary streams in places. Side roads and trails access other parts of the system, including McKinley Lake. The main boat launch is from the end of Alaganik Slough Road off of Mile 17, Copper River Highway.

Facilities: Forest Service cabins are available on the slough and McKinley Lake.

Highlights: Easy access, miles of trails, plentiful water, wildlife, and great fishing.

Main Species: SS, RS, CT, DV

The Alaganik River/Slough System is an extensive drainage of lakes, clearwater streams, and glacial sloughs in the Copper River Delta that has traditionally provided plentiful and easily-accessed salmon fishing. Much of the lower system has an abundance of open marshland with slow-moving, semi-glacial water, which is best accessed by boat. The upper system has several small, clear creeks and the main channel is fairly wide, with thick vegetation around the bank.

The U.S. Forest Service maintains cabins on the slough and lake, which are tied into the surrounding trail system. Since Alaganik Slough is so slow, even canoeists can thoroughly enjoy the area. They put in at the highway and paddle upstream to McKinley Lake and the upper system, probably the best bet for sockeye fishing, as the Alaganik itself is difficult to fish due to runoff from nearby glaciers and abundant snags.

The system receives good (awesome in some years) runs of silver salmon (late August through late September), along with significant numbers of red salmon (late June through late July), with the best fishing to be had in the slough near the boat launch (watching tides), the lower Alaganik River around the bridge, the outlet of McKinley Lake, and the mouths of inlet streams. While silvers can be taken throughout the system, red salmon are usually targeted in areas with at least some current. Cutthroat trout and Dolly Varden are also present, mostly in McKinley Lake and tributary streams. Lake fishing for them is most productive early in the season. Later in summer and fall, the lake outlet is perhaps best for targeting pre-spawning salmon and attendant trout and charr.

Martin River System

Location: Copper River Delta, 180 miles SE of Anchorage.

Access: By plane, helicopter or airboat from the town of Cordova. Floatplanes land on area lakes; wheelplanes can sometimes use the open country along the mainstem Martin River for landings.

Facilities: A Forest Service cabin is available at Martin Lake.

Highlights: Splendid scenery, abundant wildlife, and exciting, varied fishing.

Main Species: SS, RS, DV, CT

The Martin River system drains a heavily glaciated area of the coastal Chugach Range and empties into the eastern Copper River Delta. The main river is silty, originating from the Martin River

Glacier, while the tributary streams and lakes run clear and are ideal for sportfishing.

The system supports significant runs of salmon, concentrated in a few holding locations, making for fast action. Most anglers visiting this area stay at the Forest Service cabin located at the outlet of Martin Lake, as this location has some of the best fishing. However, the lower reaches of streams draining into the southern half of the lake are certainly worth a try. Other good fishing locations include the outlets of (and streams below) Little Martin and Tokun lakes, and the mouths of clearwater streams and sloughs off the Martin.

The most sought-after species is silver salmon. These flashy fighters are usually present in the latter half of August through late September, and can be caught with regularity throughout much of the system. The Martin Lake outlet downstream of the cabin is an excellent stretch of water, as the fish school up there and provide superb action, with good conditions for easy spin and flyfishing. Farther down, the outlet stream confluence with the Martin River is another great spot, as is Little Martin Lake outlet and confluence.

Red salmon, always difficult to catch, are present in good numbers in some of the tributary streams from late June through mid-July. Large Dollies are taken during the peak of the salmon runs in Martin Lake and its tributaries, along with cutthroat trout and a few rainbows. There are even some lake trout (the farthest east and south-ranging populations of the species in Alaska) in Tokun Lake, providing good fishing at the outlet from ice-out to mid-June, then later in deeper waters of the lake.

Katalla River

Location: North Gulf Coast, 190 miles SE of Anchorage.

Access: By small plane from Cordova, landing on floats in the slough or bay, or by wheelplane to a rough strip along the beach where faint trails provide upstream access. Helicopters ideal for accessing the upper river.

Facilities: None.

Highlights: Good salmon and trout fishing in a remote and isolated setting.

Main Species: SS, CT, DV

A promising, out-of-the-way salmon and trout stream, the Katalla River has perhaps the most potential of several lesser-visited coastal streams found just east of the Copper River Delta. Gathering water from sources draining the uplands between Bering Lake and the Ragged Mountains, the clear Katalla meanders down through a brushy, wet valley into the gulf at Katalla Bay. The few (mostly hunters) who have fished and explored its reaches report abundant silver and pink salmon, cutthroat trout, and Dolly Varden in a totally wild setting. For the more adventuresome, try this river in fall, as it is rumored to have a small population of steelhead trout.

Fishing spinners and spoons in the mouth and lower river with the tides is certainly one of the better ways to connect with bright salmon, but a hike upstream to check out the pools and small side creeks can yield some delightful flyfishing, especially for Dollies and cutthroats. The best time to fish would be in late summer and fall (from late July through September). Watch out for bears, they are numerous.

The Katalla is definitely worth investigating, as one of the more promising gateway streams to the vast unexplored North Gulf Coast beyond the Copper River Delta.

Bering River System

Location: North Gulf Coast, 205 miles SE of Anchorage.

Access: By small plane from Cordova, landing on beaches, gravel bars, lakes (Bering, Kushtaka), and sloughs near holding fish (spotted from the air). Some hiking (and extreme bushwhacking) necessary to reach choice fishing spots. A small, motorized raft useful for accessing some of these waters.

Facilities: No public facilities.

Highlights: Fishing for anglers with a spirit for adventure.

Main Species: SS, RS, DV

The Bering River is a fair-sized glacial system lying east of the Copper River Delta that, like the Katalla, gets little attention, but has much potential. Originating from the edge of the huge St. Elias ice fields, the silty Bering flows south to the Gulf of Alaska at Controller Bay. There are several large lakes, a few of which have clearwater streams with habitat for salmon and charr. Along with a number of small sloughs and creeks on the east side of the lower river, they hold most of the Bering's sportfish potential.

Red and silver salmon and Dolly Varden are the species most folks look for (cutthroats have been reported from parts of the drainage as well). Some of the more promising drainages to scout include Dick Creek (Bering Lake), Shepherd Creek (glacial but fishable for salmon and possibly some trout; floatplanes can land on small stretch near administrative cabin maintained by Forest Service), and Stillwater/Clear creeks (Kushtaka Lake), although just about any clearwater slough will hold salmon during the peak of the runs (late August to late September for silvers; late June to early August for reds). Bears are quite common, so caution should be used.

Recommended Lodges/Guides/Outfitters/Air taxis

Alaska Wilderness Outfitting Company: P.O. Box 1516, Cordova, AK 99574, (907) 424-5552, www.alaskawilderness.com Lodge based, guided fishing, Tebay system and Copper River delta.

Grove's Klutina River King Salmon Charters: Milepost 100.6, Old Richardson Highway, P.O. Box 236, Copper Center, AK 99573, (907) 822-5822, (800) 770-5822.

Klutina Salmon Charters & Campground: Mile 101 Old Richardson Highway, P.O. Box 78, Copper Center, AK 99573; (907) 822-3991, www.klutinacharters.com

Lee's Air Taxi Service: Box 2660, Glennallen, AK 99588, (907) 822-3343. Air taxi, Upper Copper River.

Paxson Lake Lodge: HC Box 7290, Paxson, AK 99737, (907) 822-3330.

Keystone Adventures: P.O. Box 1486, Valdez, AK 99806, (907) 835-2606, www.alaskawhitewater.com Guided floatfishing/ whitewater trips, Tonsina River.

Fishing & Flying: P.O. Box 2349, Cordova, AK 99574, (907) 424-3324. Air taxi, Copper River Delta/PWS.

Cordova Air Service: P.O. Box 528, Cordova, AK 99574, (907) 424-3289, (800) 424-7608. Air Taxi, Copper River Delta.

Ellis Air Taxi: P.O. Box 106, Glennallen, AK 99588; (907) 822-3368 www.ellisair.com Wheelplane charter service, upper Copper

River/Wrangell-St. Elias.

Cordova Auto Rentals: P.O. Box 1329, Cordova, AK 99574, (907) 424-5982, www.ptialaska.net/~cars Car and canoe rentals.

Orca Adventure Lodge: P.O. Box 2105, Cordova, AK 99574, (866) 424-6722. www.orcaadventurelodge.com Guided fishing, cabin rentals, eastern PWS and Copper River delta.

General information

Alaska Department of Natural Resources: Division of Parks and Outdoor Recreation, Mat-Su/CR Area Office, HC32 Box 6706, Wasilla, AK 99654, (907) 745-3975. For information on state facilities within Copper Basin, www.dnr.state.ak.us/parks/index.htm

Bureau of Land Management: Glennallen District Office, Box 147, Glennallen, AK 99588, (907) 822-3217. For information on public lands and facilities along Gulkana River.

Wrangell St. Elias National Park Headquarters: P.O. Box 439, Copper Center, AK 99573, (907) 822-5234.

U.S. Forest Service, Cordova Ranger District: P.O. Box 280, Cordova, AK 99574, (907) 424-7661. www.fs.fed.us/r10/chugach/cordova/index.html Information on Chugach National Forest lands and public use cabins along Copper River delta.

USGS Maps/Reference

Copper/Tanada lakes: Nabesna B-5, B-6.

Gulkana River System: Mount Hayes A-3, A-4; Gulkana A-3, A-5, B-3, B-4, B-5, C-4, C-5, C-6, D-4, D-5, D-6.

Tazlina River System: Anchorage D-1; Valdez C-6, C-7, C-8, D-6, D-7, D-8; Talkeetna Mountains A-1, A-2; Gulkana A-3, A-4, A-5, A-6.

Klutina River System: Valdez B-6, C-5, C-6, C-7, D-4, D-5, D-6.

Tonsina River System: Valdez B-3, B-4, B-5, C-2, C-3, C-4, C-5.

Tebay River System: Valdez A-1, A-2, B-1; McCarthy A-7, A-8.

Eyak River/Lake: Cordova B-5, C-5.

Alaganik Slough System: Cordova B-3, B-4.

Martin River System: Cordova B-1, B-2, B-3.

Katalla River: Cordova A-2, B-2.

Bering River System: Cordova A-1, B-1; Bering Glacier B-8.

Regulations/Information

Most waters of the Copper River drainage and Copper River delta are open to fishing year-round, all species except king salmon (January 1-July 19) on the Copper, and trout (June 15-April 14) on the Copper River delta. Most Copper River waters are single hook, artificial lure fishing only (except Gulkana, Klutina, and Tonsina rivers, and Copper River mainstem). Numerous special regulations set size and bag limits, seasons, and closed waters for king salmon and other species. Catch-and-release restrictions exist on most waters for rainbow/steelhead trout (and cutthroat trout in certain waters of Copper River delta). Always consult latest Regulations Summary for Southcentral Alaska or contact regional/field offices ADF&G for information when planning a trip to area.

Glennallen: (907) 822-3309   **Anchorage:** (907) 267-2218
Cordova: (907) 424-3212

Online info: www.sf.adfg.state.ak.us/statewide/regulations/scregs.cfm

Copper River/Delta Area Species

LOCATION	KING SALMON	RED SALMON	PINK SALMON	CHUM SALMON	SILVER SALMON	STEELHEAD	RAINBOW	CHARR	GRAYLING	LAKE TROUT	CUTTHROAT	NORTHERN PIKE	SHEEFISH	HALIBUT	LING COD	ROCK FISH	SALMON SHARK	FSHNG. PRESSURE
Copper/Tanada Lakes				✓						☺	☺							R
Gulkana River System	★	☺					R	R	☺	R	★	★						☹
Tazlina River System	☺	✓					R	R	☺	✓	★	✓						M
Klutina River System	★	★					R	R	✓	☺	☺	✓						☹
Tonsina River System	☺	☺					✓	R	✓	☺	☺	✓						M
Tebay River System	R	✓						R	★	R	✓	☺						✓
Eyak River/Lake	R	☺					★			☺				✓				☹
Alaganik River/Slough	R	☺					★			☺				☺				☹
Martin River System		☺					★	R	R	☺			✓	✓				M
Katalla River	R	R	★	✓	★	R		★			★							✓
Bering River System		☺	✓	✓	☺					☺				✓				R

	Species not present	**LL**	Landlocked species
R	Rare	**C**	Present, but fishing closed
✓	Fishable numbers (or light pressure)	**M**	Moderate pressure
☺	Good fishing	☹	Heavy pressure
★	Excellent fishing		

PRINCE WILLIAM SOUND

From the northeast coast of the Kenai Peninsula to the Copper River delta, Prince William Sound stretches in a great, mountain-rimmed arc of convoluted coastline, deep fjords, and numerous glacially carved islands that shelter its waters from the brunt of the stormy Gulf of Alaska.

A world-renowned coastal paradise of spectacularly scenic bays, rainforests, immense tidewater glaciers, and abundant marine and bird life, the sound supports very rich fisheries that include some great sport opportunities for salmon (particularly silver, chum, and pink), bottomfish, Dolly Varden charr, and the continent's westernmost cutthroat trout populations.

The coastal communities of Whittier, Valdez, Cordova, and Seward are the main hubs for accessing and fishing the sound, via either the state highways, Alaska Railroad, or Alaska Marine Highway system. (Cordova also has scheduled air connections to Anchorage and the West Coast.) Limited roads provide shorefishing opportunities around some of these coastal towns, but most of the Sound's fishing is remote and reached by boat or small plane only.

Most of the sound is totally undeveloped wilderness and managed as part of Chugach National Forest. There are 15 U.S. Forest Service public use cabins and 16 Alaska State Marine Parks (mostly undeveloped, but one near Valdez with three public use cabins) spread from the Whittier area to just outside Cordova. A full range of visitor services, including a fleet of charters, is available in each of the hubs.

Whittier/Wells Passage Area ★★★
Location: NW Prince William Sound, 65 miles east of Anchorage.

Access: By boat, foot, or kayak from the town of Whittier, or by floatplane from Anchorage.

Facilities: Forest Service cabins located at Pigot Bay, Cochrane Bay, Harrison Lagoon (Port Wells), and Culross Passage.

Highlights: Easily accessed, good Prince William Sound fishing.

Main Species: KS, SS, RS, CS, PS, DV, HT, RF

Just east of Anchorage, now accessible by road, Whittier (at the head of Passage Canal) is the convenient gateway to what many consider the best part of Prince William Sound. With picturesque, deep blue fjords, numerous sheltered islands, and countless coves, passes, rocky beaches, and bays holding good fishing possibilities, the Northwest sound is a dream come true for small craft exploration.

With few major spawning systems, Northwest Prince William Sound's salmon fishing occurs mostly in bays or near stream mouths (streams are typically short, shallow, and clear; many drain narrow, jutting peninsulas and islands), targeting runs enhanced from area hatcheries.

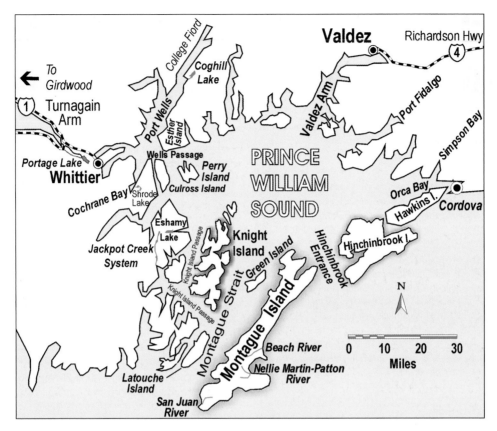

Pink salmon are by far the most common species. In July, they swarm through the sound in huge schools, invading almost any flowing body of water. (Look for bright fish early on in the season, to enjoy the best angling.) Silver salmon begin arriving sometime after the pinks (August) and provide superb action (trolling, mooching bait, and throwing chunky hardware are most effective) in bays, coves, passes, and off points around Wells Passage and Esther Island. A later run in September provides good shorefishing right in the town of Whittier. Good numbers of red and chum salmon are also present around Esther Island. A hatchery run of king salmon returns to the head of Passage Canal, providing early season action for trollers, from Esther Island into town.

Waters out of Whittier are typically very deep (quickly dropping to 600 feet or more), so bottom fishing can be a challenge. Some halibut of decent size are taken close to town, but most of the charter fleet travels to waters fronting the Gulf (Montague Strait) which are more productive for big flatfish, lingcod, and rockfish (pelagic and demersal species). Catches of deep-water rockfish species like yelloweye and short-raker, however, are the best in the sound.

Hot spots to try in the Whittier/Wells Passage area include: Whittier Docks (KS, SS), Pigot Bay (CS, PS, HT), Cochrane Bay (CS, PS, DV, HT), Long Bay (SS, PS, DV), Lake Bay (CS, PS, SS), Wells Bay (CS, PS), Passage Canal (SS, KS, PS), Harrison Lagoon (CS, PS), Unakwik Inlet (CS, PS, RS, CT, DV), Wells Passage (KS, SS, PS, CS, RF, HT), Culross Passage (SS, PS, HT, RF, DV), and Esther Passage (KS, SS, CS, PS, DV).

Coghill River

Location: NW Prince William Sound, College Fiord, 75 miles east of Anchorage.

Access: By boat from Whittier or floatplane from Anchorage.

Facilities: USFS public cabin on river.

Highlights: A unique PWS stream fishery with abundant reds, silvers, and trophy pinks.

Main Species: SS, RS, PS

The Coghill is a short Prince William Sound drainage, flowing a mere two miles from Coghill Lake to College Fiord. The upper river above the lake, however, drops out of the Mount Castner area and Dartmouth Glacier, and flows several miles through forested terrain. Much of the lower river is affected by tides, thus the salmon runs come in quickly and enter the lake without much hesitation, a fact most anglers have learned and honed their timing skills by.

Many anglers visit the Coghill in July during the great sockeye run, with good action possible using flies cast to wandering schools of fish. Yet, in some years, the pink salmon are so thick as to overshadow other game fish in the drainage. Some of these "little" salmon are quite large, often weighing six to seven pounds, with trophy catches up to ten pounds. Some weeks later, the acrobatic coho appears, but does not attract the same following as the sockeye. The fishing, however, can be very good. A wide range of techniques and tackle works, from bait to flies to hardware.

Shrode Lake System

Location: West Prince William Sound, Jackpot Bay, 90 miles SE of Anchorage.

Access: By floatplane or boat. It is a one-and-a-half-mile hike from the head of Long Bay to the lake. Undeveloped trails lead around the area.

Facilities: Forest Service cabin on the shore of Shrode Lake.

Highlights: A very isolated, picturesque, and seldom visited system with good salmon runs.

Main Species: SS, DV, RS

Situated between Culross Passage and Cochrane Bay, Shrode Lake is surrounded by 1,000-foot forest-clad mountains. The drainage consists of just one more body of water—Jack Lake—which is connected by a small stream. From the outlet of Shrode Lake, Shrode Creek runs through a heavily vegetated valley only one-and-a-half miles to narrow Long Bay, a fjord connecting to Culross Passage.

The fishing can be very good, but timing is crucial. Shrode Lake usually carries ice well into June, along with heavy snowcover sometimes, so a visit is not recommended until July. Red salmon arrive first but can be difficult to catch; anglers do far better in late summer when the silvers begin their migration. With little holding water in the small, shallow connecting stream, the best fishing is to be had at the lake outlet and mouth at Long Bay. Incoming and high tides are best as schools of salmon stack into the mouth. The creek also receives a heavy run of pink salmon in season, and charr are present in good numbers in late summer and fall.

Eshamy Lake/Lagoon

Location: West Prince William Sound, Knight Island Passage, 90 miles SE of Anchorage.

Access: By boat through Eshamy Lagoon; floatplane access also possible.

Facilities: None.

Highlights: Very productive fishery for late-season red salmon in a splendid natural setting.

Main Species: SS, RS, CT, DV

Heralded as one of the more picturesque locations in all of Southcentral Alaska, Eshamy Lake has 3,000-foot mountains lining the watershed, complete with a dense rainforest typical of the area. It is an especially productive drainage, supporting large populations of salmon—particularly sockeye.

The majority of successful anglers fish where Eshamy Creek empties into Eshamy Lagoon. (The lagoon, actually being more of a long bay with numerous hidden coves and tiny islands, is the staging area for salmon and charr moving into the system.) A late run of sockeye shows here in late July, with good fishing often lasting into the second half of August. In some years, anglers continue to catch fresh reds through September, at which time a smaller run of silvers enters the stream. This is a popular spot for boaters, who moor in the lagoon and cast to schools of fish, while admiring the scenery.

Late summer and fall anglers may come across some good Dolly Varden action, especially in the stream and the lake outlet. Additionally, some fair sea-run cutthroat trout fishing can be had, a unique opportunity for the western sound.

Knight Island Passage ★★★

Location: West Prince William Sound, 90 miles SE of Anchorage.

Access: By floatplane or boat to various lagoons, coves, beaches, and bays. (Small crafts such as pleasure boats and kayaks can be used in these sheltered waters.)

Facilities: None.

Highlights: A beautiful PWS area with abundant angling.

Main Species: SS, CS, PS, DV, BF

Like many other areas within western Prince William Sound, Knight Island Passage, between the eastern Kenai Peninsula and Knight, Chenega, Bainbridge, Evans, and Latouche islands, contains dozens of protected bays and coves and numerous clearwater streams and lakes, making it one of the finest marine sportfishing and boating destinations in Southcentral Alaska (accessed from nearby ports of Whittier or Seward).

There's a variety of fishing, including salmon, trout, charr, and bottomfish, along with abundant opportunities to set out pots for crab and shrimp. Although surfcasting can be highly productive in some locations, boat anglers mooching or trolling for salmon, or jigging for bottom fish, take the majority of the catch from most of the Passage. Though generally not the size of fish taken from waters fronting the gulf, the halibut are plentiful and easy to take on lighter tackle. Salmon are seasonally intercepted throughout the passage, and in associated bays and coves with spawning streams.

Area hot spots include: Knight Island Passage (SS, KS, PS, BF), Main Bay (CS, PS, RS, DV, HT), Ewan Bay (CS, PS, DV, HT), Jackpot Bay (SS, PS, CT, DV, HT), and Eshamy Bay/Lagoon (SS, CS, RS, PS, DV, CT, HT). Anglers who do a bit of exploring can find many great fishing locations with virtually no pressure.

Jackpot Creek System

Location: West Prince William Sound, Jackpot Bay, 100 miles SE of Anchorage.

Access: Primarily by boat through Jackpot Bay; floatplane landings on lakes also possible.

Facilities: None.

Highlights: A secluded, rarely visited stream with potentially fabulous late-season silver salmon and charr fishing.

Main Species: SS, DV

The Jackpot system is a large drainage of over a dozen lakes and ponds tied together by small and shallow clearwater streams. Surrounding mountains may reach several thousand feet, with glimpses of ice fields and tips of glaciers possible on clear days. The valley floor below, where Jackpot Creek flows, is lush and green with the dense vegetation commonly associated with the northern rainforest.

Several salmon species, as well as charr, call Jackpot home, yet relatively few are present in enough numbers to make a fishing trip there worthwhile. While pinks may swarm throughout the drainage in mid-summer, it is the prized coho that has the most potential. Lasting through August and September, the silver salmon run brings thick schools on incoming tides at the mouth of Jackpot Creek. Although it is possible to hike upstream along the creek, the most productive action is near saltwater. Dolly Varden charr are fairly abundant right after break-up and in late summer and fall. Red and chum salmon may be active in the small stream during mid-summer.

Montague Strait/Island ★★★★

Location: Southwest Prince William Sound, 100 miles SE of Anchorage.

Access: By boat from Seward or Whittier; wheelplane access possible along beaches.

Facilities: Forest Service cabins available at Green Island, Port Chalmers, Beach River, Patton Bay, Log Jam Bay, and San Juan Bay.

Highlights: The most productive bottomfish location in Prince William Sound.

Main Species: SS, PS, BF

One of the best marine locations in Prince William Sound, Montague Strait is a long, wide passage between Montague, Knight, and Latouche islands. Along with Hinchinbrook Entrance, Montague serves as a major migration corridor for salmon bound for streams deep inside the sound. There are several major bays, ports, and harbors, but the strait lacks the abundance of cutting fjords and islands that characterize most of western Prince William Sound, and is, therefore, more open and susceptible to bad weather. Boat access, from Whittier, Seward, even Valdez, is the most expedient, efficient way of reaching and fishing the strait's many locations.

Halibut run much larger than those inside, with trophies to 250 pounds or more not uncommon. Fishing shallower waters than found in most of northwest PWS, boats can more easily probe bays with salmon streams, or around small islands, points, and sandy shoals, to locate giant flatties. Other bottomfish species like rockfish and lingcod are more abundant and robust in these outer waters.

Although large numbers of salmon pass through the strait, there are relatively few streams in the area that contain substantial runs. Creeks there are typically shallow, short, and clear, with small numbers of pink and silver salmon and some Dolly Varden. Fair action for cutthroat trout may even be had in some streams on Montague Island. A boat or some type of watercraft is almost a necessity to access the best fishing, but you can do some fairly productive surf-casting near the mouths of salmon-spawning streams, like those on the southern half of Montague Island (see next three listings).

Montague area hot spots to explore include Knight Island/Bay of Isles (SS, BF), Green Island/Creek (CS, SS, PS, CT, DV, HT), Port Chalmers (HT, SS, PS, CS, CT, DV), Montague Point (BF), Hanning Bay (PS, DV), MacLeod Harbor (PS, DV), Cape Cleare (BF), San Juan Bay (SS, PS, DV), Patton Bay (SS, PS, HT), and Rocky Bay (SS).

Beach River

Location: Central Montague Island, 125 miles SE of Anchorage.

Access: By wheelplane to a short gravel strip on the beach near the river at low tide.

Facilities: Forest Service cabin by mouth.

Highlights: A very remote Gulf Coast drainage with superb salmon and charr action.

Main Species: SS, DV

Like the Nellie Martin-Patton rivers to the south, Beach River flows from the rugged spine of Montague, east through Chugach National Forest land ten miles to the exposed coast fronting the Gulf of

Alaska. The last few miles course through lowlands thick with wildlife, such as bears and a variety of waterfowl.

Like most coastal drainages, the Beach's best fishing is concentrated on the lower river near its mouth, with the few anglers that do visit timing their efforts to the tides. Big schools of strong silvers pulse into the river, often stacking up in holes and pools in great numbers. Overall peak time for these fish is the second half of August, although fish will continue to enter the drainage well into the fall. Sea-run Dolly Varden charr move into the river in late summer and are available in upstream reaches during September. Pinks flood the Beach in mid-summer, offering an option for early-season visitors.

Nellie Martin-Patton Rivers ★★★

Location: Southeast Montague Island, 120 miles SE of Anchorage.

Access: By wheelplane to beach around mouth, or along Patton Bay at low tide; boat access possible, but potentially hazardous for small craft.

Facilities: Forest Service cabin located a half-mile from beach.

Highlights: Premier PWS silver salmon fishery, great for flyfishing.

Main Species: SS, DV

The Nellie Martin-Patton rivers of southern Montague Island are popular destinations for fly-in anglers, with some of the best silver salmon fishing in Prince William Sound (abundant runs, with fish up to 18 pounds), along with large numbers of pink salmon and Dolly Varden charr. Crystal clear, with gravel and sand bottoms, long runs, and deep pools, these twin fork rivers offer great fly and spin casting possibilities. The scenery, like the fishing, is magnificent, with mountains to nearly 4,000 feet looming as a backdrop to the west.

The mouth and lower sections of both rivers are the most popular and productive areas to fish, especially on the rising tide, but Patton Bay offers good skiff fishing for silvers and pinks as well as halibut. Anglers planning a trip to these rivers should allow several days in their schedule for the possibility of bad weather and travel delays.

San Juan River

Location: South Montague Island, 125 miles SE of Anchorage.

Access: By plane or boat. Wheelplane is the safest and most practical way of reaching the river, landing on the beach nearby.

Facilities: Forest Service cabin located just south of the river.

Highlights: A very remote, little-fished river with great potential for silver salmon.

Main Species: SS

The San Juan is a very short coastal drainage on the southern tip of Montague Island, flowing only some five miles from steep mountain slopes down through a dense portion of the Chugach National Forest to a fairly wide lake, only to channel a last mile to San Juan Bay and the Gulf of Alaska. Because of its remoteness and adverse weather, the river receives light angling pressure.

While other streams offer more variety, few can match the intensity of the San Juan silver run. These large, robust fish are present in huge numbers during August and September on the lower river between the lake and the bay. Anglers fortunate to be there at the peak of the run can expect dozens of fish per day, and the drainage is perfect for flyfishing. But come prepared; inclement weather may cause travel delays, sometimes for up to several days.

Valdez/Valdez Arm ★★★★

Location: North PWS, 105 miles east of Anchorage.

Access: By car via Richardson Highway. The outer bay area is reached primarily by boat.

Facilities: Full visitor services available in Valdez.

Highlights: Perhaps the best and most consistent saltwater fishery for silver salmon in all of Southcentral Alaska, with superb deep-sea safari possibilities.

Main Species: KS, SS, PS, HT, SHK, RF

The Port of Valdez and surrounding bay and arm comprise one of the most popular road-accessible marine fishing locations in Alaska. A long curved inlet, it contains numerous clear and glacial streams draining off the Chugaches, which greatly influence its physical character and angling. In the greenish-gray, cold waters, all five species of salmon, charr, and bottomfish can be taken, but the abundant runs of lure-snapping silver and pink salmon and good-sized halibut draw anglers' attention most. (Valdez is known as the Pink Salmon Capital of the World and has three salmon derbies each summer.) The presence of the Solomon Gulch Hatchery across the bay from the town of Valdez considerably enhances the salmon fishing, in some years producing thick concentrations of returning fish and some wild action at the head of the bay. (Silvers have been known to jump into boats and up on docks there.)

Port Valdez has excellent road fishing for pinks and silvers from beaches, points, docks, and creek mouths around the bay during the peak of salmon season (July and August). But some of the best action is found in areas reached by boats or plane (Anderson, Wells, and Galena bays, the Narrows, Port Fidalgo, etc). Feeder king salmon are present in outer waters in small numbers during late winter and spring, while adult spawners return to the area through May and June. Dolly Varden charr are usually taken near the mouths of clear rivers and creeks (Robe River).

Valdez's reputation for halibut is unsurpassed in Prince William Sound, with good to excellent fishing to be had in the deeper, outer waters of Valdez Arm and adjacent bays in the eastern part of the sound, particularly in late summer and fall. Most of the charter fleet works this area down to Hinchinbrook Entrance (and beyond) for consistent and impressive catches.

Some hot spots to try for various species include Valdez Harbor (SS, PS), Valdez Narrows (SS, PS), Allison Point (SS, CS, PS), the mouth of Gold Creek (SS, PS), Glacier Island (HT), Port Fidalgo (HT, RF, SS, SHK, CS, PS, CT), Anderson Bay (SS, CS, PS), Jack Bay (HT, SS, CS, PS, DV), Sawmill Bay (CS, PS, DV, HT), Wells Bay (CS, PS), and Galena Bay (SS, CS, PS, DV, HT, RF).

Note: *Valdez hosts some of the oldest fishing derbies in Alaska, dating back to 1951. The halibut derby from late May (usually commencing Memorial Day weekend) through August awards $15,000 plus a brand new truck for the largest fish. The silver salmon derby, held throughout the month of August, offers over $65,000 in cash and prizes, with the top coho earning $15,000.*

Cordova/Orca Bay & Inlet ★★★

Location: East Prince William Sound, 135 miles east of Anchorage.

Access: By boat (there are hundreds of miles of sheltered coast-

line), or small plane (landing in bays or on long gravel beaches near salmon streams) from the town of Cordova. There are also some limited shore fishing opportunities.

Facilities: A Forest Service cabin is located at Double Bay, Hinchinbrook Island. Full visitor services available in Cordova.

Highlights: One of the more popular coastal fishing areas of Southcentral Alaska.

Main Species: KS, SS, PS, DV, SHK, BF

Orca Bay/Inlet encompasses a number of smaller bays, coves, Hawkins Island and the northeastern corner of Hinchinbrook Island. Accessed from the town of Cordova at the head of Orca Inlet, the many fine area fishing locations lie within easy reach by boat.

The major species that anglers target in the sound from Cordova are silver and pink salmon, Dolly Varden charr, and halibut, with king salmon, both feeder and terminal fish, becoming increasingly popular in late winter/spring and early summer, respectively. The better salmon action occurs at the heads of bays near spawning streams, especially those around Hawkins island, the northeast end of Hinchinbrook, and the northern section of Orca Bay. (Those small, clear-water feeder streams also offer some great spin and flycasting opportunities for salmon, Dolly Varden charr, and cutthroat trout.)

Casting from shore is most frequently done from the road system near the town of Cordova, for enhanced runs of king and silver salmon returning to locations nearby (Fleming Spit). More abundant shorefishing opportunities are available on nearby Hawkins Island.

Cordova halibut are taken in shallow waters during spring, but move deeper as the season progresses. (They may also be taken in the fall off the mouths of salmon streams in certain areas.) The most productive fishing (more and larger halibut) occurs southwest of town in the waters surrounding Hinchinbrook and out in the Gulf.

The best fishing locations in the Orca Bay/Inlet area include: the mouth of Cordova Harbor (KS, SS), Hartney Bay (KS, SS, PS), Fleming Spit (KS, SS), and the mouth of Humpback Creek (PS), near the town of Cordova; Simpson Bay (KS, SS, PS, HT, RF), Sheep Bay (SS, PS, HT, RF), and Port Gravina (SS, PS, CS, HT, SHK, RF), on the northern half of Orca; stream mouths on Hawkins Island—Hawkins Creek (PS, CT, DV) and Canoe Passage (PS, CT, DV); and Anderson Bay (PS, CT, DV), Double Bay (PS, CT, DV, HT), and Boswell Bay (PS, DV) on Hinchinbrook Island.

Note: *Much of the land surrounding Orca Inlet/Bay is privately owned. For information on location and lawful access to these lands, contact: The Eyak Corporation, 910 Lefevre, P.O. Box 340, Cordova, AK 99574, (907) 424-7161.*

Recommended Lodges/Guides/Outfitters/Air taxis

Anchor/Sportsman Inn: P.O. Box 750, Whittier, AK 99693, (907) 472-2352.

Aspen Hotel: P.O. Box 365, Valdez, AK 99686, (907) 835-4445. *www.aspenhotelsak.com*

Reluctant Fisherman Inn: P.O. Box 150, Cordova, AK 99574, (907) 424-3272, *www.reluctantfisherman.com*

Whittier Charters: 3917 Magrath Road, Bellingham, WA 98226, (360) 752-2071, *www.whittiercharters.com*

Captain Ron's Adventures: P.O. Box 3733, Homer, AK 99603;

(907) 235-4368 (winter), *www.alaskawebs.com/captainron/ fishing.htm* Multi-day fishing charters, PWS.

Orion Charters: P.O. Box 3577, Valdez, AK 99686, (907) 835.8610. *www.orioncharters.com*

Sea Sound Charters: P.O. Box 422, Cordova, AK 99574, (907) 424-5488. *www.seasoundcharters.com*

Seaview Charters: P.O. Box 331, Valdez, AK 99686, (907) 835-5115. Halibut/salmon charters, PWS.

Sound Experience: Cordova, AK, (907) 424-5988, *www.alaskaspwsx.com* Marine/freshwater fishing charters, PWS Cordova area.

Cordova Air Service: P.O. Box 528, Cordova, AK 99574, (907) 424-3289, (800) 424-7608.

Rusts Flying Service: P.O. Box 190867, Anchorage, AK 99519, (800) 544-2299, (907) 243-1595, *www.flyrusts.com* Air taxi service, western PWS.

USGS Maps/NOAA Nautical Charts Reference

Whittier/Wells Passage: Seward C-3, C-4, C-5, D-2, D-3, D-4, D-5.

Coghill River: Anchorage A-3.

Shrode Lake System: Seward C-4.

Eshamy Lake/Lagoon: Seward B-3.

Knight Island Passage: Seward A-3, A-4, B-3, B-4, C-2, C-3.

Jackpot Creek System: Seward B-4.

Montague Strait/Island: Seward A-1, A-2, A-3, B-1, B-2, B-3, C-2; Blying Sound D-1, D-2, D-3, D-4.

Beach River: Seward A-1.

Nellie Martin-Patton Rivers: Blying Sound D-1, D-2.

San Juan River: Blying Sound D-3.

Valdez/Valdez Arm: Valdez A-7, A-8; Cordova D-8; Seward D-1.

Orca Bay/Inlet: Cordova B-5, B-6, B-7; C-5, C-6, C-7, C-8.

Nautical Chart: PWS: 16700.

General Information

Chugach National Forest: 201 East Ninth Avenue, Suite 206, Anchorage, AK 99501, (907) 271-2500. Information on public lands and public use cabins within PWS, *www.fs.fed.us/r10/chugach/*

Alaska State Parks: Kenai/PWS Area Office, P.O. Box 1247, Soldotna, AK 99669, (907) 262-5581. For information on State Marine Parks and public use cabins within PWS.

Alaska Marine Highway: (800) 642-0066, *www.dot.state.ak.us/amhs/index.html* Information on state ferry service to/within PWS.

Regulations/Information

Most PWS waters are open to fishing year-round for salmon, with seasonal restrictions on halibut, lingcod, rockfish, and cutthroat trout (see regs for details). For all fresh waters, unbaited, artificial lure fishing only allowed. Always check current Regulations Summary for Southcentral Alaska and/or contact regional/field offices ADF&G for complete information when planning a fishing trip to area.

Anchorage: (907) 267-2218   **Cordova:** (907) 424-3212

Information online: *www.sf.adfg.state.ak.us/statewide/regulations/scregs.cfm*

Prince William Sound Species

LOCATION	King Salmon	Red Salmon	Pink Salmon	Chum Salmon	Silver Salmon	Steelhead	Rainbow	Cutthroat	Charr	Grayling	Lake Trout	Sheefish	Northern Pike	Halibut	Ling Cod	Rock Fish	Salmon Shark	Fshng. Pressure
Whittier/Wells Passage	☺	☺	✪	✪	✪			R	✔					☺	✔	✪	☺	☹
Coghill River	R	✪	✪	✔	☺			R	☺									M
Shrode Lake System		✔	☺	✔	☺			R	☺									✔
Eshamy Lake/Lagoon		✪	✔	✔	☺			✔	☺									M
Jackpot Creek System		✔	✪	✔	✪			✔	☺									✔
Montague Strait/Island	✔	R	✪	☺	✪			☺	✔					✪	✪	✪	☺	M
Knight Island Passage	✔	☺	✪	☺	✪			☺	☺					☺	☺	☺	✔	✔
Beach River	R	R	✪	✔	✪			R	✪									✔
Nellie Martin-Patton Rivers	R	R	✪	✔	✪			R	✪									M
San Juan River		R	✔	✔	✪			R	✔									✔
Valdez/Valdez Arm	✔	R	✪	✪	✪			R	☺					☺	✔	✔	✪	☹
Cordova/Orca Bay/Inlet	☺	R	✪	☺	✪			☺	☺					✪	☺	☺	☺	☹

Legend:

- Species not present
- **R** Rare
- ✔ Fishable numbers (or light pressure)
- ☺ Good fishing
- ✪ Excellent fishing
- **LL** Landlocked species
- **C** Present, but fishing closed
- **M** Moderate pressure
- ☹ Heavy pressure

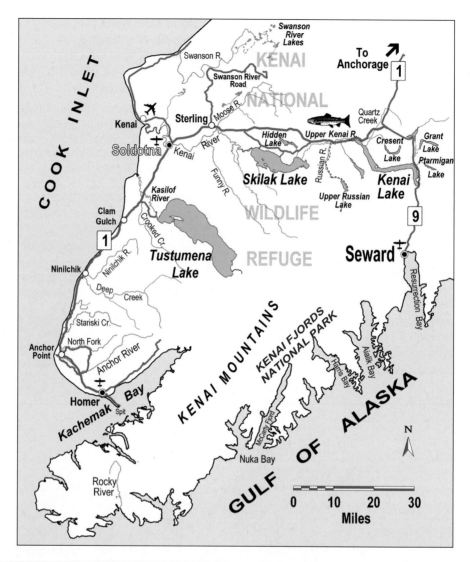

KENAI PENINSULA-COOK INLET

This area includes the waters of the Kenai Peninsula and Cook Inlet and contains some of the state's most notable marine and freshwater sport fisheries. The Kenai Peninsula is often characterized as a miniature Alaska, with its immense ice fields, turquoise glacial lakes, sparkling runoff streams, forests, fjords, and towering mountains. Its wildlife also mirrors that of the state, with some of the world's largest moose, abundant waterfowl and marine mammals, bears, and even caribou. What's more, the Kenai Peninsula and surrounding waters are amply blessed with an amazing fecundity, producing some of Alaska's most abundant and unique fishing opportunities, particularly trophy king salmon and halibut. Nearly all of it is easy to reach by boat, car, short hike, or a plane ride.

Upper Kenai River System ★★★★

Location: East Cook Inlet, Kenai Peninsula, 50 miles south of Anchorage.

Access: By car, boat, and foot via Seward and Sterling highways. Boats and rafts may be launched in several places along the Sterling Highway, which parallels the river's mainstem most of its length. Developed trails lead to remote lakes within the drainage.

Facilities: Full visitor services available along the road in the Cooper Landing area.

Highlights: One of Alaska's best road-accessible fisheries for red salmon, trophy rainbow trout, and Dolly Varden.

Main Species: SS, RS, RT, DV

The lovely upper Kenai River, with its emerald waters, scenic mountains, and forests, is one of Alaska's most popular recreation areas. It has a phenomenally productive fishery and a real wilderness character that, despite the high use of recent years, continues to thrill and amaze everyone, newcomers and seasoned Alaskans alike.

Rising from runoff streams and creeks in the Kenai Mountains, the river begins at the outlet of Kenai Lake and flows swiftly west towards Cook Inlet. Most of the river from the lake down is Class I water perfectly suited for drift fishing in boats or rafts. In the last few miles before Skilak Lake, the river enters a canyon with Class III water, which should only be negotiated by experienced boaters.

Like the lower Kenai, the upper river gets two distinct runs each of king, silver, and red salmon (it's currently closed for king salmon fishing). Silvers are primarily available during the early run from mid-August until mid-September. (The late fall/winter run is currently off limits to anglers.) Red salmon appear in abundance during mid-June to early July, from the mouth of Russian River downstream, with good to excellent action to be expected (especially near the confluence area, as these fish are bound for the Russian River drainage.) The late red run consists of mainstem and upper tributary spawning fish that are at their best from late July into early August, creating some of Alaska's best fishing for the species. The fish are typically quite large, and trophy-sized (up to 14 pounds or more) are not unusual. This is also the main spawning ground for many late-run kings (a few of which may top 100 pounds) that can be observed in late summer and fall.

Some of Alaska's best water for trophy rainbow trout (to 20 pounds) and Dolly Varden charr (to 15 pounds) can be found on the Upper Kenai, especially in September and October. Its closed waters to motorized boat traffic enhances the appeal for short drift fishing trips, easily accessed from numerous points along the Sterling Highway, which parallels the mainstem. (Try the half-day float from Kenai Lake to Jim's Landing, with a stop to fish the mouth of the Russian River along the way.)

Other angling opportunities in the Upper Kenai system include Trail Lake (RT, LT, DV); Hidden Lake (KO, RT, LT, DV); Cooper Lake (RT, DV); Vagt, Grant, and Jean lakes (RT); Crescent Lake (GR); Trail River (RT, DV); Quartz Creek (DV); Hidden Creek (RS, RT, DV); Grant Creek (SS, DV); and Ptarmigan and Daves creeks (RT, DV).

Lower Kenai River System ★★★★
Location: East Cook Inlet, Kenai Peninsula, 50 miles SW of Anchorage.

Access: By car, boat, and foot via Sterling Highway, which parallels the river more or less from Skilak Lake down to the mouth, providing extensive access for shore anglers as well as boaters.

Facilities: Full services available along the highway.

Highlights: Alaska's most popular sport fishery, and perhaps the most famous trophy salmon location in the world.

Main Species: KS, SS, RS, PS, RT, DV

The bluish-green Kenai is the queen of Alaska's rivers, with easy access, incomparable trophy fishing, and abundant salmon runs, especially in the lower river, which begins at glacial Skilak Lake and flows west 50 miles to Cook Inlet, through spruce-cottonwood forests and rolling hills.

Unlike many of the state's other rivers, the Kenai receives two distinct waves (or runs), of king, silver, and red salmon each year. King and red salmon invade the river from late spring through summer, with silver salmon running from late summer into winter.

Most of all, of course, the lower Kenai River is noted for its mammoth strain of king salmon. The current International Game Fish Association (IGFA) World Record for a sport-caught fish is over 97 pounds, taken near Soldotna in 1985. (Larger kings in excess of 100 pounds have also been sighted.) The largest fish each summer invariably go 80 to 85 pounds, with fair numbers weighing over 60 and 70 pounds. Although giant kings can be caught anytime during the season, the month of July produces by far the most fish of trophy proportion. The Kenai system has also produced numerous other world records (IGFA "All-Tackle," "line-class" and "flyrod-tippet" classes) for red and pink salmon and Dolly Varden charr, as well as a good share of Alaska's largest trophy rainbows. The state record red salmon (16 pounds) and pink salmon (12 pounds) came from the lower Kenai.

The majority of angling for king and silver salmon takes place on the far lower river below the Soldotna highway bridge, but some good fishing can also be had on the stretch of water above the bridge, particularly upstream of Naptown Rapids. Both private and guide boats, as well as a few bank fishers, actively work the area on the incoming tides using attractor lures with or without salmon roe. Back trolling and drifting are the most popular methods for kings, while anchoring up is best for silvers, especially when soaking salmon eggs or flipping spinners. The red salmon hug the riverbanks and are most susceptible in the stretch of water from Soldotna upstream to the Killey River, during the month of July. A run of trophy pink salmon often attracts considerable attention during even years, with superb action in late summer (August). Good numbers of trophy rainbow trout and sea-run Dolly Varden are taken in the first few miles of river from the Skilak Lake outlet to the mouth of the Funny River.

Local hot spots include the Moose River (KS, SS, RS, PS, RT, DV); East Fork of the Moose River (RT); Killey River (SS, PS, RT, DV); Funny River (SS, PS, RT, DV); Beaver Creek (RT, DV); King County Creek (SS, RS, RT, DV); Kelly, Peterson, Egumen, Watson, Afonas, Grebe, and Longmere lakes (RT); Union, Loon, and Sport Lakes (landlocked salmon, RT); and Scout and Arc lakes (landlocked salmon).

Russian River System ★★★★
Location: Kenai River drainage, 50 miles south of Anchorage.

Access: By car, foot, boat, and floatplane. A trail system provides access to entire drainage. The mouth is most often reached from the Sterling Highway by the way of a small ferry built to shuttle anglers across the mainstem Kenai.

Facilities: Large developed campgrounds near river mouth, Forest Service cabins on Upper and Lower Russian lakes.

Highlights: A readily-accessible, world-class stream fishery for sockeye salmon. Noted by the locals as also being good for flyfishing rainbow trout and silver salmon. Great river for sight-fishing.

Main Species: SS, RS, RT, DV

The Russian River is a major clearwater tributary of the upper Kenai River. From its headwaters high in the Kenai Mountains, it flows swift and shallow through a narrow valley lined with spruce and cottonwood. Two major lakes are formed along the way—Upper and Lower Russian. Trails follow the river along its entire length from the upper lake to the Kenai confluence (twelve miles), providing superlative hiking and access to less-visited stretches of water.

The Russian is perhaps the most visited stream of its size in Alaska, drawing anglers with its world class combination of shallow, clear waters, easy access, and dense schools of salmon (sockeye and silver) that invade every summer. The first of two large runs of red salmon enters the river in June, the second in July and August, followed by a smaller (and much less fished) run of silver salmon in August and September. It's a total carnival fishing scene during the peak of the sockeye run (particularly near its confluence with the Kenai River), but with near-perfect conditions for taking the normally tight-lipped salmon on a fly, most folks are able to get their limit (three fish), with some skilled anglers being able to catch and release up to 30 or 40 salmon in a day's worth of hard fishing.

In late summer and fall, rainbow trout and charr fishing heats up in the sections of the river associated with major salmon spawning (the mouth and river sections below the lakes). Drifted egg, flesh, and attractor patterns are most effective, but more traditional insect patterns work great early in the season. The small tributary streams of the lakes are seldom fished, but can also provide good fishing for trout and charr in late summer and fall. Since the Russian River sees an enormous amount of spawning activity in August and September, brown and black bears can be quite common, particularly along the upper river and near the campground. Use caution when fishing and tramping through the brush along the banks, especially in early morning and late evening.

Note: *The Russian was one of the first Alaska streams to see successful techniques for flyfishing sockeyes. See the chapter on red salmon for details on methods, gear, and flies used.*

Swanson River System ★★★
Location: Northeast Cook Inlet, Kenai Peninsula, 40 miles SW of Anchorage.

Access: By car and canoe/kayak/raft.

Facilities: Primitive boat launch on upper Swanson River off Swanson River Road; developed campground near river mouth accessed via North Kenai Road.

Highlights: Superb canoe access to a multitude of remote lakes containing wild populations of rainbow trout and charr.

Main Species: SS, RT, DV

The Swanson River is a slow-moving, fairly small river draining a large area of lowland lakes and swamps in the northern Kenai Peninsula. There are over 35 lakes connected to the Swanson system through tiny streams or short portages, many of them having good fishing (best in fall) for rainbow trout and Dolly Varden charr.

Extremely popular with canoeists, the Swanson River Canoe Route is easily accessed from Swan Lake Road via the Swanson River Road (put in at Paddle Lake), making for trips lasting from several days to one week. The Swanson can also be accessed at mid-river from the end of Swanson River Road; from there down to the mouth, it is an easy, two-day float and fish trip. Most of the way, the water is flat, but there are some slight rapids near the mouth. Take-out is at the Captain Cook Recreation Area and campground, about 36 miles north of the town of Kenai, along the Kenai Spur from the Sterling Highway.

Several salmon species spawn in the drainage, but it is the silvers that provide most of the fishing action on the Swanson. These fine fighters can be encountered in large schools throughout the river (especially around the confluences of streams and adjoining lakes) from mid-August through early September, but they are best fished on the lower river during incoming tides early in the season.

Lower Cook Inlet (Saltwater) ★★★★
Location: Southwest coast Kenai Peninsula, 100 miles SW of Anchorage.

Access: By boat from numerous access points along the Sterling Highway from Ninilchik to Anchor Point.

Facilities: Full visitor services readily available along Sterling Highway. Boat launches located at the mouths of the Ninilchik and Anchor rivers, Deep Creek, and surrounding beaches, including Whiskey Gulch.

Highlights: Excellent Southcentral marine fishery for trophy-sized king salmon and halibut.

Main Species: KS, SS, HT

Cook Inlet's daunting waters mix the chill gray runoff from melting glaciers with the clear-green Pacific Ocean, stirring it with strong tides and unpredictable weather. Some outstanding and unique fishing can be had, however, off the surf-swept beaches and bluffs along the western Kenai Peninsula, in a magnificent Alaska setting. On clear days, the inlet mirrors the snow-capped peaks of Mount Redoubt and Iliamna, two active volcanoes of Alaska's "ring of fire."

The inlet serves as a major migration corridor for countless fish bound for the Kenai Peninsula, the west side of the inlet, and the immense Susitna River drainage to the north. Salmon fishing is often fast and furious during the peak of the runs, with trolling being the primary method used by most anglers along the beaches (with surfcasting possible in some locations) and near stream mouths from Ninilchik south to Anchor Point.

This area is noted for its trophy king salmon and halibut fisheries, with record catches not uncommon. Halibut up to 350 pounds or more, and kings of 70 to 80 pounds plus, have been caught. (Commercial fishermen have even reported catching fish well over 100 pounds.) There are two runs of king (peak mid to late May and early July) and silver salmon (peak early to mid-August and early September). Although the action is usually best during the early runs, the late runs have larger fish. Red salmon are also abundant but, due to their reluctance to strike hardware, fishing for them is seldom better than fair. Some of the better locations for salmon in the lower Cook Inlet include the mouths of Ninilchik River, Deep Creek, Stariski Creek, and Anchor River, and areas around The Falls, Whiskey Gulch, Anchor Point, and Happy Valley.

Halibut fishing is outstanding from May into September, with these gargantuan flatfish hitting best at slack high and low tide a few miles offshore, on shoals and reefs just about anywhere along the coast of the Kenai Peninsula. The Barren and Chugach islands around Kennedy Entrance at the mouth of the inlet are good early and late season bets, and provide additional opportunity for lingcod and rockfish. For those interested in longer, overnight trips, the west side of the inlet has some phenomenal action for flatfish (try Kamishak Bay and near Augustine Volcano).

Kasilof River System ★★★

Location: Southeast Cook Inlet drainage, Kenai Peninsula, 75 miles SW of Anchorage.

Access: By car via the Sterling Highway, just south of Soldotna.

Facilities: Developed boat launches along the river, with both state-run and private campgrounds. Full services nearby on highway.

Highlights: A good boat and shore fishery for king salmon, with a little-known, late run of trophy kings in July.

Main Species: KS, SS, RS, ST, LT

The greenish-gray Kasilof River drains the immense and glacially turbid waters of Tustumena Lake (the Kenai Peninsula's largest lake), at the base of the Kenai Mountains. It provides a fairly significant amount of sportfishing in its lower reaches and clearwater tributaries, and is easily accessed. Most of the angling takes place from the Sterling Highway bridge downstream to the confluence with clear Crooked Creek (where a campground is located), a major salmon-spawning tributary. Fishing is equally productive from the bank or from a raft or driftboat.

The Kasilof is one of the most popular fisheries in all of Southcentral Alaska during the month of June, when the kings are in heavy. Two runs enter the Kasilof, the first in May and June, the second in July and August. The first run is comprised of both wild and hatchery fish, and is by far the stronger of the two. The late run is much weaker in strength, but produces larger fish of up to 60 and 70 pounds or more. Silver salmon show in good numbers in late summer and fall (mid-August through early September) and are targeted primarily in the section of river below Sterling Highway, such as the confluence with Crooked Creek. The Kasilof also has the distinction of sustaining the northernmost natural population of steelhead trout in Cook Inlet, and a small run of these fish returns every fall, to spawn in Crooked Creek the following spring.

The Kasilof system, including Tustumena Lake and its tributaries, is also one of the leading producers of red salmon in Cook Inlet, a fact bank anglers take advantage of during the run peak in early July. Due to the glacial nature of the Kasilof, bright orange yarn flies are most productive. Some really fine fishing can be had for abundant Dolly Varden charr that feed on smolt and eggs, especially in the fall and spring at the outlet and mouths of the clearwater tributaries along Tustumena Lake (accessed by side road from the Sterling Highway). Fishing the lake by boat is treacherous, due to potentially swamping winds and submerged rocks in the lake and river. Some fair to good lake trout fishing also occurs near the outlet in spring.

Ninilchik Area Streams

Location: Southeast Cook Inlet, Kenai Peninsula, 90 miles SW of Anchorage.

Access: By car from the Sterling Highway in the community of Ninilchik. The highway crosses the lower stream sections, with side roads to the lower portions of the drainages. Trails lead up and down along the streams.

Facilities: Full visitor services available in Ninilchik.

Highlights: Easily accessed, great opportunities for ocean fresh salmon and trout in a small stream setting.

Main Species: KS, SS, ST, DV

The *Ninilchik River*, in reality more of a creek than anything else, flows from the northeast, draining the lowland marshes near the coast of Kenai Peninsula. The river winds considerably, its waters consisting of a delightful combination of shallow riffles and deep holes and runs, perfect for the adventuresome angler to hike and explore the murky waters in search of quarry. Nearby *Deep Creek* (only a mile or so away from Ninilchik at the lower reaches) empties out of the Ninilchik Dome and Caribou Hills area just north of Homer and runs westward to Cook Inlet. It is the larger of the two streams and has a slightly different character than its neighbor, particularly on the lower section, with sparse vegetation, rocky beaches, and wide-open spaces. However, both streams share the attraction of being lined with dense spruce and cottonwood forests throughout the middle and upper sections.

The most prized gamefish in the Ninilchik area is, without a doubt, king salmon. Though not as heavy as their Kenai cousins to the north (these fish average 15 to 20 pounds and rarely exceed 40 pounds), it is the number of fish and early season availability that attract anglers here year after year. Good to excellent action is the norm during the peak of the runs in late May and early June. Spin fishers do well at the stream mouths, while flyfishing is the way to go on the middle and upper reaches. Good runs of silver salmon and Dolly Varden follow the kings in late summer and fall, ending with steelhead trout in late autumn.

Anglers wanting to sample some truly undisturbed fishing may want to consider hiking into the headwaters for sea-run charr and resident rainbow trout.

Many anglers take advantage of some outstanding razor clam digging on the sand beaches around the mouth of these streams. Best digging is during tides of minus two feet, or less.

Anchor River ★★★

Location: Southeast Cook Inlet, Kenai Peninsula, 115 miles SW of Anchorage.

Access: By car and foot via the Sterling Highway, from the community of Anchor Point. A side road crosses the lower river and follows it for two miles to the mouth, offering a multitude of access points. Trails lead up and down along the river.

Facilities: Full services available in nearby Anchor Point.

Highlights: Southcentral Alaska's most popular steelhead trout stream, with outstanding fishing for king and silver salmon.

Main Species: KS, SS, ST, DV

The Anchor is a small, highly productive clearwater stream of the southern Kenai Peninsula just north of Kachemak Bay. Its close proximity to Anchorage and good stream conditions give it a high amount of seasonal use. The river begins in a broad valley north of Bald Mountain and flows approximately 34 miles before emptying into Cook Inlet 16 miles northwest of Homer. Shallow and rocky for most of its length, the Anchor is a moody river, quickly turning a chocolate brown after spells of rain, but usually running clear.

The lower river is open to salmon fishing, and it is especially popular from late May to mid-June, when the king salmon arrive. The mouth of the river (where there is a nice campground) also serves as a launch point for boaters seeking salmon and halibut in the adjoining marine waters. Incoming tides are the best times to fish for fresh runs of salmon (as well as steelhead trout and Dolly Varden in season). The Anchor's first steelhead start to show up in August most years, peaking in numbers by late September and early October. Fishing can be good into November, depending on the weather. The silver run can also be heavy and productive, providing great inter-tidal sport in the latter half of August. Sea-run charr (though usually not very large) are plentiful on the lower river in July and flyfishers often report exceptional, fish-on-every-cast action.

During late summer and fall, the middle and upper river also support high numbers of Dolly Varden, along with some resident rainbows. With a little hiking, anglers can enjoy a measure of solitude and classic stream fishing conditions.

Homer/Kachemak Bay ★★★

Location: Southwest Kenai Peninsula, 125 miles southwest of Anchorage.

Access: By car and boat from Homer at the end of Sterling Highway.

Facilities: Full visitor services available in Homer and Seldovia.

Highlights: One of Southcentral's most popular, easily accessed nearshore marine fisheries.

Main Species: KS, SS, PS, HT

Beautiful Kachemak Bay, situated on the southern end of the Kenai Peninsula, provides an abundance and variety of fishing in a diverse natural setting. The north side of the bay is dominated by grassy bluffs and long sand beaches, while the south side is more rugged, with mountains, glaciers, deep valleys, and hidden coves. Along with Resurrection Bay, Kachemak Bay receives some of the greatest visitor use of any Alaska coastal destination.

In Homer, halibut is king, and one of the largest charter fleets in Alaska operates out of the port bound for more remote areas of the bay and lower Cook Inlet. Kachemak Bay is ideal for small craft, such as open skiffs and kayaks, as well as larger sport fishing vessels. It's a short run, about three to four miles straight across, from the boat launch facilities at Homer Harbor to the south side, where the majority of good angling occurs.

The clear-green waters are home to both natural and enhanced runs of salmon, in addition to a rich assemblage of shellfish and bottomfish. However, one can do quite well for salmon and charr fishing in or near stream mouths nearly anywhere in the bay, and on shoals and reefs in deeper water for halibut and rockfish. While the majority of king anglers target mature, stream-bound chinook in the outer bay from mid-May through early June, trolling for smaller "feeder" king salmon can be productive year-round in Kachemak, with some of the better fishing occurring in late winter/spring and fall. (Every March there is a winter king salmon derby held in Homer that attracts anglers from across the state.) Hot spots include Bluff Point and various areas along the southern shore, mainly Seldovia Bay, Glacier Spit, and Gull Island.

The lagoon on the Homer Spit (and Halibut Cove/Lagoon across the bay in Seldovia) has some outstanding fishing from shore for hatchery kings during the month of June. Silvers follow in August and remain well into September. Some anglers do well targeting sea-run charr off the sandy spit early in the season (May and June). A huge run of ocean-bright pinks hits Tutka Bay in July, about the same time a pulse of sockeye invades China Poot Creek.

Note: *The Homer Halibut Derby, May 1-September 30, is the largest jackpot derby in Alaska. Top contestants take home $40-50,000 in cash, with tagged fish worth up to $10,000. The winning fish generally tops 300 pounds; the record is 376 pounds.*

Rocky River

Location: Northwest Gulf of Alaska, Kenai Peninsula, 145 miles SW of Anchorage.

Access: By boat or floatplane from the towns of Homer and Seldovia.

Facilities: None.

Highlights: A remote clearwater stream with excellent silver salmon and sea-run Dolly Varden fishing.

Main Species: SS, RS, DV

Rocky River is a small, pristine watershed located on the southern tip of the Kenai Peninsula, just south of Kachemak Bay. Draining out of the Red Mountain area, the river runs a short distance south to Rocky Bay and the Gulf of Alaska. It is beautifully endowed, with thick surrounding forests, an abundance of wildlife, and water that is remarkably clear and deep, creating superb habitat for salmon (red, pink, and silver) and charr.

The most productive and popular area to fish on the Rocky is the lower river, working the big schools of anadromous fish that push into the mouth and deep holes with the incoming tides. The middle and upper sections of the river are difficult to reach, except by helicopter or hiking, but they have some great opportunities for anyone willing to do some angling prospecting. A drop-off by floatplane on Big Rocky Lake, and a hike up the old, washed-out logging road that runs along the river, is a possibility.

One of the best times of the year to visit this small river is autumn (especially September), when trophy-sized sea-run Dolly Varden charr (up to seven or eight pounds) and big silver salmon (over 15 pounds) are taken from the mouth and deep holes. There is also good fishing for red salmon early in August.

Note: *The river is on native lands; a permit is required for camping. For details, contact the Port Graham Native Corporation, P.O. Box 5569, Port Graham, AK 99603-5569, (907) 284-2212.*

Seward/Resurrection Bay ★★★★

Location: North Gulf Coast, 75 miles south of Anchorage.

Access: By car, boat, or foot via the Seward Highway.

Facilities: Full visitor services available in town of Seward.

Highlights: Alaska's most popular marine fishing destination.

Main Species: KS, SS, PS, BF

Located at the north end of Blying Sound along Kenai Peninsula's Gulf Coast, Resurrection Bay is a strikingly scenic fjord, with tantalizing greenish-clear waters, mountains, glaciers, streams, and abundant marine and shore life. Although it receives its share of bad weather from the Gulf of Alaska, the bay is fairly protected by the surrounding mountain ridges.

Boaters definitely have the edge for accessing the best fishing. Feeder kings, large halibut, and the first silvers in July are taken from Eldorado Narrows to Cape Aialik, with trolling bait (herring) the preferred method for hooking salmon, along with some mooching, jigging, and casting when feeding is concentrated. Abundant shore fishing opportunities exist as well and, during the height of the runs, very productive results can be had casting spoons, flies, and bait from the bay's beaches, docks, points, and stream mouths.

Hatchery fisheries for king salmon provide opportunities during the month of June at Lowell Creek, Seward Lagoon, and the Small Boat Harbor. Seward's world famous coho run, made up of wild and hatchery fish, hits the outer bay in heavy numbers in July, the bulk of the salmon moving steadily towards town as the season progresses. By the time the Seward Silver Salmon Derby begins in mid-August, most fish can be found in the middle and inner bay areas, with Lowell Point and the vicinity of the mouths of Resurrection River and Spring Creek being the most popular spots for fishing. Winning fish are generally between 17 and 20 pounds. Shore fishing usually becomes productive by late August and early September near the boat harbor and the mouth of streams close to town. Pinks run heavy in July and August (in even years) along with smaller numbers of reds and chums. Dolly Varden weighing up to several pounds are common in late spring and early summer; successful anglers focus efforts on stream mouths and exposed beaches.

Halibut are generally not very plentiful inside the bay itself, but can be encountered in good numbers in areas of the outer bay and surrounding waters. Charter fleets often take their clients to locations such as underwater reefs and pinnacles to find trophy-sized flatfish. Rockfish are a common catch and encountered most anywhere in the bay, perhaps especially so in the outer sections. What was once a trophy and record destination for lingcod, Resurrection Bay currently remains closed to fishing for this species. However, adjoining bays and fjords still offer great ling action, with specimens not rarely exceeding 40 pounds.

Some proven Resurrection Bay hot spot locations include: the Seward Boat Harbor area (KS, SS, PS); the mouths of Lowell Creek (KS, SS, PS), Resurrection River (SS, RS, PS), Seward Lagoon (KS, SS, RS), and 4th of July Creek (SS, CS, PS); Lowell Point (SS, PS, DV) and Tonsina Point (CS, PS, DV); Caines and Callisto heads (SS); Thumb Cove (SS, PS), Humpy Cove (SS, PS), Pony Cove (SS), Agnes Cove (SS), Porcupine Cove (SS), and Bulldog Cove (SS); Aialik Cape (KS, SS, HT, RF); Granite Cape (HT) and Resurrection Cape (HT, RF, KS, SS); Eldorado Narrows (KS, RF, SS); and Rugged Island (KS, SS, HT, RF) and Chiswell Islands (HT, RF, KS, SS).

Note: *Each year Seward hosts the largest salmon derby in Alaska, the Seward Silver Salmon Derby (held during the second and third weeks of August), with over $150,000 in prizes, including tagged fish worth $100,000. The town also hosts a smaller jackpot derby for halibut.*

WEST COOK INLET

Theodore River
Location: Upper west Cook Inlet, 30 miles west of Anchorage.

Access: By small plane to ponds or runways along lower river. Additional road access from lower runways.

Facilities: None.

Highlights: Good fishing in a remote small stream setting only minutes away by plane from Anchorage.

Main Species: KS, SS, RT

Originating near the west side of Little Mount Susitna, south of the

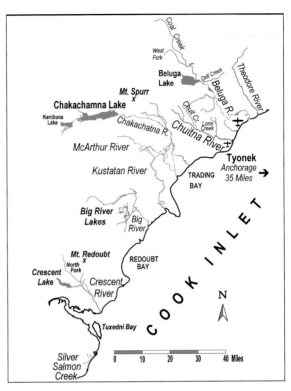

Talachulitna River, the Theodore is a small, clear stream that meanders through mixed forest and lowland brush for some 35 miles to the tidal flats of upper Cook Inlet. It's fairly productive for salmon, trout, and charr, with an abundance of holding water.

Salmon fishing is best during and after high tide in the lower river, with most anglers preferring to hike along the stream in search of likely holes and pools. Later in the season, the upper access points are better as the salmon congregate in dense schools near the spawning grounds on the middle and upper river. King salmon fishing can be quite good (catch-and-release only) in June, with silvers being abundant in August. The upper stretches of the Theodore also offer some decent trout and Dolly Varden charr action, especially in late summer and fall when the salmon are well into their spawning. Grayling are an occasional bonus. Flyfishing conditions on the upper river are quite good, with lots of rocky runs and cover.

Beluga River System
Location: NW Cook Inlet, 30 miles west of Anchorage.

Access: By floatplane from Anchorage to Beluga lakes or lower river; boat travel also possible along sections of river.

Facilities: None.

Highlights: Good fishing in a dramatically scenic location only a short flight from Anchorage.

Main Species: KS, SS, RS, RT, DV

Beluga Lake is a large, silty body of meltwater from two enormous glaciers pouring down the slopes of the Alaska Range north of Mount Spurr. The Beluga River issues from the lake and flows rapidly through a canyon down to the mudflats of Cook Inlet, 30 miles away. Though the lake and river are too silty for sportfishing, several clearwater tributary streams support moderate populations of salmon, trout, and charr, and provide some notable fishing opportunities a mere 20-minute flight from Anchorage.

While the upper and lower sections of the Beluga are slower moving and can be accessed by plane, the middle canyon sections are extremely difficult and dangerous to negotiate, even with a powerful boat. Anglers fishing the Beluga should probe the mouths of the clearwater streams for holding salmon (king, silver, and sockeye in season), with the best charr and rainbow trout water reached with a little hiking. Some of the best creeks to try are Pretty, Olsen, Drill, Scarp, and Coal. Olsen Creek can be accessed at the mouth by small wheelplane. Coal Creek, draining into the lower end of Beluga Lake, has the largest population of salmon and trout, and is easily accessed by floatplane. Try it early in the summer (late June) for kings, and later (early August) for silvers.

Chuitna River ★★★

Location: NW Cook Inlet, 40 miles west of Anchorage.

Access: By small plane or helicopter from Anchorage or Kenai. Most anglers get to the mouth of Chuitna by wheelplane, landing on the north beach. A gravel road network along the coast provides additional (albeit primitive) access to the lower river.

Facilities: Commercial lodging and guide services along river.

Highlights: The most significant westside Cook Inlet salmon and trout stream.

Main Species: KS, SS, RT

Draining the uplands between the Chakachatna and Beluga rivers, the Chuitna has clear water, deep holes, swift, rocky runs, and canyons that (along with tributaries such as Lone and Chuit creeks) offer ideal stream fishing conditions for salmon.

The mouth and lower river are the most popular spots for fishing, with the best action during and shortly after the incoming tides. Nearby Threemile Creek, which you can access from the gravel road, also offers outstanding salmon fishing. The middle and upper river contain an abundance of good holding and spawning water, along with decent populations of rainbow trout and Dolly Varden charr in late summer and fall. These sections can be reached partially by the gravel road that runs along the river, or by boat or helicopter. (Rafts can be launched from upriver and floated down to the mouth.) Some fishermen even bring their own all-terrain vehicles or dirt bikes to navigate the gravel road. Most popular times to fish the "Chuit" are in mid-June for kings and early August for silvers.

Note: *The south side of the Chuitna River is privately owned by the Tyonek Native Corporation; permits are required to access this land.*

Chakachatna-McArthur River System

Location: NW Cook Inlet, Trading Bay, 60 miles SW of Anchorage.

Access: By helicopter or wheelplane from Anchorage or Kenai.

Facilities: None.

Highlights: Excellent remote Cook Inlet fishing destination.

Main Species: KS, SS, RS

This massive coastal system drains a sizeable area of the Alaska Range within Lake Clark National Park. Of glacial origin with heavy silt loads, the rivers' sportfishing is limited to a handful of small, clear tributary streams that provide some concentrated fishing in

season, with little pressure. King salmon and silvers are the top draw, with some good angling, in places, for red salmon, along with chums, pinks, and Dolly Varden charr.

The Chakachatna River is somewhat limited in suitable locations to fish. The clear, north fork of Straight Creek is perhaps the best place to try for salmon. Small wheelplanes can land on gravel bars and ridges nearby. McArthur River has a few more streams to choose from, all of them unnamed. The better ones, more easily accessed by helicopter, are found on the flats between the two watersheds (west of Noaukta Slough). These clear streams can provide some good fishing, especially for king and silver salmon during the peak of the respective runs.

Kustatan River

Location: West Cook Inlet, Redoubt Bay, 65 miles SW of Anchorage.

Access: By small floatplane from Anchorage or Kenai to adjoining lakes along the middle section of river. Boat access into the mouth of the river also possible.

Facilities: None.

Highlights: One of the more popular and productive silver salmon streams of Cook Inlet's west side.

Main Species: SS.

Although the season is fairly short and number of species available limited, the Kustatan River of Redoubt Bay is worth mentioning for its hot silver salmon action and close proximity to Anchorage. The glacial green Kustatan drains out of the far northern part of the Aleutian Range, flowing southeast approximately 25 miles to Redoubt Bay and Cook Inlet. A good portion of the river runs gently through meadow and grassland.

Due to the glacial nature of the river, bait (salmon roe) or high-visibility attractors and spinners are most effective. Most of the fishing is done on the river near the lakes (providing easy access from drop-off points), in small tributary streams or the lower river near the mouth (an old gas field road provides access). The upper river, which is most scenic and offers still more good fishing, can be accessed via small floatplane (landing on some small lakes in the hills) or helicopter. August through early September is the best time to fish the Kustatan for the acrobatic coho.

Big River Lakes System

Location: West Cook Inlet, 70 miles SW of Anchorage.

Access: By floatplane from Anchorage or Kenai.

Facilities: None.

Highlights: One of Southcentral Alaska's top red salmon destinations, along with exceptional bear viewing.

Main Species: SS, RS

The lovely Big River Lakes area, across the inlet from Nikiski on the Kenai, has been a popular fly-in spot for years, thanks to its abundant salmon fishing in a magnificent, secluded setting. There are four connected lakes, all of glacial origin, nestled above Redoubt Bay. This system forms major habitat for salmon, particularly sockeye. In early summer, hundreds of thousands of feisty reds jam up into the lakes, creating one of Southcentral's most concentrated fishing opportunities.

The fishing is hard to beat, especially in and around the inlet/outlet streams, where sockeyes congregate from mid-June through mid-July, and aggressively strike a variety of enticements (this is one of the few places in Alaska where ocean-bright red salmon can be consistently caught on lures). Silver salmon can also be taken later in summer (August) in the mouths of clearwater tributaries along Bachatna Flats, but access is difficult. There are even some Dolly Varden and a few rainbow trout to be had. The lakes and adjoining streams are also very popular with the brown bears during fishing season, so use caution.

Crescent River/Lake

Location: West cook Inlet, 100 miles SW of Anchorage.

Access: By floatplane from Anchorage or Kenai.

Facilities: None.

Highlights: Scenic, popular fly-in fishing location, just a short hop by plane from Anchorage or Kenai.

Main Species: SS, RS, DV

Glacially tinted a beautiful blue-green, Crescent River originates from the ice fields and glaciers of central Chigmit Mountains, flowing west some 18 miles to Cook Inlet. It receives a good run of reds in July, and silvers in August, with some good fishing for Dolly Varden as well. Because it's not too remote and has great fly-in fishing for sockeye salmon, it should be considered an inexpensive, fly-in alternative to the crowded Russian River and other roadside fisheries.

The most commonly fished parts of the system are the lake outlet (a great spot for camping) and clearwater tributaries, where salmon hold in great concentrations during the peak of the runs. Spring and fall are the best times for Dolly Varden. (Keep in mind that the lake doesn't break up until the middle or last part of June.) Nearby Polly Creek has some good silver salmon fishing and outstanding razor clam digging at low tide. (Accessible by wheelplane at its mouth.)

Silver Salmon Creek

Location: West Cook Inlet, 115 miles SW of Anchorage.

Access: By floatplane, landing at either the Silver Salmon Lakes nearby, or in the narrow tidal lagoon at the mouth (very tricky).

Facilities: Commercial lodging and guide services available.

Highlights: High-quality silver salmon fishing in a most pristine setting.

Main Species: SS

Silver Salmon Creek along the lower west side of Cook Inlet is worthy of mention as a popular fly-in location for abundant coho, in season. Located almost directly across from Ninilchik on the Kenai, this short, but extremely productive, drainage is situated just south of the glacial Johnson River and Triangle Peak. It is a clearwater creek with good fishing in August and early September for bigger silvers than are generally encountered elsewhere. Red salmon and Dolly Varden are also available. The setting is quite magnificent, with deep blue water from the surrounding North Pacific absorbing the gray, glacial silt of lower Cook Inlet.

Kamishak River ★★★

Location: SW Cook Inlet, 210 miles SW of Anchorage.

Access: Difficult; floatplane landings on lower river possible (perilous with the tides), with wheelplane access limited to short gravel bars and beaches.

Facilities: None.

Highlights: Superb salmon fishing in an incredibly scenic and remote setting.

Main Species: SS, DV

On the west side of lower Cook Inlet across from Kachemak Bay lie some less-visited clearwater streams that offer good seasonal fishing for salmon and charr, along with sweeping coastal scenery and abundant wildlife. The Kamishak River is perhaps the best known of these, and it has been visited regularly over the years by the lodge crowd (particularly those from the Iliamna area), who normally fish it in late summer and early fall for silver salmon.

The Kamishak rises in the coastal mountains of Katmai National Park near the headwaters of the Naknek and flows northeast through deep valleys, picking up water from several tributaries (such as the Little Kamishak and Strike Creek) to become a fair-sized river before it spills out on the mudflats of Akumwarvik Bay. The awesome snow-covered peaks of Mount Douglas and nearby volcanic Mount Augustine enhance the rugged splendor of the surroundings, and the world-famous bear habitat of the McNeil River State Game Sanctuary is only eight miles away.

Most of the angling effort occurs on the lower river, fishing the incoming tides for fresh salmon and big, sea-run Dolly Varden charr, but there is excellent fishing and some access along the middle section (boats can be run up from the mouth.). Since the Kamishak is in an area having some of the world's most dense concentrations of brown bears, anglers should be prepared for numerous bear encounters and use extreme caution when wading smaller channels and hiking through the brush. Best time to fish it is from late August through early October. The Kamishak and nearby drainages are rumored to support small runs of steelhead trout.

Recommended Lodges/Guides/Outfitters/Air Taxis

Alaska Trout Fitters, Mile 48.2 Sterling Highway, Box 570, Cooper Landing, AK 99572, (907) 595-1212. *www.aktroutfitters.com*. Lodging, guided fishing, upper Kenai River

Kenai Cache Outfitters, Mile 52 Sterling Hwy, Cooper Landing, AK 99572, 907-595-1401, *www.kenaicache.com*. Sporting goods, lodging, guided fishing, upper Kenai River

Silent Run Driftboat Guide Service, 1803 Roosevelt Drive, Anchorage, AK 99517, 907-562-5455, *www.silentrunak.com*. Kenai River guided flyfishing, gear provided

Lands End Resort, 4786 Homer Spit Road, Homer, AK 99603, (800) 478-0400 or (907) 235-0400, *www.lands-end-resort.com*. Waterfront lodging, Homer

Anchor River Inn, P.O. Box 154, Anchor Point, AK 99556; (907) 235-8531; 800-435-8531, *www.anchorriverinn.com*. Lodging, Anchor River area

Deep Creek Sport Shop, Mile 137.3 Sterling Hwy, Ninilchik, AK 99639, 907-567-3518, *www.deepcreekfishing.com*. Fishing tackle, charters, lodging, lower Cook Inlet

Afishhunt Charters, Box 39388, Ninilchik AK 99639, 800-347-4114, *www.afishunt.com*. Charters & RV Park, lower Cook Inlet

Crackerjack Fishing Charters, PO Box 2794, Seward, AK 99664, (907) 224-2606, *www.crackerjackcharters.com*. Premier Fishing charters, Resurrection Bay

The Fish House, 1301 4th Avenue, Box 1209, Seward AK 99664, 800-257-7760, 907-224-3674, *www.thefishhouse.net*. Marine hardware/fishing tackle & charters, Resurrection Bay

Aurora Charters, Seward Small Boat Harbor, Box 241, Seward, AK 99664, 907-224-3968, *www.auroracharters.com*. Fishing charters and sightseeing, Resurrection Bay/Kenai Fjords

Homer Air, 2190 Kachemak Drive, Homer, AK 99603, 800-478-8591, (907) 235-8591, *www.Homerair.com*. Flight service, air taxi charters, Homer/Katchemak Bay

Rusts Flying Service, P.O. Box 190325, Anchorage, AK 99519, (907) 243-1595 or (800) 544-2299, *www.flyrusts.com*. Air taxi, Kenai Peninsula/Cook Inlet

Chuitna River Lodge, Beluga, Alaska 99695, 907-346-1896, *www.chuitriverlodge.com*. Lodging, guided fishing, Chuitna River

Silver Salmon Creek Lodge, P.O. Box 3234, Soldotna, AK 99669; (907) 262-4839, 888-872-5666, *www.silversalmoncreek.com*. Full service lodge, cabins, guided fishing

USGS Maps/NOAA Nautical Charts Reference

Theodore River: Tyonek A-3, B-3, B-4.

Beluga River System: Tyonek A-3, A-4, B-3, B-4, B-5, B-6, C-5, C-6.

Chuitna River: Tyonek A-4, A-5, B-5.

Chakachatna-McArthur: Lime Hills A-1, B-1; Tyonek A-5, A-6, A-7, A-8, B-7, B-8; Kenai D-5.

Kustatan River: Kenai C-5, D-6; Tyonek A-6.

Big River Lakes System: Kenai C-6, C-7, D-6, D-7.

Crescent River/Lake: Kenai B-7, B-8; Lake Clark B-1.

Silver Salmon Creek: Kenai A-8; Seldovia D-8.

Kamishak River: Afognak C-6; Mount Katmai C-1, C-2, D-1, D-2; Iliamna A-4.

Russian River System: Seward B-8.

Lower Kenai River System: Kenai A-1, B-1, B-2, B-3, B-4, C-1, C-2, C-3, C-4.

Upper Kenai River System: Seward B-6, B-7, B-8, C-6, C-7, C-8; Kenai B-1.

Kasilof River System: Kenai A-2, A-3, A-4, B-3, B-4.

Ninilchik Area Streams: Kenai A-5; Seldovia D-5.

Swanson River System: Kenai C-2, C-3, D-2, D-3.

Anchor River: Seldovia C-4, C-5, D-4, D-5.

Rocky River: Seldovia B-4.

Lower Cook Inlet: Kenai A-4, A-5, B-4; Seldovia A-5, A-6, B-6, D-5; 16640.

Kachemak Bay: Seldovia B-4, B-5, C-3, C-4, C-5, D-3, D-4; 16645; 16646.

Resurrection Bay: Seward A-7; Blying Sound C-7, D-7; 16682

General Information

Chugach National Forest: 3301 C Street, Anchorage, AK 99503, (907) 743-9500, *www.fs.fed.us/r10/chugach/* For information on Forest Service campgrounds and cabins.

Public Lands Information Center: 605 West Fourth Avenue, Suite 105, Anchorage, AK 99501, (907) 271-2737.

Alaska State Parks: 550 W 7th Ave, Suite 1260, Anchorage, AK 99501-3557,. (907) 269-8400. *www.dnr.state.ak.us/parks/* For information on state cabins, campgrounds and boat launches.

Regulations/Information

Fishing regulations throughout the Kenai Peninsula-Cook Inlet area are among the most complex in Alaska. Seasonal restrictions on fishing various sport species apply throughout, with king salmon fishing highly regulated. Restrictions, limits, and open seasons vary from drainage to drainage. Many waters are catch-and-release for rainbow trout/steelhead, and open to fishing unbaited artificial lures only. Always check current Regulations Summary for Southcentral Alaska and/or contact regional/field offices, ADF&G for complete information/updates and latest conditions when planning a fishing trip to the area.

Anchorage: (907) 267-2218 **Soldotna:** (907) 262-9368
Homer: (907) 235-8191   **Palmer:** (907) 746-6300

Online information: *www.sf.adfg.state.ak.us/statewide/ regulations/scregs.cfm*

Kenai River trophy rainbow

Kenai Peninsula/Cook Inlet Species

LOCATION	KING SALMON	RED SALMON	PINK SALMON	CHUM SALMON	SILVER SALMON	STEELHEAD	RAINBOW	CUTTHROAT	CHARR	GRAYLING	LAKE TROUT	NORTHERN PIKE	SHEEFISH	HALIBUT	LING COD	ROCK FISH	SALMON SHARK	FSHG. PRESSURE
Lower Cook Inlet Saltwater	★	✓	☺	R	☺	R			☺					★	☺		R	☹
Homer/Kachemak Bay	★	☺	★	✓	★				☺					✓	✓	✓	✓	☹
Upper Kenai River System	C	★	✓	R	☺		★		★	★	✓		R					☹
Lower Kenai River System	☺	★	★	R	★	R	☺		☺	R	✓		R					☹
Russian River System	C	★	✓		☺				★	☺	R		R					☹
Kasilof River System	☺	☺	☺	R	★	✓	R		★		✓							☹
Swanson River System	C	✓	✓	R	★		★		★									✓
Anchor River	☺	R	★	R	★	★	✓		★									☹
Ninilchik Area Streams	☺	✓	★	R	☺	✓	✓		★									☹
Resurrection Bay / Blying Sound	★	✓	☺	☺	★				☺					☺	C	☺	✓	☹
Rocky River		☺	★	✓	★				★									✓
Beluga River System	☺	☺	☺	R	★				☺		✓							✓
Chuitna River	★	✓	★	✓	★				☺		✓							M
Chakachatna / McArthur R. Systems	☺	✓	☺	☺	★						✓							✓
Kustatan River	R	✓	✓	R	★						✓							M
Big River Lakes System		★	R	R	☺					✓	✓							☹
Crescent River / Lake		★	✓	R	★				☺									✓
Silver Salmon Creek		✓	✓	R	★						✓							M
Kamishak River	✓	☺	☺	✓	★	R	R		☺									✓
Theodore River	☺	R	✓	R	☺				☺		✓	R						✓

Legend

- (blank) Species not present
- **R** Rare
- **✓** Fishable numbers (or light pressure)
- **☺** Good fishing
- **★** Excellent fishing
- **LL** Landlocked species
- **C** Present, but fishing closed
- **M** Moderate pressure
- **☹** Heavy pressure

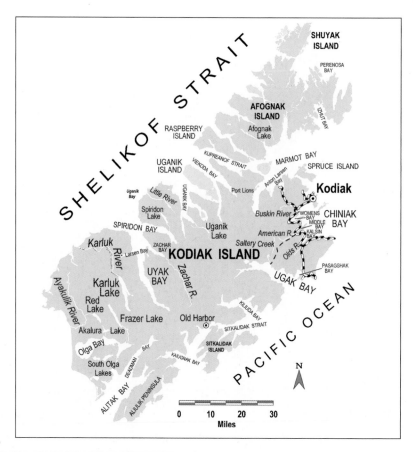

KODIAK/AFOGNAK/SHUYAK ISLANDS

Kodiak Island and its associated archipelago (16 major islands including Afognak, Shuyak, Raspberry, etc.) is a unique island complex lying just 30 miles off the coast of Katmai in the Gulf of Alaska, 90 miles south of the Kenai Peninsula. Most geographers group it with Southwest Alaska, some with Southcentral, but it really is apart from the rest of the state, with its own special character. At 3,588 square miles, the second largest island group in the U.S., the "Emerald Isle" sits at the same latitude as Scotland, and has a similar maritime climate, but with more lush vegetation and mountainous terrain. Most people know it for its giant bears, but Kodiak also has one of the richest marine environments on earth, with abundant wildlife along its coasts and an incredibly prolific fishery. Some of the most productive salmon streams in Alaska are located here, particularly for sockeye and giant silvers (to 20 pounds), along with fabulous saltwater angling, and the best steelhead fishing north of Yakutat.

With few exceptions, Kodiak's streams are short, swift, and small by mainland Alaska standards, and the countryside very mountainous and densely vegetated—definitely not the easiest country to hike and fish. Some of the best action occurs in river mouths, lagoons, and along beaches, where tides must be considered, not just for the fishing, but frequently for access as well. A short road system (82 miles) extends from the town of Kodiak (population 10,000) out along Chiniak Bay, and provides access to some of the island's better fishing opportunities (and undoubtedly the best roadside salmon streams in all of Southcentral Alaska). But, for the most part, Kodiak's rugged and remote fishing terrain is accessible by floatplane or boat only.

Two commercial air carriers provide daily connections to the mainland, and there is even state ferry service from Homer and Seward for folks who want to bring their vehicles and drive, camp, and fish along the road system. Public use cabins maintained by Kodiak Island National Wildlife Refuge (it encompasses two-thirds of the island) and Alaska State Parks, state-maintained campgrounds and recreation sites, and the usual array of privately run visitor services (B&Bs, rental cabins, fish camps, charters, wilderness lodges, etc.) complete the awesome variety of vacation options for fishermen on Alaska's most unique island.

Shuyak Island

Shuyak Island is a small (eleven by twelve miles) landmass just north of Afognak that is richly endowed with life in its myriad bays, coves, islands, and small lakes and streams. The entire coastline of the island has excellent angling potential for salmon (silver and pink mostly, with some red), charr, and bottomfish, particularly the northwest shore with its archipelago of reefs, protruding rocks, and fish-laden inlets. Angling activity for salmon and sea-run charr is concentrated in bays and inlets with streams, with August and September the most popular months. Although the numbers of fish are usually quite small, fishing can be outstanding near the mouths of these spawning streams when the runs are at their peak.

Since much of the best fishing takes place in tidal water, small skiffs, rafts or even kayaks provide the best access. Surfcasting is certainly possible at stream mouths, from points and along beaches. Salmon is the top draw around Shuyak, with some of the choice locations including Neketa, Big and Shangin bays, and Carry Inlet. All of these have spawning systems at their heads with small, but highly concentrated, runs of silver and pink salmon, as well as fair numbers of Dolly Varden and a sprinkling of reds. Fall steelhead are found in a few streams as well. Feeder king salmon are available in outlying waters, but an angler is most likely to encounter halibut there. These popular flatfish (along with lingcod and rockfish) are abundant wherever there is open water with sufficient reef and shoal structure. (Shuyak Strait between Shuyak and Afognak islands is one of the most popular areas for bottomfishing.)

Access is mostly by floatplane (landing in protected bays and coves such as Big and Neketa bays and Carry Inlet) or boat from Kodiak

or Homer. Shuyak contains more sheltered water than any other location in Kodiak, and is therefore ideally suited for kayak exploration. There are four rental cabins within the State Park, and a limited trail system for accessing some of the streams and beaches. Overall, the Shuyak Island archipelago remains one of the least visited, but most promising, destinations in the entire Kodiak area for adventure angling.

Afognak Island

Afognak Island (700 square miles), with its rugged, rocky coast, misty islands and bays, dense forests, and myriad lakes and streams, seems more a stray chunk of Southeast Alaska than the northern extension of Kodiak. Over the years, it has enjoyed a unique status among locals and visiting sportsmen as a most beautiful but challenging destination to pursue an abundant variety of fish and game. Just far enough from the mainstream to keep the crowds away, it is most frequently accessed by boat (via Anton Larson Bay and Whale Pass) or floatplane from the town of Kodiak.

Marine waters surrounding the island provide outstanding opportunities for halibut, lingcod, rockfish, and other bottom dwellers, as well as salmon that are migrating to local rivers or locations on Kodiak Island or the mainland. Some of the more productive areas targeted are Kupreanof Strait (SS, BF); Raspberry Strait (SS, HT); Whale Pass (HT, SS, KS); Marmot Bay (KS, SS, HT); Perenosa Bay (RS, SS, PS); Afognak Bay (SS, RS, HT, KS); Izhut Bay (SS, KS, HT); and the more accessible, large open bays and capes along the west side (KS, SS, BF).

For stream fishing, most of Afognak's rivers and creeks are short, rocky, and swift, with little holding water, so anglers mostly target mouths, lagoons, and lake outlets, timing efforts with the major runs and tides for most productive fishing. Almost all the island's drainages have fish in them, so don't be afraid to explore, as many an awesome day's fishing has been had in waters well off the beaten path. Some of the more promising are the creeks emptying into Paramanof South Bay (PS, DV, SS); the Little Afognak River (RS, PS, SS, DV, ST); Kitoi Lakes (SS, RS, PS, RT, KO); North Kazakof Bay streams (SS, RS, DV, ST); and the streams along the northwest coast, from Perenosa Bay to Foul Bay (SS, PS, RS).

Afognak anglers should come prepared with a variety of gear to handle everything from dabbling for Dollies in small brooks to casting in the pounding surf for big bruiser coho salmon. Although Afognak's run sizes are typically small by Alaska standards, fish are concentrated and angling pressure remains light, for an overall extremely high quality experience.

Afognak (Litnik) River/Lagoon ★★★
Location: South Afognak Island, 25 miles NW of Kodiak.

Access: By plane or boat from Kodiak.

Facilities: None.

Highlights: One of Afognak's most popular and productive fishing destinations.

Main Species: SS, RS, DV

The Afognak or Litnik River, the most productive system on Afognak Island, is located on the south end at Marmot Bay. Draining the largest body of water on the island, long and narrow Afognak Lake, the river runs east a short ways and empties into a long lagoon at Afognak Bay. It has long been a very popular and productive area salmon fishing locale, with relatively easy access.

Aside from right below the lake and the lagoon, the Afognak River has limited holding water. Most of the angling effort for silver salmon occurs in the lagoon in August when coho tend to school up with the tide. Access upstream is simplified by a small gravel four-wheeler road that parallels the river from the mouth to the lake outlet. A good strategy as the season wears on is to fish the lagoon and lower river with the tide, then head on up to the lake and work the holding water right below the outlet for the salmon that school there. Lake inlet waters like Hatchery Creek should not be overlooked, as salmon tend to mill there later in the season

The Afognak also receives a notable run of red salmon during the months of June and July. Fishing for them is best below the ADF&G weir at the head of the lagoon, or right below the lake, where they become most concentrated. Other species include abundant Dolly Varden charr (best fished in spring and late summer), some rainbow trout, and even an elusive fall run of steelhead that enter the river from September through October. As this is also world-class brown bear country, extreme caution is advised.

Marka Creek
Location: Southeast Afognak Island, 20 miles NW of town of Kodiak.

Access: By floatplane or boat from Kodiak or area lodges.

Facilities: None.

Highlights: Productive Afognak stream and lagoon fishing.

Main Species: RS, SS, PS

Marka Creek in Marka Bay, just east of the Afognak River, is another productive south Afognak stream and lagoon location. Because of its tricky access (boaters must negotiate tides and dangerous reefs to enter long, narrow, rocky Marka Bay), it doesn't get visited quite as much as other area locales, but offers abundant salmon fishing in season.

Marka is a long, shallow, rocky stream that begins in a small headwater lake deep in the center of the southern part of the island. Because of the brush and paucity of holding water, most anglers concentrate their efforts on the mouth and upper lagoon, working the tides to intercept the abundant incoming salmon (mostly sockeyes and silvers). Hardware chuckers and fly anglers do equally well in the shallow, narrow waters there. The lake outlet is another promising location, though it is seldom fished. Some Dolly Varden and a small run of fall steelhead add to the allure of this beautiful, secluded location.

Malina Creek System
Location: SW Afognak Island, 35 miles NW of Kodiak.

Access: By boat or small plane from Kodiak.

Facilities: None.

Highlights: An out of the way Afognak drainage with good fishing.

Main Species: SS, RS, DV

Malina Creek and its associated lakes form a small but productive southwest Afognak system that drains the hills on the back side of Afognak Lake, and flows west a few miles to Shelikof Strait. A rambling, rocky clearwater creek, Malina supports only moderate runs of salmon, trout, and charr, but fish tend to concentrate in a few choice locations, making for some abundant angling opportunities in season. At present, fishing pressure is relatively light.

Anglers arrive by floatplane to Lower Malina Lake (a small, abandoned cabin on Upper Malina Lake is used by hunters in the fall) and fish the outlet and inlet waters, or use small planes or boats to access the beach to fish the mouth during incoming tides (a small lagoon above tidewater creates holding water for the salmon). Mid-June through September is the period for most productive fishing, beginning with an abundant sockeye run, some chums, then huge numbers of pink salmon, followed by a prolonged run of silvers that begins in late August and continues through the fall. Dolly Varden charr are abundant during summer, and small numbers of steelhead trout run the creek in late fall as the silver run subsides. The breathtaking scenery of the Katmai coast across Shelikof Strait, and abundant marine and terrestrial life (brown bears commonly patrol the beach and lake outlet during the height of the runs, and elk are frequently seen in the surrounding hills) significantly enhance this remote small stream, beach, and lake fishing experience.

Portage Creek
Location: North Afognak Island, Discoverer Bay, 30 miles north of Kodiak.

Access: By floatplane and boat from Kodiak.

Facilities: None.

Highlights: An out-of-the-way stream with good fishing.

Main Species: SS, RS

Portage Creek is a small, shallow clearwater stream that flows from Portage Lake on northern Afognak Island to Discoverer Bay, two miles away. Since the drainage is quite small, salmon and charr populations are not very large. However, stream conditions are perfect for concentrating fish in shallow runs and pools, while the clear waters make for easy sightfishing. Flyfishing for silver and red salmon in this creek can be as good as it gets, according to several local sources.

The best locations to fish on Portage Creek are the mouth on Discoverer Bay and the lake outlet, where schools of fish tend to herd up. Most anglers fly in to the head of the bay and hike up the beach to fish the incoming tides on the lower river, especially in late summer, for silvers and Dolly Varden. The sockeyes seem more prone to hit once they are concentrated within the confines of the creek. (Sparse flies like a chartreuse Comet or Brassie work well on them.) The creek also has a small fall run of steelhead that begin showing up in September. Check with the Alaska Department of Fish and Game for the latest run conditions before heading out. As this area has quite a few brown bears patrolling during the height of the runs, caution is advised for anglers.

Pauls Lake System

Location: North Afognak Island, Perenosa Bay, 40 miles north of Kodiak.

Access: By floatplane or boat from Kodiak.

Facilities: State public use cabin on Laura Lake.

Highlights: Remote small stream and lake system with excellent salmon fishing.

Main Species: SS, RS

Like Portage Creek, the Pauls Lake system is a rather small, but very productive, clearwater drainage located on the north end of Afognak Island. Comprised of several connected lakes (including Laura and Gretchen) that empty into the east side of Perenosa Bay, Pauls Creek begins at Gretchen Lake outlet and runs several miles northwest to Laura Lake, then continues about a mile to Pauls Lake. From there, it empties into Pauls Bay, a short distance away. It is usually accessed by floatplane from Kodiak, landing either at the head of Pauls Bay, a short hike from the stream mouth, or on Pauls or Laura lakes.

The Pauls Creek system supports impressive numbers of red and silver salmon for its size, along with abundant charr, but it is quite remote so does not receive nearly as much angling effort as other Afognak locations. (It is visited mostly in August by local lodges that work the bay for silver salmon.) Fishing can be excellent at the mouth and in the surrounding bay area, or in the lake inlets and outlets, during the height of the runs. Silver salmon fishing is particularly noteworthy in the lower river and outlet of Laura Lake, while reds are best fished in the short run of creek below Pauls Lake. You'll find hordes of fat sea-run Dollies in the upper parts of the system late in the season. The creek system also has a little-fished fall run of steelhead. Most of the effort is from local lodges day-fishing the bay and outlet stream, which leaves much untouched potential for varied, small stream and lake fishing in a remote, magnificent setting.

KODIAK ROAD SYSTEM

Chiniak Bay ★★★★

Location: NE Kodiak Island, 250 miles SW of Anchorage.

Access: By boat from Kodiak (weather permitting, can be navigated by almost any size craft, with harbor and road network from Spruce Cape to Cape Chiniak providing ample launching locations).

Facilities: Full range of visitor services available in town of Kodiak.

Highlights: Kodiak's main recreational saltwater fishery.

Main Species: KS, SS, BF

Chiniak Bay, surrounding the town of Kodiak and the island's only highway system, is the most popular recreational marine fishery on Kodiak Island. Its numerous islands and lesser bays contain important salmon/trout streams, and its rich offshore waters are a haven for salmon, halibut, lingcod, and rockfish. Lush, green mountain slopes drop dramatically into the bay's clear blue waters, making for an idyllic Alaska setting. Despite its high use, Chiniak Bay manages to hold its own year after year.

The bay has long been known to be a year-round feeding ground for chinook, but it was not until the early '90s that a fishery developed to catch these dime-bright brutes. About 12 to 20 pounds on average, they are plentiful in the middle and outer parts of Chiniak (Cape Chiniak and Buoy Four are two of the more popular locations), providing action year-round, with a peak from May to October.

Large runs of pink salmon invade the bay in late summer, followed by waves of acrobatic silvers that perk up the action into fall. Best fishing is from boats, working bays with rivers, but angling from shore along beaches near the mouths of spawning streams can also be productive for salmon (and Dolly Varden charr). The action can be especially good working the hatchery-enhanced fisheries at Mill Bay (SS), Mayflower Beach (SS), and Monashka Bay (KS). A small number of sockeye and chum salmon are also taken in Chiniak saltwater, mostly incidentally while fishing coho or chinook.

Halibut and other bottom species lurk on reefs and shoals in the deeper waters of the outer bay and are especially abundant during the summer months.

Hot spot locations around Chiniak Bay include Monashka Bay (PS, KS, DV), Mill Bay (KS, SS), Womens Bay (SS, PS, DV), Middle Bay (SS, PS, DV), Kalsin Bay (SS, PS, HT, DV), Isthmus Bay (PS, DV), Long and Woody islands (KS, HT), Pinnacle Rock (KS, BF), Cape Spruce (KS, HT), Cape Chiniak (KS, HT), Williams Reef (BF), and Buoy Four (KS, HT).

Buskin River ★★★★

Location: NE Kodiak Island, 5 miles SW of town of Kodiak.

Access: By car from Kodiak via road system.

Facilities: State Recreational Site with camping off Rezanof Drive.

Highlights: Kodiak's major stream fishery.

Main Species: RS, PS, SS, DV

The clear-flowing Buskin, located on Chiniak Bay just southwest of the town of Kodiak, is the most popular fishery on the island (supporting nearly half of Kodiak's total sportfishing effort), with easy access and abundant salmon (red, pink, and silver) and Dolly Varden charr.

The Buskin system drains a fairly small valley between Pyramid and Erskine mountains, and a small lake of the same name located a few miles above Chiniak Bay. The medium-sized river is gravel-bottomed and brushy, with plenty of holding water and good sight-fishing possibilities. Since the Buskin is located along the road system so close to town, it receives its fair share of angling pressure from locals, as well as from outside anglers with limited time or funds to enjoy the Kodiak area.

The Buskin is perhaps best known for its amazing Dolly Varden fishing. Scads of outmigrating fish are typically caught right after break-up (in April and May) on small silver spinners, spoons, and smolt pattern flies, while fattened, prime fish enter the river from mid-summer through fall and succumb mostly to bright flies and spinners. Some very nice runs of red salmon enter the Buskin in June and July, creating one of Kodiak's most significant, easily accessed sockeye fisheries. Next to the sea-run Dollies, however, silvers are the most sought-after fish, entering the Buskin in mid-August and continuing into September. Because of regulations, the early part of this fishery is restricted to the mouth and lagoon, while later on (in mid-September) it opens up to include the entire river.

American River

Location: NE Kodiak Island, 12 miles SW of town of Kodiak.

Access: By car from Kodiak; Rezanof Drive crosses lower river, with trails providing additional access; Saltery Cove Road follows middle and upper river for several miles, crossing in two places.

Facilities: None.

Highlights: A great stream for silver salmon and Dollies.

Main Species: SS, PS, DV

The clear American River originates near Center Mountain and runs east through a forested valley to Middle Bay, a small inlet connected to Chiniak Bay. Moderately fast, with good stream fishing conditions, the American has several small tributary creeks and lakes, and provides one of the most extensive and popular salmon/charr fisheries on the Kodiak road system.

The American, from midsummer through late fall, hosts large runs of silver, chum, and pink salmon. The abundance of the smallish humpbacked salmon can be staggering, so much that anglers wishing to target the flashy silvers sometimes delay their fishing until late in the season (September), when the pinks thin out.

The American is also a major spawning ground for sea-run Dollies, which become quite abundant in the fall. Although the fish are not very large, typically about 10 to 15 inches, their concentrations make for top-notch action, definitely worth checking out if you're fishing the Kodiak road system in late summer or fall.

Olds River System

Location: Northeast Kodiak Island, 15 miles south of Kodiak.

Access: By car via Rezanof Drive West from Kodiak to lower river. Limited trail access to mouth and upstream areas.

Facilities: None.

Highlights: Another great road-accessible Kodiak salmon stream.

Main Species: SS, PS, DV

Olds River is a road-accessible, clearwater stream draining into Kalsin Bay, on the south side of Chiniak, approximately 15 miles southwest of Kodiak. Its headwaters originate near Marin Range, and there are a few small lakes connected to the system. Like other productive road streams of Chiniak Bay, the Olds receives moderate to heavy pressure from local and visiting anglers, but holds up with especially good fishing for pink and silver salmon, as well as Dolly Varden charr.

Winding through a narrow, heavily forested valley, the upper and middle sections of the Olds are fairly fast-flowing, while the lower river is slower and wider, especially in its last mile, where a major tributary, Kalsin Creek, joins in from the south. Most people access the lower river via Rezanof Drive West and fish salmon there or in the mouth, working the incoming tides for bright fish. During low water, conditions are good for sight-fishing.

In addition to great silver and pink salmon runs, the Olds gets a healthy run of spawning Dolly Varden in autumn (September and October). These colorful charr brighten up the fishing along the entire river. Like the American, the Olds makes a popular one-day destination for anyone sampling the fishing along the Kodiak road system, with adjacent Kalsin Bay holding some of the more popular and productive salmon and halibut waters in Chiniak Bay.

Pasagshak River System ★★★★

Location: NE Kodiak Island, 25 miles south of town of Kodiak.

Access: By car via Rezanof Drive West and Pasagshak Road to State Recreation Site near mouth. Several trails exist along creek.

Facilities: Campground at State Recreation Site.

Highlights: Kodiak's most famous silver salmon stream.

Main Species: SS, RS, DV

The Pasagshak River is one of the most famous and visited streams on Kodiak Island, with clear, wide waters that are easy to fish and amazingly productive for salmon and Dolly Varden charr.

Originating from the south slopes of Marin Range, the headwaters drain into Lake Rose Tead. From there, the river flows only two miles to Ugak Bay. The beach area around the mouth is the hot spot on the Pasagshak and, as is common on most coastal streams, incoming tides usually bring the best fishing for snappy, bright schools of salmon and charr. Of particular note is the river's trophy silver salmon fishery. Thousands of above-average-sized coho invade the Pasagshak every fall (late August through September), with ample opportunities for fish weighing in the mid-teens, and occasional specimens to 18 and 20 pounds or more. Many diehard anglers still use salmon roe clusters, but flies and hardware take a good share of these big Pasagshak silvers.

A strong red salmon run usually occurs in early to midsummer; they're best taken in the shallow, faster sections of the river. Abundant pink salmon usually follow the reds, but they can be caught anywhere, although the mouth is probably the most popular area. Dolly Varden are another Pasagshak highlight. The prime times are during the spring outmigration from Lake Rose Tead right after break-up, and again in late summer and fall as the fish return fat, bright, and full of fight from the salt of Pasagshak and Ugak bays.

Saltery River ★★★

Location: Northeast Kodiak Island, 25 miles SW of town of Kodiak.

Access: By car via Rezanof Drive and Saltery Cove Road (four-wheel recommended); also by plane or boat to Saltery Cove.

Facilities: Private lodge in area.

Highlights: An excellent, road-accessible salmon stream.

Main Species: SS, RS, DV

The Saltery River begins on the south slopes of Center Mountain and flows into Ugak Bay. It is one of the more outstanding Kodiak road streams, fairly remote even though it lies along the road system, and noted for superb silver and red salmon fishing and abundant Dolly Varden charr.

The river above Saltery Lake runs swift and straight, but down below it slows considerably and meanders through a flat valley before reaching Saltery Cove. It is beautiful, crystal-clear water, with many deep holes, riffles, and runs, and a bottom of fine gravel. Wildlife is abundant in the area and the scenery pleasing.

The majority of anglers fish the river's noteworthy silver and red salmon runs (some of the best along the road system). The reds are the first to arrive, in early July, and spice up the action for flyfishers until August. Next come the silvers later in the month. They are hefty fish, many weighing into the teens, and can be caught from tidewater all the way up to the lake outlet. Along with the Buskin and Pasagshak, the Saltery also provides some of the best spring Dolly Varden action along the Kodiak road system, as thousands of fish move out of Saltery Lake on their way to the ocean. This fishery turns on again later in the season (from late summer through fall), as fat Dollies return to the river to feed on salmon eggs and prepare for spawning and overwintering. The upper river, just above the lake, is a major salmon spawning area and one of the best places to find thick schools of voracious charr. Fair to good Dolly fishing can also be enjoyed all summer long in the cove, using narrow silver spoons, herring strips, or small diving plugs.

Ugak Bay

Location: Northeast Kodiak Island, 25 miles south of Kodiak.

Access: By car, boat, or plane. Road access (and boat launch) via Saltery Cove Road or Pasaghak Road.

Facilities: Campground, private lodge, and guide services in area.

Highlights: Easily accessed, productive nearshore fishing location.

Main Species: KS, SS, PS, DV, HT

Ugak Bay is a pristine outlet to the Gulf of Alaska, located just south of Chiniak Bay, its shores contained within Kodiak National Wildlife Refuge. A fairly deep, clear bay with a diverse bottom structure accommodating a variety of fish species, Ugak is a popular angling and recreation destination for locals and visitors alike, accessible by road, water or air. The outer bay is surrounded by forested mountains and hills, while the inner bay has deep-cutting valleys and some snow-covered peaks, making for a beautiful setting.

A handful of clearwater streams empties into Ugak, most with significant runs of salmon and charr that provide good fishing for boaters and surfcasters alike. Be aware that strong east winds from the Gulf of Alaska can turn outer Ugak into a whirlpool of whitewater, although its more protected bays and coves are generally calmer, and on good weather days are a pleasure to fish. Large schools of silver and pink salmon traveling close to shore can be seen and targeted (late summer-fall), and halibut tend to be on the aggressive side. There is also a developing feeder king salmon fishery in the outer bay. Dolly Varden action is best during late spring and again in late summer, when these sea-run charr forage the points, beaches, and stream mouths in search of outmigrating or spawning salmon.

Suggested areas for boaters include Saltery Cove, Portage Bay, Pasagshak Bay, and Eagle Harbor for salmon and charr, and the reefs and shoals of their moderately deep waters for bottomfish. Surfcasters do well at the mouths of the Saltery and Pasagshak rivers, and the mouths of streams draining into Portage Cove and Eagle Harbor.

KODIAK REMOTE

Uganik River System ★★★

Location: Northwest Kodiak Island, 35 miles west of Kodiak.

Access: By floatplane from town of Kodiak to Uganik Lake. Boat, raft, or kayak for additional access to productive parts of system, including lower river and mouth.

Facilities: Refuge recreation cabin available on Uganik Lake.

Highlights: One of Kodiak's best remote fishing locations.

Main Species: SS, RS, DV, RT

The Uganik River System is one of the most productive on Kodiak. Gathering water from some of the highest peaks on the central part of the island, its several arms empty into Uganik Lake, from which the river then flows northwest to the east arm of Uganik Bay. The fishing can be superb—some of Kodiak's finest—with abundant, huge silver salmon and incredible numbers of Dolly Varden. Some of the largest silvers on Kodiak originate here, with fish regularly caught in the middle and upper teens, and occasionally to 20 pounds.

The majority of anglers who fish the Uganik system fly in by floatplane and target the lake outlet and nearby water by hiking. Some even float the entire short river with raft or kayak, taking out in the tidal water of east Uganik Bay by floatplane. (It can be floated in a half to two days, depending on how hard you work the water.) The upper river above Uganik Lake, with its tributaries, can also be productive, but it is more difficult to access.

The Uganik also supports healthy runs of red and pink salmon. (Fishing for pinks is better on the lower Uganik, while reds can be taken throughout the system.) Some big rainbows are also taken in the lake and upper river, and there is a small, elusive run of fall steelhead.

Little River

Location: Northwest Kodiak Island, 50 miles west of Kodiak.

Access: By floatplane or boat from Kodiak or area lodges.

Facilities: Refuge recreation cabin located at Little River Lake.

Highlights: A remote location with high quality angling.

Main Species: RS, SS, DV

The Little River system is located on the lobe peninsula between Spiridon and Uganik bays, on Kodiak's west side. For its size, it has significant runs of salmon (all species except king), along with abundant Dolly Varden fishing, and is out of the way enough to provide a potentially high quality experience.

Beginning at Little River Lake and scattered headwaters, Little

River runs clear and fast, joining numerous tributaries, for approximately 9 miles before emptying into unsheltered waters along Shelikof Strait. Because of its location and terrain, it's not that easy to reach or fish. Small planes or boats (weather permitting) can usually access the beach by the mouth, where fishermen can intercept salmon (reds in June-July; silvers in September) in the small lagoon or holding areas in the lower river. Another option is to fly into the lake and work the outlet waters and stretch of river below the lake and tributary creeks, searching for schools of silver and red salmon (in season) in the holding water. Dolly Varden are abundant on the upper river and the outlet early and late in the season, and a small run of steelhead trout can be encountered during the fall months.

Uyak Bay

Location: West Kodiak island, 60 miles west of town of Kodiak.

Access: By plane or boat from Kodiak or area lodges.

Facilities: Private lodges, guided fishing available in area.

Highlights: Excellent Kodiak remote marine fishing location.

Main Species: KS, SS, PS, HT

Uyak Bay, fronting Shelikof Strait, 50 miles west of the town of Kodiak, is a long, clear fjord that almost bisects the island. Surrounded by steep mountain slopes and impenetrable brush and forests (part of Kodiak National Wildlife Refuge), Uyak is home to abundant marine life—fish, waterfowl, seals, otters, and whales—along with a healthy brown bear population that stalks its beaches and streams in search of food. Some of Kodiak's largest river systems drain into these and adjacent waters, assuring anglers of excellent salmon fishing. Larsen Bay, on the northwest side of Uyak, has traditionally served as the main hub and access point for the bay and the nearby, ever-popular Karluk River drainage.

The greater bay area between Rocky Point and Cape Kuliuk encompasses 34 streams and rivers, some of which are small and crystal-clear, while others are large, but glacial and turbid. Almost without exception, these systems all support fish runs of varying size. The best way to explore these numerous prospects is by boat, though surfcasting can be quite productive around the better stream locations. (Traditional points of access for wheel and/or floatplane support have been Larsen, Spiridon, Amook, and Zachar bays.)

Salmon, especially silvers and pinks, are abundant in season throughout much of Uyak and, depending on time, are best encountered in deeper, outer waters or in the smaller bays near stream mouths. Spiridon Bay and Zachar Bay receive heavy runs, and anglers do very well in and around these areas. Feeder king salmon can be taken twelve months of the year, with the larger, prespawners available as early as late April.

Halibut fishing is said to be some of the best on Kodiak, according to local sources, with an abundance of flatties, many of three-digit size, taken every season in waters nearshore and around reefs, shoals, points, and islands in the outer bay. Several area lodges offer tantalizing packages that combine stream fishing along the incomparable Karluk River with saltwater excursions into the bay.

Sitkalidak Island/Strait

Location: Southeast Kodiak Island, 50 miles SW of town of Kodiak.

Access: By boat or small plane from Kodiak or area lodges.

Facilities: Private lodging and charters available in Old Harbor.

Highlights: An out-of-the-way, extremely productive near shore marine fishing location.

Main Species: KS, SS, PS, BF

On Kodiak's remote southeast side, by the village of Old Harbor, lies Sitkalidak Strait, a sheltered pass containing numerous bays and points and some very productive fishing, owing to its location, structure of its coastline, and abundant forage.

Prespawning salmon (mostly king and silver) veer off their north Pacific migration routes, utilizing the rich waters around Sitkalidak Island to feed and fatten before making their final surge to natal rivers in mainland Alaska and Canada, creating abundant sport fishing opportunities. Feeder king salmon are available year-round, but the fishing for big, bright hogs bound for Cook Inlet and other points along the coast kicks in during late spring (May) and continues through June, with many fish over 50 pounds taken in shallow, nearshore waters. Big silvers show up in late July and provide steady action through August into September. Trolled herring and lures are the most productive methods for taking both species.

Bottomfishing is equally impressive, with plentiful halibut, a variety of rockfish species, and big lingcod available inshore along the strait and associated bays, reefs, and points. The outer waters, especially those to the south, hold virtually untouched fishing and chances for record catches. Best times are from April through September.

Old Harbor is accessed by scheduled commercial flights daily from the town of Kodiak. Some B&Bs, a local fishing lodge, and several boat charters comprise the area's visitor facilities. Just far enough off the beaten path to escape any real fishing pressure, this obscure part of Kodiak has great promise for anyone seeking superlative marine fishing in an uncrowded, magnificent setting.

Karluk River System ★★★★

Location: Southwest Kodiak Island, 65 miles SW of town of Kodiak.

Access: By small plane or boat from Kodiak or area lodges.

Facilities: Private cabins with guided fishing available.

Highlights: Kodiak's premier stream fishing destination.

Main Species: RS, KS, SS, DV, ST

The Karluk River is Kodiak's largest and most productive drainage. The island's most popular fly-in location, it is world famous for its amazing salmon and steelhead runs, and ranks among the finest fishing streams in Alaska, particularly for flyfishing.

The river's extensive mountain headwaters—nearly a dozen clearwater tributaries draining deep-cut valleys—gather at Karluk Lake, in a spectacular setting. From there, the main river flows north 22 miles to Shelikof Strait. It is clear, fairly good-sized, fast flowing, and not too deep—rated Class I water for rafting and kayaking. The upper and middle river sections run through marshlands and open country in the Kodiak National Wildlife Refuge, while the lower river cuts a narrow canyon and eventually widens into Karluk Lagoon.

The Karluk is one of the most fecund systems of its size in all the world, with significant runs of all five salmon species (particularly sockeye, pink and coho) in addition to Alaska's most prolific runs of steelhead north of Yakutat. Along with the neighboring Ayakulik River, it contains Kodiak's only real stream fishing for chinook, which kicks off the sportfishing season in June, along with the start of the Karluk's heavy sockeye runs (continuing well into July). By late July, pink salmon are in the lower river and, shortly after, silvers and the first of the fall steelhead begin showing up.

The lagoon and lower river are the most popular areas to target bright salmon early in the season. (They are usually accessed by plane from Kodiak or boat from the town of Karluk across the lagoon.) Later in the season, anglers will fish the middle river section, known as the "Portage" area (reached by trail via Larsen Bay), or the Karluk Lake outlet, to intercept migrating fish. Steelhead fishing is done mostly in late September and October from the Portage area downstream, where many fish tend to congregate. The Karluk's abundant Dolly Varden charr provide mostly incidental fishing excitement throughout the season, but they can be targeted in spring, late summer, and fall at the lagoon and in tributaries around the lake (like the Thumb River).

A very popular and productive way to sample the action on the Karluk is by raft. The river lends itself perfectly for a leisurely float trip of two to five days, depending on the put-in (either at the lake or Portage). Most of the Karluk is wide and fairly shallow (one to four feet), with good holding areas noticeably scarce on some sections of the river (especially below Portage). Good campsites and firewood are even harder to find.

Note: *A land-use permit, available from Kodiak National Wildlife Refuge, is required to sportfish the Karluk. Contact Kodiak National Wildlife Refuge, 1390 Buskin River Road, Kodiak, AK 99615 (888) 408-3514, www.r7.fws.gov/KarlukRiverApp/ for details.*

Ayakulik (Red) River System ★★★★
Location: Southwest Kodiak Island, 80 miles SW of town of Kodiak.

Access: By floatplane from town of Kodiak to Red Lake, Red River outlet, or points along Ayakulik River (Bear Creek vicinity); limited trails exist along parts of drainage.

Facilities: None.

Highlights: One of Kodiak's most outstanding streams.

Main Species: KS, RS, SS, DV, ST

The Ayakulik or Red River on the southwest corner of the island is generally conceded to have, along with the Karluk, the best stream fishing on Kodiak. Like its exalted neighbor, the Ayakulik is blessed with a proliferation of salmon—all five species—as well as abundant charr and steelhead. Considerably smaller than the Karluk, it has comparable stream conditions, and it doesn't get anywhere near as much visitation.

The Ayakulik meanders through a shallow valley above Olga Bay, surrounded by rolling green hills, tiny lakes, and marshlands. A series of small tributary streams draining the slopes of nearby mountains helps shape the river's character, especially Red River, flowing out of Red Lake, which contributes significantly to the Ayakulik sportfishery.

Salmon fishing kicks off on the lower river (below the Red River confluence, near Bear Creek) in early June, starting with king salmon. It trails off in the fall with deep-bodied silvers and steelhead. In between, there is nonstop action for red and pink salmon. The Ayakulik is especially noted for its king salmon fishing, which in many ways outclasses that found on the Karluk (more fish, better

flyfishing conditions, and less people). The red run has two components, just like on the Karluk: one in June, the other in July. Pink salmon, as most everywhere else on the island, swarm the lower part of Ayakulik in midsummer alongside less numerous chums. Dolly Varden are available most anytime to fill in the brief gaps between salmon runs. The Ayakulik fall steelhead run is about half the size of the Karluk's, but is more spread out along the river. That diffusion, plus the river's smaller size, makes for some outstanding fishing. A small population of rainbow trout also lives in Red Lake.

Most folks fish the Ayakulik just below the Red River confluence, near Bear Creek, which is accessible by floatplane. The river makes an excellent float trip of three to five days duration, from Red Lake or the Red River put-in.

Akalura Lake/Creek
Location: Southwest Kodiak Island, 80 miles SW of town of Kodiak.

Access: By boat or floatplane from Kodiak or nearby lodges, to Akalura Lake or creek mouth at Cannery Cove.

Facilities: None.

Highlights: A small, out-of-the-way, very productive drainage.

Main Species: RS, SS, DV

Akalura Lake and its adjoining creek is one of the smaller, but more productive, drainages of south Kodiak Island. Located on Olga Bay, just south of Red Lake, Akalura Lake is only two-and-a-half miles wide and shaped like a triangle. The brushy outlet stream is swift and clear, and empties into Cannery Cove two miles away.

Although not much in size, the Akalura drainage has some concentrated fishing. Silver salmon are thick around the creek mouth during incoming tides in the fall, as are pink salmon and Dolly Varden earlier in the season. A smaller run of red salmon also moves into the area in early summer and provides some good flyfishing at the mouth at Cannery Cove and lake outlet. The lake has some native rainbow trout providing fair fishing in the spring and fall, but the real show at Akalura is the silver salmon fishing. It's a popular spot with the fly-in lodge crowd, who often stop to check the fishing on their way to the Karluk or Ayakulik.

Dog Salmon (Frazer) River System ★★★
Location: Southern Kodiak Island, 80 miles SW of town of Kodiak.

Access: By floatplane from Kodiak or area lodges, to Frazer Lake outlet or flats at mouth of river; trails along creek lead upstream from mouth.

Facilities: Refuge cabins located on the north end of the lake and on a small tributary lake west of the outlet.

Highlights: An outstanding remote Kodiak salmon fishing location.

Main Species: CS, RS, PS, SS, DV

Dog Salmon River, also known as Frazer River, drains the second largest lake on Kodiak Island, Frazer, which is situated between Karluk and Red lakes. Along with its fabulous neighbors, the Karluk and Ayakulik rivers, the Fraser is one of the island's most productive salmon systems, particularly for sockeye and chum.

This fast and rocky river flows about eleven miles from the lake to the east end of Olga Bay, with a set of falls about a mile below the outlet. Many anglers fish the system through Frazer Lake, working the section of river above the falls for silvers and reds. A handful of tributaries, many of them with small lakes at their headwaters, drains into Frazer Lake and the Dog Salmon River. Wildlife, especially bears, is abundant. On the lower reaches near the mouth, the river slows in an area known as Dog Salmon Flats and the main channel splits.

True to its name, Dog Salmon River has Kodiak's prime chum salmon fishing. In July, incoming tides push huge numbers of the sea-bright calicos into the river mouth, creating exceptional angling opportunities. Red and pink salmon also return in great numbers about that time to spawn in the drainage, along with a notable silver run in the fall. And, like so many other productive island streams, the Dog Salmon has a super abundance of Dolly Varden charr, to the point of being a nuisance at times. There are also small numbers of king salmon (fishing for them is prohibited) and steelhead trout.

Olga Lakes System

Location: South Kodiak Island, 90 miles SW of town of Kodiak.

Access: By floatplane from Kodiak or area lodges, to lake outlets (upper and lower) or mouth of Olga Creek on Olga Bay.

Facilities: None.

Highlights: Great fishing in an out-of-the-way location.

Main Species: RS, PS, SS, DV

The Olga Lakes, on lower Olga Bay on the south part of the island, are also known as South Olga Lakes or Upper Station Lakes. These twin bodies of water are connected by a short, wide channel, with Olga Creek, a narrow and slow stream, as their primary outlet to saltwater. Though not a large system, Olga Lakes offers a variety of superb fishing experiences—lake, small stream, and tidal water—in fabulous, salmon-rich Olga Bay.

At the mouth, huge schools of red salmon throng beginning in late June and continuing into July, followed by vast numbers of pinks, then silvers later in the fall. (There is another red run in September as well.)

Each tide brings in more fresh, bright salmon, creating opportunities for fishing that can equal the best anywhere on the island. Sea-run Dollies can be taken in the salt off the creek mouth all season, and in the river from midsummer on. The outlet of Lower Olga Lake is another prime fishing location for salmon, Dolly Varden charr, and even a few rainbows.

Recommended Lodges/Guides/Outfitters/Air taxis

Port William Wilderness Lodge: P.O. Box 670556, Chugiak, AK 99567, (907) 688-2253. Lodge-based guided fishing, Shuyak Island.

Kodiak Discoveries: P.O. Box 8972, Kodiak, AK 99615, (907) 486-8972, *www.tomstick.com* Lodge-based guided fishing, Afognak Island.

Kodiak Island Charters: P.O. Box 3750, Kodiak, AK 99615, (907) 486-5380, *www.ptialaska.net/~urascal* King/silver salmon and halibut charters, Chiniak Bay.

Zachar Bay Lodge: P.O. Box 2609, Kodiak, AK 99615, (800) 693-2333, (907) 486-4120, *www.zacharbay.com* Lodge-based, guided fishing, Uyak Bay and beyond.

Shelikof Lodge: P.O. Box 774, 211 Thorsheim, Kodiak, AK 99615, (907) 486-4141. Overnight lodging, Kodiak.

Buskin River Inn: 1395 Airport Road, Kodiak, AK 99615, (800) 544-2202, (907) 487-2700, *www.kodiakadventure.com*

Kalsin Bay Inn: Mile 29 Chiniak Road, P.O. Box 1696, Kodiak, AK 99615, (907) 486-2659, *http://chiniak.net/kalsin/* Lodge-based, guided fishing, Olds River/Kalsin Bay.

Kodiak Combos: P.O. Box 141, Old Harbor, AK 99643, (907) 286-2252, *www.kodiakcombos.com* Salmon and bottomfish charters, Sitkalidak Strait.

Saltery Lake Lodge: 1516 Larch Street, Kodiak, AK 99615, (907) 486-7083 or (800) 770-5037, *www.salterylake.com*

Kodiak Kamps: 311 Upper Mill Bay Rd., P.O. Box 4111, Kodiak, AK 99615, (907) 486-5333. Complete outdoor equipment rentals.

Rent-a-Heap: 508 Marine Way, PO Box 1221, Kodiak, AK 99615, (907) 486-8550. Car rentals, Kodiak road system.

Andrews Airways: P.O. Box 1037, Kodiak, AK 99615, (907) 487-2566, *www.andrewairways.com* Float and wheel plane air taxi, Kodiak Island.

Sea Hawk Air: P.O. Box 3561, Kodiak, AK 99615, (800) 770-4295 or (907) 486-8282, *www.seahawkair.com*

Cub Air: P.O. Box 1616, Kodiak, AK 99615, (907) 486-5851.

USGS Maps/NOAA Nautical Charts Reference

Shuyak Island: Afognak B-2, C-1, C-2, C-3; 16604, 16605.

Chiniak Bay: Kodiak C-1, D-1, D-2; 16595, 16593.

Ugak Bay: Kodiak B-1, B-2, B-3, B-4, C-3; 16593.

Uyak Bay: Kodiak B-5, B-6, C-6; Karluk C-1; 16598.

Sitkalidak Island/Strait: Kodiak A-4, A-5; 16592.

Portage Creek: Afognak B-2.

Pauls Creek System: Afognak B-1, B-2.

Afognak (Litnik) River/Lagoon: Afognak A-3.

Marka Creek: Afognak A-2, A-3.

Malina Creek: Afognak A-4.

Uganik River System: Kodiak C-4, C-5.

Little River/ Lakes: Kodiak D-5, D-6.

Buskin River: Kodiak D-2.

American River: Kodiak C-2.

Olds River System: Kodiak C-2.

Pasagshak River: Kodiak B-1.

Saltery River: Kodiak C-3.

Karluk River System: Karluk B-1, C-1, C-2; Kodiak B-6.

Ayakulik River System: Karluk A-1, A-2, B-1, B-2.

Akalura Lake/Creek: Karluk A-1.

Dog Salmon (Fraser) River System: Karluk A-1, B-1.

Olga Lake System: Karluk A-1, A-2.

General Information

Alaska State Parks: Kodiak District, 1400 Abercrombie Drive, Kodiak, AK 99615, (907) 486-6339, *www.dnr.state.ak.us/parks/aspbro/charts/kodiak.htm* Public use cabins and other state public facilities within Kodiak area.

Kodiak National Wildlife Refuge: 1390 Buskin River Road, Kodiak, AK 99615, (907) 487-2600, *http://kodiak.fws.gov* Refuge lands and public use cabins within Kodiak.

Alaska Marine Highway: P.O. Box 703, 100 Marine Way, Kodiak, AK 99615, (800) 526-6731, *www.akferry.com* for information on and reservations for Alaska State Ferry service to Kodiak.

Kodiak Island Convention & Visitors Bureau: 100 Marine Way, Kodiak, AK 99615, (800) 789-4782, (907) 486-4782, *www.kodiak.org*

Regulations/Information

Most Kodiak freshwaters are open to fishing all species, year-round, except for rainbow/steelhead trout (closed in spring, most flowing waters). Almost all Kodiak saltwaters open year-round, all species except lingcod (closed Jan. thru June) and halibut (closed Jan.). Always consult current Kodiak Regulations Summary and/or contact the Alaska Department of Fish and Game, Kodiak office, 211 Mission Road, Kodiak AK 99615, (907) 486-1880 for complete information when planning a trip to the area.

Online info: *www.sf.adfg.state.ak.us/statewide/regulations/kodregs.cfm*

KODIAK SPECIES

LOCATION	KING SALMON	RED SALMON	PINK SALMON	CHUM SALMON	SILVER SALMON	STEELHEAD	RAINBOW	CUTTHROAT	GRAYLING	LAKE TROUT	CHARR	SHEEFISH	HALIBUT	LING COD	ROCK FISH	SALMON SHARK	FSHG. PRESSURE
Shuyak Island	✓	✓	☺	R	★	✓					★		★	★	★	✓	✓
Afognak River	R	★	☺	R	★	✓	✓				★						M
Marka Creek		☺	★	✓	★	✓					☺						✓
Malina Creek	R	★	★	R	★	✓	✓				★						✓
Portage Creek System	R	★	★	R	★	✓	R				★						✓
Pauls Lake System	R	★	☺	R	★	✓	✓				★						✓
Chiniak Bay	★	✓	☺	R	★	R					✓		★	★	☺	☺	☹
Ugak Bay	✓	✓	★	✓	★	✓					✓		★	✓	☺	✓	M
Uyak Bay	☺	R	★	R	★	R					✓		★	✓	☺	✓	M
Uganik River	R	☺	☺	R	★	✓	☺				★						✓
Little River System	R	☺	☺	☺	☺	✓					☺						✓
Buskin River	R	★	★	R	☺	R					★						☹
American River		R	★	✓	☺						☺						☹
Olds River		R	★	✓	★						☺						M
Pasagshak River	C	★	★	R	★						★						☹
Sitkalidak Island/Strait	★	R	☺	☺	★						☺		★	★	★	✓	✓
Saltery River		★	★	R	★	✓					★						M
Karluk River	★	★	★	✓	★	☺					★						☹
Ayakulik River	★	★	★	✓	★	☺					★						✓
Akalura Lake/Creek		☺	★	R	★			✓			☺						✓
Dog Salmon River	C	★	★	★	☺	✓					☺						✓
Upper Station (Olga) Lakes		★	★	R	★	R	✓				☺						✓

Not present
R Rare
✓ Fishable numbers (or light pressure)
☺ Good fishing
★ Excellent fishing

LL Landlocked species
C Present, but fishing closed
M Moderate pressure
☹ Heavy pressure

Arctic
Alaska

The Arctic National Wildlife Refuge, or ANWR (pronounced "anwar"), as it is called, is located in Alaska's most remote corner—the easternmost Brooks Range and coastal plain that abut the northern Yukon border. The size of several eastern states, this pristine reserve is noted for its wildlife and oil potential, but it isn't your typical destination for flyfishing. But, for the man (or woman) who comes prepared, it is not without its pleasant surprises.

On the third morning of an extended backpacking and rafting odyssey into the heart of this last great wilderness, you and your tripmates mount a ridge to afford a better view of the surrounding country. While your buddies glass the distant tundra for animals, your eyes divert to some much more tantalizing goings-on nearby, in a set of beaver ponds right below.

There, in crystal placid waters, you'd swear are the unmistakable forms of grayling—BIG grayling—swimming lazily about and slurping flies. There must be a dozen or more of them, all of impressive size, and you'd bet your bottom dollar not a single one has tasted metal. In the farthest pond—if your eyes aren't playing tricks on you—there swims an absolute behemoth, dwarfing the others, with an enormous, flamboyant dorsal fin that swirls about with each move like an unfurling banner. Surely this is a dream, you tell yourself, pulse quickening as you remember the four-piece tucked away in your pack.

You're all set to charge down the rocky slope with your flyrod, when some movement on the edge of the closest pond stops you in your tracks. A young grizzly bear is excavating a large beaver lodge there, in hopes of making a meal of one or more of the fat occupants. (Never mind that the rodents have all exited through their underwater escape routes and are curiously eyeing him from the deep safety of the pond.) Unlike the mild-mannered bruins that ply the fish-filled waters of the southern coasts, these northernmost mountain grizzlies are known to be short-tempered and highly unpredictable. You wisely sit this one out, watching your giant sailfin swim in dreamy circles, oblivious to the commotion. But patience comes easy in these surroundings. There is time enough for that bear to learn about beavers and time too, in these long, arctic summer days, for you to chase the grayling of your dreams. If you can just remember where you put those doggone flies!

Charr fishing on the Kongakut River,
Arctic National Wildlife Refuge

341

Unmatched solitude and wild fishing on a remote, North Slope mountain lake

The 700-mile arc of the Brooks Range, like a great wall, isolates Alaska's northernmost region from the climate, vegetation, and human development of the Interior and southern coast. From the crest of these great mountains, north to the Beaufort and Chukchi seas, lies Alaska's true Arctic or "North Slope," the state's most remote, inhospitable, and least-visited region. Offering limited fishing variety and a short open-water season, with expensive access and notoriously difficult weather, the Slope certainly can't compete solely as an angling destination with Alaska's gentler and more endowed regions. But it does have Alaska's most pristine backcountry and wildest rivers, along with unique fishing opportunities. For those adventurous souls willing to take it on, the rewards to be had on the rivers, lakes, tundra, and mountains of Alaska's Arctic go far beyond the fishing.

COUNTRY, CLIMATE & FISHING CONDITIONS

The broad, flat, treeless coastal plain is the major feature most people associate with this region. Underlaid with permanently frozen ground, with poor drainage, much of this area is covered with small, shallow, similarly oriented "thaw" lakes, most of which are barren of fish populations (Teshekpuk and the central coastal plain lakes are the exceptions). The rivers are almost all north-flowing, rapid-runoff streams, originating in the highlands to the south. The more outstanding ones, clear and spring-fed, along with a handful of scattered, deep mountain lakes, provide most of the region's better fishing opportunities.

The extreme climate limits the fishing potential. Intense (to minus 30 to 50°F.) cold, darkness, and constant winds predominate for much of the year. Ice can reach a thickness of seven feet and persist into July in some areas, with many shallow rivers and lakes freezing solid by winter's end. Scant precipitation— eight inches or less for most of the region—creates rapidly fluctuating and turbid water conditions in most of the streams, many of which can practically dry up after the spring thaw. All this doesn't bode well for fish, many of which are at their limits of environmental tolerance this far north. Chums and pinks are found only sporadically, while other types of salmon are practically nonexistent. The charrs—Arctic, Dolly Varden and lake trout—along with the plucky grayling, are the only sportfish that really thrive, providing most of the region's fishing opportunities. A few northern pike, with whitefish and some burbot, round out the region's species variety.

The season for good fishing conditions and decent weather is amazingly short, usually from mid-June through August in this most northern and remote province. Stream and lake conditions vary with the weather from year to year, so frequent checks with local contacts beforehand, and alternative trip plans, are requisite to safety and success.

ACCESS, SERVICES & COSTS

Except for a few scattered villages and some oil industry facilities, Alaska's Arctic is virtually uninhabited. Access from the outer world is almost exclusively by plane (from Bettles or Fairbanks), except via the North Slope Haul Road (also known as the Dalton Highway), which bisects the region from Prudhoe Bay to Atigun Pass (see more on the Dalton Highway and its fishing locations in the section that follows). Distances in the Arctic are great; services and facilities extremely limited and expensive. (Expect to pay more than anywhere else in Alaska.) There are no fishing lodges, permanent outpost camps, or floatplane air taxis based in the region at present. Guided float and backpacking trips, and some limited tent camp operations at a few of the major lake locations, represent virtually the only guided fishing options currently available. Some of the major air taxis serving the region also do a limited amount of outfitting, renting gear like rafts, kayaks, and canoes for unguided adventures. (See the listings at the back of the next section for more details.)

The town of Bettles (pop. 36), on the south slope of the Brooks Range, is the main hub for air travel into the western and central Arctic, while Fairbanks (and, to a lesser extent, the villages of Fort Yukon and Arctic

Arctic: Alaska's most awesome wildlife region

Village) serves as the main jumping-off point for adventures into the easternmost part of the region.

If all this puts you off from even considering Alaska's Arctic, be assured that its not as bad as it sounds, but you must come well prepared. Few places on earth can be so unforgiving, and nowhere in Alaska will you be more isolated. Only highly experienced wilderness trekkers, armed with the finest quality gear and a meticulous expedition plan, should attempt this region without the assistance of an experienced guide, and they should consult thoroughly and frequently with local contacts for details and updates on local conditions, particularly when doing a float down one of the region's volatile rivers.

COSTS

RT Air: ANC-FBKS: $127; ANC-Deadhorse: $600; FBKS-Bettles: $240.
Lodging (Umiat): $200/night.
Jetboat Rentals (Umiat): $65/hr.
Raft Rentals: $280-350/wk; Canoe rentals: $245-270/wk.
Guided Float/Backpacking Trips: $250-400/day/person.
Guided Remote Base Camp Fishing: $400-550/day/person.
Unguided Float/Backpacking Trips: $175-250/day/person.
Air Taxi: Cessna 185: $300-385/hr.; Cessna 206-207: 280-$385/hr.; Navaho: $650/hr.; Beaver: $585-650/hr.; Helio-Courier: $300-400/hr.

WHAT TO EXPECT

Arctic maritime to Arctic continental climate conditions prevail. Ice break-up generally comes in late May or early June, but can be delayed into July in the higher elevation lakes and in certain areas along the coast, while freeze-up can begin as early as mid-September. From late May through August, you can expect sunny and reasonably temperate weather, with temperatures in the 40s to 70s (°F), even climbing to the 80s in the foothills, but come prepared for damp, cold winds, extended fog, and even snow at any time. (This is especially true along the coast, where the advancing and retreating ice pack greatly affects the weather.) Swarms of mosquitoes and other biting insects infest the inland tundra during the warmer months of June and July, making head nets, bug jackets, and repellent mandatory.

ARCTIC RUN TIMING

SPECIES	JAN	FEB	MAR	APR	MAY	JUN	JUL	AUG	SEP	OCT	NOV	DEC
Grayling												
Lake Trout												
Charr												
Northern Pike												
Chum Salmon												
Pink Salmon												

▬▬▬ Available   ▬▬▬ Peak

Note: Time periods shown in blue are for bright fish in the case of salmon entering rivers, or for general availability in saltwater or resident species (freshwater). Peak sportfishing periods are shown in red. Run timing can vary among different areas within the region. Always check local contacts for run timing specifics for locations you intend to fish.

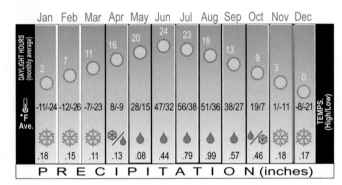

	Jan	Feb	Mar	Apr	May	Jun	Jul	Aug	Sep	Oct	Nov	Dec
DAYLIGHT HOURS (monthly average)	2	7	11	16	20	24	23	18	13	9	3	0
°F Ave. TEMPS. (High/Low)	-11/-24	-12/-26	-7/-23	8/-9	28/15	47/32	56/38	51/36	38/27	19/7	1/-11	-8/-21
PRECIPITATION (inches)	.18	.15	.11	.13	.08	.44	.79	.99	.57	.46	.18	.17

Grayling action on the Hulahula River

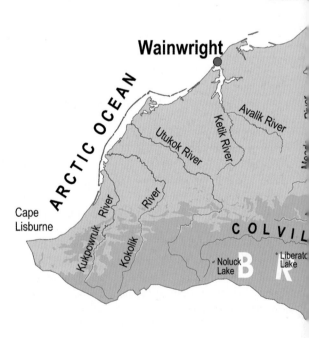

ARCTIC FISHING HIGHLIGHTS

While the Arctic's sportfishing certainly won't win any awards for diversity, most of its streams and lakes get little or no pressure, and offer potentially very high-quality wild fishing, particularly for lake trout, big charr, and grayling. Countless lakes and streams beckon with the promise of virgin angling, but the price of getting in and out is high, and the window of opportunity for good weather and open water very narrow.

A headwater float down one of the many fine rivers of the region, like the tributaries of the Colville (Killik, Anaktuvuk, Nigu/Etivluk, etc.), the Ivishak, Canning, Hulahula, and Kongakut, is perhaps the most exciting way of experiencing the exemplary wilderness and underutilized fishing opportunities of the region. Numerous lake locations, among the most pristine in all of Alaska, make fine destinations for extended camp, hike, and fish adventures, while some of the state's best roadside fishing can be reached from the 414-mile Dalton highway.

Laker from North Slope foothill lake

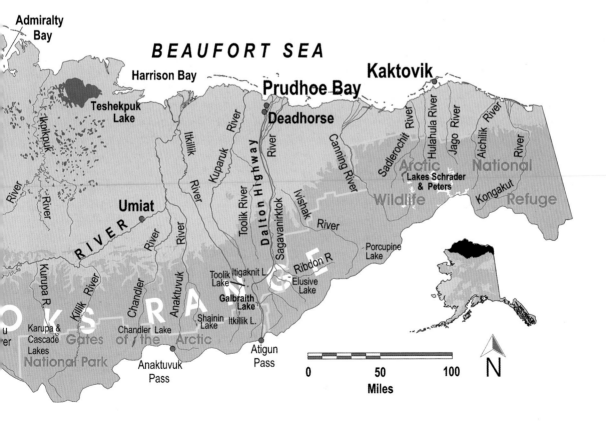

With its awesome vistas, pristine waters, and isolation, Alaska's Arctic can
provide high-quality wilderness adventures that include great angling.

WESTERN CENTRAL SLOPE

The barren coastal plain predominates (to 115 miles inland) in the western and central Arctic slope, with expansive wet tundra, winding rivers, and thousands of shallow lakes. Significant sportfishing possibilities are limited to the giant Colville River system and certain lakes (many unnamed) near the coast, between the Colville and Ikpikpuk rivers. Because of the isolation and difficulty of access, these waters see little visitation at present, but have noteworthy potential for high-quality wild fishing (lake trout, grayling, charr, and some rare salmon). Access is from Bettles, Deadhorse, Umiat, or Barrow.

(Note: Presently there are no air taxis services with floatplanes on the North Slope. Floatplanes from south slope hubs can refuel at Umiat and access many central slope locations.)

Teshekpuk Lake
Location: Central Arctic coastal plain, 430 miles NW of Fairbanks.

Access: By snowmachine from Barrow, or floatplane (via Umiat) from south slope hubs.

Facilities: None.

Highlights: One of the Arctic's least visited but most promising lake trout fisheries.

Main Species: GR, LT

Teshekpuk Lake, west of Harrison Bay, 75 miles SW of Barrow, is the largest body of water on Alaska's North Slope—25 miles across and 315 square miles in area. An important waterfowl breeding site, it is also an anomaly (along with other nearby lakes east of the lower Ikpikpuk River) among thousands of shallow, barren, coastal plain thaw lakes, for its substantial numbers of grayling and hefty lake trout (which are considerably larger-than-average sized, according to ADF&G and locals who fish there). For anyone seeking largely untouched, concentrated lake trout opportunities, with the potential for large fish, Teshekpuk and neighboring Ikpikpuk Lakes are certainly worth a visit.

Central Coastal Plain Lakes
Location: Central Arctic coastal plain, 415 miles NW of Fairbanks.

Access: By private floatplane via Umiat, or floatplane charter from south slope hubs.

Facilities: None.

Highlights: An unexplored frontier of wild lake trout fishing.

Main Species: GR, LT

The Ikpikpuk River flows 200 miles, from headwaters in the foothills of the Brooks Range onto the coastal plain, and into Smith Bay, west of Teshekpuk Lake. It is sluggish and shallow, with tea-colored water and only an occasional grayling or northern pike to tempt anglers. Of greater interest are the dozens of small, unnamed lakes lying east of the river in the central coastal plain, south of Teshekpuk and west of the Colville River. All of the lakes are relatively shallow, but the deeper ones (depths greater than 20 feet) support fish pop-

ulations. Like Teshekpuk, many of these lakes contain abundant grayling and good-sized lake trout. These are remote and expensive waters to access, but offer virtually unexploited, exciting fishing possibilities.

Colville River ★★★
Location: Western Arctic coastal plain, 335 miles NW of Fairbanks.

Access: By floatplane from Bettles to headwaters; lower river by boat from Umiat.

Facilities: Limited services (fuel, lodging, air strip, boat transport) at Umiat on lower river.

Highlights: The Arctic Slope's major river system, with good fishing for a variety of species.

Main Species: CHR, GR, CS

The Colville River is the largest river on the Arctic Slope. Over 420 miles (the seventh largest river in Alaska) from its extensive headwaters in the Brooks Range to its mouth on the Beaufort Sea, it drains 29% of the coastal plain in its mainstem and numerous meandering tributaries. It supports a remarkable diversity and abundance of fish for a river this far north (20 species total), with charr, chum and pink salmon, grayling, lake trout, whitefish, and others found in its vast reaches. Fish are most abundant in the mainstem (Itkillik River to Umiat), and mouths and lower sections of the tributaries. (Killik, Anaktuvuk, Chandler, and Itkillik rivers contain the best stream fishing, particularly for big charr and grayling.)

Not much real sportfishing occurs on the Colville, except by locals or occasional hunters and kayakers. It's a big river with deep, long pools—not easy to fish unless you know your way around. Because of its length, the river is seldom floated in its entirety from its headwaters, but a few of the tributaries can be run by kayak or raft, usually in early summer when the water is high.

NORTH SLOPE FOOTHILL & MOUNTAIN LAKES

Considering the major ice-scouring the Brooks Range received during the last periods of glaciation, surprisingly few glacial lakes of any size exist in the mountains and foothills north of the divide. Most of the North Slope foothill and mountain lakes that support fish populations are small, deep catch basins, lying at the headwaters of tributary streams of large rivers, like the vast Colville River System. Almost all of these lakes have abundant lake trout, grayling, and charr and can provide some outstanding fishing adventure, especially when combined with raft or kayak floats down the rivers they are associated with. The open-water season is short, however; the elevation and latitude of most of these lakes generally results in ice cover from early October (if not before) until late June.

Karupa and Cascade Lakes
Location: Central North Slope, 515 miles NW of Anchorage.

Access: By floatplane from Bettles.

Facilities: None.

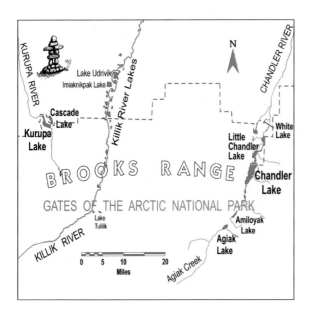

Highlights: Two of the North Slope's prettiest mountain lakes, with excellent fishing.

Main Species: CHR, GR, LT

Lovely Karupa and Cascade lakes, twin headwaters for the Karupa River, lie in the high mountains of Gates of the Arctic National Park, about 15 miles west of the upper Killik River. These lakes are small, but very deep (more than 120 feet), making them two of the deepest lakes in the Brooks Range. The lakes' milky turquoise waters provide good to excellent fishing for lake trout and landlocked charr, with abundant grayling in the inlet and outlet streams. Traditional sites for Eskimo hunters intercepting migrating caribou, these lakes aren't visited much by anglers because of their isolation and elevation (3,000 feet), but they are certainly among the more outstanding small mountain lakes on the North Slope.

Cascade Lake lies on the other side of a high ridge, about a mile northeast of Karupa, and is connected to it by a short gorge at its southern end. Cascade is smaller (about two miles long), but higher in elevation by 500 feet than its twin, Karupa, and usually has more abundant fishing and clearer water. The outlet stream is noted for its fine grayling fishing, and there are nice beaches for camping.

Chandler Lakes

Location: Central North Slope, 274 miles NW of Fairbanks.

Access: By floatplane from Bettles.

Facilities: No developed public facilities.

Highlights: A popular North Slope lake area with good fishing.

Main Species: CHR, GR, LT

On the edge of Gates of the Arctic National Park, 26 miles west of Anaktuvuk Pass, lies lovely Chandler Lake. In a beautiful setting at nearly 3,000 feet elevation, it is the largest mountain lake on the North Slope (five miles long). Along with several other good fishing lakes (Little Chandler, White, and Amiloyak lakes), it forms the headwaters of the Chandler River. Chandler Lake is known for its fine lake trout and landlocked charr fishing, with larger fish (including

lakers up to 30 pounds) more common than in most other mountain lakes of the region. Grayling are also abundant in the inlet and outlet streams.

Amiloyak is the uppermost lake in the Chandler chain, situated in a valley near the Continental Divide, about seven miles southwest of Chandler Lake. It is small, less than two miles long, but has excellent fishing for lake trout (up to 20 pounds) and landlocked charr (up to six pounds), with some grayling in several tributary creeks. You can also hike to fish nearby *Agiak Lake*, two miles on the other side of the divide. *Little Chandler* lies to the north, adjacent to and a tributary of the big lake, connected by a short outlet. It has good fishing, too. *White Lake* lies in a bowl off the river, a few miles northwest of Big Chandler. It also has good lake trout and charr populations. Being situated at this high an elevation, this far north, these waters have a very limited amount of ice-free time.

Killik River Lakes

Location: Central North Slope, 490 miles NW of Anchorage.

Access: Headwaters by small plane from Bettles; pickup by boat on Colville River from Umiat or small plane from other North Slope hubs.

Facilities: None.

Highlights: One of more popular North Slope drainages, with good float fishing potential.

Main Species: CHR, GR, LT, NP

The Killik is one of the better-known North Slope rivers, with a reputation for outstanding float trip possibilities. The river begins in the Brooks Range, in Gates of the Arctic National Park, then flows 105 miles north to the Colville River. As it emerges from the mountains, the upper river area encompasses quite a few small, clustered lakes (Udrivik, Imiaknikpak, Kaniksrak, and Tululik) that are moderately deep and hold lake trout and charr, along with some of the Slope's few opportunities for northern pike. Grayling are abundant in all the streams. The wildlife viewing and hiking along the river are quite noteworthy. Below the lakes, the Killik picks up steam, with canyons, rapids (some rated Class II and Class III), and heavily braided sections, so continuing down to the Colville by raft or kayak is certainly an exciting option.

Anaktuvuk River/Lakes

Location: Central Brooks Range, 260 miles NW of Fairbanks.

Access: Headwaters by small plane from Bettles; pick-up on Colville River by boat from Umiat or small plane from other north slope hubs.

Facilities: None.

Highlights: Important North Slope river with good fishing potential.

Main Species: CHR, GR, LT

The Anaktuvuk is the second largest tributary of the Colville River. One of the more significant North Slope rivers, it has good fish populations (sea-run charr, grayling, and lake trout), and great importance to the central Brooks Range Eskimo (Nunamuit), who have utilized the fish and caribou of the upper river valley for thousands of years. The river rises in the Endicott Mountains (on the edge of Gates of the Arctic National Preserve), and flows 135 miles to the Colville. Numerous small and moderately deep lakes (Tulugak, lower Anayak, Irgnyivik, Natvakruak, etc.), nearly all with good lake trout and grayling fishing, lie along the upper river valley. The swift and braided Anaktuvuk River, known for abundant, big grayling and charr, can be floated during higher water (which occurs in July, generally, but check with air taxis for the latest conditions) down to the Colville for an exciting, rewarding trip.

Shainin or **Willow Lake** is located 22 miles northeast of Anaktuvuk Pass, at the head of the Kanayut River, a major tributary of the Anaktuvuk River. It is a small but pretty alpine lake (elevation 2,700 feet), with milky blue, deep water and abundant grayling and lake trout, even some charr. It doesn't get fished much, except by a few Eskimo hunters, but it's worth considering if you're planning a trip to the Anaktuvuk area. Folks who have fished it report outstanding catches from August through early September.

Itkillik Lake

Location: Central Brooks Range, 270 miles NW of Fairbanks.

Access: By floatplane from Bettles; also winter trail from the Dalton Highway at Galbraith Lake.

Facilities: None.

Highlights: A well-known Brooks Range lake with good fishing for lake trout and grayling.

Main Species: CHR, GR LT

Itkillik Lake has been one of the more popular foothill lake sites, owing to its proximity to the Dalton Highway (just 15 miles west of Pump Station #4) and good fishing. Slightly smaller than Shainin Lake, noted above, Itkillik is located within Gates of the Arctic National Preserve, where it heads a river by the same name that drains into the Colville River, 220 miles south. Fishing has always been good for lake trout and grayling, but it has been hit more in recent years by folks who access lakes north of Atigun Pass by snowmachine from the Dalton Highway (there is a winter trail leading from Galbraith Lake) in late winter/early spring.

DALTON HIGHWAY

The 414-mile Dalton Highway, or North Slope Haul Road, was built in 1974 by Alyeska Pipeline Service Company to facilitate construction and maintenance of the Trans-Alaska Pipeline. Originally reserved for support services and oil field personnel, the Dalton, south of Disaster Creek (Dietrich Camp, milepost 211), was opened to the general public in June of 1981, with travel restrictions along the remainder lifted in 1995. Sportfishing for all species, except salmon, is now allowed along the road corridor (five miles on each side).

The Dalton, north of Atigun Pass, provides limited access to a number of North Slope lakes and rivers, including the Toolik, Galbraith, and Campsite lakes areas and the Kuparuk, Toolik, and Sagavanirktok rivers. Fishing opportunities for lake trout, charr, and grayling are plentiful in most of these waters, especially for folks who take the initiative to explore beyond the immediate reaches of the road. For instance, there are dozens of small, fish-filled lakes that lie within hiking distance of

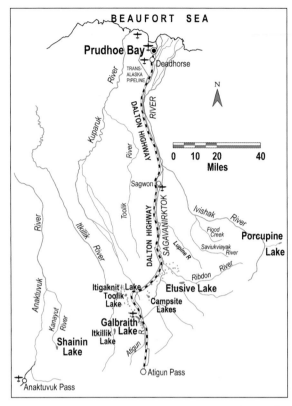

the highway, between Pump Stations #3 and #4. The Sagavanirktok River, a prime drainage for large sea-run charr, can be reached from certain points north of Pump Station #3. With an inflatable raft or canoe, the possibilities are almost limitless.

Adventuresome anglers planning on traveling this primitive road should come prepared, however, for a shortage of services (Mile 56, 175, and 414 only) and facilities (Mile 56, 60, 115, 175, and 180 only), along with hazardous driving with dust, flying rocks, and barreling 18-wheelers. The most popular time to travel the Dalton for fishing is from July through mid-September, with late spring (April) snowmachine ice-fishing safaris becoming increasingly popular.

Note: *always check latest road conditions beforehand with the Alaska Department of Transportation, (800) 478-7675, before traveling the Dalton Highway.*

Galbraith Lakes ★★★

Location: Central Brooks Range, 250 miles north of Fairbanks, adjacent to mileposts 270 to 276 on the Dalton Highway near Pump Station #4.

Access: By small plane from Bettles or Coldfoot, or by hiking from the Dalton Highway.

Facilities: No developed public facilities.

Highlights: Easily accessible lakes with good seasonal fishing for lake trout, charr, and grayling.

Main Species: CHR, GR, LT

Galbraith, Tee, and Atigun lakes lie in the lower Atigun River Valley, adjacent to the west side of the Dalton Highway near Pump Station #4 (mileposts 270 to 276), approximately 250 miles north of Fairbanks. Situated at 2,600-foot elevation, these are mountain lakes, with beautiful scenery and fairly abundant fishing, but with a limited season of open water. Galbraith has always been the most productive and popular of these waters, with good seasonal catches of lake trout and landlocked charr. The other two lakes, the largest of a group of lakes along the upper Atigun River, contain good fishing as well (with grayling available in the river). All these lakes have had a fair amount of fishing pressure since the highway was opened, but are still worth visiting. They are reached by a short hike from the highway or by small plane to an airstrip just west (one-and-a-half miles) of Galbraith Lake. The best time to fish these waters is from late June through early July, and in August.

Toolik and Itagaknit Lakes

Location: Approximately 257 miles north of Fairbanks, adjacent to milepost 284 on the Dalton Highway.

Access: Toolik Lake has a short access road leading from highway and nearby airstrip.

Facilities: No developed public facilities.

Highlights: A popular Dalton Highway lake area with good seasonal fishing for lake trout and grayling.

Main Species: CHR, GR, LT

Toolik and Itagaknit are the largest of a group of clustered lakes along the upper Kuparuk River drainage, just a short distance west of the Dalton Highway at milepost 284. Small, but deep (up to 100 feet), the lakes and their numerous connecting streams have good populations of grayling, and small to medium-sized lake trout and charr. Because of access, Toolik and, to a lesser extent, Itagaknit, have seen some use. But with a little hiking and exploring (best times are spring or fall), you can tap into some of the lesser fished, more productive lakes and streams.

Campsite Lakes

Location: Five miles south of the Dalton Highway, twelve miles east of Toolik Lake.

Access: By hike-in trail from the Dalton Highway at milepost 295.

Facilities: None.

Highlights: Easy hike-in lakes with decent lake trout and charr fishing.

Main Species: CHR, GR, LT

The Campsite Lakes area, located approximately twelve miles east of Toolik Lake, includes a dozen or more small, fairly deep lakes clustered along upper Oksrukuyik Creek, a tributary of the Saga-vanirktok. Nearly all have fish in them—abundant lake trout, land-locked charr, grayling, and even burbot. Campsite Lake is the largest and most popular of the group. They all can be reached by trail (about five miles long) from the Dalton Highway. Along with the Toolik and Galbraith lakes, they offer the Dalton's best opportunities for road-accessible lake trout and charr fishing.

Elusive Lake

Location: Central Brooks Range, twelve miles east of the Dalton Highway, 260 miles north of Fairbanks.

Access: By small plane from Arctic Village, Bettles, or Coldfoot; winter trail access by snowmachine from the Dalton Highway.

Facilities: None.

Highlights: A noteworthy North Slope lake fishing destination.

Main Species: GR, LT

Elusive Lake is located in the Ribdon River Valley, twelve miles east of the Dalton Highway, approximately 260 miles north of Fairbanks. Usually accessed by wheelplane (there's a gravel strip on the east end of the lake), it can also be easily reached during winter via a snowmachine trail from a highway maintenance camp on the Dalton, making it one of the more popular foothill lakes for ice fishing (lake trout), especially in late winter and early spring, with catches to 20 pounds not uncommon.

Kuparuk River ★★★

Location: North flowing drainage, west of the Sagavanirktok River, approximately five miles east of Toolik Lake.

Access: By foot trail from the Dalton Highway.

Facilities: No developed public facilities.

Highlights: One of the North Slope's best grayling rivers, with excellent flyfishing.

Main Species: GR, LT

The most popular grayling fishery on the North Slope, the Kuparuk River flows west of the Sagavanirktok River, 180 miles north to the Beaufort Sea. It is easily accessed along its upper east fork from the Dalton Highway, where it crosses the river about six miles beyond Toolik Lake Road at milepost 290. The Kuparuk has great flyfishing along its swift, clear, rocky upper reaches and, by North Slope standards, the grayling are plentiful and big. Farther upstream lies a small headwater lake of the same name, which is known to have abundant lake trout.

Sagavanirktok River ★★★

Location: Central Arctic Slope, 300 miles north of Fairbanks.

Access: By small plane to the upper river (Atigun River or upper mainstem) from Coldfoot, Bettles, or Deadhorse; access is also possible from the Dalton Highway at several points.

Facilities: No developed public facilities.

Highlights: An easily accessible North Slope river with noteworthy fishing for trophy charr.

Main Species: CHR, GR

The Sagavanirktok, or "Sag," is one North Slope river most folks have heard of, since it's closely associated with the Dalton Highway—it follows the river for some 100 miles. It has a reputation as an exciting whitewater float. And, as the North Slope's most significant drainage for sea-run charr, with major overwintering and spawning habitat in its deep pools and miles of spring-fed tributaries, the Sag has great potential as a trophy fishery (with average size three to five pounds, and fish up to 10 pounds or more).

The Sag is wide, rocky and swift (Class I mostly, with some Class II and Class III stretches), with extensive braids for most of its length. It rises in the Philip Smith Mountains of the Arctic National Wildlife

Refuge, flowing south for 175 miles before emptying into the Beaufort Sea east of Prudhoe. It has 20 tributaries, some, like the Ivishak River (see listing), with exceptional qualities, including substantial sportfishing potential. The best thing about the Sag is its easy access. You can reach some of the more remote headwaters by small plane, but most folks access the mainstem (and Atigun River) from the Dalton Highway at numerous locations (north of Pump Station #3; Mileposts 253, 271, 325; Happy Valley; etc.), hiking and fishing the river or putting in with raft or kayak for a short float to takeout points below (Franklin Bluffs or Deadhorse).

The lower Sag is commonly fished by oil field workers who access the numerous channels, sloughs, and pools with excellent results. The charr begin their fall spawning inmigrations sometime in early August; the best time to fish the river is probably from mid-August into the first part of September. The Sagavanirktok also offers some fine grayling and occasional lake trout catches.

EASTERN ARCTIC SLOPE

From the Canning River east to the Canadian border, the land becomes significantly more varied in form and character than the rest of the Arctic Slope. The highest peaks of the Brooks Range, running north to east, crowd out the coastal plain to a narrow strip of rolling tundra less than ten miles wide at the border, and give rise to some of Arctic's most significant rivers. This area, perhaps best known for its superlative wilderness (the 19-million-acre Arctic National Wildlife Refuge, the nation's largest, including eight million acres of designated wilderness) and wildlife (caribou, musk-ox, polar bear, and wolves), also has quite a few outstanding sportfishing possibilities for trophy-sized charr, grayling, and lake trout. Access is from Arctic Village, Kaktovik, and Prudhoe Bay.

Ivishak River ★★★
Location: Arctic coastal plain, 320 miles north of Fairbanks.
Access: Small plane to headwaters or lower river; highway access possible to takeout points along Sagavanirktok River.
Facilities: None.
Highlights: An outstanding North Slope river with excellent trophy charr fishing.
Main Species: CHR, GR

The Ivishak Wild and Scenic River is one of the North Slope's premier float trip streams, making for an outstanding wilderness voyage that can be finished on the Sagavanirktok River. It is also the Sagavanirktok's most significant tributary for big sea-run charr, with abundant spawning and wintering populations and excellent sportfishing potential.

You can fly into the headwaters located in the Philip Smith Mountains by small plane, making landings on gravel bars. Or take a floatplane to Porcupine Lake and enjoy some good lake trout fishing, then float down (some dragging of the boats will be necessary right below the lake in low water conditions) through a beautiful

canyon to the foothills and the flat coastal plain. There's a strip near the confluence of the Echooka River where you can take out, or you can continue down to the Sagavanirktok (approximately 92 miles below the lake) for a five to seven-day trip. Scenery, hiking, and wildlife viewing (bear, wolf, Dall sheep) opportunities are excellent on the upper river, as is the fishing, making this one of the best all-around trips on the North Slope. The best time to fish the Ivishak for big charr is in August but, like all Slope rivers, you should check with local air taxis for conditions before making final arrangements.

Canning River
Location: Eastern Arctic coastal plain, 350 miles north of Fairbanks.
Access: By wheelplane from Kaktovik or Arctic Village.
Facilities: None.
Highlights: A great North Slope float river with good charr fishing.
Main Species: CHR, GR

The Canning River certainly deserves mention among the North Slope's better options for sportfishing, as it supports an abundant sea-run charr population with numerous headwater springs for overwintering survival. It begins in the steep recesses of the Philip Smith Mountains of the Arctic National Wildlife Refuge (ANWR), flowing north 120 miles to Camden Bay, west of Kaktovik. It's a whitewater river, nothing major (Class I and Class II), but heavily braided and silty along most of its mainstem below the mountains. Most folks who float it put in somewhere along the upper Marsh Fork, where the water is clear, then float, fish, and camp down to the confluence, with a pick-up somewhere below along gravel bars in the river's middle or lower section, above the broad and braided delta.

Fishing is good for big charr and grayling all along the upper river in late summer, and it's a pretty float with awesome mountain scenery and lots of wildlife, well worth the time and expense of getting in and out. This trip is a great way to experience the wonders of the Arctic National Wildlife Refuge along with some superb fishing.

Lakes Schrader and Peters
Location: Arctic National Wildlife Refuge, 325 miles NE of Fairbanks.
Access: By small plane from Kaktovik or Arctic Village.
Facilities: None.
Highlights: An Arctic National Wildlife Refuge lake system with excellent fishing.
Main Species: CHR, GR, LT

Lakes Schrader and Peters are well off the beaten path, even for the remote Arctic Slope. Seldom visited except by locals (mostly from Kaktovik), these deep and lovely twin lakes at the headwaters of the Sadlerochit River in the Arctic National Wildlife Refuge are reputed to have some of the best trophy lake trout and landlocked charr fishing on the Slope. Fish in the 20 to 30-pound range are possible, especially in the spring.

Access is expensive, with a small plane fly-in usually from Arctic Village or Kaktovik, landing at a small gravel strip or on the lakes (with floats). Kaktovik residents visit the lakes mostly in late spring, by snowmachine. The ice doesn't melt until late June, so the open-water season is quite short.

Kongakut River ★★★

Location: Eastern Arctic coastal plain, 335 miles NE of Fairbanks.

Access: By wheelplane from Kaktovik, Arctic Village, Fairbanks, or other area hubs.

Facilities: None.

Highlights: The most popular river in ANWR, with outstanding sea-run charr and grayling fishing.

Main Species: CHR, GR

It would be remiss not to list the Kongakut among the North Slope's better fishing rivers, even though this drainage certainly needs no more attention. Hidden in Alaska's most remote northeast corner, the "Kong" has seen quite a bit of visitation the last 15 years or so from folks eager to experience all the wild, delicate values of the Arctic coastal plain threatened by oil exploration.

An extraordinary river, the Kong flows swift and clear through the rugged heart of some of Alaska's wildest country where, with any luck, you can catch glimpses of caribou, wolves, even musk-ox, while you float through "a pristine mountain setting of great aesthetic value" (USFWS description). The fishing is very good; everyone who floats this river is impressed, rating the charr and grayling fishery of exceptional quality (the average Kongakut charr is larger in size than those encountered in any other North Slope river).

But it is an expensive, serious trip for only the most seasoned of wilderness rafters, involving long flights from Kaktovik, Arctic Village, or other area hubs to gravel bar put-ins along the headwaters, then 8-10 days of floating down to the lower river, and take-out via plane from Kaktovik. Best time to float for optimum fishing, weather, and stream conditions is from late June through early August.

Recommended Lodges/Air Taxis/Guides/Outfitters

Umiat Lodge: 2700 S. Cushman, Fairbanks, AK 99701, (907) 322-7040, (907) 452-6631, *www.umiat.com* Lodging, meals, boat rentals, fuel, 5,900-foot airstrip, lower Colville River.

Wright Air Service: P.O. Box 60142, Fairbanks, AK 99706, (907) 474-0502. North Slope air taxi.

Alaska Flyers: Walt Audi, P.O. Box 67, Kaktovik, AK 99747, (640) 6324. Air taxi, Arctic National Wildlife Refuge.

Bettles Lodge/Air Service: P.O. Box 27, Bettles, AK 99726, (800) 770-5111, (907) 692-5111, *www.bettleslodge.com* Lodging, outfitting, air taxi, Brooks Range.

Brooks Range Aviation: P.O. Box 10, Bettles, AK 99726, (692) 5444, (800) 692-5443. *www.brooksrange.com*

Yukon Air Service: P.O. Box 84107, Fairbanks, AK 99708, (907) 479-3993 (winter), (907) 662-2445 (summer).

Cape Smythe Air Service: P.O. Box 340091, Deadhorse, AK 99734, (907) 659-2743.

Sourdough Outfitters: P.O. Box 26066, Bettles, AK 99726, (907) 692-5252, *www.sourdoughoutfitters.com* Guided/unguided float fish trips, Brooks Range.

ABEC's Alaska Adventures: 1550 Alpine Vista Court, Fairbanks, AK 99712, (877) or (907) 424-8907, *www.abecalaska.com* Guided float/backpacking trips, Brooks Range and ANWR.

Pristine Ventures: P.O. Box 83909, Fairbanks, AK 99708, (907) 451-4366, *www.pristineventures.com* Guided float trips.

USGS Maps Reference

Teshekpuk Lake: Teshekpuk B-1, B-2, C-1, C-2; Harrison Bay C-5.

Central Coastal Plain Lakes: Teshekpuk A-1, A-2, A-3, B-1, B-2, B-3; Harrison Bay A-4, A-5, B-4, B-5; Umiat C-5, D-5.

Colville River: Misheguk Mountain C-2, C-3, D-2, D-3; Utukok River A-1, A-2; Lookout Ridge A-4, A-5; Howard Pass D-1, D-2, D-3, D-4; Killik River D-5; Ikpikpuk River A-1, A-2, A-3, A-4, A-5; Umiat A-5, B-3, B-4, B-5, C-3, D-3; Harrison Bay A-2, A-3, B-1, B-2.

Karupa & Cascade Lakes: Killik River B-3.

Chandler Lakes: Chandler Lake A-5, B-5.

Killik River Lakes: Killik River A-2, A-3, B-2, C-2, D-1; Ikpikpuk River A-2.

Anaktuvuk River & Lakes: Chandler Lake A-3, B-3, C-2, C-3, D-2, D-3.

Itkillik Lake: Philip Smith Mountains B-5.

Elusive Lake: Philip Smith Mountains C-3.

Galbraith Lakes: Philip Smith Mountains B-5, B-4.

Toolik & Itagaknit Lakes: Philip Smith Mountains C-5.

Campsite Lakes: Philip Smith Mountains C-4.

Kuparuk River: Philip Smith Mountains C-4, C-5, D-5; Sagavanirktok A-5, C-5, D-5; Umiat A-1, B-1, C-1; Beechey Point A-4, B-4.

Sagavanirktok River: Philip Smith Mountains A-4, B-4, B-5, C-3, C-4, D-3, D-4; Sagavanirktok A-3, A-4, B-3, C-3, D-3; Beechey Point A-2, A-3, B-2, B-3.

Ivishak River: Arctic C-5, D-5; Sagavanirktok A-1, A-2, B-2, B-3; Philip Smith Mountains C-1, D-1.

Canning River: Arctic C-4, C-5, D-3, D-4; Mt. Michelson A-3, A-4, B-4, C-4, D-4; Flaxman Island A-4, A-5.

Lakes Schrader & Peters: Mount Michelson B-2.

Kongakut River: Table Mountain D-2, D-3, D-4; Demarcation Point A-1, A-2, B-1, B-2, C-2, D-2.

General Information

Arctic National Wildlife Refuge (ANWR): 101 12th Ave., Rm. 236, Box 20, Fairbanks, AK 99701, (907) 456-0250, h*ttp://arctic.fws.gov/index.htm*

Gates of the Arctic National Park and Preserve: National Park Service; 201 First Avenue, Fairbanks, AK 99701, (907) 457-5752, *www.nps.gov/gaar/*

Alaska Department of Transportation: Northern Region Headquarters; 2301 Peger Road, Fairbanks, AK 99709, (907) 451-2206, *www.dot.state.ak.us/*

Regulations/Information

Alaska's North Slope drainages are open to fishing year-round, all species, with few restrictions other than along the Trans-Alaska Pipeline Corridor (extending five miles on either side of Dalton Highway), which is closed to all salmon fishing and taking of lake trout, with size restrictions on grayling. Consult current Regulations Summary for Region III or contact regional/field office of ADF&G for latest info when planning a fishing trip to region.

Fairbanks: (907) 459-7207   **Barrow:** (907) 852-3464

Online: *www.sf.adfg.state.ak.us/statewide/regulations/aykregs.cfm*

Arctic Species

LOCATION	KING SALMON	RED SALMON	PINK SALMON	CHUM SALMON	SILVER SALMON	STEELHEAD	RAINBOW	CUTTHROAT	CHAR	GRAYLING	LAKE TROUT	SHEEFISH	NORTHERN PIKE	HALIBUT	LINGCOD	ROCKFISH	SALMON SHARK	FSHG. PRESSURE
Teshekpuk Lake										☺	★							R
Central Coastal Plain Lakes										✓	★		R					R
Colville River	R		R	R					★	★	✓							R
Karupa/Cascade Lakes									☺	★	☺							R
Chandler Lakes									★	★	★							R
Killik River Lakes									☺	★	☺	✓						R
Anaktuvuk River/Lakes			R	R					★	★	☺							R
Shainin Lake									☺	☺	☺							R
Itkillik Lake									☺	☺	☺							R
Galbraith Lakes									☺	★	☺							✓
Toolik/Itagaknit Lakes									☺	☺	☺							M
Campsite Lakes									☺	☺	☺							M
Elusive Lake										☺	★							R
Kuparuk River										★	✓							✓
Sagavanirktok River			C	C					★	☺	✓							M
Ivishak River									★	☺	✓							R
Canning River			R	R					★	☺								R
Lakes Schrader/Peters									★	☺	★							R
Kongakut River									★	☺								✓

Legend:

	Species not present
R	Rare
✓	Fishable numbers (or light pressure)
☺	Good fishing
★	Excellent fishing
LL	Landlocked species
C	Present, but fishing closed
M	Moderate pressure
☹	Heavy pressure

Southeast Alaska

Imagine a vacation destination where you spend quiet mornings stalking wild steelhead on small, secluded streams; then, after lunch, boat out to scenic bays and fjords, clip on downriggers, and hunt fat feeder kings or jig for giant halibut. You thrill to frequent sightings of whales, eagles, sea otters, and beach-roaming bears, along the densely forested coastline. At day's end, arms weary, you feast on a cornucopia of delights harvested from the clear, cold waters: chunks of batter-dipped halibut, grilled salmon, rockfish, and succulent shrimp and crab pulled fresh from the pot. Later on, around the fire, the next day's anticipation is stoked with talk of exciting fishing adventure, like flights into nearby mountain lakes, where the cutthroat trout and Dolly Varden run thick and hungry, furious to the fly.

Believe it or not, such a place does exist, beyond the realm of anglers' dreams—along the magnificent coastline, islands, and sheltered passages that make up the Southeast panhandle of Alaska. This narrow (120-mile-wide), long strip of land wedged between the Pacific and the coast of British Columbia contains, without a doubt, some of the most fabulous country anywhere for sport anglers. Nowhere else can you find such variety and abundance of world-class opportunities for steelhead and cutthroat trout, saltwater salmon, halibut, rockfish, Dolly Varden, and others—all within easy reach by boat or plane from a half dozen communities scattered along the coast. With its misty forests, snow-capped mountains, quaint fishing towns, and colorful totems, this unique region has always had a mystique all its own. One visit and you may find, like so many others, that Southeast is your port of call for a lifetime of fishing adventure.

Heading out, Misty Fjords
National Monument

355

Flyfishing the Chilkoot River, northern Southeast

2005 Michael DeYoung/AlaskaStock.com

COUNTRY, CLIMATE & FISHING CONDITIONS

From Dixon Entrance, which divides Canada's Queen Charlotte Islands from their neighboring American counterparts, north and west in an enormous arc to Icy Cape, the Southeast panhandle stretches nearly 600 miles. Within this region lies an impressive and dynamic landscape, shaped by the powerful forces of nature and nurtured by a benign climate. Isolated from the rest of Alaska, Southeast has a unique character and fisheries unlike those found elsewhere along the coast.

This is the land of temperate rain forests, with most of the coast cloaked in dense stands of hemlock, cedar, and spruce, encompassing the 17-million-acre, Tongass National Forest, the largest in the nation. An archipelago of hundreds of islands (including the third largest in the U.S.—Prince of Wales), with countless straits, sounds, bays, and fjords, this region, along with the adjacent coast of southern British Columbia, comprises the only real significant sheltered habitat along the entire wave-battered, rocky

north Pacific. As such, it is a rich haven for a diversity of marine wildlife, from seabirds to whales to salmon. (The abundance of easily available resources gave rise to a vibrant native culture, with a rich mythology still very much alive today.)

With its glaciers and abundant rain and snow, this coastal paradise is further enhanced with thousands of lakes, streams, and ponds, most of them containing sportfish of some kind. Much of the region's more exemplary wilderness is protected in national parks, monuments, wildernesses, and preserves, among them some of our nation's most spectacularly scenic, like Glacier Bay and Misty Fjords.

Southeast's climate is mild, especially compared to the rest of Alaska. Warmed in winter and cooled in summer by the maritime influence of the Pacific, conditions here can be surprisingly more favorable to outdoor activities than in some locations in the lower 48 states. (Compare the January or July average temperature here with that of Chicago, for instance.) The abundant "liquid sunshine" that naysayers cite as the

A humpback whale breaches in Frederick Sound. Southeast's magnificently scenic coast and abundant wildlife are a plus for anglers.

Just as much, if not more, fishing effort in Southeast takes place in saltwater, in conditions that can vary tremendously, from one location to the next, or from day to day, even. You can troll familiar drags in calm straits along the Inside Passage, soak bait in quiet, sheltered bays anywhere along the coast or, if weather allows, jig in the productive, rocky, surging waters fronting the north Pacific. As in most of coastal Alaska, but even more so, the weather and ocean conditions will greatly influence fishing plans. For your safety and enjoyment, the services of an experienced guide or charter boat captain are highly recommended, especially for novices.

ACCESS, SERVICES & COSTS

The region's close proximity to the outside world and its well-developed network of transportation and services adds immeasurably to its appeal as a vacation destination. Although there are no outside road connections to most of the panhandle (Hyder, Haines, and Skagway on the mainland are the exceptions), the major hubs like Juneau, Ketchikan, and Sitka are all serviced daily by commercial jets linking with the West Coast and the rest of Alaska. Local air taxis provide scheduled or charter flights to most outlying towns, and a well-established state ferry service further links the communities along the panhandle.

With a limited road network, (other than the short highways leading out from major communities, or gravel logging roads in some areas) access to many of the better fishing locations is by boat or small plane only. Numerous hiking trails exist throughout Southeast, some providing access to prime fishing waters. A very well-known and extensive system of public-use cabins is maintained by the U.S. Forest Service throughout the region, many located at or near the most popular lake and stream locations, with skiffs usually included for fishing.

You'll find a burgeoning visitor services industry in Southeast to help make your stay there productive and most memorable. Spurred by the rapid growth of tourism in recent years (especially from cruise ships that ply the Inside Passage with great numbers of visitors eager to sample the fabled fishing), there now exists a bewildering array of wilderness lodges, family-style fishing camps, bed and breakfasts, fishing charters, guides, air taxis, boat and yacht rentals, floating hotels, etc., offering a diversity of experiences perhaps unmatched anywhere else in Alaska.

region's main drawback, seldom prevents anyone, adequately prepared, from enjoying the bounty of outdoor recreation possibilities.

Like much of Alaska's southern coast, Southeast has streams that, with few exceptions (the large, transboundary glacial systems mostly), are short, high gradient, and small compared to most drainages on the mainland. Their swift, rocky nature and abundant surrounding vegetation make them much more difficult to negotiate then streams elsewhere in Alaska, as newcomers to this part of the state are quick to realize. Because of this and the lack of holding water, most of the fishing in these creeks takes place at mouths or in tidal lagoons. With abundant rainfall and snowpack, these streams can fluctuate greatly through the season, especially during periods of abnormal precipitation (or rare drought).

More advantageous are the numerous Southeast waters with associated lakes, which typically have more consistent stream flows and better fishing (the lakes greatly enhance productivity of trout and salmon populations). The more fecund of these lake and stream systems, like the McDonald and Naha near Ketchikan, Thorne and Karta of Prince of Wales Island, Kadake near Petersburg, Sitkoh near Sitka, Situk near Yakutat, and a few others, are some of the most popular freshwater angling destinations in the region.

WHAT TO EXPECT

Temperate maritime climate: visitors should come prepared for mild, moist weather, with cloudy, cool days the norm. Temperatures in summer range from the mid 50s to the upper 60s (°F), with highs into the 70s possible, when the sun shines. Winters are mild, with temperatures ranging from the teens to the lower 40s, and snow or rain likely. Southeast weather is unpredictable and ever-changing. Areas in the vicinity of large glaciers are subject to fog or strong, cold winds that can sweep down at any time of year. Marine anglers can likewise expect chilling winds even during the warmest parts of the summer. Precipitation is extremely varied within the region (from 30 to over 200 inches a year), but follows the same trend prevalent most elsewhere in Alaska: spring and early summer (from April to July) are the driest, sunniest parts of the year, while fall and early winter (from October to January) are the cloudiest and most stormy.

Because of the mild climate, fishing season typically begins earlier and continues later than elsewhere, with an extended open-water period allowing for freshwater fishing all year in some areas. (Higher elevation lakes and some locations in northern Southeast ice over much the same as Alaska waters do elsewhere.)

COSTS:

RT Air: Seattle to Ketchikan, Sitka, Juneau: $338-460.
Guided, Deluxe Lodge: $616-931/person/day.
Guided, Family Style Lodge: $350-521/person/day.
Unguided Lodge: $167-665/person/day.
Fly-in Guided Fishing: Half day, $320-400/person; full day $425-750/person.
Boat Charter: Half day $125-150/person; full day $175-250/person.
Yacht Charter: $400-600/person/day.
Lodging: $60-175/night, single room.
Remote Lodging: $185-275/person/day.
B & B: $60-150/person/night.
Remote Cabins: $50-215/person/day.
Boat Rentals: $90-280/day.
Car Rentals: $49.95-99.95/day.
Air Taxi: Cessna 180-185: $310-400/hr; Cessna 206: $320-380/hr; Beech Bonanza: $300/hr; Beaver: $480-550 /hr; Otter: $780-1100/hr.

SOUTHEAST SALTWATER RUN TIMING

SPECIES	JAN	FEB	MAR	APR	MAY	JUN	JUL	AUG	SEP	OCT	NOV	DEC
King Salmon												
Silver Salmon												
Red Salmon												
Chum Salmon												
Pink Salmon												
Halibut												
Rockfish												
Salmon Shark												
Ling Cod												

SOUTHEAST FRESHWATER RUN TIMING

SPECIES	JAN	FEB	MAR	APR	MAY	JUN	JUL	AUG	SEP	OCT	NOV	DEC
King Salmon												
Silver Salmon												
Red Salmon												
Chum Salmon												
Pink Salmon												
Steelhead												
Rainbow Trout												
Cutthroat Trout												
Dolly Varden												
Grayling												

▬ Available   ▬ Peak

Note: Time periods shown are for bright salmon entering rivers, or for general availability of nearshore (saltwater) or resident (freshwater) species. Run timing can vary among different areas within region. Check local contacts for run timing specifics of locations you intend to fish.

Southeast's famous totem poles and other artifacts are evidence of a vibrant native culture.

	Jan	Feb	Mar	Apr	May	Jun	Jul	Aug	Sep	Oct	Nov	Dec
DAYLIGHT HOURS (monthly average)	7 ½	9 ½	11 ¾	14 ¼	16 ½	17 ¾	17	15 ¼	12 ¾	10 ½	8 ¼	7
°F Ave. TEMPS. (High/Low)	35/25	38/27	41/30	48/34	54/41	59/47	62/50	63/49	57/43	49/37	41/30	37/30
PRECIPITATION (inches)	9.48	8.14	8	7	6.5	5.1	5.5	8.5	12.9	16.6	11.3	10.9

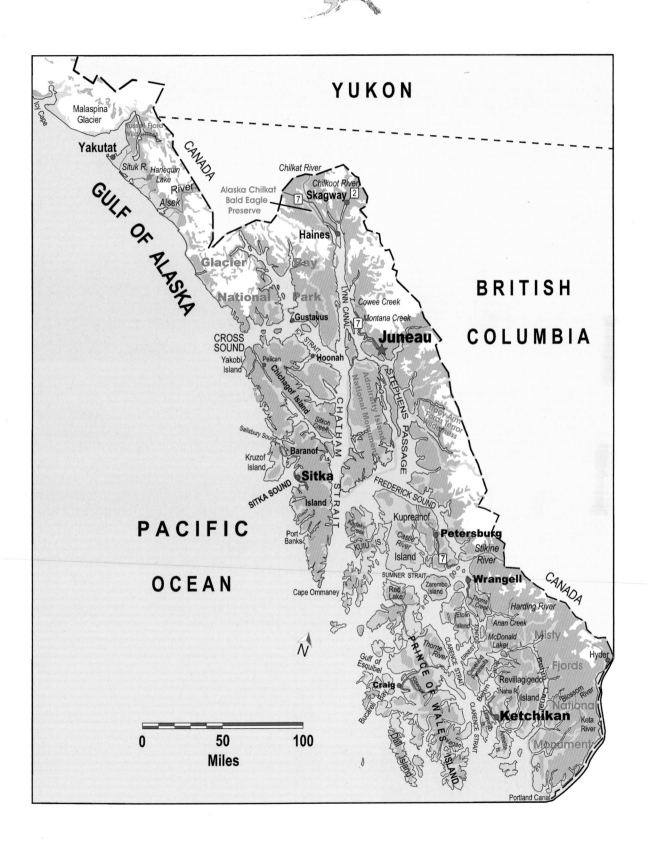

YUKON

Icy Cape

Malaspina Glacier

Russell Fiord Wilderness

Yakutat

Situk R.

Harlequin Lake

River

Alsek

CANADA

Chilkat River

Chilkoot River

Alaska Chilkat Bald Eagle Preserve

[7] **Skagway** [2]

Haines

GULF OF ALASKA

Glacier Bay

National Park

Cowee Creek

Montana Creek

[7]

Juneau

BRITISH

COLUMBIA

•Gustavus

CROSS SOUND

Yakobi Island

Pelican

Hoonah

ICY STRAIT

LYNN CANAL

Admiralty Island National Monument

STEPHENS PASSAGE

Tracy Arm Fords Terror Wilderness

Chichagof Island

Sitkoh Creek

CHATHAM STRAIT

Salisbury Sound

Kruzof Island

Baranof

Sitka

Island

FREDERICK SOUND

SITKA SOUND

Kupreanof

Port Banks

Kadake Creek

Castle River

Island

PACIFIC

KUIU IS.

Petersburg

Stikine River

[7]

OCEAN

SUMNER STRAIT

Cape Ommaney

Red Lake

Zarembo Island

Wrangell

CANADA

Thoms Creek

Harding River

Etolin Island

Anan Creek

Misty

McDonald Lake

Fjords

Hyder

Thorne River

CLARENCE STRAIT

ERNEST SOUND

Cleveland Peninsula

Bradfield Canal

Naha R.

Revillagigedo

Blossom River

Island

National

Gulf of Esquibel

PRINCE OF WALES ISLAND

Karta River

Keta River

Craig

Bucareli Bay

CLARENCE STRAIT

Ketchikan

Monument

Annette Is.

N

Kegan

Dall Island

Portland Canal

0   50   100

Miles

Hot saltwater salmon action, northern Southeast

Southeast—wild steelhead mecca of Alaska

Trophy saltwater king, west coast Prince of Wales Island

SOUTHEAST FISHING HIGHLIGHTS

As an angling destination, Southeast Alaska has so much to offer that one can only wonder why folks would want to fish anywhere else. For one thing, it has far and away Alaska's most abundant and varied marine fishing opportunities, with quite a few world-famous salmon and halibut locations. (Communities here continually vie for "world's best salmon and halibut fishing" distinction.) Terminal hatchery fisheries have augmented or created quite a few fishing opportunities along the coast, many within easy reach.

Southeast is also the state's wild steelhead mecca, with hundreds of identified streams containing the species, quite a few of them enjoying world-class distinction. (With a little exploration, you can have one all to yourself.) Cutthroat trout and Dolly Varden charr, similarly, are found throughout the region in thousands of streams, lakes, and ponds, providing added highlights to nearly every fishing excursion, no matter what time of year. (And with Southeast's mild climate, you can enjoy the longest fishing season in Alaska.)

Trophy anglers will find plenty of opportunities in the region. Most of the state's largest specimens of silver and chum salmon, steelhead and cutthroat trout, and several species of rockfish come from Southeast's waters. On an exotic note, the region contains Alaska's only opportunities for fishing eastern brook trout, *Salvelinus fontinalis*, from stockings that were done years ago, along with a few rare watersheds containing Arctic grayling.

KETCHIKAN/PRINCE OF WALES

The Ketchikan/Prince of Wales area, from Dixon Entrance to Ernest Sound, includes the Revillagigedo, Annette, Gravina, and Prince of Wales Island complexes, along with part of the Cleveland Peninsula, Behm Canal, Clarence Strait, and Misty Fjords National Monument. It has some of Alaska's most significant marine and freshwater fisheries, particularly for salmon, steelhead, and cutthroat trout.

This is famous saltwater trolling country (the "Salmon Capitol of the World") with a major charter fleet working the waters of West Behm Canal, Tongass Narrows, and Clarence Strait for king and coho salmon. The extremely productive outside waters are usually targeted for salmon and halibut by lodges and guides from Prince of Wales (Klawock, Waterfall, Craig, Thorne Bay). Most of the area's recreational effort, however, occurs near Ketchikan, from Clover Pass to Mountain Point.

The Ketchikan area is also known for its unique and outstanding freshwater angling opportunities. Southeast's finest lakes (including Wilson, Humpback, and Manzanita) are located here, along with Alaska's best trophy cutthroat and kokanee possibilities, and some rare isolated populations of Arctic grayling and brook trout.

Prince of Wales Island, the largest island in Southeast (over 2600 square miles), has abundant, high-quality streamfishing—some of the best in Alaska—including world-famous steelhead rivers like the Karta, Klawock, and Thorne. An extensive network (1400 miles) of logging roads and state highways connects many of the great locations, with trails providing additional access. The island's road system is linked to Ketchikan and other coastal communities by the Alaska State Marine Highway System and Inter-Island Ferry, with terminal facilities at Hollis, on the east side of the island. Anglers can drive, hike, or boat in practically any direction and reach superb fishing for steelhead, cutthroat, rainbow trout, Dolly Varden, and silver and red salmon.

Ketchikan, the main hub (population 14,000) is a major cruise ship port and offers a full range of visitor services and facilities. It is linked to Washington state and the rest of Alaska by daily jet service and ferries of the Alaska Marine Highway System. Local air taxis provide connections to outlying communities and many of the remote locations listed in this section.

As part of the Tongass National Forest, the area has dozens of remote public-use cabins, shelters, and campgrounds maintained by the U.S. Forest Service, many of them in or near fishing locations listed in this section. There are also a few state marine parks and recreation sites.

PRINCE OF WALES ISLAND/SURROUNDING WATERS

Salmon Bay Lake ★★★

Location: North Prince of Wales Island, 40 miles south of Petersburg.

Access: By floatplane (or boat) from Wrangell, Petersburg, Thorne Bay, or other area hubs. A trail from the cabin at the north end of lake leads along the outlet stream one-and-eight-tenths miles to Salmon Bay.

Facilities: A Forest Service public use cabin is located near lake outlet.

Highlights: A well-known, scenic hotspot for good salmon and cutthroat trout fishing.

Main Species: RS, SS, CT, ST

Draining into upper Clarence Strait through Salmon Bay on the northeast tip of Prince of Wales Island, the Salmon Bay Lake drainage is one of the better known, but lesser visited, Prince of Wales locations for high quality salmon and trout fishing. It receives most of its fishing pressure from locals from nearby Petersburg and Wrangell.

Surrounded by mountains and dense forests, this scenic lake has a good sockeye run, one if its major attractions. Reds enter the stream and Salmon Bay Lake in mid to late summer (mid-July into August), with most successful anglers concentrating efforts on the outlet and shallower stretches of the stream right above the bay. Later on (September), a good run of coho shows up and continues running through most of the fall; along with the red salmon, they are the most sought-after species in the drainage. The Salmon Bay Lake outlet, the deeper holes in the outlet stream, and the mouth are the best locations to encounter this punchy fighter.

Steelhead trout enter the drainage in two distinct runs, one in spring, one in late fall, with the spring run receiving the most attention from anglers who work the entire length of the outlet stream with good results. Sea-run cutthroat trout, Dolly Varden, and resident rainbow can be taken as well, especially in early summer and fall, from the lake's inlet and outlet waters.

Red Bay Lake

Location: North Prince of Wales Island, 40 miles SW of Petersburg.

Access: By car via Forest Road 20 from Thorne Bay to lower outlet stream (or parking lot/trailhead and eight-tenths of a mile hike, to lake), or boat or plane from Petersburg, Wrangell, or Klawock.

Facilities: A Forest Service public-use cabin is available at the lake.

Highlights: Exceptional scenery, isolation, and outstanding stream and lake fishing.

Main Species: RS, SS, CT, RT

Situated on the northern tip of Prince of Wales Island, Red Bay Lake is fairly small (only two miles long and about a half mile wide) but highly scenic, with a short outlet stream connecting it to Red Bay and Sumner Strait. It has a good variety of sport fish, with outstanding fishing at times, making it a very desirable location for anglers wanting a secluded, high-quality experience.

Starting in spring, migrating cutthroat trout and Dolly Varden are taken from the lake outlet area and head of Red Bay. Fishing with ultralight gear or light fly rods is ideal, as these fish will reach two to three pounds. Resident rainbows running about the same size are

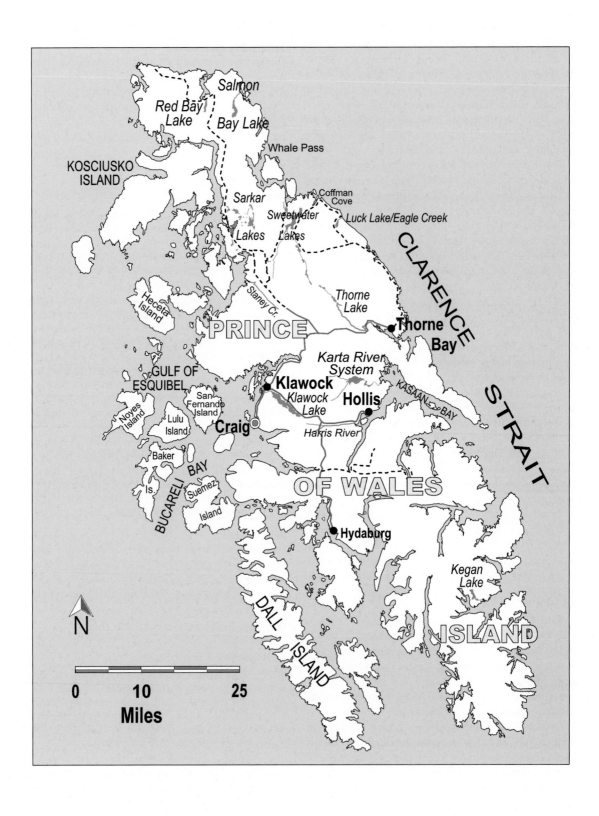

active in all areas of the lake. Additionally, a small spring run of steelhead trout is available, with fair to good fishing in the outlet stream. (A tributary entering from the northeast will also hold significant numbers of fish.)

After a short break in the spring fishery, decent runs of red, chum, and pink salmon begin in mid to late summer (from mid-July on) and provide variety and excitement from the lake outlet to tidewater. (Reds are the most sought-after, and may be pursued effectively with sparse bucktail flies in faster flowing, shallow stream sections.) A few weeks later, silver salmon jam the small outlet stream all the way up into the lake, sustaining the fishing action into the fall. As the salmon are running, cutthroat trout and Dolly Varden will move into the drainage from salt water and begin feeding actively, creating still more angling opportunities.

Getting around the lake is difficult without a boat, because of the rugged nature of the shoreline and heavy timber (the Forest Service provides a skiff at the lake by the trail leading from the road for folks who have reserved the cabin). Aside from an unmaintained old trail leading up from salt water, access to the outlet is restricted to the road crossing by tidewater or boat from the lake.

Sarkar Lakes System

Location: Northwest Prince of Wales Island, 75 miles NW of Ketchikan.

Access: By plane (to Sarkar Lake), car (via road from Craig/Klawock), or boat from Craig or Klawock via Cristoval Channel, Gulf of Esquibel, and Tuxekan Passage to Sarkar Cove.

Facilities: A Forest Service public-use cabin is located at Sarkar Lake.

Highlights: A beautiful location with great canoe potential and excellent salmon and trout fishing.

Main Species: SS, RS, DV, CT

The Sarkar Lakes system consists of a network of 19 lakes and ponds of varying sizes, and two major tributary streams that drain into El Capitan Passage and Sea Otter Sound. Sarkar Lake, the first in the drainage, is the gateway to area fishing and has a Forest Service public use cabin on the northeast shore. Despite the somewhat brown water, salmon, trout, and charr are abundant in the lakes and streams and offer outstanding action from late spring through fall.

Sarkar Lake is tidally influenced, with mostly brackish water. It can be entered on a high tide with a skiff from Sarkar Cove, otherwise there are rapids that impede boat travel. The short outlet stream and Sarkar Cove serve as a staging area for the system's substantial runs of silver (mid-August), along with chum, pink, and good numbers of red salmon (June to mid-July). Some of the better action occurs by the road crossing at the head of the cove, or in the lakes (Sarkar, Finger, Raven, etc.) by the inlets and outlets.

Sea-run cutthroat trout and Dolly Varden overwinter in the system and outmigrate in late spring, with good fishing possible. Anglers wise enough to bring a canoe can portage and navigate throughout much of the system and enjoy some outstanding fishing. (With heavily timbered shorelines and scant trails, many of the lakes are hard to fish from shore.) Both spring and fall runs of steelhead trout occur in the Sarkar.

Sweetwater Lake System ★★★

Location: NE Prince of Wales Island, 50 miles SW of Petersburg.

Access: By floatplane from Petersburg/Wrangell or Ketchikan; or by national forest road from Thorne Bay.

Facilities: Two forest service public-use cabins, at Sweetwater and Barnes lakes.

Highlights: A famous area destination, with canoe route and excellent lake and stream fishing.

Main Species: SS, RS, ST, RT, CT, DV

Emptying into Lake Bay in northern Clarence Strait, the Sweetwater System consists of dozens of interconnected lakes and ponds, of varying sizes, draining the northeast interior of Prince of Wales Island. Due to the heavy muskeg in the drainage, Sweetwater is largely tannic brown, but angling is very good overall, with a satisfying variety of species available. With all the good water in this drainage, a visitor can spend weeks exploring and fishing different areas, from headwaters down to the tidal zone (especially with a canoe or kayak).

The first important game fish to invade Sweetwater in the spring is steelhead trout. These flashy fighters are at their best in the outlets for Sweetwater and Barnes lakes, but can also be encountered in many other flowing waters of the system, including Hatchery and Logjam creeks. Resident rainbow trout are present in the main lake and in its tributaries, along with sea-run cutthroats and Dolly Varden. The lower end of the lakes and inlet streams have traditionally been the hot spots for them, particularly in spring and fall.

Later on in the season, red and silver salmon begin to show in large numbers. Sweetwater has perfect conditions for taking these fine sport fish; anglers do well for them in Indian Creek, Gold and Galligan Lagoon, and the lower sections and mouths of other outlet waters. While the sockeyes come through in one big push (in July), there are two distinct runs of coho in the system. The first run occurs primarily during July and August, while the second run hits its peak in September and continues into October. Only small numbers of chum and pink salmon show every year, in late summer, with fishing action reported fair for pinks, at times.

Luck Lake/Eagle Creek ★★★

Location: East Prince of Wales Island, Clarence Strait, 60 miles NW of Ketchikan.

Access: By car via logging road from Coffman Cove or Thorne Bay; also by floatplane from Ketchikan. Spur roads and trails provide additional access.

Facilities: None.

Highlights: Another well-known, fine POW lake and stream fishing destination.

Main Species: SS, CT, RT, ST

Luck Lake and its outlet, Eagle Creek, on the east side of the island just down the coast from Coffman Cove, is a well-known lake and stream system of significant sportfish potential. This scenic location has been a traditional getaway spot for locals to camp, hunt deer, and fish for salmon (mostly coho) and trout (steelhead and cutthroat).

The fair-sized, but short (less than two miles long), swift outlet stream, Eagle Creek, is superb flyfishing water, where anglers target steelhead (mostly spring-run) and salmon (silvers and reds) with great results. From the bridge below the outlet down to the mouth is the most productive stretch.

The major inlet, Luck Creek, presents a different scenario for flyfishing, but yields some great trout fishing (both sea-run and resident cutts and rainbows), especially in the spring. Logging roads provide access to most of it.

Staney Creek ★★★
Location: Tuxekan Passage, West Prince of Wales Island, 65 miles west of Ketchikan.
Access: By car from Klawock, Craig, or Hollis via highway and logging roads; can also be reached by boat from area hubs.
Facilities: Forest Service public use cabin and two campgrounds along river.
Highlights: A very well-known, easily accessed POW steelhead and salmon stream.
Main Species: SS, ST, DV

Staney Creek flows 20 miles west, from central Prince of Wales Island into Tuxekan Passage. With its size and different forks, it is a significant producer of salmon and steelhead, and one of the island's better streams for flyfishing that is easily accessible from the road system.

The creek was fished for years by locals for its outstanding runs of silver, chum, and pink salmon. Extensive logging in the area brought road access to much of the drainage and increased attention from steelheaders, who target the fine spring run. Dolly Varden and a few cutthroat trout round out the mix of sport species available.

Unlike some other high gradient streams on the island, the muskeg-colored Staney holds a variety of good water for the flyfisherman. Much of it lies on the lower south fork, below where it divides into several tributary forks. Most anglers work the stream from this point down, accessing it from the logging roads and/or trails leading along the creek. The stretch from the lower campground (above the horseshoe bend in the river) down to the cabin by the mouth gets heavily fished.

Gulf of Esquibel/Outside Waters ★★★★
Location: West coast Prince of Wales Island, 75 miles west of Ketchikan.
Access: By boat from Klawock, Craig, or area lodges, or by floatplane from Ketchikan.
Facilities: Commercial lodging, fuel, water, and guide services available locally.
Highlights: A traditional local favorite for salmon and halibut.
Main Species: KS, SS, BF

The west coast of Prince of Wales Island has traditionally been one of the most productive salmon and bottomfish areas in all of Southeast Alaska. With numerous islands and an abundance of marine life, the Gulf of Esquibel and surrounding waters form an active feeding ground for fish bound for watersheds on Prince of Wales Island and the mainland. Very little shore fishing takes place in this area, with most effort expended by boaters from Craig and Klawock. Points of interest include the Heceta and Maurelle islands

and, of course, Noyes Island for big kings (50 to 70 pounds possible) and silver and pink salmon. Halibut are caught year-round, with the action best during summer in 100-300 feet depths around the outside islands (Noyes, Baker, Warren, Heceta, etc.), where trophy catches to 350 pounds or more are possible. Other gamefish worth considering include rockfish, lingcod, cod, and flounder. Fair numbers of Dolly Varden can be found off mouths of clearwater streams.

For anglers wanting to spice up their visit, area waters also teem with shrimp and crab, so come prepared to set pots for these tasty shellfish prior to going salmon and halibut fishing. The natural beauty found in and around this vast archipelago of islands is breathtaking.

Some of the more productive locations in and around the gulf for salmon and halibut include: Noyes Island (Saint Nicholas Point/Channel, Cape Addington, Shaft Rock, Roller and Steamboat bays, and Cape Ulitka); Saint Joseph Island; Sonora Passage; Maurelle Islands (San Lorenzo, Turtle, Sonora, Flotilla, Esquibel, and Hendida/Pesquera islands, Hole-In-The-Wall, Anguilla Bay); Saint Phillip Island; Heceta Island (Point Desconocida, Warm Chuck Inlet, Cape Lynch, Gull, and Camp islands, and Port Alice); Portilla Channel; San Fernando Island (Point Garcia, Hermagos Island, and San Cristoval Channel).

Bucareli Bay ★★★
Location: West coast Prince of Wales Island, 65 miles west of Ketchikan.
Access: By boat (or floatplane) from Klawock, Craig, or area lodges.
Facilities: A Forest Service public use cabin is available at Point Amargura on the southern tip of San Fernando Island.
Highlights: A favorite saltwater destination of local fishing guides.
Main Species: KS, SS, BF

Bucareli Bay is, without a doubt, one of the more scenic and popular saltwater fishing locations on Prince of Wales Island. The bay area includes the ever-popular San Alberto Bay just outside Klawock, and Craig and surrounding larger islands, such as Suemez, Baker, Lulu, and San Fernando.

A favorite of residents from the nearby communities, Bucareli provides year-round catches of feeder king salmon, and some outstanding action for mature pre-spawners up to 70 pounds in late spring and early summer. Except for a few individuals moving up the Klawock River, there are virtually no king salmon spawning streams on the island; the vast majority of fish are actually heading for mainland locations, and are caught when feeding heavily along the surf-swept coast.

The salmon delivering the hottest action around Bucareli Bay is actually the spunky silver. From mid-summer into fall, anglers target these flashy fighters as they feed heavily and prepare to enter the area, as well as more distant streams. The best fishing occurs right outside the communities of Klawock and Craig. In between the king and silver runs, large numbers of pink salmon flood the area.

Halibut and other bottomfish are best pursued in summer in the outside waters surrounding the bay, such as the backside of Suemez or Baker Islands, or nearby Dall Island.

Proven hot spots in and around Bucareli Bay include: Baker Island

(Veta and Fortaleza bays, Cape Bartolome, Point Fortaleza, Port San Antonio, Point San Roque, Port Asumcion, Veta/Outer and Granite points, Cape Chirikof, and Point Maria); Saint Ignace Island; Port Real Marina; Suemez Island (Cape Felix, Port Santa Cruz, Cabras, and Ridge islands, Port Dolores, and Point Verde); Ulloa Channel; Point San Antonio; Joe Island/Cape Flores; Port Estrella; Point Providence; Point Lomas; Port Caldera; San Juan Bautista Island (Diamond Point, Balandra Island, and Point Eugenia); Trocadero Bay; Doyle Bay/Culebrina Island; Coronados Island; Port Saint Nicholas; Cape Suspiro; Ursua Channel; San Fernando Island (Point Colocano, Cruz Pass, Point Amargura, Fern Point, and Point Cuerbo), and San Alberto Bay (Fish Egg, Sombrero, Abbess, and Ballena islands, San Cristoval Channel, Klawock Inlet, and Crab Bay).

Klawock River ★★★★

Location: West Prince of Wales Island, 55 miles west of Ketchikan.

Access: By road or trail from Klawock (both follow river from mouth up to lake); floatplane access possible from Ketchikan to Klawock Lake.

Facilities: Full services available in nearby towns of Klawock and Craig.

Highlights: One of Prince of Wales Island's most famous steelhead and salmon locales.

Main Species: SS, RS, ST, CT, DV

Seven-mile-long Klawock Lake is beautifully situated in a valley between Sunnahae Mountain and Pin Peak, near the community of Klawock on the island's west coast. The Klawock River heads at the lake and runs approximately a mile west into the tidal water of Klawock Inlet of San Alberto Bay. The light-brown, muskeg filtered waters are considered to be some of the top salmon and steelhead producing on Prince of Wales Island and receive quite a bit of angling attention during the peak of the runs.

The most sought-after gamefishes in the Klawock are silvers and steelhead trout. Silvers run heavy in fall (September), followed by a smaller run of steelhead trout. The sea-run rainbows continue to trickle in throughout the winter months before a sizable showing of spring-run fish arrives sometime around the first of March. A July run of reds, an August run of pink salmon, and a fall run of chums also grab anglers' interest. Good rainbow trout action may be had in the lake and at the mouth of inlet streams (Threemile and Hatchery creeks and ten others).

As is the case with many streams in Southeast Alaska, the Klawock's salmon and trout seem to be quite sensitive to water levels and often time their entrance into the river accordingly. During a portion of the summer, the Klawock may run slow and clear, but once the late summer and fall rains begin and the water rises, fishing really heats up.

Harris River

Location: East central Prince of Wales Island, Twelvemile Arm, Kasaan Bay, 40 miles NW of Ketchikan.

Access: By car from Hollis or Klawock via highways 924 or 913 and spur logging roads. Trails provide additional access along lower river.

Facilities: Campground on highway 924, 11 miles from Hollis; limited services available in nearby Hollis.

Highlights: A significant, easily accessed POW salmon/steelhead stream.

Main Species: SS, ST, DV

The 14-mile Harris River, flowing east into Harris River Bay near Hollis, is an important stream worth checking out by anyone who makes his way to Prince of Wales Island.

Located near the center of the island, and largely accessible by road, this drainage has long been a significant salmon (mostly coho) and steelhead trout producer.

The Hollis Road (state highway 924), Hydaburg Road (913), and spur logging roads provide multiple access points (there is a bridge crossing about eight miles out of town, with logging roads leading up and down river), augmented with intermittent trails along the lower river.

The Harris has traditionally been fished by locals for its fine run of coho in the fall; it also gets a good influx of sea-run Dolly Varden in late summer. A significant spring steelhead run occurs, but the Harris with its many logjams, shallow riffles, and intermittent pools is not easily fished except during higher water. Most anglers work down from logging road or trail access points several miles to a mile above tidewater, and do well in the deeper pools and other holding areas of the lower river. Good fishing areas in the upper river above the bridge are harder to come by.

Thorne River System ★★★★

Location: East Prince of Wales Island, 45 miles NW of Ketchikan.

Access: By car from Klawock, Craig, or Thorne Bay (via state highway 929) to lower river two miles from mouth or tributaries; by foot on creekside trails; also by floatplane or boat from Ketchikan.

Facilities: Forest Service public-use cabin available at Control Lake; limited visitor services available in nearby Thorne Bay.

Highlights: A world-famous Prince of Wales steelhead and salmon stream.

Main Species: SS, ST, CT, DV

The largest river system on Prince of Wales, the Thorne drains some 28 lakes and ponds of varying size, covering a substantial part of the central island. It's also one of the most accessible prime fishing locations in the Ketchikan/POW area, since a good part of it can be reached by plane, boat, car, and on foot.

Draining into Thorne Bay and Clarence Strait on the east side of Prince of Wales, the mainstem and North Fork total about 30 miles in length, and support spring and fall runs of wild steelhead, salmon, cutthroat and rainbow trout, and Dolly Varden charr.

The fishing season usually kicks off in late March, with the arrival of the first spring steelies, followed by schools of sea-run cutthroat trout and Dolly Varden in April and May. Summer first brings sockeye, pink, and chum, then later silver salmon (mid-August), which invade the river into the fall months. In late September and October, the action picks up with inmigrating sea-run "cutts" and Dollies and a well-known run of fall steelhead that continues into early winter.

Most anglers fish the Thorne from the banks, hitting the major pools along the lower river from the road or from trails leading up and down stream. The Thorne can also be floatfished for most its length.

Put-in is by floatplane at Thorne Lake, with take-outs at the road crossing and at the boat launch near Thorne Bay. The distances are approximately eight and fifteen river miles respectively, or a good one to two-day float. This is an excellent option, allowing anglers to sample sections of the Thorne that receive little pressure. There is also a canoe route that covers a substantial part of the drainage with a few portages. The trip takes about three days.

Lakes and streams of the upper drainage generally have poor to fair trout and charr fishing, with good numbers of spawning salmon; for this reason, most anglers concentrate their efforts from Thorne Lake down the mainstem to Thorne Bay. For additional variety, try the marine fisheries for salmon and halibut in adjacent Thorne Bay and Clarence Strait.

Karta River System ★★★★
Location: East Prince of Wales Island, 45 miles west of Ketchikan.
Access: By floatplane or boat from Ketchikan or area lodges. A trail leads from the mouth upstream to the lakes.
Facilities: Four Forest Service public-use cabins are available along system.
Highlights: One of the most productive and famous trout, salmon, and steelhead rivers in SSE.
Main Species: SS, RS, ST, RT, CT, DV

For an angler wishing to sample some of the best freshwater fishing in southern Southeast Alaska, particularly for steelhead, the Karta River must be given serious consideration. Situated at the head of Kasaan Bay in the central portion of Prince of Wales Island, the ten-mile long Karta River drains two major lakes (Karta and Salmon) and several smaller ones. Part of the Karta River Wilderness, the area also offers excellent hiking in addition to its well-known fishing opportunities. (The U.S. Forest Service has opened up the area considerably by constructing an extensive trail network, taking anglers into the midst of this world-class fishery.)

Starting in early spring and continuing into late fall, the Karta offers consistent, outstanding streamfishing for trout, charr, and salmon, especially steelhead and sockeyes. Thousands of bright reds enter (July to mid-August) the system in most years, providing some of Southeast's best flyfishing opportunities for the species. The Karta's steelies come in spring and fall runs. Spin and baitcasting with drift bobbers, jigs, spinners, etc., and flyfishing attractor, egg, and forage patterns are most popular, with April, May, and October the best times. Karta anglers also target fairly abundant silver and pink salmon, rainbows, and fall and spring runs of sea-run Dolly Varden and cutthroat trout. Best areas to fish are downstream of the short stretch of waterfalls below Karta Lake, the mouth of the river, the outlet of Salmon Lake and dropoff along the north shore, and the mouths of Andersen and McGilvery Creeks (Salmon Lake).

Area trails begin at Karta Bay, where anglers can moor their boats at the beach near the first Forest Service cabin, and extend upstream along the tea-colored river to Karta Lake and the second public-use cabin. The trail then leads to the north shore of Salmon Lake and the third Forest Service cabin. From there, the trail continues along the lake and up Andersen Creek, a major tributary. The fourth Forest Service cabin is located at the mouth of McGilvery Creek in the southwest corner of Salmon Lake.

Kegan Lake System
Location: South Prince of Wales Island, 25 miles SW of Ketchikan.
Access: By floatplane or boat from Ketchikan; a trail leads from Kegan Cove along river to outlet of Kegan Lake.
Facilities: Forest Service public-use cabins located at Kegan Cove and 200 yards downstream from Kegan Lake.
Highlights: A well-known Prince of Wales destination for good trout and salmon fishing.
Main Species: SS, RS, CT, DV

Situated along Moira Sound on south Prince of Wales Island, the Kegan River and Lake area has been a popular recreational destination for years. The stream itself is short, less than a mile long, and runs from Kegan Lake to Kegan Cove. All of the areas are accessible by foot; a well-developed trail parallels the drainage through an old-growth forest.

The tea-colored waters of the creek and lake host healthy numbers of wild salmon, trout, and charr, with additional opportunities for salmon and halibut just off the mouth of Kegan Cove. During the height of the river's runs, anglers can fish the entire length, from the outlet of Kegan Lake downstream to Kegan Cove, often with very good results. (Schools of fish often stage in the cove and lake outlet and are very susceptible at such times.)

Good fishing begins in July with reds and pinks, and continues into October with silvers, cutthroats, and rainbows. Visitors from local towns and from around the country come to experience the first-class fishing, with a stay in a comfortable cabin only yards away from the action. A spring run of bright steelhead trout also enters the river, peaking in April and May, drawing considerable attention.

Kegan Lake offers good opportunities for cutthroat and charr, with excellent rainbow trout fishing reported at times. A lightweight canoe comes in handy to reach the more inaccessible parts of the drainage. (On the northeast shore, a tributary stream draining four other lakes in the system serves as a holding/feeding area and is a good spot to try.)

Lower Clarence Strait
Location: Along east Prince of Wales Island, west of Etolin Island, 15 miles west of Ketchikan.
Access: By boat or floatplane from Ketchikan, Wrangell, and area lodges and towns.
Facilities: Forest Service public-use cabins are available at Karta Bay and Trollers Cove (Kasaan Bay), Phocena Bay (Gravina Island) and Kegan Cove (Moira Sound).
Highlights: One of Southeast's better marine fishing locations for salmon and bottomfish.
Main Species: KS, SS, BF

Lower Clarence Strait includes all waters south of Thorne Bay and the north tip of the Cleveland Peninsula. Like Icy Strait in the Juneau region, Clarence Strait is a major migration channel and feeding ground for salmon, trout, charr, and halibut bound for other locations (the west coast of Prince of Wales Island, Behm Canal, Revillagigedo Island, and Ernest Sound). A gorgeous marine haven of fjords, islands, reefs, and steep, forest-clad slopes dropping into crystal-clear waters, Clarence is a favorite playground for anglers from Ketchikan and beyond, world-famous for having some of the best marine fishing in Alaska.

Most angling effort is aimed at the more popular sport species, such as king and silver salmon and halibut, but the strait has good numbers of other salmon and bottomfish species as well. Feeder kings are available year-round, as they are most everywhere in Southeast. The better fishing action takes place in early summer, when big concentrations of pre-spawners invade the cool, blue waters of lower Clarence on their way to the mainland. Occasional catches up to 60 and 70 pounds or more have been recorded, with the typical king averaging 15 to 25 pounds.

Silver salmon permeate the strait throughout late summer and into fall, with specimens up to 20 pounds possible. They typically feed heavily early in the season, and are targeted mainly by boaters around the traditional holding locations such as points and breakwater beaches. Later, bays, narrows, and shorelines in the vicinity of clearwater rivers and streams produce good catches.

Although not the most sought-after salmon, chums and pinks are undoubtedly the most numerous. Ocean-bright pinks, a few of trophy size, provide excellent action on light tackle all along the coast, but primarily near spawning streams. Record-size chums—some between 20 and 30 pounds—have been hoisted from locations near Gravina Island and the mouth of Behm Canal during the months of June and July.

Lower Clarence Strait also offers some of Ketchikan's best action for bottomfish, all summer long, including some flatties that occasionally exceed 300 pounds, as well as rockfish and lingcod.

Hot spot locations to focus on for salmon and halibut are as follows: Tolstoi Point; Tolstoi Bay; Cleveland Peninsula (Lemesurier, Niblack, and Caamano points, Meyers Chuck, and Ship Island); Grindall Passage; Grindall Island/Approach Point; Kasaan Bay (Patterson/High islands, Island, Skowl, Baker, and Outer points, Skowl and Twelvemile arms, Saltery Cove, and Mills and Karta bays); Twenty Fathom Bank; Clover Point; Skin Island; West/South arms; Cholmondeley Sound; Outer Cholmondeley Sound; Trollers Cove; Chasina Point; South Chasina Point; Windy Point; Guard Islands; Wedge Islands; Outer Moira Sound (Moira Rock, Moira Island, Rip Point, Polk Island, and Outer Kendrick Bay); Outer McLean Arm/McLean Point; Stone Rock; Cape Chacon; Percy Island; Bee Rocks; Hassler Reef; West Rock, and Club Rocks.

REVILLAGIGEDO ISLAND/BEHM CANAL

McDonald Lake System ★★★★
Location: West Behm Canal, 45 miles north of Ketchikan.

Access: By floatplane (to McDonald Lake or Yes Bay at the mouth of Wolverine Creek) or boat (via Behm Canal and Yes Bay to outlet stream) from Ketchikan; foot trails from Yes Bay to McDonald Lake.

Facilities: Commercial lodging and Forest Service public-use cabin are available at Wolverine Creek and McDonald Lake.

Highlights: A famous SSE fishing location, noted for excellent sockeye and silver salmon action.

Main Species: SS, RS, ST, RT, CT, DV

The McDonald Lake system is one of the richest freshwater fish-

eries in the Ketchikan area, attracting considerable attention from anglers near and far. Situated on the scenic Cleveland Peninsula, the system consists of eight lakes, of which McDonald is the largest. Good to excellent angling for all the popular game species of the region is the norm in McDonald's lakes and streams.

A healthy run of bright spring steelhead kicks off the fishing season in April, closely followed by sea-run cutthroat and Dolly Varden, in addition to good spring fishing for resident rainbow trout. Summer brings returning hordes of red, pink, and chum salmon. The sockeye run is made up of both wild and hatchery fish. Their sheer numbers often flood Wolverine Creek, creating some of Southeast's best flyfishing conditions for the species. In fall, a late run of large silver salmon keeps the action going.

The tinted waters of this drainage are home to distinct, late-running stocks of sockeye salmon, which usually enter Wolverine Creek and McDonald Lake a month later than in most other area waters (August, early September). Additionally, the area has a population of trophy pink salmon commonly weighing six to eight pounds, with specimens up to ten pounds possible.

The Forest Service cabin at McDonald Lake provides anglers with access to the lake outlet and all of Wolverine Creek via the trail network that extends to Yes Bay. A canoe or inflatable is a definite plus, but you can do fairly well just wading and hiking. Wolverine Creek flows rather fast and is quite brushy, making for some challenging flyfishing. From the northern end of McDonald Lake, a trail leads upstream from an abandoned fish hatchery, along Walker Creek, the major system tributary.

Naha River System ★★★★
Location: West Revillagigedo Island, 25 miles north of Ketchikan.

Access: By floatplane (to lakes Heckman and Patching, or mouth at Roosevelt Lagoon) or boat from Ketchikan or area lodges. Trails lead from Roosevelt Lagoon to the river and upstream into the system.

Facilities: Four Forest Service cabins are located in the system at Jordan (one), Heckman (two), and Patching (one) lakes.

Highlights: One of southern Southeast's premier sportfishing systems for salmon and trout fishing.

Main Species: SS, RS, ST, CT, GR

The Naha River system, like the Karta and the Thorne, is another very significant sportfishing location in southern Southeast. Flowing out of Orton Lake in the central part of Revillagigedo Island, 25 miles north of Ketchikan, the Naha is more than 17 miles long and annexes eight small but deep lakes along its way to Naha Bay and Behm Canal. Fishing is good to excellent in both the river and lakes. Silver and red salmon, steelhead (both spring and fall runs), and cutthroat trout are the top draws.

The Naha has a variety of water for anglers to test their skills on. Tidally influenced Roosevelt Lagoon, a major holding area for migratory fish, is known for its pink salmon fishing. From the lagoon, a well-developed and popular trail (the Naha River Trail) leads to the river and adjoining lakes, for a variety of superb fishing. Jordan Lake, the first lake in the system, has a Forest Service cabin, along with some of the Naha's best fishing for cutthroat, steelhead and rainbow trout, Dollies, and coho. Try the outlet and the river above and below the lake for steelhead.

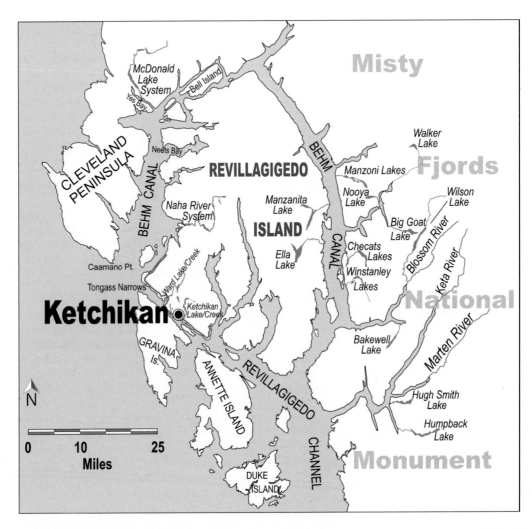

Next is Heckman Lake, with two public-use cabins and great trout fishing (try the outlet and Naha River below lake). Beyond Heckman is Patching Lake, the largest, deepest lake in the system, with two cabins. Salmon can't make it up this far because of a barrier waterfall, but cutthroat trout do very well, with trophy fish up to six pounds available in Patching's deep waters. Try the outlet above the falls for small trout; bigger fish are best pursued from a boat or raft. The lake also has a few kokanee and Arctic grayling. Farther on are Chamberlain, Snow, and Orton lakes, all mountain headwater lakes beautifully situated and offering some of Southeast's rare opportunities for Arctic grayling (from stocking done in the 1960s).

Chums and pinks are more prevalent in the lower system, while silvers and reds will be scattered throughout the drainage. The best fishing is below the lake outlets, near inlet streams, and in holding areas of the mainstem between lakes.

Ward Lake System
Location: Southwest Revillagigedo Island drainage, five miles NW of Ketchikan.

Access: By car from Ketchikan via Ward Lake Road to Ward Lake (with trails continuing to the upper drainage), or via North Tongass Highway to Ward Creek just above Ward Cove.

Facilities: Fuel, water, convenience store, and two campgrounds nearby.

Highlights: A great do-it-yourself, one-day Ketchikan area fishing location.

Main Species: SS, PS, ST, DV

The Ward Lake system originates on the north side of Slide Ridge and runs south to Ward Cove and Tongass Narrows. There are four lakes in the system, Ward, Connell, Talbot, and Perseverance, all of which are popular with anglers and other recreationists in the Ketchikan area. (Combination hiking and fishing trips are popular in this scenic, heavily forested area.) Tea-colored Ward Creek is host to numbers of salmon, trout, and charr, offering good to excellent fishing within a few minutes' drive of Ketchikan.

The most abundant and sought-after species are silver and pink salmon, steelhead trout, and Dolly Varden charr. These are targeted mostly between April and October, providing a high-yield fishery comprised of both natural and hatchery fish. The creek's sizable spring run of steelhead migrates in from the salt at roughly the same time overwintering Dollies move out of the system, providing some exciting fishing in April and May. Later on in July, a strong run of coho enters the creek, followed by a much smaller fall run in September and October. (The summer fish are primarily hatchery stock and contribute significantly to area marine fisheries.) A small run of red salmon destined for Ward Lake offers fair flyfishing.

The better salmon and steelhead fishing is found at the Ward Lake inlet and in the creek above. Since the drainage is in a fairly developed area of Southeast, access is no problem, with ample parking and trails available to anglers. In the upper system, Connell and Talbot lakes are also road/trail accessible, with good opportunities for Dolly Varden and fair numbers of cutthroat trout. Perseverance Lake has a population of stocked brook trout. For an angler with a day or two to kill in the Ketchikan area, the Ward Lake system is highly recommended.

Ketchikan Creek System
Location: Southwest Revillagigedo Island drainage, Ketchikan area.

Access: By car or foot from Ketchikan via the South Tongass Highway; trail access to upper stream sections and Ketchikan Lakes.

Facilities: Full visitor services/facilities available in town of Ketchikan.

Highlights: The best city angling in all of Southeast Alaska.

Main Species: SS, ST, DV

Like the Ward Lake System, swift, clear-flowing Ketchikan Creek originates from several mountain lakes just north of town. (There are four lakes, of which Ketchikan Lake is the largest.) Surrounded by picturesque mountain scenery, with trail access, this extremely popular recreation area at times has good fishing for salmon and steelhead, and is worth investigating if you're in the area.

Most of the fishing effort occurs on lower Ketchikan Creek from the mouth at Thomas Basin in Tongass Narrows to a mile upstream. Here, every season, local anglers intercept runs of salmon and trout. A fall run of silver salmon keeps the action going strong until October. For variety, anglers can try their flyfishing skills on the creek's steelhead trout in spring and fall (a smaller run). Dolly Varden show up at roughly the same times.

Keep in mind, these waters are heavily regulated, with a season that usually runs September 15 to May 15, unless opened earlier by emergency order. Fishing though, when it occurs, can be good. While there are many far superior Southeast locations, few can match the easy accessibility of the stream that runs through the middle of Ketchikan. If you've only got a few hours in this Southeast waterfront town, give Ketchikan Creek a try.

Gravina Island/Tongass Narrows
Location: Southwest of Revillagigedo Island, Ketchikan area.

Access: By boat, kayak, or floatplane from Ketchikan.

Facilities: Full visitor services/facilities, including boat rentals/launching, available in Ketchikan. A public-use cabin is also available at Phocena Bay on the southern end of Gravina Island.

Highlights: An all-time local favorite for salmon and bottomfish, only minutes from Ketchikan.

Main Species: KS, SS, CS, PS, HB

Gravina Island lies to the south and west of giant Revillagigedo Island, along fish-rich Clarence Strait. Part of Tongass National Forest, it is heavily wooded with 17 small creeks streaming down its green slopes, most of them with at least one or more sportfish species present. But it is not the stream-fishing opportunities that the island is noted for, but rather its phenomenal marine fishery. Its western coastline lies along the path of tens of thousands of salmon bound for rivers, streams, and lakes in the region, with good numbers of halibut actively feeding just offshore. Tongass Narrows, along the island's other side, supports both natural and hatchery runs of all five salmon species, plus native charr and bottomfish.

Trophy-size silver salmon abound in late summer and early fall, with fish in the upper teens not unusual, and a 20-pounder always a possibility. Chum salmon of similar size cruise the island's beaches also, particularly on the west side. Pinks are found all around the island, but seem more noticeable in the Tongass Narrows, where major spawning runs headed for the Ward Lake system and Ketchikan Creek school up in shallow, near-shore areas. King salmon are available as feeder and mature fish, with locals reporting catches throughout the year. (Pre-spawners are dominant in late spring and early summer.)

Anglers wanting more variety can try for sea-run Dolly Varden along the east side of the island or in Tongass Narrows (Ward Cove), or anywhere a clearwater stream flows into salt water. For bottomfish, the west side of Gravina is a traditional halibut hole, with fish over 100 pounds caught every so often, along with a healthy mix of lingcod, rockfish, and other bottomfish species. Set pots for crab in the bays of Nichols Passage.

One of the most attractive features about fishing the marine waters around Gravina is the accessibility. Only minutes from the town of Ketchikan, anglers can easily reach some of the state's most productive salmon fishing sites for trolling, mooching, and even surfcasting along Tongass Narrows (especially from the shores of Revillagigedo Island).

Hot spots around the island for salmon, charr, and halibut include: Clarence Strait (Vallenar and South Vallenar points, Grant and Nelson coves, Phocena Rocks, and Vallenar Bay); Nichols Passage (Gravina, Blank, and Bostwick points, Blank and Bostwick inlets, Stomach Bay, Dall Head, Blank islands, and Point McCartey) and Tongass Narrows (Pennock Island, Point Higgins, and Ward Cove).

West Behm Canal ★★★
Location: Along west Revillagigedo Island, 20 miles north of Ketchikan.

Access: By boat or floatplane from Ketchikan or area lodges. The western Canal can be reached via Tongass Narrows, and the eastern through the upper sections of Revillagigedo Channel.

Facilities: Private lodge and guide services available at Yes Bay, with Forest Service public-use cabins located at Helm Bay, Blind Pass, and Anchor Pass.

Highlights: One of Alaska's premier saltwater fishing locations, renowned for superior salmon and halibut and trophy-sized fish.

Main Species: KS, SS, CS, HB

World-famous Behm Canal completely separates Revillagigedo

Island from the mainland. It serves as a conduit for fish bound for numerous area lakes and streams, which include some of Southeast Alaska's most significant spawning systems (such as the Naha River, Wolverine Creek/McDonald Lake, and the Chickamin and Unuk rivers). Sportfishing is concentrated around the points along the outer and upper areas of West Behm Canal (around the southern tip of the Cleveland Peninsula and Bell Island).

Silver salmon regularly grab the limelight as huge (up to 20-plus pounds), aggressive fish make their way through the clear waters of the canal for island and mainland spawning grounds. In some years, the fish are so numerous that anglers can hook dozens in a single day. King salmon fishing is also very productive, with the bulk of the catch hauled out of the outer canal near Clarence Strait. Although feeders can be taken year-round, mature pre-spawners become available during early summer.

If you're looking for a trophy, West Behm Canal is definitely the place to go. Consistent catches of chums between 18 and 25 pounds are reported from the outer and upper canal, with the current state record fish (32 pounds) taken from Caamano Point on the Cleveland Peninsula. July is the best month. Neets Bay is great for hatchery chums and silvers in early fall. Trophy pinks are available as well, with typical catches of five or six pounds, and up to ten pounds or more possible. It should also be noted that the world record steelhead trout (42 pounds, 3 ounces) was caught in West Behm near Bell Island.

Halibut fishing is good in the deeper parts of Behm throughout the season, and in a few of the bays near salmon spawning streams in late summer and fall. Rockfish, Dolly Varden, other bottomfish species as well as crab are also available.

Hot spots for salmon and halibut in West Behm include: Cleveland Peninsula (Caamano Point, Bond, Outer Smuggler, Helm, Spacious and Yes bays, Helm Point, Wadding Cove, and Point Francis); Revillagigedo Island (Point Higgins, Survey, Indian and Chin/Nose/Brow points, Betton Island/Clover Passage, Tatoosh, Back, Grant, and Stack islands, Bushy Point/Cove, and Naha and Neets bays); Gedney Island; Hassler Island/Pass; Black Island; and Bell Island/Behm Narrows.

Revillagigedo Channel

Location: Along south Revillagigedo Island, ten miles SE of Ketchikan.

Access: By boat or floatplane from Ketchikan or area lodges. The channel also provides boat access to George and Carroll inlets, Thorne Arm, east Behm Canal, Duke Island, and Boca de Quadra.

Facilities: Commercial lodging, boat launch, fuel, and water are available at Mountain Point on Revillagigedo Island.

Highlights: A highly productive intercept fishery, one of the best in southern Southeast.

Main Species: KS, SS, HB

Revillagigedo Channel is an important salmon feeding and migration route located south of Revillagigedo Island, between Annette Island and the mainland. The outer channel borders Dixon Entrance near Canada. Anadromous fish heading for mainland rivers and island streams pass through the channel in substantial numbers, and are mainly targeted by sportfishing fleets out of Ketchikan.

Salmon and halibut dominate the fishery. Feeder kings weighing between 10 and 30 pounds can be taken year-round in the channel's clear waters, while larger, mature specimens up to 60 or 70 pounds are taken in early summer. (Many of these mature kings are bound for the glacial Chickamin River in east Behm Canal, a major spawning system for southeast Alaska.)

Silver and pink salmon are the most prolific species in Revillagigedo Channel. These fish can be particularly abundant in late summer and fall, and are best targeted fairly close to shore near bays or coastlines with spawning streams. Cohos weighing in the teens are not unusual. Reds and chums run heavy at times, but are taken much less frequently than silvers and pinks by sport anglers. As with many other major saltwater locations in Southeast, Revillagigedo Channel produces some decent halibut fishing at times, with additional opportunities for rockfish, lingcod, and even shellfish.

The scenery is fantastic, with inlets cutting far into mainland mountain ranges and islands, and an abundance of marine wildlife. (The eastern half of Revillagigedo Channel is part of Misty Fjords National Monument Wilderness.) Although not as popular with recreational users as nearby Clarence Strait or West Behm Canal, the channel has some fabulous sportfishing potential for anglers willing to take the time to explore, particularly the outer Revillagigedo for bottomfish and the mainland bays for salmon. (If exploring in this area, note private property around Annette Island Indian Reservation.) Favorite areas are Mountain Point near Ketchikan and outer East Behm Canal.

The following are known hot spots for salmon and halibut in Revillagigedo Channel: Revillagigedo Island (Mountain Point, Lucky Cove, Cone Island/Point, Herring Bay, California Head, Carroll Point/Ice House Cove, and Thorne Arm); Behm Canal (Point Alava, Alava Bay, and Point Sykes); Slate Island; Quadra Point; White Reef; Kah Shakes Point; Snail Rock; Black Rock; House Rock; Foggy Bay; Foggy Point; Lakekta Point; Humpy Point; Tree Point; Cape Fox/Fox Island; Mary Island; and Duke Island (Duke Point, Kelp Island, and East Island).

MISTY FJORDS NATIONAL MONUMENT WILDERNESS

Misty Fjords National Monument Wilderness, on the mainland and east Revillagigedo Island, is an area of incredible scenic beauty, encompassing some two million acres of almost entirely untouched old-growth rainforest complete with sinuous fjords, long, twisting valleys, and exposed ridges. Rugged mountains rise up to 3,000-4,000 feet from the deep fjords , decorated with numerous glaciers, ice fields, and rushing waterfalls. Here one will find large populations of wildlife and clearwater lakes teeming with salmon, trout, charr, and even the southernmost populations of grayling in Alaska.

Manzanita/Ella Lakes

Location: Misty Fjords National Monument Wilderness, east Revillagigedo Island, 25 to 35 miles NE of Ketchikan.

Access: By floatplane or boat (to stream mouths draining lakes, with a few developed trails available) from Ketchikan or area lodges.

Facilities: Four Forest Service public-use cabins; two on Manzanita (northwest and south ends) and two on Ella (north end and northwest arm) lakes. Manzanita Bay also has a shelter.

Highlights: A great area for combination hike-in and small-stream and lake fishing.

Main Species: SS, KO, CT, DV

On the western side of the monument, on Revillagigedo Island, lie the lake systems of Manzanita and Ella, surrounded by tall mountain peaks and lush, green valleys containing spruce and hemlock. There, anglers will find four species of salmon (except kings) and exceptional opportunities for cutthroat trout, charr, and steelhead.

Manzanita Lake is perhaps the most visited of the waters, supporting excellent numbers of cutthroat trout, kokanee, and Dolly Varden charr. A developed trail follows the outlet stream, Manzanita Creek, from the lake down to Manzanita Bay (about three-and-a-half miles). Anglers can take advantage of this access by trying their luck for runs of silver, red, pink, and chum salmon. The lower stream near its mouth is best. Sea-run cutthroat trout provide excellent action in the stream as well.

Ella Lake, just south of Manzanita, has fair to good runs of silver, pink, and chum salmon, in addition to excellent opportunities for large cutthroat, kokanee, and Dolly Varden charr. The salmon fishing is most productive in the outlet stream, Ella Creek, which is paralleled by a trail from the lake down to Ella Bay and Behm Canal (three-and-a-half miles). For the freshest coho, try the creek mouth on incoming tides.

Another angling possibility is to boat over to the mouth of ***Grace Creek,*** north of Manzanita Bay, which supports a small run of spring steelhead trout.

East Side Behm Canal Lake Systems ★★★★
Location: Misty Fjords National Monument Wilderness, 30 to 50 miles east/northeast of Ketchikan.

Access: Mainly by floatplane (landing on area lakes) or boat (to stream mouths draining lakes) from Ketchikan, with a few developed trails available.

Facilities: Forest Service cabins are located on Big Goat, Upper Checats, Winstanley, and Bakewell lakes. Shelters can be found on Nooya Lake and west end of Winstanley Lake.

Highlights: Superb lake fishing for trout and charr in the remote and scenic Misty Fjords National Monument Wilderness.

Main Species: SS, KO, ST, RT, CT, DV, GR

There are seven main lake systems in this area of the monument wilderness. All offer good to excellent fishing for native species, with additional opportunities for some decent salmon in outlet streams, particularly in the lower reaches near saltwater. The scenic qualities of the area are world-famous, with great hiking to match.

The northernmost lake of the Behm Canal lake complex is ***Walker Lake,*** a small body of water draining into Rudyerd Bay. Rainbow trout are abundant, with some large specimens available, as access is limited and angling pressure very low. Salmon (silver, chum, pink) and steelhead run in season and are complemented with healthy populations of cutthroat trout and Dolly Varden charr.

Big Goat Lake in Rudyerd Bay, provides anglers with the unique chance of tangling with Arctic grayling, a species introduced to the

lake years ago. The population thrived, and action is good in the lake as well as in the larger tributary streams.

Nooya Lake, also connected to Rudyerd Bay, has some great action for sea-run Dolly Varden charr, and is known to be a major overwintering spot for the species. The stream draining the lake has populations of silver, pink, and chum salmon, all of which provide the best sport near tidewater.

The Manzoni Lake system consists of four small lakes connected by Granite Creek, a small stream draining into Behm Canal. As with Big Goat Lake, Manzoni is stocked with grayling and offers good to excellent fishing from summer into fall.

Upper Checats Lake is known for its good population of large rainbow trout. Salmon (silver, chum, pink) also enter the lake, but are best caught in the lower reaches of the outlet stream (Checats Creek) between Lower Checats Lake and Checats Cove. A trail from the cove to the lower lake provides angling access. A small run of steelhead trout enters the creek in the spring.

Winstanley Lake represents a two-lake system draining into the south end of Shoalwater Pass and Behm Canal. The lake itself offers good angling for kokanee and cutthroat trout, while the outlet stream is better for sea-run salmon (silver, pink, chum), and steelhead and rainbow trout. As usual, fish near salt water for brightest salmon. Upper Winstanley Creek above Winstanley Lake has some productive cutthroat trout fishing in late summer and fall.

The last lake in the area is ***Bakewell***, a long and narrow body of water connecting to Bakewell Arm and Smeaton Bay. It is recognized as one of the best locations for cutthroat trout, with some specimens reaching trophy proportions. Flyfishing is superb. Bakewell Creek draining the lake supports runs of sea-run cutthroat and salmon (silver, red, pink, chum), with opportunities considered very good. Anglers will find the lower stream near the salt most productive for fishing as there are some pronounced holes and runs concentrating the fish. In season, look for spring steelhead as well.

If the opportunity arises, angling for halibut and other bottomfish is considered excellent near the mouths of outlet streams and adjoining bays and coves.

Wilson-Blossom River Systems ★★★
Location: Misty Fjords National Monument Wilderness, 45 miles east of Ketchikan.

Access: By floatplane or boat from Ketchikan or area lodges.

Facilities: Two Forest Service cabins are available, at the north and south ends of Wilson Lake.

Highlights: Premier trophy cutthroat waters matched with very good silver salmon action in fall.

Main Species: SS, KO, CT, DV.

The twin drainages of Wilson and Blossom are splendidly situated within Misty Fjords National Monument and Wilderness, one of the most beautiful scenic areas of Southeastern Alaska. A prolific growth of rainforest and abundant wildlife, amidst numerous ragged mountain peaks stretching to thousands of feet, make it a coveted location to pursue salmon and trout.

Wilson Lake is a clearwater drainage long known for its trophy cutthroat trout potential, with good to excellent catch-and-release opportunities in spring and fall. As a matter of fact, three out of the top four largest sportcaught specimens of the species have come from this lake, including the eight-pound-plus state record. There is a strong run of sea-run cutthroat in Wilson River during the month of May as well. In addition, the lake supports good populations of kokanee and Dolly Varden. Fishers seeking to do battle with silver salmon won't walk away disappointed. The river sports a large run of this species.

Just a few miles east of Wilson lies **Blossom River**. This runoff drainage has a more wild approach than its neighbor, as access is more difficult and facilities nonexistent. However, the few anglers that do brave the autumn season on the Blossom are richly rewarded with some outstanding angling for silver salmon.

Boca de Quadra Systems ★★★

Location: Misty Fjords National Monument Wilderness, Boca de Quadra, 50 miles SE of Ketchikan.

Access: By floatplane or boat from Ketchikan or area lodges.

Facilities: Two Forest Service cabins, one at Hugh Smith Lake, the other at Humpback Lake. Commercial lodge located on Mink Bay.

Highlights: Exceptional opportunities for true wilderness fishing excursions for salmon and trout.

Main Species: SS, RS, ST, CT, DV

The Boca de Quadra area represents one of the least visited parts of the Tongass National Forest. It is a vast recreational paradise containing fertile lakes and a myriad of small streams and rivers. Most systems drain out of the east, from the Rousseau Range and the Peabody Mountains, and include some top angling destinations like the Hugh Smith and Humpback lake systems and Marten River.

Flowing into the mouth of Mink Bay at the mid-section of Boca de Quadra is **Sockeye Creek**, a short (quarter-mile long) stream draining well-known **Hugh Smith Lake**. The creek supports four species of salmon (no kings), with red and silver salmon and steelhead trout being the favored targets of most anglers during the summer and fall months. The lake itself is famed for trophy cutthroats and good fishing for rainbow trout and Dolly Varden charr. One may also find schools of salmon at the mouths of streams draining into the lake in season.

At the head of Mink Bay is **Humpback Creek and Lake**. Excellent fishing for large sea-run cutthroat trout and Dolly Varden charr may be had during the spring and fall in the creek, with additional opportunities for good silver salmon action at the mouth and lower one mile of the creek in September. A spring and much smaller fall run of steelhead are available. (The stream has good flyfishing conditions.) Starting at the mouth of Humpback Creek, a marked trail follows the north side of the stream about three miles to the west end of Humpback Lake. This long and narrow clearwater alpine lake has a reputation for very productive fishing for cutthroat trout and Dolly Varden charr, especially near the outlets of tributary streams.

Marten River at, the head of Marten Arm, is home to a multitude of gamefish species, with particular highlight some strong runs of silver salmon and a small spring run of steelhead. Expect very good action in a true wilderness setting with little angling pressure.

In addition to freshwater angling, there is excellent action for salmon, halibut, and other bottomfish in the marine waters throughout Boca de Quadra.

Recommended Lodges/Guides/Outfitters/Air taxis

Fireweed Lodge: P.O. Box 116, Klawock, AK 99925, (907) 755-2936, *www.fireweedlodge.com* Lodge-based salmon/halibut fishing, POW.

Blue Water Charters: P.O. Box 8276, Ketchikan, AK 99901, (907) 225-1271. Saltwater salmon charters, Ketchikan area.

Advanced Charters (Eagle Creek Lodge): P.O. Box 7555, Ketchikan, AK, 99901, (866) HALIBUT, (907) 225-7535, *www.advancedcharters.com* Fishing charters and lodge packages.

Boardwalk Wilderness Lodge: P.O. Box 19121, Thorne Bay, AK 99919, (907) 828-3918, (800) 764-3918, *www.boardwalk lodge.com* Lodge-based, guided fishing, POW.

Classic Alaska Charters: P.O. Box 6117, Ketchikan, AK 99901, (907) 225-0608, *www.classicalaskacharters.com* Custom marine/freshwater guided fishing excursions, Ketchikan area.

Experience One Charters: 3857 Fairview, Ketchikan, AK 99901, (907) 225-2343, *www.experienceonecharters.com* Half day and full day fishing charters.

Island Wings Air Service: P.O. Box 7432, Ketchikan, AK 99901, (888) 854-2444, (907) 225-2444, *www.islandwings.com* Fly-out guide service/air taxi charters, Misty Fjords.

Northern Lights Charters: P.O. Box 793, Ward Cove, AK 99928, (888) 550-8488, (907) 247-8488, *www.ketchikanfishing.net*

Klawock Bay Charters: P.O. Box 145, Klawock, AK 99925, (907) 755-2329.

Kupreanof Flying Service: P.O. Box 768, Petersburg, AK 99833, (907) 772-3396. Air taxi, POW.

Last Frontier Charters: P.O. Box 19443, Thorne Bay, AK 99919, (907) 828-3989.

Prince of Wales Sportfishing: P.O. Box 748, Craig, AK 99921, (888) 943-4746, *www.princeofwalessportfishing.com* Fully guided, freshwater/marine adventures, POW.

Salmon Falls Resort: P.O. Box 5700, Ketchikan, AK 99901, (800) 247-9059, (907) 225-2752, *www.salmonfallsresort.net* Luxury lodge-based guided/unguided fishing.

Sonny Campbell's Fishing Charters (The Cedars Lodge): P.O. Box 8889, Ketchikan, AK 99901, (907) 247-2315, *www.alaskasportfishing.com*

Taquan Air: 1007 Water St., Ketchikan, AK 99901, (907) 225-8800, (800) 770-8800, *www.taquanair.com* Air taxi, Ketchikan/POW.

Yes Bay Lodge: P.O. Box 8660, Ketchikan, AK 99901, (800) 999-0784, (907) 225-7906, *www.yesbay.com* Lodge-based, guided fishing packages, West Behm Canal.

Shaub-Ellison Tires & Fuel: 1507 E. Craig Highway, Craig, AK, 99921, (907) 826-3450. Car rentals, fuel, POW.

Sunnahae Lodge: P.O. Box 90, Craig, AK 99921, (800) 524-3442. *www.sunnahaelodge.com* Lodge-based fishing, POW.

Shoreline Charters: P.O. Box 549, Craig, AK 99921, *www.shorelinecharters.com* Guided fishing, POW.

Sweet Success Charters: Ketchikan, AK 99901, (907) 225-6819, (907) 723-5271.

General information

Alaska Department of Fish and Game: Sportfish Division, 2030 Sea Level Drive, Suite 205, Ketchikan, AK 99901, (907) 225-2859.

Prince of Wales Chamber of Commerce: P.O. Box 490, Klawock, AK 99925, (907) 755-2626, *www.princeofwalescoc.org*

Tongass National Forest, Craig Ranger District: P.O. Box 500, Craig, AK 99921, (907) 826-3271, *www.fs.fed.us/r10/tongass/*

Ketchikan Chamber of Commerce: P.O. Box 5957, Ketchikan, AK 99901, (907) 225-3184, *www.ketchikanchamber.com*

Tongass National Forest: 648 Mission Street, Federal Building, Ketchikan, AK 99901-6591, (907) 225-3101, *www.fs.fed.us/r10/tongass/*

Misty Fjords National Monument: 3031 Tongass Avenue, Ketchikan, AK 99901-5743, (907) 225-2148.

USGS Maps/NOAA Nautical Charts Reference

Gulf of Esquibel: Craig B-5, B-6, C-4, C-5, C-6, D-4, D-5, D-6; 17404.

Bucareli Bay: Craig A-5, B-3, B-4, B-5, B-6, C-3, C-4; 17405, 17406.

Lower Clarence Strait: Craig A-1, A-2, B-1, B-2, B-3, C-1, C-2, D-1, D-2; Ketchikan A-5, A-6, B-6, C-6; Dixon Entrance C-1, D-1; Prince Rupert D-5, D-6; 17426, 17432,17436.

Gravina Island/Tongass Narrows: Ketchikan A-6, B-5, B-6; 17428, 17430.

West Behm Canal: Ketchikan B-6, C-5, C-6, D-5, D-6; Craig C-1; 17422.

Revillagigedo Channel: Ketchikan A-2, A-3, A-4, A-5, B-2, B-3, B-4, B-5; Prince Rupert D-3, D-4; 17434.

Sarkar River System: Craig D-4; Petersburg A-4.

Klawock River: Craig B-3, C-3, C-4.

Harris River: Craig B-3.

Staney Creek: Craig C-4, D-4.

Sweetwater Lake System: Craig D-3, D-4; Petersburg A-4.

Red Bay Lake: Petersburg A-4, B-4.

Salmon Bay Lake: Petersburg A-4, B-4.

Thorne River System: Craig C-2, C-3, D-2, D-3.

Luck Lake/Eagle Creek: Craig D-3.

Karta River System: Craig C-2, C-3.

Kegan River System: Craig A-1.

McDonald Lake System: Ketchikan D-6; Bradfield Canal A-6.

Naha River System: Ketchikan C-5.

Ward Lake System: Ketchikan B-5, B-6.

Ketchikan Creek System: Ketchikan B-5.

Manzanita Lake: Ketchikan C-4.

Ella Lake: Ketchikan C-4, B-4.

Bakewell Lake: Ketchikan B-2.

Winstanley Lake: Ketchikan B-3.

Checats Lakes: Ketchikan B-3.

Manzoni Lakes: Ketchikan C-3.

Nooya Lake: Ketchikan C-3.

Big Goat Lake: Ketchikan C-2.

Walker Lake: Ketchikan C-2, D-3.

Blossom River: Ketchikan B-2, C-2.

Wilson Lake/River: Ketchikan B-2, C-2.

Hugh Smith Lake: Ketchikan A-3.

Humpback Lake/Creek: Ketchikan A-2.

Marten River: Ketchikan A-2, B-1, B-2.

Regulations/Information

Special regulations for trout (steelhead, cutthroat, and rainbow) and salmon fishing apply to many Ketchikan/POW waters, fresh and salt. Always contact local or regional office, ADF&G or consult latest Sportfishing Regulations Summary for Region I, Southeast Alaska, when making plans for fishing the area.

Douglas: (907) 465-4320   **Ketchikan:** (907) 225-2859
Craig: (907) 826-2498

Online info: *www.sf.adfg.state.ak.us/statewide/regulations/seregs.cfm*

Ketchikan/POW Species

Location	King Salmon	Red Salmon	Pink Salmon	Chum Salmon	Silver Salmon	Steelhead	Rainbow	Cutthroat	Charr	Grayling	Lake Trout	Sheefish	Northern Pike	Halibut	Ling Cod	Rock Fish	Salmon Shark	Fishing Pressure
Gulf of Esquibel	★	✓	★	☺	★	✓		✓						☺	☺	☺	R	M
Bucareli Bay	☺	✓	★	✓	★	✓		✓						☺	☺	☺	R	M
Lower Clarence Strait	☺	☺	★	☺	☺	✓		✓						☺	☺	☺	R	M
Gravina Island/Tongass Narrows	☺	✓	☺	☺	☺	R		R						☺	✓	✓	R	☹
West Behm Canal	☺	☺	☺	★	☺	✓		✓						☺	✓	✓	R	☹
Revillagigedo Channel	☺	✓	☺	☺	☺	R		R						☺	✓	✓	R	☹
Sarkar Lakes		☺	☺	☺	☺	☺	✓	☺	☺									✓
Klawock River System	C	☺	☺	☺	★	★	★	☺	☺									M
Harris River	R	☺	☺	☺	★	☺	R	✓	☺									M
Staney Creek	✓	☺	☺	☺	★	★	✓	✓	☺									M
Sweetwater Lakes		☺	✓	✓	★	☺	☺	☺	☺									M
Red Bay Lake		★	☺	✓	☺	☺	★	☺	☺									✓
Salmon Bay Lake		☺	☺	✓	☺	☺	☺	☺	☺									✓
Thorne River System		☺	☺	☺	★	★	✓	☺	★									M
Luck Lake/Eagle Creek		☺	☺	✓	☺	★	★	★	☺									M
Karta River System		★	☺	✓	☺	★	★	★	★									M
Kegan Lake/Creek		☺	☺	✓	☺	✓	☺	☺	☺									✓
McDonald Lake System		★	★	☺	☺	☺	★	☺	☺									M
Naha River System		☺	★	☺	☺	★	☺	☺	☺				✓					☹
Ward Lake System		✓	★	R	☺	☺	✓	✓	☺									☹
Ketchikan Creek System	C	✓	☺	✓	☺	✓		✓	☺									☹
Manzanita/Ella Lakes	LL	☺	☺	☺	✓	★	☺											M
East Side Behm Canal Lake Systems	LL	☺	✓	☺	✓	★	★	☺	☺									M
Wilson/Blossom Rivers	LL	☺	✓	☺	✓	★	☺											M
Boca de Quadra Systems		★	☺	✓	☺	✓	☺	★	☺									M

Legend:

   Species not present
R Rare
✓ Fishable numbers (or light pressure)
☺ Good fishing
★ Excellent fishing

LL Landlocked species
C Present, but fishing closed
M Moderate pressure
H Heavy pressure

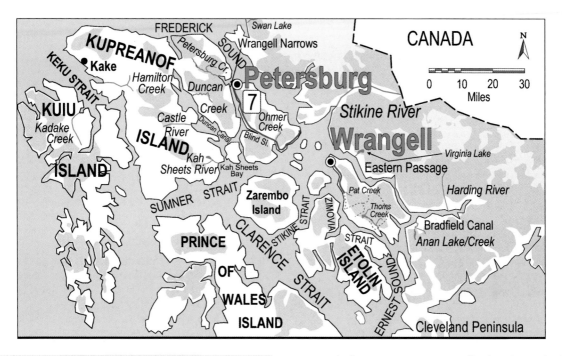

PETERSBURG/WRANGELL

The Petersburg/Wrangell area, from Cape Fanshaw to the Cleveland Peninsula, encompasses numerous islands, including Kupreanof, Kuiu, Etolin, Wrangell, and Zarembo, along with the Stikine Wilderness on the mainland, and a preponderance of straits, channels, sounds, and bays. With its abundance of rugged coastline, sheltered waters, and dozens of small lakes and streams, this area has significant opportunities for high-quality marine and freshwater fishing, which are probably unequalled for variety anywhere in Southeast.

All five species of salmon occur here. As elsewhere, most of the effort for king and coho takes place in salt water as an intercept fishery (the giant Stikine River is far and away the largest spawning destination in the area). Frederick Sound and Wrangell Narrows, Eastern Passage, and Zimovia and Stikine straits are the most frequently fished marine areas, also providing opportunities for some bottomfish (mostly halibut and a few rockfish). New opportunities for both king and coho have been created by the local hatchery (Crystal Lake). Some of the better locations to target these hatchery (and wild stock) fisheries are: Blind River/Slough, Anita Bay, lower Duncan Canal, and the mouths of Petersburg and Falls creeks.

Roads leading out from the three major communities (Petersburg, pop. 3300; Wrangell, pop. 2600; Kake,

pop. 700) allow access to many quality locations—both fresh and salt water. Some of the more outstanding of these are: Thoms Lake and Creek system, 39 miles south of Wrangell (ST, RS, CT, DV, SS); Blind River and Blind Slough, 15 miles southeast of Petersburg (KS, SS, CT, DV); Pat Creek and Pat Lake, 11 miles south of Wrangell (SS, PS, CT, DV); the Zimovia and Mitkof Highway shorelines (SS, PS, DV, CT); Hamilton Creek, 13 miles south of Kake (ST, SS, CT, DV); and Ohmer Creek, south of Petersburg (ST, SS, DV, CT). An extensive network of old logging roads and trails throughout the area provides additional access to many remote fishing locations.

The U.S. Forest Service maintains 42 public-use cabins and nine shelters on many of the better secluded lake, stream, and bay locations which lie in Tongass National Forest. Steelhead, cutthroat trout, and Dolly Varden are the main attractions, with some high-quality salmon (silver, pink, chum) and rainbow trout fishing also available in some systems. Petersburg and Kadake creeks, Castle River, and the Anan, Marten, Swan, Virginia, and Eagle Lake systems are some of the more noteworthy ones. Both Petersburg and Wrangell are serviced by daily jet flights connecting to Juneau, Seattle, and Anchorage, and all three towns are linked by the ferries of the Alaska Marine Highway System.

PETERSBURG VICINITY

Ohmer Creek

Location: Mitkof Island, 21 miles south of Petersburg.

Access: By car via Mitkof Highway.

Facilities: USFS campground located next to highway, near mouth of stream.

Highlights: Petersburg's top roadside stream attraction.

Main Species: PS, CS, SS, CT, ST

Ohmer Creek is perhaps the best of several (Falls and Bear creeks being the others) road-accessible creeks on Mitkof Island, a short distance south of town. Like Petersburg Creek, it is a heavily fished, easily reached clearwater stream that makes a fine spot for folks with limited time or resources.

Situated on the mountainous southern end of Mitkof Island, 21 miles south of town, Ohmer Creek is a relatively small drainage that empties into Blind Slough. Salmon fishing is one of the stream's main attractions, with late summer runs of chums and pinks and a fairly large number of silver salmon entering the river in fall. Local anglers tend to favor the river's lower section, including the mouth, for intercepting the brightest, feistiest fish.

Other fine species available are sea-run cutthroat trout and Dolly Varden, offering steady action near the road crossing and other spots. A small run of native steelhead trout also shows up in spring, with fair fishing to be expected during the peak in May.

Petersburg Creek ★★★

Location: Eastern Kupreanof Island, five miles west of Petersburg.

Access: By floatplane/boat from Petersburg or Wrangell. Planes land at Petersburg Lake; boats reach creek mouth with a 15-ft. tide via Wrangell Narrows; from there a 6 1/2-mile trail leads to the lake.

Facilities: A USFS cabin is located at the SE end of Petersburg Lake.

Highlights: A tremendously popular Petersburg stream fishing location for steelhead and salmon.

Main Species: SS, ST, CT, DV

Located on the Lindberg Peninsula of Kupreanof Island, just across from the town of Petersburg, Petersburg Lake and Creek are very popular recreation areas that get heavily fished by locals during the height of the salmon and steelhead runs. The lower stream is lined by the crests of Petersburg Mountain and Del Monte Peak, adding considerable scenic appeal. As part of the Petersburg Creek-Duncan Saltchuck Wilderness, this area offers some fairly high-quality lake and streamfishing possibilities in combination with trail excursions (Petersburg Lake Trail and Portage Mountain Trail).

Clear and fairly fast, the creek is best known for its spring steelhead run, which grabs anglers' attention earlier in the season. Petersburg Creek steelies tend toward being some of the largest in Southeast, with a few exceptional fish up to 20 pounds or more possible. A brief showing of sockeye salmon presents another angling opportunity during the midsummer lull; fish for them from the lake down in late July. Slightly later, the creek often sees good numbers of chums and pinks. And, starting in late summer and continuing until late fall, abundant silver salmon enter the system. Sea-run cutthroats, Dollies, and resident rainbows are taken in Petersburg Lake, particularly during the spring and fall months.

Swan Lake

Location: Thomas Bay, 18 miles NE of Petersburg.

Access: By plane from Petersburg; also boat access to Cascade Creek.

Facilities: Forest Service cabin at east end of lake.

Highlights: A famous Petersburg area lake location.

Main Species: RT, DV

A short way across Frederick Sound from Petersburg, Swan lake has always been one of the more popular area lake destinations, for its scenery, wildlife, public-use cabin, and decent trout fishing.

Lying over 1500 feet above sea level on the mainland, two-and-a-half miles from tidewater east of Thomas Bay, the lake is situated in a deep canyon basin rimmed by impressive peaks topping 5000 feet, a gorgeous alpine area immensely popular with hikers, photographers, and goat hunters. But it is the trout fishing—rainbows originally stocked there years ago—that really adds appeal for anyone wanting a high quality, fly-in lake experience that's close to town.

Known at one time for their size, Swan Lake's 'bows won't stretch anyone's stringer these days. (Fish in the twelve inch class are more the rule.) But they're plentiful and they're easy to catch, with the possibility of an outsized 20-incher if you get lucky.

Because of the steep topography, it is nearly impossible to walk around the lake or fish from shore, except at the outlet and inlet, so a boat (there are two on the lake provided by USFS) is essential for getting around. Hiking access adds other possibilities, as there is a crude, steep trail leading from the outlet (Cascade Creek) down to Falls Lake (which also has some rainbow trout fishing and a skiff and shelter) and the lower creek and falls (right above tidewater), ending at Thomas Bay, approximately four-and-a-half miles below Swan Lake. (There is another USFS public-use cabin on the bay not far from the trailhead.) The lower barrier falls keeps other species out of the system, but Dolly Varden can sometimes be taken at the mouth of Cascade Creek.

Because of the elevation and nearby glaciers, Swan Lake is usually not ice-free until late June or early July, and freezes sometime in late October. It can sometimes get weathered in for days, delaying floatplane pick-ups, so it is wise to plan for an extended stay.

Wrangell Narrows/Duncan Canal

Location: SE Kupreanof Island, running directly west and south of Petersburg.

Access: By boat from Petersburg; floatplane and limited road access (Mitkof Hwy) also possible.

Facilities: Seven Forest Service cabins available in area: Kah Sheets Bay, Beecher Pass, Harvey Lake, Breiland Slough, Castle River/Flats (two), and Saltchuck.

Highlights: A very productive, easily accessed Petersburg marine fishing destination.

Main Species: KS, SS, CS, PS, DV, CT

Wrangell Narrows separates Mitkof Island from the larger Kupreanof Island, just west of Petersburg. Stretching from Frederick Sound in the north to Sumner Strait in the south, the narrows averages only about a mile in width. Duncan Canal, a fairly long, wide fjord that cuts deep into the center of Kupreanof Island, connects with Wrangell Narrows at Woewodski Island near Sumner Strait. With the proximity of Petersburg, both serve as major recreational waters for boating and angling, providing one of the most intense marine sportfisheries in southern Southeast, along with access to some notable stream angling locations.

King salmon are the most favored target. Feeders can be taken consistently every day of the year at the outer ends of Wrangell Narrows, and a large hatchery run of these fish returns every season to the mouth of Blind Slough (the intertidal outlet of Crystal Creek) on Mitkof Island, 15 miles south of town. An enhanced run of silvers mixed in with wild stocks offers fast action in late summer and fall in the slough and adjoining Blind River and, in varying amounts, throughout the narrows and Duncan Canal as well. Although primarily a boat fishery early in the season, it can be fished with good results by shore anglers later on. Chum and pink salmon are also taken frequently near the mouths of rivers and streams.

Sea-run cutthroat trout and Dolly Varden are spread throughout the narrows and canal in fair numbers, and are usually caught at the mouths of Petersburg, Falls, and Duncan Saltchuck creeks, as well as along points and beaches in the vicinity. Small runs of steelhead populate some of the streams along the canal (Castle River, Towers Creek, Taylor Creek) and narrows (Falls Creek) providing additional possibilities for angling. Halibut fishing is done predominantly at the north and south ends of the narrows; some smaller fish may be hauled out of deeper parts of Duncan Canal in mid-season.

The main fishing areas for salmon and halibut in Wrangell Narrows and Duncan Canal include: Kupreanof Island—Prolewy, Mountain, Finger, and North points; Mitkof Island—Petersburg Harbor, Scow Bay, Danger, Blind, and December points, Blind Slough and Point Alexander; Duncan Canal—Whiskey Pass/Butterworth Island, Castle Islands, and Saltchuck; and Woody Island.

Duncan Creek/Saltchuck

Location: Central Kupreanof Island, 11 miles west of Petersburg.

Access: By plane or boat from Petersburg or Wrangell. Boat access via Wrangell Narrows or Sumner Strait to Duncan Canal and Saltchuck. (A rock rapids blocks boat access to saltchuck except during tides of 17 feet or more).

Facilities: A Forest service public-use cabin on the east side of saltchuck.

Highlights: A famous area locale for cutthroat trout and steelhead.

Main Species: CT, ST, DV, SS

This short, productive creek and saltchuck lie at the head of Duncan Canal in the central part of Kupreanof Island, a short distance west of Petersburg. Long known for outstanding sea-run cutthroat trout fishing, it draws locals and visitors alike to its waters each spring and fall with light spin tackle and flyrods, to try for above average numbers of these popular fighters.

Due to the draining of muskeg around the Bohemian Range, the creek usually has a tannic-brown color, especially after heavy rains, but it still fishes well. The lower part of the creek offers the best fishing conditions, having fewer logjams and many fair-sized pools interspersed with shallow riffles. Sea-run Dolly Varden are frequently taken there in spring and late summer-fall, with substantial

catches made on egg and attractor pattern flies or flashy spinners (also spoons fished off the mouth of the creek).

Steelhead trout enter the drainage in spring, offering a few weeks of top-notch flyfishing excitement (late April to mid-May). Most successful anglers fish the tides on the lower creek sections, intercepting these robust sea-run rainbows on their way upstream to spawning areas. Other important species include silver salmon and rainbow trout. The lower river and mouth in September are best for coho, while the upper sections harbor the best rainbow opportunities. Additionally, some chum and pink salmon can be enticed into striking flashy hardware right above the mouth in late summer.

Castle River ★★★

Location: South Kupreanof Island, 20 miles SW of Petersburg.

Access: From Petersburg or Wrangell by floatplane or boat (via Wrangell Narrows or Sumner Strait to Duncan Canal). A tide of at least 15 feet required to access mouth of river.

Facilities: Two Forest Service public-use cabins; one at mouth of river and the other on flats northeast.

Highlights: An important Petersburg area steelhead and silver salmon stream.

Main Species: ST, SS, CT, DV

Flowing into west Duncan Canal on south Kupreanof Island, 20 miles from Petersburg, Castle River is a tannic-brown stream surrounded by muskeg, rain forests, and rolling hills. Small in size, the river is nonetheless one of the most productive streams of the area, known best for silver salmon and steelhead trout.

Most anglers access the drainage at the mouth, then fish and hike upstream. The first major gamefish of the season are spring-run steelhead trout. They are best intercepted early on in the first few miles of the river, fishing the tides. Later on, anglers do better by hiking to holes and runs on the middle Castle. Resident rainbows, as well as sea-run cutthroat trout and Dolly Varden, are also available from spring through fall.

Silver salmon begin running in August and continue until October, and inspire a fair amount of angling effort in the Castle. Chum and pink salmon also show in large numbers, but a little earlier than the coho. As is the case most anywhere, brighter fish are generally taken at the mouth or in the lower river.

Eastern Frederick Sound

Location: Northeast coast Kupreanof/Mitkof islands, 650 miles SE of Anchorage.

Access: By boat from Petersburg or Wrangell (via Sumner Strait and Wrangell Narrows or, if tides permit, Dry Strait on the Stikine River Flats); floatplane access to protected bays and coves.

Facilities: Three Forest Service cabins: Cascade Creek, Spurt Cove, West Point at mouth of Portage Bay.

Highlights: A traditional, local marine hotspot.

Main Species: KS, SS, PS, DV, HT

Separating Kupreanof and Mitkof islands from the mainland, eastern Frederick Sound includes all waters from Cape Fanshaw and Pinta Point in the west, to Stikine River flats in the southeast. It is a breathtaking area of dense coastal forests, deeply incised valleys, enormous tidewater glaciers, and an abundance of fish and marine life. Seasoned marine boaters, primarily from Petersburg, enjoy a fishery that has been producing good catches for generations. King and silver salmon and halibut are by far the most popular available species, and subject to intense harvest efforts during the summer and fall months.

Chinook, present year-round, are most numerous in late spring and early summer (late April through June), as wild runs head to spawning areas up the Stikine River and hatchery fish returning to release sites in the Wrangell Narrows pass through in full force. While they average 15 to 25 pounds, larger fish to 50 or 60 pounds are sometimes taken. By July, as the best king fishing declines, things start to heat back up with the return of pink salmon. These scrappy fighters are taken in inshore waters everywhere, particularly near and in the mouths of clearwater streams. (Look for numbers of chum salmon, cutthroat trout, and Dolly Varden at the same time.) Silvers are the last of the salmon to show, and continue to arrive through most of autumn.

Halibut fishing is rated as good, with decent-sized flatfish taken throughout the Sound, but especially abundant in areas with appropriate bottom structure (bars, dropoffs, mounts, etc.) or in the vicinity of salmon streams later in the season. Jigging is the most popular angling method, but a fair number are taken incidentally while fishing for other species, especially salmon. It is worthwhile to note that the lower southeast section of Frederick Sound may get cloudy with glacial silt in summer. This is due to the heavy discharge from the nearby Stikine River. When the weather cools, the runoff generally subsides completely and the sound becomes clear blue again.

Frederick Sound is regarded by most folks as a day-trip fishery, but longer stays are possible by mooring off beaches and stream mouths in protected bays and coves. Some of the proven fishing locations for halibut and salmon include: Cape Fanshaw/Fanshaw Bay; the northwest coast of Kupreanof Island (Pinta Point, Schooner Island, Big Creek, and Portage Bay); Farragut, Thomas, and LeConte bays on the mainland; Cape Strait; and Beacon, Frederick, and Vandeput points.

PETERSBURG REMOTE

Keku Strait

Location: Between NW Kupreanof and Kuiu islands, 35 miles west of Petersburg.

Access: By boat from village of Kake or by boat/floatplane from Petersburg; some area streams can be accessed by logging roads.

Facilities: Limited services available in nearby Kake; three Forest Service cabins along strait.

Highlights: Outstanding, out-of-the-way marine/stream fishing.

Main Species: KS, SS, BF, CT, DV, ST

Keku Strait separates Kupreanof and Kuiu islands, from Chatham Strait and Frederick Sound on its north end, to Sumner Strait in the south. With its numerous sheltered islands and bays, it has been a traditional rich fishing grounds for salmon and halibut that feed and stage during their seasonal movements through inside waters. Numerous streams containing salmon and trout populations empty into the strait, some receiving little attention.

From Kake, the main fishing community (pop. 700), access via logging roads or by small boat can put anglers into some outstanding, lesser-fished stream and marine locations in and around western Kupreanof and northeast Kuiu islands. Predominant species include king/silver salmon, halibut, steelhead, cutthroat trout, and Dolly Varden charr. Services presently are limited to a few charters and local overnight lodges/B&Bs, with car rentals available.

Marine fishing in the adjacent waters of Keku Strait is excellent for salmon and halibut. Feeder kings can be taken year round within a short boat ride of town, with the larger prespawning fish (up to 50 pounds) available from mid-April into July. Trolling is the predominant method, but some anglers do well mooching and even jigging in certain areas. Silver salmon fishing, both in the waters of the strait and numerous feeder streams, is another area highlight, providing great fishing in late summer and fall.

Halibut fishing is best done out in the more open waters fronting Chatham or Sumner straits early in the season, with the big flatfish moving in closer and shallower as summer progresses. Jigging and bait fishing are equally productive, and large catches are still possible, though not as abundant as in years past. Other bottomfish. like rockfish and lingcod, are best fished in the strait's outer waters.

Some of the hotspots along Keku Strait are: Keku, Hamilton, Conclusion, and Entrance islands (KS, SS); Kadake Bay/Creek (SS, ST, CT, DV); Hamilton Bay/Creek (SS, ST, DV); Big John Bay/Creek (SS, ST, CT, DV); Irish Creek (SS, ST, CT, DV); Tunehean Creek (SS, ST, CT, DV); Kushneahin Creek (SS, RS, CT, DV, ST); Camden Point (KS, SS); Cornwallis Point (KS, SS, BF); Point Macartney (KS, SS, BF).

Hamilton Creek

Location: Western Kupreanof Island, 13 miles south of Kake.

Access: By one-mile trail from FR 6040 along Hamilton Bay; parts of upper drainage also reached by spur logging roads.

Facilities: None.

Highlights: A more out-of-the-way stream with great fishing potential.

Main Species: SS, CT, DV, ST

Hamilton Creek is one of the most significant drainages in the Petersburg area for its size and fish potential. It drains a large area of muskeg and small headwater lakes on the northwest side of Kupreanof Island and empties into Hamilton Bay, south of the village of Kake. A longtime hotspot for locals, with its proximity to town, ease of access, and good salmon and trout fishing, it should not be overlooked by anyone wanting a slightly off-the-beaten path, high quality stream fishing experience.

Hamilton is fairly wide and shallow, interspersed with moderately deep pools along much of its lower stretches (below the confluence of the three major forks, approximately ten miles upstream), where most anglers concentrate their efforts. A trail leading from the logging road to the lower river continues along the banks and provides access to most of the best fishing water. The creek is best known for its excellent flyfishing conditions and good spring steelhead (April-May) and cutthroat trout fishing. It gets an outstanding run of late summer-fall silver salmon and healthy numbers of inmigrating Dolly Varden. Small numbers of fall steelhead liven up the action as fishing wanes late in the year.

Kadake Creek ★★★★

Location: Northern Kuiu Island, 45 miles west of Petersburg.

Access: Plane or boat (access to mouth of creek requires 18-foot tide) from Petersburg or Wrangell. Parts of drainage can be accessed by logging roads.

Facilities: Forest Service public-use cabin at Kadake Bay.

Highlights: One of Southeast's top steelhead streams.

Main Species: ST, SS, CT, DV

Located on the north end of Kuiu Island, Kadake Creek is a fair-sized drainage, comprised of numerous tributaries, that empties into Kadake Bay and Keku Strait. For years it has been one of southern Southeast's more significant angling destinations, with abundant salmon, cutthroat trout, a good run of spring steelhead, and perfect stream fishing conditions.

There are four small headwater lakes that feed two major forks. Due to muskeg in the area, the water runs slightly brown in color. Most angling effort takes place on the lower creek below the forks, where the best holding water is. Anglers usually work the tides at the mouth at Kadake Bay, moving upstream to search for holding fish after the crest of the tide. A big spring run of steelhead and hungry cutthroat trout open the season every year in April and May. July and August bring chum and pink salmon into the system. Fishing the tides at the mouth usually produces the most and brightest fish.

Coho invade Kadake beginning in late summer and continuing into October. (Look for inmigrating cutthroats and Dollies along with the salmon, especially around spawning beds.) There are some resident rainbow trout in the upper and middle sections of Kadake Creek, but they are seldom targeted. Also, a very small run of fall steelhead may be present in the latter part of November.

Kah Sheets River ★★★

Location: Southeast Kupreanof Island, 25 miles SW of Petersburg.

Access: Floatplane or boat from Petersburg or Wrangell. Boaters go through Wrangell Narrows/lower Duncan Canal or Summner Strait to Kah Sheets Bay. A 14-foot tide is required to reach trailhead (two-and-three-quarter mile trail to lake) at Kah Sheets Bay.

Facilities: Two Forest Service public-use cabins; one at lake outlet, the other on bay near river mouth.

Highlights: One of SSE's better steelhead/salmon streams.

Main Species: ST, SS, CT, DV

Kah Sheets River is a lightly tannic-stained stream draining into Kah Sheets Bay and upper Sumner Strait on the southeast tip of Kupreanof. Only about two miles long, the river is easily fished along its entire length, from tidewater to the outlet of Kah Sheets Lake, via a well-marked trail. From near and far, anglers come to experience one of the best streams in southern Southeast for silver salmon and steelhead trout.

Like other drainages on Kupreanof Island, Kah Sheets has a vibrant run of spring steelies. They can be taken anywhere on the river, with the best success reported on incoming tides near the mouth early in the run, and in the upper river just below the lake later on. Resident rainbows are found in the lake, giving anglers with canoes or inflatables some action during spring and fall months. Sea-run cutthroat trout and Dolly Varden are also present in varying numbers throughout the season.

The Kah Sheets also has a reputation for its ballistic coho. Large schools of these fighters enter the river in August and stay into October. They are taken from Kah Sheets Bay clear up into the lake. Earlier trips in midsummer can be productive for hefty chum salmon and spunky pinks. (A small run of reds also occurs, with the best opportunities found in the river's faster-flowing stretches.)

Upper Sumner Strait

Location: Between upper POW and Kupreanof/Mitkof islands, 25 miles south of Petersburg.

Access: By boat from Petersburg or Wrangell; floatplane access in protected bays/coves.

Facilities: A Forest Service cabin at head of Kah Sheets Bay is the nearest public facility.

Highlights: A favorite location for great salmon and bottomfish.

Main Species: KS, SS, DV, CT, BF

Upper Sumner Strait stretches from the Stikine River Flats to Point Baker (the northwest tip of Prince of Wales Island) and Point Barrie (the southwest corner of Kupreanof Island). Like certain other straits and passages in Southeast, Sumner is a major migration channel for salmon bound for spawning systems on area islands and the mainland (the Stikine River being the major contributing system). Also, bottomfish use the strait in summer as an active feeding ground. It is common knowledge that some of the best marine sportfishing opportunities in southern Southeast may be found off the strait's beaches, points, reefs, shoals, and stream mouths, particularly those near outside waters.

King salmon are a prime target for strait fishermen, primarily in spring and early summer when mature fish move through, but persevering anglers can catch smaller feeder kings year-round. (The waters near Petersburg and Wrangell receive the most attention from charter fleets, but some really good fishing can be had from Clarence Strait to Point Baker.) Silver salmon provide the main action in late summer-fall, from just about anywhere along the shoreline. Some sea-run cutthroat trout and Dolly Varden add to the fare in late spring and summer, off the mouths of clearwater streams and adjoining points and beaches (Red, Totem, and Kah Sheets bays; St. John Harbor).

Bottomfishing is popular during the warmer months, with halibut the obvious favorite. Available throughout the year (except in January, during the statewide closure), early summer is the preferred time to go after huge flatties up to 200 pounds or more. Areas near the eastern end of Sumner Strait are most productive this time of year, with fish averaging between 20 and 75 pounds.

Like other straits and passages around the mouth of the glacial Stikine River, the eastern end of Sumner may get silty at times, especially during the warm summer months when runoff peaks. From late fall into spring, however, the entire strait is usually clear blue.

Hot spots for salmon, charr, and halibut include: the northern end of Prince of Wales Island (Point Baker, Merryfield and Red bays, and Point Colpoys); The Eye Opener; McArthur Reef; Level Islands; White Rock; Zarembo Island (Vichnefski Rock, Saint John and Baht harbors, and Low and Craig points); Kupreanof Island (Outer Kah Sheets Bay/Lung Island); Mitkof Island (Midway, Wilson and Station islands, Point Alexander, Banana Point, Outer Blind Slough, and Point Howe); Vank Island; Two Tree Island; Sokolof Island; Greys Island/Pass; Rynda Island; Kadin Island; and Liesnoi Island.

WRANGELL VICINITY

Pat Creek & Lake
Location: NW Wrangell Island, eleven miles south of Wrangell.

Access: By car eleven miles south on Zimovia Highway to Pat Creek Landing; unimproved road parallels creek to Pat Lake/headwaters.

Facilities: None.

Highlights: A good roadside Wrangell area stream, perfect for folks with limited time/resources.

Main Species: CT, DV, SS

Pat Creek and Lake has been a perennial favorite among local anglers, lying just south of town along the highway, and offering decent angling for trout and salmon. Small, as Southeast streams go, the creek drains a small valley on the northwest side of Kupreanof and feeds a small lake not far from where it empties into Zimovia Strait. A trail and road follow the creek up to the lake, providing easy access to the best water.

Sea-run cutthroat trout and Dolly Varden have been the major draws for anglers, along with a few steelhead, providing some of the best spring fishing within close reach of Wrangell. A good run of silver salmon makes the creek quite popular in the fall.

Thoms Creek System ★★★
Location: SW Wrangell Island, 21 miles south of Wrangell.

Access: By car, boat, and floatplane. Lower creek reached by FR 6265 to 6270 to 6299. Trail (one-and-four-tenths miles) to lake reached by FR 6265 to 6290. Boat/floatplane access to mouth at State Marine Park.

Facilities: Thoms Place State Marine Park at mouth; USFS recreation site at creek crossing of FR 6299.

Highlights: Wrangell's most productive roadside stream.

Main Species: RS, SS, CT, DV

The Thoms Creek drainage is a small, road-accessible system that drains into Zimovia Strait on the south end of Wrangell Island, about 21 miles south of town. Three lakes comprise the heart of the drainage, with Thoms being the largest and most visited. As a fair amount of muskeg is present, the water is slightly tannic-stained. The system is a favorite destination among locals, known for its surprisingly good catches of some of the more sought-after gamefishes of the region.

Thoms Creek has a reputation for some of the best red salmon fishing in the Petersburg/ Wrangell area. Although they don't really return in very large numbers, the sockeyes concentrate in dense schools, making for great streamfishing opportunities, particularly flyfishing. The action is usually best on the lower stream near the road crossing and at the mouth, especially during the height of the run. Chums and pinks are also present in fishable numbers and provide some excitement just as the sockeyes begin tapering off. Later in the fall, a strong showing of chunky silver salmon puts the capper on the salmon season, with good fishing to be expected from tidewater up to the lakes well into November.

The creek also has cutthroat trout (sea-run and resident) and Dolly Varden, with the best fishing generally in spring and fall in Thoms Lake (and Little Thoms Lake below) and the lower stream sections. The mouth of Thoms Creek at Thoms Place can also yield some fairly good results during the summer months. Resident rainbow trout are available in the upper stream drainage.

Many visiting anglers fish the system from the road crossing but, in recent years, it has become increasingly popular to moor a boat at Thoms Place State Marine Park at the mouth of Thoms Creek, then fish the intertidal area for schools of salmon.

Eastern Passage
Location: NE of Wrangell Island, 35 miles SE of Petersburg.

Access: By boat from Wrangell, but also from Petersburg via Wrangell Narrows and Sumner Strait or, if tides permit, through Dry Strait at Stikine River Flats.

Facilities: A Forest Service public-use cabin is located on the mainland at Berg Bay.

Highlights: One of the main Petersburg/Wrangell area fishing destinations.

Main Species: KS, SS, CS, DV

Long and narrow, Eastern Passage, parting Wrangell Island from the mainland, stretches from Stikine River Flats to Ernest Sound and Bradfield Canal. Part of Tongass National Forest, the highly scenic surroundings—dense evergreens, lush valleys, and snow-capped mountains (some of which rise up to 5,300 feet)—add appeal to the area's great fishing potential. Along with Stikine and Zimovia straits, the Passage is a main local destination for salmon.

Eastern Passage receives substantial numbers of salmon. The northern section yields native fish bound for the glacial Stikine River while, on the southern end, at outer Blake Channel, anglers do well intercepting schools of fish heading for Bradfield Canal drainages. Mature, prespawning kings become abundant in late spring and early summer, with immature feeders scattered throughout year-round. "The Narrows," a half-mile-wide chute separating the Passage from Blake Channel, is a major feeder king attraction from November to April. (A Forest Service cabin in Berg Bay, only a few miles away, makes a fine point of access.) Large spawner kings up to 40 or 50 pounds are taken in June and July at the south end. Later in the summer anglers begin taking more and more silver salmon as the smaller pinks peak in area waters. Running into October and even November in some locations, these fall coho are right behind the kings in popularity and attract considerable angling attention. Chum salmon are usually only caught incidentally and, along with Dolly Varden, they can provide fair angling for anyone with a little patience. Halibut are most predictably hooked in moderately deep water around the north and south ends of Eastern Passage, and range between 15 and 60 pounds with occasional larger catches.

Hot spots along Eastern Passage include: Babbler Point, The Narrows, Wrangell Island (Point Highfield and Earl West Cove), and Blake Channel/Island.

Virginia Lake System
Location: Mainland, eight miles east of Wrangell across Eastern Passage.

Access: By boat or floatplane from Wrangell/Petersburg.

Facilities: Forest Service cabin at NE end of lake (wheelchair accessible).

Highlights: A famous Wrangell semi-remote lake/stream destination with a variety of fishing.

Main Species: CT, DV, RS

Located on the other side of Eastern Passage, a short plane or boat ride from town, the Virginia Lake system has always been one of the Wrangell area's most popular destinations, perfect for a quick getaway to a lovely, secluded lake and stream setting. A small lake (1/2 by 2 miles) situated a mere hundred feet above sea level, Virginia has a long history of trophy cutthroat fishing. Though today it takes quite a bit of effort to turn up fish of any size, Virginia's cutts are still abundant enough to provide good angling. Dolly Varden, sockeye salmon, and kokanee add variety to the mix.

Most of the lake shoreline is steep-sided with overhanging trees, very hard to fish (or get around) without a boat, except at the outlet and the shallow deltas below the two main inlets. (These areas are some of the lake's prime fishing spots, however.) Like in all classic SE cutthroat lakes, Virginia's larger trout are best pursued by trolling, using spoons or plugs pulled along the steep dropoffs.

The outlet, Mill Creek, empties into Eastern Passage a short ways down from lake. Most of the red salmon fishing occurs there, below the falls right above tidewater. (This falls and several others on the creek hinder passage of most anadromous species.) A one-mile, well maintained USFS trail provides access.

Stikine River System ★★★

Location: Mainland, east of Mitkof Island, 30 miles SE of Petersburg.

Access: By boat from Petersburg or Wrangell via Dry Strait or Eastern Passage (tide of at least 14 feet required to cross Stikine River Flats). Small plane access possible in select locations.

Facilities: There are thirteen Forest Service public-use cabins along the drainage and surrounding flats.

Highlights: A colossal drainage with awesome adventure angling possibilities.

Main Species: CS, SS, PS, CT, DV

The Stikine River is an immense, 330-mile-long glacial system originating from the snow and ice-bound Cassiar Mountains in British Columbia, Canada. The largest trans-boundary river in Southeast, only the last 30 to 35 miles of it lies within Alaska, fanning out into a huge, sandy delta at the head of Sumner Strait and Frederick Sound just east of Mitkof Island. Part of the Stikine-Leconte Wilderness, the river is dramatically scenic, with ice-capped mountain peaks soaring over 4,000 feet, steep gorges, and forested valleys and tidewater glaciers. Wildlife is particularly abundant and there are many historical and geologic areas of interest along its banks, even some hot springs.

With its vast number of tributary lakes and clearwater streams supporting significant salmon, charr, and trout populations, the Stikine is a giant of untapped sportfishing potential, waiting for adventurous anglers with the time and means to explore its many productive waters.

Since the river carries a heavy silt load most of the year, almost all sportfishing takes place at the confluences of clearwater streams and sloughs. The largest and most popular tributary among local anglers is Andrew Creek, on the south bank only a few miles above tidewater. Another, but slightly smaller, stream is nearby Government Creek, situated near the mouth. Both of these receive a fair amount of angling pressure during the height of salmon runs in summer and fall.

Although it has a substantial run of large king salmon (from May through July), the Stikine, like most freshwater drainages in Southeast, is closed to fishing for the species, leaving most fish to head unimpeded into major spawning streams in Canada. (A personal use king salmon fishery is sometimes open on this river if returns are high; check with the Petersburg ADF&G office for current status.) Good numbers of silvers, chums, and pinks, along with smaller numbers of reds, are also present throughout the lower drainage, and provide the bulk of angling activity. Dolly Varden are available and seasonally abundant (best in late summer to fall), and there are even occasional cutthroat and rainbow trout taken. (Some may be found in the mainstem Stikine from late fall to early spring, when the river clears for lack of meltwater.) The best areas to fish in the summer are clearwater sloughs and creek mouths. Steelhead are rumored to be available, but elusive; apparently they are concentrated in tributaries farther upriver.

There are many options for adventure angling on this impressive drainage. It can be floated by kayak, raft, or canoe, with a put-in usually at Telegraph Creek (150 miles above tidewater), which can be accessed via the Cassiar Highway (B.C) or at other points along the river by small float or wheelplane, conditions permitting. This is ideal, as it allows anglers to sample countless opportunities for good angling in clear tributary creeks, streams, lakes, and sloughs on the way down. It is also possible to jet boat upriver from Wrangell to camp and fish, or float down. Since this is a true wilderness river with a volatile nature and extensive tidal flats at the lower end, employing the services of a local guide is highly recommended.

Zimovia Strait

Location: SW of Wrangell Island, NE of Etolin Island, 35 miles SE of Petersburg.

Access: Primarily by boat from Wrangell Harbor; limited access from road network south of town; also floatplane access possible to protected waters in strait.

Facilities: Full services available in nearby Wrangell.

Highlights: A very popular and productive Wrangell area fishing destination.

Main Species: KS, SS, PS, RS, CT, DV

Zimovia Strait lies between the islands of Etolin and Wrangell, just south of the town of Wrangell. The rolling green hills and occasional peaks lend scenic contrast to the strait's deep blue waters. With great fishing and abundant marine wildlife, it is an attractive and very popular recreation area within easy reach of town.

Zimovia is slightly narrower and longer than Stikine Strait. Like the Stikine, it can get cloudy in its upper end during summer hot spells due to glacial outwash from the giant Stikine River but, generally, it is clear most of the year. King salmon are the most sought-after species there. Feeders can be caught year-round, with the best action from October into May or June, when the big spawners heading for the mainland take over. (Most of the salmon that pass through the strait are headed for clearwater tributaries of the Stikine, with some bound for smaller local streams like Thoms and Pat creeks.) A new hatchery release site at Anita Bay should augment the fishery. Silver salmon arrive soon after and stay from late summer into fall, with a few fish available into November at the south end of the strait. Very good pink and red salmon, cutthroat trout, and Dolly Varden fishing are possible at times at the mouth of Thoms Creek in Thoms Place. Halibut are primarily caught at the outer ends of Zimovia Strait in deeper water, with the best action in early summer.

Good locations for salmon, charr, and halibut along Zimovia Strait are: Wrangell Island (Thoms Place, Nemo and Cemetery points, Pat Creek Landing, Bluffs/Shoemaker Bay, and Wrangell Harbor); Etolin Island (Olive Cove, Anita Point, Anita Bay, and Chichagof Pass); Woronkofski Island (Elephants Nose/Woronkofski Point); and Young Rock.

Stikine Strait

Location: NE of Etolin Island, 35 miles south of Petersburg.

Access: By boat from Wrangell or from Petersburg via Wrangell Narrows and Sumner Strait.

Facilities: A USFS public-use cabin is located at Steamer Bay.

Highlights: One of the most productive Petersburg/Wrangell area marine locations.

Main Species: KS, SS, BF

Stikine Strait separates Zarembo Island from the larger Etolin Island, connecting Sumner and Clarence straits near Wrangell. Serving as one of the main pathways for returning salmon and other species bound for the glacial Stikine River (and other area streams), Stikine Strait is one of the most productive Southeast fishing locations, especially for king and silver salmon and halibut.

Despite the fact that the northern part of the strait may at times carry a silt load from the nearby Stikine River (particularly during the hot summer months), the fishery does yield consistent catches throughout the season. King salmon, present year-round, are primarily taken in late spring and early summer when large prespawners cruise through the area. Following these salmon monarchs, silvers begin to show up in July and are caught into October. Pinks and sea-run Dollies are not particularly abundant, but can offer fair action, at times, when encountered in numbers near stream mouths.

Halibut fishing is good, with the best catches coming from the north section of Stikine bordering Sumner Strait. Good anglers can find flatties any day of the year (except during the January closure), but most success occurs in early summer when fish are in shallower water. Various other species of bottomfish are available, as well as outstanding crab, clams, and abalone in near-shore waters (said to be some of the best for the Wrangell and Petersburg area).

Hot spots for salmon and halibut include: Etolin Island (Point Harrington/Steamer Bay, The Bend, Chichagof Pass, Steamer Point, and Quiet Harbor); Zarembo Island (Point Nesbitt, Meter Bight, Fritter Cove, South Point, and Roosevelt Harbor); Vank Island (Mud Bay and Neal Point); and Woronkofski Island (Elephants Nose, Woronkofski and Reef points, Sunrise Creek, Point Ancon, and Drag Island).

WRANGELL REMOTE

Upper Clarence Strait ★★★

Location: Between northeast POW Island and SW Etolin and Zarembo islands, 50 miles south of Petersburg.

Access: By boat from Petersburg (via Wrangell Strait) or Wrangell (via Stikine Strait).

Facilities: Two Forest Service cabins: Steamer Bay on Etolin Island and Barnes Lake on POW.

Highlights: One of SSE's major marine fishing locations.

Main Species: KS, SS, PS, CT, DV, BF

Upper Clarence Strait runs along the northeast side of Prince of Wales, and southwest side of Zarembo and Etolin islands, down to Lemesurier Point/Meyers Chuck on the Cleveland Peninsula. The surrounding land is covered by dense rain forests, with a multitude of wildlife present. Frequented by boaters from the Ketchikan, Petersburg, and Wrangell areas, the strait is one of the better marine fisheries in Alaska, as it serves as a major migration and feeding corridor for salmon and bottomfish.

The strait is a wonderland of islands, reefs, hidden bays, and coves, with clearwater streams that have substantial numbers of anadromous fish species. Some of the more important drainages (see individual listings in the Ketchikan/POW section) include Salmon Bay Lake and Sweetwater Lake in the Kashevarof Passage area, and Thorne River in Thorne Bay, but fish destined for spawning rivers in Ernest Sound, Sumner Strait, and even the vast Stikine River system flood upper Clarence Strait in season.

King salmon, always a favorite and always present in the form of immature feeders, are at their best in late spring and early summer (mid-May to mid-June), when the large prespawners move through on their way to destinations to the east and north. Silver salmon, the next most sought-after species, are usually taken during late summer and fall by trolling and casting in the bays of the strait (especially those containing spawning streams). Schools of pink salmon may be encountered at times near the mouths of spawning streams as well. You can expect some sea-run cutthroat trout and Dolly Varden when fishing these areas for salmon.

Halibut are common, and are mainly targeted in waters of moderate to shallow depth during the summer months, though some fish are present in deeper parts of the strait year-round. Lingcod and rockfish opportunities abound, among the best in all of southern Southeast.

Frequented hot spots for salmon, charr, and bottomfish include: Prince of Wales Island (Point Colpoys, Bay, Ratz and Narrow points, Outer Salmon Bay, Exchange Cove/Island, Thorne Island/Whale Passage, Stevenson Island, Coffman Cove/Island, and Ratz Harbor); Rookery Island; Tide Island; Zarembo Island (McNamara Point, Snow Passage, and Point Nesbitt); Kashevarof Islands (Bushy, Shrubby, and Blashke islands); Rose Rock; Rose Island; Seal Rock; and Key Reef.

Ernest Sound

Location: Between SE Etolin/Wrangell islands and mainland.

Access: By boat from Wrangell via Zimovia Strait, or Ketchikan via Tongass Narrows and Clarence Strait; floatplane access possible in protected waters.

Facilities: One Forest Service cabin located at Frosty Bay.

Highlights: An area marine fishery of high potential.

Main Species: KS, SS, PS, CS, HT

Ernest Sound is bordered by the Cleveland Peninsula and the mainland in the east, and Etolin and Wrangell islands in the west. Situated within Tongass National Forest, the Sound is very scenic, with a multitude of bays, coves, and jutting points set among snow-clad mountains and forested valleys. Although it is not mentioned much outside of Petersburg, the Sound has great angling potential for a variety of sought-after game species.

The central and outer areas of Ernest Sound are regarded as a highly productive marine fishery for salmon and halibut. Trolling or mooching for king salmon is done year-round, but success rates are much higher in early summer for mature prespawners. Some of these monarchs eventually head up a few of the rivers draining into Bradfield Canal, but most continue on to other areas farther north.

With a great number of clear rivers and streams flowing into Ernest Sound and connecting waters, angling for other salmon species is highly productive. In midsummer, look for schools of dime-bright chum and pink salmon on their way to Bradfield Canal. (Anan Bay receives a tremendous run of pinks, and is regarded as one of the best locations in Southeast for the species. It also has trophy chum salmon up to 20 pounds or more.)

Silver salmon are present from late summer through fall, with a few fresh fish still available in November. The Sound is a good area to intercept these battlers, with larger concentrations of fish near the mouths of spawning streams. Halibut are available in deeper parts of the Sound, and fair numbers of cutthroat trout and Dolly Varden cruise the shorelines near salmon streams in late spring and early summer.

Some proven hot spot locations around Ernest Sound for salmon, charr, and halibut include: Peterson, Westerly, Easterly, Deer, Found, Niblack, Stone, and Onslow islands; Point Peters; Wrangell Island (Fools Inlet and Southeast Cove/Thoms Point); Seward Passage; Bradfield Canal and Cleveland Peninsula (Lemesurier, Magnetic, Eaton, and Watkins points, Vixen Inlet, Point Warde, Lemly Rocks, Union and Emerald bays, and Cannery Creek).

Harding River

Location: North Bradfield Canal, 40 miles SE of Wrangell.

Access: By boat or floatplane from Wrangell, Petersburg or Ketchikan. Boats use Eastern Passage and Blake Channel or Ernest Sound to reach mouth in Bradfield Canal.

Facilities: A USFS public-use cabin located at mouth of river.

Highlights: One of the more significant mainland rivers in SSE for sportfishing.

Main Species: CS, SS, CT, DV

This fairly remote river is located on the mainland near the head of Bradfield Canal. It begins in the high glaciers of the coastal range and cuts through a forested valley surrounded by 3,000-foot snow-capped mountain ridges. Its clear waters support strong runs of salmon and healthy populations of trout and charr, which get only moderate pressure from anglers.

Most visitors utilize the cabin at the mouth to fish the river. A small lake, Fall Lake, and barrier falls lie several miles upstream. The river below is swift and wide, with boulder-strewn rapids, riffles, and nice holding pools. It is there that anglers do best, concentrating their efforts around the tides.

For salmon, the Harding is noted for its good fall run of silvers and midsummer run of above-average-sized chums. Although perhaps not as potentially large as fish taken from the Keta River of Revillagigedo Channel, Harding's trophy chums can weigh as much as 20 pounds or more. A small run of king salmon also enters the river in early summer, but they are currently off-limits to anglers. Pinks are not abundant in this drainage.

As far as other species go, some resident rainbows and a few spring steelhead are available, usually offering only fair fishing, with better numbers of sea-run cutthroat trout and Dolly Varden present in early spring and again during the salmon spawning runs in late summer and fall.

Anan Creek System

Location: South Bradfield Canal, 35 miles SE of Wrangell.

Access: By boat or floatplane (land at headwater lakes, Anan and Boulder) from Wrangell, Petersburg or Ketchikan. Boaters access mouth via Eastern Passage and Blake Channel or Ernest Sound. Trail leads from Anan Bay to Anan Lake outlet (restricted to travel during height of salmon runs, June 15 to Sept. 15, because of bears, check with USFS for details).

Facilities: Forest Service public-use cabin at Anan Bay and one (with skiff) on south end of Anan Lake.

Highlights: An outstanding recreational area with excellent fishing.

Main Species: PS, SS, CT, DV, ST

Perhaps best known for its dense bear population, the Anan Creek system is also an excellent stream for sportfishing. Its fairly accessible, clear waters offer a wide variety of species in pleasant forest surroundings. There are two major lakes in the system—Anan and Boulder—with another dozen smaller lakes spread throughout the headwaters (comprised of a main and east fork). Salmon, trout, and charr are relatively abundant, providing anglers with exciting fishing in a small stream setting.

Emptying into Bradfield Canal southeast of Wrangell, the Anan receives a good number of visitors, primarily outdoor enthusiasts and photographers hoping to catch a glimpse of the area's famous bear population. (A platform has been built expressly for the purpose of viewing these creatures in their natural environment.)

But the fishing on Anan Creek is great. A big run of pink salmon enters the creek in late summer, along with a fair showing of chums. "Fish on every cast" action is common during the peak of the runs, with the brightest fish taken near salt water. Later on in fall, a run of silvers arrives and continues through October into November. For this species, the lower portion of Anan Creek and the mouth is best, but fish may also be taken out of the Anan and Boulder Lake inlets and outlets (as well as the connecting stream) as the season progresses.

Little effort is directed toward the spring run of steelhead trout in the system, though fishing can be quite good during some years. (Runs tend to be more extended than elsewhere, with good fishing continuing into June.) Resident rainbow are also found in Anan and Boulder lakes and inlet streams, while sea-run cutthroat trout and Dolly Varden are found throughout the system.

Recommended Lodges/Guides/Outfitters/Air taxis

Regal Alaskan Charters: Cornell Bean Jr., P.O. Box 503, Kake, Alaska 99830, (907) 785-3245. Boat charters, Keku Strait.

Waterfront Lodge: P.O. Box 222, Kake, AK 99830, (907) 785-3472. Lodging, car rentals, charters.

Tenacious Charters: P.O. Box 1542, Wrangell, AK 99929, (907) 874-3723. Wrangell area charters.

Kupreanof Flying Service: P.O. Box 768, Petersburg, AK 99833, (907) 772-3396.

Pacific Wing Air Charters: P.O. Box 1560, Petersburg, AK 99833, (907) 772-4258, *www.pacificwing.com*

Nordic Air: P.O. Box 1752, Petersburg, AK 99833, (907) 772-3535.

General Information

Alaska Department of Fish and Game: Sportfish Division, P.O. Box 667, Petersburg, AK 99833, (907) 772-3801.

City of Wrangell: P.O. Box 531, Wrangell, AK 99929, (907) 874-2381, *www.wrangell.com.*

Tongass National Forest, Petersburg Ranger District: P.O. Box 1328, Petersburg, AK 99833, (907) 772-3871, *www.fs.fed.us/r10/ tongass/districts/petersburg*

Petersburg Visitor Information: P.O. Box 649, Petersburg, AK, (907) 772-3646, *www.petersburg.org/*

Tongass National Forest, Wrangell Ranger District: P.O. Box 51, Wrangell, AK, 99929, (907) 874-2323, *www.fs.fed.us/ r10/tongass/districts/wrangell*

USGS Maps/NOAA Charts Reference

Eastern Frederick Sound: Sumdum A-3, A-4, A-5, A-6; Petersburg C-2, C-3, D-2, D-3, D-4; 17367, 17377.

Wrangell Narrows/Duncan Canal: Petersburg C-3, C-4, D-3, D-4, D-5; 17375.

Upper Sumner Strait: Petersburg B-2, B-3, B-4, B-5, C-2, C-3, C-4; 17382.

Keku Strait: Petersburg B-6, C-6, D-6; Port Alexander D-1; 17368, 17372.

Upper Clarence Strait: Petersburg A-2, A-3, A-4, B-3, B-4; Craig D-1, D-2, D-3; 17382.

Stikine Strait: Petersburg A-2, A-3, B-2, B-3; 17382.

Ernest Sound: Bradfield Canal A-5, A-6; Petersburg A-1; Ketchikan D-6; Craig C-1, D-1, D-2; 17385.

Zimovia Strait: Petersburg A-1, A-2, B-1, B-2; 17385.

Eastern Passage: Petersburg B-1, B-2, C-1, C-2; Bradfield Canal A-6, B-6; 17385.

Hamilton Creek: Petersburg D-5, D-6.

Swan Lake: Sumdum A-3.

Kadake Creek: Petersburg D-6; Port Alexander C-1.

Duncan Saltchuck Creek: Petersburg D-4, D-5.

Castle River: Petersburg C-4, C-5.

Kah Sheets River: Petersburg C-4, C-5.

Petersburg Creek: Petersburg D-4.

Ohmer Creek: Petersburg C-3.

Stikine River System: Bradfield Canal C-6, D-6; Petersburg C-1, C-2, D-1.

Virginia Lake System: Petersburg B-1.

Pat Creek: Petersburg B-1, B-2.

Thoms Creek System: Petersburg A-1.

Harding River: Bradfield Canal A-5, B-5, B-6.

Anan Creek System: Bradfield Canal A-5, A-6.

Regulations/Information

Most Petersburg/Wrangell waters are open to fishing year-round for most species (see Regulations for regionwide exceptions), with special regulations for Blind Slough, Gray's Passage, and high use and trophy cutthroat trout lakes. Always consult current Regulations Summary for Region 1, Southeast Alaska, or contact regional or local offices of ADF&G for latest information when planning a fishing trip to the area.

Douglas: (907) 465-4320   **Petersburg:** (907) 772-3801

Online info: *www.sf.adfg.state.ak.us/statewide/regulations/ seregs.cfm*

Stikine River

Petersburg/Wrangell Species

LOCATION	King Salmon	Red Salmon	Pink Salmon	Chum Salmon	Silver Salmon	Steelhead	Rainbow	Cutthroat	Grayling	Charr	Lake Trout	Sheefish	Northern Pike	Halibut	Ling Cod	Rock Fish	Salmon Shark	Fshg. Pressure
Eastern Frederick Sound	☺	R	☺	✓	☺	R		✓		✓				★	✓	✓	✓	M
Keku Strait	★	✓	☺	☺	★	R		✓		✓				★	✓	☺	✓	✓
Wrangell Narrows/Duncan Canal	★	R	☺	☺	★	R		✓		✓				☺	R	R	R	☹
Upper Sumner Strait	☺	R	☺	✓	☺	R		✓		✓				★	★	★	✓	M
Upper Clarence Strait	☺	R	✓	✓	☺	R		R		✓				★	★	★	☺	✓
Stikine Strait	☺	R	✓	R	☺	R		R		✓				☺	✓	✓	R	M
Zimovia Strait	★	☺	☺	✓	☺	R		☺		☺				☺	R	R	R	☹
Eastern Passage	☺	R	☺	R	☺	R		R		✓				☺	R	R	✓	☹
Ernest Sound	☺	R	★	☺	☺	R		✓		✓				☺	✓	✓	☺	M
Kadake Creek			☺	☺	☺	☺	☺	R	☺	☺								✓
Duncan Saltchuck	R	R	✓	✓	☺	☺	✓	☺		☺								☹
Castle River			☺	☺	☺	☺	☺	☺		☺								M
Kah Sheets River		✓	☺	☺	☺	☺	☺	☺		☺								M
Petersburg Creek			☺	☺	☺	☺	☺	☺		☺								☹
Ohmer Creek			☺	☺	☺	✓	R	☺		☺								☹
Stikine River System	C	✓	☺	☺	☺	☺	☺	☺		☺								✓
Thoms Creek System			☺	✓	✓	☺	✓	☺		☺								☹
Harding River	C	R	R	★	☺	✓	✓	☺		☺								✓
Anan Creek System			☺	★	✓	☺	✓	✓	☺	☺								✓
Hamilton Creek			R	★	✓	★	☺	R	☺	☺								✓
Swan Lake							★	R		✓								M
Pat Creek				R	☺		☺	R	☺	✓								☹
Virginia Lake System		✓					R	R	☺	R								☹

Legend:

- (blank) Species not present
- R Rare
- ✓ Found in fishable numbers (or light pressure)
- ☺ Good fishing
- ★ Excellent fishing
- LL Landlocked species
- C Species present, fishing closed
- M Moderate fishing pressure
- ☹ Heavy fishing pressure

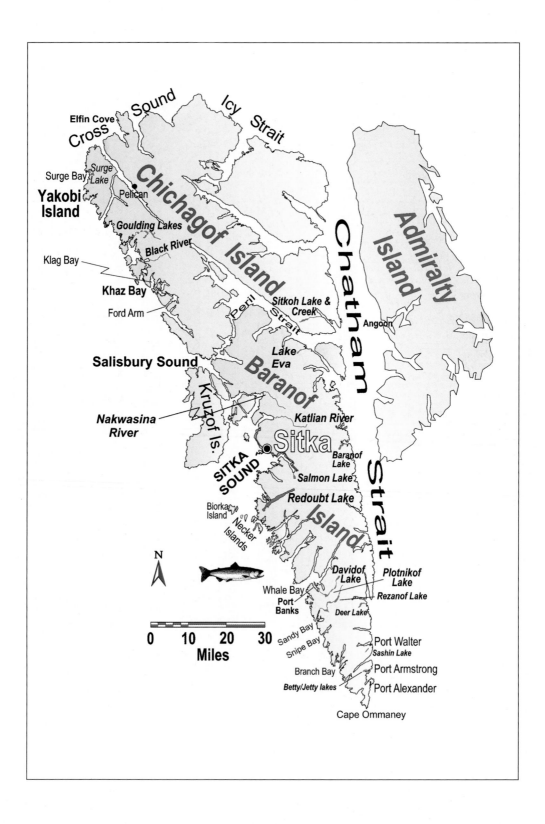

SITKA

The Sitka area encompasses some significant freshwater and marine locations on and around Baranof and western Yakobi and Chichagof islands. Important species include king and silver salmon, halibut, lingcod, rockfish, steelhead, cutthroat trout, and Dolly Varden charr.

Sitka, the main hub (pop. 8,000), harbors a burgeoning charter fleet that services the largest recreational marine fishery in all of Southeast Alaska. Most of the serious salmon effort targets the productive outer coast, where big kings—some of the largest in Southeast—and coho are intercepted on their way to spawning destinations in Alaska, Canada, and beyond. (Sitka catch rates for salmon are the highest in the region.) A considerable amount of this fishing is done around Sitka, Salisbury and Nakwasina sounds, and Katlian Bay. Sitka's strategic location also puts it in reach of some of the most productive bottomfish areas in all of Southeast, with record catches always a possibility.

A limited road system (15 miles) leads north and south along the coast from Sitka and provides access to some seasonally productive shorefishing (Starrigavan Bay) and a few popular roadside streams (such as Starrigavan Creek and Indian River). Species most often taken are Dolly Varden and silver and pink salmon. Area lakes (Blue, Beaver, and Thimbleberry) offer some fair to good fishing for rainbow trout, Dollies, and even rare brook trout and grayling. More remote and productive are the prestigious locations of the Sitkoh, Lake Eva, Redoubt, and Port Banks systems. (The Forest Service maintains over two dozen remote public-use cabins and numerous shelters at or near many of these better lake and stream locations.)

Daily jet service connecting to Anchorage, Seattle, Juneau, and Ketchikan, along with Alaska Marine Highway System ferries to and from the rest of the panhandle, put Sitka's superlative fishing within easy reach.

Sitka Sound ★★★★
Location: West Baranof Island, 580 miles SE of Anchorage.
Access: By boat or car from Sitka.
Facilities: Full visitor services are available in Sitka.
Highlights: One of the most productive marine fisheries in SE.
Main Species: KS, SS, DV, BF

Located on the west side of Baranof Island, Sitka Sound has one of the best marine fisheries in all of Southeast Alaska. Fronting the open waters of the North Pacific, with abundant forage and sheltered waters, it attracts feeding and migrating fish from offshore areas beyond reach of the rest of the panhandle.

Hungry salmon (all species common except reds) and charr cruise the blue depths of the Sound starting in May and continuing into October. (Feeder king salmon weighing 15 to 20 pounds are available any day of the year, but are most abundant during this time.) Mature prespawning kings bound for mainland rivers and streams near and far are commonly intercepted in early summer (mid-May into June) and may reach a hefty 70 pounds or more, while trophy coho (July into September) are another distinct possibility, with some specimens reaching 20 pounds. The king and coho salmon action is concentrated around the Sound's numerous islands, points, rocks, reefs, coves, and bays. Dolly Varden are taken off beaches and points around town, with major populations of these sea-run charr inhabiting areas in the northern part of Sitka Sound, such as Nakwasina Sound and Katlian Bay.

There is good bottomfish angling in the middle and outer bay areas, though many serious sport anglers (and all charter boat captains, as required by Sitka Sound Special Use Area regulations, June through August) now venture beyond the fringes to lesser-fished waters along the outer coast of Baranof and Chichagof islands. Halibut are present year-round, but are larger in size and much more numerous during the warmer months. Early and very late in the season, the outer waters of the Sound produce the best halibut catches, while late summer and early fall see these giants closer to town and in shallower water.

Westerly swells and southerly winds frequently make the waters of the Sound treacherous. On calm days, however, it is one of Southeast's most idyllic settings, with its many small islands and bays, and impressive, 3,200-foot, snow-capped Mount Edgecumbe, adorning the west side on Kruzof Island, across from Sitka.

The best way to reach the Sound's more productive fishing areas is by boat, although surfcasting is possible along Sitka's road system, from either Halibut Point or Sawmill Creek roads. When the weather cooperates, kayaking is a popular option for enjoying the inner parts of Sitka Sound.

Hot spot locations for salmon, charr, and halibut in and around the Sound include: Necker Islands (Biorka Channel and Biorka, Legma, Elovoi, and Golf islands); Saint Lazaria Island; Vitskari Rocks/Island; Eastern Channel; Sheldon Jackson Hatchery; Silver Bay; Kasiana Island/Western Channel; Middle/Crow Island; Inner Point; Hayward Strait; Magoun Island; Olga Strait; Lisianski Point; Starrigavan Bay; Katlian Bay; Krestof Sound (Halleck, Neva, and Whitestone points); and Nakwasina Sound.

Salisbury Sound/Peril Strait ★★★
Location: Northwest Baranof Island, 25 miles from Sitka.
Access: By boat and floatplane from Sitka.
Facilities: No developed public facilities.
Highlights: A favorite location of Sitka's charter fleet.
Main Species: KS, SS, HT, DV

The large islands of Chichagof and Baranof are separated by long and narrow Peril Strait. Less than a mile wide in places, the strait is an active feeding and migration route for fish bound for terminal areas in inside waters. On its west end, it opens into Salisbury Sound, a tremendously productive area between Kruzof and Chichagof islands that offers some of the best saltwater angling in the Sitka area. Both are favored locations for Sitka's charter fleet.

On the west end of the strait, in Salisbury Sound, the most sought-after sportfish include king and silver salmon and halibut. Kings up to 60 or 70 pounds are possible in early summer (from mid-May through mid-June), while feeder fish are available any time of the year. Behemoth halibut to 300 pounds are taken throughout the summer months. In late summer and fall (from the second half of August on), anglers are busy with the huge coho destined for nearby streams and lakes.

Peril Strait always seems to have some kind of fishing action to offer. Though the big, mature kings are not particularly abundant as in outside waters, feeders weighing 10 to 25 pounds are common. They are targeted by anglers in the narrower sections, in Hoonah Sound and on the outer edge at Chatham Strait. Two major fish-producing waters drain into Peril Strait: Lake Eva and Sitkoh Creek. Both have good populations of silver, chum and pink salmon, sea-run cutthroat trout, and Dolly Varden, as well as other game species. Sitkoh Bay is especially favored for mixed-creel catches.

Anglers usually access the area through the protected waters of upper Sitka Sound and Olga and Neva straits from Sitka, or by crossing Chatham Strait into Peril Strait from Angoon on Admiralty Island. Floatplanes can also be used to reach many locations. While there are no developed public facilities, some lakes in the immediate area have Forest Service cabins.

Hot spots for salmon, trout, charr, and halibut include: Fortuna Strait/Klokachef Island; Kruzof Island (Point Kruzof and Kalinin Point); Sinitsin Island; Scraggy Island; Kakul Narrows; Big Island; Baranof Island (Point Kakul, Saint John Baptist Bay, Fish Bay, Pogibshi and Elizabeth points, Outer Rodman Bay, Hanus Bay, and Saook Point/Bay); Povorotni Island; Chichagof Island (Poison Cove, Sitkoh, and Florence bays, Point Craven, and Morris Reef).

Salmon Lake

Location: West central Baranof Island, head of Silver Bay, eleven miles SE of Sitka.

Access: By plane or boat (to mooring buoy at head of Silver Bay) from Sitka; trail access from Silver Bay.

Facilities: Forest Service public-use cabin at lake.

Highlights: A great day trip destination near Sitka.

Main Species: SS, DV, CT

This small system located near Sitka is one of several popular local destinations that offer easily accessed, decent stream and lake fishing in a secluded setting of mountains and old-growth forest. It makes a great day trip for folks with limited time.

Salmon Lake is small and shallow (only about a mile long by a quarter-mile wide and 60 feet deep maximum). There are inlet waters at the southeast corner of the lake, and the outlet stream runs from the north end only a short distance before dumping into Silver Bay.

Most anglers fish this system for Dolly Varden and coho salmon. A considerable number of charr overwinter there, making for good fishing in the spring after ice-out. The coho run begins in late August and continues into October. The system also supports small runs of sockeye, chum, and pink salmon. Trout fishing is fair for cutthroats, an occasional rainbow, and a few steelhead as well.

Most of the fishing is done at the lake, targeting the outlet and inlet areas, or down at the lagoon on Silver Bay. The outlet stream is very small, with almost no holding water except right below the lake and at the mouth. A short trail leads from the head of Silver Bay to the lake and continues on to Redoubt Lake, about five miles.

Katlian River ★★★

Location: West Baranof Island, eleven miles NE of Sitka.

Access: By boat from Sitka, via upper Sitka Sound and Katlian Bay, accessing the mouth of the Katlian River at high tide.

Facilities: No developed public facilities.

Highlights: Southeast Dolly Varden charr fishing at its best.

Main Species: CS, DV, PS, SS

The Katlian River, one of Sitka's best streams for big Dolly Varden, is located at the head of Katlian Bay in upper Sitka Sound, where it drains a mountainous, heavily forested region of central Baranof Island. In the east, mountain peaks can be seen towering over 4,600 feet high, bearing ice and snow fields. Although it's not a particularly large river, the Katlian supports good runs of salmon and a population of trophy sea-run Dolly Varden charr.

Fairly shallow, with lots of riffles and some deeper pools, the Katlian has perfect spawning habitat for salmon. It receives substantial numbers of chums and pinks in August and a smaller showing of silvers in late September, peaking in October. It is common for these fish to stage off the mouth of the river for several days (to a couple of weeks) before moving into fresh water. Expect fair to good action for silvers and chums, but hot action for pinks.

Most anglers fish for salmon at the head of Katlian Bay, focusing their attention on the river, when Dolly Varden begin entering in fishable numbers around the first of July. It is a popular fishery, since many of these charr tend to be on the heavy side; two to four pounds is fairly common, though you may find an occasional lunker up to eight pounds. Look for trophy charr in holes, sloughs, or tailouts near spawning salmon on the lower river for best results. Fly-fishing conditions on the Katlian are ideal.

Nakwasina River ★★★

Location: Northwest Baranof Island, 15 miles north of Sitka.

Access: By boat from Sitka, via Sitka and Nakwasina sounds.

Facilities: No developed public facilities.

Highlights: Another premier location for Dolly Varden charr.

Main Species: CS, DV, PS, SS

The Nakwasina is one of Southeast's premier locations for stream Dolly Varden fishing. It flows into Nakwasina Sound on the upper part of Sitka Sound. Although the upper river sections are fast and rocky, extending high into the surrounding mountains (well over 2,000 feet), the lower section is ideal for angling. A fairly small river, shallow in many places, the Nakwasina is a prime spawning ground for salmon, but most anglers come to this clearwater stream for its healthy run of large sea-run Dolly Varden charr.

These bright fish, some as large as eight pounds (or more), enter Nakwasina starting in early summer and are present until fall, offering exceptional fly and spin casting opportunities. The best fishing traditionally coincides with the large return of chum and pink salmon (July and August), as Dollies feed heavily on eggs. (Egg pattern flies, attractors, and bright spoons and spinners work best, obviously.) A late run of big silver salmon, peaking in late October, enters the river but, in the Nakwasina, these fish begin their spawning soon after entering fresh water. Near tidewater or at the river mouth early on in the run is best for some fair to good fishing.

The river's banks are ideal for walking and casting. You can spot-cast toward schools of salmon and pick up the Dolly Varden stacked up behind them, especially in the deep holes on the lower river near salt water. (This is particularly effective on the Nakwasina, with many big fish taken this way.) Anglers focusing on Nakwasina Sound off the river mouth will find superb silver and pink salmon and Dolly Varden fishing.

Lake Eva

Location: Northeast Baranof Island, 20 miles NE of Sitka.

Access: By floatplane or boat from Sitka and Angoon, with trail access along outlet to lake.

Facilities: A Forest Service cabin (wheelchair accessible) and public shelter are located on the lake.

Highlights: Scenic, remote Sitka area lake destination, famous for good salmon and trout fishing.

Main Species: CT, DV, PS, RS, SS

A well-known, remote Sitka-area fishing site, Lake Eva is located in a particularly scenic part of Baranof Island, about 20 miles northeast of town. Snow-capped mountains loom to the southwest, and the blue waters of narrow Peril Strait lie just a few miles to the north. A small stream drains the lake and pours into Hanus Bay, providing passage for salmon, trout, and charr (along with a small spring run of steelhead). Although the drainage is relatively small, it is a very appealing destination due to its surroundings, closeness to Sitka, and reputation for productive fishing.

Only about two miles long, Lake Eva offers good opportunities for cutthroat trout and Dolly Varden. Though not of trophy proportions, the fish are plentiful and aggressive. The mouths of inlet streams are concentration areas in fall, as is the lake outlet in spring and early summer. The outlet stream is good during the annual migration periods. Its mouth at Hanus Bay can be productive all summer.

Salmon are popular with anglers visiting the area and can be caught from midsummer into fall almost anywhere in the drainage. The lake outlet, the outlet stream, and its mouth at Hanus Bay are the most productive locations. (Pinks are most abundant, followed by silvers and reds, with a few chums mixed in.)

The Forest Service cabin on the north shore is popular among a wide range of recreational users. Built for the physically challenged, many elderly and wheelchair-restricted visitors make use of its unique facilities to enjoy the great outdoors. A fishing platform is available (and a small skiff), and a public shelter is located at the lake inlet where the Hanus Bay Trail ends.

The lake can be accessed by floatplane or boat from Sitka and Angoon. Drop-offs are usually made by plane near the lake outlet, while boaters moor in Hanus Bay and hike the Hanus Bay Trail about a mile to Lake Eva.

Baranof Lake

Location: East central Baranof Island, head of Warm Springs Bay, 18 miles east of Sitka.

Access: By plane or boat from Sitka.

Facilities: Forest Service public-use cabin at lake; private hot springs resort nearby.

Highlights: One of the most popular cutthroat trout lakes in SE.

Main Species: CT

Located 18 miles east of Sitka on the east side of Baranof Island above Warm Springs Bay, lovely Baranof Lake is one of the most visited Sitka area lake sites, popular for its proximity to town, magnificent setting, adjacent hot springs, and good cutthroat trout fishing.

Accessible by floatplane or boat (via Warm Springs Bay with a half-mile hike up a boardwalk trail leading from the hot springs above Baranof village at head of bay), this deep, convoluted two-and-a-half-mile lake nestled in the mountains has historically been a very productive cutthroat trout fishery, despite its high use over the years. Although the fish are not anywhere near trophy size, they make up for it in abundance and beautiful coloration.

The lake draws its water from numerous runoff sources, the largest being the Baranof River, which empties into the southwest end near the Forest Service cabin. The short outlet stream at the northeast end of the lake cascades down an impressive barrier falls at the head of Warm Springs Bay, effectively preventing any migration of anadromous species.

Fishing is best at the west end of the lake, especially by the mouth of the Baranof River and along drop-offs from shore. Flyfishing can be especially productive during hatches in the warmer months, while ultralight spin fishermen do best in spring and fall working the deep waters of the lake with small spoons.

Because of the heavy vegetation and steep slopes, hiking the shore is difficult, if not impossible, so a boat or inflatable is the only real way of working the lake. (There is a skiff at the USFS cabin for anglers staying there.) The hot springs attracts quite a bit of visitation, particularly from the cruise ships during tourist season, so for serious anglers wanting solitude and the best fishing, the cabin and west end of the lake are the only way to go.

Sitkoh Creek/Lake ★★★★

Location: Southeast Chichagof Island, 35 miles NE of Sitka.

Access: By plane or boat from Sitka or area lodges.

Facilities: Two Forest Service cabins are available, on the west and east ends of Sitkoh Lake.

Highlights: One of Southeast's most famous steelhead locations.

Main Species: SS, ST, DV

One of Southeast's premier steelhead streams, Sitkoh Creek/Lake is nestled in a picturesque valley in the Moore Mountains of Chichagof Island, about 35 miles northeast of Sitka. The landscape is shrouded in thick, rainforest vegetation, with 2,500-foot peaks surrounding the lake. It is a small water body, about two-and-a-half miles long, and the creek draining it into Sitkoh Bay not much longer. But the clear and highly productive waters of the drainage have long been a major attraction for salmon and trout enthusiasts, with good chances to spot bears feeding on fish in the stream during late summer and fall.

The Sitkoh supports the most substantial population of steelhead in the Sitka area. The spring run (mid-April into May) of these large sea-run rainbows (averaging 9 to 11 pounds) receives the most attention, but there is a much smaller late autumn run as well. They are best intercepted in holding areas along the lower river. (The stream is brushy with plenty of windfall, but offers some classic fly-fishing, in spots.) Silver salmon, thick in late summer and fall (from late August through mid-September) are also best fished in the lower reaches of the creek or in the bay around the mouth (where, farther out in deeper waters, halibut can be taken). Anglers looking for less robust sport can find an abundance of cutthroat trout, rainbows, and Dolly Varden. Spring, late summer, and fall are particularly good times to try for these other species.

Access is usually by plane or boat from Sitka or area lodges. Float-planes can land on Sitkoh Lake or use the Chatham Seaplane Base in Sitkoh Bay. From the seaplane base, a rough forest road network provides access to the lake. For those accessing through Sitkoh Bay by boat via Peril Strait, a trail begins at the mouth of Sitkoh Creek and leads four-and-three-tenths miles along the north side of the stream to a Forest Service cabin at the Sitkoh Lake outlet (another cabin is available on the other side of the lake as well).

Redoubt Lake

Location: Central Baranof Island, ten miles south of Sitka.

Access: By floatplane or boat from Sitka; by foot from Silver Bay via trail.

Facilities: USFS public cabin located at the NE end of the lake.

Highlights: A famous Sitka area lake and stream location for salmon and trout fishing.

Main Species: RS, SS, DV, CT

A very popular lake and stream fishing location, Redoubt Lake is a clear, narrow, ten-mile-long lake in the heart of Baranof Island, a 15-minute flight from Sitka. Mountains ranging to 3,500 feet, topped with snowfields, hem the north and south shores, with their steep cliffs dropping almost vertically into the water. Small streams pour off the forested slopes, creating magnificent waterfalls. This area, considered one of the better spots around Sitka for salmon and trout, receives a fair amount of angling pressure.

Healthy runs of silver and red salmon arrive in the drainage in mid-summer and last well into fall. Successful anglers concentrate their efforts in three specific areas: the falls below Redoubt Lake—a temporary barrier for migrating fish, it creates a haven for spin and flycasting, particularly for tackle-busting coho and sockeye salmon; the lake outlet—a very good location, especially for schooling silvers; and the mouth of Redoubt Creek near the Forest Service cabin (northeast end of the lake).

Resident species such as rainbow, Dolly Varden, and cutthroat trout offer very good action, particularly in spring (May) and fall (September and October), but can be taken quite readily through the summer in deeper parts of the lake near the inlet and outlet. When the salmon spawn in autumn, target these magnificent gamefishes near the inlet stream. A few steelhead also make their way into the system.

Access is usually by floatplane from Sitka. (Drop-off near the channel connecting the lake to salt water, or at the cabin near the lake inlet.) Another option is to hike in via the rough Redoubt Lake Trail (five miles long) from Silver Bay. The lake can also be reached by small boat or kayak from Redoubt Bay through the channel into the west end of the lake. Some portaging is required for the latter option (a set of falls must be crossed prior to reaching the lake).

SOUTH BARANOF

Traveling south, Baranof Island's topography becomes even more rugged and dramatic. Long, narrow, curved fjords carve in from the coast, accentuating impressive, snow-covered peaks that rise abruptly from shore. Numerous alpine lakes feed streams that cascade down from these headlands into the dense forests and brush of one of the wettest zones of southeast Alaska (200 plus inches of precipitation a year).

Some of these lakes are barren, but many have trout populations (RT/ CT), with salmon seasonally abundant in bays and lower gradient feeder streams. The surging ocean waters and rocky, broken coastline provide perfect refuge for a variety of fish species, and the potential for great catches of salmon, halibut, lingcod, and rockfish is there for anglers willing to brave the challenging conditions along the open west side.

Many of the stream and lake locations can be accessed by boat, but most folks use floatplanes from Sitka to reach the more alpine lakes. Primitive trails provide additional access in some locations, and there are Forest Service cabins on a few of the more popular lakes. Other than that, a saltwater outpost camp at Whale Bay and a small sportfishing lodge at Port Alexander are the area's only visitor's facilities. Because of the weather and remoteness, many of the good fishing opportunities in south Baranof receive very little pressure.

Port Banks System ★★★

Location: Southwest Baranof Island, 40 miles SE of Sitka.

Access: By plane or boat from Sitka.

Facilities: Two Forest Service cabins are available at the inlets of Plotnikof and Davidof lakes.

Highlights: A famous Sitka area location for trout and salmon.

Main Species: SS, RT, ST

Situated within the South Baranof Wilderness, 40 miles southeast of Sitka, the Port Banks System of Whale Bay is one of the most scenic (and productive) fishing locations on the entire island. High mountain ridges and snow-covered peaks (some reaching 4,000 feet or more) surround two deep connected lakes (Plotnikof and Davidof), providing spectacular views on clear days.

Quite unique for Southeast fisheries, the Port Banks drainage receives a summer run of silver salmon and an extended run of spring steelhead trout. Starting as early as the Fourth of July and continuing into September, bright cohos enter the system in large numbers, providing outstanding action for anglers taking the time to fish and explore its waters. Although most salmon fishing takes place at the mouth of the Plotnikof River (below the falls right above tidewater), silvers may be taken just about anywhere within the Port Banks system later in the season. Elusive steelhead filter into Port Banks beginning in April, with ocean-fresh fish still arriving into July (or later) in some years. Early in the season, anglers do best near tidewater at Port Banks while, later on, action peaks at the outlets of Plotnikof and Davidof lakes.

Both lakes have rainbows, but Plotnikof is especially productive, with decent-sized fish possible, especially in spring and fall. (The outlets, inlets, and Plotnikof River are the best areas to target) Dolly Varden and a small population of kokanee exist in Plotnikof Lake.

Port Banks can be accessed by floatplane or boat (via Whale Bay) from Sitka. A rough, two-and-a-half-mile trail follows the Plotnikof River from tidewater up to the lake outlet. Another short (one-and-two-tenths miles) trail connects Davidof Lake with upper Plotnikof. Both lakes have a Forest Service cabin with small skiff.

Rezanof Lakes

Location: Southwest Baranof Island, 38 miles SE of Sitka.

Access: By plane or boat from Sitka.

Facilities: No public facilities.

Highlights: A more remote Sitka area lake destination with good trout fishing.

Main Species: SS, RT

The Rezanof Lakes system lies just south of Port Banks and consists of four interconnected lakes that drain into Sandy Bay. Access is by floatplane from Sitka. Rezanof, the main lake—long, narrow and deep—and Lonief (Gar) Lake—right above the bay—have the best fishing for rainbow trout of fair size. Best areas to hit are the outlet and inlet waters, especially in the spring. (The higher elevation lakes generally aren't ice-free until June—check with air taxis for current conditions before heading out.) Poor trails connect the lakes, and hiking and fishing the shorelines may not be possible in some locations (lower Kvoustof). Below the large waterfall, on the Lonief outlet at Sandy Bay, salmon and Dollies can be taken.

Other nearby areas with high sportfish potential on south Baranof are: *Sashin Lake* (RT), on the east side of Baranof, reached by short trail from Little Port Walter; *Deer Lake* (big RT; SS in outlet), south of Patterson Bay; *Betty/Jetty lakes* (RT) near Port Armstrong; *Branch Bay* (KS, SS, BF, with excellent SS, RS, DV, CT in feeder streams/lakes of lesser bays—-Redfish, Big Branch, Little Branch); *Snipe Bay* (KS, SS); *Whale Bay* (KS, SS, BF, and salmon/trout/charr in streams and lakes of lesser bays and arms).

Chatham Strait ★★★★

Location: Along eastern Baranof and Chichagof islands.

Access: By plane or boat from Sitka, Angoon, or area lodges.

Facilities: No public facilities; limited services available at Angoon.

Highlights: A major, historically significant fishing area.

Main Species: KS, SS, CS, BF

Long Chatham Strait separates Chichagof and Baranof islands from Admiralty, Kupreanof, and Kuiu islands. An historically important area for salmon and herring fishing, its productive and mostly sheltered waters support rich forage for abundant local fisheries, in addition to being a major migration route for salmon returning to spawning sites in northern Southeast. Terminal releases from three area hatcheries along the strait now significantly augment the fishing for king, coho, and chum salmon. Because of its remoteness, most of the strait doesn't get too much sportfishing pressure, despite its abundant angling opportunities.

Salmon fishing is a top draw for area lodges operating out of Angoon, Warm Springs Bay, and south Baranof. King salmon are available year-round, with the best action concentrated from late spring (late May) well into summer (late July), with fish up to 50 pounds possible (they generally do not run as large as fish in outside waters). Trolled and mooched herring are the most preferred enticements by area anglers. Chum salmon, abundant in the strait from early summer on, are taken incidentally or targeted by anglers in the know. (See saltwater salmon chapter for details on fishing saltwater chums.) Silvers begin appearing in the strait in early July and continue into the fall, with abundant catches quite the norm from local wild runs and substantial hatchery enhancements from Hidden Falls and Port Armstrong. All exposed points, islands, reefs, and mouths of bays (especially those with spawning streams) throughout the strait are good areas to intercept these flashy fighters.

Halibut and other bottom fish, like lings and rockfish, are abundant, but are at best pursued in the more open waters in lower Chatham Strait. There you can expect large, multi-species catches, and fish of trophy potential, though the weather and tides can create difficult and sometimes hazardous conditions. Streams and lakes along the strait add yet another dimension of fishing possibilities for cutthroat and rainbow trout, Dolly Varden charr, and steelhead.

Some of the more productive areas to try along Chatham Strait are: Marble Cove, Parker Point, Basket Bay, Morris Reef, Kelp Bay, Kootznahoo Head/Inlet, Chaik Bay, Whitewater Bay, Kaznyku Bay, Takatz Bay (hatchery release site), Wilson Cove, Yasha Island, Warm Springs Bay, Patterson Bay/Mist Cove (hatchery release site), Red Bluff Bay, Gut Bay, Little Port Walters and Port Armstrong (both hatchery release sites), Cape Ommaney, and Kuiu Island (Port Malmesbury, Pt. Ellis/Tebenkof Bay, Bay of Pillars).

West Chichagof/Yakobi Islands ★★★

The West Chichagof/Yakobi area is a remote, seldom-visited wilderness with an extremely rugged coastline containing many sheltered and interconnected bays, and numerous streams and lakes of high sportfish potential. The province of commercial fishermen, miners, and a few hunters, it has only recently been explored by recreationists, mostly kayakers, who paddle and camp along the protected tidal waters and occasionally sample the abundant fishing.

Access can be difficult and expensive. With good weather and proper timing for tides, watercraft from Pelican, Elfin Cove, Hoonah, or even Sitka can make safe passage through the gauntlet of big swells and countless islands, reefs, and kelp beds that guard this area. Floatplanes from Juneau or Sitka can land in the bays or area lakes. A limited trail system augments access in some of the more frequented bay and stream/lake locations. Save for a few scattered Forest Service cabins, there are no developed public facilities.

Salmon are plentiful in nearly all the major bays, with cutthroat and rainbow trout and Dolly Varden charr found in most of the streams and associated lakes. There are even steelhead in a few systems. Some of the more promising areas along this challenging west side of Chichagof/Yakobi worthy of investigation:

Picturesque *Surge Lake* (RS, SS, DV and RT) at the head of Surge Bay on west Yakobi, 80 miles NW of Sitka, barely above tide level but easily negotiated by kayak or canoe; *Goulding Lakes System*

(CT, RT, DV, ST), a series of lakes and connecting streams accessed by short trail from the head of Goulding Harbor, with a Forest Service cabin on north shore of Otter Lake; *Khaz Bay* (KS, SS, BF); *Klag Bay* (RS, SS, CT, DV), one of the most productive areas on Chichagof, containing lakes and outlet streams feeding the bay and adjoining Anna and Sister lakes; *Ford Arm* (RS, SS, DV, ST), another very productive bay with small lake at head and three-quarter-mile outlet stream; and *Black River* (SS, DV, CT), at the head of Black Bay.

Recommended Lodges/Guides/Outfitters/Air taxis

Baranof Wilderness Lodge: P.O. Box 42, Norden, CA 95724, (800) 613-6551, *www.flyfishalaska.com* Lodge-based guided fishing, eastern Baranof Island/Chatham Strait.

Alaska Getaway Charters: 1009 Halibut Point Road, Sitka, AK 99835, (866) 944-3474, *www.alaskagetaway.net*

Flyaway Fly Shop: 300A Harbor Drive, Sitka 99835, (877) 747-7301, *www.alaskanflyshop.com* Fly shop and Sitka Sound charters.

Fisherman's Inn: P.O. Box 8092, Port Alexander, AK 99836, (907) 568-2399, *www.fishermensinn.com* Lodge-based guided fishing, lower Baranof Island/Chatham Strait.

Chatham Strait Charters: P.O. Box 8044, Port Alexander, AK 99836, (907) 568-2227, *www.chathamstraitcharters.com*

Harris Air: 400 Airport Road, Sitka AK 99835, *www.harrisaircraft.com* Air taxi service, Sitka area.

Ward Air: 8991 Yandukin Drive, International Airport, Juneau, AK 99801, (907) 789-9150 or (800) 478-9150, *www.wardair.com* Air taxi, Chichagof, Baranof islands.

Whalers Cove Lodge: P.O. Box 101, Angoon, AK 99820, (800) 423-3123 or (907) 788-3123, *www.whalerscovelodge.com* Lodge-based guided/unguided fishing, Chatham Strait/Admiralty Island.

General Information

Alaska Department of Fish and Game: 304 Lake Street, Room 103, Sitka, AK 99835, (907) 747-5355.

Sitka Convention & Visitors Bureau: P.O. Box 1226, Sitka, AK 99835, (907) 747-5940, *www.sitka.org*

Tongass National Forest, Sitka Ranger District: 204 Siginaka Way, Sitka, AK 99835, (907) 747-4220, *www.fs.fed.us/r10/tongass/districts/ sitka/sitka.html*

Alaska Marine Highway System: 6858 Glacier Hwy, Juneau AK 99801, (800) 642-0066, *www.dot.state.ak.us/amhs/index.html*

USGS Maps/NOAA Charts Reference

Salisbury Sound/Peril Strait: Sitka B-3, B-4, B-5, B-6, C-3, C-4, C-5, C-6; 17323, 17338.

Sitka Sound: Sitka A-4, A-5, A-6, B-5, B-6; Port Alexander D-4, D-5; 17324-17327.

Salmon Lake: Port Alexander D-4; Sitka A-4.

Sitkoh Creek/Lake: Sitka B-3, B-4, C-3.

Lake Eva: Sitka B-4.

Baranof Lake: Sitka A-3.

Nakwasina River: Sitka A-4, B-4.

Katlian River: Sitka A-4.

Redoubt Lake: Port Alexander D-4.

Surge Bay/Lake: Mt. Fairweather A-2; Sitka D-8; 17303.

Goulding Lakes System: Sitka D-7.

Khaz Bay: Sitka C-7; 17322.

Klag Bay/Lakes: Sitka C-7; 17322.

Ford Arm/Lakes: Sitka C-6; 17322.

Black River: Sitka C-6, C-7.

Port Banks System: Port Alexander C-3; 17328.

Rezanof Lakes: Port Alexander B-3, B-4, C-3.

Branch Bay: Port Alexander B-3, B-4; 17330.

Whale Bay: Port Alexander C-3, C-4; 17328.

Chatham Strait: Port Alexander A-2, B-2, C-2, D-2, D-3; Sitka A-2, A-3, B-2, B-3, C-2, C-3, D-3, D-4; Juneau A-3; 17320, 17331-339, 17341, 17370, 17376.

Regulations/Information

With few exceptions (see General Regulations for Southeast), fishing in the Sitka area is open year-round, all species, fresh and salt waters. Various restrictions apply to certain areas like Sitka Sound (Special Use Area designation), Sitkoh Bay/Creek, Indian River, Starrigavan Creek, etc. Always consult current ADF&G Regulations Summary for Southeast (Region 1) or contact regional or field offices for complete information when planning a fishing trip to area.

Juneau: (907) 465-4180   **Sitka:** (907) 747-5355

Online info: *www.sf.adfg.state.ak.us/statewide/regulations/ seregs.cfm*

Sitka Harbor

Sitka Area Species

LOCATION	King Salmon	Red Salmon	Pink Salmon	Chum Salmon	Silver Salmon	Steelhead	Rainbow	Cutthroat	Char	Grayling	Lake Trout	Sheefish	Northern Pike	Halibut	Ling Cod	Rock Fish	Salmon Shark	Fshg. Pressure
Salisbury Sound / Peril Strait	☺	R	☺	✓	★	R		☺	☺					★	★	★	✓	☹
Sitka Sound	★	R	★	☺	★	R		✓	☺					★	★	★	✓	☹
Sitkoh Creek / Lake			C	★	✓	☺	★	☺	☺									☹
Salmon Lake	C	☺	☺	✓	☺	✓	✓	★	☺									☹
Lake Eva		☺	☺	R	☺	R		☺	☺									☹
Nakwasina River			☺	☺	☺				★									☹
Katlian River			★	☺	☺				★									☹
Baranof Lake								★	☺									☹
Surge Lake			★	☺	☺	★	✓	✓	☺									✓
Goulding Lake System						R	✓	☺	☺									✓
Khaz Bay	☺	✓	☺	☺	☺									☺	☺	☺		✓
Klag Bay/Lake			★	☺	✓	★	✓	✓	☺									✓
Ford Arm/Lake			☺	★	★	★	☺	☺	☺									✓
Black River			✓	☺	✓	★	R		☺	☺								✓
Redoubt Lake	C	★	☺	✓	★	R	☺	☺	☺									M
Port Banks System		LL				★	☺	☺	☺									M
Rezanof Lakes System							✓		★		✓							M
Whale Bay	★	✓	☺	☺	★	R			R					★	★	★		M
Branch Bay/Streams	☺	★	☺	☺	★	✓	✓	☺	☺					☺	☺	☺		✓
Chatham Strait	★	R	✓	☺	★	R			R					★	★	★	☺	✓

Legend

- Species not present
- **R** Rare
- **✓** Fishable numbers (or light pressure)
- **☺** Good fishing
- **★** Excellent fishing
- **LL** Landlocked species
- **C** Present, but fishing closed
- **M** Moderate pressure
- **☹** Heavy pressure

NORTHERN SOUTHEAST ALASKA

Northern Southeast Alaska encompasses the portion of the panhandle from Cape Fairweather to Frederick Sound, and includes Admiralty Island, the northern half of Chichagof Island, Icy Strait, Glacier Bay, Lynn Canal, and Stephens Passage. Five salmon species, halibut, steelhead, cutthroat trout, and Dolly Varden charr are the main fish found here. In some systems, kokanee (and even some rare brook trout and grayling) are found. Most of the fishing is done by boats in salt water, targeting bottomfish and millions of salmon that migrate to inland waters each year. But hundreds of freshwater streams and some lovely lakes, particularly on Admiralty Island, present abundant freshwater fishing options too.

A wide variety of services is available throughout the area, providing all types of fishing options for visiting or resident anglers. There are full-service lodges specializing in stays of a week or more, charter boats that do daily or multi-day trips, and flyfishing guides offering remote fly-out options. For the do-it-yourself angler, there are bareboat charters, skiff and kayak rentals, air charters, remote public use cabins, marine parks, and roadside angling in all the towns and villages. These services allow folks a chance to sample the true essence of a wild fishing experience in Southeast Alaska. Fishermen can easily spread out in the plentiful waters, find a stream, ocean reef, or pristine lake all to themselves, and enjoy world-class angling in some of the most beautiful surroundings on Earth.

Upper Lynn Canal

Location: Haines and Skagway area, 25 miles NW of Juneau.

Access: Primarily by boat from Haines, Skagway, or Juneau. Shore fishing possible from the road system in Haines and Juneau.

Facilities: Full services available locally.

Highlights: A popular northern Southeast fishing location for a variety of species.

Main Species: KS, SS, DV, HT

A very picturesque Alaska marine setting surrounding Haines and Skagway, Upper Lynn Canal offers good fishing for salmon and Dolly Varden. Bordered by the snow-clad Chilkat Range to the west, Takshanuk Mountains to the north, and Chilkoot Range and the Coast Mountains to the east, the Upper Lynn Canal area encompasses Chilkat, Chilkoot, Lutak, and Taiya inlets—four significant fjords within Tongass National Forest—and the coastline south to Berner's Bay. The many glacial rivers and creeks pouring into the north end of Lynn Canal give its water a greenish-gray tint. Though perhaps not as productive as waters to the west or south, upper Lynn Canal holds some great fishing. Numerous clearwater streams feed into the canal, all of which receive strong runs of salmon and charr, and the Chilkat and Chilkoot Rivers provide perhaps the best late-season freshwater salmon fisheries in Southeast Alaska.

Feeder king salmon are available year-round, and early in the summer (beginning the first half of June), mature prespawners migrate through on their way to local rivers. In recent years, hatchery production in Skagway has bolstered king salmon returns, sometimes resulting in outstanding catch rates, particularly in the last three weeks of August. There are several hotspots to try for king salmon near Haines: just outside of town along the Chilkat Peninsula, at Taiya Point, and along the rock wall in Chilkoot Inlet near the Katzehin River. The entire shore of Taiya Inlet can also be very good, all the way up to the town of Skagway, particularly when the hatchery fish move through. However, this stretch of water is often affected by winds that barrel down the inlet from the north, so boaters are advised to be cautious.

A strong pink salmon run arrives about midsummer, keeping anglers busy from late July through early August. Chilkat Inlet and Berner's Bay are the best places to catch these ocean-fresh pinks. Lutak Inlet and Tank Farm Point near the Haines ferry terminal are also good spots; knowledgeable anglers usually fish on the incoming tide and troll slowly or cast from shore with pink-colored lures.

Silvers show up in fall (from late August through late September) and are present until the snow flies. Near Haines, the best spots to intercept silvers bound for area waters are at the southernmost Chilkat Islands and the shoreline near the mouth of Lutak Inlet. Farther south in Lynn Canal, the southern tip of Sullivan Island and Point Sherman north of Berner's Bay are also productive.

Although present year-round, halibut are at their best in late summer. Fishing in the upper end of Lynn Canal near Haines and Skagway has declined in recent years, so anglers looking for a decent chance at these bottomfish venture farther south to the outer areas of the Chilkat Islands, and along the coast to William Henry and Berner's bays. Sea-run Dolly Varden are present and offer good action in early summer (June and July) along beaches and points of

the Chilkat Peninsula and Berner's Bay.

The upper Lynn Canal is perfect for day trips out of Haines, Skagway, or Juneau for the angler short on time or just wanting to sample a little bit of Alaska's renowned fishing. Chilkat and Chilkoot inlets and area waters are fished by boat out of Haines and Skagway, while the southern canal around Berner's Bay is accessible by boat out of Juneau. A public boat launch facility in Echo Cove provides the best access for Berner's Bay. Shore fishing is possible from the road system in Haines (Mud Bay Road) and Juneau (Juneau Veterans Memorial/Glacier Highway). Charter boats are easily available in Skagway or Juneau, but fairly difficult to find in Haines.

Chilkat River System

Location: North Lynn Canal drainage, 85 miles NW of Juneau.

Access: By car from Haines or Canada; Chilkat Lake also accessed by floatplane from Haines.

Facilities: Full services available in Haines and at points along the Haines Highway.

Highlights: One of NSE's prime stream fishing and wildlife viewing destinations.

Main Species: CS, SS, CT, DV

Emptying into Upper Lynn Canal at the town of Haines, the Chilkat River System is noted for fine late fall fishing for chum and silver salmon, spring and late fall fishing for Dolly Varden, and unique bald eagle viewing opportunities in a magnificent setting.

It originates high in the Coast Mountains of Canada and flows south to Chilkat Inlet and Lynn Canal. Quite braided, it cuts a valley between the Takshanuk and Takhinsha Mountains, and is joined by several major glacial tributaries, including the Klehini and Tsirku rivers. Since the river is glacially fed, the Chilkat runs heavy with silt in the warm summer months, effectively limiting angling opportunities to clearwater tributary lakes and streams. However, during the cooler months of the year from about late September to mid-April, the river runs semi-clear and is very fishable, particularly in some of the side-water sloughs. A large section of the Chilkat River Valley has been designated the Alaska Chilkat Bald Eagle Preserve. Thousands of these majestic birds gather each fall along the river to feed on a late run of chum and silver salmon.

The prime time to fish the mainstem Chilkat is late fall, particularly in October, as the silt settles and the river clears, revealing a heavy run of chum salmon. Many anglers prefer to target this species near tidewater on the lower river, as chances of catching brighter fish are better. An area along the highway by the airport is a favored chum hot spot, but fish may be taken just about anywhere, upstream to the Tsirku River confluence. Big, bright silvers are available at the same time and are present in small numbers into February. Also, in late autumn and early spring, angling for Dolly Varden is a favorite local pastime as overwintering fish begin to actively feed. A very small winter run of steelhead trout spawn in the Chilkat as well.

The outlets of Chilkat and Mosquito lakes are good for fall silvers and fair for reds. Cutthroat trout fishing is great in local lakes, especially after break-up and prior to freeze-up, but fish are present year-round. Pink salmon run in small clearwater streams of the

Chilkat in late summer. Stocked, but very small, grayling may be found in Herman Lake by Klehini River.

Access is by car from Haines or Canada via the Haines Highway, which parallels much of the middle and lower river, then follows a major tributary, the Klehini River, to the Canadian border. A few side roads lead to tributary streams and lakes, such as Mosquito Lake. The lakes are also accessible by floatplane from Haines.

Chilkoot River System

Location: North Lynn Canal drainage, 85 miles NW of Juneau.

Access: By car, a few miles from Haines.

Facilities: Commercial lodging and campground by the river and lake outlet. Full services available in nearby Haines.

Highlights: Another NSE major stream fishing destination.

Main Species: SS, DV RS

The most popular river in the Haines area, the Chilkoot offers good spring fishing for Dolly Varden, late summer action for pinks, and fall silver salmon. This semi-glacial river emerges from a series of ice fields high in the Coast Mountains above Haines and flows south to Chilkoot Lake, continuing on to Lutak Inlet. Above Chilkoot Lake, the river is fairly fast and narrow, with several tributaries from the surrounding mountains. The lower river, however, is wider and not as swift, with plenty of deep holes and runs. From the lake down to tidewater, the river is only a little over a mile long; most of the sport fishery takes place there. Boulders and rocks are scattered throughout the Chilkoot, providing excellent fish habitat. A state recreation site lies by the outlet of Chilkoot Lake to accommodate the considerable visitor load during the height of the salmon and charr migrations.

Like neighboring Chilkat River, the emerald Chilkoot draws considerable attention from northern Southeast Alaska and Canada anglers because of its easy access and beautiful setting. The fishing is often very good, with silver and red salmon and Dolly Varden charr the main targets. Silver salmon are taken all along the lower river, from the mouth upstream to (and including) the outlet of Chilkoot Lake. This late run of coho (in the first half of October) consists of large fish, with many taken in the mid-teens and some specimens of 18 pounds or more.

Good numbers of red salmon enter the river in two separate runs: one in June and July, another in August. Action for reds is said to be only fair, as the fish are usually finicky about anglers' offerings, but they have been known to consistently strike red or orange flies and sponge balls. Pink salmon also fill the river in late summer (the second half of August), and are much easier to catch. Dolly Varden are available year-round, but the best fishing for these sea-run charr occurs in spring (April and May) at the lake outlet, as the fish gather in large schools preparing for outmigration. Many charr are also caught in late summer and fall after returning from the ocean. Every year, a few stray king salmon show up in the Chilkoot from nearby hatchery release sites.

The Chilkoot can be accessed by car, and is just a few miles from Haines. The Haines Highway parallels the entire lower river and ends at the outlet of Chilkoot Lake. There are pull-offs along the road, with several trails leading to various sections of the river and lake.

JUNEAU AREA

A long with Ketchikan and Sitka, this is one of the major saltwater angling hubs for Southeast Alaska, with some excellent marine fisheries. Most of the salmon angling targets fish bound for important spawning systems, like the Taku and Chilkat rivers, as well as the hundreds of small streams in the region. Hatcheries significantly enhance local runs and create new angling opportunities. Halibut are fairly plentiful, and light-tackle enthusiasts do very well with Dolly Varden charr.

With well-developed harbors and boat launch facilities, and a rather extensive road system, Juneau has numerous opportunities for boat, marine beach, and freshwater fishing, although some of the roadside locations can be fairly crowded at peak season. Much of the saltwater angling is done only minutes away from the harbors at locations in Upper Stephens Passage, Gastineau Channel, Favorite and Saginaw channels, and Lower Lynn Canal. Farther afield, ventures as far as Icy Strait or Lower Stephens Passage are commonly made, often with spectacular results. The productive outer waters of Cross Sound, Chichagof, and Glacier Bay are more effectively accessed from surrounding towns like Elfin Cove, Gustavus, and Hoonah.

Favorite and Saginaw Channels ★★★

Location: North of Admiralty Island, 25 miles west of Juneau.

Access: Primarily by boat from the Juneau area to Shelter Island and "The Breadline;" surf casting also possible from locations along the highway system.

Facilities: Full services, including boat rentals and launch, available in Juneau, Auke Bay, and Dotsons Landing.

Highlights: Major area attraction for salmon and halibut fishing.

Main Species: KS, SS, CT, DV, HT

For several decades, the waters of Favorite and Saginaw channels between Admiralty Island and the mainland have been a major attraction for Juneau area anglers. Nine-mile-long Shelter Island creates the two channels that connect Lynn Canal and Stephens Passage. Huge numbers of migrating and feeding salmon and bottomfish move through every season and are harvested by sport fishing fleets.

The best way to enjoy this fishery is by boat (usually accessed from launches along Glacier Highway, from Juneau to Berner's Bay). Favorite and Saginaw channels are perfect for one-day trips out of Juneau. Boat launch facilities in Auke Bay, Douglas, North Douglas Island, and Amalga Harbor are the most convenient facilities for people trailering boats. Developed harbors with floating piers are located in downtown Juneau, Douglas, Auke Bay, and Tee Harbor.

Feeder king salmon are available all year, but the best action for kings occurs from the first part of May through early June when mature spawners move through. Silvers are abundant beginning late July through mid-September. Chum salmon arrive in great numbers in mid-July and are especially numerous in Favorite Channel near Amalga Harbor and Eagle Beach. Good numbers of charr and a few cutthroat trout are found along the beaches, primarily in the springtime and early summer when they feed on juvenile salmon (note that Dolly Varden fishing is prohibited in salt water near the mouth of Eagle River and in Auke Bay all of April and May).

Generally, the west side and south end of Shelter Island, and all along the mainland coast of Favorite Channel, are top locations for king and silver salmon, while mid-channel islands and reefs are great for halibut. "The Breadline," stretching from Tee Harbor to the Shrine of St. Therese, is a longtime favorite trolling drag, especially in May; many kings are also taken in Tee Harbor itself early in the year. Other favorite spots for early kings include North Pass (between Shelter and Lincoln Island) and Point Retreat at the tip of Admiralty Island. Later in the summer, good spots to try for feeder kings include south Shelter Island, Barlow Point, Point Retreat, Aaron and Benjamin islands, and Poundstone Reef. Some of the best silver salmon action is also found around Shelter Island, particularly at South Shelter, Favorite Reef, North Pass, and Handtroller's Cove. Lincoln Island, Lena Point, and Point Retreat are also very good for silvers.

Upper Stephens Passage

Location: North of Admiralty Island, ten miles south of Juneau.

Access: By boat and car from Juneau.

Facilities: Full services, including boat launch and rentals, available in and around Juneau area.

Highlights: Major area marine fishing destination.

Main Species: KS, SS, DV, HT

Another great location for boat trips out of Juneau, Upper Stephens Passage is a fairly narrow body of water extending from Shelter Island and Favorite and Saginaw channels in the north, to the mouth of Taku Inlet in the south, separating Admiralty Island from Douglas Island and the mainland.

Area fish populations are healthy and strong in Upper Stephens Passage, with a mix of natural and hatchery-enhanced runs of salmon returning to its semi-glacial waters. Feeder kings (10 to 15 pounds) are available throughout the year, with peak abundance in midsummer, while mature fish (20 to 25 pounds) are at their best from mid-May until mid-June. The prespawning, wild kings are bound for the Taku River at the head of Taku Inlet; adult hatchery fish are primarily destined for Juneau-area release sites. Large hatchery-enhanced runs of silver, chum, and pink salmon also flood the upper passage starting in July and continuing until October. Boaters and surfcasters can both enjoy these runs, with offshore areas producing best early in the season, and near-shore locations proving better later on. Although chum salmon are only caught incidentally out in the open sea, action can be quite good at the terminal fisheries.

Other species popular with local anglers include Dolly Varden and halibut. Sea-run Dollies are present along beaches and stream mouths through much of spring and early summer, and halibut and other bottomfish are taken in deeper parts of the passage all summer long. A few cutthroat trout are also available and usually taken while fishing for charr.

Anglers looking for fast action on short trips out of Juneau are well advised to look into the fisheries of Upper Stephens Passage around Douglas and Admiralty Islands. Locations along the shores of Admiralty Island and the nearby mainland are strictly for boaters, but several roads extending out from Juneau can be used to reach good surfcasting spots (Glacier, North Douglas, and Douglas highways, Egan Drive, and Thane Road). The abundance of hotspots in this area includes: Admiralty Island (Point Symons, Piling Point, Scull Island, Young Bay, Point Young, Stink Creek, False Point Arden, and Point Arden); Auke Bay and Point Louisa; Gibby and Georges Rocks off Douglas Island; the west and south sides of Douglas Island (Outer, False Outer, Middle and Inner points, Point Hilda, White Marker, and Icy Point); and Taku Inlet (at Point Bishop and Waterfall, on the south side of the inlet).

Gastineau Channel

Location: Between Juneau and Douglas Island.

Access: By boat and car from Juneau.

Facilities: Full services, including boat launches and rentals, available in and around Juneau area.

Highlights: A Juneau-area main salmon fishing location.

Main Species: KS, SS, CS, DV

Some of Juneau's most accessible and productive salmon angling is just off the road system in the brackish water of Gastineau Channel, which separates Douglas Island from the mainland. The channel has two completely different characters: on the northern end, from the mouth of the Mendenhall River to Salmon Creek, it is a shallow channel coursing through intertidal wetlands. Only navigable by boat at high tides, it shrinks to no more than a small saltwater "river" at low tide, lending itself to wade fishing by anglers who venture out onto the wetlands before the tide changes. South of Salmon Creek, however, the channel becomes a deepwater trench; fishing from a boat is more common here, especially at the southernmost end of the channel where it joins Upper Stephens Passage.

Wild fish, as well as tens of thousands of king, coho, pink, and chum salmon from the Macaulay Hatchery, pass through the channel each summer, providing steady action from June to mid-October. King salmon arrive first; the run is spread out fairly evenly from mid-June through July. They are followed by enormous numbers of chums, which fill the channel from July to mid-August. (The best time to fish for these underrated bruisers is the two-week period from the end of July through the first week of August.) Beginning in mid-August, silvers begin to show up, with peak catches occurring during the first two weeks of September and hot fishing lasting all the way into October.

The most popular place to hook into these fish is at the public dock near the Macaulay Hatchery off Egan Drive. It's a busy place, and for good reason—thousands of pounds of salmon are harvested here each summer. Note that snagging is legal in salt water in Alaska, and current regulations allow snagging from the dock (this may change in the near future). Snaggers also commonly fish the shore near the dock. Anglers seeking more solitude can find excellent beach fishing nearby at the mouth of **Salmon Creek**, just north of Macaulay Hatchery, or at **Sheep Creek**, three miles south of downtown Juneau on Thane Road. The best fishing usually occurs at lower stages of the tide when schools of cruising and milling salmon are more accessible. Wearing hip boots or chest waders is a good idea. South of Sheep Creek, saltwater trolling along the steep rocky beaches is very good, especially for king salmon in late May and early June. Dupont and Point Salisbury are the most productive spots, and anglers working trolling or mooching rigs commonly land kings over 30 pounds.

Dolly Varden fishing is also good throughout Gastineau Channel. In May and early June, voracious Dollies cruise the channel feeding on juvenile salmon and mycid shrimp. Small lures and flies that imitate salmon fry are effective; retrieve them fast to excite marauding fish into striking. Later in the summer, Dollies move into the riffles of Salmon and Sheep creeks to feed on salmon eggs. Egg imitations fished behind the sluggish spawning salmon can almost always trigger strikes from these opportunistic charr.

Fish Creek, a small clear stream off the North Douglas Highway, is another favorite in the Gastineau Channel system. There is a good run of wild pink and chum salmon here, with fair numbers of Dolly Varden present in the summer months, and a few cohos in the fall. What draws most anglers to Fish Creek, however, are the king salmon that nose into the lower sections of the stream in July and early August. These are hatchery fish that mill in the intertidal area before ascending the stream on incoming tides, providing one of Juneau's most popular fisheries. An old gravel pit, now filled with water and lined with trees, is connected to Fish Creek just above the intertidal zone; big kings make their way into here as well, and anglers prowl the banks, casting lures to cruising fish. People do well with a variety of lures, but spinners retrieved slowly are perhaps the most effective way to hook up at either the pond or the creek mouth. The creek mouth is also an excellent place for flyfishermen to have a chance to do battle with big, bruiser king salmon.

Three miles past Fish Creek out the North Douglas Highway is the rocky beach of *Picnic Cove*, another very popular spot to intercept king salmon migrating to Fish Creek and Gastineau Channel. From mid-May until the end of June, anglers line the shore of the cove, throwing all kinds of lures and rigged herring. Success can be sporadic, but when the fish are in, dozens of beautiful kings are taken each day. Most people who fish here agree that early-morning hours with an incoming tide is the best time to catch a big king.

Although many people fish the Picnic Cove / Fish Creek area from shore, boaters commonly troll these hotspots as well—especially when the kings are running in June. Slower-than-normal trolling speeds are best when fishing these terminal areas, with hoochie and flasher rigs almost always productive, as well as herring rigged to troll well at slow speeds. As mentioned, chum salmon are Southeast Alaska's most underrated sportfish, and the Picnic Cove area is an excellent place to find them. Blue or purple flashers with small pink or black hoochies are recommended by charter boat captains who know how to fool these tough fish. The easiest access for boaters is at a public boat launch facility just off the North Douglas Highway past Fish Creek.

Cowee Creek/Echo Cove

Location: Southeast Lynn Canal, 35 miles NW of Juneau.

Access: By car from Juneau.

Facilities: No developed public facilities.

Highlights: The best fishing stream on Juneau's road system.

Main Species: SS, PS, CS, DV

Situated close to Juneau at the bottom of Lynn Canal, and offering consistent fishing with easy road access, Cowee Creek and Echo Cove are two favorite locations among the local angling community. Healthy runs of three species of salmon, and charr, are present at various times from early summer to late fall.

Cowee Creek is semi-glacial, running clear in the winter and early spring, then becoming somewhat turbid in the warm summer months, and finally clearing again later in the autumn. A heavy run of pink salmon (the latter half of July) always draws crowds to this popular stream, but early summer chums (from late June through early July) and fall silvers (in mid-September) are also very popular. Dolly Varden move into the stream during the early part of summer (June and July) and yield good action on light tackle. A small spring run of steelhead trout spawns in the creek as well, and a few pan-sized cutthroat trout occasionally add to the creel.

Most anglers park at the Glacier Highway bridge and walk either up or downstream, but the lower two miles of the creek, which runs through an open tall-grass meadow in Point Bridget State Park, is also accessible by walking the Point Bridget trail. The trailhead is located just off the Glacier Highway approximately two miles southwest of the Cowee Creek bridge.

Anglers in the know find bright fish in the holes and runs near the mouth during incoming and high tides, and in areas farther upstream a few hours after the tide. Schools of fresh salmon can be intercepted at these locations on their way to the spawning grounds higher up in the valley.

Echo Cove, located just north of Cowee Creek at the end of the Juneau road system, is also popular with anglers, particularly for Dolly Varden in May and June, and in late July when schools of bright pink salmon migrate through. There is a public boat launch facility here, providing boaters access to the cove and to Berner's Bay and Lynn Canal. The Echo Cove shoreline provides easy walking, and anglers do well casting lures and flies from the beach. Small pink-colored lures and flies fished slowly can be deadly for pink salmon in salt water locations like Echo Cove.

Montana Creek

Location: Mainland drainage, Juneau area.

Access: By car from Juneau, off Mendenhall Loop and Montana Creek roads.

Facilities: No developed public facilities; full services available nearby.

Highlights: Another major Juneau roadside fishing stream.

Main Species: SS, PS, DV, CS

A favorite spot for local fishermen, Montana Creek is a small clearwater stream draining out of valleys near Stroller White and McGinnis mountains, not far from Juneau. It is short, only about ten miles long, with many riffles and some deep holes and runs. About two miles downstream from Mendenhall Loop Road it joins the silty Mendenhall River, originating from its namesake lake and glacier.

Its clear waters support healthy fish populations, with excellent opportunities for salmon and charr. Pink salmon and Dolly Varden are plentiful throughout most stream sections in July, while small schools of silver and chum salmon are encountered later in the deeper parts of the lower Montana. For brighter salmon, try the last few miles of water above the mouth; fish the second half of September for silvers and first part of July for chums.

Montana Creek is great for anglers who enjoy sight-fishing, as schools of salmon are easy to spot and cast to. Dolly Varden are commonly found below the redds of spawning salmon; egg patterns are very effective. There are three main access points for Montana Creek. To fish the lower section and mouth, there is a trail from the parking lot at Brotherhood Bridge off the Glacier Highway; for the middle sections, access is provided by trails leading up or downstream from the Montana Creek bridge on the Mendenhall Loop Road; and for the headwaters, anglers should drive to the end of Montana Creek Road and walk upstream. Some of the best fishing can be found by exploring the more remote sections of the stream away from these access points. For those with some spare time in or around Juneau, Montana Creek is good for a trip lasting a few hours to a day.

Turner Lake ★★★

Location: Mainland, 22 miles east of Juneau.

Access: By floatplane or boat from Juneau.

Facilities: Forest Service cabins are available at the west and east ends of the lake.

Highlights: One of northern Southeast's prime trophy cutthroat waters.

Main Species: CT, DV, KO

Turner Lake is a deep, clear blue body of water, beautifully situated among tall snow-capped peaks in Tongass National Forest, 22 miles east of Juneau on the east side of Taku Inlet. Bound by steep cliffs with cascading waterfalls, and surrounded with thick stands of spruce, the lake is certainly one of the most scenic locations in all of Southeast Alaska, noted also for its premier cutthroat trout fishing.

Although most trout are in the 10 to 16-inch range, some may reach three to four pounds, with a few as large as five pounds or even more. (The largest recorded trout from Turner was a six-pound, seven-ounce cutthroat.) To preserve this remarkable fishery (a three-pound cutthroat may be twelve years old), Turner Lake has been designated a special trophy cutthroat water with catch-and-release fishing only, and bait prohibited.

Kokanee, the pan-sized, landlocked sockeye salmon that provide the main forage for the lake's big cutthroat, are abundant in Turner and pursued as a sportfish year-round, although the best action occurs in late spring and summer. Dolly Varden provide additional excitement.

Fishing for all species is quite good overall, but the action is usually best just after break-up and before freeze-up, particularly at the lake outlet and near any of the waterfalls.

A boat is nearly indispensable for fishing the lake, as the spectacular shoreline is made up almost entirely of sheer cliffs that plunge directly into deep water; except for a few small places, wading or walking the shore is impossible. Trolling is the proven method for big trout, with successful anglers making sure their lures are presented just above the cold thermocline layer. Casting lures can also be effective, particularly near the downed timber at the lake outlet or

near any of the stream inlets. Small skiffs are available for use at either of the two the Forest Service cabins (see below).

Turner Creek, which is the outlet stream at the west end of the lake, is only about three-quarters of a mile long but it carries a large volume of beautifully clear water rushing over a mostly gravel bottom. Near the lake, there is a barrier falls preventing upstream movement of anadromous fish. Fishing anywhere below the falls is good for catches of charr and pink salmon. The best times to hit it are from about midsummer through September, with small spinners and bright attractor flies the best enticements. You will need chest waders to fish the river effectively.

Turner Lake is primarily accessed by a short floatplane hop from Juneau. Most visitors land near the lake outlet or on the lake shore near one of the two Forest Service cabins (one on the east end, one on the west end). Some anglers, however, choose to access the lake by boat via Taku Inlet, where a trail leads to Turner Lake along Turner Creek.

Icy Strait ★★★★

Location: North of Chichagof Island, 35 miles west of Juneau.

Access: By boat (or plane) from Juneau or Gustavus, Hoonah or Elfin Cove.

Facilities: Commercial lodging, guide services available locally.

Highlights: NSE's premier saltwater fishing destination.

Main Species: KS, SS, CS, HT

Icy Strait's cold, blue waters split Chichagof Island from the mainland and the Chilkat Mountain Range, bordering world-famous Glacier Bay National Park and Wilderness. Ten to 15 miles wide and 55 miles long, connecting Cross Sound with Chatham Strait, it serves as the largest migrational corridor for mainland-bound salmon in northern Southeast. Millions of salmon pour through to inland spawning streams from April to October. It is also an active feeding ground for halibut and other bottomfish, and teems with a variety of marine animals, particularly whales, birds, and seals, attracting substantial numbers of visitors to view and photograph them. The productivity of these waters is nothing less than astounding; Icy Strait is regarded by many anglers, guides and biologists, as one of the top saltwater fishing destinations in all of Alaska.

Most anglers arrive by boat, guided or private, from the Juneau area or the surrounding towns of Hoonah and Gustavus. Kings, silvers, and halibut are undoubtedly the favorite target species, with excellent action almost guaranteed. Smaller feeder kings are available year-round, but the larger mainland spawners show up in early May and entertain anglers until mid-June.

The late summer silver salmon fishing is especially noteworthy, having considerable trophy potential. (The current state record fish, a 26-pounder, was taken from Icy Strait, and many silvers over 20 pounds are caught there every season.) Halibut are plentiful and excellent catches of both large slabs and smaller "chickens" are taken, especially from mid-summer on into September when the fish move into moderately shallow water. (The former state record fish, a 440-pounder, was pulled from the bottom here, and flatties over 300 pounds are caught yearly.) Limit catches are common.

Other species not to be ignored are chum and pink salmon. A flood of ocean-bright pinks comes through in mid-summer, a portion of them plugging the streams flowing into Icy Strait, with the remainder migrating through to other spawning grounds farther inside the Southeast Archipelago. Just before the pinks peak in area waters, huge runs of chums arrive and provide one of Alaska's few consistent saltwater fisheries for the species.

Many parts of Icy Strait have well-deserved reputations as salmon hotspots. These include: Point Dundas and North and South Passages near Lemesurier Island, Point Adolphus, Pleasant Island (cohos, primarily), the "Homeshore" from Excursion Inlet to Point Couverden (especially for king salmon early in the summer), Point Sophia at Port Frederick, Point Couverden at the junction of Icy Strait and Chatham Strait, and the shoreline from Whitestone Harbor to Point Augusta.

Hotspots for halibut typically occur along reefs and drop-offs, or at the entrances of saltwater inlets and bays. Knowledgeable anglers examine the bottom structure, remembering that tidal currents strongly affect fish behavior. (Halibut and other bottomfish are usually found "downstream" of bottom structure, waiting behind reefs or near tidal eddies for feed to drift by.) Similarly, fishing the mouths of inlets and bays is usually more productive near the drop-offs and on outgoing tides, as bait gets flushed out into more open water. Keeping this in mind, some of the best places to hook into a big halibut in Icy Strait include: Mud Bay and Idaho Inlet, Lemesurier Island (especially the south side), Pleasant Island reef and Hanus and Spasski reefs, Halibut Island and Sisters islands near Port Frederick, and Point Couverden/Rocky Island.

Glacier Bay National Park

Location: 60 miles SE of Yakutat, 420 miles SE of Anchorage.

Access: By boat from nearby marine hubs or by car from Bartlett Cove or village of Gustavus.

Facilities: Full services available locally.

Highlights: World famous scenic destination with good fishing.

Main Species: SS, RS, DV, HT

Many visitors to Glacier Bay National Park will pass through the park headquarters at Bartlett Cove or visit the village of Gustavus, which is connected to Bartlett Cove by a ten-mile paved road. There are good saltwater and freshwater fishing options here that are perfect for the visitor who wants to spend a day or two angling while visiting the park and its surrounding areas.

Glacier Bay itself is a huge, deep body of water with many individual bays and inlets extending far into the Fairweather mountain range. It is especially noted for its tidewater glaciers and the raw, awe-inspiring scenery of massive ice floes and scoured rock cliffs that drop steeply into the ocean. The abundance of glacial runoff makes the water in Glacier Bay turbid and bluish-colored. Although salmon return to many of the streams in Glacier Bay, more productive fishing occurs outside the bay in nearby Icy Strait. An exception to this is in the springtime, primarily from mid to late May, when good numbers of pre-spawning king salmon migrate through the lower sections of the bay. As usual, anglers look for concentrations of baitfish to determine where they are most likely to find these prized fish. Hotspots include the outer shoreline of Geikie Inlet, Tlingit Point, and Fingers Bay.

There is also good halibut fishing in parts of Glacier Bay. Anglers

wishing to blend sight-seeing in the park with a chance at a big flatfish should concentrate their efforts on the shoals, reefs, and trenches in Sitakaday Narrows (there is heavy tide current here, fishing is best at slack tide) and near Young, Strawberry, and Willoughby islands. Beardslee Entrance is also a good spot.

The ***Bartlett River*** outside of Bartlett Cove may be the best freshwater stream in the area. Located in the park, it provides a quality fishery with a good run of sockeyes (one of the largest runs in Icy Strait area) pinks, and cohos. Some good-sized Dolly Varden charr and a few cutthroat trout are also present, and in late April and May a small run of steelhead also ascends the river. Accessible by either a two-mile trail or a half-hour kayak paddle from Bartlett Cove (only non-motorized boats are allowed in this portion of Glacier Bay Park), the best fishing usually occurs above the lower quarter-mile of the river where the water is strongly affected by the tide, running fairly deep with a moderate current at higher stages of the tide. Note that Bartlett Lake, east of Bartlett River, is not a fishing destination. It is essentially landlocked and no fish other than sticklebacks are known to inhabit it.

Flowing through Gustavus, the ***Salmon River*** is another freshwater fishing option; it is a low-gradient stream offering mainly pink and chum salmon fishing, but also has good numbers of Dolly Varden for light-tackle enthusiasts, and coho salmon in late August and September. The best fishing occurs below the Salmon River bridge; convenient access is at the public park adjacent to the Gustavus Community Association building. Anglers should be aware that much of the lower river passes through private property and should limit their fishing and walking to within the high-water level of the stream banks.

Cross Sound ★★★★
Location: 75 miles west of Juneau.

Access: By boat from Gustavus, Hoonah, Elfin Cove, and Juneau.

Facilities: Full services including transient small boat harbor, available in community of Elfin Cove.

Highlights: Along with Icy Strait, the premier NSE marine angling destination.

Main Species: KS, SS, BF

Located just 75 miles west of Juneau, Cross Sound is an angler's mecca, with perhaps the best saltwater fishing and marine wildlife viewing in northern Southeast Alaska. A fairly wide passage between Chichagof Island, Yakobi Island, and the Glacier Bay National Park mainland, it joins several large bays, with islands of all sizes scattered along its edges. Brady Glacier, a huge mass of ice dropping into Taylor Bay in the northern part of Cross Sound, contributes to the water's greenish tint.

Much of the area is within Tongass National Forest, and home to incredible populations of marine wildlife and fish. As the major entry into northern Southeast's inside waters (it fronts the Gulf of Alaska), Cross Sound, along with adjacent Icy Strait, is the largest conduit for migrating salmon bound for spawning streams throughout the region, and attracts numerous predators such as seals, sea lions, whales, sharks, birds and, of course, sport anglers.

Because of its unsheltered location, the area's weather can often be unpredictable, and anglers venturing into these waters must be prepared for the unexpected. Aside from that, fishing in Cross Sound can be fantastic for salmon and bottomfish. Anglers work the area by boat, concentrating their efforts on obvious lies and feeding grounds, such as points, tidal rips, and narrow passages for salmon, and shoals, reefs, and the bases of underwater cliffs for halibut and other bottomfish.

Feeder kings and halibut are present year-round, but are more frequently caught from spring to fall. Mature, prespawning kings arrive in late spring and early summer (from May through June), offering some of the best action in the region, while huge schools of silvers (mid-July through August), and impressive numbers of ocean-bright chum (first half of July) and pink salmon (second half of July) provide excitement in late summer. "Barn-door" halibut are active in the sound from spring into fall (May through September), as concentrations of these flatfish move into shallow water to feed. Fishing is outstanding, with many trophy fish taken and record-size catches possible. Good numbers of lingcod and rockfish are available as well; anglers should look for underwater pinnacles and reefs for these fish. Jigging with Buzz Bombs or Point Wilson Darts often produces a mixed bag catch of both bottomfish and salmon.

Most of the fishing for chinook occurs "outside," off the rocky and islet-studded outer coast of Yakobi Island. Popular and proven locations include the waters just outside Deer and Graves Harbors, Surge Bay, and Hocktaheen and Bingham Coves. Either trolling or mooching is effective. When the weather prevents travel to the outer coast, anglers concentrate their efforts in the more protected waters farther inside the sound. And from mid-July through September, when schools of cohos, chums, and pinks pass through the area, there is often no need to travel to the outer coast to find plenty of fish; anglers easily fill their limits in the waters near Lisianski Strait and Port Althorp. Locations such as Soapstone Point, Point Lucan, Three Hill Island, North and South Inian passes, and Point Wimbledon not only provide excellent angling opportunities, but offer exceptional marine mammal viewing as well.

Freshwater fishing opportunities are also available along Cross Sound, although they are not nearly as popular as saltwater angling. Freshwater anglers with fly and spinning gear target mainly pink and chum salmon and Dolly Varden charr. Some of the largest and most productive rivers in the area are the *Trail River* flowing into Idaho Inlet, the *Hoktaheen River* and lake system on Yakobi Island, and *Lisianski River* in Lisianski Inlet.

The quaint little community of Elfin Cove provides the closest land-based facilities, offering fuel and food, a small general store, and a good harbor for transient boaters. Several fishing lodges operate out of Elfin Cove, with facilities that range in capacity from 4 to 14 guests. Other anglers who fish Cross Sound come by boat from local communities such as Gustavus and Hoonah; a few come from as far away as Juneau.

Tenakee Inlet

Location: Eastern side Chichagof Island, 40 miles SW of Juneau.

Access: By boat from Juneau or Tenakee Springs.

Facilities: Limited facilities available in Tenakee Springs.

Highlights: An outstanding NSE fishing location.

Main Species: CS, PS, SS, HT

Located 40 miles southwest of Juneau and extending deeply into the eastern shore of Chichagof Island, Tenakee Inlet has long been a favorite destination for boating anglers in northern Southeast. Its principal attractions are the rustic, picturesque village of Tenakee Springs, with its harbor and available goods and services to cruising fishermen, including a public hot springs and the productive waters of the inlet, which provide outstanding salmon and halibut fishing.

For salmon, this is primarily pink and chum country; the numerous streams flowing into Tenakee Inlet support enormous numbers of these fish, and the ecosystem is driven by their presence. Spend a day on any of the streams in late July or August and you will be virtually guaranteed to see bears, eagles, otters, marten, and a whole host of other animals and birds, most of them drawn to the fecundity provided by the spawning and dying salmon. And, on a medium-weight rod, the bright, fresh salmon and charr that have recently entered the stream will provide you with plenty of action. By mid-September, decent numbers of cohos also arrive to spawn in inlet streams.

Most fishermen in Tenakee Inlet, however, fish from a boat and concentrate their efforts on migrating king salmon in the early summer, then switch to cohos beginning mid-July. The best trolling and mooching spots are in the outer waters of the inlet, close to Chatham Strait. Both East and South Passage points at the mouth of the inlet are the preferred locations, but when the weather gets rough, or time is limited, anglers also do well fishing the tide rips and points of land farther up the inlet at Cannery Point or at Corner Point east of Corner Bay.

Halibut are also found on the underwater shelves and reefs at the entrance of Tenakee Inlet, but there is also some very good fishing in the bays of the inlet, especially late in the summer after the salmon have arrived. Good-sized fish of 30 to 50 pounds are regularly taken in Saltery, Crab, and Seal bays, with leviathans over 100 pounds not that uncommon. Try drifting with bait or large jigs at the drop-offs near the stream mouths.

Lower Stephens Passage ★★★

Location: Between eastern Admiralty Island and mainland, 20-80 miles SE of Juneau.

Access: By boat or floatplane from Juneau or Petersburg via Frederick Sound.

Facilities: Forest Service cabins available at Church Bite in Gambier Bay, and at Donkey Bay in Pybus Bay.

Highlights: More remote, lesser fished NSE location with a variety of great marine and stream fishing.

Main Species: KS, SS, DV, CT, HT

Lower Stephens Passage encompasses the waters between the mainland and the eastern shore of Admiralty Island, from Taku Inlet south to Fredrick Sound. It includes the popular tourist destination of Tracy Arm on the mainland, and some important and productive fishing spots for Juneau-based anglers on daytrips. But the southernmost reaches of Lower Stephens Passage beyond Tracy Arm are some of the more remote and lightly fished areas in northern Southeast (accessed by boat from Juneau or Petersburg via Frederick Sound, or by floatplane from either hub), seeing far fewer fishermen than Icy Strait, Upper Stephens Passage, or Lynn Canal.

Anglers typically fish the northern portion of Lower Stephens Passage on day trips out of Juneau, but those who travel farther south are usually on a live-aboard boat, which can be chartered in Juneau either bareboat or with a crew, and usually mix plenty of sight-seeing with their fishing. Some of the best whale watching and marine mammal viewing in all of Southeast Alaska exists in the southern end of Lower Stephens Passage, which anglers should note for more than one reason. Not only do these awe-inspiring creatures add tremendous esthetic value to a fishing trip, they are also found here because the waters are rich in marine life and, where baitfish are found, so are gamefish.

As with most of Southeast Alaska, halibut, coho, and king salmon are the most sought-after fish in Lower Stephens Passage. Some of the more popular trolling drags close to Juneau are found off Admiralty Island at Doty Cove and Cove Point, and on the mainland shore near Taku Harbor at Grave Point, Suicide Cove, Circle Point, and Stockade Point. These places are particularly good in May and early June when king salmon pass on their way up the Taku River; later in the summer, they are also good for feeder kings. There is a state marine park in Taku Harbor, with a float for boaters to tie up to and an access ramp to shore.

Farther south on the Admiralty Island side, other good trolling or mooching spots can be found along the Glass Peninsula, particularly Station Point, South Island, Twin Point, and Point Hugh. Gambier and Pybus bays provide good harbors, and the salmon fishing off the mouths of these bays and near the Brothers Islands can be outstanding, particularly for king salmon. Halibut, rockfish, and lingcod are also found in good numbers here, both in the bays and near the reefs and islands in Stephens Passage.

The mainland side of Stephens Passage is dominated by major fjords that cut deeply into the steep coastline, usually with glaciers or glacially-fed rivers at their terminus. Port Snettisham, Tracy Arm, and Endicott Arm are the largest of these magnificent bodies of water. Typically, the fjords themselves are deep trenches of glacially-tinged water but, at their entrances where they open into Stephens Passage, there are usually islands and underwater shelves —places where knowledgeable anglers concentrate their efforts for both salmon and halibut. This holds true for the waters off Windham Bay and Port Houghton as well.

There are some excellent freshwater streams in Lower Stephens Passage, the best of which are found on the remote mainland south of Tracy and Endicott Arms. The **Chuck River**, flowing into Windham Bay, is a jewel of a stream, with heavy runs of chums, cohos and, especially, pink salmon. Dolly Varden also run thick beginning the first part of July, and sea-run cutthroat trout fishing can be excellent in the river and along the beaches early in the summer. The lower one-and-a-half miles of river is easily negotiable; upstream from there the river passes through a mile-long section of steep-walled canyon. Anglers exploring the Chuck River should respect the private property, originally part of one of the first gold mining operations in Alaska, that is located along the lower portion of this lovely stream. **Taylor Creek**, across Windham Bay from the Chuck River, is another good place to find plenty of light-tackle opportunities for charr, sea-run trout, and salmon. Fishing is best at the mouth of the stream where it empties into the bay. Windham

Bay itself is an excellent anchorage for boaters.

Farther south, the streams that flow into Port Houghton are equally productive. The **Sandborn River** in Sandborn Canal and the **Rusty River**, which flows into the salt chuck at the terminus of Port Houghton, are excellent fishing streams. The Rusty runs semiglacial in the summertime, particularly in warm weather, but it contains runs of all five species of salmon—even a few kings. Gravel bars are wide and the walking is easy on this river. In both the Sandborn and Rusty, wildlife is plentiful and anglers will have the satisfaction of fishing streams seldom visited by others. Each of these rivers, along with the Chuck River, also supports decent runs of steelhead in late April and May.

People who venture this far south in Stephens Passage will probably notice the ravaged landscape of Hobart Bay, site of massive clear-cuts made in the 1980s and 1990s on Alaska Native Corporation land. This is probably the only blemish in this otherwise pristine part of Southeast Alaska, but timber harvesters have jealously eyed the untouched timber in Port Houghton, and the Forest Service has started to plan timber sales for the area. Remember that when you pass through here.

ADMIRALTY ISLAND

The principal waterways of northern Southeast Alaska are defined by the geography of the mainland and the three largest islands: Admiralty, Baranof, and Chichagof. Called "Kootznahoo" or "fortress of the bears" in the local Tlingit native language, Admiralty Island is the largest of the three main islands. Its eastern shore is separated from the mainland by Upper and Lower Stephens Passage; to the south, it is bounded by the large inland waterway of Frederick Sound, while its western and northern shores lie on Chatham Strait.

For the most part, Admiralty Island is as unspoiled and lovely as it ever was; the majority of the island—some 950,000 acres—is managed as a wilderness area within the Tongass National Forest. This is the pristine environment that makes angling on Admiralty both productive and pleasing. The streams, lakes, estuaries, and saltwater shores are lined with towering old-growth forests and lush vegetation that helps support a plethora of fish, birds, and wildlife, including one of the highest concentrations of brown bears in the world. Pack Creek, a small stream on the northern end of Seymour Canal, is a notable Admiralty Island visitor destination. Each summer, 15 to 20 brown bears congregate here to feed on the heavy run of chum and pink salmon that ascend this small stream. Limited numbers of visitors are allowed each day to view the bears under carefully controlled conditions.

Most of the angling effort on Admiralty is concentrated in two general areas: along the island's northeastern shores in the vicinity of Juneau, and near the village of Angoon, which is the only town on the island. But even at these places conditions are seldom crowded, and virtually everywhere else on the rest of the island, angling in solitude is the norm.

As is typical throughout Southeast Alaska, salmon, Dolly Varden charr, and bottomfish can be caught literally anywhere along the Admiralty shoreline; it's just that some locations are better than others. (See the listings on Upper and Lower Stephens passage and Chatham Strait for a summary of proven hotspots.) Freshwater angling is notable on Admiralty Island for its abundance of lakes with excellent cutthroat trout fishing. Most of the lakes are found in the southern one-third of the island along the popular Cross-Admiralty Canoe Route (see next listing). Kathleen and Florence lakes on the northwestern side of the island also have good trout fishing, but the drainages in this part of the island are privately owned and have been ravaged by clearcut logging. If your preference is to fish in an unspoiled Alaska environment, it's best to skip these lakes.

Outside of the Kathleen/Florence drainages, there are rich and intact salmon streams flowing out of practically every mountain valley on Admiralty Island. Most of these waters are mere creeks, yet their fecundity can be astonishing; streams like these are the "heart and soul" of salmon production in Southeast. Some of the larger and more productive systems on Admiralty include Wheeler Creek at Hawk Inlet, Hasselborg Creek in Mitchell Bay, and King Salmon River, Windfall Creek, and Mole River on Seymour Canal.

Cross-Admiralty Canoe Route/Kootznahoo Inlet ★★★

Location: 50 miles NE of Sitka.

Access: By floatplane from Juneau or Sitka.

Facilities: Forest Service cabins and shelters available on several of the lakes; lodging, guiding services and canoe rentals available in village of Angoon.

Highlights: One of SE's great canoe fishing locations.

Main Species of Interest: KS, CT, DV, HT

The beautiful lakes, streams, and saltwater estuaries of the cross-Admiralty Island canoe route offer one of northern Southeast's most unique angling and outdoor travel experiences. Located in the unspoiled Kootznahoo Wilderness Area, many of the lakes in this part of Admiralty Island are connected by small streams and portage trails, linking Mole Harbor on the east side of the island with Mitchell Bay and Kootznahoo Inlet on the west side. The canoeing is outstanding, and Forest Service public-use cabins and shelters are available on several of the lakes, which can provide excellent cutthroat trout fishing. Salmon and sea-run trout and charr are available in the estuaries and lower reaches of the streams near salt water, providing still more variety. Nearby are even more remote and lovely lakes, nearly all with healthy populations of cutthroat trout. Solitude at these lakes is almost guaranteed, wildlife is abundant

and, combined with the pristine old-growth forest surroundings, it would be hard to find a more tranquil and esthetically pleasing place to spend a few days fishing.

There are two routes for people who want to paddle and portage the entire distance across Admiralty Island. Each begins or ends at Mole Harbor and Kootznahoo Inlet, but the longer route, which involves an additional portage, passes through **Thayer Lake**, a large lake with cutthroat trout and landlocked Dolly Varden charr. Thayer Lake is the only body of water in the area with private development on it; there is a small lodge that specializes in wildlife viewing, but offers fishing trips as well.

Apart from canoeing the entire route across Admiralty, many people enjoy relaxing trips to one of the many lakes in the area, particularly those with Forest Service public-use cabins on them. The more popular locations include **Hasselborg Lake**, the largest lake in the system, and **Distin**, **Davidson**, **Jims**, and **Guerin** lakes. All are accessible by float plane and all have good numbers of trout (from May to September); a few of the lakes also have some kokanee and charr. Hasselborg Lake occasionally produces trophy cutthroats of four to five pounds, and a few trophies are taken out of the other lakes as well. Fishing can also be worthwhile in the small inlet and outlet streams during summer months. (Warning: cutthroat trout in Southeast Alaska are a fragile resource and easily over-fished; regulations vary between the lakes—check regulation book carefully.)

Mole River, at the eastern end of the canoe route in Mole Harbor, contains good runs of salmon and sea-run Dolly Varden. Although it is located just off the canoe route, it is a remote stream that seldom sees fishermen. As with most streams in Southeast, the best fishing begins above the large tidal flats at the mouth of the river. The north bank of the river offers the easiest walking. Be advised that Admiralty Island is noted for its large population of brown bears, and remote, productive streams like Mole River invariably attract their share of bruins.

Flowing west from Hasselborg Lake, **Hasselborg Creek** empties into **Salt Lake**, a brackish body of water at the head of Mitchell Bay. It has excellent angling potential, with the lower portion offering sea-run trout, charr, and good runs of salmon (a barrier falls about two miles upstream from Salt Lake blocks anadromous fish from the rest of the drainage). Starting in July and continuing into October, red, chum, pink, and silver salmon move into the stream, with good action available for all species. Note, this is one of the few freshwater streams in the area that is regularly visited by fishing guides from the nearby village of Angoon.

Salt Lake is separated from Mitchell Bay only by "The Falls," a narrow chute of water that is impassable to boaters at low tide (canoeists can easily portage it). Salmon school in this area before entering the spawning streams farther up in the system. Mitchell Bay itself is part of Kootznahoo Inlet, a very protected body of water off Chatham Strait; with its many nooks and canals, it offers good action for salmon. Feeder king salmon and halibut are available in the outer inlet near Angoon and Chatham. Kootznahoo Inlet is a wonderful paddling destination, but parts of it have very tricky and dangerous tidal currents, so extreme caution is advised if traversing these waters by kayak or small powerboat. It's best to travel through the narrowest canals during high slack tide.

The village of Angoon, at the west end of Kootznahoo Inlet, is used by many people to access the fishing in the inlet, or to start or finish a cross-Admiralty canoe trip. From Angoon, there are daily air connections to Juneau, and ferries from the Alaska Marine Highway system come to town once or twice a week. A well-run fishing lodge operates there and offers guided or unguided trips into Kootznahoo Inlet and Mitchell Bay, and to the excellent saltwater salmon and halibut angling just outside the inlet in Chatham Strait.

Coho and chinook salmon are particularly abundant in Chatham Strait near Angoon. Fishermen with boats seldom need to venture far from the trolling drags near town; the stretch of water from Danger Point, at the entrance of Kootznahoo Inlet, to the western shore of Killisnoo Island is an excellent spot. Peak season for "feeder" chinook is from mid-June through August, while large schools of cohos pass through from mid-July through September.

Recommended Lodges/Guides/Outfitters/Air Taxis

Haines Tackle Company: (Carmine DeFranco, owner) Box 765, Haines AK 99827, (907) 766-2255.

Cross Sound Lodge: (Elfin Cove), P.O. Box 1167, Haines, AK 99827, (800) 323-5346, *www.crosssoundlodge.com*

Icy Strait Adventures: P.O. Box 13, Elfin Cove, Alaska 99825, (907) 239-2255, *www.icystraitadventures.com*

Shearwater Lodge & Charters: P.O. Box 57 Elfin Cove, AK 99825, (907) 239-2223.

Gustavus Marine Charter: P.O. Box 81, Gustavus, AK 99826, (907) 697-2233, *www.gustavusmarinecharters.com*

Thayer Lake Lodge: P.O. Box 8897, Ketchikan, AK 99901, (907)247-8897, *www.alaskabearviewing.com* Admiralty Island fishing and bear viewing.

Whaler's Cove Lodge: P.O. Box 101, Angoon, AK 99820, (800) 423-3123, *www.whalerscovelodge.com* Guided/unguided fishing.

Glacier Bay Country Inn: P.O. Box 5, Gustavus, AK 99826, (800) 628-0912, *www.glacierbayalaska.com* Gustavus lodging and fishing.

Bear Creek Outfitters: 9723 Trappers Lane, Juneau, AK 99801, (907) 789-3914, *www.flyfishsoutheast.com* Fly-out flyfishing.

Juneau Flyfishing Goods: 175 South Franklin Street, Juneau, AK 99801, (907) 586-3754, *www.juneauflyfishinggoods.com*

Alaska Boat and Kayak: 6105 Thame Rd., Juneau, AK 99801, (907) 586-8220, *www.juneaukayak.com* Boat and kayak rentals.

Silver King Marine Charters: P.O. Box 210003, Auke Bay, AK 99821, (907) 789-0165. Juneau charters.

Auke Bay Sportfishing and Sightseeing Charters: 9111 Miner Court, Juneau, AK 99801, (800) 586-6945, *www.experience alaska.com*

Flywater Adventures: P.O. Box 33245, Juneau, AK 99803, (907) 789-5977, *www.flywateradventures.com* Marine and freshwater flyfishing expeditions, NSE.

Ward Air: 8991 Yandukin Drive, Juneau, AK 99801, (800) 478-9150 or (907) 789-9150, *www.wardair.com*

Nordic Tugs: P.O. Box 020006, Juneau, AK 99802, (907) 586-2844. Bareboat charters.

General information

Alaska Department of Fish & Game: Sport Fish Division, P.O. Box 240020, Douglas, AK 99824-0020, (907) 465-4270.

Tongass National Forest, Juneau Ranger District: 8465 Old Dairy Road, Juneau, AK 99801-8041, (907) 586-8800. *www.fs.fed.us/ r10/tongass/*

Admiralty Island National Monument: 8461 Old Dairy Road, Juneau, AK 99801-8041, (907) 586-8790, *www.fs.fed.us/r10/tongass/districts/admiralty/*

Glacier Bay National Park and Preserve: P.O. Box 140, Gustavus, AK 99826-0140, (907) 697-2230, *www.nps.gov/glba/*

Haines Visitor Bureau: P.O. Box 530, Haines, AK 99827, (800) 458-3579 or (907) 766-2234, *www.haines,ak.us/*

Juneau Convention & Visitor Bureau: One Sealaska Plaza, #305, Juneau, AK 99801, (800) 587-2201, *www.traveljuneau.com*

USGS Maps/NOAA Charts Reference

Cross Sound: Mount Fairweather A-1, A-2, A-3, B-2, B-3; 17302.

Icy Strait: Mount Fairweather A-1, B-1, B-2; Juneau A-3, A-4, A-5, A-6, B-4, B-5, B-6; 17302, 17316.

Glacier Bay: Juneau B-5, B-6, C-5, C-6, D-6; Mt. Fairweather C-1, C-2, D-1, D-2, D-3, D-4; Skagway A-5, A-6; 17318.

Bartlett River: Juneau B-6, C-6.

Salmon River: Juneau B-6.

Upper Lynn Canal: Skagway A-1, A-2, B-1, B-2; 17317.

Chilkat River System: Skagway A-2, A-3, B-2, B-3, B-4, C-3, C-4.

Chilkoot River System: Skagway B-2, B-3, C-3.

Gastineau Channel: Juneau A-1, B-2; 17315.

Favorite/Saginaw Channels: Juneau B-3, C-3; 17316.

Cowee Creek/Echo Cove: Juneau C-3.

Montana Creek: Juneau B-2, B-3.

Turner Lake: Taku River B-6.

Tenakee Inlet: Sitka D-3, D-4, D-5, D-6, C-4, C-5; 17320.

Stephens Passage: Juneau A-1, A-2, A-3, B-1, B-2, B-3; Taku River A-6; Sitka B-1, C-1, D-1; Sumdum B-4, B-5, B-6, C-3, C-4, C-5, C-6, D-4, D-5, D-6; 17300, 17360.

Chuck River: Sumdum C-4, C-5.

Rusty River: Sumdum B-4.

Sandborn River: Sumdum A-4.

Cross-Admiralty Island Canoe Route/Kootznahoo Inlet: Sitka B-1, B-2, C-1, C-2, D-1, D-2.

Regulations/Information

Special regulations setting seasons, size/bag limits, open waters, fishing methods, etc., apply to many NSE waters—fresh and salt. There are regionwide seasonal restrictions on halibut and lingcod fishing and a ban on king salmon fishing in fresh water. Consult current Regulations Summary for Region I, SE Alaska or contact ADF&G regional (Douglas) or field offices for complete information.

Douglas: (907) 465-4270   **Haines:** (907) 766-3638

Online info: *www.sf.adfg.state.ak.us/statewide/regulations/seregs.cfm*

Northern Southeast Species

LOCATION	King Salmon	Red Salmon	Pink Salmon	Chum Salmon	Silver Salmon	Steelhead	Rainbow	Cutthroat	Charr	Grayling	Lake Trout	Sheefish	Northern Pike	Halibut	Ling Cod	Rock Fish	Salmon Shark	Fshg. Pressure
Glacier Bay	☺	R	✓	✓	☺	R			✓					☺	✓	✓	✓	M
Bartlett River		☺	☺	✓	★	✓		✓	☺									✓
Salmon River		R	☺	☺	✓	R		R	☺									M
Cross Sound	★	R	★	★	★	R		R	✓					★	★	★	☺	M
Icy Strait	★	R	★	★	★	R		R	✓					★	★	★	☺	M
Upper Lynn Canal	☺	R	☺	☺	☺	R		R	✓						R	✓	R	☹
Chilkat River System	C	✓	★	★	☺	R		☺	★									☹
Chilkoot River System	C	☺	☺	R	☺	R		R	★									☹
Gastineau Channel	★	R	★	★	★	R		R	☺					✓	R	R	R	☹
Favorite/Saginaw Channels	★	R	★	★	★	R		R	☺					☺	R	✓	R	☹
Cowee Creek/Echo Cove	C	R	★	★	☺	✓		✓	☺									☹
Montana Creek	C	R	★	☺	☺	R		R	★									M
Upper Stephans Passage	★	R	★	★	★	R		R	☺					★	☺	☺	R	M
Lower Stephans Passage	★	R	★	★	★	R		R	☺					★	☺	☺	☺	✓
Chuck River	C	R	★	★	★	✓		★	★									✓
Rusty River	C	R	★	★	☺	✓		✓	☺									✓
Sandborn River	C	R	★	★	☺	✓		✓	☺									✓
Turner Lake		LL	☺					✓	★	☺								M
Tenakee Inlet	✓	R	★	★	☺	R		R	☺					☺	R	✓	R	✓
Cross Admiralty Canoe Route	R	✓	☺	☺	☺	R		★	☺									✓

Legend:

	Not present	**LL**	Landlocked species
R	Rare	**C**	Present, but fishing closed
✓	Fishable numbers (or light pressure)	**M**	Moderate pressure
☺	Good fishing	☹	Heavy pressure
★	Excellent fishing		

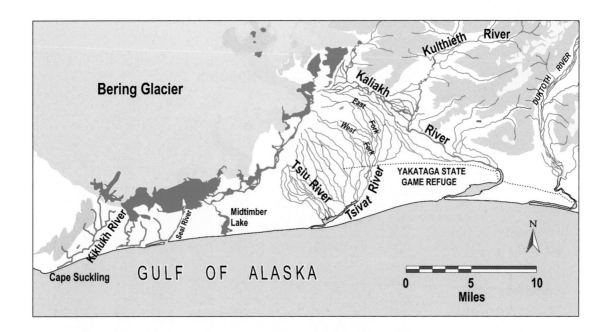

NORTH GULF COAST/YAKUTAT

Between Cape Suckling and Glacier Bay, the wild and stormy North Gulf Coast beckons with some fabulous and sometimes unexploited fishing possibilities. A remote expanse of enormous glaciers and colossal mountains (the St. Elias Range, with peaks up to 19,850 feet) that drop abruptly to coastal flatlands and deserted beaches, this area, with its short, braided streams, surprisingly holds some of Alaska's finest steelhead and silver salmon fishing. Except for the immediate area surrounding Yakutat and the famed Kiklukh and Tsiu systems, it receives comparatively little visitation, despite its awesome sportfishing potential.

Most of these locations are extremely remote and difficult to reach, requiring expensive trips by small plane or boat from Cordova or Yakutat. Highly unpredictable, potentially extreme weather complicates logistics. But the species available include trophy silver salmon, locally abundant steelhead, cutthroat and rainbow trout, sockeyes, Dolly Varden and, in protected inshore waters, even some king salmon and bottomfish. The phenomenal angling potential combined with spellbinding scenery makes this a paradise for the adventure angler.

Kiklukh/Tsiu/Tsivat Rivers ★★★★
Location: North Gulf of Alaska, 125-145 miles NW of Yakutat.
Access: By wheelplane from Cordova or Yakutat to beach strips or sand/gravel bars by rivers.

Facilities: Lodging, guided fishing available locally.
Highlights: Some of the Gulf Coast's finest silver salmon streams.
Main Species: SS, CT

One of the Gulf Coast's most productive areas lies in the flats just east of Cape Suckling, in an extensive system of short, braided, gravelly streams and ponds rising in runoff and upwellings from the enormous Bering Glacier. Lying well off the beaten path, these streams are usually reached by small plane from Cordova, landing along beaches at the mouth. Despite the expense and difficulty of access, they are especially noteworthy for their prolific salmon runs and great fly-fishing.

The **Kiklukh**, also known as Eightmile Creek, is one of them. It begins in and above the Suckling Hills and flows through extensive marshland in its upper sections before reaching timber and gravel beaches surrounding its terminus. Strong runs of silver salmon flood in every fall from the Gulf Coast, and the river's clear, rushing waters and long runs make perfect conditions for sight fishing these sea-bright brutes. The lower river is especially noted for flyfishing. Earlier in the season, the Kiklukh River also has a good showing of sea-run cutthroat trout in the 10 to 20-inch range. A short way east lies the **Tsiu/Tsivat** system, an even more notable Gulf Coast silver salmon destination. This expansive, braided drainage in the heart of Yakataga State Game Refuge includes at least a dozen tributary streams and numerous small ponds that create perfect spawning habitat for major runs of silver salmon. Phenomenally productive for its size, it has been hailed as one of the best coho fishing locations in Alaska by area guides, writers, and biologists.

The shallow **Tsiu** rushes from upwellings in its headwaters through forests and open meadows until joining the **Tsivat** in a giant lagoon popular for fly fishing. There, the vegetation begins to disappear, with the final two miles of the river winding through extensive flats resembling the Sahara Desert, complete with sand dunes—certainly not your typical Alaska stream surroundings.

The run begins in August, peaks during September, and tapers off in October. At the peak of the influx, these waters churn with bright, aggressive coho that like to hit big surface patterns. A much smaller run of red salmon earlier in the season provides good action for anglers in the know. Bright yarn and sparse bucktail flies are the most productive enticements to use.

While salmon occupy most of the thoughts and energy of anglers visiting the Tsiu, the drainage also receives scantily fished spring and fall runs of steelhead, while the Tsivat has resident rainbows and cutthroat trout.

Both the Kikhlukh and Tsiu/Tsivat Rivers have remote fishing camps with full guide services. Anglers from as far away as Anchorage commonly fly in for a day's fishing on these renowned streams.

Kaliakh River System ★★★

Location: North Gulf of Alaska, 115 miles NW of Yakutat.

Access: By plane from Cordova or Yakutat.

Facilities: No developed public facilities.

Highlights: Out-of-the-way Gulf Coast drainage with outstanding fishing potential.

Main Species: SS, CT

The Kaliakh is a fairly large, silt-laden river system originating from the Robinson Mountains and the vast Bering Glacier, east of Cape Suckling. Numerous clear-water tributaries feed it, providing ideal habitat for sportfish, particularly silver salmon. With its most productive fishing grounds far upstream from the river mouth, fishing the Kaliakh is more complicated than the more accessible Kiklukh or Tsiu rivers, but the rewards of fine fishing in the solitude of one of the least visited streams on the North Gulf Coast can be worth the effort.

Anglers with the time and resources to venture to this isolated drainage will discover awesome silver salmon and sea-run cutthroat trout fishing. Both species are found throughout the Kaliakh, and are encountered in the clear water sloughs, backwaters, and streams. The ***Kulthieth River***, flowing into the midsection of the main river, is a particular hotspot for silvers and is often jammed with these sleek fighters during the peak of the run. (The lower Kulthieth is somewhat glacial, but the middle and upper sections usually run clear and are very fishable.) Cohos arrive here in full force toward the middle of September, bringing dynamite action.

Another major tributary, the clear ***Chiuki River***, or Stink Creek, is best known for its trophy-sized cutthroat trout. In summer and fall it is possible there to hook "cutts" up to four and five pounds, with silver salmon fishing unparalleled at the mouth during the first part of September.

Wheel planes from Cordova or Yakutat can land on gravel bars along clear water streams, and boats powered with outboard jet units are sometimes used to access the middle and upper reaches. A primitive road leads from Cape Yakataga, crosses the mainstem Kaliakh River, and runs up into the foothills with access to a few smaller tributaries.

Yakutat Bay ★★★★

Location: North Gulf of Alaska, Yakutat area, 350 miles SE of Anchorage.

Access: By boat or car from Yakutat.

Facilities: Full services available in the community of Yakutat.

Highlights: One of the most productive marine fishing locations in all of SE.

Main Species: KS, SS, BF

Yakutat Bay is located north of Cape Fairweather in a spectacular setting. On the west, colossal glaciers (Malaspina, Hubbard, and others) spill down from the St. Elias Range—the highest range of coastal mountains in the world—emptying their silty load into the waters of the bay. The east side, however, has small islands, bays, coves, and a few streams flowing clear into the green of Yakutat Bay. The town of Yakutat (connected by regular jet flights to the lower 48) provides an ideal jumping-off point to explore these waters.

Bottom-fishing and saltwater salmon angling are both popular here. In years past, Yakutat was mostly a local fishery, but its appeal is broadening as anglers familiar with the region's salmon and trout streams discover more variety and excitement in nearby marine waters. Halibut, lingcod, and rockfish are very plentiful in the Yakutat area; some of the best fishing occurs off the reefs, moraines, and pinnacles in the deeper parts of the bay and in the Gulf of Alaska. These places provide perfect habitat for bottomfish, and anglers haul in many halibut in the 20 to 60-pound range, with occasional catches up to 300 pounds.

There is excellent salmon fishing on the east side of the bay and off the mouths of rivers draining into the Gulf. Some feeder kings are available year-round in area waters, with mature kings taken in early summer prior to entering major spawning systems such as the Situk and Alsek rivers. The Yakutat area streams have some of the finest sportfishing for silver salmon in all Alaska; large schools of these tackle-busters cruise the shorelines near town, particularly off the west side of Khantak Island and Point Carew, awaiting the heavy fall rains that push them into freshwater. Pink salmon, cutthroat trout, and Dolly Varden are also present in the marine waters of Yakutat, and offer fair to good fishing during summer.

While enjoying the world-class area stream fisheries for salmon and trout, you might want to give Yakutat Bay a try for some great halibut jigging and salmon trolling. Boats can be launched from the Yakutat harbor or mouth of the Situk River, and guided trips are easy to arrange. Forest Road 9962 provides vehicle access to the Ocean Cape area. You will be hard-pressed to find such superior saltwater angling in a more magnificent setting.

Situk River System ★★★★

Location: North Gulf of Alaska, five miles east of Yakutat.

Access: By car, boat, or floatplane from Yakutat.

Facilities: Full services, including boat launches, available. Forest Service cabins are located on Situk Lake and Situk River.

Highlights: World-famous steelhead location.

Main Species: ST, KS, SS, RS

The Situk River of Yakutat certainly isn't lacking notoriety among the world angling fraternity. Small in size, it is a giant of unbelievably productive fishing for a variety of prized sport species, particularly

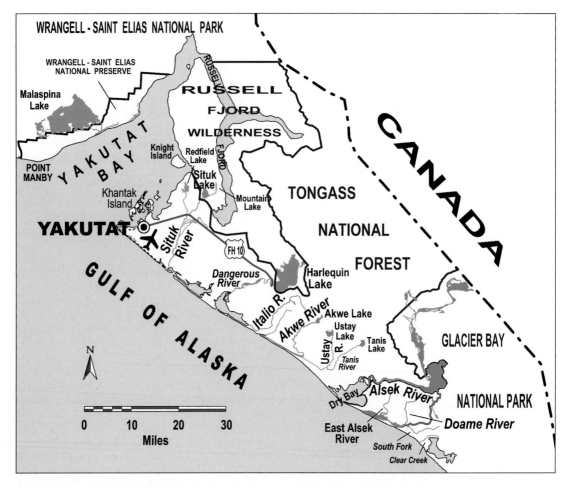

steelhead and salmon. With its easy access, it has been an extremely popular destination for years. Draining three headwater lakes near Russell Fjord in Tongass National Forest, the Situk runs clear, through the wooded Yakutat Forelands into the Gulf of Alaska, some 18 miles away. Small and brushy, it does have some excellent stretches for fly and spin casting, particularly the lower end and outlets of the lakes.

The Situk has become a legend for its abundant spring and fall runs of steelhead trout. These stocks are wild fish that offer some of the most exciting fishing available for the species, with runs numbering upwards of 8,000 fish in good years. The river receives a major influx of sea-run rainbows in September and October, but the more abundant and spunky spring steelhead (April and May) give the Situk its claim to fame.

Large salmon runs are also present in the Situk from June into October, providing some of Southeast's best stream fishing. In June and July, kings averaging 25 pounds mix with flotillas of red salmon that completely pack certain stretches of the system. Pinks jam in later on, followed in late August by a run of silver salmon that produces some of the highest catch rates in Alaska, including some of

trophy-size (20 to 23 pounds) from time to time, adding yet more appeal to this sizzling hot fishery. Cutthroat, rainbow trout, and Dolly Varden are taken incidentally, with the best areas to target being the adjoining Situk, Redfield, and Mountain lakes.

There are several ways to sample the superb Situk. Most anglers begin by fishing either the lower river (accessible by road from Yakutat; additional gravel roads along the coast provide access to the estuary at the mouth. The Lost River, another productive coho stream, also empties into the estuary) or sections of river up and downstream from 9-Mile Bridge (nine miles out of town on Forest Highway 10). Both these areas have well-used trails for hiking along the river. A popular option is to rent a boat in town and float and fish the 13-mile section from 9-Mile Bridge to the landing at the mouth of the river, a trip that can be done in one to three days. Yet another possibility is to fly into one of the Forest Service cabins at either Situk Lake or the middle Situk and fish and/or float downstream. (Float planes for Situk Lake are available only for clients of the Yakutat Lodge.) No matter how you decide to fish it, the Situk is definitely a "must do" river for anyone aspiring to sample the best of the Gulf Coast's stream fishing.

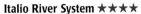

Italio River System ★★★★
Location: North Gulf of Alaska, 25 miles SE of Yakutat.

Access: By small wheelplane or boat from Yakutat.

Facilities: Forest Service cabin available a few miles from lower main river.

Highlights: World-famous silver salmon stream fishing location.

Main Species: SS, CT

Draining a broad area 23 miles southeast of Yakutat, between the Akwe and Dangerous Rivers, the clear-flowing waters of the Italio system are some of the premier silver salmon stream destinations in Southeast Alaska, with a consistent history of yielding trophy-sized fish (20 pounds or more). Next to the Situk River, the Italio System is the most popular coho destination in the Yakutat area. Fish it in the fall someday and you'll understand why.

Comprising several branches and tributaries, the river has changed its configuration over the years due to erosion and seismic activity. There are three main branches, popularly referred to as the "Middle," the "Old" and the "New" Italio. Sharing much of the same headwaters, the Middle and Old branches are a spiderweb of small tributaries that flows out into the Dangerous River Delta, whereas the New Italio flows 16 miles from the outlet of Italio Lake into the lower Akwe River. Silver salmon is the most sought-after and abundant species in the system, with runs that begin in August. The fishing doesn't peak until September, however, when thousands of these powerful salmonids move in from the Gulf of Alaska following heavy fall rains. Lasting well into October (and beyond), the Italio's famous silver run typically yields catches weighing in the mid to upper teens, with some 20 to 23-pound fish not uncommon. (The Italio and Akwe are reputed to have the largest silver salmon in the state, on average.)

Pink salmon, Dolly Varden, cutthroat trout, and even a few rainbows are present throughout the system. Trout fishing can be especially good in some of the small, secluded lakes that require overland hiking to reach. There is also a good steelhead run in the New Italio, which, due to its more difficult access, is seldom fished. Sockeyes are also present in good numbers in the New Italio; even a few king salmon enter the river in June and early July.

Wheel planes from Yakutat have traditionally accessed a strip along the Middle Italio. There is a Forest Service cabin there, offering front door fishing. From the Middle Italio, it is possible to hike about two miles to the New Italio, with the best walking along the dry former riverbed. There is also an outfitter's camp near the Middle Italio airstrip, offering full guide services.

Adventurous anglers have been known to drive from Yakutat to the end of Forest Highway 10 at the Dangerous River, then hike four miles to the New Italio headwaters, carrying an inflatable canoe or small raft. The float downriver offers a true wilderness experience, through pristine stretches of river seldom fished, with a final pick-up by airplane on the Akwe River or Middle Italio.

Akwe River System ★★★
Location: North Gulf of Alaska, 32 miles SE of Yakutat.

Access: By plane or boat from Yakutat.

Facilities: Forest Service cabin on nearby Square Lake, a tributary lake to the Ustay River.

Highlights: A more remote Gulf Coast stream with exceptional angling potential.

Main Species: SS, CT, DV, RS

The glacially tinged, green waters of the Akwe originate from Akwe Lake at the base of the Brabazon Range, 32 miles southeast of Yakutat. Since glaciers and snowfields dominate the mountainous terrain at the headwaters, there can be a fair amount of silt in the river during the summer months. Heavy rains also affect the Akwe more than neighboring rivers, temporarily discoloring the water. However, the river, along with several clear water tributaries, can provide anglers with some terrific fishing, particularly for huge coho salmon. Very few anglers venture to the Akwe, despite its excellent potential.

After meandering through forests and marshlands, the Akwe (for the last seven miles) parallels the sandy beaches of the Gulf Coast, where it widens into a shallow slough with a gentle current. As salmon, trout, and charr move through this section, angling can be excellent, despite the relatively cloudy water. Near its outlet into the ocean, the Akwe joins the crystal-clear New Italio, forming one of the most productive fishing holes on the river. Just upstream from the Italio/Akwe confluence, Back Creek also flows into the Akwe. A clear water tributary, Back Creek provides yet one more productive fishing hole on the Akwe system.

A large run of silver salmon is available every fall, along with a sizable population of cutthroat trout, and fair numbers of reds (June through July) and Dolly Varden charr. Fishing for both cohos and cutthroats is considered to be excellent, but knowing anglers concentrate on the mouths of clear streams and sloughs to get the best action possible. Around the first of June, a few king salmon can even be picked up on the lower few miles of river. Sockeyes are present from mid-June through July.

The Akwe does not produce the number of fish that neighboring systems do, but it receives much less angling pressure. It can offer outstanding fishing during the height of the season, especially in late summer and fall.

Wheel planes from Yakutat access the river by landing on an airstrip about six miles upriver from the mouth. Shallow-draft boats and canoes can negotiate the river, particularly the lower slough. A couple of outfitters have camps on the Akwe, and offer guide services.

East Alsek River
Location: North Gulf of Alaska, 60 miles SE of Yakutat.

Access: By wheelplane or boat from Yakutat.

Facilities: Forest Service cabin available along river.

Highlights: A remote river with awesome fishing potential.

Main Species: KS, RS, SS

The East Alsek River, or East River, is a short coastal drainage just a few miles south of the vast Alsek River system, located in Glacier Bay National Preserve. Originating as upwelling water in the flat forelands near the Alsek River, the upper river has a spring creek-like character, consisting of a series of ponds with slight current separated by short stretches of riffles. The river eventually joins the Doame River to form a large shallow lagoon, where schools of sockeye, chum, and silver salmon mature before moving upriver to spawn. The final three miles of river winds through open sand flats, paralleling the ocean before emptying into the Gulf of Alaska.

Although East River sockeye runs have declined from highly productive years in the mid to late 1980s (local biologists believe this is due to changing physical characteristics of the river), there are still plenty of these feisty fighters to occupy anglers. The run arrives later than other systems in the Yakutat area, peaking around the first part of August, with above-average-sized fish (seven pounds) available to flyfishermen. If conditions and timing are right, anglers will find king salmon in the lower river in the first part of June. These fish, bound for the Alsek River, have temporarily strayed into the clear East River, providing for a potentially unique experience of fishing for huge, ocean-bright chinooks in a small river within sight of the pounding Gulf of Alaska surf.

The only substantial run of chum salmon around Yakutat is found here as well, with this species particularly abundant on the lower river in late summer. Later in fall, a good run of cohos puts on a finale for this exquisite fishery.

A Forest Service cabin with an airstrip on the west side of the river provides access to the middle and upper sections. Also, the lower river near the mouth has gravel beaches ideal for landings. Hiking and tractor trails lead along the river. Two small, full-service fishing lodges are located on the middle river near the lagoon and provide fishing options for both the East and Doame Rivers. This is a developing fishery with high potential, especially for flyfishing. It's destined, no doubt, to become one of the new hotspots in the Yakutat sub-region, considering access is relatively easy and inexpensive.

Doame River System ★★★

Location: North Gulf of Alaska, 65 miles SE of Yakutat.

Access: By small plane from Yakutat.

Facilities: No developed public facilities.

Highlights: Remote, unexploited salmon stream of high potential.

Main Species: SS, RS, CT

The Doame River system originates from a series of small lakes and streams in the Deception Hills in Glacier Bay National Park and Preserve, only a few miles south of the glacial Alsek River. Meandering through a densely wooded region, its crystal-blue waters are perfectly suited for angling, especially sight-fishing the river's large schools of salmon as they move upstream from hole to hole. The Doame eventually flows out of the woods across a shallow, open flats before joining the East Alsek River. Virtually an untapped fishery because of its fairly difficult access, the pretty Doame offers a high-quality experience of angling, solitude, and abundant wildlife.

The Doame receives strong runs of silver and red salmon, along with a few chums. The Doame's sockeyes arrive about a month earlier than those of the East Alsek, and are slightly smaller. While they are not quite so numerous they, nonetheless, present a delightful challenge. Silver salmon fishing on the Doame is much better, with substantial runs. They are available, like the reds, throughout the length of the river, and are most abundant during late summer and fall. Some worthwhile fishing for cutthroat and rainbow trout is also reported from the system, not only from the lakes of the upper drainage but from the lower river sections as well.

The Doame is usually accessed by wheelplanes that land on gravel bars along the river and beaches near the mouth. Upper Doame Lake is suitable for smaller floatplanes, but caution is advised. In years past, the spectacular Situk and Italio fisheries nearby have overshadowed the Doame. But as more people search out new, uncrowded territory, this "sleeper," like the East Alsek, will gain increasing notoriety for high-quality stream fishing in a remote and very scenic setting.

Recommended Lodges/Guides/Outfitters/Air taxis

Glacier Bear Lodge: P.O. Box 303, Yakutat, AK 99689, (866) 425-6343, (907) 784-3202, *www.glacierbearlodge.com* Lodging, boat rentals, guided fishing.

Yakutat Lodge: P.O. Box 287, Yakutat, AK 99689, (800) YAKUTAT, (907) 784-3232, *www.yakutatlodge.com* Guided/unguided lodge-based fishing.

Leonard's Landing Lodge: P.O. Box 282, Yakutat, AK 99689, (907) 784-3245, *www.leonardslanding.com* Lodging, boat/car rentals, guided fishing.

John & Fran Latham: P.O. Box 254, Yakutat, AK 99689, (907) 784-3287, *www.johnlatham.com* Guided fishing, bed & breakfast, and vacation rentals

George Davis Fishing Adventures: (800) 950-5133. Fishing tours, Icy Cape.

Orca Adventure Lodge: Box 2105, Cordova, AK 99574, (866) 424-ORCA, *www.orcaadventurelodge.com* North Gulf Coast, remote fishing.

Tsivat River Lodge: P.O. Box 2562, Cordova, AK 99574, (800) 424-1607, *www.tsivatriverlodge.com*

Dierick's Tsiu River Lodge: P.O. Box 421, Yakutat, AK 99689, (907) 784-3625.

Johnny's East River Lodge: (907) 463-1288, *www.johnnyseastriverlodge.com* Remote lodge, guided fishing, and tours.

Italio River Adventures: P.O. Box 210, Yakutat, AK 99689, (907) 784-3697, *www.italio.com* Remote fishing camp and tours.

Sea Raven Charters: P.O. Box 342, Yakutat, AK 99689, (800) 826-5362, *www.ksfisheries.com* Yakutat Bay boat charters.

Ross Marine Tours: Box 371, Yakutat, AK 99689, (253) 373-9787, (907) 784-3698, *www.rossmarinetours.com* Yakutat Bay boat charters.

Alsek Air: P.O. Box 489, Yakutat, AK 99689, (907) 786-3231. Yakutat air taxi service.

Air Juneau: P.O. Box 326, Yakutat, AK 99689, (907) 786-3831. Yakutat air taxi service.

Fishing & Flying: P.O. Box 2349, Cordova, AK 99574, (907) 424-3324. Air taxi service, Gulf Coast.

General Information

Alaska Department of Fish & Game: Sport Fish Division, P.O. Box 49, Yakutat, AK 99689, (907) 784-3222.

USFS, Yakutat Ranger District: P.O. Box 327, Yakutat, AK 99689, (907) 784-3359. *www.fs.fed.us/r10/tongass/*

Glacier Bay National Park/Preserve: P.O. Box 140, Gustavus, AK 99826, (907) 697-2230, *www.nps.gov/glba*

USGS Maps/NOAA Charts Reference

Kiklukh River: Bering Glacier A-7, A-8.
Tsiu/Tsivat Rivers: Bering Glacier A-6.
Kaliakh River System: Bering Glacier A-5, A-6.
Yakutat Bay: Mount Saint Elias A-4, A-5, C-4, C-5, C-6, C-7, D-4, D-5, D-6; 16761.
Situk River System: Yakutat B-5, C-4, C-5.
Italio River System: Yakutat B-3, B-4.
Akwe River System: Yakutat A-3, B-3.
East Alsek River: Yakutat A-1, A-2.
Doame River System: Yakutat A-1.

Regulations/Information

A few special fishing regulations exist for the Gulf Coast/Yakutat area. (Seasonal restrictions for halibut and lingcod exist as regionwide regulations.) Freshwater drainages are seasonal single hook, unbaited lure fishing only, November 16 to September 14, with 36-inch min. size for steelhead. (Additional restrictions apply for Situk River—see regs.) Consult current Regulations Summary for Region I, SE Alaska, or contact regional/field offices, ADF&G for information.

Douglas: (907) 465-4270   **Yakutat:** (907) 784-3222

Online Info: *www.sf.adfg.state.ak.us/statewide/regulations/seregs.cfm*

North Gulf Coast/Yakutat Species

LOCATION	KING SALMON	RED SALMON	PINK SALMON	CHUM SALMON	SILVER SALMON	STEELHEAD	RAINBOW	CUTTHROAT	GRAYLING	CHARR	LAKE TROUT	NORTHERN PIKE	SHEEFISH	HALIBUT	LING COD	ROCK FISH	SALMON SHARK	FSHG. PRESSURE
Yakutat Bay	☺	R	✓	R	★	R		✓		✓				★	☺	☺	✓	✓
Kiklukh River	R	☺	✓	R	★	R	✓	★		✓								M
Tsiu/Tsivat River	R	✓	✓	R	★	✓	✓	☺		✓								M
Kaliakh River	R	R	✓	R	★	✓	✓	★		✓								✓
Situk River System	☺	★	★	R	★	★	✓	✓		☺								☹
Italio River System	R	✓	☺	R	★	☺	☺	☺		☺								M
Akwe River System	✓	☺	✓	R	★	R	✓	★		☺								✓
East Alsek River	☺	★	R	☺	★	R	✓	✓		☺								✓
Doame River System	R	☺	✓	✓	★	R	☺	☺		☺								✓

Legend:
- (blank) Not present
- **R** Rare
- ✓ Fishable numbers (or light pressure)
- ☺ Good fishing
- ★ Excellent fishing
- **LL** Landlocked species
- **C** Present, but fishing closed
- **M** Moderate pressure
- ☹ Heavy pressure

Alaska Fly Patterns

In the pages that follow are shown and briefly described most of the traditional (and a few less well known) flies for Alaska. These have been in use for quite some time and are considered the core group of patterns from which are derived the countless variations currently available in flyshops and catalogs.

Many of these patterns come from the Pacific Northwest, or elsewhere, and have been put into use with slight or no modifications in Alaska waters. Others are unique Alaska creations, developed by tyers for local conditions, that were found to be effective throughout the state and gained widespread acceptance. A few are considered specialty patterns, most too new to be included in the essential group of traditional patterns for Alaska, but very popular and gaining acceptance. Anyone planning a flyfishing trip to Alaska, whether it be to Southeast or the Arctic, would be wise to fill his/her flyboxes with more than a few of the patterns shown. (Be sure to consult the various species chapters in this book for information on the most productive flies.)

Alaska patterns can be grouped, most broadly, by whether or not they imitate a natural food item (natural versus attractor patterns). Those that mimic something natural can be further classified by the type of forage they represent (egg/flesh; traditional forage—fry, smolt, leech, etc.; and insect nymph/larva/adult), and/or the manner in which they are presented (dry as opposed to wet flies). Not all flies, and certainly not some of the more notorious Alaska patterns, fit neatly into these categories; there are some patterns that truly defy any kind of classification. For convenience, all the traditional Alaska saltwater patterns, whether attractor or forage, are grouped together in this chapter, as are the Alaska specialty flies.

More advanced anglers who enjoy tying flies should use these patterns only as guidelines. Learn the feeding habits and behavior of your favorite species, then experiment and create your own "classics" that are just as effective, less expensive, and infinitely more satisfying to use. With the many new materials available today, the possibilities are endless.

Attractor Patterns

A broad, catch-all group of flies that trigger instinctive, aggressive responses in predatory gamefish, with their bright colors and tantalizing action. Like forage imitations, they are effective in a wide range of conditions.

McNally Magnum: A large, bright attractor streamer used for northern pike and sheefish. Hook size 1/0-2.

Egg Sucking Leech: The most versatile pattern in the Alaska flyfisher's arsenal. Deadly on all trout and salmon. Hook size 2-8.

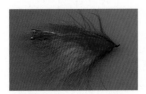

Alaskabou: One of several marabou fly adaptations for Alaska and a standard for king, silver, and chum salmon; also good for pike. Hook size 3/0-4.

Alaska Mary Ann: A true Alaska classic, originally tied for Northwest sheefish, but a good all around attractor for salmon, trout, and charr as well. Hook size 1/0-6.

Purple Peril: A classic Northwest steelhead pattern used for Alaska steelies and salmon. Hook size 1/0-6.

Spruce: A classic baitfish-like attractor fished in Alaska for all predatory freshwater species. Hook size 2-6.

Supervisor: An eastern trout and charr classic used widely in Alaska, especially the bucktail attractor version shown, has great effect on salmon as well. Hook size 1/0-6.

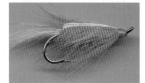

Sparkle Shrimp: An extremely effective, versatile Northwest standard that is deadly on Alaska's king and silver salmon, steelhead, cutthroat trout, and charr. Hook size 2-8.

Yarn Fly: A simple fly that can be tied in different colors to tempt Alaska sockeyes, trout, and charr. Hook size 2-6.

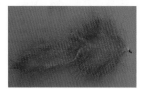

Bunny Fly: Extremely versatile, productive, rabbit-fur attractor. Tied in various ways and colors for salmon and trout. Hook size 3/0-6.

Polar Shrimp: A Pacific Northwest steelhead standard that became one of the most productive Alaska trout and charr patterns. Hook size 2-8.

Russian River: A well-known Alaska classic. Don't fish the Kenai River without it if you expect to catch sockeye salmon. (Also good for SS.) Hook size 2-6.

Comet: A versatile, deep-sinking attractor tied in various colors and styles for all Alaska salmon, trout, and charr. Hook size 2-8.

Coronation: A Pacific Northwest salmon trolling fly that works well on Alaska rainbows and salmon. Hook size 1/0-6.

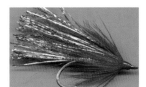

Flash Fly: Versatile and extremely productive for salmon, particularly chums and silvers. Oversize versions are good for king and northern pike. Hook size 3/0-6.

Pink Sparkler: A unique Alaska attractor developed for charr and rainbow trout, will also take salmon. Hook size 2-6.

Sockeye Willie: A specialty creation tied for Alaska sockeyes that has seen widespread use across SC and SW Alaska. Hook size 2-6.

Sockeye Charlie: A shad fly variation used in various colors with great results around Bristol Bay and Southcentral. Hook size 2-6.

Sockeye Orange: Well- known, very effective, sparse bucktail sockeye fly, can be tied in various colors. Hook size 2-8.

Sportsman Special: A classic from the Kenai Peninsula that became one of the first popular bucktail sockeye salmon flies. Hook size 2-6.

Black Ghost: An eastern classic bait streamer, used in Alaska for lake trout (and other charr) and sheefish. Hook size 1/0-6.

Gray Ghost: Another smelt imitation streamer from the East that is useful for charr, sheefish, and trout. Hook size 1/0-6.

White Ghost: This ghost fly is useful for all Alaska predatory resident species. Hook size 1/0-6.

Coho Fly: A Pacific Northwest salmon standard that has morphed into many variations for Alaska's salmon and trout. Hook size 1/0-6.

Copper & Orange: A Northwest Alaska creation effective for charr, trout, and grayling. Hook size 2-6.

Fall Favorite: A West Coast standard that is very productive for all Alaska trout and charr. Hook size 2-6.

Green Butt Skunk: A variation of a classic West Coast steelhead pattern that does famously well on Alaska steelhead. Hook size 2-8.

Woolly Bugger: One of the most famous and widely used patterns in Alaska, tied in various colors and materials, for all trout, charr, and salmon. Hook size 2-6.

Popsicle: Another famous Alaska marabou fly variation used for salmon. Hook size 3/0-4.

Rajah: A sparse Northwest steelhead pattern that is very effective on Alaska steelhead, rainbows, and charr. Hook size 4-8.

Everglow: A gaudy attractor used in various colors with great effect on Alaska salmon and trout (steelhead and rainbows). Hook size 3/0-4.

Mickey Finn: A classic streamer used to great effect on all Alaska game species. Hook size 2-8.

Matuka: A New Zealand pattern that made its way up north. A versatile attractor for all Alaska game species. Hook size 1/0-6.

Krystal Bullet: A unique Alaska attractor tied in various colors, used primarily for trout, charr, grayling, and some salmon. Hook size 4-8.

Zonker: Extremely popular and versatile, in its many variations (like the Egg Sucking Zonker, Psycho Zonker, etc.) and different sizes, is used for all game species. Hook size 1/0-6.

Skykomish Sunrise: A famous Northwest pattern that produces great results on Alaska steelhead, rainbows, charr, and grayling. Hook size 2-6.

Boss: Very well-known and widely used Northwest pattern usually tied similar to the Comet, in different colors, for Alaska salmon, trout, and charr. Hook size 2-6.

Montana Brassie: An effective pattern used to elicit strikes from Alaska trout, charr, and sockeye salmon. Hook size 4-8.

Wet Fly Patterns
(nymph/larva/emerger)

This important group includes many early season insect forage items for Alaska's trout, charr, and grayling, plus a few perennially effective attractor style nymphs.

Brassie Nymph: Extremely versatile and productive attractor nymph for wide range of Alaska species. Hook size 8-14.

Pheasant Tail Nymph: A necessary nymph pattern for every Alaska trout angler's flybox, shown in the bead head version. Great for grayling, too. Hook size 12-14.

Caddis Larva: An important nymph pattern for early season Alaska trout, charr, and grayling, tied in several color variations. Hook size 8-14.

Mosquito Emerger: The mosquito, in its various life phases, is a very important food source for grayling and small trout. Hook size 14-16.

Teeny Nymph: A useful attractor nymph tied in various colors to appeal to most Alaska game species (salmon, trout, and grayling). Hook size 4-12.

Zug Bug: A standard nymph pattern that is very useful in Alaska for trout, grayling, and charr. Hook size 8-12.

Bitch Creek: Another trout classic widely used in Alaska for rainbows, charr, and grayling. Hook size 4-10.

Woolly Worm: Another classic. Very popular in Alaska for trout, tied in various colors for different conditions. Hook size 4-14.

Black Stonefly Nymph: A trout classic, used at times very effectively on Alaska rainbows, charr, and grayling. Hook size 6-12.

Brown Caddis Nymph: Another versatile caddis pattern, used in Bristol Bay and Southcentral for early season trout. Hook size 8-12.

Brown Emerger: A classic pattern used everywhere with good results in Alaska's trout waters. Hook size 10-14.

Caddis Case: An important, spring/summer fly for Alaska rainbows and grayling. Hook size 6-12.

Dragonfly Nymph: An important trout forage in the weedy lakes of Southcentral and elsewhere. Hook size 4.

Gold Ribbed Hare's Ear: A famous, versatile nymph pattern used to great effect on Alaska's trout, charr, and grayling. Hook size 10-14.

Egg/Flesh Patterns

Flies tied to imitate salmon roe or flesh. They are extremely effective for all Alaska trout (including steelhead), charr, and grayling late in the season when the rivers are pumped full of spawning salmon.

Wiggletail: A versatile pattern, can be tied as either an attractor or egg pattern (shown here). Hook size 1/0-6.

Carcass Fly: A Bunny Fly variant, the Carcass simulates a drifting chunk of salmon flesh, particularly tempting to trout very late in the season. Hook size 2-6.

King Caviar: This giant Alaska version of the Glo Bug, also known as Fat Freddy, is used for king salmon. Hook size 3/0-2.

Battle Creek: Pacific Northwest salmon/steelhead pattern. Can be fished as an attractor. A productive, late season drift pattern for big trout, charr, and grayling. Hook size 2-6.

Cluster Fly: A great late season drift pattern for big trout, also productive for king salmon. Hook sizes 1/0-6.

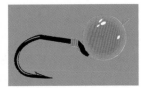

Bead Egg: This plastic, lifelike egg imitation has become one of Alaska's most productive (and economical) late season trout (and CHR, GR) patterns. Hook size 8-10.

Babine Special: A Pacific Northwest classic, two-egg, drift pattern used widely in Alaska for trout, grayling, and charr. Tied in different colors and style variations, in hook size 2-6.

Marabou Flesh Fly: This is the marabou wing version of the classic late season drift pattern for trout, charr, and grayling. Hook size 2-6.

Glo Bug: The original egg pattern, this puff of chenille on an egg hook, tied in a mind-boggling array of colors, is the fall fishing standard for all Alaska trout fanatics. Hook size 6-10.

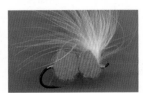

Two Egg Sperm Fly: Very similar to the Babine Special, the Two Egg, in different colors, is an essential part of the trout angler's late season arsenal. Hook size 2-6.

Forage Patterns

The most effective flies for Alaska's resident predators over a wide range of conditions, because they mimic important Alaska prey species, such as sculpins, young salmon, and leeches.

Alaska Smolt: A variation of the basic smolt pattern, used for Alaska's trout, charr, and sheefish. Hook size 2-6.

Alevin: Tied to mimic the fragile, emerging stage of newly hatched salmon. Its many variations are spring trout standards, also good for charr and grayling. Hook size 6-12.

Black Nose Dace: A minnow imitation designed for waters down south, this pattern works well in Alaska for trout and charr. Hook size 2-6.

Maggot: An important food item of salmon carcass scavengers, this forage has various imitations that are very effective for Alaska's late season trout and charr. Hook size 6-10.

Minnow: A widely used, generic forage imitation tied in many ways, this versatile pattern appeals to all Alaska trout, charr, and grayling. Hook size 2-8.

Muddler Minnow: One of the great classic forage patterns for all North America's trout and charr, this fly belongs in every Alaska angler's flybox. Hook size 2-8.

Parr Fly: Tied to mimic the larger pre-smolt phase of young salmon and trout, this is another fly not to leave home without, for all your spring trout fishing. Hook size 2-6.

Fry: A versatile pattern with many variations; simulates juvenile salmon. Along with the Smolt, it is the standard for all spring trout fishing in Alaska. Hook size 4-10.

Scud: In various colors mimics very important forage for Alaska's lake rainbows, charr, and grayling. Hook size 10-16.

Thunder Creek: Extremely effective fly used across southern Alaska's "trout belt" for rainbows, cutthroat, grayling, and charr. Hook size 4-10.

Blue Smolt: The classic smolt pattern, used everywhere, including Alaska, to imitate small forage for a variety of gamefish species. Hook size 2-6.

Bristol Bay Smolt: Another unique Alaska smolt variation, especially good on rainbows and charr. Hook size 2-6.

Katmai Smolt: An Alaska classic, tied for fishing the famous trout lakes and streams of the north Alaska Peninsula. Hook size 2-6.

Leech: Another true classic for all time, this pattern can be tied in a million ways to appeal to all Alaska's game species. Hook size 1/0-8.

Dry Fly Patterns

These should be included in every Alaska angler's flybox, for grayling and those special situations when trout, charr, and salmon can be taken with surface presentations (see species chapters for details).

Adams: One of the most widely used dry patterns in existence, don't fish Alaska without some in your flybox (for RT, DV, GR). Hook size 10-14.

Black Gnat: Another very important forage insect and the quintessential fly for Alaska's grayling. Hook size 10-16.

Bomber: A classic, super dry used down south for steelies, but mostly for big rainbows and silver salmon in Alaska. Hook size 4-8.

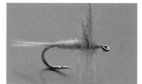

Cahill: An important and widely used trout pattern, useful for Alaska rainbows and grayling. Hook size 10-18.

Elk Wing Caddis: One of the most versatile dry flies in existence, a great floater and very effective for Alaska rainbows (GR too). Hook size 8-14.

Gray Wulff: One of the standard dry fly patterns for Alaska, used for rainbows and grayling, hook size 8-14.

Irresistible: Like the Bomber, an incomparable, highly visible floater, used to entice big trout and grayling in Alaska. Hook size 6-14.

Midge: A classic pattern for finicky Alaska lake rainbows and grayling. Hook size 12-18.

Mosquito: Anybody who has fished Alaska during the warmer months knows how important this pattern is. Hook size 10-16.

Royal Coachman: One of the true classic dries, highly visible and very useful in coaxing trout and grayling to the surface. Hook size 10-16.

Royal Wulff: A popular Wulff variation used widely for trout, grayling, and charr. Hook size 6-14.

Humpy: A great fly for Alaska, particularly surface feeding rainbows (also GR). Hook size 10-14.

Bivisible: A versatile, high-profile dry pattern tied in various colors; a favorite for Alaska rainbows. Hook size 8-12.

Griffith's Gnat: A great midge pattern for graying and trout. Hook size 12-16.

Saltwater Patterns

Traditional Northwest bait imitation streamers, a few classic saltwater attractors, and some unique, highly effective Alaska creations make up this group. Many can be used in tidewater or even streams or lakes for salmon, trout, or charr.

Candlefish: A very important forage. The fly is tied in many ways throughout the Pacific Northwest, and used in Alaska for all salt game species. Hook size 1/0-6.

Deceiver: Famous saltwater attractor, with many variations; very effective for Alaska salmon (fresh and salt) and bottomfish. Hook size 5/0-4.

Amphipod: A Northwest standard, tied various ways to imitate different kinds of shrimplike plankton. Used in Alaska for saltwater salmon. Hook size 4-8.

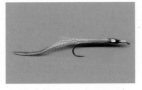

Needlefish: Another important forage pattern, tied all kinds of ways, and an essential fly for the Alaska saltwater angler. Hook size 2-6.

Baitfish: A generic pattern tied in almost infinite ways, simulating a range of fair-sized baitfish forage. Great for Alaska salmon, halibut, and lingcod. Hook size 5/0-1/0.

Alaska Candlefish: An Alaska version of the Pacific Northwest standard, useful in both fresh and salt for all salmon, trout, and charr. Hook size 1/0-6.

Clouser Minnow: Along with the Deceiver, possibly the most widely used saltwater attractor, useful for all Alaska saltwater game species. Hook size 3/0-4.

Crab: Another important fly, resembling a most essential item in the food chain. Good for Alaska's bottomfish (and salmon). Hook size 3/0-6.

Euphausid: A Northwest standard, simulating certain plankton, this fly can be used in Alaska for salmon (pink, chum, silver, and red). Hook sizes 4-10.

Halibut Flesh Fly: This giant, tandem hook fly mimics a big chunk of drifting salmon flesh that late season halibut crave. Hook size 5/0-3/0.

Salmon Trolling Fly: A traditional Northwest coho fly that can be used with great effect in Alaska. Hook size 5/0-1/0.

Sandlance: A great Northwest baitfish pattern tied various ways, especially useful for Alaska salmon and halibut. Hook size 3/0-4.

Seaducer: Classic saltwater pattern, tied many ways. Useful in Alaska for all bottomfish, salmon, and northern pike. Hook size 5/0-4.

Shrimp: A classic pattern tied in many ways and colors to mimic important food for all game species along north Pacific (especially salmon). Hook size 2-10.

Squid: An essential fly for Alaska salt water, with many variations. Especially useful for salmon, halibut, and lingcod. Hook size 3/0-2.

Tarpon Fly: The classic attractor tied in many variations. Can be used for Alaska salmon, bottomfish, and northern pike. Hook size 5/0-2.

Whistler: Another great saltwater pattern that can be very effective for Alaska's bottomfish, salmon, and other species. Hook size 5/0-1/0.

Salmon Treat: An Alaska baitfish/attractor pattern for salmon. Tied in various ways and colors. Hook size 3/0-2.

Herring: The quintessential saltwater baitfish pattern, useful in all conditions for Alaska salmon, halibut, and lingcod. Hook size 5/0-1/0.

Crazy Charlie: The famous flats fly, used in several variations in Alaska for a wide range of salt and freshwater species (all salmon and rockfish). Hook size 2-8.

Lambuth Candlefish: A classic Northwest salmon pattern that works well in Alaska. Hook size 3/0-2.

Specialty Patterns

An arbitrary group of flies created for a special set of conditions or species, such as topwater or diving patterns for pike, oversize attractors for big king salmon, or forage imitations for halibut, lingcod, or rockfish.

Pike McMurderer: A unique surface fly with irresistible action, used for pike in Alaska. Hook size 5/0-1/0.

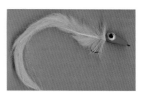

Pike Slider: A unique creation with tantalizing action for northern pike. Hook size 5/0-1/0.

Dahlberg Diver: One of the best known of many topwater/diving creations used to entice Alaska's big northern pike. Hook size 3/0-1/0.

Weaver's Deep Six: A very effective, highly visible pattern for rockfish. Hook size 1/0-4.

D's Minnow: A fly designed to mimic a whitefish, forage for Alaska's northern pike and sheefish. Hook size 3/0.

Outrageous: A not-too-commonly-used, but very effective, gaudy, tarpon tied attractor for Alaska salmon and pike. Hook size 3/0-4.

Mouse: The most famous Alaska "dry fly." Tied with fur or spun deer hair, it is the best thing going for big rainbows and pike. Hook size 1/0-4.

Pink Pollywog: A notorious spun deer hair creation for topwater fishing Alaska silver salmon, pike, and rainbows. Hook size 1/0-4.

Popper: A broad group of topwater "flies" of varying design, materials, and colors, used for everything from pike to silver salmon to big rainbows. Hook size 2-6.

Reynolds Pike Fly: A great pattern for northern pike throughout the northland. Hook size 3/0-2.

Baby Rockfish: An essential forage imitation for lingcod. Hook size 3/0-1/0.

Sea Snake: A potent attractor designed to incite strikes from big halibut and lingcod. Hook size 5/0-3/0.

Lake Snake: A specialty fly for big Alaska northern pike. Hook size 3/0-1/0.

Greenling: An effective forage imitation for large lingcod. Hook size 5/0-3/0.

Planning a successful fishing vacation in Alaska

It takes considerable time and advance preparation. Although a few folks leave it up to luck and somehow manage to make the right choices and connections to have a decent vacation, a great many more make the long trek up north each summer only to find disappointment and/or frustration, as their vacations turn out a little or a lot less than expected, because they did not adequately plan or prepare.

A certain measure of the blame lies with Alaska's tourist industry which, to lure travelers in today's super-competitive world market, often helps promote unrealistic expectations with hyped-up literature, extravagant promotions, or big talk over the phone. (Despite what you might be inclined to believe, most Alaska tourist business operators are honest professionals who would just as soon poke themselves in the eye than sell you a trip or service you won't be happy with.) As a consumer, however, the ultimate responsibility for getting the kind of Alaska fishing vacation you deserve is yours alone. No one can read your mind or know your heart in order to deliver the arrangements and the fishing that are right for you. Like shopping for a car, planning a successful Alaska fishing vacation is a process that begins with identifying what you want, surveying the available market, asking the right questions, "kicking some tires," and then bargaining with prospective businesses. The end result is a signed contract, delivery of the "goods," and, hopefully, two satisfied parties. What follows are some fundamental points to keep in mind that can make the whole process more efficient and ultimately more satisfying:

KNOW WHAT YOU WANT/LEARN WHAT'S AVAILABLE

It's important as a first step to determine the kind of fishing experience(s) you are most interested in. Like so many others, you may have an Alaska fishing dream that burns bright and long in your heart. Perhaps this desire has articulated into something specific, such as catching a big king salmon, a trophy rainbow trout, or a monster halibut. Or maybe you just want to catch fish until your arms fall off or sample the potpourri of delights available along Alaska's incomparable coastline. If you're really adventurous, your designs on the Alaska dream may entail camping and hiking in the wilderness, with some great stream or lake fishing on the side.

To be ultimately satisfied and avoid disappointment, however, your expectations should be tempered by a realistic assessment of your budget and time constraints, the level of accommodations and service you require, your taste for adventure, and a basic understanding of what Alaska has to offer in the way of fishing and services.

To do this right requires a considerable amount of self education. You can begin by reading this book in its entirety (and other Alaska publications listed in the back of this book), and browsing through sporting literature for material on Alaska fishing. Libraries, bookstores, sport shops, and the Internet are the most obvious places to search for this information. Don't overlook the public agencies listed throughout this book for trip planning materials they may have to offer. You should also try to talk to anyone you know who has fished Alaska, and make a point of attending one of the winter trade shows near you to chat with lodge owners, guides, air taxis, and outfitters. You may even find some interesting and relevant television and radio broadcasts on your local channels or cable, from time to time. The more general background you have on Alaska—its geography, climate, history, culture, economy, wildlife, etc.—the better you can plan, execute, and enjoy a fishing vacation that is everything you want it to be. It's the ultimate trip insurance.

You should do your research and planning well ahead of time, so you can begin making arrangements early in the year (January through March) in which you plan to vacation, for best selection on services and accommodations. (Some of Alaska's premier operations start booking up twelve months or more, in advance, with the prime dates quickly taken.)

To help you stay focused in your research and planning, compile a list of the important things you want from your vacation—species and type of fishing desired, preferred accommodations, meal requirements,

budget constraints, etc.—and work through each and every item as you consider possibilities.

Armed with realistic vacation goals and a broad, if cursory, familiarity with what Alaska has to offer, you can begin to narrow your choices. There are services and facilities that cater to every whim and desire imaginable as far as fishing in Alaska goes, and usually you can home in on those that initially interest you by way of magazines, vacation planners, travel guides, travel agencies, visitors bureaus, Internet searches, sportfishing organizations, trade shows, and word-of-mouth. Preliminary contact by phone, fax, mail (both electronic or postal), or in person, will further narrow down your selection.

NEGOTIATING WITH TOURIST SERVICES

When you deal with Alaska tourist businesses, it is vital to be forthcoming and honest. Begin by telling them everything they need to know to determine if what they provide is most suited to your needs. Naturally, the details will vary depending on the service; it isn't necessary, obviously, to spill your guts when talking to a B&B or RV rental agency, but it can't hurt to mention what brings you to their area, for they may be able to provide valuable information or contacts that you would be unaware of otherwise.

When talking to lodge owners, guides, air taxis, outfitters, and any other high ticket operators, don't be shy. Get answers to your satisfaction for anything you may have questions on. And don't consider doing business with anyone who hesitates to give you information or tries to intimidate you in any way. Most reputable people in the business enjoy talking with someone who knows enough to ask intelligent questions, and wouldn't think of putting them off because of their inquisitiveness or meticulousness with details. Some important points to remember:

• Are you interacting with an owner, manager, guide, or booking agent? It is important to deal directly, whenever possible, with the people who will be ultimately responsible for your arrangements, as they are best capable of answering any questions or concerns you have, and will be most committed to seeing that you are satisfied.

• Make sure you discuss exactly what is to be provided in the way of transportation, accommodations, meals, guide service, gear, alcoholic beverages, licenses, gratuities, etc. Don't assume anything. Many wilderness lodges, for instance, include in their fee, air taxi to and from a major hub, which can be a considerable sum of money in some cases. And some offer basic packages that may or may not include daily guide service or fly-outs to remote fishing locations. Many lodges, guide services, and charters provide all needed fishing gear; some charge a nominal rental fee. (You may decide, as extra insurance, to bring your own gear. Make sure that is okay with the operator.) Ask about tipping the guides and staff; as a general rule, it's not unreasonable to leave up to 10% of the lodge fee as a gratuity.

- How large an operation are you dealing with? Some of the more successful Alaska businesses have morphed into "industrial tourism" operations, handling large numbers of clients to maximize profits. While they are certainly efficient and very competitively priced, their services lack the intimacy and flexibility of the smaller operators. (Generally, for lodges, if you inquire how many rods per week they handle, the smaller, high-quality operations will be in the 6 to 12 range.)

- Inquire about special packages, or (if applicable) senior, military, group, spouse, or preseason discounts. You may be able to save considerable money by compromising your plans somewhat. Make sure to ask about any cancellation policies that may apply if for some reason you are not able to fulfill your vacation plans.

- Be humble. Listen to and learn from each and every person you contact along the way about local fishing conditions, available services, accommodations, etc., as the information they provide is extremely valuable, no matter who you decide to do business with. Be open to suggestions and advice about your vacation from those who know more. And be sure to thank everyone for their time spent interacting with you. Dealing with the public takes up a lion's share of time (and patience) when you are a tourist operator, and the vast majority of encounters don't result in any business. It's nice to know your knowledge and experience are appreciated.

Narrowing Down the Choices

Shop Around: In most areas of Alaska, the choices are usually many for basic services. The more remote

The services of a reputable guide can greatly increase your success and enjoyment of Alaska's fishing, especially for anglers new to Alaska.

or specialized the service, the more exclusive the operations become. But if you find several services offering similar rates, and they check out equally in some of the other criteria mentioned earlier, the smaller business will usually, but not always, be the better choice in providing personal service and satisfaction. Don't be afraid to trust your intuition if you cannot decide on which service to use.

Get and Check References: As part of the narrowing down process, be sure to ask your prospective guide, outfitter, lodge owner, or air taxi for a list of former clients to contact for reference. Also ask if they are endorsed by any professional or industry organization. Any operator who balks at your requests or cannot provide suitable references should be immediately dismissed from consideration. When you contact some of these references, ask them about the fishing, accommodations, services, etc., and whether they would recommend the operator. Naturally, any ambiguous or negative responses should be cause for concern and doubt as to whether this is the person or organization with whom to do business.

Clinching the Deal

When it comes time to plunk down your hard-earned green on a particular lodge, outfitter, guide, or what-have-you, be sure to get a contractual agreement in writing for all services, equipment, accommodations and/or arrangements to be provided and the fees charged, to the specifications previously discussed and your satisfaction. Read over the contract carefully

Mosquitoes—Alaska's world class infestations plague anglers throughout the state during the warmest months.

of items to include on any personal gear inventory:

Layered clothing for warmth (synthetics, wool or silk)
Expedition quality raingear with hood
High quality sunglasses, preferably polarized
Sunscreen
Bug spray (minimum 25% Deet)
Water repellent hiking boots with several pairs socks
Small pocket knife
Matches or lighter
Good fishing hat with sun visor
Wool or synthetic cap for cooler days
Fingerless wool or synthetic gloves
Small flashlight/extra batteries & bulb (for late summer/fall)
Small Nalgene bottle for drinking water

Timing Considerations

Despite what you might be inclined to believe from some of the travel literature, Alaska's fishing is not a continuous "fish in the bucket" cornucopia of angling opportunity, at least not in any one location. The fishing, even here, has its ups and downs, with some very real and distinct advantages to each part of the season—from early spring to late fall—some of which have little to do with fishing but can affect your vacation significantly in other ways.

The big question, of course, is one of fish availability and how it fits in with your schedule and desires. If you've never been to Alaska, it's probably wise to plan a trip for early in the season (mid-May to early July) so as to enjoy the best of the chinook salmon fishing. Then again, if you couldn't care less about the king of salmon and want to stalk fall coho or fat rainbows, you should plan on coming up later on, in August or September.

Seasoned Alaska anglers can fine-tune their timing to partake of the peak periods for a variety of species (for instance, early September for big rainbows, coho, and charr). The choices are many, and certainly not easy to make, but below is a general summary of the best times to fish the major species throughout Alaska. Keep in mind that wide variations in run timing exist from region to region (consult the run timing charts within the various region overviews in this book), even among certain streams within an area, so it's wise to inquire with reputable sources, like the Alaska Department of Fish and Game, or local guides or air taxis, for accurate details.

before signing, and discuss any discrepancies or unclear areas you find in the wording. This is most important, as the written agreement is the legally binding document that holds the provider to deliver everything specified. It's your guarantee of getting what you paid for.

Once you've committed to a services contract with an operator you feel best about, it's time to give them your absolute trust and attention in following their recommendations for your travel arrangements, equipment, and any other trip preparations. Don't show up without any of the gear they recommend, and don't bring anything not specified unless you clear it beforehand with your trip mentors. Remember, these folks are professionals who know Alaska conditions and the fishing like nobody's business, so heed their instructions carefully or you may regret it later.

Gearing Up

Having the right clothing and gear for your Alaska fishing vacation is vital to your safety and enjoyment. Much of what you bring will depend on the time of year, area you fish, and kind of fishing adventure you are going on. If you are fishing with a guide or lodge, they will provide a gear list, but the following is a list

General Run Timing For Alaska

Rainbow Trout: early June; late August to early October
Steelhead: April and May; late September to mid-November
Grayling: mid-May to mid-September
Northern Pike: late May to early October
Cutthroat Trout: May to June; and August to October
Charr: April to June; and August to October
King Salmon: May to mid-July
Red Salmon: mid-June to late July
Chum Salmon: late June to early September
Pink Salmon: mid-July to mid-August
Silver Salmon: early August to early October
Halibut: late May to early September
Rockfish: late May to October
Lingcod: late May to November
Salmon Shark: July to September
Sheefish: April to October
Lake Trout: May to early July; late August to October

Other Considerations

There are some other factors to be aware of that can affect your fishing vacation, things they don't mention in the brochures or magazines for fear of turning people off. Things like the bugs and bum weather. Alaska has its share of both. But did you know that there is a "peak period" for each? The notorious Alaska mosquito and its allies generally come out in greatest force during the warmest time of year (June and July). A trip in August or early September, while offering some of the best fishing of the season, also provides respite from the swarming hordes that plague anglers incessantly earlier in the season.

Weather, always a factor in Alaska, has a historical tendency to be more benign (drier and calmer) in the spring and early summer throughout most of the state, deteriorating through late summer and fall, although it can vary dramatically from year to year. If you're planning an Arctic or Northwest trip, keep in mind that the season is effectively over by early September in most years.

Another very important thing not to overlook, especially if you're planning a camping or floatfishing trip, is the extreme variation in daylight throughout the season. A trip in June or early July will offer long hours of daylight, for almost nonstop fishing and leisurely camping, while the same outing in late September will have 12 hours of legitimate darkness, making for a much different pace, with considerably less time for fishing and setting up camp. These great fluctuations of light are even more pronounced in the Northwest and Arctic regions.

ALASKA SPORTFISHING SERVICES & ACCOMMODATIONS

Lodges

Lodges are a celebrated part of that potent Alaska fishing mystique. While the best of them can certainly deliver an experience that is hard to duplicate any other way, there is a wide variety of services and accommodations available to suit the different needs and budgets of fishermen of all persuasions. If you're considering a lodge stay, it makes sense to know the main types of facilities available, what they offer, and their range of costs.

Deluxe Lodges: These are the cream of Alaska's lodging and service facilities, usually in prime, remote waterfront locations in the best parts of Bristol Bay, the Southeast panhandle and Southcentral Alaska, with awesome fishing right out the door or not too far away. These custom operations feature plush accommodations, daily fly-outs or boat excursions to Alaska's best fishing, the most experienced guides, gourmet food, and a rather exclusive clientele to rub shoulders with. Some go even further with on-site fly-fishing seminars, European chefs, in-house tackle shops and fly-tying benches, open bar, and more. Itineraries and schedules are usually fixed, with regular hours for fishing and dining. Expect to pay for all the luxury and service, however, usually from $4,200 to $6,000 per week (or more) per person.

Family-Style Lodges: These lodges are a step down in luxury from the big glamour establishments, but they still offer outstanding service and accommodations, without all the frills. Some of the better ones pride themselves—and rightfully so—on delivering more real fishing time than any custom lodge. Located in remote or semi-remote areas, many in Southcentral and Southeast, (and a few in Southwest) these less-costly facilities usually offer fly-outs or boat fishing packages, bunk-style or small, shared cabin accommodations, and informal, family-style dining with plenty of good food. Fishing can be outstanding, depending on the location, time of year, quality of the guides, and other factors. Research and referrals are generally the best ways to locate the better operations. Costs vary from $2,500 to $4,000 (or more) per week per person.

Fishing Camps/Tent Lodges: These are the real basic, streamside, lakeside, or bayside facilities catering to hard-core anglers, with accommodations that range from bunkhouses to small cabins to heated tents or even large boats or barges. Fishing is usually done from shore or from skiffs. The rustic ambience is usually enhanced by plentiful, home-style food, and lots of fishing opportunities (24 hours a day if desired) in some of the best fishing locations in Alaska. Some of these operations are truly unique, set in areas far off the beaten path and run by remarkable individuals, locals usually, who can deliver more than your money's worth in abundant fishing and overall quality of experience. Many also offer unguided packages as outfitters, providing camps/cabins already set up in choice locations, with skiffs. Again, as with the family-style lodges, the best way to locate a reputable operation is by word of mouth and research. Prices vary from $1,000 to $2,500 per week, per person, depending on location, time of year, and accommodations/services provided.

Hotels, Inns, B&Bs

Alaska has seen a tremendous increase in recent years in the number and variety of overnight accommodations facilities available in and around the major hubs. Everything from fancy four-star hotels to rustic country inns, or cozy home-based B&Bs, offer visitors a wide range of lodging options, many also offering packages that include local guided fishing or related services. Prices vary widely, from $50 to $250 per night per person, depending on location, accommodations, and time of year. Magazines, travel guides, the Alaska Vacation Planner, visitors bureaus, the Internet, and contacts listed in the locations section of this book are good sources for locating appropriate accommodations for your vacation itinerary.

Public Use Cabins

Scattered throughout Alaska's widespread public lands, particularly those along the coast , are numerous public use cabins that are available for rent at a small fee (usually $35 per night or less). They provide a viable alternative for do-it-yourself vacations, as many are located along or near prime fishing destinations in national forests, refuges and monuments, or state or BLM land. Most are administered/maintained by the U.S. Forest Service and are weathertight log or A-frame style cabins, with wooden bunks that sleep four people (or more), tables, oil or wood stoves, and benches. Many on lakes include small skiffs for the use of occupants. Basic equipment—splitting mauls, saws, and brooms—is usually provided, but not bed-

Rustic, family-style lodges, such as this operation on Kodiak Island, provide modest amenities, good food, and often unlimited fishing opportunities at affordable rates.

ding, fuel, kitchen utensils, food, or drinking water. Information on cabins located in prime fishing areas can be found in the locations descriptions section of this book.

ALASKA GUIDES & OUTFITTERS

Alaska's guides and outfitters have often been cast as a maverick lot, reputedly drinking and swearing too much, lying outrageously, and otherwise not presenting very high standards of professionalism. While this may have been more true years ago, the Alaska guides and outfitters of today are dedicated professionals with high standards of ethics, competing in an industry that demands much in time and personal commitment.

You'll find them to be an extremely diverse and likeable bunch, for the most part, eager to share their knowledge and love of Alaska's incomparable fishing. The many services they provide cover the full range of visitor activities related to fishing, but can be summarized briefly as follows:

Short-Trip Guides: Far and away the greatest number of guides in Alaska offer services that cater to the shorter, flexible itineraries of today's visitor. Usually hanging a shingle in the more populous regions, like Southcentral's Kenai Peninsula or the larger communities of Southeast, these guides offer a variety of short-trip options ranging from a half-day to several days fishing, using boat, small plane, car, or foot access. Accommodations, if provided, are simple, often at small cabins, bed and breakfasts, hotels, tent camps, or on-board vessels. Some meals and gear are usually provided. This diverse group includes the many charter boat captains, river guides, and quite a few small air taxi operators across Alaska, many offering unguided outfitting options as well. Advance reservations are preferred, but last-minute inquiries can usually be accommodated. Prices usually range from $125 to $150 per person for a half day fishing to $400 per person (or more) for a full day, depending on the location and the services provided.

Wilderness Guides: The real thing, the hard-core cadre of the Alaska guiding profession, wilderness guides generally represent the highest level of training, education, and commitment within the Alaska sportfishing industry. Many have college degrees, wilderness emergency medical training, and other qualifications. Most of them operate out of the major hubs such as Juneau, Anchorage, Fairbanks, Dillingham, Nome, Kotzebue, and Bettles, and offer trips that range in length from 3 to 14 days. They handle everything from float trips to spike camps, usually offering unguided outfitting options as well. Reservations generally must be made well in advance, although they can sometimes fit folks in at the last minute. The better operations can provide some of Alaska's finest wilderness fishing experiences, with personalized service, outstanding professionalism, and itineraries in some of the state's best areas, like Bristol Bay, Northwest, Interior, southern Southeast, and the North Gulf Coast. Prices vary from $250 to $400 (or more) per day per person, usually all-inclusive (covering transportation, meals, guided fishing, and everything else to and from the point of departure).

Outfitters: Today's Alaska outfitters run the gamut of services and rentals to provide a full spectrum of possibilities for exciting, less expensive vacations. Fishermen can arrange to use rafts, boats, yachts, cabins, cars, tent camps, even camping gear and fishing tackle, on a daily or weekly basis. In addition to the regular outfitter or rental services located in most of the major hubs, many of the more established guide, lodge, and air taxi businesses provide outfitting to customers as part of their business, so check when inquiring about their service. (See the locations chapters for listings and descriptions of available services.)

Rates vary from region to region, but generally expect to pay from $75-150 per day for a small boat or raft, with a slight discount for weekly rental. Larger boats and yachts go for $250-600 per day per person, with usually a four to six-person minimum for the larger craft. Keep in mind that with high air cargo

Exploring headwaters of a remote stream in Southwest Alaska. Float trips are an exciting way to experience some of the state's best backcountry fishing.

rates, it may be more prudent to pay higher rates on site with air taxi or local outfitters than to ship gear from one of the major hubs.

Float Trips

Perhaps the most unique and exciting way to experience Alaska's wild rivers and fishing is to float down from headwaters in lightweight rafts or kayaks. While certainly not an option for everyone, float trips offer some distinct advantages over fly-ins, camps, and lodges. For one, the float trip offers an intimate river experience, traveling through remote sections which few can access by any other means. The entire length of the river can be fished, and schedules and streamside camps allow for convenient, 24-hour-a-day access to prime areas like salmon-spawning beds, where the rainbow trout, charr, and grayling are abundant and hungry. Variety and catch rates on float trips are unequalled.

Since no mechanized equipment is used, the entire trip is one of peaceful immersion in the sounds and sights of the wilderness, with wildlife frequently sighted during the downstream journey. The downside to the float-trip experience can be the weather, with particularly foul stretches hampering comfort and overall enjoyment. High-quality equipment—tents, raingear, and footwear—is essential, as are maps, bear protection, and wilderness survival and boating skills. The services of an experienced guide are highly recommended, and fees charged range from $250 to $500 per day per person, all-inclusive.

(Prices are greatly influenced by location, as some trips require extensive travel by small plane.) The best rivers for float fishing in Alaska are in the Bristol and lower Kuskokwim Bays of the Southwest region.

Bush Pilots & Air Taxis

If you had to pick the most romantic figures in the whole Alaska sportfishing scene, it would surely be the intrepid souls who brave Alaska's fickle skies to shuttle the people and supplies that make it all happen— the bush pilots. Steadfast and reliable through thick and thin, they keep everyone on schedule during the busy summer season, which is not an easy job in a place so vast and primitive. Your average Alaska bush pilot also knows the local fishing like no one else you'll meet, so it is definitely to your advantage to get on his good side and cultivate a working relationship with him, especially if you plan on returning for more adventure.

Float planes are indispensible for accessing Alaska's most remote fishing locations. The DeHavilland Beaver, shown here, is the undisputed workhorse of Alaska's bush plane fleet.

Most air taxis bill by the hour, which can vary from $150-500 or more, depending on the size of plane used (fees usually include return flight time). Many of the larger air taxis charge a standard seat fare for destinations on their daily/weekly flight schedule, or offer per person package prices for drop-offs and pick-ups at popular locations. (Be sure to check weight restrictions on these fares.)

A variety of interesting craft is in service all across Alaska, but the real workhorses are the single-engine Cessnas, Pipers, and DeHavillands, which have proven their versatility and reliability over the years in the most challenging conditions. Since most of Alaska's better stream and lake locations involve some flying to reach them, air transportation is usually a significant part of total trip costs. If you are planning a do-it-yourself excursion, some of the ways you can keep air taxi costs down are:

- *Travel with a small group:* Usually two to four people is an ideal group size for lowering per-person costs and achieving higher efficiency, not to mention the time saved in spreading the work load. You'll also have much more fun if you go with a group of buddies.

- *Use scheduled commercial flights* whenever possible: You can buy a ticket to just about any village or town in even the most remote parts of Alaska on the regularly scheduled flights offered by the major air carriers (shipping your gear as cargo), then contract with local flight services for arrangements to and from nearby fishing locations. Careful planning and research are required, but this can save you a bundle over chartering small planes from major hubs like Anchorage or Fairbanks.

- *Shop around:* Have a definite idea of the number in your party, the kind of trip you have in mind, and the rivers, lakes, or bays you wish to fish before you contact anyone for preliminary arrangements. If possible, get quotes from at least two other services. Air taxis have different planes and rates vary; some can even save you money on the backhaul if they've got flights already going to the area you're interested in.

- *Go light:* The number-one mistake among tourists in general, and the bane of every bush pilot, has to be the excessive amount of gear most people bring for a trip. Limit yourself to 40 to 50 pounds of personal gear—clothes, sleeping bag, fishing equipment, and camera—and streamline your equipment list to a bare minimum. (If you're traveling with a group, coordinate your planning to avoid duplication of gear.) You'll save money (cargo costs these days run 50 to 70 cents per pound one way from Anchorage to the state's better fishing areas), and enjoy your trip more with less gear to lug around.

Alaska Fishing Ethics

Familiarize yourself with current Alaska fishing regulations, and please obey all bag limits and restrictions. Report all violators: call 1-800-478-3377.

Respect the rights of property owners along rivers, streams, and lakes by contacting them, if possible, before you trespass on their lands. Some of their addresses are given in the destination descriptions.

Keep only the fish you intend to eat or take for mounting; practice proper catch-and-release techniques whenever possible.

Be courteous to other anglers and respect their right to privacy.

Tread lightly – use minimum impact camping techniques and please don't litter!

CATCH AND RELEASE FISHING TECHNIQUES

With increasing fishing pressure each year, the preservation of Alaska's high quality sport-fishing will depend upon more anglers choosing to practice effective minimum impact, catch-and-release fishing techniques. The following are some important points to remember about fishing gear, techniques, and fish handling, if you want to maximize chances for survival:

Tackle

Use sufficiently strong line to bring your catch in quickly.

Fish caught with flies or lures survive more often than fish caught with bait.

Don't use treble hooks! Single hooks penetrate deeper, hold better, and damage fish less than trebles. (They also snag much less.)

Use the correct hook size. Hooks too small may be taken deeply by fish; hooks too large can cause severe damage and death to fish.

Use barbless or micro-barb hooks, or pinch barbs down on regular hooks with pliers.

Landing Your Catch

Land your fish as carefully and quickly as possible.

Keep only the fish you truly need.

Do not remove from water any fish you intend to release.

Do not let fish flop in shallow water, over rocks, or on dry land.

Use nets made with soft or knotless mesh; do not lift fish out of water.

Handling Your Catch

Keep the fish in the water at all times.

Cradle the fish gently with both hands, one under its belly, one near its tail.

Keep your fingers out of and away from the gills.

Use wet cloth gloves or wet your hands when handling fish.

Never squeeze the fish.

Removing the Hook

Remove the hook quickly and gently, keeping the fish in the water.

Use long-nosed pliers or a hemostat to grip the shank and back the hook out.

When a fish is hooked deeply, cut the line near the hook.

Use steel hooks that will quickly rust out; avoid using stainless steel hooks.

Cut your line rather than injure an active fish.

Reviving Your Catch

Support the fish in slow current and let it work its gills to revive.

Gently move an exhausted fish back and forth until its gills are working properly and it maintains its balance.

Large fish may take some time to revive.

Releasing Your Catch

When the fish recovers and attempts to swim out of your hands, let it go.

Any fish bleeding heavily, or that does not revive after a few minutes, should be kept.

THE IMPROVED CLINCH KNOT

This is probably the most common knot used. It is easy to learn, will not slip, and gives nearly 100% line strength. It can be used to connect hooks, lures, or terminal tackle to your line.

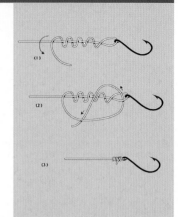

1. Pass line through eye of hook, swivel, or lure ring, bend back and make five turns around taut standing end (immobilize hook/lure/swivel).

2. Pass end of line through first loop above hook, swivel or lure, then back through larger loop, as shown.

3. Wet knot for lubrication, then slowly cinch down by pulling both ends of line. Use thumbnail to work coils down snug to hook eye, swivel, or lure ring, while pulling hard on line ends. Trim tag end.

THE PALOMAR KNOT

The Palomar Knot is another very commonly used knot. It is probably the easiest knot to tie correctly and is rated the strongest knot by the International Game Fish Association. It provides one of the best knots known to hold terminal tackle.

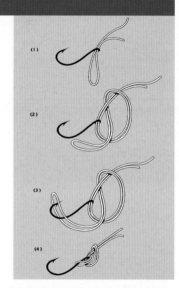

1. Double about four inches of line and pass the loop through the eye.

2. Let the hook hang loose and tie an overhand knot in doubled line. Avoid twisting the lines and don't tighten the knot.

3. Pull the loop of line enough to pass it over the hook, swivel, or lure. Make sure the loop passes completely over this attachment.

4. Pull both tag end and standing line to tighten. Clip about 1/8" from the knot.

THE HOOK SNELL

Where a hook has an offset eye, this allows for an efficient "straight" pull of the hook's point.

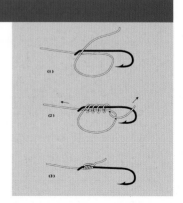

1. Thread the line through the eye about six inches. Form a loop and hold it against the shank of the hook.

2. Make five or six turns through the loop and around the hook shank.

3. Close the knot and tighten by pulling the standing line in one direction and the hook in the other. Trim the tag end.

Knots for Alaska Anglers

THE BLOOD KNOT

A very important and widely used knot for joining two lines of roughly the same diameter, especially useful for making leaders for flyfishing.

1. Lay the ends of the lines alongside each other, overlapping about six inches of line. Hold the lines at the midpoint. Take five turns around the standing line with the tag end and bring the end back between the two strands, where they are being held.

2. Hold this part of the knot in position while the other tag is wound around the standing line in the opposite direction and also brought back between the strands. The two tags should protrude from the knot in opposite directions (as shown).

3. Wet the knot, then pull up slowly on the two standing lines, taking care that the two ends do not back out of their positions. The turns will gather into loops as they come together. Use thumbnails to push coils tightly together as knot cinches down.

4. Clip tag ends to 1/16" of knot.

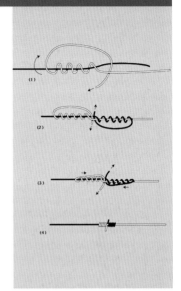

THE SURGEON'S KNOT

The Surgeon's Knot is, as the name implies, a knot used by doctors in the operating room. It's easy to learn (it can even be tied in the dark) and reliable. It's useful for joining a heavier monofilament (or fluorocarbon) leader to a lighter monofilament main line.

1. Lay six to eight inches of line and leader parallel and overlapping.

2. Using the two lines, tie an overhand knot.

3. Proceed to tie a second overhand knot.

4. Pull both lines in opposing directions to gather and tighten the knot. Trim the ends of the line.

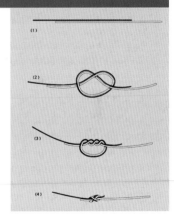

THE PERFECTION LOOP KNOT

This well-known knot is one of several used to attach lures with a loop, allowing for free movement. Especially useful for flyfishermen.

1. Tie overhand knot in line before passing end through eye of hook or lure ring. Loop line back through open overhand knot as shown.

2. Adjust loop, as in a slip knot, by pulling standing end. Bring end around standing line and tuck back in overhand knot as shown.

3. Draw knot tight. Trim end.

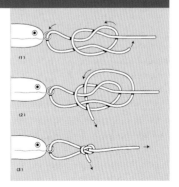

THE ALBRIGHT KNOT

Another strong knot to join lines of dissimilar materials or diameter. Especially useful for flyfishermen.

1. Make a bend or bight in thicker line (fly line) and draw thinner line (leader) end alongside and begin wrapping toward end of bight, as shown.

2. Wrap tightly and carefully so each turn is cinched snug to next, using left thumb and forefinger to pinch wraps while winding with right hand.

3. Make 7 to 10 wrapping turns (depending on thickness of line), then pass end of line through bight. Slide wraps toward end of bight using left thumb and forefinger while pulling both ends of lighter (leader) line.

4. Pull looped fly line and leader ends to draw knot down, using left thumbnail to push wraps tightly together on end of bight. Clip tag end to about 1/16" of knot.

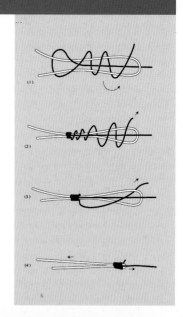

THE NAIL KNOT

One of the most important knots for connecting two dissimilar lines, like fly line and leader material.

1. Bring opposing ends of line in parallel to each other and draw about six inches of the smaller diameter line (leader) beyond end of larger line (fly line) and lay it along fly line with small (4d) nail or short piece of drinking straw or tubing, as shown.

2. Begin binding end of leader material, wrapping tightly around nail (or tube) and fly line as shown. Complete six wraps, using thumb and forefinger to keep them tight and close together.

3. Slip working end back in alongside of nail or into end of straw until it emerges through, under all loops, as shown. Grab working end and withdraw nail or straw.

4. While still holding wraps between thumb and forefinger, slowly tighten both ends of line until all slack is out of knot (you may have to use your mouth to grip one end of line). Open thumb and forefinger, then use thumbnail to slide wraps snug to each other while pulling both ends of line to cinch knot tight. Trim (to about 1/16") leader tag end and excess fly line protruding beyond knot.

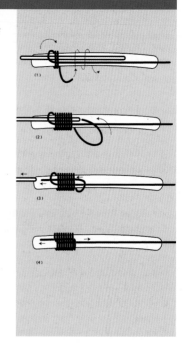

THE UNI KNOT

Another universal, very strong knot for making terminal connections. Also can be used for connecting line or backing to a reel.

1. Run six inches or more of line through eye and fold back parallel against standing line.

2. Bring end back toward eye and make six wraps around parallel lines as shown, then pass end through larger loop.

3. Wet knot, then pull standing line (keeping hook or lure fast) to draw knot down.

4. Cinch knot down all the way to eye, by pulling both ends of line. Use thumbnail to push coils down tight. Trim tag end.

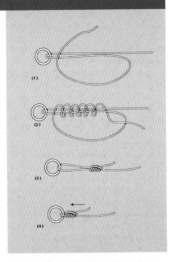

THE BIMINI TWIST KNOT

A very fancy big game loop knot used for joining leaders where the utmost strength and shock resistance is needed.

1. The line is doubled into a loop or bight two to three feet long, and 20-30 twists are made.

2. Loop is pulled forcibly outward while holding standing end of line taut, compressing twists . (This will entail the help of a partner or use of knees or feet to pull out sides of loop.)

3. As loop is forced outward and twists compress, overlapping counter-turns will begin at upper end and work down to end of bight, as shown. Keep standing end taught, while feeding working end of line and pulling loop out until counterturns reach end of twists.

4. Finish knot with two half hitches. Pull tight, trim tag end.

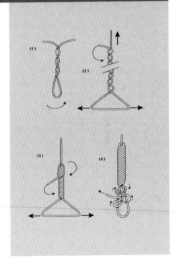

ROUND FISH FILLETING

1. Lay clean fish on cutting board. Take a long (9" blade recommended) and sharp fillet knife, and starting at anal vent, work tip up along middle of belly, slicing fish open. (Use tip of knife only—do not plunge blade into fish, as this will rupture digestive organs and spill contents, possibly ruining meat.)

2. Carefully cut (down to backbone only) around gill plate and down to belly cut, detouring around side fins. Do not pierce digestive organs!

3. Insert fillet knife at right angle to fish and carefully begin fillet cut along backbone, as shown. Make sure knife tip protrudes beyond belly cut and does not cut meat or organs. Work knife slowly at first, making sure blade is close to back bone. Hold top of fish with other hand as you push and pull blade toward tail. Cut fillet all the way to base of tail fins and separate from fish. Flip fillet over and carefully cut around and remove belly and anal fins.

4. With fillet still skin side down, remove rib bones by working knife tip under top of rib cage, and pressing bones up with other hand to help separate them from meat. Slice ribs away from meat and continue until all bones are removed.

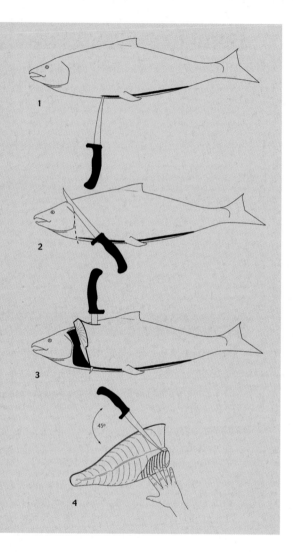

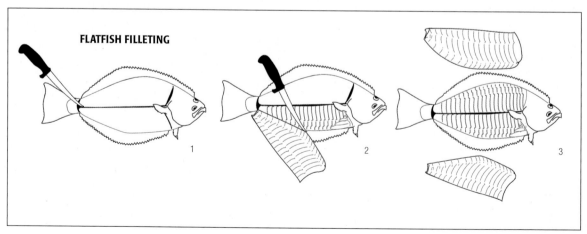

FLATFISH FILLETING

434

Alaska Fish Filleting & Steaking

Fish Steaking

1. Lay clean fish on cutting board and slit fish along belly from vent to throat, taking great care not to puncture organs.

2-3. Sever spine and head behind gills, but leave organs attached (cut around side fins down to belly slit). Remove head and gills with trailing organs. Rinse inside body cavity, using a spoon or your thumb to remove clotted blood from along the backbone. Make sure all blood and viscera are removed from body cavity. Pat dry.

4. Using fillet knife, carefully cut away fins from belly, removing as little flesh as possible.

5. Using a sharp, stout-bladed knife, make vertical steak cuts 1 1/2 to 2 inches apart, through flesh, backbone, and skin of the fish (as shown). Continue steaking to the base of the tail.

Flatfish Filleting

1. Lay clean halibut (or other flatfish) on a cutting board, head up as shown. Make a cut (to backbone only) from just behind head down to tail (roughly following lateral line) and another along cheeks to top and bottom fins (as shown).

2. Go back to the start of the cuts behind the head and carefully begin cutting away flesh from ribs, toward the bottom of the fish, as shown. Grab edge of fillet with one hand as you slice with the other. (Short slices with tip held along bone work best.) Keep slicing and peeling away fillet until you reach the edge of the fins, then cut through skin and detach fillet.

3. Repeat cut with the other fillet on topsides. Flip fish over and repeat all steps above. You will have a total of four fillets when you are done. Skin may be left on or removed, depending on thickness of fillet and preferred cooking method.

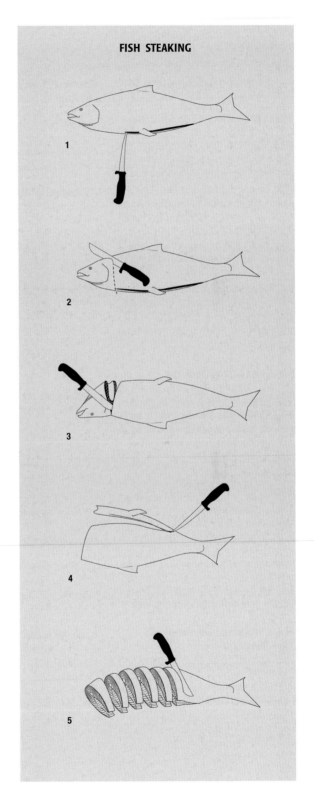

FISH STEAKING

1

2

3

4

5

Alaska Department of Fish and Game
P.O. Box 25526, Juneau, AK 99802-5526, (907) 465-4112, (907) 465-3088 (fax). Info on sportfish resources in Alaska. *www.sf.adfg.state.ak.us/statewide/sf_home.cfm*

Alaska Public Lands Information Center
605 West Fourth Avenue, Suite 105, Anchorage, AK 99501-5162. (907) 271-2737, *www.nps.gov/aplic/*. Information on Alaska's state and national parks, refuges, and forests.

U.S. Forest Service Alaska Region
PO Box 21628, Juneau, AK 99802-1628, (907) 586-8806, *www.fs.fed.us/r10* Information on Alaska's national forests, including fishing resources and cabin rentals.

Bureau of Land Management
222 W Seventh Ave., Box 13, Anchorage, AK 99513, (907) 271-5960, *www.blm.gov/ak*. Information on wild and scenic rivers, campgrounds, waysides, and public use cabins on undesignated federal land.

PUBLICATIONS

Alaska Vacation Planner
Alaska Travel Industry Association
2600 Cordova Street, #201, Anchorage, AK 99503, *www.travelalaska.com*
Useful trip planning information for the entire state, including addresses of local visitor services and contacts. For further information, send for the free *Alaska Vacation Planner*.

Alaska Wilderness Recreation and Tourism Association
2207 Spenard Road #201, Anchorage, AK 99503, (907) 258-3171, *www.awrta.org/*
Produces a member list and directory of the better Alaska fishing guides and outfitters.

The Alaska Roadside Anglers' Guide
Fishing Alaska Publications
P.O. Box 90557, Anchorage, AK 99509, *www.roadsideangler.com.*
Publisher of a comprehensive guidebook to fishing all Alaska roadside waters, with information on over 750 locations.

Fly Patterns of Alaska
Frank Amato Publications
P.O. Box 82112, Portland, OR 97282
(800) 541-9498, *www.amatobooks.com*
Fly Patterns of Alaska is a color desktop reference of Alaska fly patterns.

Alaska Atlas and Gazetteer
Delorme
Two Delorme Drive, P.O. Box 298
Yarmouth, ME 04096
(800) 561-5105, *www.delorme.com*
A handy, bound atlas of topographic maps on the entire state.

The Complete Book of Fishing Knots
Globe Pequot Press
246 Goose Lane, P.O. Box 480
Guilford, CT 06437
(888) 249-7586, *www.globepequot.com*
A thorough, easy-to-follow guide to knots, by Geoffrey Budworth.

SERVICES & GEAR

Alaska Wildwater
P.O. Box 110615
Anchorage, AK 99511
(907) 345-4308
Statewide equipment rentals, including rafts, tents, and kayaks.

Alaska Raft & Kayak
401 West Tudor Road
Anchorage, AK 99503
(907) 561-7238
www.alaskaraftandkayak.com
Statewide equipment rentals, including rafts, tents, and kayaks.

Bristol Bay Flies
P. O. Box 88600
Steilacoom, WA 98388-0647
(253) 584-9601, *www.bristolbayflies.com*
Fiy patterns for Alaska fishing.

World Wide Angler
2375 E 63rd Ave. #2
Anchorage, AK 99507
907-561-0662, www.akflyshop.com
Alaska's premier flyshop.

Mt. View Sports Center
3838 Old Seward Highway
Anchorage, AK 99503
(907) 563-8600, *www.mtviewsports.com*
Alaska's most complete tackle and sporting goods store.

Mossy's Fly Shop
750 West Dimond Blvd
Anchorage, Alaska 99515
907-770-2666, *www.mossysflyshop.com*
Anchorage's newest and most modern fly shop.

ORGANIZATIONS

International Game Fish Association
300 Gulf Stream Way
Dania Beach, FL 33004
(954) 922-4212, *www.igfa.org/*
International organization devoted to promoting sportfishing, conservation, and the keeping of game fish records.

Trout Unlimited
Membership Department
1300 N. 17th Street, #500
Arlington, VA 22209-3801
www.tu.org/index.asp
America's leading non-profit coldwater fisheries conservation organization.

Index for Alaska Fishing